Oak Grove
3.19.1977

Malden Center
12.27.1975

MALDEN CENTER

Wellington
9.6.1975

Assembly
9.2.2014

Sullivan Sq
4.7.1975

Community
College
4.7.1975

To Haverhill

Everett Extension

Everett
3.15.1919
4.4.1975 closed

Sullivan Sq
6.10.1901
4.4.1975 closed

Thompson Sq
5.22.1902
4.4.1975 closed

City Sq
6.10.1901
4.4.1975 closed

Charlestown
Bridge 11.27.1899

Chelsea

CHELSEA

Bellingham Sq

Box District

Eastern Ave

To Newburyport, Rockport

Wonderland
6.19.1954

Revere Beach
6.19.1954

Beachmont
6.19.1954

Suffolk Downs
4.2.1952

Orient Heights
1.5.1952

Wood Island
1.5.1952 Day Sq
10.21.1954 Wood Island Park
1967 renamed

Somerville

GLX

Lechmere
7.10.1922

Science Park/West End
6.20.1955 Science Park
2009 renamed

Cambridge St. Portal
1916-1952

East Cambridge Extension 6.1.1912

Haymarket-North Extension

NORTH STATION
Causeway St.
Elevated

North Station
6.1.1912 elevated North Station West
6.25.2005 elevated closed
1967 renamed
11.12.2005 subway

Haymarket Portal
8.18.1898 streetcar

North Station
6.10.1901 elevated
4.17.1975 subway

Battery St
8.22.1901
10.1.1938 closed

Airport
1.5.1952

Maverick
12.30.1907

Terminal C

Terminal E

Logan
Airport

Terminal B

Terminal A

Bowdoin
3.18.1916

Beacon Hill Tunnel 3.23.1916

East Boston Tunnel Ext.

Haymarket Portal
11.30.1908 rapid transit

Adams Sq
8.19.1898
1963 closed

America's
First Subway
Tremont St.
Subway

Haymarket
9.3.1898 Haymarket Sq
11.30.1908 NB Union; SB Friend
1.26.1967 renamed

Court St
12.30.1904; 1912 closed

Government Center
9.3.1898 upper level Scollay Sq
3.18.1916 lower level Scollay Under
10.28.1963 renamed

East Boston Tunnel 12.30.1904

Silver Line SL3 4.21.2018

Ted Williams Tunnel

Park St
9.1.1897
3.23.1912 Park St Under

State
12.30.1904 upper level Devonshire
11.30.1908 lower level NB State
11.30.1908 middle level SB Milk
1.25.1967 renamed

State St
8.22.1901; 10.1.1938 closed

Aquarium
4.5.1906 Atlantic Ave; 2.13.1967 renamed

Rowes Wharf
8.22.1901
10.1.1938 closed

Harbor St

Tide St

23 Dry Dock Ave

27 Dry Dock Ave

Washington St. Tunnel

Tremont St. Subway

Dorchester Tunnel

Downtown Crossing
11.30.1908 upper level NB Summer
upper level SB opened as Winter
4.4.1915 lower level Washington
1.23.1967 renamed Washington
6.1985 Downtown Crossing/Washington

Atlantic Avenue Elevated

Courthouse

World Trade
Center

Silver Line Way

Silver Line Phase II 12.17.2004

DESIGN
CENTER

Black Falcon Ave

88 Black
Falcon Ave

Chinatown
11.30.1908 NB Essex
SB Boylston
2.11.1967 renamed Essex
6.1985 Chinatown/Essex

To Nubian

South Station 8.22.1901; 10.1.1938 closed

South Station
12.3.1916 South Station Under
1967 renamed
12.17.2004 opened for Silver Line

SOUTH
STATION

E. 1st St

M St

City Point

3.29.2009 discontinued

To South Station/
Boylston

Beach St
8.22.1901
7.4.1919 closed

Broadway
12.15.1917
10.14.1919 underground streetcar level closed

Center
opened
renamed

South Cove Tunnel
Elevated

Ash St. Portal

Herald St

East Berkeley St

Union Park St

Newton St

Worcester Sq

Mass. Ave

Lenox St

Melnea Cass Blvd

Nubian
1.7.2002 Dudley
2.13.2020 renamed

Dover St
6.10.1901
5.1.1987 closed

Northampton St
6.10.1901
5.1.1987 closed

Washington St. Elevated

Silver Line Phase I 7.20.2002

Andrew
6.29.1918

JFK/UMass

JFK/UMass
11.5.1927 Columbia
12.2.1982 renamed JFK/UMass
6.1985 renamed JFK/UMass/Columbia

North Quincy

Dudley
St

Egelston Sq
11.11.1909
5.1.1987 closed

West Hills Extension

Green St
11.11.1909
1967 renamed Green
5.1.1987 closed

Savin Hill
9.1.1928

Fields
Corner
11.5.1927

Shawmut
9.1.1928

Ashmont
9.1.1928

South Shore Extension 9.1.1971

Dorchester Tunnel Extension

QUINCY
CENTER

Wollaston

Quincy Center

Quincy Adams
9.1983

Braintree Extension

To Greenbush

Braintree
3.22.1980

BRAINTREE

Hills 11.11.1909 elevated
5.4.1987 subway

Mattapan High-Speed line 12.21.1929

Cedar Grove

Mattapan

Capen St

Valley Rd

Central Ave

Milton

Butler

To Forge Park/495

To Middleborough, Lakeville,
Kingston, and Plymouth

Boston in Transit

Boston in Transit

Mapping the History of
Public Transportation in The Hub

STEVEN BEAUCHER

The MIT Press

CAMBRIDGE, MASSACHUSETTS

LONDON, ENGLAND

This book was set in Belizio by David Berlow. Printed and bound in China.

Library of Congress Cataloging-in-Publication Data
Names: Beaucher, Steven, author.
Title: Boston in transit : mapping the history of public transportation in the hub / Steven Beaucher.
Description: Cambridge, Massachusetts : The MIT Press, [2023] | "Reprint previous title: Boston in Transit: Mapping the History of Public Transportation in The Hub (self-published ebook)"—ECIP details information. | Includes bibliographical references and index.
Identifiers: LCCN 2022019898 | ISBN 9780262048071 (hardcover)
Subjects: LCSH: Massachusetts Bay Transportation Authority—History. | Transportation—Massachusetts—Boston—History. | Urban transportation—Massachusetts—Boston—History. | Local transit—Massachusetts—Boston—History.
Classification: LCC HE310.B6 B33 2023 | DDC 388.409744/61—dc23/eng/20220609
LC record available at https://lccn.loc.gov/2022019898

10 9 8 7 6 5 4 3 2 1

Contents

Preface

My earliest experiences with public transportation in Boston took place in the 1980s. I grew up in the Merrimack Valley community of Chelmsford, just as the town was completing the transition from New England village to bedroom community. In my early teens, I began to venture to Lowell's Gallagher Transportation Terminal to catch MBTA commuter rail trains to Boston. The commuter rail was my escape from suburbia.

My arrivals at Boston's well-worn North Station transitioned into hours riding the trolleys and rapid transit trains of the T. Beyond my youthful excitement over being in the big city, I was stimulated by the infrastructure that facilitated my movement around town. Questions swirled in my head. How old was this trolley I was riding? How long had this station been here? Why was a certain platform no longer used? What is that old map on the wall with station names I do not recognize? I came to learn the answers to many of my questions, but not before obtaining a degree in architecture, studying urban history with vigor, practicing architecture in Greater Boston, and launching my antique map and transit artifact business, WardMaps.

I created *Boston in Transit* because I needed it. Initially, I sought to create a quick-reference guide to help me establish basic information about items I was collecting and dealing in at WardMaps. Though I had assembled a comprehensive library of research materials, it was frustrating to remember which resource to check, if one existed at all. I came to realize that nobody had put Boston's entire history of public transportation, from 1630 through today, into a single, bookshelf-ready volume. During my years of dealing in antique maps and transit artifacts, I have been asked countless times "What book is the best history of the T?" and "What book do you recommend on the history of public transportation in Boston?" While I could rattle off titles about various aspects of Boston's transit history, I could never point to one, definitive publication. So, beyond my personal desire for a summarized history, I knew others were seeking *Boston in Transit*.

I spent six years researching, writing, and editing *Boston in Transit*. I read a ton. I collected a ton more. I mined archives and collections, both public and private. I sought visuals of the uncommon variety, photographs not yet published, maps and ephemera not yet digitized. As I read more, dug deeper into historic collections, and assembled a body of unparalleled research, *Boston in Transit* evolved from a simple summary into an encyclopedic tome.

Boston in Transit is for the historian seeking a one-stop reference. It is for the Bostonian looking to know their city a bit more intimately. It is for the visitor to Boston seeking to return home with a single resource. For all audiences, *Boston in Transit* is intended as a gateway to further research and exploration of Boston's nearly four hundred years of public transportation history.

Steven Beaucher
Cambridge, Massachusetts
January 2020

Introduction

Public transportation moves people, is available to the general public, and is established, regulated, or sanctioned by a governmental body. Public transportation modes, infrastructure, and policies are developed with public funds, private resources, or both.

Boston in Transit tells the history of public transportation infrastructure — the vehicles, lines, and stations — that facilitated the movement of Bostonians between 1630 and today. It is a record of what was built, who built it, and why. It introduces the entities and people that created, funded, operated, and utilized public transit in Greater Boston for nearly four centuries. *Boston in Transit* details evolutions in public transportation technologies from water-based and horse-drawn conveyances of the seventeenth and eighteenth centuries, to steam-powered and railed transportation systems of the nineteenth century, to the multi-modal publicly-controlled system overseen by the MBTA today.

The story is broken down into nine chapters, each with a high-level topical focus. As arranged, the chapters follow an overarching chronological sequence. Each chapter's title serves as a signpost for the segment of history covered within. While each chapter may be digested independently, a cover to cover read allows the reader to build upon concepts explained earlier in the narrative.

Throughout *Boston in Transit* an unprecedented collection of graphics complements the textual narrative. Maps, photographs, and ephemera make the book as visually engaging as it is factually enlightening. Many graphics are reproduced for the first time or have been digitized expressly for this publication. A curated selection of maps spanning over three hundred years provides a running cartographic record. Architectural and engineering drawings reveal designs for lines, stations, and vehicles. Photographs bring specific places, transit equipment, and times into direct view. Brochures, pamphlets, guidebooks, timetables, and tickets complete the picture, revealing how transit was marketed, navigated, and utilized over the centuries.

Boston In Transit is intended to be a first-stop reference. As no one volume can cover all aspects of any subject of history, *Boston in Transit* stands as an unprecedented gateway. It is a portal for the reader to pass through as they begin a journey of exploration of the rich history of public transportation in The Hub of the Universe.

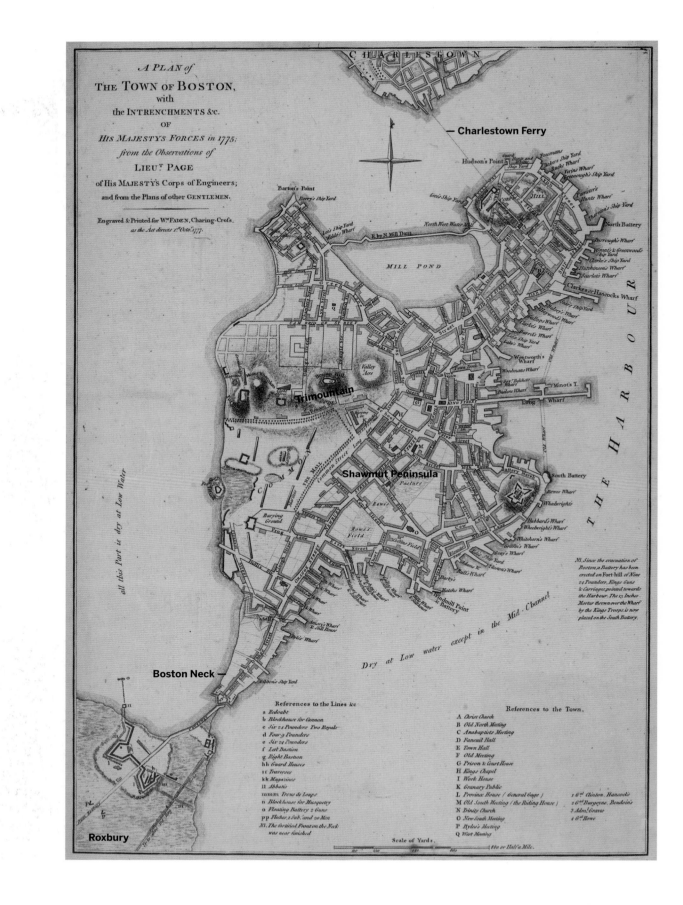

A PLAN of
THE TOWN OF BOSTON,
with
the INTRENCHMENTS &c.
OF
HIS MAJESTYS FORCES in 1775:
from the Observations of
LIEUT. PAGE
of His MAJESTYS Corps of Engineers;
and from the Plans of other GENTLEMEN.

Engraved & Printed for Wm FADEN, Charing-Cross,
as the Act directs 1st Octr. 1777.

Charlestown Ferry

Trimountain

Shawmut Peninsula

Boston Neck

Roxbury

all this Part is dry at Low Water

MILL POND

THE HARBOUR

Dry at Low water except in the Mid-Channel

NB. Since the evacuation of
Boston, a Battery has been
erected on Fort hill of Nine
24 Pounders, Kings Guns
& Carriages, pointed towards
the Harbour. The 13 Inches
Mortar thrown over the Wharf
by the Kings Troops, is now
placed on the South Battery.

References to the Lines &c
a Redoubt
b Blockhouse for Cannon
c Six 24 Pounders Two Royals
d Four 9 Pounders
e Six 24 Pounders
f Left Bastion
g Right Bastion
hh Guard Houses
ii Traverses
kk Magazines
ll Abbatis
mmm Trous de Loups
n Blockhouse for Musquetry
o Floating Battery 2 Guns
pp Flechs, 1 Sub, and 20 Men
N1. The fortified Front on the Neck
was near finished

References to the Town.
A Christ Church
B Old North Meeting
C Anabaptists Meeting
D Faneuil Hall
E Town Hall
F Old Meeting
G Prison & Court House
H Kings Chapel
I Work House
K Granary Public
L Province House (General Gage)
M Old South Meeting (the Riding House)
N Trinity Church
O New South Meeting
P Byles's Meeting
Q West Meeting

1 Gl. Clinton, Hancocks
2 Gl. Burgoyne, Bowdoin's
3 Adm. Graves
4 Gl. Howe

Scale of Yards

880 or Half a Mile.

CHAPTER 1

Making Connections:
Early Public Transportation for Boston

The Massachusetts Bay Company Arrives

Public transportation for Boston is as old as the city itself, originating in 1630. In that year, approximately 700 English citizens operating as the Massachusetts Bay Company migrated to New England. Along the shores of their company's namesake bay, the colonists established a puritanical version of English civilization, an aspect of which was reliable transportation.

The Massachusetts Bay Company did not arrive at lands devoid of existing settlement. Indigenous people had long lived, farmed, fished, and transported themselves throughout the region. The Massachusett ("Those of the Great Hill") utilized waterways and ancient footpaths, known as "traces." The first Europeans to settle in New England built upon existing networks of canoeable waters, portages between waterways, and countless miles of traces.

In advance of the Massachusetts Bay Company, a few Europeans established themselves around Massachusetts Bay. Samuel Maverick set up on Noddle's Island (now part of East Boston) in 1624. Captain Wallaston (evolved to Wollaston) settled in 1625 on land that became Braintree. By the mid-1620s, Reverend William Blaxton (evolved to Blackstone) established himself on a peninsula at the head of Massachusetts Bay.

The spit of land upon which Blaxton lived and farmed was known to indigenous people as "Shawmut." Though the word is most often translated to mean "Place of Clear Waters," a scholar argued in 1867 that Shawmut was essentially a word for "Where There is Going by Boat" or simply "Crossing Place." These generally disregarded translations, if accurate, confirm that Shawmut was a named part of the local transportation network of indigenous peoples.

In Blaxton's time, the Shawmut Peninsula was dominated by what European colonists and traders called Trimountaine (Anglicized as Trimountain), a ridge with three distinct peaks visible from throughout Massachusetts Bay (Figure 1.2). Likewise, Trimountain (evolved to Tremont) offered views from the Shawmut Peninsula far out across the bay.

The Massachusetts Bay Company colonists who arrived in 1630, first made landfall along the northern reaches of Massachusetts Bay, at the English settlement of Naumkeag (now Salem). After a few months, the group relocated southward, to a peninsula less then a mile north of the Shawmut, between the confluence of the Charles River, Mystic River, and Massachusetts Bay. On the western edge of that headland, the colonists worked to rebuild the failed English settlement of Mishawam (evolved to Mishawum), renaming it to Charlestown in the process.

Throughout the summer of 1630, some Massachusetts Bay Company colonists decamped from Charlestown and moved south, across the Charles River onto the Shawmut Peninsula. A larger dispersion occurred after the summer ended. Reacting to months of disease, lack of reliable fresh water, and a rumored foreign invasion, most left Charlestown. By the end of 1630, the colonists settled places that became Watertown, Medford, Roxbury, and Saugus.

On September 7, 1630, the Massachusetts Bay Company decreed that Trimountain be renamed Boston, the name of an English town from which some members hailed. By the end of the month, Watertown and Boston were the largest settlements around Massachusetts Bay, with Boston hosting

Figure 1.1 Boston and the Shawmut Peninsula, 1775

A British military engineer mapped Boston and the city's militarization by the British at the eve of the American Revolution. Important transit links are shown. The Charlestown Ferry runs between "Ferry Way," in Boston's North End, and Charlestown (top). Boston Neck connects the Shawmut Peninsula with Roxbury (bottom) and mainland North America.

approximately 150 persons. With their population spread around Massachusetts Bay and its feeder rivers, the colonists worked to establish systems of governance and facilitate movement between their nascent towns.

Following their charter, Massachusetts Bay Company colonists began to govern colonial Boston with a General Court. The General Court elected from its ranks a governor, a deputy governor, and a Court of Assistants. The first governor of the Massachusetts Bay Colony to oversee Boston was John Winthrop. Initially, the General Court only met four times a year, typically handling only the most significant issues. The Court of Assistants served as day-to-day lawmaker, regulator, and judiciary. The Great and General Court designated Boston as the capitol of the Massachusetts Bay Colony in 1632. The Great and General Court evolved into the General Court of The Commonwealth of Massachusetts, today's legislature of the state of Massachusetts. Throughout the history of Boston, Massachusetts's General Court and governor's office have regularly joined forces with city government to affect the creation, development, and improvement of public transportation for the city and the region.

At the time of the arrival of the Massachusetts Bay Company onto its shores, the Shawmut Peninsula was, at its extremes, two miles wide and four miles long. The only dry land connection between Boston and the rest of North America was a narrow isthmus referred to as "The Neck." Trails of indigenous people extended inland from Boston Neck, linking navigable waterways and reaching far into the interior of North America. Traces were Boston's first overland pathways. Except for slender Boston Neck, the Shawmut Peninsula was entirely surrounded by tidal waters. Boston was essentially an island. A map of Boston published at the time of the American Revolution, and some 150 years after the arrival of the Massachusetts Bay Company (Figure 1.1), shows the Shawmut Peninsula still tenuously connected to the mainland by only The Neck.

In the seventeenth and eighteenth centuries, walking across Boston took less than an hour. Travelling overland between the Shawmut Peninsula and settlements around Massachusetts Bay required significantly more time, often many hours. Marine travel was the fastest and most direct way for people to move between points around the bay; indigenous people and early settlers employed canoes (Figure 1.2), and later, colonists introduced

barges and boats. Europeans expanded Native American traces for their own uses, at first for heavy foot travel, then for travel with horses, and later, into roads to support wheeled vehicles. Scores of decades elapsed before overland travel around Massachusetts Bay was as direct or expedient as water travel. Hence, the first example of public transportation in Boston came by sea.

The Charlestown Ferry

English colonial governments in seventeenth century New England recognized public transportation infrastructure as vital to the economic well-being, security, and livability of their young communities. Colonial documents record early forms of public transportation around Massachusetts Bay. Plymouth Colony, located approximately forty miles south of Boston, was established by English settlers in the early 1620s. Plymouth Colony decreed in 1639 that trees be felled and placed as footbridges across local rivers and streams. In their early years, both Plymouth and Massachusetts Bay Colonies established simple canoe ferries where water crossings were too broad for felled trees.

Within months of establishing themselves on the Shawmut Peninsula, the Massachusetts Bay Company sought to facilitate movement between Charlestown and Boston. At its first meeting in Boston, held on November 9, 1630, the Court of Assistants agreed to solicit for a person to establish and operate a ferry across the Charles River. The Court approved an initial ferry fare of one pence per person. By summer 1631, the Charlestown Ferry, Boston's first public transit line, was up and running. In June, the General Court confirmed Edward Converse as the ferry's operator and approved a new fare structure. Individuals paid two pence each way, while two or more people travelling together each paid one pence. The route of the Charlestown Ferry is represented as a dotted line crossing the Charles River at the top of Page's map of 1775 (Figure 1.1). In November 1636, the General Court granted Converse the exclusive right to operate the "Great Ferry" for three years. It also required Converse to provide an adequate level of service and pay forty pounds rent, quarterly, back to the Massachusetts Bay Colony. The 1636 arrangement set fares for the ferry at two pence per person or swine, one pence per goat or per person travelling in a group of two or more, and six pence per cow or horse. The General Court also granted Converse the

Figure 1.2 The Shawmut Peninsula in the 1600s
The three peaks of Trimountain provide a backdrop for canoes, the earliest mode of transport on Massachusetts Bay.

ability to charge, at his discretion, a reasonable fare for travel on the ferry before sunrise or after sunset.

The General Court awarded the Charlestown Ferry franchise to various operators during a span of 150 years. In 1640 the General Court required that income from the Great Ferry be granted to Harvard College in perpetuity. This subsidy arrangement remained in place for 146 years. A portion of a 1728 map of Boston (Figure 1.3) shows the "Ferry" as a rowboat with passengers. In time, boats capable of carrying carriages and flocks of livestock were deployed.

The Winnisimmet Ferry

Once Boston came into being, transportation links between the new town and the pre-existing settlement of Salem became increasingly important. The most direct route consisted of a ferry between the Shawmut Peninsula and Winnisimmet Landing (now part of the city of Chelsea) coupled with a series of foot paths linking Winnisimmet and

Salem. Purely overland travel between Boston and Winnisimmet was a circuitous journey that was miles and hours longer than the direct route that incorporated the ferry.

Less than a year after establishing Boston, the General Court recognized in 1631 that Thomas Willins had established a ferry connecting Boston, Charlestown, and Winnisimmet. The route of Willins' ferry between the Shawmut Peninsula and Winnisimmet was less than a quarter of the distance of the overland route between the same points. Seeking to preserve the marine connection, and the shortcut it offered between Boston and Winnisimmet, Massachusetts' colonial government granted the ferry to Willins "forever." A few years later, colonial documents record that Samuel Maverick was in control of the ferry from September 3, 1634 until February 27, 1635. During that time, Maverick was based on Noddle's Island and owned lands at Winnisimmet. The name of East Boston's Maverick Square recalls Maverick, Noddle's Island's permanent earliest English settler.

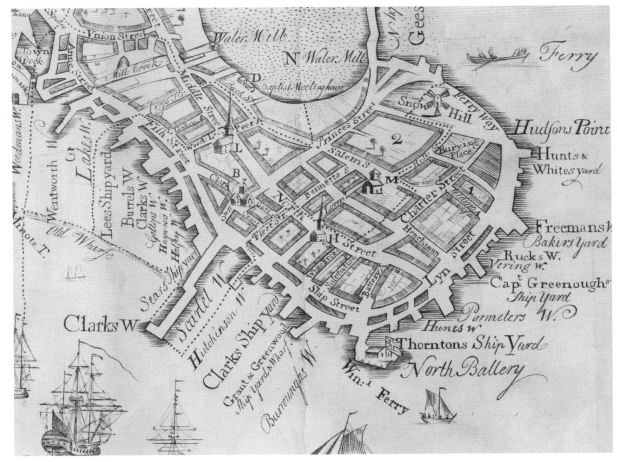

Figure 1.3 Mapping Boston's First Public Ferries, 1728
A portion of Will Burgis's 1728 map of Boston depicts the Charlestown Ferry as a small boat next to the word "Ferry" (top right). The text "Win:¹ Ferry" trails behind a modest boat rigged with sails. This may represent the Winnisimmet Ferry.

The Winnisimmet Ferry served Noddle's Island regularly until the East Boston Ferry began regular operation in the middle of the nineteenth century.

Various persons operated the Winnisimmet Ferry throughout the seventeenth and eighteenth centuries. During that time, the General Court set rates and established rules for operation for the service. In January 1635, the General Court selected Thomas Marshall to operate a ferry from "Milne Point" in Boston's North End to Charlestown and Winnisimmet. The General Court set fares for Marshall's operation at six pence for a single rider and two pence for riders in groups of two or more persons. In 1711 the General Court required Winnisimmet Ferry operations consist of at least three boats, with one vessel always to be "passing on the water." The General Court required the boats be rowed by "able, sober persons" from sunrise until eight o'clock, from October 1 through April 1, or nine o'clock, from April 1 through October 1.

By 1798 the Winnisimmet Ferry was serving Boston from the foot of North Street in the North End. In *The History of East Boston*, William H. Sumner mentioned Henry Howell Williams as "lessee, and afterward the owner of the ancient ferry between Boston and Winnisimmet, the both of which stopped at Noddle's Island on their passage from one place to another." Sumner mentioned that in the early nineteenth century, after Williams's

death, his heirs sold the ferry and its modest, sail-powered vessels to the Winnisimmet Ferry Company.

The Winnisimmet Ferry Company ended service to Noddle's Island in the mid-1830s. The discontinuance coincided with the arrival of boats of the East Boston Ferry Company. The October–November 1836 edition of *Badger & Porter's Stage Register* recorded that the "Chelsea" ferry operated with three boats. Nathaniel Dearborn's *Boston Notions* counted 547,750 passengers (a daily average of 6,709 passengers) carried by the "Chelsea Ferry" in 1847. In time, the Winnisimmet Ferry Company disposed of its sailboats and upgraded to steam-powered ferries to move people and vehicles across Boston Harbor. An 1856 view depicts a steam-powered vessel of the Winnisimmet Ferry in action (Figure 1.5). Foot passengers purchased paper tickets to ride on the ferry (Figure 1.4).

A ferry linking Boston with Winnisimmet crossed Boston Harbor for 286 years. An 1888 map of Boston, depicts the "Ferry to Winnisim[m]et" linking Boston's North End with Winnisimmet Landing (Figure 1.6). The Winnisimmet Ferry Company controlled the service until 1917, when declining ridership caused it to cease operations. A 1917 map of Boston's North End shows the Winnisimmet Ferry landing at the foot of Hanover Street

Figure 1.4 Winnisimmet Ferry Tickets, Undated
Winnisimmet Ferry "foot pass" tickets bear the Winnisimmet Company name and an image of a steam-powered ferry. The rear face of a foot pass (bottom) bears the company's initials.

Figure 1.5 Winnisimmet Ferry, 1856
A steam-powered boat (left) plies Chelsea Creek between Winnisimmet Landing in Chelsea (in the distance) and Boston's North End (out of view to the left).

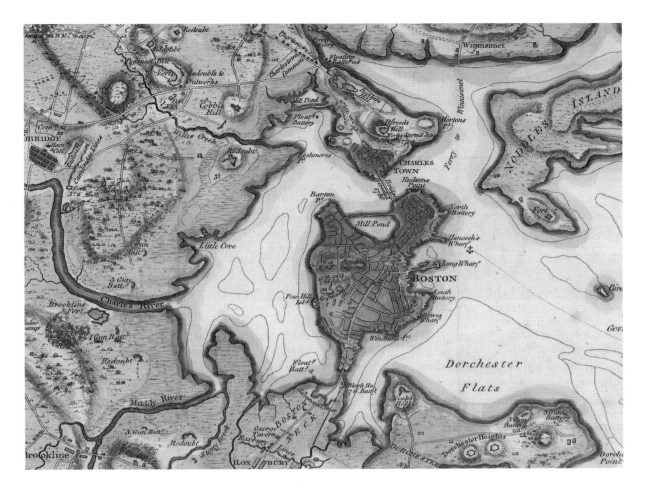

Figure 1.6 Boston and Environs, 1788
A map shows Boston two years after the opening of the
Charles River Bridge, labeled "Bridge erected 1786" (middle).
On the far left is Cambridge. On the right is Noddle's Island. At
the top of the map is Winnisimmet, connected by the "Ferry to
Winnisimmet" to Boston and the Shawmut Peninsula.

(Figure 5.99). The site now lies within United States
Coast Guard Base Boston.

In 1631, the same year that it first regulated the
Winnisimmet Ferry, the General Court approved
the colonial government's purchase of a portion of
Reverend Blaxton's lands on the west side of the
Shawmut Peninsula. The tract stretched from the
lower slopes of Trimountain to the tidal waters of
the Charles River. The General Court set aside the
land for common use by all Bostonians, thereby
establishing the first public park within a nascent
America. At the end of the nineteenth century,
Boston Common became the site of a landmark
piece of Boston's public transportation infrastructure—America's first public transit subway (see
Chapter 3).

The Charles River Bridge
Performance of Boston's early ferries was subject to
regularly hostile weather and rough sea conditions.
In summer, glaring sun or driving rain beat down
onto ferry passengers, many of whom were exposed
to the elements. In winter, ice and snow prevented
ferries from operating for days or weeks at a time.
The 1701 *Clough's Almanac* describes one Boston
winter when "all the bay was frozen over quite out
to sea" and ferries did not cross the harbor for two
months. Despite their drawbacks, Boston's ferries
continued gaining more riders. Between 1630 and
1775 the population of Boston increased from less
than 100 to approximately 16,000. Correspondingly, ferry travel became increasingly vital and
crowded. To mitigate often jam-packed or inoperable ferries, the General Court discussed, as early
as 1720, replacing the Charlestown Ferry with a
bridge across the Charles River. Eventually, a bridge
between Boston and Charlestown became a reality,
but over sixty-five years after the initial discussions.

Construction of the Charles River Bridge
commenced in 1785. The bridge opened to the public
on June 17, 1786. After Boston Neck, the Charles
River Bridge became Boston's second non-marine
connection between the Shawmut Peninsula and the

Figure 1.7 The Charles River Bridge, 1789
Shown three years after its inauguration, the Charles River Bridge was the first bridge to connect Boston with Charlestown. It replaced the Charlestown Ferry and stood until 1899, when it was replaced by the Charlestown Bridge.

mainland. The "Bridge erected 1786" is prominently called out on an 1888 map of the city (Figure 1.6). A view of the forty-two-foot-wide span, complete with lanterns that illuminated its wooden deck at night, was published in *Massachusetts Magazine* in 1789 (Figure 1.7). In that same year, George Washington visited Boston for the first time as President of the United States. The President's procession crossed Boston Neck and followed Orange, Newbury, and Marlborough Streets. Marking Washington's visit, Boston renamed the streets collectively to Washington Street. In combination with Boston Neck and the Shawmut Peninsula, the Charles River Bridge provided the most direct overland route between the south and north shores of Massachusetts Bay.

Public Coaches
Colonial-era ferries traversing the waters around Boston were complimented on land by vehicles transporting goods and people. Documents prepared by Boston's colonial government mention carts and wagons for the movement of goods, while carriages, chaises, chariots, landaus, and sedan chairs carried people. Conservative Bostonians of the late 1600s reserved particular hate for the sedan chair, which they eschewed as an ostentatious vehicle "inspired by the devil." The same colonists enacted many a law to keep Bostonians subjugated under their puritanical rule, going so far as to ban most travel within the city on Sundays.

Figure 1.8 Stagecoach, Photographed in 1929
A nineteenth century stagecoach is posed in front of Newburyport's Garrison Inn.

Figure 1.9 Stagecoach, Photographed Circa 1920s
Passengers and the driver wave from a stagecoach typical of those used in nineteenth century New England.

Figure 1.10 Stagecoach Newspaper Ad, Circa 1820s

In developing areas of seventeenth century colonial America, covered wagons for goods evolved into enclosed coaches for the transportation of people and small parcels such as mail. Early American coaches were functional, certainly not constructed for comfort. They were essentially wagons with one or more hard benches. The earliest written reference to a "coach" in Massachusetts colonial records appeared in 1669.

From the late seventeenth to the late nineteenth centuries, Bostonians with financial means owned or hired private horse-drawn carriages or similar vehicles. Those with less means, along with visitors to the city, hired public carriages or coaches. By the end of the first quarter of the eighteenth century, for-hire public coaches had become the backbone of overland, public transportation in Boston and around Massachusetts Bay.

A typical, horse-drawn public coach of eighteenth and nineteenth century America consisted of a cab, a supporting frame, and at least two axles, each with two wheels (Figure 1.8 and Figure 1.9). The cab sheltered passengers from the elements and had a typical capacity of four to six people. Some coaches featured benches atop or behind the cab. The driver sat on an open bench above the front of the cab where he overlooked and controlled a team of two or more horses that pulled the coach.

A ride in a public coach was a physically jarring experience. Passengers were jostled inside the cab as the coach rambled along rut-filled roads at a typical rate of five miles per hour. Bruises, nausea, and bloody wounds were regularly incurred by travelers. The driver and passengers seated in the exterior benches fared worse, being directly exposed to glaring sun, driving rain, freezing snow, blowing dust, and splattering mud.

America's primitive road network was a hindrance to consistent, speedy movement of coaches. When rain turned primitive roads into muddy troughs, coach travel was brought to a crawl or halted altogether. Where a bridge had yet to be constructed at a river too deep to drive through, a coach could cross via a ferry. Early coach ferries were nothing more than two large canoes lashed together, each supporting two wheels of the coach. At ferries of limited capacity, passengers exited and the driver unhitched the horses; the horses, the coach, the driver, and the passengers each took their turn crossing on the ferry. In colder months, coaches were outfitted with wood runners, essentially skis for coaches. During winter, horse-drawn sleighs shared snow-covered roads with coaches outfitted with runners.

After the American Revolution, coach companies established regular, long distance service. Longer runs were typically broken down into segments, each known as a stage. The length of a stage was determined by either the distance that could be travelled in one day, the location of an inn where coach passengers could receive overnight lodging between stages, or the range that a team of horses could work before tiring. Coaches operating in stage service were called "stagecoach" or simply "stages" for short. Under ideal road and weather conditions, stagecoaches achieved speeds of twelve miles an hour. Travel at half that speed was more typical on early roads. Many stagecoaches were referred to as "mail stages" because they provided delivery of the mail in addition to transporting paying passengers. The exchange of mail among colonial settlements led directly to improvements of Native American trails into all-season roads and the development of coaches into vehicles for efficient movement of people and baggage.

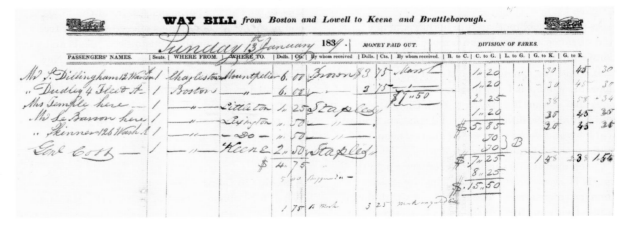

Figure 1.11 Stagecoach Way Bill, Monday, January 14, 1839
From left to right, columns organize passenger names, quantity of seats, place of embarkation, destination, money paid, and fare breakdowns. The way bill tracks all pertinent information for one day's journey of a stagecoach operating between Keene, New Hampshire, and Boston.

Figure 1.12 Concord Coach "Ipswich," Built 1852
This stagecoach was designed for performance, with robust construction, a cab that could be sealed from the elements, and suspension engineered for increased comfort. A bench sits atop the rear storage area (left). The driver sat on the open bench at the front (right), from where they oversaw the horses.

Boston's first regular stagecoach service connected the city with Newburyport and Portsmouth, New Hampshire. It was launched by Bartholomew Stavers in the early 1760s. In May 1763 Stavers christened his service "The Portsmouth Flying Stagecoach" and carried six passengers per trip. The fares from Boston were nine shillings to Newburyport or thirteen shillings and six pence to Portsmouth. The Flying Stagecoach left Boston early on Friday mornings and took nearly two days to reach Portsmouth. Passengers lodged at an inn between the journey's two stages. Return trips departed Portsmouth on Tuesday mornings. Stavers maintained his coach and horses in Charlestown. His customers used the Charlestown Ferry to cross from Boston's North End to where they boarded the Flying Stagecoach in Charlestown.

Boston's first long distance stagecoach service, in place by 1788, operated between Boston and New Haven, Connecticut. The service was provided by two stagecoaches, each with a team of six horses. Fares on New England stagecoaches were typically collected by drivers, who completed waybills to record riders, destinations, and fares collected (Figure 1.11).

As stage travel increased in both frequency and distance, coaches became more reliable and comfortable, with increasingly robust construction, improved springs, upholstered interiors, and operable windows. Long distance stagecoaches, like ones that served Boston, New York City, Albany, and Buffalo, featured cabs of solid construction and windows and doors that sealed shut to keep out rain, snow, and mud (Figure 1.12).

Coach operations serving Boston grew significantly between 1790 and 1830. The 1796 *Boston Directory* mentioned: "The number of the different stages that run through the week from this town

is upward of 20, eight years ago there were only three." Of the two dozen stages listed in the 1798 *Boston Directory*, two were dedicated to local travel within Boston, Dorchester, Cambridge, Roxbury, and Brookline. The balance connected Boston with cities and towns throughout Massachusetts, along with out of state points including Albany, Portsmouth, and Providence. The 1803 *Boston Directory* listed just over two dozen local and long distance stages serving Boston. Three years later, the number listed exceeded three dozen.

The War of 1812 brought marine traffic along the coast of the United States to a near standstill. Denied their historic sea routes, America turned to wheeled vehicles to move people and goods overland like never before. Correspondingly, the country's road network underwent unprecedented upgrading and expansion. Improved roads carried an ever-increasing number of stagecoaches, so much so that by the early 1820s many routes experienced a glut of service. In one local example, stage companies competed furiously to move people between Boston and Providence. Typical travel time was five hours each way. The average one-way fare was $3.00. During fierce price wars of the 1820s, competing stage companies offered virtually free travel by paying for their customers' meals and wine at inns along the way. Into the next decade, New England's improved road network and stage services continued to grow. By 1832, a stagecoach was in operation between Boston and New York City. The trip took forty-one hours and the fare was $11.00 each way, bruised knees free of charge.

A Bridge to Cambridge
When it established Boston in 1630, the Massachusetts Bay Company also resolved to create

"New Towne" (New Town), an intended new home for their colonial government. The colonists selected a site to the northwest of the Shawmut Peninsula, approximately three miles up the Charles River from Boston. New Town never replaced Boston as the seat of government; instead, it became a hub of higher education. By 1634 the General Court sanctioned the creation of the first institution of higher learning in Colonial America, provisionally named "New College." By 1638 the General Court decreed that New College be sited in New Town. Within two years, and after a local minister John Harvard who had attended college in Cambridge, England bequeathed his collection of books along with funds to New College, the school was renamed Harvard College and New Town had been renamed Cambridge. After the establishment of Harvard College, Massachusetts colonists worked to improve transportation connections between Boston and Cambridge.

Prior to 1793, there were two primary routes to travel between the Shawmut Peninsula and Harvard College. One was an indirect, multi-mile overland route. The other and more direct route incorporated a ferry across the Charles River, from Boston's West End to the Old Port section of Cambridge. The latter was linked to Harvard by local Cambridge roads. The ferry was forever replaced on November 23, 1793, when the West Boston Bridge opened to the public.

The West Boston Bridge completed a nearly straight line link between downtown Boston and Harvard College. It was constructed with private financing and under a public charter. The structure was forty feet wide and 3,400 feet long, including causeways and a central span supported by 180 piers. Within two years of opening, the $77,000 West Boston Bridge carried an eight person coach that ran twice daily between Boston and Cambridge. A printed view from the middle of the nineteenth century depicts foot traffic and horse-drawn vehicles crossing the bridge (Figure 1.13).

As it had done previously with the Charles River Bridge, the General Court designated the West Boston Bridge as a means to subsidize higher education, requiring proprietors of the West Boston Bridge to collect tolls and remit three hundred pounds of their income each year, for forty years, to Harvard College. By 1850, tolls charged for passage over the West Boston Bridge were one cent per person on foot, five cents for a one-horse vehicle, and ten cents for a two-horse vehicle. Tolls on the bridge were abolished at the end of January 1858.

The Omnibus

Two hundred years after Boston's establishment, in 1830, the city's population exceeded 60,000 persons for the first time. Outgrowing the limits of the Shawmut Peninsula, Bostonians had long been creating "new" land from tidal waters surrounding their city. Land reclamation was often achieved via "wharving," the process of erecting wharves or sinking ships, and then filling the gaps between them with earthen fill, rubble, and trash. As Boston's footprint and population continued to grow, the city's modes of transit evolved to carry more people, with increased frequency, and over longer distances. The 1832 *Boston Directory* listed ninety-nine stagecoach routes emanating from Boston. A fall 1836 stagecoach register listed a steam boat operating between Boston and Hingham every day

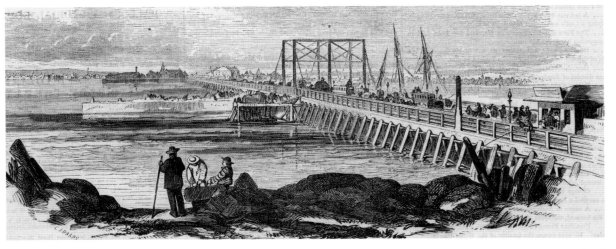

Figure 1.13 The West Boston Bridge, 1855
The West Boston Bridge, shown just after a major rebuilding, is jammed with foot traffic and horse-drawn vehicles. A toll house is shown at the far right. Approximately mid-way across the river is an operable draw, marked by tall structures. The draw opened to allow vessels to pass along the Charles River. The West Boston Bridge was in use from 1793 until 1906.

except Sunday. The ferry to Hingham departed Boston's North End at 9:30 a.m., 1:00 p.m., and 4:30 p.m. *Phelps's Traveller's Guide Through the United States* for 1850 listed long distance stages departing Boston for New Bedford, Cape Cod Light, Newport (RI), Keene (NH), Dover (NH), Portsmouth (NH), Albany (NY), and Saratoga Sprints (NY). Each made at least one stop in a Boston neighborhood or town contiguous with the city. *Phelps's* guide noted the Middlesex Canal as a twenty-seven mile link between Charlestown and Lowell.

On the streets of Boston, coach companies added more stages to accommodate more people, but because a coach was a vehicle with a capacity limited by design they could not operate larger coaches. The width of a coach was limited by the strength of its axles and what could pass along narrow and crowded city streets. A typical coach serving Boston at the start of the nineteenth century carried no more than six or eight people within the cab. As coach travel became more popular, coach companies sought to increase the number of passengers they could carry using a single team of horses. Since they were unable to build enormous coaches, which would be subject to snapped axles or becoming wedged in a narrow street, they brought a new vehicle to the streets of Boston—the omnibus.

Omnibus means "all-carrying-vehicle." The first American omnibuses were constructed in the early nineteenth century. Designs of the vehicles were based on those of horse-drawn vehicles which operated in the streets of Paris as early as the 1660s. Like a coach, an omnibus was composed of a passenger cab mounted onto axles with wheels and was pulled by one or more horses (Figure 1.14). The salient difference between a coach and an omnibus was the configuration of the cab. Whereas a coach cab had two doors, one on each side, an omnibus cab had one door, centered at its rear and aligned with the cab's center aisle (Figure 1.15). A typical omnibus seated a dozen passengers, more than double the capacity of a typical coach. Omnibus passengers sat on open benches that bracketed the cab's aisle and wrapped two to three sides of the cab's interior. Additional riders could stand or stoop between the benches. An omnibus driver sat on a bench high upon the front of the cab. From his perch he controlled the horses and hand brake. Behind the driver, baggage was transported on the roof of the cab.

The single rear door and center-aisle configuration of omnibuses allowed the vehicles to be constructed and operated with lengths and capacities greater than those of coaches. Despite being longer than coaches, omnibuses were not significantly wider than stages. This made standard omnibuses essentially as operable as coaches along Boston's nineteenth century streets.

Massive omnibuses, called barges, were the length of two or more standard omnibuses. Barges were capable of transporting dozens of passengers

Figure 1.15 Stephenson Omnibus, Built Circa 1865

A classic omnibus features drop-down windows for ventilation, benches along both sides of the cab interior, and painted landscapes adorning the interior above each window. The exterior is signed "Stevens House," a resort in Vermont that operated the vehicle. The vehicle was produced by the "Henry Ford of omnibus manufacturers," John Stephenson of New York City.

Figure 1.16 Roxbury Coaches Metal Ticket, 1837

Figure 1.17 Maverick Coach Metal Ticket, 1837

at a time. Due to their size, barges were typically relegated to use beyond narrow city streets or for special occasions. They often served resort locations or were chartered by large groups. The 1881 *Stranger's Guide to Boston* stated: "Barges leave Bowdoin Square to connect with all the harbor and excursion boats…on Atlantic Avenue."

The English and the French brought regular omnibus service to European cities in the 1820s. At the beginning of the 1830s, and after debuting the prototype omnibus "Accommodation" along Manhattan's Broadway, in 1829, Abraham Brower deployed additional omnibuses in New York City. The first omnibus in regular operation in Boston was most likely the "Governor Brooks." As early as 1833, the vehicle served a line started by Brooks Bowman in 1826. Making use of Washington Street and Boston Neck, the Governor Brooks travelled between Roxbury and the Winnisimmet Ferry landing in Boston's North End. The vehicle was drawn by four horses and scheduled to make each round-trip in two and a half hours.

One of Boston's earliest omnibus operations was established by Horace King, who took over Bowman's hourly coach line that had run between Boston and Roxbury since 1826. King added two omnibuses to the line by 1832. Soon thereafter, King consolidated omnibus lines in Boston into what became known as "King's Lines." As early as 1834, the first regular omnibus service between Boston and Cambridge was up and running. The omnibuses

soon ran hourly, with a one-way fare of ten cents. Ridership grew on the line and omnibuses soon departed on the half hour. The 1841 *Boston Almanac* listed omnibuses running hourly, from 8:00 a.m. to 8:00 p.m., between Brattle Street in Boston and Harvard Square in Cambridge, and half hourly, from 7:30 a.m. to 8:00 p.m., between Boston, Cambridge, and Cambridgeport.

Omnibuses operated by Hawthorne's Lines served the depots of the Boston & Lowell, Eastern, and Fitchburg Railroads. The fare was four cents. Hawthorne's Lines were started by Jacob H. Hawthorne, who, in 1851, took over an existing line. Hawthorne expanded the service to traverse Boston Neck, serve the steam railroad depots along Causeway Street, and access Charlestown via the Warren Bridge. After the Charles River Bridge, the Warren Bridge was the second span to link Boston with Charlestown. It opened to the public on December 25, 1828 alongside the older 1786-built structure.

In 1837, to commemorate the opening of its newest line, Roxbury Coaches sold metal tickets to paying riders. Upon boarding a Roxbury Coaches vehicle, a patron surrendered their "token," in lieu of cash, to the driver. Resembling a small coin, the metal ticket displayed "Roxbury Coaches" on one face and "New Line 1837" on the other (Figure 1.16). Maverick Coaches of East Boston issued its own metal ticket in 1837 (Figure 1.17). The Maverick Coaches and Roxbury Coaches metal tickets are the earliest metal tokens issued for travel on public transportation in Boston.

Before 1851, typical omnibus fares were fifteen cents for travel between Boston and Cambridge, and eighteen and three-quarter cents for travel between Boston and Medford. With one omnibus a transit company was able to collect more fare revenue than was possible with a single, smaller coach. The additional revenue generated by omnibuses allowed coach companies to replace coaches with omnibuses, purchase new omnibuses, and eventually phase out coaches altogether.

As operators replaced or augmented coaches with omnibuses, new omnibus companies were formed, and new routes established. The 1844 *Boston Almanac* listed eighteen omnibus routes radiating from Boston to points as far south as Weymouth, as far north as Woburn, and as far west as Newton Upper Falls (Figure 1.18). Nearly a decade later, the 1853 *Boston Almanac* listed no fewer than thirty omnibus routes, with many exclusively servicing destinations within Boston's city limits (Figure 1.19). Dearborn's *Boston Notions* recorded omnibuses carrying 1.1 million passengers across Boston, Cambridge, Charlestown, and Roxbury in 1847. In that same year, public carriages transported approximately 125,200 people, or just over eleven percent of the riding public.

Contrasting with stagecoaches, which typically operated between established terminals, did not regularly make unscheduled intermediate stops, and often required advance reservations, omnibuses served multiple stops along a route and picked up passengers on demand. In Boston, Horace King operated smaller capacity omnibuses making many stops, in coordination with larger capacity omnibuses making limited stops, all along the same route. The use of metal tickets, which sped up fare collection and boarding, made multiple, local stops more feasible. With the omnibus, three core aspects of modern public transportation arrived in Boston: tokens for transit, center-aisle transit vehicles, and coordinated local and express service.

At the beginning of the 1850s, the omnibus was the dominant mode of local, in-street public transportation in Boston. Views published in *Gleason's Pictorial Drawing-Room Companion* at the time depict horse-drawn carriages, coaches, and omnibuses passing along Tremont Street, between Boston Common and Court Street (Figure 1.20 and Figure 1.21).

Bringing Steam Railroads to Boston

At the beginning of the nineteenth century, the industrial revolution sparked to life in Massachusetts. Mechanized manufacturing, initially powered by moving water, and later by steam, propagated throughout the Commonwealth. Towns located at natural river falls, including Waltham, Lowell, Lawrence, and Worcester, became new centers of industrial production; Boston lost its seat as the exclusive center of manufacturing in New England. Across Massachusetts, baggage wagons, stagecoaches, canal boats, and ships transported raw materials, manufactured goods, and people between new and established centers of commerce. Stagecoaches regularly travelled 100 miles in eighteen hours. Baggage wagons moved four to five tons the same distance. Movement along the Middlesex Canal, which linked Boston with Lowell, took twelve hours. The atmosphere of unprecedented industrialization and need for improved connectivity between factory and worker, between towns new and old, and between markets and suppliers was primed for a new mode of transportation, the steam railroad.

During the 1820s, in America and the United Kingdom experiments with horses drawing cars along metal rails proved that goods and people could be moved longer distances, in less time, and with less effort than with baggage wagons, stagecoaches, or canal boats. Even with the iron horse on Boston's horizon, the Commonwealth still thought canals could be the future of transportation for Massachusetts. In early 1825, the General Court established a commission to study the design and construction of a canal from Boston Harbor to New York's Hudson River.

The canal commission appeared on the heels of recent canal openings in the American northeast. Locally, the twenty-seven mile long Middlesex Canal opened in 1803. With twenty locks, the thirty-foot-wide canal facilitated the movement of goods and people between the mills of Lowell and the port of Boston. The Erie Canal spanned New York State and opened in 1825, the same year the Massachusetts Canal Commission was established. The Erie Canal, in combination with the Hudson River on one end and the Great Lakes on the other, connected the interior of North America to the port of New York City. The Erie Canal provided for the nation what the Middlesex Canal did for trade and transportation in the eastern portion of Massachusetts.

The Commonwealth's canal commission released a report on November 11, 1826, articulating the

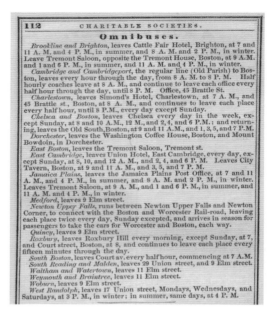

Figure 1.18 Omnibus Listings in the 1844
Boston Almanac Omnibus routes serving Greater Boston are organized by destination.

Figure 1.19 Omnibus Listings in the 1853 *Boston Almanac* As early as 1850, reflecting the increasing number of omnibuses operating in Boston, the listing of omnibus lines in the *Boston Almanac* was revised from a long list of destinations and departing times (Figure 1.18) to a simplified list of places served accompanied by departure locations.

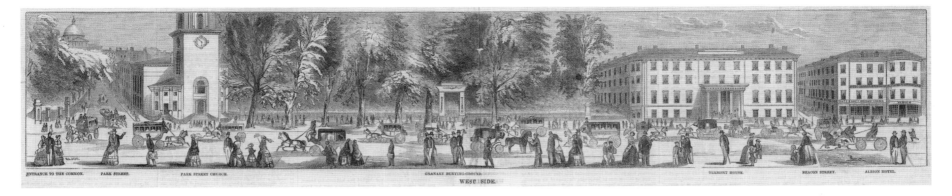

Figure 1.20 West Side of Tremont Street, Early 1850s

Horse-drawn carriages, coaches, and omnibuses travel between Boston Common (far left) and Scollay Square (out of view far right). Omnibuses, distinguishable from coaches by their lack of side doors, are signed for Jamaica Plain and Brookline. By the end of the 1850s, tracks for horse railroads would appear along this stretch of Tremont Street. Figure 1.21 shows the opposite side of the street.

Figure 1.21 East Side of Tremont Street, Early 1850s

Private coaches, public coaches, and omnibuses travel along Tremont Street past the Boston Museum (left), King's Chapel (middle), and Tremont Temple (right). The publisher of this and an opposing view (Figure 1.20) of Tremont Street was housed in "Gleason's Publishing Hall" (right).

massive engineering and construction efforts that a trans-Massachusetts Canal would require. Rapid developments in railroad technology, in combination with predicted outlandish costs and distinct technical challenges (the canal would have required the engineering and construction of some 200 canal locks, some to be located on the slopes of the Berkshire Hills), caused support for a trans-Massachusetts canal to evaporate.

Within four months of completion of the canal report, on March 2, 1827, the General Court established a Board of Commissioners of Internal Improvements to explore the feasibility of constructing a railroad, in lieu of a canal, between Boston and Albany. Water-filled ditches were out and steel rails were in. The board was tasked with exploring not only a railroad running west from Boston to Albany, but also a railroad linking Boston with Providence. After less than a year of study, in January 1828 the commissioners completed a report for a proposed railroad between Boston and Providence. The report featured a fold-out survey map depicting two proposed routes (Figure 1.22).

A few months after the release of the 1828 report, the General Court appointed a nine-person Board of Directors of Internal Improvements. The Directors released a final report on the railroad from Boston to Albany on January 16, 1829. The "Report of the Board of Directors of the State of Massachusetts on the Practicability and Expediency of a Rail-Road from Boston to the Hudson River, and from Boston to Providence" was accompanied by a pair of maps depicting proposed routes for a railroad from Boston to Albany. The first map covered the eastern half of the route, from Boston to Springfield (Figure 1.23). The second map covered the Springfield to Albany section. The 1828 and 1829 reports referenced "railroad mania" that gripped England around 1825. As the 1820s became the 1830s, railroad mania gripped Massachusetts.

Boston Mayor Harrison Gray Otis, spoke during his January 5, 1829 inaugural address to the Boston City Council:

> Another object, however, is lately brought into view by the spirit of the age we live in, the importance of which, if within reach of the city, it would not be easy to exaggerate—a communication with the country by railway.

The mayor went on to articulate how the continued economic prosperity of cities in Massachusetts,

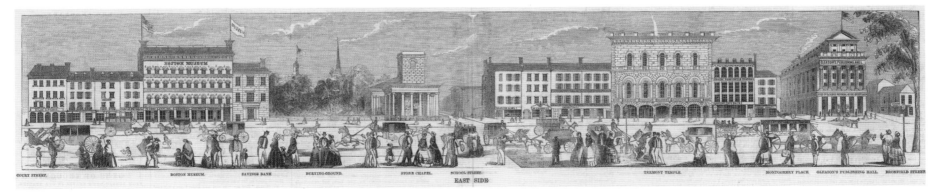

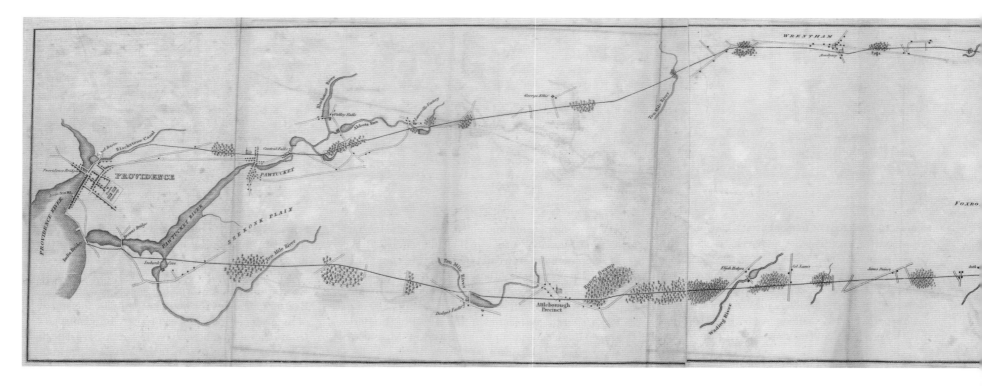

Figure 1.22 Boston to Providence Railroad Survey, 1828

Published by the state-appointed Board of Commissioners of Internal Improvement, a map depicts two possible routes for a railroad connecting Boston (far right) with Providence, Rhode Island (far left). A western route runs along the top of the map. An eastern route runs along the bottom of the map. This is the earliest "topographic strip map . . . showing a railroad survey" in the Library of Congress' map collections.

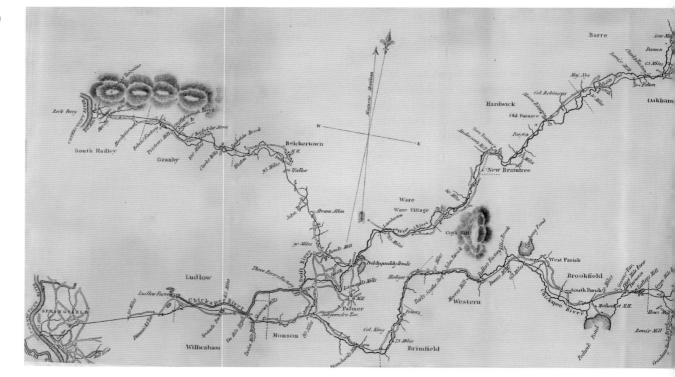

Figure 1.23 Boston to Albany Railroad Survey, 1828

A portion of a survey map shows the eastern sections of proposed routes for a railroad connecting Boston (right) and Albany, New York. On the top half of the drawing, a northern route runs through Watertown and Sudbury. On the lower portion, a southern route runs via Natick and Worcester.

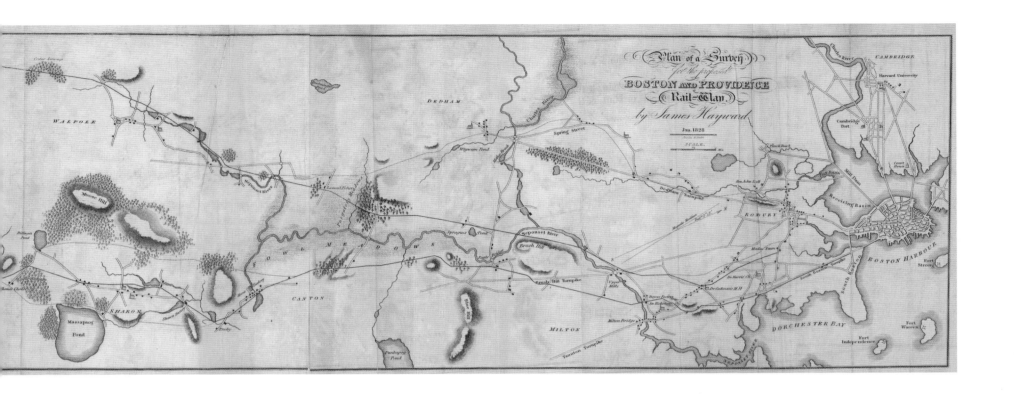

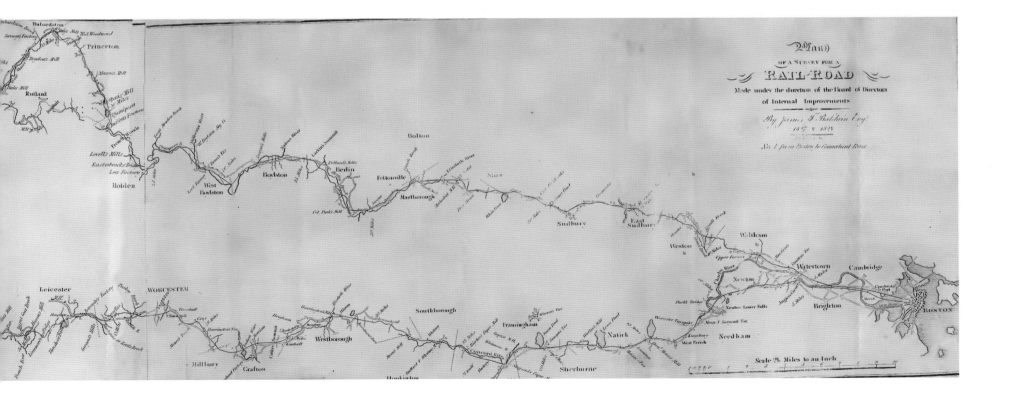

especially Boston, might be diminished without "intercommunication with each other and with our sister states by methods which they adopt, or we shall be left insulated." Otis continued:

> The question will arise, and we must prepare to meet it, not whether railroads are subjects of lucrative speculation, but whether they be not indispensable to save this state and city from insignificance and decay.

The mayor's heralding of railroads as a necessity for the economic health and prosperity of Boston was supported by the city's citizens. Bostonians overwhelmingly supported (3,000 votes in favor versus 60 opposed) two public ballot questions in 1829 resolving that Massachusetts should fund and construct two railroads: one between Boston and the Hudson River near Albany; and another, between Boston and the Pawtucket River near Providence. Via connections with boats traveling the Hudson River at Albany, the western railroad would connect Boston with the Erie Canal, and by extension, the interior of North America. The southern railroad would strengthen Boston's connection with the growing manufacturing hubs at Pawtucket and Providence in Rhode Island, allowing Boston to compete directly with the manufacturing hub of Worcester, which, since 1828, had been connected directly to the port of Providence by the Blackstone Canal.

The Granite Railway

Three years before the release of the final report of the Directors of Internal Improvements, in 1826, the General Court granted a charter to the Granite Railway Company. The Granite Railway, the Commonwealth's first railroad, was established approximately eight miles south of the Massachusetts State House, in the city of Quincy. The Granite Railway Company was created to quarry granite for the Bunker Hill Monument in Charlestown. Along its Granite Railway, the company transported stone from its Quincy quarries to the Neponset River, approximately three miles away. At the river, the stone was loaded onto boats for transport to Charlestown. Later, Quincy granite was exported to points all along the eastern seaboard.

The Commonwealth granted the Granite Railway Company the right to take private property in order to secure new rights-of-way for its trackage. This right was granted to subsequent railroad companies

charted by Massachusetts and is the mechanism that allowed hundreds of miles of new roads of rail to crisscross the state. The charter of the Granite Railway Company featured language requiring the company to allow the public to transport their own stone, should they so wish, via the Granite Railway. The concept that railroads should be treated like turnpikes or other rights-of-way created from state-sanctioned condemnation of private property and that anyone should be allowed to operate along privately constructed rails was codified in the Commonwealth's early railroad charters, including that of the Boston & Lowell Railroad (Boston & Lowell). But the logistical nightmare of unscheduled and uncoordinated vehicles utilizing a single track nullified the practical operation of public vehicles on private railroads. Railroad companies were those best suited to control operations of vehicles and trains on their lines.

The Granite Railway was an industrial operation, never providing passenger service or operating far beyond the Quincy city limits. The Granite Railway commenced operations with horses pulling loads (Figure 1.24) on October 7, 1826. Four years later, the company added a branch line to serve a new quarry. The branch ran up a steep slope which

Figure 1.24 Envisioning The Granite Railway, 1883
A woodcut print depicts a primitive train of Granite Railway cars pulled by a pair of horses. Each car supports blocks of granite suspended beneath their axles.

Figure 1.25 The Granite Railway Incline Restored, 1934
At the top of the incline, primitive railroad cars were loaded with granite. The cars were then lowered down the "tracks" under the control of a central cable. The tracks, more like guideways, were supported by granite cross-ties. The paved area and improved guideways shown post-date the initial operation of the railway.

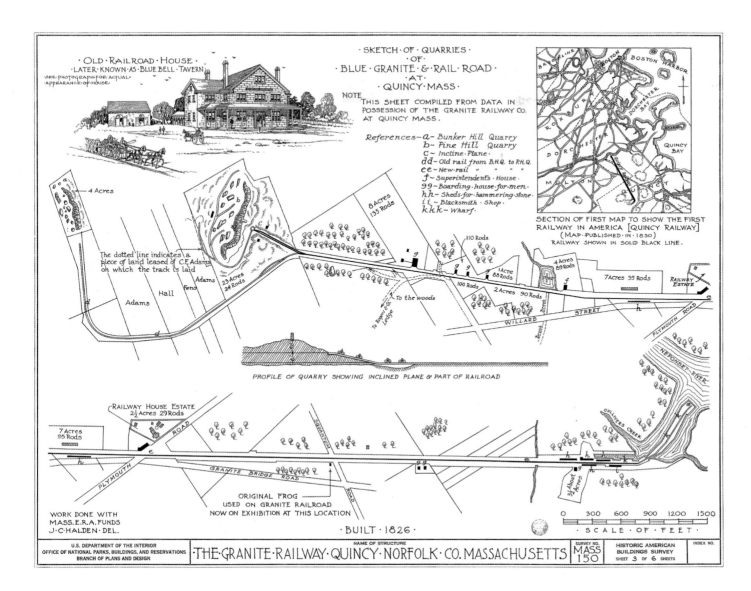

Figure 1.26 The Granite Railway in Quincy

Prepared in 1934 by the Historic American Building Survey, a sheet of drawings details the route and location in relation to Boston (inset map at top right), of the Granite Railway in Quincy. The railway facilitated the movement of granite from Bunker Hill Quarry (left; labeled "a") to a wharf on the Neponset River (bottom right; labeled "k").

became known as "the incline" (Figure 1.25). On the incline, cars loaded with granite were lowered down from a hilltop quarry; empty cars were raised up with the assistance of a steam-powered cable mechanism. The cars travelled along iron guideways anchored to granite sleepers on the ground. Through its use of the incline, the Granite Railway Company validated that the operation of cars along fixed metal rails was a viable means to move massive loads, even up a steep grade.

The incline in Quincy was an improved version of what were most likely America's first two railroad-like operations, both of which appeared in Boston. In *A History of Travel in America*, Seymour Dunbar mentioned an inclined plane operated on the slope of Beacon Hill in 1795. The plane featured tracks of

wooden rails, set two feet apart, upon which cars descended loaded from a kiln and ascended empty with an assist from a cable hoist system. Dunbar also described "[a] short railway built in Boston by Silas Whitney near the location of the previous inclined plane...intended to facilitate the movement of horse-drawn wagons." The two operations were not used to transport paying passengers.

The Historic American Building Survey (HABS) prepared drawings to memorialize Quincy's Granite Railway in 1934 (Figure 1.26). The Granite Railway was the subject of a HABS survey because of the pioneering engineering of Gridley Bryant, the genius behind the design and construction of the project. Per Bryant's designs, the initial segments of track consisted of three inch wide by one quarter inch thick strap iron set upon three inch wide wood rails. The rails were secured to granite cross ties, each measuring nearly one foot square by seven and a half feet in length. Spaced approximately eight feet apart, the cross ties sat upon two continuous stone walls, each two feet wide and two feet deep. The walls were set into trenches deep enough to limit movement from ground freeze and thaw cycles. Bryant designed a railroad turntable for turning rail cars and track switches for aligning trains onto one of two diverging tracks. Bryant did not patent his engineering solutions. After being developed at the Granite Railway, turntables and switches were adopted by other railroads and became standard railroad technology.

Four years after the 1826 opening of the Granite Railway, American railroads began to carry people in addition to materials and goods. The Baltimore & Ohio Railroad opened its first segment of track, along which it operated one of America's first railed passenger service in early 1830. A single car with the capacity of a few dozen passengers was pulled along rails by a horse at approximately fifteen miles per hour.

Some fifty years after its opening, a defunct Granite Railway was purchased by the Old Colony Railroad (Old Colony). Much of the right-of-way of the Quincy operation was recycled by the Old Colony into its Granite Branch, off its line from Boston to Plymouth. Much later, the incline of the Granite Railway, along with quarries it once served, were purchased by the Metropolitan District Commission (now the Massachusetts Department of Conservation and Recreation) in 1985. The incline remains a monument to primitive yet influential railroading in America.

Roads of Rail for Boston

In February 1825, the first steam locomotive to operate along metal rails in America traversed an experimental track in Hoboken, New Jersey. The vehicle was built by John Stevens, an American, who on February 6, 1815 received America's first charter for a railroad. The operations in Hoboken were just the beginning for steam railroading.

In the late 1820s and early 1830s, American steam railroad companies, mostly located in New York and the mid-Atlantic states, experimented with steam locomotives as replacements for horses pulling cars along rails. At the same time, complimenting experiments in England lead to a breakthrough. In October 1829, the newly-opened Liverpool &

Manchester Railway held a competition for steam locomotive designers. The prize was the right to produce locomotives for the company. George Stephenson's "Rocket," the only entry to successfully complete what became know as "The Rainhill Trials," pulled a train of thirteen tons at an average speed of fifteen miles per hour. Running solo, the steam-powered locomotive reached top speeds of approximately thirty-five miles per hour. The Rocket proved the viability of a steam locomotive in railroad operation.

Inspired by the success of Stephenson's Rocket, both Europeans and Americans began to construct steam locomotives and railroads in earnest. Thousands of miles of new railroads were constructed by private companies throughout the United States during the 1830s, 1840s, and 1850s. Boston became the hub of an unprecedented network of steam railroad lines during that time. Under the heading "Railroads Diverging from Boston," the 1846 *Boston Almanac* listed one dozen steam railroads operating within Massachusetts, with seven serving Boston directly. It proclaimed: "The whole state is brought so near within our reach that it may be, without exaggeration, termed the suburbs of the city."

Boston's second railroad to serve paying passengers was the Boston & Lowell, opened to the public in May 1835 with infrastructure similar to that of the Quincy Railway; sunken stone walls supported granite ties, which, in turn, supported iron rails. The Boston & Lowell's tracks were distinctly different from those of the Granite Railway with their primitive construction. Instead of strap iron supported by wood, the Boston & Lowell's rails were solid iron. The tracks had a "fish-belly" profile, giving them enough integrity to span between each tie and support the load of a train. After realizing that the stone walls and granite tie system was over engineered against ground movement, and that early trains were being damaged by the unforgivably rigid track system, the Boston & Lowell replaced its stone walls and sleepers with crushed stone ballast and wood ties. The fish-belly tracks were spiked to the wood ties. In time, iron tracks gave way to steel, which, along with wooden ties and crushed stone ballast, became standard railroad technology.

Early Steam Railroad Coaches

In its most basic form, a steam railroad train consisted of a connected lineup of steam-powered locomotive, tender, and one or more cars for transporting people or goods. Wheels of the locomotive,

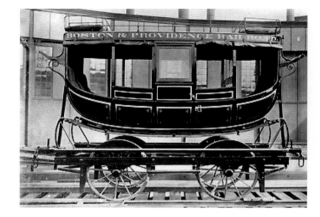

Figure 1.27 Early Steam Railroad Coach, Constructed 1833
A passenger coach built and used by the Boston & Providence Railroad stands on display at the World's Colombian Exposition in Chicago in 1893.

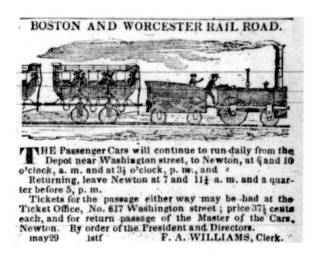

Figure 1.28 Boston & Worcester Railroad Ad, 1834
Printed in the May 29, 1834 edition of the *Boston Courier*, an advertisement depicts a train consisting of a primitive steam locomotive (right), a tender (middle), and stagecoach-type passengers coaches (left).

Figure 1.29 Boston & Maine Railroad Print Ad, 1861

tender, and cars were flanged, allowing the wheels to follow the inside of the rails and keep the train on the tracks. The car in which passengers rode was a coach, a name borrowed directly from stagecoaches. Some of the earliest steam railroad coaches were actual stagecoach cabs installed upon a framework and supported by wheels flanged for railroad operation.

The first coaches built new for steam railroad use were slightly larger versions of stagecoach cabs, with side doors and rounded bottoms at the front and back (Figure 1.27). The Boston & Lowell's earliest coaches each had three passenger compartments, each accessed via doors installed on the sides of the car (Figure 1.28). Early railroad coaches were not waterproofed nor well-ventilated. Windows did not always open nor always close. Boston's earliest steam railroad coaches retained their original stagecoach handbrakes and driver's seats. From the driver's seat, a brakeman manually operated the hand brake for that car.

The unluckiest passengers in early steam railroad coaches were subject to a special piece of hell known as a "snake's head." Primitive iron rails were prone to snapping under the weight of early trains. In rare cases, a broken rail coiled upwards, directly into the bottom of a moving coach. As the train continued to move, the iron rail was drawn through the floor of the coach, often impaling or otherwise injuring passengers. Until the train stopped or the rail snapped again, the broken rail continued to coil up into the coach like a snake with a devastating bite.

Early railroad coaches lacked robust springs and were linked to other cars in a train with primitive couplers. Jerky movements were the norm. Early coupler mechanisms lacked the "give" provided by today's automatic couplers when a train starts or stops and slack is taken up or distributed throughout a train. A ride in an early steam railroad coach was not significantly more comfortable than that in a stagecoach, but the experience was an improvement. In *Steelways of New England*, Alvin F. Harlow recalled:

> [Stagecoaches] rocking crazily behind galloping horses were upset in the night by fallen trees or washouts, crashed through flimsy bridges, were occasionally wrecked by half-drunken drivers, locked wheels with other coaches while racing and when to smash, or their brakes failed on steep grades and they piled up in the ditch; always with casualties, not infrequently with lost of life. It was asserted that upon the smooth, almost level track of a railroad, this sort of thing would never happen.

The form of steam railroad coaches evolved during the 1840s and 1850s, away from that of stagecoaches and to that of a simple box, similar in proportions to a shoe box (Figure 1.29 and Figure 1.30). A typical "box coach" of the time had a length of thirty to forty feet, a width of eight feet, and an internal clearance for passengers of approximately six-and-a-half feet.

Figure 1.30 Eastern Railroad Train, November 2, 1848
A train composed of a box coach (left), tender (middle), and locomotive (right) of the Eastern Railroad pauses to accept passengers at Salem Depot. The locomotive "Sagamore" sports a stack intended to reduce the amount of fire-starting cinders released as the train travelled along its track.

By the end of the 1850s, steam railroad coaches were outfitted with basic conveniences (Figure 1.31). Initially, in-coach heating was provided by a coal or wood stove, an imperfect system. The stove overheated the customers near it and did little to warm the riders at the opposite end of the car. Interior lighting was at first provided by candles, and later, whale oil lamps. Kerosene lamps replaced whale oil lamps before electric lights became the norm.

Early box coaches featured wooden benches, some without supports for riders' backs. Seating evolved to become more comfortable, with backrests, upholstery, and a convenient arrangement, arranged on two sides of a center aisle. Box coaches featured doors at their extreme ends. Just as center-aisle design allowed omnibuses to carry more passengers than stagecoaches, the configuration of box coaches allowed each to carry more passengers than stagecoach-type railroad coaches.

Early Steam Railroad Locomotives

A steam locomotive derives its power for propulsion from the burning of wood or coal inside of a fire box, which, in turn, converts water to steam within a boiler. Controlled release of pressurized steam from the boiler moves a piston and turns the locomotive's driving wheels, known as drivers. The earliest and mostly experimental locomotives consisted of a fire box, a boiler, drive gears, and flanged wheels supported by a chassis (Figure 1.32). Once steam locomotives began to be deployed for more than a

few miles, they required more space for fuel and water. A tender, towed immediately behind a steam locomotive, contained water for the boiler and fuel for the firebox.

A nineteenth century steam train required a team of people to operate. The engineer controlled the speed and direction (forward or reverse) of the locomotive. A fireman monitored the transfer of fuels into the firebox and water into the boiler. Together, the engineer and fireman orchestrated the operation of all locomotive systems. During the first decades of steam railroad operations, the engineer and fireman worked on platforms at the back of the locomotive and front of the tender. They had no practical protection from the elements, nor the smoke, steam, and cinders released by the locomotive.

A brakeman, or brakemen, operated hand brakes on each car of early trains. A brakeman's job required great balance and concentration, as it required the brakeman to move from car top to car top to individually operate each car's hand brake. Developments in hand-brake technology, including the Hodge Hand Brake and Stevens Brake of 1849 and 1851, respectively, improved the efficiency of manual breaking.

In time, brakemen disappeared from the roofs of trains. Westinghouse's air brake was patented in 1869. It was improved upon in 1871 by the vacuum brake. Hand brakes were eventually replaced by automatic braking systems controlled by the engineer, who administered the addition or removal of

Figure 1.32 Boston Locomotive Works Ad, 1852
The Boston Locomotive Works constructed steam locomotives under various corporate names from 1839 to 1889. The company fabricated their machines in Boston's South End, on a site between Harrison Avenue and Albany Street.

Figure 1.33 Hinkley & Williams Works Ad, 1860
A locomotive with a semi-enclosed compartment for the engineer and fireman is joined with its tender.

pressurized air to control the breaking of an entire train.

The role of train conductor originated during the nineteenth century. The conductor was the captain of their train, and as such, responsible for the freight and passengers being transported. Conductors often served as an onboard ticket agent or railroad company customer service representative.

In 1834 the Boston & Lowell imported its first steam locomotive, designed and manufactured in England by George Stephenson, of "Rocket" fame. The apparatus was shipped across the Atlantic to the Port of Boston. There, it was disassembled and transported to Lowell via the Middlesex Canal. The locomotive, named "Stephenson" in honor of its designer, first pulled a train of fare-paying customers from Lowell to Boston on June 24, 1835. On that day, regular service commenced with two morning departures from Lowell and two afternoon departures from Boston. Commuter rail had arrived in Boston, at least for the residents of Lowell. By fall 1836, the Boston & Lowell was operating five daily departures from Lowell.

By the 1850s, typical steam locomotives were manufactured with protective enclosures for the engineer and fireman (Figure 1.33). While form still followed function in locomotive design, exteriors of locomotives of the 1850s–70s were commonly accented with polished metal fixtures and finely detailed with painting and lettering (Figure 1.34). Engineers took pride in maintaining the appearance and performance of such locomotives. For over a quarter century, Boston's steam locomotives were named after people and places associated with the railroad along which they operated. By

the late nineteenth century, most locomotives were simply numbered, since organizing massive fleets of vehicles was easier with numbers.

The Boston & Worcester Railroad

The first company to provide steam railroad passenger service in Boston was the Boston & Worcester Railroad (Boston & Worcester), chartered on June 23, 1831. In the following year, the Boston & Worcester began constructing a main line between its namesake cities. The Boston & Worcester built westward from Boston. As it completed a portion of the line, the railroad opened service along that segment. The first steam locomotive used in Boston & Worcester passenger service was named Meteor.

The Boston & Worcester operated test trains carrying passengers from Boston on April 7 and 8, 1834. Freshly installed iron rails broke repeatedly, delaying the second day's train. After repairing its rails, the Boston & Worcester ran a six car excursion train carrying a score of passengers on April 15. A day later, the company launched regular service between Boston and West Newton. Two locomotives were dispatched, with each pulling a train. Boston's newspapers recorded approximately 120 passengers traveling in six cars over the nine mile route in just under a half an hour. The average speed of the train was approximately twenty miles per hour. The fare was thirty-seven and a half cents. Newspaper advertisements for the Boston & Worcester's nascent service appeared in the May 12, 1834 editions of Boston's *Daily Advertiser* and *Patriot*. The same advertisement appeared in the *Boston Courier* as early as May 29 (Figure 1.28). By September 21,

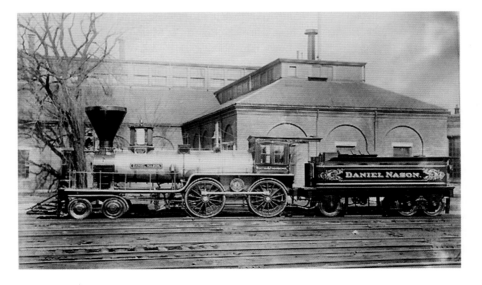

Figure 1.34 Locomotive "Daniel Nason," Circa 1860
A typical example of a mid-nineteenth century American steam locomotive and tender, the Daniel Nason was built and used by the Boston & Providence. An 1836 stage register listed Daniel Nason as the Master of Transportation for the Boston & Providence.

WORCESTER RAILROAD DEPOT.

Figure 1.35 Boston & Worcester's Boston Depot, 1855
A view published in a pictorial newspaper reveals the busy train hall of the Boston & Worcester's second Boston depot. A train of box-type coaches occupies one track (left), while, in the distance, a steam locomotive sits on the other (center).

the Boston & Worcester provided service between Boston and Hopkinton, where, on the previous day, the company held a celebration. In front of two hundred VIP passengers who detrained for a banquet, the Boston & Worcester paraded a train with a military band playing from atop the roofs of seven passenger coaches.

The Boston & Worcester was operating trains along its entire mainline by the end of June 1835. The company delayed formal opening ceremonies until the following month to coincide with Fourth of July celebrations. Trains made the forty-four mile trip between Boston and Worcester in approximately two and three-quarter hours, including time for intermediate stops. Initially, the railroad employed four steam locomotives and coaches. Each coach carried approximately two dozen passengers. By the end of 1835, the Boston & Worcester transported over 1,500 passengers a day.

The Boston & Worcester's second Boston passenger terminal opened on Beach Street on November 7, 1836. The terminal became a busy place, being the starting point for all rail journeys from Boston westward. Within a portion of the station opened alongside the initial segment in 1846, two tracks served platforms within a two-story train hall (Figure 1.35). The exterior of the depot resembled an extra-long New England church, complete with a peaked roof and wood-framed tower. (Figure 1.37). The fall 1836 *Badger & Porter's Stage Register* listed Boston & Worcester trains

departing from both Boston and Worcester at 7:00 a.m. and 3:00 p.m. Each pair of morning and afternoon trains met at Framingham. A ticket from Boston to Worcester cost $1.50.

Mapping Boston's Earliest Steam Railroads
Other steam railroad companies followed the Boston & Worcester, establishing service between Boston and surrounding communities. By the end of the 1830s, steam railroad lines radiated from Boston along the North Shore, into the Merrimack Valley, across the Worcester Hills, and into Rhode Island (Figure 1.38). By 1855, eight steam railroad companies provided service to and from Boston. These were the Boston & Maine, Eastern, Boston & Lowell, Fitchburg, Boston & Worcester, Boston & New York Central, Boston & Providence, and Old Colony Railroads. The main lines established by these eight railroads became the foundation of Boston's modern commuter rail network. Advertisements with schedules and fares for Boston's steam railroads regularly appeared in the *Boston Directory* (Figure 1.39).

More bridges were erected across the waters surrounding the Shawmut Peninsula in the first two decades of the nineteenth century than had been constructed in the preceding two centuries. The South Boston Bridge opened in July 1805. The 1,550 foot long span connected Boston Neck with South Boston. Craigie's Bridge (a.k.a. Canal Bridge)

Figure 1.36 Boston & Worcester Railroad Ticket
An undated paper ticket for travel in a second class car on the Boston & Worcester to Natick.

connected Boston's West End to Lechmere Point in East Cambridge in 1809. The Mill Dam (a.k.a. Western Avenue) opened on July 2, 1821. The Warren Bridge, opened in 1828, was the first toll-free bridge to link Boston with Charlestown. The Free Bridge, another toll-free span, crossed the Fort Point Channel and opened in December 1828.

In the 1830s, steam railroad companies constructed a plethora of bridges and causeways to bring their tracks and trains into Boston.

Figure 1.37 Boston & Worcester Railroad Print Ad, 1864

An advertisement from the 1864 *Boston Directory* depicts the Boston & Worcester's second Boston passenger terminal.

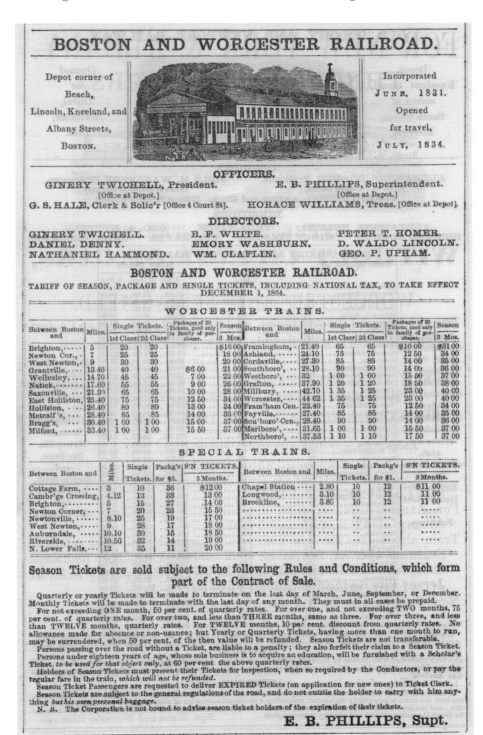

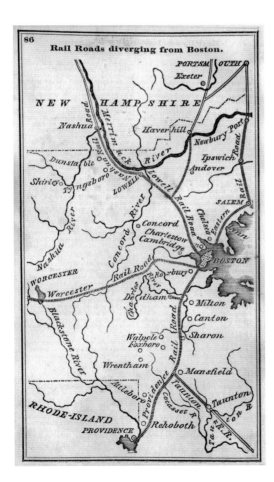

Figure 1.38 Mapping Boston's First Railroads, 1840

On a pocket-sized *Boston Almanac* map, lines of the Boston & Lowell, Boston & Worcester, and Boston & Providence Railroads extend from Boston Proper. From East Boston, the Eastern Railroad runs northward.

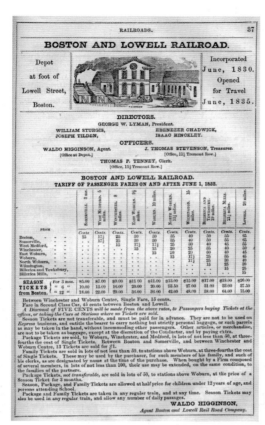

Figure 1.39 (Left) Steam Railroad Company Print Ads, 1852
The 1852 *Boston Directory* contained full page advertisements for each steam railroad serving Boston. A similar broadside, for the Boston & Worcester Railroad published in 1864, is shown in Figure 1.37.

Figure 1.40 (Opp.) Mapping Boston's Connections, 1842
Less than a decade after the first steam railroad arrived on the Shawmut Peninsula, a map shows Boston tied to the mainland by three steam railroad lines. The combination railroad line and harbor ferry of the "Eastern Railway" connects East Boston with the Shawmut Peninsula. The "Lowell Railway," parallel to Craigie's Bridge, extends from Cambridge into Boston. The causeways of the "Worcester Railway" and "Providence Railway" cross like an "X" in the middle of the Back Bay, near the "Mill Dam" causeway (now Beacon Street). Beyond steam railroad lines, multiple bridges and ferry lines link Boston with surrounding communities.

Charlestown

Winnisimmet Ferry

East Cambridge

Charles River Bridge

Warren Bridge

Craigie's Bridge

East Boston

West Boston Bridge

East Boston Ferry

Shawmut Peninsula

Mill Dam

Back Bay

Boston Neck

BOSTON

WITH

CHARLESTOWN AND ROXBURY.

SCALE.

POPULATION 85,000

Under the Superintendence of the Society for the Diffusion of Useful Knowledge.

Figure 1.41 Trains Crossing Boston's Back Bay, 1835
A Boston & Providence passenger train (foreground) travels across the "dizzy bridge" towards Boston, crowned by the dome of the Massachusetts State House (top center). A Boston & Worcester train (far left) heads away from the city. This view was engraved and published by John Barber one year after the Boston & Providence brought the first passenger train service to Boston.

The lines of two steam railroads, the Boston & Worcester and the Boston & Providence, crossed each other in the middle of the Back Bay (Figure 1.41). Along the Boston & Providence's narrow causeway was a short section of track supported by wood pilings known as the "dizzy bridge." At high tide, when the tidal flats on both sides of the causeway flooded, passengers in a train traversing the bridge felt like they were travelling across the surface of the water. The combination of the swaying motion of early coaches, deflections of iron rails as the train moved over the bridge, and a sublime view across an overwhelming expanse of water led to passengers experiencing dizziness.

By the early 1840s, the Shawmut Peninsula was connected to the mainland via three railroad viaducts, six road bridges and causeways, multiple ferry lines, and streets on a widened Boston Neck (Figure 1.40). The Neck had been widened through wharving and landfill projects to accommodate new streets and urban development, including an 1832 extension of Tremont Street running parallel to Washington Street. The 1840s saw maps and guides published to represent Greater Boston's growing steam railroad network. A railroad map of New England, published nine years after the 1840 *Boston Almanac* map, accompanied an 1849 edition of the *Pathfinder Railway Guide for The New England States*. On the 1849 map (Figure 1.42), Boston lies at the center of the densest part of the region's burgeoning railroad network. The *Pathfinder Railway Guide*, started by George K. Snow & Company of Boston, was first published in July 1849. Iterations and revised editions of *Pathfinder* guides, including *ABC Pathfinder*, *Baby Pathfinder*, and *Snow's Pathfinder*, were published into the twentieth century. Snow's

publications were indispensable guides and document the growth of America's railroad network (Figure 1.43).

J. H. Colton & Company's (Colton's) 1857 "Map of Boston and Adjacent Cities" (Figure 1.44) shows Boston fifteen years after the 1842 map. On Colton's map, sinuous steam railroad lines traverse waterways onto the Shawmut Peninsula. There, each terminates at a depot. While city plans like those by the SDUK and by Colton represented steam railroad lines in reasonable detail, the earliest maps produced by railroad companies themselves were often nothing more than line diagrams listing stations along a route, typically published to accompany schedules. However, by the end of the nineteenth century, steam railroads produced not only line maps but also elaborate and beautifully designed maps, often to accompany marketing brochures and promotional guide books (Figure 4.15).

In 1869, the same year that the golden spikes were driven in Utah to complete America's first transcontinental railroad, Massachusetts established its Board of Railroad Commissioners, the first entity created by the Commonwealth to be dedicated to the regulation of the state's burgeoning railroad industry. In its first annual report, published in 1870, the Railroad Commissioners mentioned: "Massachusetts is already, as compared with other parts of this continent, and even with Europe, not deficient in railroad facilities." The commissioners backed up their statement with a table that listed Massachusetts having one mile of railroad for every 5.47 square miles of territory, a density of track to land area higher than any state or country in the world at the time.

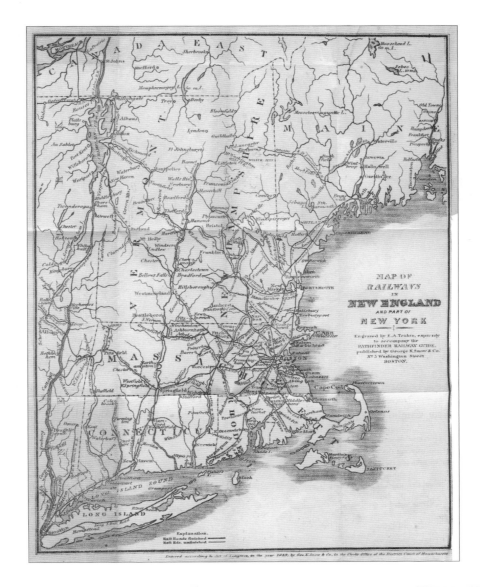

Figure 1.42 Pathfinder New England Railroad Map, 1849

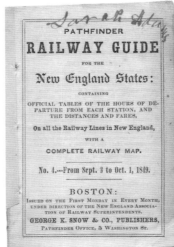
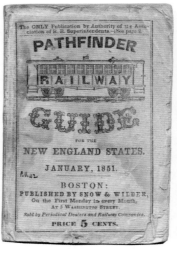

Figure 1.43 Pathfinder Guide Covers, 1849–58

The cover of the January 1851 *Pathfinder Railway Guide for the New England States* (middle) features an early, box-type passenger coach. The May 1858 *Snow's Pathfinder Railway Guide* (right) sports a classic steam locomotive of the 1850s.

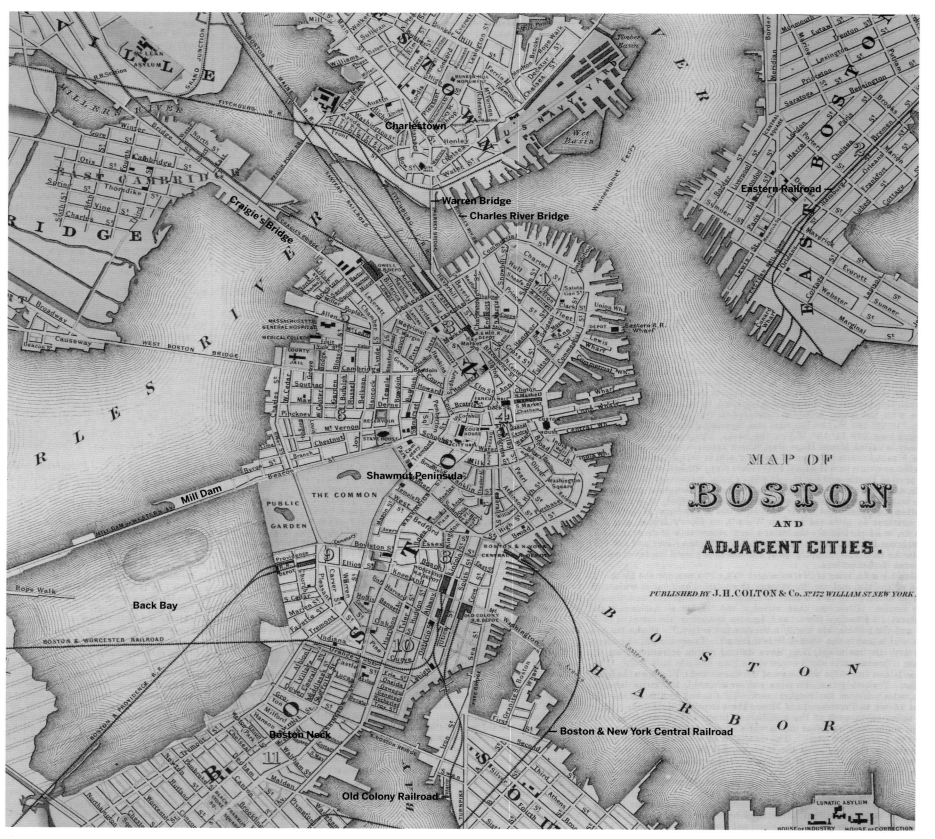

Charlestown

Warren Bridge

Charles River Bridge

Craigie's Bridge

Eastern Railroad

Mill Dam

Shawmut Peninsula

Back Bay

Boston Neck

Boston & New York Central Railroad

Old Colony Railroad

MAP OF

BOSTON

AND

ADJACENT CITIES.

PUBLISHED BY J.H.COLTON & Co. Nº172 WILLIAM Sᵗ NEW YORK.

Figure 1.44 Mapping Boston's Railroad Connections, 1857
From the north (top left) lines of the Boston & Lowell, Boston & Maine, and Fitchburg Railroads cross the Charles River into Boston and terminate around Causeway Street. From the west (left bottom), lines of the Boston & Worcester and Boston & Providence Railroads cross the Back Bay onto the Shawmut Peninsula. From the south (bottom center), lines of the Boston & New York Central and Old Colony Railroads cross South Bay and Fort Point Channel, respectively. From East Boston via Charlestown (top), the Eastern Railroad's line reaches Causeway Street, between the lines of the Boston & Lowell and Boston & Maine.

The East Boston Ferries

Before the 1830s, a decade that brought steam railroads to Boston, ferry service between the Shawmut Peninsula and East Boston was provided by independent boat owners and operators of the ferries to and from Winnisimmet. Nearly two centuries earlier, in 1637, the General Court approved Edward Bendall as operator of a ferry between Boston and Noddle's Island. Two hundred years later, regular and dedicated ferry service between Boston and Noddle's Island, by then known as East Boston, came into being.

Sumner's *History of East Boston* recorded the East Boston Ferry Company starting regular trips between Boston and East Boston in 1835. The ferry landing in East Boston was located on land owned by the East Boston Company, the first developer of much of East Boston. As a means of improving access to their lands under development, the East Boston Company provided land for ferry operations near the Maverick House Hotel.

The majority of the shares of the East Boston Ferry Company were owned by the Eastern Railroad Company (Eastern) in 1835. The early paths and roads, and later the Salem Turnpike, that linked Boston and Salem were augmented by steel rails in 1838, when the Eastern opened

its line from East Boston to Salem. The Eastern was one hundred percent in control of the East Boston Ferry Company by 1842. A map from that year (Figure 1.40) reveals an "East Boston Ferry" running from Lewis Wharf in the North End to "Steam Boat Landing" in East Boston. Steam Boat Landing was located at the end of the largest wharf in East Boston, Lewis Wharf. Today, Lewis Street traces the historic centerline of the wharf. Located next to Steam Boat Landing was the city terminal of the Eastern. The railroad's depot and ferry terminal in East Boston were strategically located to offer patrons a quick transfer between trains and ferries.

A new wharf was constructed along the North End waterfront during 1845 and 1846. Located between Sargent's and Lewis Wharves, the new structure opened with two ferry slips, one for the East Boston Ferry and another for the Eastern Railroad Ferry. The new slips and parallel routes of the two ferries are depicted on an 1850 map (Figure 1.45). Just like the steam railroads, the operations of the East Boston Ferry sold season passes (Figure 1.46).

Massachusetts approved a private company to operate a ferry to East Boston in 1853–54. It was branded the "People's Ferry," distinguishing it from

Figure 1.45 Mapping the East Boston Ferries, 1850
The parallel routes of the East Boston Ferry and Eastern Railroad Ferry serve Boston's North End at contiguous slips. In East Boston, the ferries serve neighboring wharves.

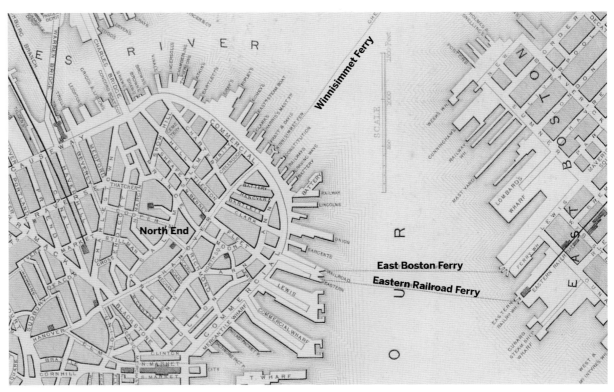

the privately-owned East Boston Ferry. An 1874 map of the East Boston waterfront reveals the terminals for both the People's and East Boston Ferries (Figure 1.47). On the map, the People's Ferry is labeled "North Ferry" and the East Boston Ferry no longer shares a wharf with the Eastern Railroad's passenger depot. After April 1854, when it began to run trains into and out of passenger terminals in downtown Boston, the Eastern no longer ferried its riders across Boston Harbor and closed its waterfront passenger depot in East Boston.

After the city of Boston purchased the terminals of the People's and East Boston Ferries 1859, the former quickly became known as the South Ferry, distinguishing it from the North Ferry. After months of discussion, and despite vigorous protests

from officials and citizens of East Boston, the city closed the North Ferry in 1933. A year after the closure of the North Ferry, Boston opened its city-built Sumner Tunnel between the North End and East Boston. The Sumner was Boston's first trans-harbor automobile tunnel. Beneath the harbor, it joined the East Boston Tunnel, opened for streetcar service at the end of 1904 and converted to rapid transit service in 1924.

In 1937, the *Boston Daily Globe* reported Boston providing service on the South Ferry route with a boat constructed in 1906. The coal-burning, steam-powered vessel made its crossing in seven minutes. Throughout the 1940s and early 1950s, the foot passenger fare on the South Ferry was a penny. The October 6, 1946 *Boston Daily Globe* articulated that the remaining active South Ferry boat, the Daniel

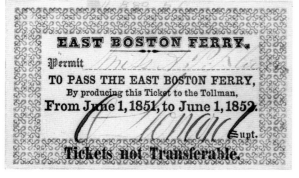

Figure 1.46 East Boston Ferry Season ticket, 1851–52

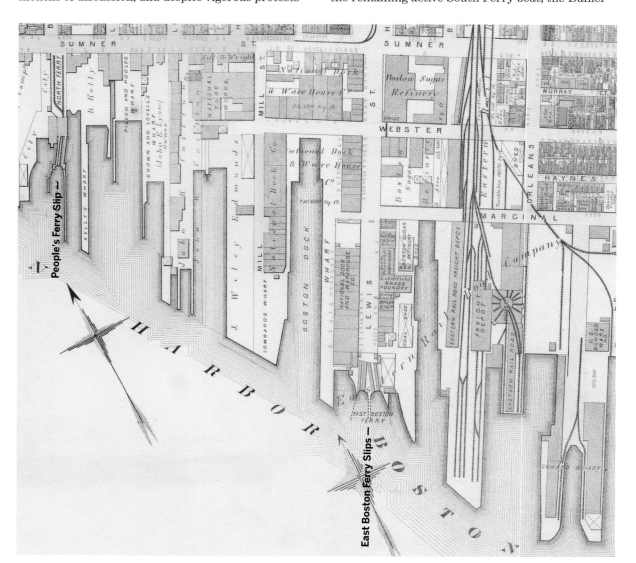

Figure 1.47 Mapping the Ferries in East Boston, 1874

A real estate map of the East Boston waterfront depicts the People's Ferry (left) and the East Boston Ferry (right). The People's Ferry is also labeled North Ferry. In time, the East Boston Ferry shown became the South Ferry.

Figure 1.48 Ferrying to East Boston, February 3, 1934
City of Boston ferry Daniel A. MacCormack arrives at its East Boston terminal. The terminal's two slips (right) are spanned by structures supporting gangways used by cars and people to board and deboard the ferries.

A. MacCormack, made two trips per hour, from 8:00 a.m. to 10:00 p.m. The MacCormack was a coal-burning, propeller-driven craft that carried over 1,000 people and approximately 250 vehicles daily (Figure 1.48).

After years of losing its riders to the automobile and transit tunnels, and running the South Ferry at a yearly financial loss of hundreds of thousands of dollars, Boston abandoned the South Ferry in 1952. Taken two years earlier, a photograph captures city ferry Charles C. Donoghue in action (Figure 1.49). A massive fire destroyed the shuttered South Ferry building on the Boston side in 1961. In that same year, the state-built Callahan Tunnel opened to vehicular traffic alongside the Sumner Tunnel, doubling capacity for rubber-tired traffic travelling beneath the harbor.

Horse Railroads

Just under a century before Boston terminated its East Boston ferry service, in the mid-1850s, the city's population surpassed 150,000. At the time, half of Bostonians were foreign-born immigrants and many lacked the resources to own private carriages and stable the horses they required. Simultaneously, trade and commerce brought hordes of long and short term visitors. More people in Boston needed public transportation than ever before. In the mid-1850s, responding to both unprecedented demand for local transportation and developments in steam railroad technology, entrepreneurs brought a new mode of public transportation to the streets of Boston—the horse railroad.

Horse railroads were similar to steam railroads in that they featured cars with flanged metal wheels

propelled along fixed metal tracks. Like steam railroads, horse railroads required less force to move the same load than a stagecoach or omnibus. Less friction existed between a horsecar's flanged metal wheels and metal tracks than plain wheels bouncing along irregular road surfaces. Unlike most steam railroad lines, horse railroad lines typically followed city streets and public ways. Tracks were held flush with finished road surfaces by sleepers, ties, and other, sometimes complex, sub-surface structural members. Boston's horse railroads were the city's first street railways. They typically lacked the dedicated rights-of-way that allowed steam railroads to carry trains of multiple cars. Horse railroad trains of multiple streetcars snaking along Boston's narrow streets and twisting lanes was not feasible. With some exceptions, single car service was the norm for Boston's horse railroads.

Horse railroad passengers rode in cars pulled by one or more horses. Horsecars were Boston's first streetcars. Early horsecars had the capacity of approximately 20–25 people (similar to larger omnibuses) and the form of early, box-type steam railroad coaches. They were typically sixteen feet long, lacked heating, and were illuminated within by oil lamps. A driver at the front of each horsecar controlled the equine power.

The core infrastructure of a horse railroad, just as it was for a steam railroad, was its trackage. Wherever a track branched off from another, a short movable segment of rails, known as a set of points, existed to permit cars to continue along the main track or onto the branching track. A set of points was moved to "switch" a horsecar between tracks. The operation of switches in horse railroading, pioneered at the Quincy Granite Railroad, was

Figure 1.49 Boston Ferry Charles C. Donoghue, Circa 1950

typically achieved manually. On some of Boston's horse railroads, horses themselves operated switches equipped with a special metal plate. Upon approaching the equine-operable switch, a horse depressed the plate with its hoof and proceeded to pull its horsecar onto the appropriate track. Most railroad switches were manually operated until the widespread use of remote-operated electric switches in the twentieth century.

The Cambridge Railroad

In 1832 the New York & Harlem Railroad Company opened America's first horse railroad to operate urban streetcars. The company's initial segment of line ran along The Bowery in Manhattan. Transit historian Foster M. Palmer, in *Horse Car, Trolley and Subway*, outlined America's subsequent horse railroad line openings: one serving New Orleans in 1835, multiple serving New York City in the 1850s, one in Brooklyn in 1854, the "Chemin de Fer Améri-cain" (American Railroad) serving Paris in 1855, and one launched in Cambridge in 1856, the Cam-bridge Railroad.

Massachusetts began to grant charters to compa-nies seeking to build and operate horse railroads in the early 1850s. The first two companies to receive charters from the Commonwealth did so in 1853. Of the two companies, one proposed to connect Boston with Roxbury. The other, sought to connect Boston with Cambridge. The Boston to Roxbury company received its charter in May 1853. At the time, Roxbury was still an independent municipality and had yet to be annexed by Boston. Though the Boston to Cambridge company received its charter a mere few days after that of the Roxbury company, the Cambridge Railroad Company (Cambridge Railroad), at it was named, was the first to provide horsecar service, and therefore streetcar service, in Boston.

The Cambridge Railroad came into being as a speculative, for-profit venture. Its founding group of investors anticipated people would prefer riding within a horsecar along smooth rails than inside of a coach or omnibus bouncing over city streets. Construction of the Cambridge Railroad commenced on September 1, 1855. The Cambridge Railroad then leased its unfinished horse railroad to the Union Railway Company (Union Railway), also of Cambridge, a company better capitalized to complete and operate the new horse railroad. By January 1, 1856, all of the significant coach and omnibus lines in Cambridge were consolidated by the Union Railway. The Union Railway operated omnibus service while the Cambridge Railroad was under construction. Though the Cambridge Rail-road was leased to the Union Railway, the latter operated the horse railroad under the Cambridge Railroad name.

With five horsecars purchased from the Brooklyn City Railroad, the Cambridge Railroad opened to the public on March 26, 1856. Three days later, the *Cambridge Chronicle* reported that on the first day of service horsecars operated from Bowdoin Square, in Boston's West End, and over the West Boston Bridge to Cambridgeport. Each car seated twenty-four people and had room for additional persons standing. The *Cambridge Chronicle* recounted:

> Fifty persons can be drawn in a car, by two horses, with more ease and comfort than can half that number in an omnibus, drawn by *four* horses. The trial thus far proves that the cars can make much better time than the omnibuses as they can be stopped and started easier, and drawn over the road at a more rapid speed, with less danger from accidents of any kind.

To generate interest in its speculative project, the Cambridge Railroad offered free rides during the first weeks of service (Figure 1.50). Within a week of commencing operations, the Cambridge Rail-road was carrying two thousand people a day. The company had fifteen former Brooklyn horsecars in operation by April 19, 1856. By May, the Cambridge Railroad extended operations westward, across Cambridge into Harvard Square. The Cambridge Railroad began charging fares on June 1, 1856. A one-way ride from Harvard Square to Boston cost ten cents. Horsecars traversed the three mile route from Harvard Square to Bowdoin Square in approximately twenty-five minutes.

The front page of the June 7, 1856 edition of *Ballou's Pictorial* was dedicated to the Cambridge Railroad (Figure 1.51), an operation just over two months old. In the year before the article was published, M. M. Ballou, an editor of *Gleason's Pictorial*, took over *Gleason's* and rechristened it with his name. According to the June 7 article, the Cambridge Railroad was operating fifteen horsecars and had extended its rails from Harvard Square (Figure 1.52) westward, to Watertown, and north-ward, towards Somerville. The extension to the north ran along North Street (now Massachusetts Avenue) to Porter's Hotel. The Porter House gave its name to the Porter House Steak as well as the

Figure 1.50 Cambridge Railroad Ticket, Circa 1856
Two faces of a paper ticket for "free" travel on a horsecar of the Cambridge Railroad Company.

BALLOU'S PICTORIAL

M. M. BALLOU, { CORNER OF TREMONT AND BROMFIELD STS. BOSTON, SATURDAY, JUNE 7, 1856. $3,00 PER ANNUM. 6 CENTS SINGLE. } VOL. X., No. 23.—WHOLE No. 257.

THE CAMBRIDGE HORSE RAILROAD.

We present our readers on this page with an accurate view from the pencil of Mr. Hill, taken in Bowdoin Square, in front of the Revere House, depicting that admirable hotel, with some of the adjacent buildings and stores, and exhibiting prominently, in the foreground, the cars of the Cambridge Horse Railroad, just at present an interesting locomotive novelty. The tracks are now laid as far as Mount Auburn, between four and five miles from this city, with a branch extending to Porter's Hotel in Old Cambridge, and over these fifteen cars, drawn each by two horses, make their regular trips during the day and evening. The receipts of each car are stated to be about forty dollars a day. Mr. Stiles, the superintendent, has proved himself an admirable manager, being always on hand and personally attending to the comfort of passengers and the interest of the road. The road cost, we are informed, about three hundred thousand dollars, and is built in a substantial manner. The establishment of this road is another proof of the progressive spirit of the day. Only a few years ago, there was no regular public communication between the city proper and its suburbs. If a man wished to go to Roxbury, for instance, he had either to hire a private vehicle at a heavy expense, or to perform the journey—for it is quite a journey—on foot. Then came the Roxbury Hourly—an insane scheme, the old fogies deemed it. These worthy and venerable gentlemen shook their sage heads, and predicted all sorts of uncomfortable consequences from the lightning speed of the rising generation. But the speculation succeeded; the coaches were multiplied; patronage poured in, and Roxbury began to fill up with people, who felt crowded in our little city, and desired elbow room and air for their residences. Now all the suburbs are connected with the city, either by railroad, by steam cars, or by omnibusses. The whole aspect of our surroundings is changed. In the place of barren and unproductive hills, covered with rocks and pines, we have beautiful tracts of cultivated land, parcelled out into gardens and lawns, and beautified with tasteful and neat residences, from the costly villa of the semi-millionaire, to the snug little cottage of the mechanic or laboring man. This change has been the result of improved means of intercommunication between the city and the environs. Omnibus life is quite a feature in our social system. The omnibusses are commodious and elegant, with fine horses, and driven by accomplished "whips." They radiate in all directions. Horse railroads are an advance on omnibusses. For some years they have been in successful operation in New York city, and also in Brooklyn and Williamsburg, where the generous width of the streets permits their employment without detriment to any interest. They can never be introduced to a similar extent in Boston, because the founders of this village, never dreaming of its possible magnitude, were excessively economical in laying out the town thoroughfares. Our widest avenue within the limits of the city proper is too contracted for the vehicular tide which flows through it already. Washington Street must be relieved of the pressure on it, and before long, Tremont Street will suffer from the crowd. Still, there is no reason why several of the surrounding towns should not be connected with the city by horse railroads. There can be no doubt that they would do a lucrative business. The success of the Cambridge road may be considered as a fixed fact. Besides those whose business compels them to ride in them to and fro, thousands of citizens weekly will avail themselves of this cheap and comfortable means of transport, to go forth and breathe the fresh air, and enjoy the beautiful scenery of the environs. Mount Auburn itself, with its quiet shades and soothing influences, is an attraction; while beyond it and around it are scenes of exquisite rural beauty, which amply repay an occasional visit.

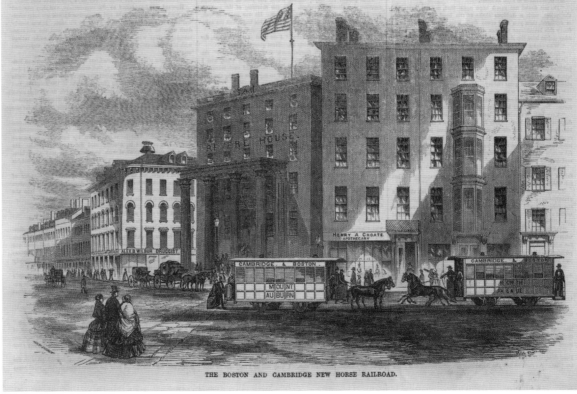

THE BOSTON AND CAMBRIDGE NEW HORSE RAILROAD.

Figure 1.51 Front Page News in 1856

The front page of the June 7, 1856 edition of *Ballou's Pictorial* was dedicated to the Cambridge Railroad. Below the text of the article, a view shows Cambridge Railroad horsecars operating in Boston's Bowdoin Square.

Figure 1.52 Harvard Square, Circa 1858

An early Cambridge Railroad horsecar signed for "Cambridge & Boston" (far left) pauses at Harvard Square. A large tree (center) occupies the center of Harvard Square and future site of the main head house for Harvard Station of the Cambridge Subway.

Figure 1.53 Horsecar at Mount Auburn Cemetery, Circa 1860

A Cambridge Railroad horsecar pauses at the cemetery's main gate. The car's driver stands on the front vestibule holding the horses' reins.

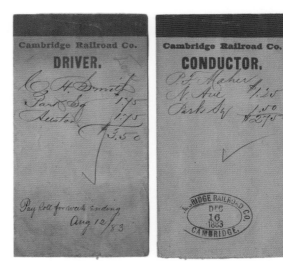

Figure 1.54 Cambridge Railroad Collection Envelopes, 1883

Each of two envelopes, one for use by a horsecar driver (left) and one for use by a conductor (right), feature a list of cash collections and an associated date.

intersection of streets immediately to the east of the hotel. Porter Square remains a hub of railed transit activity.

The Cambridge Railroad reached Mount Auburn Cemetery in 1856. The cemetery lay at the far western edge of Cambridge and approximately four and a half miles from Boston's Bowdoin Square. Cambridge Railroad horsecars serviced a stop at the cemetery's main gate (Figure 1.53). Mount Auburn Cemetery opened in 1831 as America's first "garden cemetery." Visiting the cemetery and its park-like setting was a popular pastime for late nineteenth century Bostonians. The Cambridge Railroad was the most convenient means of public transportation

between downtown Boston, Harvard Square, and Mount Auburn Cemetery.

In self-promoting publications, the Cambridge Railroad described landmarks passengers passed as they rode from Boston to the cemetery. Its *Handbook for Passengers Over the Cambridge Railroad with a description of Mount Auburn Cemetery* went through multiple editions, a testament to its usefulness in soliciting and enlightening streetcar customers. A map in the 1858 edition notes a storefront "station" for Cambridge Railroad patrons in Harvard Square. As late as 1883, an iteration of the *Handbook* was published by Moses King, a producer of guide books who began publishing while attending

Figure 1.55 Metropolitan Railroad Ad, 1858

Under a rendering of an early, boxy horsecar, a print ad features a brief history of the Metropolitan's lines and provides a schedule of cars operating between points in Roxbury, Boston, and West Roxbury. The ad mentions night service running between Boston and Guild's Hall in Roxbury.

Figure 1.56 Metropolitan Railroad Horsecar, Circa 1860s

Figure 1.57 Horsecars on Tremont Street, 1856

People rush to board a Metropolitan Railroad horsecar (left). The Tremont Hotel (right) marked the downtown terminus of the Metropolitan Railroad's first streetcar line.

Harvard College. King went on to become a prominent publisher of detailed and visually-rich guide books of Boston, New York City, and Philadelphia, most packed with views or photographs. Editions of *King's Handbook of Boston* remain valuable and contain detailed records of Boston's public transportation infrastructure during the last quarter of the nineteenth and first decade of the twentieth century.

The Cambridge Railroad was a definitive financial success, allowing its parent company, the Union Railway, to expand operations. At the end of 1860, just four years after opening its first line, the Union Railway employed a fleet of some fifty horsecars, stabled approximately 500 horses, operated around 275 daily trips, and carried approximately 8,000 passengers per day. Fifteen years later, an 1875 schedule listed Cambridge Railroad horsecars leaving Harvard Square for Boston every seven minutes, more frequently during rush hours.

The Metropolitan Railroad

The company chartered in 1853 to build a horse railroad from Boston to Roxbury finally opened its first line to the public in September 1856. The Metropolitan Railroad (Metropolitan) was the second company to transport paying customers via horsecar through the streets of Boston. Initially, Metropolitan horsecars ran from the company's Boston terminus, located in front of the Tremont House Hotel on Tremont Street, to the Norfolk House Hotel in Roxbury. Early schedules listed cars running from sunrise to midnight with two minute headways. The fare was five cents. The profitable Metropolitan grew to provide service twenty-four hours a day, with three to four cars running each hour between midnight and sunrise hours.

Each of the Metropolitan's earliest horsecars (Figure 1.56) seated a couple of dozen passengers and had proportions similar to early cars of the Cambridge Railroad. For a time, the Metropolitan's main offices were located in the same building as those of *Ballou's Pictorial*, on Tremont Street opposite the Park Street Church. On more than one occasion, *Ballou's Pictorial* featured Metropolitan horsecars on its front page (Figure 1.57). In its January 31, 1857 edition, the newspaper raved about the horse railroad opened by its neighbor:

Thus far, the Metropolitan Railroad has worked admirably. In no other way could the traveling demand be met. Not only have cars carried more passengers than the omnibuses ever did, but the

Figure 1.58 Bowdoin Square, April 25, 1857
A Metropolitan Railroad open-top horsecar (right) and a closed horsecar (left) pass among coaches and pedestrians in front of the Winthrop House Hotel in Bowdoin Square.

Figure 1.59 Metropolitan Railroad Schedule Card, 1861
A two-sided schedule card, effective June 7, 1861, lists Metropolitan Railroad horsecars operating between Dorchester and Boston via Warren Street and Grove Hall.

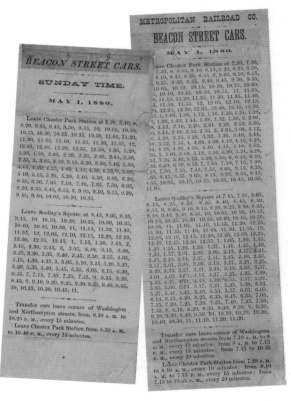

ease of running, the facility of getting in and out of them, and the frequency of their trips, fulling meet with all the wants and desires of the public.

Of the streetcars operated by the Metropolitan, a few lacked any fixed roof (Figure 1.58). The company pioneered the operation of such open-top streetcars in Boston.

After the opening of the Metropolitan, additional horse railroad companies came into being and opened their own lines. One linked Boston with Charlestown in 1857. Another connected Boston with South Boston in 1858. Omnibuses previously made those connections, as coaches had before them. In 1857, the Lynn & Boston Railroad Company (Lynn & Boston) opened a horse railroad linking Boston with Lynn, a city located approximately ten miles to the northeast of the Shawmut Peninsula.

The Metropolitan expanded rapidly. After two years of operation, it had twelve miles of street railway in service. The company operated forty-two miles of track in late 1865. At the end of the following year, the Metropolitan had forty-four horsecars and 516 horses. Growth of the company

continued. In its annual report for its fiscal year ending November 1870, the Metropolitan listed 170 horsecars and 914 horses in inventory. Its annual report for 1881 listed over 2,770 horses in company stables. Between December 30, 1857 and November 30, 1858, the Metropolitan carried over four and a half million passengers. Between the end of 1869 and the end of November 1870, the company transported nearly fifteen million people. During its fiscal year for 1883, the Metropolitan transported just over thirty-two million passengers.

The Metropolitan brought in significant revenue from fares, real estate, and other sources. The company sold enough manure from its horses in 1860 alone to cover nearly half the cost of corporate salaries for that year. The Metropolitan used its financial might to purchase other horse railroad companies. It bought the West Roxbury Railway in 1862, the Dorchester Railway and Dorchester Extension Railways in 1863, and the Suffolk and Dorchester & Roxbury Railways in 1864. Schedule cards for Metropolitan streetcars from years bracketing the period of acquisitions are shown in Figure 1.59 and Figure 1.60.

Figure 1.60 Metropolitan Railroad Schedule Card, 1880

Figure 1.61 Metropolitan Railroad Tickets, Circa 1870

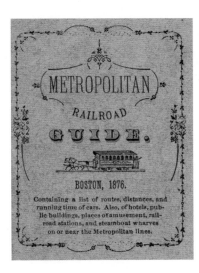

Figure 1.62 Metropolitan Railroad Guide, 1876

Figure 1.63 Horsecar at the North Ferry, Circa 1860s
A Metropolitan Railroad horsecar (center) has turned and is ready to accept passengers at the North Ferry terminal in Boston's North End.

Throughout Boston in the late 1850s and early to mid-1860s, financially weaker horse railroad companies were merged with, leased to, or purchased by newer or financially stronger companies. By 1865 only four companies remained in effective control of street railway operations in Boston. The Metropolitan served Boston, Roxbury, Dorchester, and West Roxbury. The South Boston Railroad served Boston and South Boston. The Middlesex Railroad served Boston, Charlestown, Somerville, and Medford. The Cambridge Railroad served Boston, Cambridge, Somerville, and Brighton. Though the Lynn & Boston did reach downtown Boston using rights it had to operate its cars over the Middlesex Railroad's tracks, the company did not own its own tracks in the heart of the city proper.

After the consolidations of the mid-1860s, the Metropolitan came to control most of Boston's key routes, including those that served the city's steam railroad depots and ferry terminals (Figure 1.63). The company issued miniature guides to its growing network into the 1880s (Figure 1.62).

Proliferation and consolidation of horse railroads in Greater Boston accelerated the decades long demise of the region's coach and omnibus operations. King's omnibus empire fell apart in 1856–57 amidst mismanagement and an economic downturn. King's Lines, along with other omnibus operations in Boston, were purchased by the Metropolitan, who operated them to augment horse railroad operations. The 1873 *New England: A Handbook for Travellers* announced: "Horse-cars traverse the city in all directions." The guide indicated horsecars departing "every few minutes" from Tremont Street, Bowdoin Square, and Scollay Square, serving dozens of local destinations and serving "20 routes to the western suburbs." The guide mentioned only two omnibus routes. Carriages were described as functioning like modern taxis, with "a tariff of fares" hung in each and charging the following rates: "50 cts. each passenger within the city proper; from South of Dover Street to the North End, $1."

City Directory & Almanac Maps

Prior to the arrival of horse railroads, maps of Boston tended to lack depictions of street-running public transportation modes, such as stagecoaches or omnibuses. Steam railroad lines appeared on maps of Boston as soon as the iron horse arrived in the 1830s. After the opening of the Cambridge and Metropolitan Railroads in 1856, maps of Boston and surrounding communities began to depict horse railroad lines. Still, a map explicitly designed and published as a cartographic aid for navigating modes of public transit had yet to take shape for Boston. The first publicly available, portable, paper maps to depict streetcar lines of Boston and surrounding communities were prepared not by horse railroad companies, but by existing book and map publishers, including those behind city almanacs and directories.

Throughout the nineteenth century, maps of Boston, Cambridge, and surrounding cities accompanied city directories and almanacs, published yearly. City directories and almanacs listed basic data about governmental bodies, businesses, citizens, and local modes of transportation.

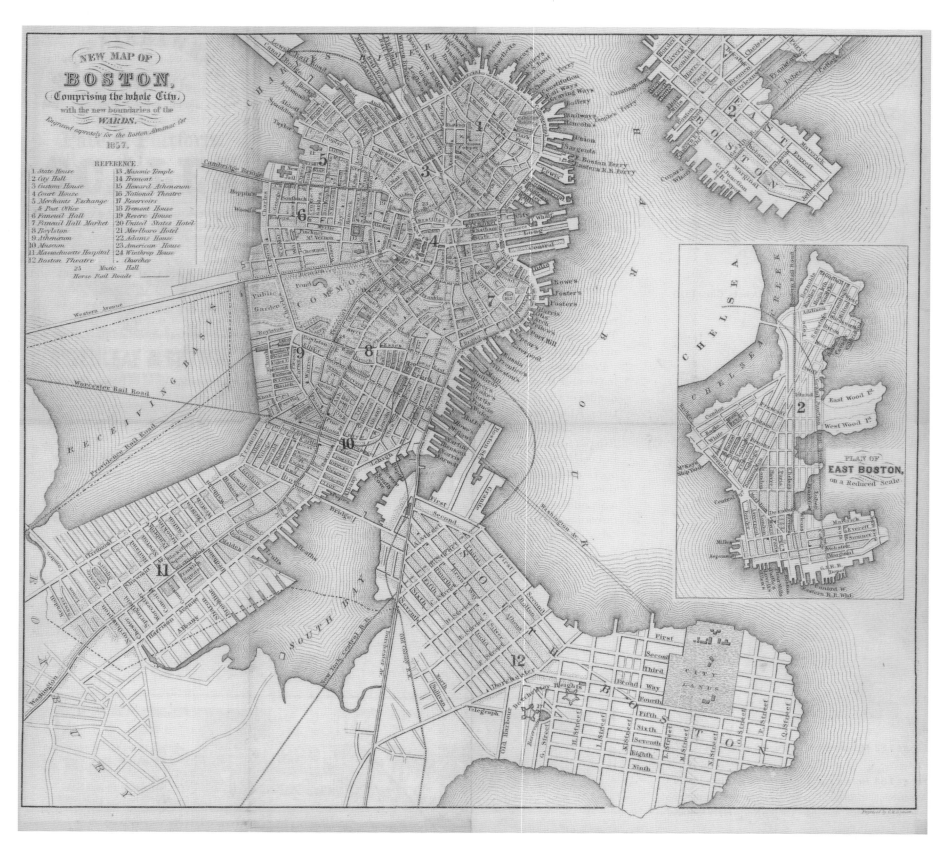

Figure 1.64 Boston Directory Map, 1857

The lines of eight independent steam railroad companies span local waterways and link Boston with surrounding communities. No fewer than three horse railroad lines radiate from downtown into surrounding neighborhoods. A double line traces the tracks of the Cambridge Railroad from the intersection of Cambridge and Court Streets, along Cambridge Street, and across the Charles River via the West Boston Bridge. A double line traces the Metropolitan from the intersection of Court Street and Tremont Row, along Tremont and Washington Streets, and into Roxbury.

Figure 1.65 Cambridge Almanac Map, 1856

Cambridge Railroad horsecar lines traverse Cambridge, from Mount Auburn Cemetery (bottom left) to the Charles River (right).

Almanacs and directories for Boston, Cambridge, and Roxbury, especially those published before the 1880s, came out in a pocket-sized format. With their information about public transportation, including lists of omnibus routes, breakdowns of streetcar routes by operator, lists of places to board street-cars, details about steam railroad depots and routes, and maps showing steam and horse railroad lines and depots, the pocket-sized volumes were go-to, portable tools for anyone traveling around Boston.

The first edition of the *Boston Directory* was published in 1789. The 1857 edition of the *Boston Almanac* was the first to contain a map depicting horse railroads (Figure 1.64). It was engraved by G. W. Boynton, a prolific Boston-based engraver of the later half of the nineteenth century. Compared with Page's 1775 map (Figure 1.1), Boynton's 1857

map reveals a significantly expanded footprint of Boston, the result of land reclamation around the Shawmut Peninsula and Boston's annexation of South Boston and East Boston in 1804 and 1836, respectively. The year of the map, 1857, was also the year of incorporation of the Winnisimmet Street Railway Company, operators of a horse railroad serving Winnisimmet Landing in Chelsea. In time, the company was leased to the Lynn & Boston.

The 1856 *Cambridge Almanac* map (Figure 1.65) was published in the same year as the opening of the Cambridge Railroad. The sixth edition of the *Roxbury Directory* was published in 1858 by Adams, Sampson & Company, publishers of directories for Boston, Charlestown, and Lowell, among others. Some editions of the *Boston Almanac* included

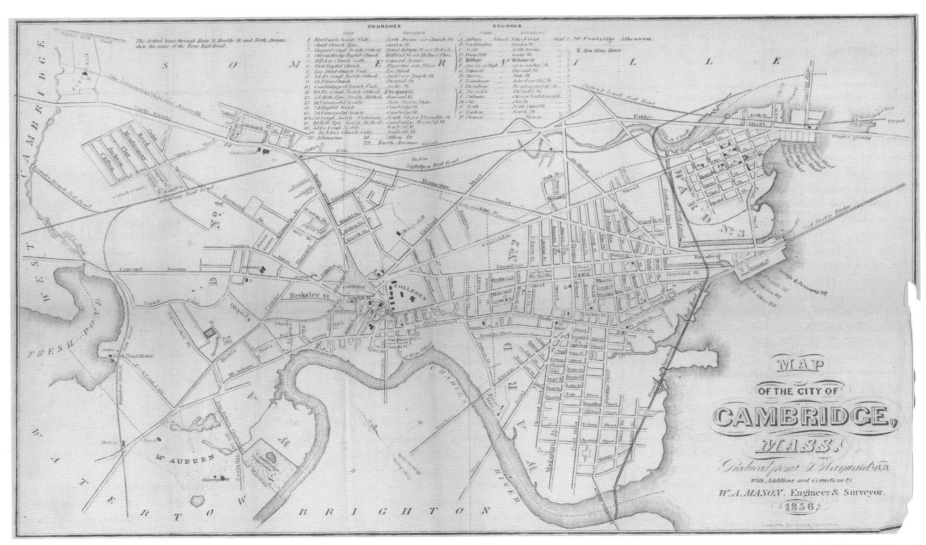

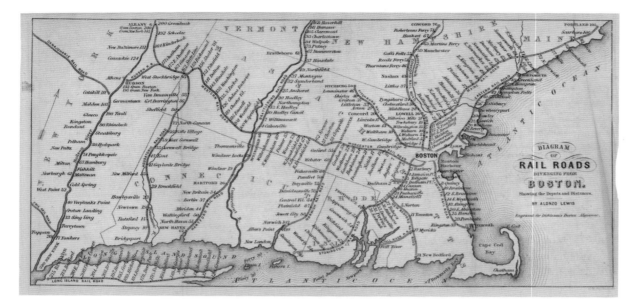

Figure 1.66 Map of Railroads Serving Boston, 1846
Along each railroad line, subtle differences in typography delineate terminals from intermediate stations. Little geographic detail exists for areas of dry land, but shorelines, major rivers, and railroad lines are given strong and equal weight.

maps of Boston's Regional steam railroad network (Figure 1.66).

Navigating Boston's Early Street Railways

Boston's horse railroad operators did not commonly produce public maps showing all horsecar lines. They had little incentive to advertise the lines or destinations of competitors. For their own riders, however, they did provide non-cartographic navigation aids, including schedule cards. On their cars, companies applied destination signage, route signage, and color-coding, improving upon signage and color-coding practices pioneered by coach, omnibus, and steam railroad operators. The Cambridge Railroad applied text to its cars indicating such destinations as "Boston," "Cambridge," and "Mount Auburn." Metropolitan horsecars wore signage for "Brookline" and "Boston & Roxbury."

Beyond destination and route signage, horse railroad companies applied didactic colors and embellishments to their cars. Horsecars serving the same neighborhood were painted the same color. Cars operating from the same car barn were painted with a unique accent color or adorned with an identifying scrollwork design. Within its first year of operations, the Metropolitan painted its Roxbury cars a straw color, its Dorchester cars blue, edged with gold, and its Boston Neck cars red. To augment vehicle color-coding at night, horsecar companies installed colored lamps onto cars. The Metropolitan installed green lights on its Roxbury cars and red lights on its Boston Neck cars. As horse railroad

companies amassed large fleets of vehicles, they applied a unique number to each of their cars. The numbering facilitated inventory tracking, routing, and scheduling of the vehicles.

Today, vehicles of the Massachusetts Bay Transportation Authority (MBTA) feature the devices standardized by early streetcar companies. Destination signage, often accompanied by a route number or letter, is located on the front or side of rapid transit trains, light rail vehicles, trackless trolleys, and buses. The MBTA color-codes its vehicles by type, mode, and route, not by destination, as was done by the horse railroad operators. Vehicle numbering remains a vital practice.

Complimenting the horse railroad data and maps contained within city directories and almanacs were horse railroad guide books. One of the earliest such publications for Boston was the May 1862 edition of *Russell's Horse Railroad Guide for Boston and Vicinity*. According to Russell, he intended to update and reissue his guide monthly. A page from the guide (Figure 1.67) lists Cambridge Railroad lines departing from Boston, organized by destination. Russell's guide exclusively listed horse railroad routes and schedules. It lacked any type of map.

The 1887 *Boston Horse and Street Railroad Guide* grouped street railway routes by operating company. The guide featured an indexing system to direct readers to the proper page for a specific route, each of which was assigned a number. Though the 1887 guide contained no maps, it did include diagrams of individual horsecar lines. Three pages from the 1887 guide describe Cambridge

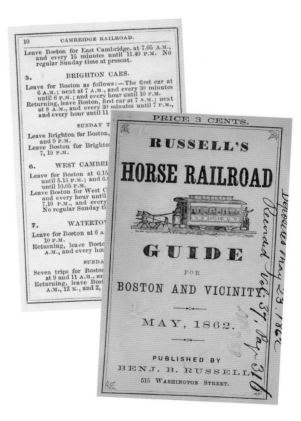

Figure 1.67 Pocket-sized Horse Railroad Guide, 1862
The title page (right) and portion of a listing for Cambridge Railroad horsecar routes (left) from the May 1862 edition of *Russell's Horse Railroad Guide*.

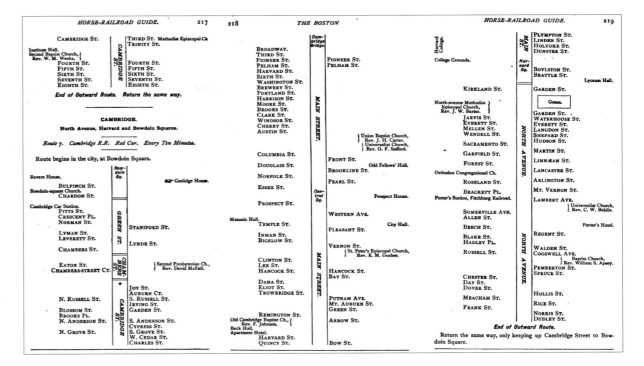

Figure 1.68 Cambridge Railroad Horsecar Route 7, 1887

Three pages from The Boston Horse and Street Railroad Guide diagram Cambridge Railroad horsecar service between Boston's Bowdoin Square and North Cambridge. On the leftmost sheet, the route's number is accompanied by the color and frequency of service. Following the basic data is the route's diagram, to be read from top to bottom of each sheet. Two vertical lines, each representing an edge of a street along which Route 7 followed, form a spine for the diagram. Names of each route's streets are printed along the middle of the spine. Arranged in relative order along either side of the spine are the names of cross streets and landmarks along the route.

Railroad "Route 7" serving "North Avenue, Harvard and Bowdoin Squares" (Figure 1.68). The Route 7 diagram, along with others in the 1887 guide, was an early example of a transit line map. Before the arrival of horse railroads, steam railroads prepared similar route diagrams to accompany timetables and schedules. While steam railroad line maps typically represented long distances, horse railroad route diagrams, like those in the 1887 guide, were devices of hyper-local representation.

Boston's First Transit System Maps

In 1865, a Cambridge-based civil engineer, J. G. Chase, produced a pair of maps that are among the earliest comprehensive public transit maps for Boston. One map in the pair (Figure 1.69) represents Greater Boston at the scale of one and one half inches to the mile, covering a broad geographic area around Massachusetts Bay, from as far north as Lynn to as far south as Quincy. The other map in the pair (Figure 1.70) covers Boston, Charlestown, South Boston, and most of East Boston. It includes much of Cambridge, Somerville, and Brookline. At a scale of five inches to the mile, the map is similar to Boynton's maps prepared for the *Boston Almanac*.

Both of Chase's 1865 maps feature concentric circles drawn at a quarter mile scale increments. The center of the circles is not city hall, nor the state house, as was common on Boston maps of

similar vintage, but as Chase notes: "Distances are Given in 1/4 mile Circles, from Scollay's Building; Junction of Tremont, Court and Cornhill Streets." In 1865 Scollay Square was, as continued to be for subsequent decades, the epicenter of street railway traffic for Boston.

Chase's maps were useful cartographic resources for anyone traveling via the street railways and steam railroads of Greater Boston; they fit into a pocket and could be unfolded on demand. Portability is key to the utility of any transit map.

Chase's simultaneous publication of two maps focusing on modes of transit serving the public, with one showing the urban core in detail and another covering Greater Boston at a smaller scale, was unprecedented in Boston. Chase's pair of maps are antecedents for maps produced by operators of public transportation in Greater Boston since 1865. Folding paper system maps of the Boston Elevated Railway Company (BERy) (Figure 6.53 and Figure 6.56), the Metropolitan Transit Authority (MTA) (Figure 6.57), and the MBTA (Figure 9.29) all featured a regional map with an inset map of downtown Boston. Since the early 1970s, the MBTA has produced a pair of maps, one of Greater Boston and one of the core of its system.

Figure 1.69 Chase's Railroad Map of Greater Boston, 1865
The complete map (above) and portion reproduced at 1:1 (left) are shown. Steam railroad lines (in black) and street railway lines (in red) weave across a map that was a companion to a larger scale map of Boston and its immediate vicinity (Figure 1.70).

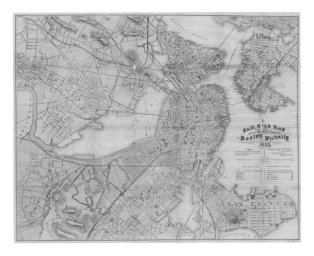

Figure 1.70 Chase's Railroad Map of Boston, 1865

The complete map (above) and portion reproduced at 1:1 (right) are shown. The map represents roads, steam railroads, horse railroads, harbor ferries, bridges, and causeways linking Boston with contiguous communities. One line type represents steam railroad lines. Another line type, colored, represents horse railroad lines of the Metropolitan, Cambridge, Middlesex, Broadway, and Lynn & Boston Railroads. The map was published simultaneously with a map of Greater Boston (Figure 1.69).

The Horsecar Matures

By the 1880s, the boxy horsecars of the 1850s and 1860s were replaced on the streets of Boston by cars that, for the most part, fell into one of two categories, closed-type or open-type. Closed-type streetcars featured fully enclosed passenger compartments with windows, vestibules at the front and rear, and a center-aisle configuration (Figure 1.71). Passengers entered a closed-type car through the rear vestibule. A closed car's driver stood on the front vestibule. Open-type streetcars lacked fully enclosed passenger compartments (Figure 1.72). Passenger sat on benches that spanned the width of each open-type. People boarded an open-type car by stepping onto one of the running boards on the long side of the car and then sliding onto one of the benches. If the benches were full, or for short trips, riders could hang onto a pole mounted on the side of the car and ride the running boards.

The population of Boston exceeded 362,000 in 1880. In that same year, thousands of horses pulled hundreds of horsecars along miles of streetcar tracks. A year later, the 1881 *Stranger's Guide to Boston* described the city's horse railroad network:

> The street-railway system in Boston is quite extensive, and remarkably well conducted, although controlled by a few companies; ... each strives to put forward the best accommodations for the public; consequently the cars are neat,

clean, and attractive, and generally first-class. All parts of the city can be reached by a ride in the street-cars. They can be always found at every railroad depot, and at some of the steamboat wharfs; so the traveller can at all times be sure of transportation from his place of arrival to his place of destination, if not by one direct ride, at most by one transfer ticket. Over one hundred and forty miles of track are now laid in the city of Boston, by the following railroad companies: [the Metropolitan, Highland, Union, Middlesex, South Boston, and Lynn & Boston].

The 1881 guide listed horse railroad rules "intended for the comfort, convenience and safety of passengers," including prohibitions on entering or exiting a horsecar by way of the front platform, riding on the steps, chatting with the driver, boarding a moving car, being disorderly, riding while intoxicated, soliciting, and bringing a dog on board. Smoking was banned "excepting on the three rear seats of the open cars." Children were required to pay full fare if "occupying seats which may be required for other passengers."

The 1881 guide listed routes operated by the six horse railroad companies serving Boston. The longest route was the eleven and one half mile long "Lynn and Boston Line," along which cars took just under two hours to make a one-way trip. The first car departed from Lynn at 8:30 a.m., and

Figure 1.71 Closed-type Horsecar, Circa Mid-1890s
West End car number 1497 pauses at Washington Street Car House in Brighton. The car is a typical closed-type, featuring an enclosed passenger compartment and open vestibules at each end. The West End never electrified the car and sold it in 1902.

Figure 1.72 Open-type Horsecar, Circa 1860–80
Metropolitan Railroad open-type car number 24 poses with employees, some standing on the running boards.

from Scollay Square at 8:20 a.m. Cars ran hourly until the late evening. The second longest route was the Union Railway's "Oak Square Line," from Oak Square in Brighton to the Providence Railroad depot downtown. Running time for the eight mile long route was one hour and ten minutes each way. Cars departed from Oak Square every half hour, from 6:00 a.m. until 10:30 p.m., and from the Providence Railroad depot every half hour, from 7:00 a.m. until 11:40 p.m. The majority of the routes operated on ten, fifteen, or thirty minute headways. A few routes had five minute headways, forty minute headways, or longer.

In addition to the daytime routes, the 1881 guide listed four routes of "night cars," all operated by the Metropolitan and running between downtown Boston and Roxbury. Outbound night cars departed from the Tremont House on Tremont Street hourly, from 1:00 a.m. until 6:00 a.m., and from State Street at the bottom of each hour, from 12:30 a.m. until 5:30 a.m. Inbound cars departed from Tremont Crossing at the bottom of each hour, from 12:30 a.m. until 5:30 a.m., and from the intersection of Washington and Dudley Streets hourly, from midnight until 5:00 a.m.

During the horse railroad era, coach companies continued to operate in Boston. The 1881 *Stranger's Guide* listed the "Citizen's Line" running

a vehicle every three minutes, from morning until late evening, connecting Northampton Street in Boston's South End with Salem Street in Charlestown. The "People's Line" ran every ten minutes, from 7 a.m. to 8 p.m., connecting Summer Street in Boston with Inman Square in Cambridge. The "People's Line" also linked Summer Street with Rowe's Wharf. "People's Coaches" connected Upham's Corner and Neponset, both in Dorchester, with cars operating every half hour. The guide mentioned that "Barges leave Bowdoin Square to connect with all the harbor and excursion boats, and the Lynn and Revere Beach Railroad on Atlantic Avenue."

The 1883 *King's Dictionary of Boston* listed seven companies providing horsecar service in Boston. These were the Metropolitan, Cambridge, Middlesex, Lynn & Boston, and South Boston Railroads. King also listed the Highland Street Railway and Charles River Street Railway Companies, established in 1872 and 1882, respectively. By the end of the 1880s, all of the horse railroad companies listed by King, except for the Lynn & Boston, were consolidated under the control of a single company, one that brought not only the broomstick train, but a unified electric streetcar network to The Hub.

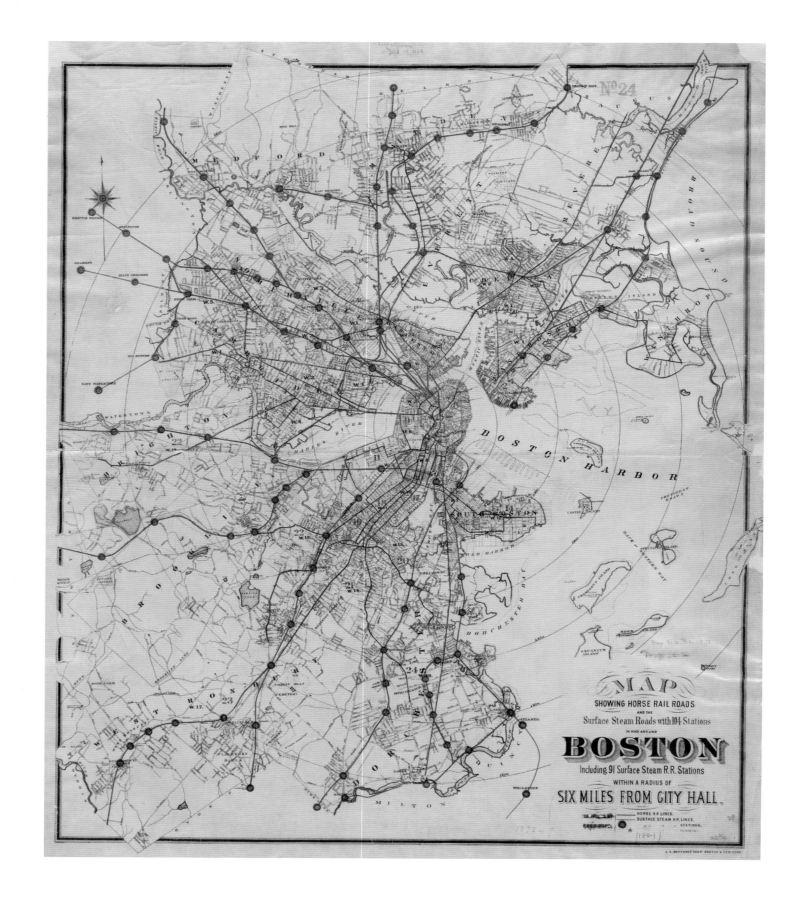

N.º 24

MAP
SHOWING HORSE RAIL ROADS
AND THE
Surface Steam Roads with 104 Stations
IN AND AROUND
BOSTON
Including 91 Surface Steam R.R. Stations
WITHIN A RADIUS OF
SIX MILES FROM CITY HALL.

CHAPTER 2

Unification and Electrification: Trolleys Take Hold

Henry Whitney's Streetcar Suburb

Street railway companies constructed new lines not only to move people through existing urban areas, but as a means of attracting people to areas of new development. As publicly funded interstate highways fostered the growth of Boston's automobile suburbs in the twentieth century, privately financed streetcar lines facilitated the development of Boston's "streetcar suburbs" in the latter half of the nineteenth and early part of the twentieth centuries. Streetcar companies often had financial connections with, or even direct control over, lands developed along their lines. One such company was the West End Land Company, formed in 1886 to develop lands in Brookline, a town contiguous with Boston's western border.

Movement of the public between Boston and Brookline was facilitated by stagecoaches by 1798. Steam railroads first linked the two communities in 1848. The Brookline Railroad and Brookline & Back Bay Railroad were charted in 1857 and 1866, respectively. Omnibus service was established between Brookline's Coolidge Corner and downtown Boston in 1838. Horsecar lines of the Metropolitan Railroad reached Coolidge Corner by the end of 1884.

Henry M. Whitney, a Massachusetts native residing in Brookline, was the industrialist behind the West End Land Company. Since 1870, he was the second generation to oversee the successful, Boston-based Metropolitan Steamship Company. The company's ships linked Boston and New York City via the waters of the Atlantic. As early as the 1860s, Whitney began purchasing land to develop around Brookline's Beacon Street. The road was laid out during 1850 and 1851 as an extension of Boston's fashionable street of the same name.

In order to increase the desirability of his Beacon Street lands to developers, Whitney proposed widening the fifty-foot-wide country road in Brookline to an avenue approximately 200 feet wide. Whitney envisioned a grand boulevard with separate paths for horse-drawn carriages, horses, bicycles, and pedestrians, with a horse railroad line running down the central reservation, all to maximize the value of his lands. To facilitate acceptance of his street-widening project by Brookline, Whitney not only donated portions of his own property to be used for the expanded right-of-way, he also paid half of the anticipated cost of the street widening.

Seeking an end product of the highest caliber, Whitney solicited designs from Frederick Law Olmsted. Mr. Olmsted, who provided plans for Beacon Street in 1886, is considered the grandfather of the modern practice of landscape architecture. He remains renowned for his designs for urban parkland across America, including Boston's Emerald Necklace and Commonwealth Avenue, as well as New York City's Central Park. While the final design of Whitney's Beacon Street project ended up being only 160 feet wide and lacked planned bridle and bicycling paths, the final design did include a new horse railroad line.

The West End Street Railway Company

The West End Street Railway Company (West End) was incorporated in January 1887 to construct and operate horse railroad lines serving Brookline, including the centerpiece of Whitney's Beacon Street project. After receiving approval from the Brookline selectman, the West End began construction at Coolidge Corner on August 20, 1887.

Figure 2.1 Boston's Horse and Steam Railroads, 1876
A large format map shows Boston being served by a web of steam railroad lines (red) and horse railroads lines (green). Colored circles denote 104 steam railroad stations. Unlike Chase's maps of 1865 (Figure 1.69 and Figure 1.70), which denote distances from Scollay's Building, this map places Boston City Hall at the center of concentric distance markings.

The company completed laying tracks along Beacon Street to the Boston city line by the end of the year. The West End then established a second horsecar line along Brookline's Harvard Street. The line extended to Allston, a part of Brighton. Annexed by

Boston in 1874, Brighton sat between Brookline and the Charles River. By April 1888, West End tracks were in place to Westchester Park (now Massachusetts Avenue) in Boston's Back Bay. On May 21, the West End was running ten-minute horsecar service

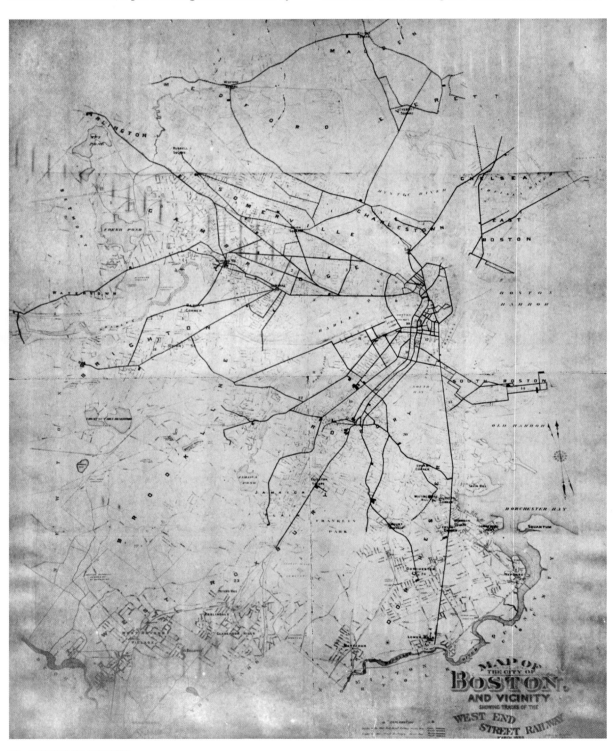

Figure 2.2 Mapping the West En[...]
A rare map depicts the track netw[...]
1888, less than a year after the co[...]
horse railroads operating in Bosto[...]
End lines extend through Cambri[...]
and Malden. South of the city, mo[...]
at the Boston city limits. West of [...]
Brookline and Watertown.

Figure 2.3 West End Street Railway Co. Tickets, Circa 1890

An "Inward Check" (bottom) and "Outward Check" (middle) were valid for travel on specified streetcars from Roxbury Crossing and only on the day issued. A red ticket (top) was valid only on the date and until the time stamped on its right side. It was valid for travel on any "car taken at the ferry on Boston side."

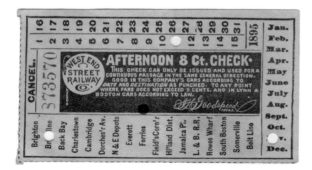

Figure 2.4 West End Afternoon Eight Cent Ticket, 1895

A West End Street Railway Company paper ticket is marked for travel on November 11, 1895, towards Brookline, and where "any point where the fare does not exceed five cents."

between Coolidge Corner and Allston, via Harvard Street. The first West End horsecar ran along the Beacon Street line on June 1.

The improvement of Beacon Street, in conjunction with the new horse railroad lines in Brookline, directly contributed to the financial successes of Whitney and his companies, including the West End. The Coolidge Corner neighborhood of Brookline, located at a crossroads and midway along the revamped boulevard, experienced significant development in the 1890s. Lands along Beacon Street were developed with single family homes, apartment blocks, and residential subdivisions. The legacies of Whitney's Beacon Street project remain in place today. Though parking spaces for automobiles have consumed much of the central reservation of Beacon Street, streetcar tracks remain the spine of the grand avenue.

The West End Takes All

The financial success of Whitney's Beacon Street project hinged on there being an unhindered connection between the West End's horse railroad lines with the existing lines of the Metropolitan Railroad (Metropolitan) at Coolidge Corner in Brookline and the Cambridge Railroad in Brighton. The Metropolitan, whose system dominated Boston, resisted cooperating with the West End, viewing Whitney's startup as a threat to its business. Attempting to foil the West End, the Metropolitan and the Cambridge Railroads entertained joining forces to fight Whitney. Responding to the hostile atmosphere, and seeing no other alternative, Whitney and the West End's backers purchased controlling interests in not only the Metropolitan and Cambridge Railroads, but also the South Boston, Charles River, and Boston Consolidated Railroads, the latter of which was formed by the merger of the Highland Street Railroad and the Middlesex Railroad Companies in 1886.

By the end of 1887, the West End was in effective control of the majority of the horse railroads serving Boston (Figure 2.2). To ensure smooth transitions of each company into the West End fold, the West End appointed managers and presidents of the formerly independent companies to upper management positions within its own organization. In the last quarter of 1888, the West End organized its fresh streetcar empire into nine divisions. Divisions one through seven each oversaw operations within a particular geographic area. Each divisional service area corresponded roughly with one previously

covered by a company consumed by the West End. Division eight focused on operations in downtown Boston. In time, division nine came into being to oversee the West End and Boston's first electric streetcar operations.

After its takeover of the horse railroads serving Boston, the West End dominated street-running public transportation in The Hub. In his book, *Streetcars of Boston Vol. 1*, O. R. Cummings described the West End after consolidation as "the largest horse railroad system under a unified management in the world." The first annual report of the West End, issued on September 30, 1888, articulated the scope of Boston's unified street railway system, listing over 225 miles of horse railroad owned and operated, over eighty-four million passengers carried, nearly fourteen million miles run, and over 1.8 million trips taken.

The consolidation of Boston's street railway operations under the West End benefited the riding public. Competition was quelled between horsecars of different companies racing recklessly through the streets to pick up passengers. Streetcar traffic jams, caused when competing lines flooded the same area with cars, were reduced. West End streetcars operated longer distances over consolidated lines, extending the range of a single ride for customers and reducing the amount of transfers required. The West End implemented a single fare, thereby eliminating the multiple fares incurred by riders who previously utilized the cars of different companies to complete a single trip. For travel within its broad system the West End issued paper tickets, some known as "checks," in addition to collecting cash fares. Tickets were precise in where and when they allowed a ticket holder to travel (Figure 2.3). An 1895 paper ticket with a menu to be punched by a conductor, very much like those developed by steam railroads, is shown in Figure 2.4.

Speaking to West End stockholders in the company's first annual report, Whitney stated:

> We think also that the community generally are pleased with the results of the consolidation. Blockades have become infrequent, some needed long lines have been established, and the cars run under a better system than was possible under a divided management.

Whitney also alluded to what became a quantum leap in how the public was transported around Boston—the transition from horsepower to electricity: "Should any other system of motive power come into use, the advantages to the community of this consolidation will be still more apparent." One other system of motive power—electricity—indeed came into use in Boston, and the West End pioneered its large scale application in public transportation for America.

From Horsepower to Electric Traction

At the end of its first calendar year of consolidated operations, 1888, the West End owned 7,684 horses and operated 1,584 horsecars. It was an operation of unprecedented size, requiring significant financial and physical resources to sustain. Horses needed to be purchased, trained, fed, stabled, and disposed of. With a typical cost of $75 to $125 each, the animals came from Vermont, New York, and Canada. One employee alone purchased over 100,000 horses during his tenure. Hay for the horses arrived from fields around Massachusetts. West End farriers re-shoed company horses every three to four weeks. The company typically staffed one farrier for every seven horses. The army of farriers was complemented by doctors and an in-house veterinary department. A horse lasted five to eight years in service on the West End. The company sold worn-out live horses at auction, at an average price of $30 each.

At a horse railroad, buildings housing streetcars were called barns, just like the often contiguous buildings for the stabling of horses. After its takeover of Boston's horse railroad companies, and their respective car and horse barns, the West End became one of the largest owners of real estate in Greater Boston. With substantial equine, vehicle, and real estate holdings came substantial maintenance costs and property taxes. Looking to maximize efficiencies early on, and in the spirit of statements made by Whitney in the West End's 1888 annual report, the West End explored replacing horses with a more cost-effective motive power.

By the 1880s, viable means for conveying streetcars without horses, including electric traction motors and continuously moving underground cables, had already been developed or implemented successfully outside of Boston. Electric-motor and cable-propelled streetcars did away with horses and their limited speed, jerky starts, olfactory disturbances, feed costs, manure, need to be changed out upon tiring, and land required for stabling.

A cable-propelled streetcar operates along fixed tracks and makes frequent stops along city streets, just like a horsecar. But unlike a horsecar, a cable car is dragged along its tracks by an under-street continuously moving cable. A cable car driver operates a mechanism to connect or disconnect their car from the cable. When connected, a cable car moves in the direction of the continuously moving cable. The cable follows a narrow trench in the ground, centered between the tracks, and running beneath the longitudinal center line of the cable car. A cable station at the end of a cable car line keeps the cable moving via massive wheels spun by steam-powered or electric motors. A cable car driver applies brakes to keep their car from moving when it is disconnected from the cable and they are paused to pick up or drop off passengers.

The first public cable car network in the United States came into being in San Francisco. What began as one line in 1873, expanded into a network of twenty-three lines with fifty miles of track. The system was decimated by the great earthquake of 1906. Today, the San Francisco Municipal Railway (MUNI) continues to operate three cable car lines with the last manually-operated cable cars providing daily revenue service in the world. New York City once had an expansive cable car network, none of which remains in use. Boston never saw the introduction of a cable car transit system.

America's first public transit street railway powered by electricity opened in 1884. In Cleveland, Ohio, an underground conduit concealing a third-rail-like electric power source was used in lieu of an overhead power wire. Streetcars tapped into and drew electric current from the underground conduit to power their electric traction motors. After Cleveland, a similar system was installed in Allegheny, Pennsylvania. The company that provided the conduit for Cleveland became the Bentley-Knight Company. In Massachusetts, on July 2, 1888, the Lynn & Boston started regular operation of one of Massachusetts' earliest electric street railway lines. Called the "Highland Circuit Route," the line served the city of Lynn.

Of America's early electric street railway operations, one was developed and installed in Richmond, Virginia by inventor and entrepreneur Frank J. Sprague. Because of his pioneering work with electric motors and power distribution systems for streetcars in Richmond and beyond, Sprague became known as "The Father of Electric Traction." In Richmond, and after months of intense on-site construction, engineering, and testing by Sprague and his team, the Richmond Union Passenger Railway opened to paying customers on February 2,

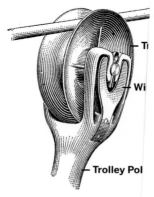

Figure 2.5 Trolley Wheel Mal
A trolley wheel is held in place
trolley pole. The pole and its w
trolley wire by a mechanism m

1888. Later that year, Henry Whitney came down from Boston and personally inspected Richmond's twelve mile long system and its streetcars propelled by Sprague's newly-developed electric traction motors. After a visit to also inspect Allegheny's underground conduit technology and additional correspondence with Sprague, Whitney became convinced that electric traction was the ideal replacement for the West End's massive collection of equine-powered horsecars.

The West End Brings Trolleys to Boston

On July 17, 1888, the West End awarded the Sprague Electric Railway & Motor Company an initial contract to implement its technology for the West End in Brookline and Boston. A day before the awarding of the contract, Brookline selectmen held a hearing to review the West End's intention to install an electric power system for its streetcars. At the meeting, Henry Whitney advocated eloquently that his company be permitted to install trolley wires over and along city streets. On August 18, and with popular support from their constituents, the Brookline selectmen approved installation of trolley wire along Beacon Street.

Before the word "trolley" became interchangeable with the terms streetcar, light rail vehicle (LRV), or tram (a term more commonly used for urban streetcars outside of the United States), the word

described a roof-mounted mechanism that delivered electric current from trolley wire to an electric streetcar. Early trolley systems made contact with trolley wire via a trolley wheel, held in place at the top of a trolley pole (Figure 2.5). The wheel, pole, and rooftop elements at the bottom of the pole were collectively known as the trolley. Trolley poles extended from the rooftop of streetcars and were raised or lowered manually. From a streetcar's trolley mechanism, electricity flowed into the car's wiring where it provided power for electric lights, heaters, and traction motors. The motors, located beneath the floor of the car, turned a streetcars' wheels and provided the vehicle with tractive power.

As improved mechanisms for connecting streetcars to trolley wire came into being, trolley wheels disappeared from the top of trolley poles, but not before the word "trolley" became synonymous with the electric streetcar vehicle itself. The Boston Elevated Railway Company (BERy), successor to the West End, explained in its August 1926 employee newsletter that the average life of a trolley wheel was four months or six to seven thousand miles, and that the company was using approximately nine-thousand of the twenty-one pound metal wheels per year.

Aspects of the West End's Beacon Street electric streetcar line were rendered in the January 1889 issue of *The Street Railway Journal* (Figure 2.6). Along the line, trolley wire was suspended above

BEACON STREET WEST FROM HARVARD STREET.

Figure 2.6 Beacon Street Electric Streetcar Line, 1889
Trolley wires are supported by cross-wires attached to trackside poles (above). Two of the West End's earliest electric streetcars (right) feature vestibules reading "Brookline & Brighton," locales served by each. Each car's side displays "Beacon St. Brookline," the route along which each ran. Wooden signs of the roofs display additional destination and route information.

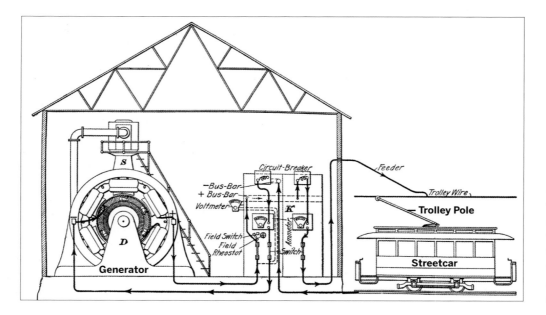

Figure 2.7 Direct Current Circuit f[...]
From left to right are: the generator ([...]
powered by coal-burning steam boile[...]
circuit breakers; and the trolley wire [...]
tracks. The generator and controls a[...]
station. Direct current (DC), created [...]
flows out of the power station and al[...]
trolley wheel and pole, DC power run[...]
to the internal wiring of the streetcar[...]
act as the ground, completing the cir[...]
station.

two parallel tracks. The West End's Beacon Street trolley wires provided direct current (DC) power for company streetcars. Figure 2.7 and its accompanying caption explain the essential components of DC power generation and transmission for electric streetcars.

Unlike Brookline, Boston initially prohibited overhead trolley wires in the Back Bay, the neighborhood through which the West End intended to run its new electric streetcars to and from downtown Boston. Where trolley wire was prohibited, the West End contracted Bentley-Knight to install underground electric conduits. Upon their completion along Boylston and other Back Bay streets, the conduits provided West End cars with power from below. Each streetcar tapped the power source with a retractable plough extending from beneath its traction motors (Figure 2.8). Inside of the conduit, the plough made contact with and drew current from energized metal conductors. The fixed conductors were the underground equivalent of an overhead trolley wire. As a streetcar dragged its plough along the conductors within the conduit, electricity was transmitted through, up, and into the car's electrical system.

When viewed from above, each conduit looked like a narrow slot in the road surface bound by metal protection rails. A conduit was similar in appearance to the in-street slot protecting the moving cable utilized by cable cars. West End cars made the changeover from trolley wire to underground conduit during a brief stop to allow the driver to lower the car's trolley pole, breaking contact with the trolley wire, and extend the car's ploughs into the conduit, making contact with the conductors. Conversely, the car's driver raised the ploughs and trolley pole when the car made the transition from conduit and back to trolley wire.

After installing conduit in the Back Bay and overhead wires in Brookline throughout December 1888 and into early January 1889, the West End performed test runs of Boston's first electric streetcars. The company operated a test run on January 2, 1889, as recorded in the January 3 *Boston Daily Globe*:

> The first car left the car house at Allston yesterday about 2 o'clock, and came into Park square at 2:50. Here it speedily filled with passengers, curiosity seekers, all of them, several West End officials and newspaper man....the car left Park square....From Charles street to Dartmouth street the street was lined with interested beholders. The advent of the car had been heralded, and all were waiting with eager expectancy. The majority seemed pleased.... Even the horses on passing cars seemed pleased, thinking evidently that they were at last to have a respite from their daily drudgery. Others, however, reared and plunged, amazed probably at the car moving along so easily, and not being drawn by their fellow creatures....Ipswich street was reached at 3:07, 14 minutes run from Park square....Here the change is made from the conduit to the overhead system...(sic).

The car arrived at its destination in Allston at 3:30 p.m., just short of an hour after leaving Park Square. The West End launched regular, electric streetcar service between Park Square and Coolidge Corner, in the middle of January 1889. The *Boston Daily Globe* reported on January 13: "The new Boylston street Back Bay line will run twelve-minute trips Saturday, starting at 9:24 a.m. Last car will leave at 8 p.m." Five days later, on January 18, the *Boston Daily Globe* provided additional service details:

> ...tomorrow...the Oak square, Brighton, and Park square electric cars will run as follows: Leave Oak square at 5:30 a.m., 6 a.m., and return every 15 minutes until 10:30 p.m. Returning, leave Park square at 6:20 a.m., 6:50 a.m., and every 15 minutes until [late evening] (sic).

The January 18 article listed cars operating every fifteen minutes on Sundays and confirmed that the West End had discontinued horsecar service along its the newly electrified lines.

The underground conduit system used by the West End in the Back Bay was flawed by design. Snow and ice easily jammed the narrow slot and kept the plough from consistently making contact with the conductors. Virtually any metal object dropped into the conduit slot, including coins, caused a short circuit at the conductors and brought electric streetcars in the Back Bay to a halt. Hunting down and removing the offending object took considerable time. On April 10, the *Boston Daily Globe* reported on a malfunctioning section of conduit in the Back Bay. A team of horses drawing a carriage on the Boylston Street bridge over the Boston & Albany Railroad (Boston & Albany) tracks was electrocuted upon making contact with the conduit. The shrieking horses were released by firemen and the driver of the carriage, but not before all parties received some unwanted jolts. The horses and their rescuers escaped without significant injury, but the failings of the conduit system were eventually recognized by Boston. In May 1889, the city approved a request by the West End to replace its Back Bay conduits with overhead trolley wire. In early July, the West End discontinued use of underground conduits. After summer 1889, trolleys operated exclusively under wire in Boston.

The West End opened a second electrified streetcar line to the public on February 16, 1889. The line connected Cambridge's Harvard Square with Boston's Bowdoin Square, tracing the route of the line opened by the Cambridge Railroad in 1856 (see Chapter 1). The West End extended electric streetcar service from Harvard Square into Arlington on July 6, 1889. The West End contracted electrification of the line to the Thomson-Houston Electric Company, which had recently absorbed the Bentley-Knight Company. Thomson-Houston merged with the Edison General Electric Company (founded by Thomas Edison, which took over the Sprague Electric Railway & Motor Company) in 1892 to form the General Electric Company. General Electric, a company with deep roots in the early electrification of public transportation in Boston, relocated its corporate headquarters to the city in 2016–17.

As the West End deployed more and more electric streetcars, the company was keen to educate riders where to board one of its trolleys. The West End's circa 1890 *Strangers' Guide* instructed:

> Stopping places are designated by a white band painted around the middle section of pole supporting trolley wire nearest to the proper stopping place, on the right hand side of the street,

Figure 2.8 Streetcar Motor and Underground Conduit, 1889
A cross-sectional drawing reveals the configuration of the conduit (bottom right) through which runs a plough attached to an electric bus bar beneath a streetcar. The plough draws current from conductors within the conduit, transmits it via the bus bar to the electric traction motor (center), which in turn rotates the wheels (left and right) to propel the streetcar.

when facing in the direction the car is going; stops at street intersections being at the further cross-walk. When two white poles stand opposite, stops are made going in either direction. Cars will *not stop at stopping places unless signalled* by persons wishing to board or leave the car (sic).

Power Stations Come Online

The West End was a private company, established to not only move the public, but to generate profit for its investors. A circa 1900 West End bond certificate features an electric streetcar overtaking a somewhat startled pair of horses pulling a carriage (Figure 2.9). The West End was selling more than bonds. It was marketing the future.

When it launched regular electric streetcar service in 1889, the West End was among the first large public transit operator in America to devote significant resources to converting from horse-power to electric traction. Of the approximately 21,750 streetcars and 6,000 miles of street railways operated throughout the United States at the time, more than ninety-nine percent of the cars and over ninety percent of the miles were operated via

literal horsepower. When it moved forward with electrification, the West End was so ahead of the curve that it was forced to contend with few viable sources of electricity from which it could draw to power its cars. To augment the limited electricity it did purchase from commercial suppliers, the West End constructed its own power stations, the first of which was erected in Allston, .

The Allston Power Station powered the West End's Beacon Street and connected streetcar lines with 500 volts DC. Steam-powered engines turned two dynamos (generators), each rated for 80,000 watts. A smoke stack towered one hundred feet above a brick power house. DC power flowed out of the power house along silicone-bronze, overhead conductor wires. The Allston Power Station was constructed next door to, and along with, a new building for electric streetcars (Figure 2.10). The nearly 100 feet long and eighty feet deep car house accommodated twenty-four of the West End's earliest electric streetcars (Figure 2.11). Each car had a typical maximum operating speed of less than fifteen miles per hour.

A year after powering up a massive new power plant, its Central Power Station, the West End

Allston Power Station and Car House, Circa 1890
d's Allston Power Station (marked by the tall
) and Car House (right; with trolleys peaking out
was the first power plant and car house complex
from the ground up for electric streetcar opera-
on.

closed its Allston Power Station in 1897. The
Central Power Station was erected in Boston's
South End. The site of the new facility was previously occupied by the Hinkley Locomotive Works, a
manufacturer of steam locomotives that opened in
1840. In the first half of the 1840s, when it was doing
business as Hinkley & Drury, the locomotive builder
produced the first three steam locomotives of the

Old Colony Railroad. During the 1850s, Hinkley's
operation was known as the Boston Locomotive
Works. The company did business in the 1860s as
Hinkley & Williams. The Hinkley company ceased
operations in early 1889. In July, the company
sold its South End property to the West End. The
Central Power Station covered more than an acre
on the former Hinkley property. Maps from 1874

Boston's Earliest Electric Streetcar, 1889
eet Railway Company car #443, constructed as
1888 by the Newburyport Car Manufacturing
as converted by the West End to electric traction

(Figure 2.12) and 1898 (Figure 2.13) depict the site of the Central Power Station before and during the plant's existence.

The West End fired up the Central Power Station with three 2,000 horsepower engines in 1896. A year later, the station churned out power with an additional five engines, massive machines that occupied a cavernous space (Figure 2.14). Water for the station's boilers flowed into the facility through massive underground pipes that ran between it and South Bay, a finger of Boston Harbor located just across Albany Street from the plant. Above ground, coal for the boilers arrived on ships and barges atop the same waters. Along Albany Street, coal for the power station was off-loaded and stored in a coal

pocket before being consumed. The Central Power Station was full of extremes. Its two main smoke-stacks were each over 250 feet tall, some thirty feet taller than the Bunker Hill Monument. The order for the belts used to transmit power from its boiler-powered steam engines to its dynamos was the largest order for such equipment yet taken. The following was written in the *The Street Railway Journal* about the Central Power Station:

It is justly a matter of pride with Boston people that the largest and most thoroughly equipped electrical power plant on the face of the globe is located in their city, and that what is by all odds the most comprehensive system of electrical

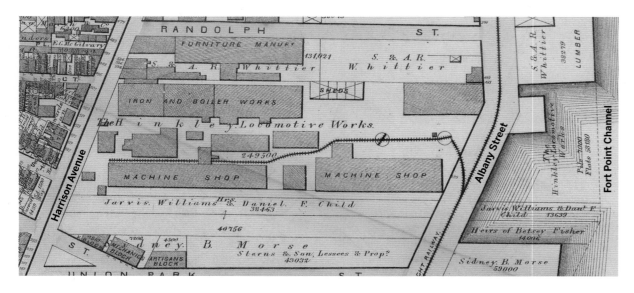

Figure 2.12 Future Site of the Central Power Station, 1874
A real estate map of Boston's South End shows the complex in use by the Hinkley Locomotive Works (center).

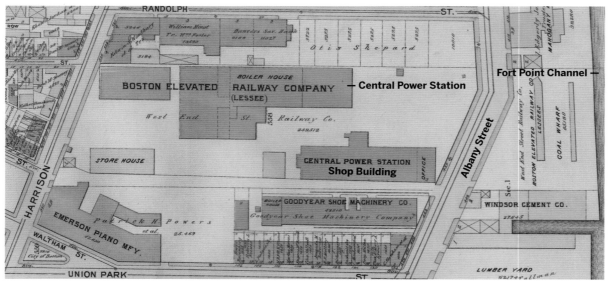

Figure 2.13 Mapping the Central Power Station, 1898
A real estate map of Boston's South End shows the Central Power Station, initially opened by the West End, labeled "Boiler House." The "Coal Wharf" on the edge of the South Bay (far right) is where the fossil fuel for the power station's steam boilers was off loaded from barges.

street railways in the world is to be credited to the 'Hub of the Universe.'

The Central Power Station was upgraded and improved by the West End, and later, by its successor, the BERy. A photograph (Figure 2.15) reveals the Harrison Avenue side of the plant in 1925, when the BERy was its operator. Full time operation of the Central Power Station ceased on February 26, 1930 when the BERy, after bringing newer power plants online, relegated the South End facility to standby service. The BERy closed the Central Power Station for good on July 1, 1932. In early 1941, the massive smokestacks were dismantled from the top down, by hand.

Central Power Station, Circa Late 1890s

...shed on the cover of the BERy's October 1931 ...agazine, depicts the interior of the West End's ...r Station as it was in the late 1890s.

Central Power Station Complex, 1925

...nokestack rises from the Central Power Station, ...by the West End and by the time of this photo- ...l by the BERy. The landmark stack, nor the second ...ostly conceals, no longer stands tall. The main ...ain, having undergone adaptive reuse.

Figure 2.16 Twenty-Foot Electric Streetcar, Circa 1892
West End built car number 97 in 1892. "West Somerville" is painted on the side, indicating the car's outbound destination from Boston. The four-faced, wood sign mounted to the long side of the roof reads "Scollay Sq," the car's inbound destination, and "via Highland Avenue & Medford St," the car's route.

Figure 2.17 West End Number 1 Streetcar, Circa 1892
West End car number 1537 at Copley Square. A twenty-five-foot, closed-type electric streetcar, the vehicle was constructed by the Newburyport Car Company in 1891.

Figure 2.18 West End Number 1 Streetcar, Circa 1891
The interior of West End car number 331, a twenty-five-foot, closed-type electric streetcar built in 1890.

Electric Streetcars for Boston

During the 1890s, after technological and commercial success with its Beacon Street and Cambridge electric streetcar lines, the West End embarked on a system-wide conversion from horsepower to electric traction. Existing horsecars were electrified or disposed of and new streetcars were ordered with electric traction motors. At the time, typical closed-type horsecars owned by the West End were sixteen feet long and had a rated capacity of approximately two dozen passengers. The West End's first closed-type electric cars were either sixteen-foot horsecars converted to electric traction or sixteen-foot cars ordered new. As electric motors became more powerful, the West End brought larger electric streetcars onto the streets. Twenty-foot models were ordered new or built in-house by splicing together two sixteen-foot cars (Figure 2.16).

Combined, the West End and the BERy purchased over 1,200 twenty-five-foot, closed-type electric streetcars. The twenty-five-foot cars mostly fell into one of four types, Number 1, 2, 3, and spliced. Figure 2.17 shows the exterior and Figure 2.18 exposes the interior of a West End Number 1 twenty-five-footer. The West End ordered 150 Number 1 cars in 1890. The last Number 1 was scrapped in 1927. The West End acquired 240 Number 2 twenty-five-footer cars (Figure 2.19) during 1891. The last remaining Number 2 was disposed of by the Metropolitan Transit Authority

(MTA) in 1952. Number 3 cars were put into service by the West End and the BERy between 1895 and 1900. They were gone from the streets of Boston by the end of the 1920s. After the West End, the BERy proceeded to operate larger and larger closed-type cars, employing twenty-six-and-one-half-foot closed cars during 1903–30, then, thirty-four-foot-four-inch cars during 1921–29.

Prior to electrification, typical open-type horsecars seated thirty-five to forty passengers on seven or eight benches. After electrification, during the 1890s, the West End brought to Boston open-type cars with seven, eight, nine, ten, and even twelve benches. Twelve-bench models (Figure 2.20) were used by the company for heavily travelled summer routes, just as horse-drawn barges had been deployed.

BERy Number 3 Streetcar, Circa 1900

-foot, closed-type car, number 1636 was by St. Louis Car Co. in 1899.

West End Twelve-Bench Streetcar, Circa 1890

r number 1906, built in 1890 by the Newburyport ', is signed for "Arlington Heights" at its front and mbridge & Arlington" along the long side of its destinations for the car when it ran outbound.

The November 1891 *Street Railway Journal* contained a description of a double-deck streetcar used by the West End for forty days in 1891–92. The towering car (Figure 2.21) was constructed by Pullman and ran along Main Street and North Avenue (now Massachusetts Avenue) in Cambridge. The interior of the two-story vehicle was finished with fine woods and upholstered seats. Windows were glazed with crystal glass. Doors featured embossed glass panels. An electric seating

Figure 2.21 West End Double-deck Streetcar, Circa 1891

Figure 2.22 BERy Articulated Car, 1912
Paused at Bennett Street, Cambridge, car number 405 consisted of two, twenty-foot streetcars reworked and joined together with a new, central compartment.

Boarding a Snake Car at Harvard Square, 1912

...atchful gaze of the conductor, a patron steps into ...ompartment of BERy articulated car number 405. ...hand-hold pole, the conductor monitors the fare ...ductor controlled the deployment or retraction of ...step (bottom), as well as the opening and closing ...at the center of the car.

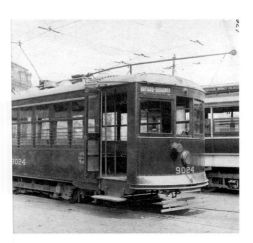

BERy Birney Car #9024, August 2, 1920

indicator displayed available upper level seats to those boarding the car at the base of twin spiral staircases.

Other Boston streetcars of creative design included articulated cars, also called "snake cars," and compact, Birney "safety" cars. Each articulated car was essentially two twenty or twenty-five-foot, single-truck streetcars joined together with a new, elevator cab-like compartment (Figure 2.22). The formerly independent streetcars each lost one of their two vestibules to accommodate their conversion into a single articulated car. Flexible joints, located where each end of the middle compartment met one of the streetcar bodies, allowed a snake car to attenuate, or "snake," around curves. The central compartment featured the passenger entrance and exit doors, housed a conductor, and contained a fixed fare box at its center (Figure 2.23). Boston's articulated cars were home grown, designed, and patented by the BERy's superintendent of rolling stock and shops, John Lindall. A ride in a snake car was often rough for passengers and the conductor alike. Heavily loaded or fast-moving snake cars vibrated and nearly scraped the ground as they bounced along. As Lindall's articulated cars trundled down Boston's streets, they were mocked as "two rooms and a bath." It was not until the 1970s that a smooth-running fleet of articulated streetcars arrived in Boston.

Boston's Birney cars were lighter than earlier electric streetcars and significantly shorter than articulated cars. Birney cars were designed by the Stone & Webster Company's lead streetcar engineer Charles Birney. Unlike most streetcars of its day, Birney cars required one operator each. Lightweight construction and single man operation made Birneys economical to purchase and operate. Birney cars brought increased safety to the streets of Boston. Each car featured a dead man handle, that, if released by the operator, automatically cut power to the car and deployed the brakes. From 1917 to 1937 the BERy deployed approximately eighty Birney "safety" cars (Figure 2.24), often as replacements for obsolete or larger cars that required a crew of two to operate.

Parlor cars were streetcars of high design, typically deployed for special purposes, including company meetings, line inspection trips, and charter trips. They were not intended for revenue service. The West End received a pair of custom-built parlor cars in 1894. Numbered 924 (Figure 2.25 and Figure 2.26) and 925, the cars were twenty-foot types, painted black with gold and dark red accents. Under roofs with leaded glass monitor windows, the interiors of cars 924 and 925 featured mahogany panels, elaborate draperies, plush carpeting, and twenty upholstered chairs. The cars were available for private charter, earning non-fare revenue for the West End when not being used by company management. After being relegated to work car

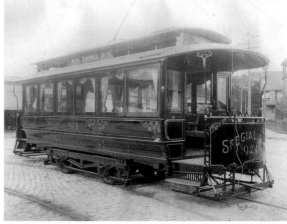

Figure 2.25 West End Parlor Car #924, 1896

Figure 2.26 Interior of West End Parlor Car #924, 1896

Figure 2.27 BERy Parlor Car #101, Circa 1905

Interior of BERy Parlor Car #101, Circa 1905
st extravagantly furnished streetcar was used
General Bancroft for inspection cruises around the
m. Despite heavy use by the General, the car was
fter Bancroft's departure.

BERy Snow Plow #101, Circa 1900
roft, president of the Boston Elevated Railway
ses with a streetcar snowplow tailored for his use.

duty from the 1920s through the early 1950s, 924 was scrapped and 925 moved into the collection of Maine's Seashore Trolley Museum. Complimenting its parlor cars, the West End converted a closed-type horsecar into a private director's car in 1895.

Boston's penultimate parlor car was the BERy's car number 101 (Figure 2.27), the pride and joy of General William A. Bancroft, president of the BERy from October 1899 until September 1916. Previously, Bancroft was the superintendent of the Cambridge Railroad in 1885 and the Mayor of Cambridge from 1893 to 1896. A multi-hour tour of the BERy's system on a Sunday was a regular event for Bancroft, who sometimes brought his family along for the ride.

Transit historian O. R. Cummings described BERy's car number 101 as, "a masterpiece of the carbuilder's art." G. C. Kuhlman Car Company constructed the unique vehicle for the BERy in 1904. The thirty-seven-foot car was powered by four, sixty-five horsepower General Electric traction motors. Cummings recalled the 101 as, "[the] fastest car ever owned by the Boston Elevated." The car was designed to achieve speeds of fifty-five miles per hour, making it more akin to a high-speed interurban streetcar, not a city-running trolley. Cummings recalled that one BERy motorman pushed car number 101 beyond seventy miles per hour in the salt marshes between East Boston and Lynn.

The exterior of car 101 was painted black with red accents and gilt lettering. Leaded glass transom windows allowed light to flow into an interior fitted with mahogany panels, bass fixtures, silk drapes, and heavy carpet (Figure 2.28). Seven revolving arm chairs of mahogany and leather were each outfitted with a heater at their base. Oversize windows and glazed doors allowed for nearly unobstructed views out, useful on track inspection trips taken by management. With the addition of extra chairs, car 101 comfortably transported forty people in style.

Besides Kuhlman-built parlor car 101, Bancroft had access to a second BERy car numbered 101, a streetcar snowplow (Figure 2.29). Bancroft often rode in snowplow 101 to inspect snow removal operations being undertaken by BERy employees. Snowplow 101 was one of hundreds of service or work cars deployed by the BERy. Work cars included cranes, plows, spreaders, pump cars, flat cars, dump cars, and inspection cars.

Citing safety concerns, in 1900, the General Court passed a law requiring closed vestibules on all streetcars operating within Massachusetts. For

a few years, the BERy hid behind an exception and attempted to convince the state it did not have to submit to the law. At the end of spring 1902, the Board of Railroad Commissioners confirmed that the BERy indeed was required to comply with the statute. After the decree, open vestibule streetcars disappeared from the streets of Boston and the BERy worked to enclose vestibules on existing cars and ordered new cars without open vestibules.

When the West End consolidated horse railroad operations in 1887, it amassed a fleet of horsecars painted a rainbow of color schemes. The cars of the Metropolitan Railroad alone were each painted one of no fewer than ten different hues. Cars of the South Boston Railroad came in one of four color variants. During its first full year of consolidated operations, the West End implemented a program of repainting and renumbering existing cars as well as ordering new cars with standardized colors and predetermined numbers. With some exceptions, cars of each West End division were each painted a specific color scheme and assigned to a specific block of numbers. The circa 1890 West End *Strangers' Guide* articulated the specific colors of West End streetcars:

> Cars are colored according to the district from which they come. Thus: Dark green cars embrace Franklin Park, Grove Hall, Dorchester, Bartlett Street, Egleston Square, Forest Hills and Norfolk House. Lemon yellow cars embrace Tremont Street, Jamaica Plain, Columbus Avenue, and Belt Line cars. Dark blue cars embrace Dorchester Avenue, Field's Corner, Neponset, Milton and Meeting-House Hill lines. Scarlet cars all pertain to South Boston Division. Chrome yellow cars cover Charlestown, Somerville, Winter Hill, Medford, Malden, Everett and Bunker Hill lines. Crimson cars embrace all Cambridge lines, including West Somerville, Union Square, Somerville via East Cambridge, Newton, Watertown and Arlington. Pea green car, one line running to Back Bay District.... All cars in East Boston are orange-colored, running to Jeffries Point, Winthrop Junction and Chelsea.

Divisional colors remained in use by West End successor, the BERy, until 1909, when the BERy began painting cars green with white trim.

The West End applied destination signage to existing and new streetcars, with some exceptions, as follows. Principle outbound destinations from Boston were painted in large letter onto car

Figure 2.30 BERy Employees at Grove Hall, Circa 1890s
BERy motormen and conductors pose in front of Grove Hall Station and Car House. The station housed a public waiting room and offices for streetcar operations.

broadsides and inside the glass roof monitors. Additional destination information was generally displayed on wood signs mounted over the ends of car roof hoods. Detailed route or destination information was generally displayed on wood signs installed upon the sides of roof hoods. Additional destination information appeared on vestibule skirts at car ends. Beyond thoughtful paint, numbering, and signage schemes for its streetcars, the BERy formalized the public face of its operations with smartly uniformed employees (Figure 2.30).

More Power
The percentage of West End passenger receipts from electric streetcars exceeded those from horse-cars (fifty-three percent from electric streetcars and forty-seven percent from horsecars) for the first time in 1892. The ratio rose to 80:20 in favor of electric streetcars in 1893, and 96:4 in 1895. By September 30, 1896, the only West End horsecars transporting revenue customers trundled along tracks in the Back Bay; only one percent of the West End's network operated under direct horse-power. The last West End horsecar serving the public in Boston ran on Marlborough Street on December 24, 1900. After that, trolley wire reigned

supreme over the streetcars of Boston. Twenty-five years after its last horse retired from revenue service, and after its electric streetcar network had grown significantly, the BERy estimated that "it would require 167,000 horses to handle the passengers who now ride in the Boston District."

As the West End's web of trolley wires grew, so too did its electricity generation and transmission infrastructure. By 1897, power for the West End's electric streetcar network was generated at seven company-owned power stations. These were located in Boston's South End, South Boston, Dorchester, East Cambridge, Harvard Square, Charlestown, and East Boston. Complimenting the power plants was a network of strategically-placed electrical substations. The network of power plants and substations provided and distributed DC power to trolley wires of the West End's system. Successor to the West End, the BERy, improved and replaced the power plants and substations of the West End. The BERy constructed new plants, including its Lincoln Wharf Power Station in Boston's North End (Figure 2.31 and Figure 2.32), its Harvard Square Power Station in Cambridge, and its South Boston Power Station.

The electricity generated by the West End, and later the BERy, was produced by generators spun by massive engines. The engines were turned by the

Lincoln Wharf Power Station, Circa 1908

of the BERy's Lincoln Wharf Power Station is Boston's North End. The plant's stack is complete.

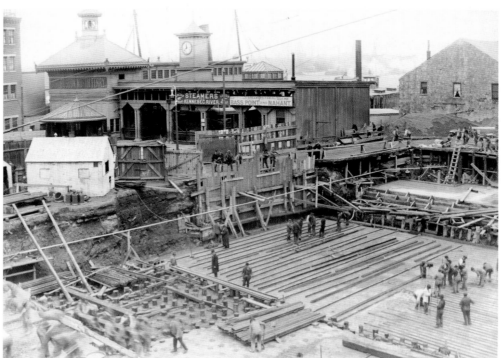

Building a Power Station, December 17, 1908

coln Wharf Power Station was constructed upon oden piles, each driven deep into mud and clay. f the piles are exposed as builders work on the foundations. The city of Boston's North Ferry e background of the scene.

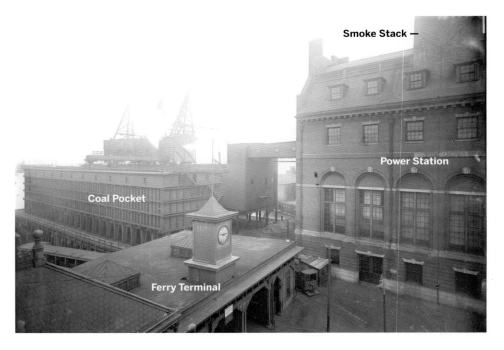

Smoke Stack —

Power Station

Coal Pocket

Ferry Terminal

Figure 2.33 Lincoln Wharf Power Station, December 17, 1908
Cranes perch atop the massive, timber-frame coal pocket (left) where coal was stockpiled before being transferred into the BERy's Lincoln Wharf Power Station (right). Mechanisms, concealed by an enclosed bridge (center), moved the coal from the pocket into the plant, where the coal was used to fire massive boilers. A clock tower crowns the Boston terminal of the North Ferry (bottom).

force of steam, generated by giant boilers, mostly fired by coal. A 1908 photograph shows the massive coal pocket used to store coal and supply the boilers at the Lincoln Wharf Power Station (Figure 2.33). The BERy recorded burning over 260,000 tons of coal in 1923 alone. With the electricity generated during that year, the company carried over 382 million riders, or as the company broadcast in a radio talk given in 1924:

> That is more than twice as many passengers as are carried on all the lines of the New England steam railroads. That is nearly four times the population of the entire United States. To carry this traffic 54,049,665 car miles were operated during 1923, which is equivalent to 109 round trips to the moon and over half the distance to the sun.

During the twentieth century, most of Boston's public transit power stations were converted from providing DC to alternating current (AC) power, and new generators arrived to produce exclusively AC. Before being transmitted to wire or third rail for pick up by transit vehicles, AC (provided by the power plants and substations) was converted to DC (powering the majority of streetcars, trackless trolleys, and rapid transit trains) by transformers located throughout the system.

The Broomstick Train

The proliferation of electric streetcars in 1890s Boston was unprecedented. The novel application of electricity to public transportation locomotion left many people mystified by streetcars being propelled without the aid of horses. Horses pulling a coach, an omnibus, or a horsecar was always straightforward and explainable. Electric streetcars, drawing their unseen power of propulsion from a skinny pole connected to a thin wire suspended in the air, were a bit mysterious. Concealed electric traction motors beneath streetcars did their work out of sight, unlike horses clippety-clopping down the street.

Recognizing the newness of electric streetcars, and recalling Massachusetts Bay's notorious colonial-era hysteria, during which colonists sentenced people to death as witches, Oliver Wendell Holmes penned: "The Broomstick Train or The Return of The Witches" (Figure 2.34). With his 1890 poem, the Cambridge-born Holmes waxed about supernatural forces exerting their will through witches and magically propelling electric streetcars along Boston's streets. Holmes likened trolley poles drawing power from overhead trolley wires to witches' broomsticks drawing on dark, unseen forces. With the line, "But the string is held by a careful man," Holmes reassured his readers that the motorman tending the cord that raised and lowered the trolley pole was indeed of this earth, and in fact the one in control of the electric streetcar.

LOOK out! Look out, boys! Clear the Track!
The witches are here! They've all come back!
They hanged them high, --No use! No use!
What cares a witch for a hangman's noose?
They buried them deep, but they would n't lie sill,
For cats and witches are hard to kill;
They swore they should n't and would n't die, --
Books said they did, but they lie! they lie!

Since then on many a car you'll see
A broomstick plain as plain can be;
On every stick there 's a witch astride,--
The string you see to her leg is tied.
She will do a mischief if she can,
But the string is held by a careful man,
And whenever the evil-minded witch
Would cut some caper, he gives a twitch.
As for the hag, you can't see her,
But hark! you can hear her black cat's purr,
And now and then, as a car goes by,
You may catch a gleam from her wicked eye.

Figure 2.34 "The Broomstick Train" Poem, 1890
The first and last stanzas of Oliver Wendell Holmes' poem relating supernatural forces and Boston's earliest electric streetcars.

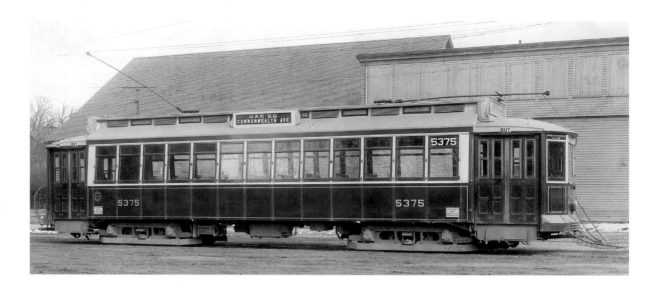

Semi-convertible Streetcar, March 11, 1914

...re in Brighton, BERy car number 5375 sits parked
...losed and steps retracted. Signage above the
...nates points of entrance or exit for riders. A large
...on the roof displays "Oak Sq." and "Common-
...' a destination and route, respectively.

Semi-convertible Streetcars

The electrification of Boston's streetcar network
allowed the BERy to deploy a plethora of electric
streetcar models. A large and evolving fleet offered
the BERy flexibility of deployment anywhere trolley wire had been strung. After years of operating
simple closed-type and open-type cars, the BERy
brought a new streetcar type to Boston, the semi-
convertible. Semi-convertibles were essentially
closed-type streetcars with window sashes that
could be fixed in an open position during pleasant
weather. The BERy launched its first semi-convertible car, a home-grown experimental model, in 1905.
Later that year, the first of what would become
a fleet of some forty Type 1 semi-convertibles

arrived. In the following year, the BERy added a
fifty-car fleet of Type 2 semi-convertibles. The
BERy received a fresh fleet of 100 Type 3 semi-
convertibles during late 1907 and early 1908. Type 1s
were approximately forty-three feet long, accommodated four dozen passengers seated, and were rated
to carry 140 riders. Types 2 and 3 both measured
forty-five feet long and had a capacity of 150 people.
By the early 1930s, all Type 1, 2, and 3 semi-convertibles were either scrapped or were no longer being
used in revenue service.

The 1910s saw the BERy bring online 275 Type
4 Semi-convertibles. The Type 4s (Figure 2.35 and
Figure 2.36) became the BERy's workhorse streetcars of the 1920s and 1930s. A typical Type 4 was

BERy Semi-convertible Streetcar #5453

...4 semi-convertible streetcar, with doors open
...tended, sits at Park Street Car House. From roof-
...n boxes, rollsign curtains call out destinations
...d "Andrew" served by the car.

powered by fifty horsepower traction motors. Straps for standees hung from the ceiling (Figure 2.37). Window sashes raised out of and lowered back into a pocket in the car's body. Each car featured a dedicated area for the conductor. Space for the motorman could be enclosed with a movable series of panels.

Upon the roof of each Type 4, four sign boxes displayed destination and route information. Each box enclosed one rollsign curtain used to display the car's terminal destination, sometimes accompanied by a route number or a major thoroughfare followed by the car. Most route numbers were three digits in length. The rollsign within each box was turned to

display one set of destination and route information from a fixed list. While earlier types of BERy semi-convertibles were retrofitted with rollsign boxes, Type 4 semi-convertibles were typically manufactured with sign boxes installed.

By the end of the 1910s, the BERy configured Type 4s to tow a streetcar that lacked traction motors and known as a trailer. The lack of a motorman in the trailer freed up more space for fare-paying riders. Type 4 trailers were center-entrance type cars, the floor at the center of which was lower at the car's middle, where the doors were located. The configuration reduced the amount of steps at the doors, expediting movement of people into and

Figure 2.37 Semi-convertible Streetcar, September 7, 1911
All seats are taken within BERy Type 4 Semi-convertible streetcar number 5198.

Figure 2.38 Interior of BERy Center-entrance Trailer #7001
Rigid wooden seats occupy the raised front and rear seating areas. The conductor's control stand and fare box lie at the middle of the depressed central area.

BERy Center-entrance Streetcars, 1927

 rain of center-entrance motor cars in MU opera-
 to pick up passengers on Commonwealth Avenue.
 ortion of the first car, an army of suited men
 ward. The train is signed for the Tremont Street
 Commonwealth Avenue.

Center-entrance Streetcars, 1941

 y center-entrance cars signed for Fenway Park
 to pull into Kenmore Station and consume a crowd
 ox game.

out of the car. A conductor sat at a fare box in the depressed section (Figure 2.38). Approximately 225 Type 4 trailers were utilized by the BERy from 1915 to 1944.

Powered versions of center-entrance streetcars were employed in Boston from 1916 to 1953, initially by the BERy, and later, by the MTA. Center-entrance motor cars were each equipped with four, forty horsepower motors. The motor cars were of the semi-convertible type, with window sashes that could be raised from and lowered into pockets. Each car measured approximately forty-eight feet long. Like their non-powered trailer cousins, center-entrance motor cars featured a depressed central portion where the doors and fare box were located. Boston's center-entrance motor cars wore 6000,

6100, 6200, and 6300-series numbers. Trailers wore 7000 and 7100-series numbers.

Many center-entrance cars were deployed in multiple unit (MU) operation (Figure 2.39). One, two, or more cars were joined and operated as a train, to combine tractive effort and increase passenger capacity. Despite having a rated capacity of 150–175 riders (depending on the model and alterations to each car) each center-entrance car often carried many more people. Referred to as "crowd swallowers," center-entrance cars were deployed in long lines along Commonwealth Avenue awaiting to consume crowds emerging from baseball games at Braves Field. Trains of center-entrance cars also scooped up crowds at Kenmore Station after Red Sox home games (Figure 2.40) and at North Station when the Bruins were in town.

Streetcar Post Offices

From 1895 until 1915, the West End, and later the BERy, operated streetcars to transport and process the U.S. Mail. Specially outfitted cars ran between post offices and delivery points in and around Boston. The first streetcars to carry mail in Boston operated like stagecoaches once did, carrying pouches of mail for the Postal Service for a fee. As the post office expanded mail service on electric streetcar lines, streetcar companies deployed cars partially or completely dedicated to mail operations (Figure 2.41 and Figure 2.42). The West End operated eleven mail cars. Later, the BERy operated from ten to twelve mail cars (Figure 2.43).

A streetcar upon which mail was received, sorted, and distributed for delivery was a Railway Post Office (RPO), literally a post office on wheels. Streetcar RPOs, which typically featured an exterior mail slot for customer use, had counterparts on the steam railroads. While steam railroad RPOs regularly travelled long distances and served large geographic areas, streetcar RPOs typically serviced local routes in populated areas. After the first successful operation of streetcar RPOs in Saint Louis in 1891, the list of cities with streetcar RPOs grew to fourteen, including Boston. Though some long distance interurban streetcar RPOs operated in the U.S. as late as 1950, operation of urban

Figure 2.41 Copley Square, Circa Late 1890s

A panoramic view of Copley Square, in Boston's Back Bay, captures an electric streetcar (left) and BERy mail car number 1300 (middle) in Boston's Back Bay neighborhood. Trinity Church and the Museum of Fine Arts preside over the scene.

Figure 2.42 BERy Mail Car #410, Circa 1905

This was one of the first eight streetcars converted to mail service by the West End in 1895. All were former Metropolitan Railroad streetcars. By 1905, the BERy owned the car.

Figure 2.43 U.S. Mail Wagon and Streetcar, May 6, 1907

An RPO streetcar (right), a post office wagon (middle), and postal workers (left) pose on Water Street, outside of Boston's main post office (far left).

streetcar RPOs in America wrapped up by the end of the 1940s. While trucks took over the shuttling of mail within American cities, steam railroads transported the mail across America throughout much of the twentieth century.

Mapping the West End

A public transit system of the size and complexity of the West End's could not function effectively without maps. The company produced maps for regulatory review, to survey its real estate, to document its lines, and to layout proposed improvements to its network. In 1887, the West End produced one of the earliest maps in which a tunnel for streetcars, a public transit subway, was proposed for Boston. The map (Figure 2.44) represented Henry Whitney's vision for improving public transportation in Boston. A decade after the map's publication, the proposed tunnel became realized as the Tremont Street Subway.

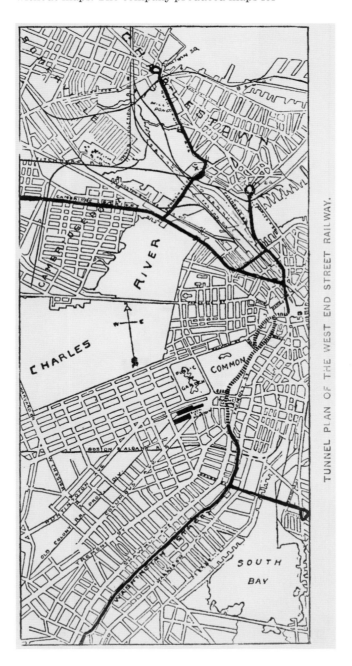

The West End's Tunnel Plan, 1887

...es represent proposed public transit trunk lines, ...potentially elevated or surface lines by the West ...shed lines passing through downtown indicate ...els or subways.

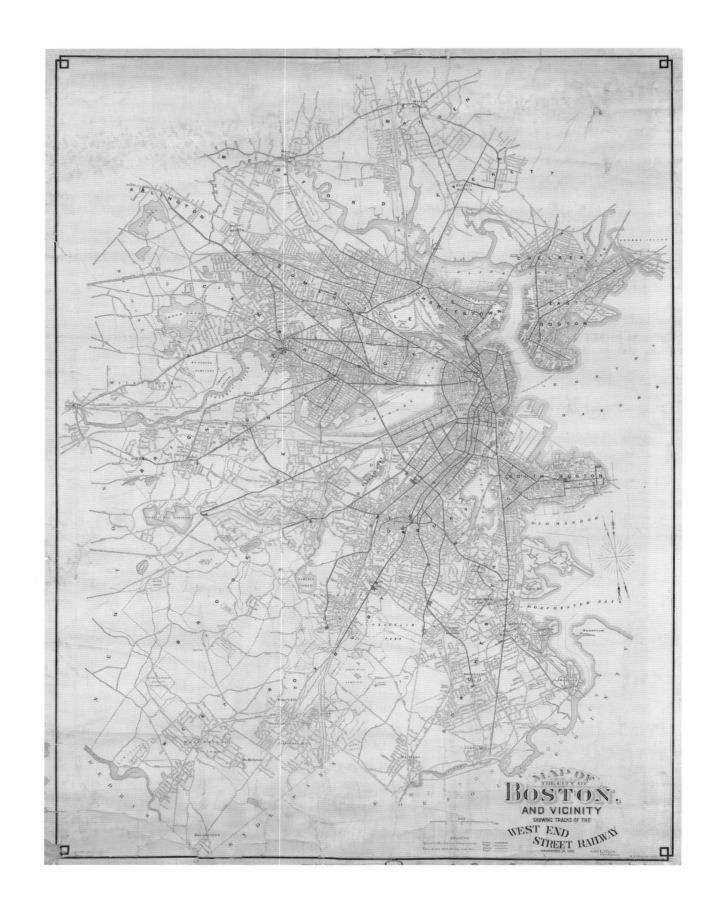

(Opp.) The West End System, December 19, 1891
...es of the West End are highlighted in red. Solid
...shed lines represent stretches of double track and
...respectively. Street railway lines of other compa-
...esented in yellow.

Harvard Bridge, 1905
...etcars share the Harvard Bridge with a horse-
...1. The bridge is fourteen years old in this image.

West End Track Plan Sheet Number 17, 1892
...icks, each represented by a single white line, wind
...ay and Adams Squares (right). The tracks trace
...Washington Streets and what today is Downtown
...t). Street names are marked and lengths of track
...noted in increments of a mile.

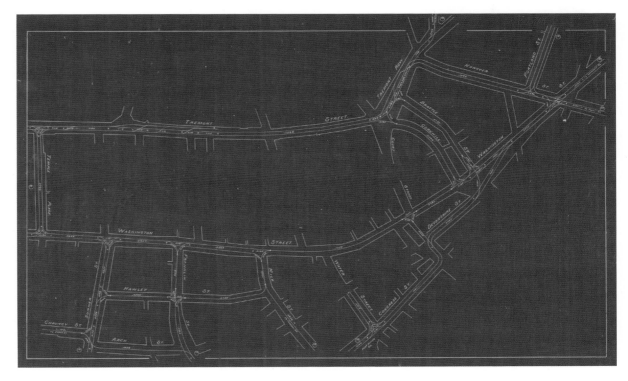

West End Guide, Circa Early 1890s
...street railway guide produced by the West End
...here at its original size. The miniature guide was
...extremely portable proportion.

The West End regularly produced a regional
streetcar map of its network. Typically titled
"Map of Boston and Vicinity Showing Tracks
of the West End Street Railway Company," the
map featured base cartography by Boston map
maker George H. Walker. An early edition, dated
March 1888 (Figure 2.2), was published less than
a year after the West End consolidated Boston's
streetcar companies. A December 19, 1891 edition
(Figure 2.45) included thirty miles of track added
to the West End's network since publication of the
March 1888 map. At the center of the 1891 map, a
red streetcar line crosses the Charles River Basin
via the Harvard Bridge (Figure 2.46), opened on
September 1, 1891.

Beyond maps of proposed and existing streetcar
lines, the West End produced track plans
(Figure 2.47) and guide books (Figure 2.48), the
former of which were engineering drawings that
allowed it to precisely document its rails. A comprehensive set of track plans was continuously kept
up to date by the West End's in-house engineers.
After the West End, the BERy, MTA, and MBTA all
maintained track maps of their respective systems.

Mapping the Regional Streetcar Network
Complementing the West End and successor streetcar systems serving Greater Boston was a broader
network, composed of multiple independent street

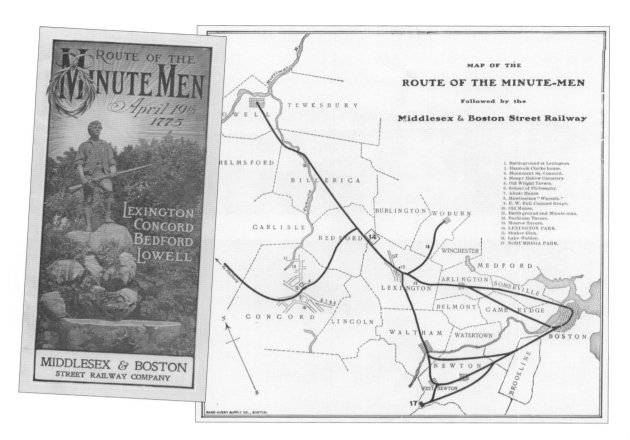

Figure 2.49 **Middlesex & Boston Brochure, Undated**
Middlesex & Boston streetcars connected Boston, Newton, Lowell, Concord, and points between.

Figure 2.50 **Trolley Trips Cover, 1901**
A trolley guide focused on destinations around Boston including Salem, the Blue Hills, and Hampton Beach, NH.

Figure 2.51 **South Shore Trolley Trips Cover, 1898**
"Pilgrims" regard a streetcar on the cover of a trolley guide to Boston's South Shore, including Plymouth.

railways. The scope of Boston's regional streetcar network was described in Karl Baedeker's 1889 *Guide to the United States*: "tramways (nearly all electric) traverse the principle streets and run into the various suburbs." By transferring between the lines of the different street railways, people could travel around Greater Boston, throughout New England, and well beyond.

To solicit readers, street railway company-issued maps often accompanied promotional guides. The Middlesex & Boston Street Railway Company (Middlesex & Boston), whose lines ran northwest from Boston, published such a guide. The *Route of the Minute Men* (Figure 2.49) contained a map of Middlesex & Boston lines as well as photographs and descriptions of towns and historic sites along the lines.

Popular publications for streetcar travel around Greater Boston were trolley guide books, published by various companies with titles that included *Trolley Trips* (Figure 2.50), *South Shore Trolley Trips* (Figure 2.51), *Derrah's Official Street Railway Guide*, and *By Trolley Through Western New England* (Figure 2.52). Trolley guides typically featured maps and information about specific streetcar networks or routes. *Trolley Trips Through Southern New*

England was packed full of maps and schedules for street railways operating between Boston and New York City. It listed fares required to reach various cities and towns, contained route descriptions, and featured photographs of destinations reachable by streetcar.

The "Map of the Street Railways in Eastern Massachusetts," published by R. H. Derrah in 1896, depicts Boston at the center of a tangle of street railway and steam railroad lines (Figure 2.53). Derrah's map also represented the first standard gauge steam railroad line to be converted to electric train service in America. Prior to the conversion, electric traction technology along rails was exclusively used only by streetcars. The converted railroad line ran from Nantasket Junction on Boston's South Shore to Pemberton Point in Hull. It was electrified by the New York, New Haven & Hartford Railroad in summer 1895. The railroad successfully operated large open-type passenger coaches, similar to open-type streetcars, through tidal marshes and along the shore.

Trolley guides were in wide circulation by the turn of the twentieth century. A prime example was the *Official Street Railway Guide of New England: Trolley Wayfinder*, published by the New England

Trolley Guide Book Covers, 1904; 1900; 1902

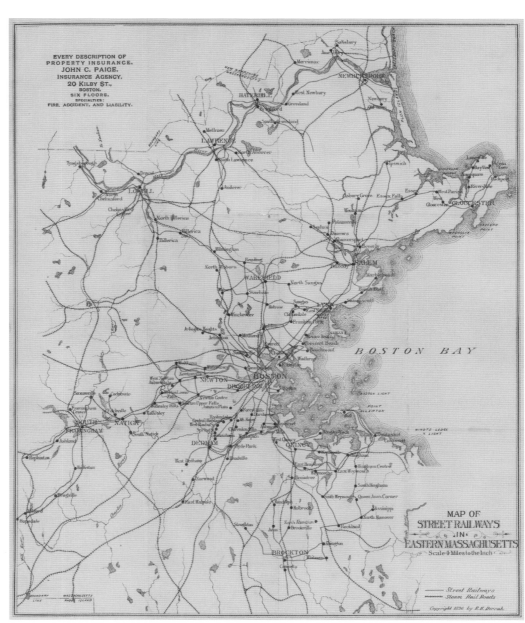

Derrah's Street Railway Map, 1896

...ds the center of a web of street railways (red lines)
...ailroads (black lines with ticks).

Street Railway Club (Figure 2.54). The multi-page guide was foldable to pocket-size. The Club revised and reissued the publication, typically on a yearly basis. The 1909 guide featured thirty-two tables, each listing fares, distances, and travel times between major points as well as intermediate stops. It was crammed full of street railway maps (Figure 2.55–Figure 2.58). A table for the trip from Boston to Gloucester provided data about the journey, including a map, a list of stops along the route, travel times between points, and a list of fares (Figure 2.59).

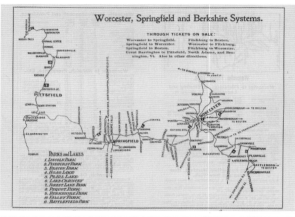

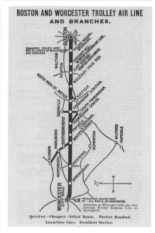

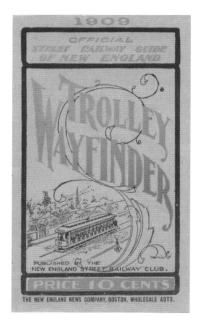

Figure 2.54 Trolley Wayfinder Cover, 1909

Figure 2.55 Trolley Wayfinder Maps and Cover, 1909
Clockwise, from top left, are maps of street railways serving metro-west Boston, central and western Massachusetts, southern New Hampshire, Boston's southwestern suburbs, and towns between Boston and Worcester.

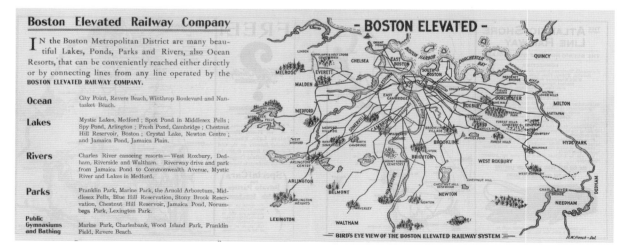

Figure 2.56 BERy Map from Trolley Wayfinder, 1909
The network of the BERy was the linchpin between the systems of the Boston & Northern Street Railway Company (Figure 2.57) and Old Colony Northern Street Railway Company (Figure 2.58).

Boston & Northern Map, 1909

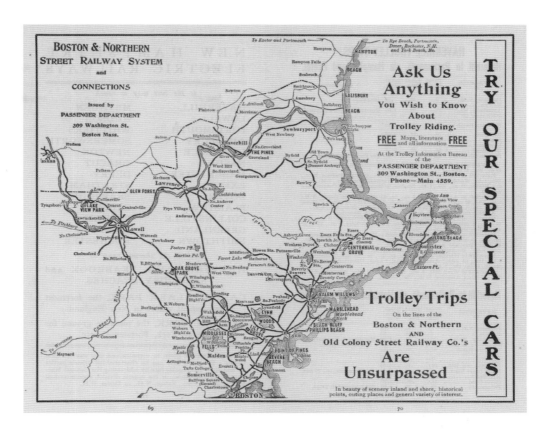

Old Colony Street Railway Map, 1909

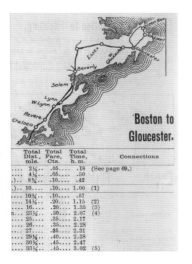

Boston to Gloucester.

Total Dist. mls.	Total Fare, Cts.	Total Time, h. m.	Connections
.... 2¾...	.05....	.18	(See page 69.)
.... 4½...	.05....	.50	
.)... 8¾...	.10....	.42	
.).. 10....	.10....	1.00	(1)
... 10¾...	.10....	.57	
... 14½...	.20....	1.15	(2)
... 16....	.20....	1.35	(3)
...n 23¾...	.50....	2.07	(4)
... 25....	.35....	2.17	
... 26....	.35....	2.28	
... 27....	.35....	2.31	
... 29¾...	.40....	2.38	
... 30¾...	.45....	2.47	
... 33½...	.45....	3.02	(5)

Table 12 from Trolley Wayfinder, 1909

ition of *Trolley Wayfinder* designated itself as the
et Railway Guide of New England." Table 12 is one
thirty in the guide. The table, for a trolley trip from
oucester, features a map, a list of stops, distance
and fare details.

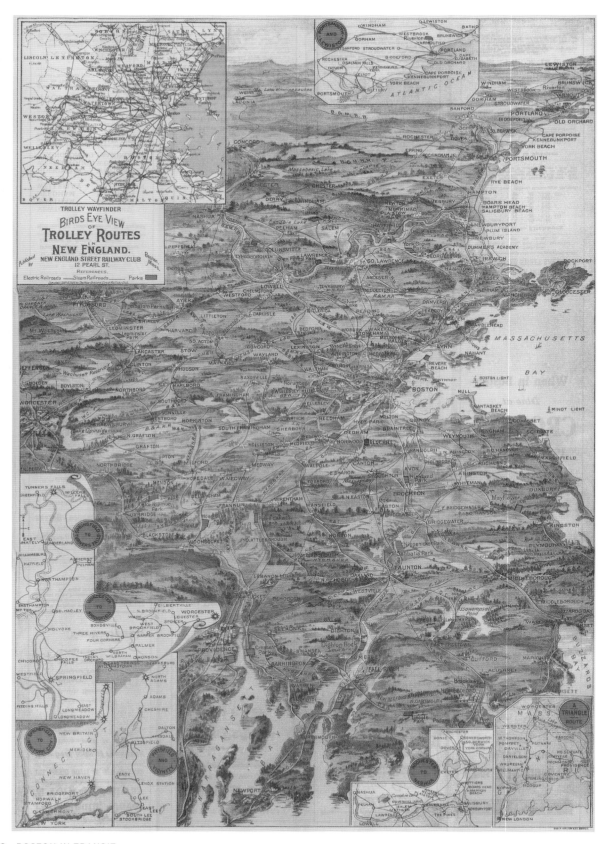

Figure 2.60 Trolley Routes in New England, 1905

A bird's eye view shows streetcar lines connecting cities, towns, and trolley parks from Southern Maine (top) to Rhode Island (bottom). Trolley parks are marked by red boxes connected to a streetcar line, also highlighted in red.

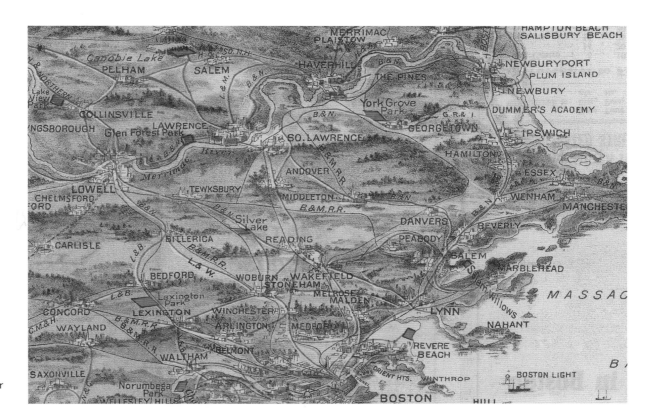

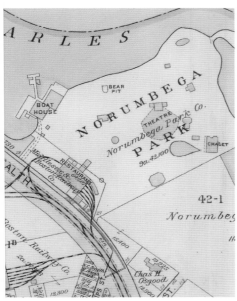

Published concurrently with trolley guide books
were large format maps of Boston's regional
streetcar network. A colorful example is the "Birds
Eye View of Trolley Routes In New England"
(Figure 2.60), published in 1905 by the New England
Street Railway Club. The map was produced in
a news-stand-ready format, folded and enclosed
in a protective cover. The view unfolded to show
the lines of street railways serving Rhode Island,
eastern Connecticut, eastern Massachusetts,
southern New Hampshire, and southern Maine.

Trolley Parks for Amusement

To encourage ridership on Saturdays and Sundays,
when there was a lack of workday commuters on
their trolleys, street railway companies established
parks to serve as weekend destinations for riders.
The companies often located their parks at the end
of their streetcar lines, where land was inexpensive
and ridership was low. Many started as simple land-
scaped gardens. Some evolved from modest green
spaces to attraction-rich centers of leisure-time
amusement, featuring zoos, carousels, and midways.
By the early twentieth century, trolley parks were
popular and busy destinations unto themselves,

fulfilling the goals of street railway companies to
increase off-peak traffic.

The 1905 "Birds Eye View of Trolley Routes
In New England" (Figure 2.60) records scores
of trolley parks. An enlarged portion of the view
(Figure 2.61) shows no fewer than four trolley parks
in Northwest Greater Boston. Near the top of the
enlarged view is "Canobie Lake," created by the
Northeast Street Railway Company in 1902. Near
the bottom of the image is "Norumbega," opened
by the Commonwealth Avenue Street Railway in
1897. Both parks grew in popularity as the twentieth
century progressed. During the height of patronage
at Norumbega, special cars were run by Commonwealth Avenue Street Railway, and successor
company Middlesex & Boston, to serve crowds
seeking the amusements at the popular park.
Figure 2.62, a 1917 real estate map of the Auburn-
dale section of Newton, depicts the facilities of the
Middlesex & Boston at Norumbega. Some of the
trolley parks developed by street railway companies remained in operation long after the streetcar
tracks serving them were removed. Norumbega
remained in operation until 1963. Canobie Lake
Park remains vibrant and open, a legacy of the age
of Boston's regional streetcar network.

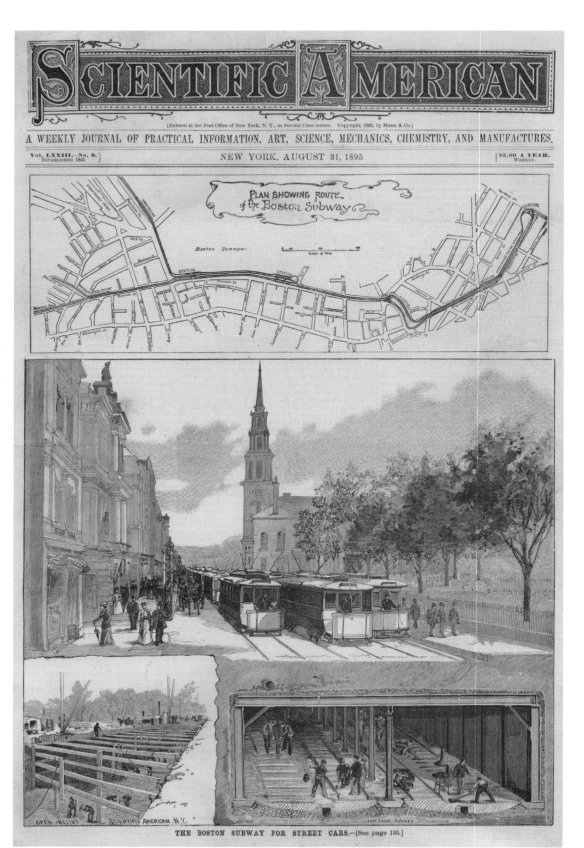

Figure 3.1 Front Page News, August 31, 1895

Scientific American anticipated Boston's subway project with a front page article. Graphics map the subway (top), show the streetcar traffic problem on Tremont Street (middle), and diagram construction of tunnels.

CHAPTER 3

America's First Subway

Epicenter Scollay Square

Boston's Scollay Square took its name from that of a block of buildings, one of which was owned by William Scollay as early as 1795. By the early 1830s, Scollay's Buildings, as the entire block became known, stood like a monolith packed with commercial tenants at the intersection of Tremont Street, Court Street, and Cornhill. From 1825 until 1838, *Badger & Porter's Stage Register* was published from offices at the corner of Court Street and Cornhill, directly opposite Scollay's Buildings. The city of Boston adopted Scollay Square as the official name for the area in 1838.

At the end of the 1850s, horse railroad construction was exploding across Boston. The city was forced to contend with excessive horsecar traffic downtown, especially along Tremont Street between Scollay Square and Boylston Street. Responding to the crisis, on January 18, 1858, Boston passed an ordinance limiting horse railroads from stopping their streetcars on Tremont Street, near Scollay Square or alongside Boston Common between 6:00 a.m. and 8:00 p.m. The city limited necessary stops to no more than one minute in duration. Then, in 1864, the General Court further addressed horsecar congestion at Scollay Square, requiring horse railroads to provide facilities for patrons who were

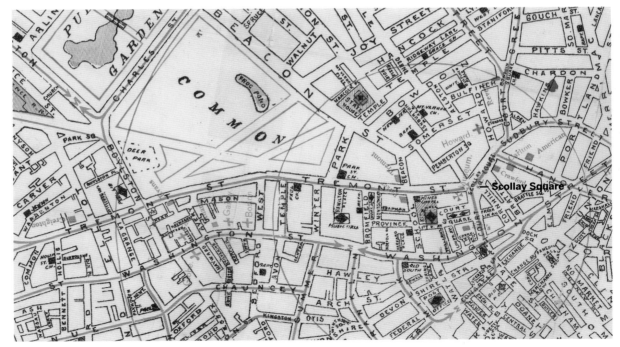

Figure 3.2 Horse Railroad Lines in Downtown Boston, 1880
Horse railroad lines, highlighted in red, trace various downtown streets. At the intersection of Court Street, Tremont Street, and Cornhill (right), a red iron cross marks Scollay Square, the epicenter of streetcar traffic for the city. Turquoise squares and crosses denote theaters and hotels.

often forced to wait outside without proper shelter. Chapter 229, Section 25, of the Statutes of 1864 articulated:

> The several street railway corporations whose cars are…run upon routes approaching Scollay's buildings, in the city of Boston, and going past or from the same by return tracks, shall unite in providing reasonable station accommodations, at or near the site of said building, for all passengers having occasion to take or leave the cars, or exchange cars, at that point.

By the middle of the 1860s, Scollay's Buildings wore signage marking it as the location of the Middlesex Railroad Company's horsecar "station" (Figure 3.3). The entire block was encircled by horse railroad lines (Figure 3.4 and Figure 3.5). The 1869 *Stranger's New Guide Through Boston* confirmed Scollay's Buildings as the focal point for Boston's streetcar lines:

> At this place, the horse-cars from Roxbury, East Boston, South Boston, Charlestown, and Chelsea…arrive and depart every few minutes during the day and evening; and at this general "station" of these roads (the "office" being in the basement of Scollay's Building…), there is in constant attendance an employe[e] of the roads, who announces from time to time, as they come

and go, the direction and place to which each car is destined.

> [From Scollay's Building]…at any hour of the day or evening, he will find conveyance in first-class cars, attended by gentlemanly conductors, over good roads, to his destination, at a cost of a few cents for the trip.

The city purchased Scollay's Buildings in 1870. Shortly thereafter, Boston demolished the block to expand Court Street and Tremont Row so that they better accommodated street traffic (Figure 3.6). While the opening of Scollay Square and double-tracking of Tremont Street alongside Boston Common allowed streetcars to pass each other, it did not keep unchecked quantities of streetcars moving traffic-free. In 1880, Boston erected a statute of Colonial Governor John Winthrop in the middle of Scollay Square. There, Winthrop stood sentinel over Boston's growing streetcar traffic situation until being relocated during construction of Boston's solution to those traffic woes, a subway.

Streetcar Blockade

In the early 1890s, tens of thousands of people boarded onto, de-boarded from, and interchanged between streetcars at Scollay Square and Tremont Street along Boston Common. So many streetcars

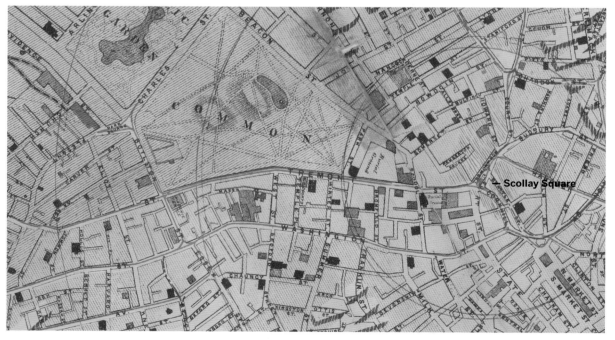

Figure 3.3 Scollay's Buildings, South Side, Circa 1860s
A busy block, Scollay's Buildings housed a waiting area and office for streetcars of the Middlesex Railroad, as called out by the lowermost sign on the building.

Figure 3.4 Horse Railroad Lines in Downtown Boston, 1865
On an enlarged portion of Chase's 1865 map of central Boston (Figure 1.70), red lines represent horse railroad tracks. Double tracks following Tremont Street and alongside Boston Common handled streetcar traffic between Scollay Square (right) and Boylston Street (left). This enlargement is oriented to coordinate with the portion of Hobbs's 1880 map covering the same area (Figure 3.2).

Figure 3.5 Scollay's Buildings, North Side, Circa 1860
This photograph was taken sometime between the late 1850s, after the installation of horse railroad tracks around Scollay's Buildings (center), and 1870, when the city of Boston purchased the block of structures in order to demolish it.

converged in the area at the same time that they created massive traffic jams. Karl Baedeker's 1893 *Guide to the United States* recounted how "the extraordinary congestion of the main business-streets of Boston makes the electric tramway somewhat of an absurdity in the centre of the city" (sic). At certain times of day, Tremont Street between Scollay Square and Boylston Street grew thick with streetcars unable to pass one another on the limited number of available tracks.

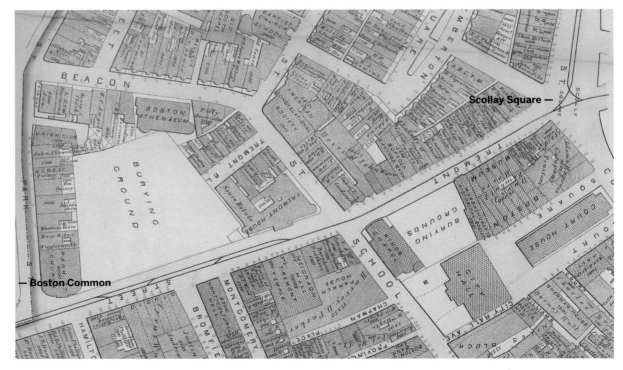

Figure 3.6 Scollay Square and Tremont Street, 1874
Published shorty after the removal of Scollay's Buildings, a 1874 real estate map depicts horsecar lines (solid black lines) running through Scollay Square and along Tremont Street. The double tracks running in front of the Burying Ground are the same ones represented on Hobbs's 1880 map (Figure 3.2) and Chase's 1865 map (Figure 3.4).

Streetcar traffic on Tremont Street often congealed into parallel lines of slow moving cars or stopped all together. When it was not possible for omnibuses, carriages, or pedestrians to navigate a street due to streetcar traffic at a standstill, a "streetcar blockade" existed (Figure 3.7).

Swift Transit For Boston

Responding to Boston's growing street traffic problems, including regular streetcar blockades, Henry Curtis Spalding published a pamphlet titled: "Local Transportation for Boston: Comprising Swift Transit by Tunnel Railways Connecting Together the Tracks of all the Steam Railroads and Rapid Transit by the Aid of Subways, Relieving the Streets in the Business Centre from Their Tramway Burden." Behind the lengthy title, Spalding laid out how tunnels under downtown Boston might allow steam trains and streetcars unhindered and continuous passage beneath the city's crowded streets.

For steam railroad trains, Spalding proposed tunnels connecting the railroad lines radiating from the northern and southern edges of downtown.

One tunnel would cross under the Charles between Cambridge and Boston's Allston neighborhood. Other tunnels would extend directly beneath downtown. In the twentieth century, a proposed crosstown railroad tunnel linking tracks at South Station and North Station became known as the North–South Rail Link. To date, a subterranean railroad link across Boston remains unbuilt.

For streetcars, Spalding proposed public transit subways, complete with underground stations. In time, tunnels proposed by Spalding became realized as the Tremont Street Subway, the Washington Street Tunnel, and the Beacon Hill Tunnel. To free up city streets for general traffic, Spalding went so far as to suggest removing a significant portion of the surface streetcar tracks from Boston's downtown and Back Bay neighborhoods.

A Plan for Public Transportation

In the same year that Spalding published his treatise on swift transit, state and city joined forces to create a comprehensive plan for the growth of transportation in Greater Boston. In furtherance,

Figure 3.7 Streetcar Blockade, July 12, 1895
Streetcars crowd three parallel tracks on Tremont Street. The lines of streetcars trails off into the distance toward Scollay Square.

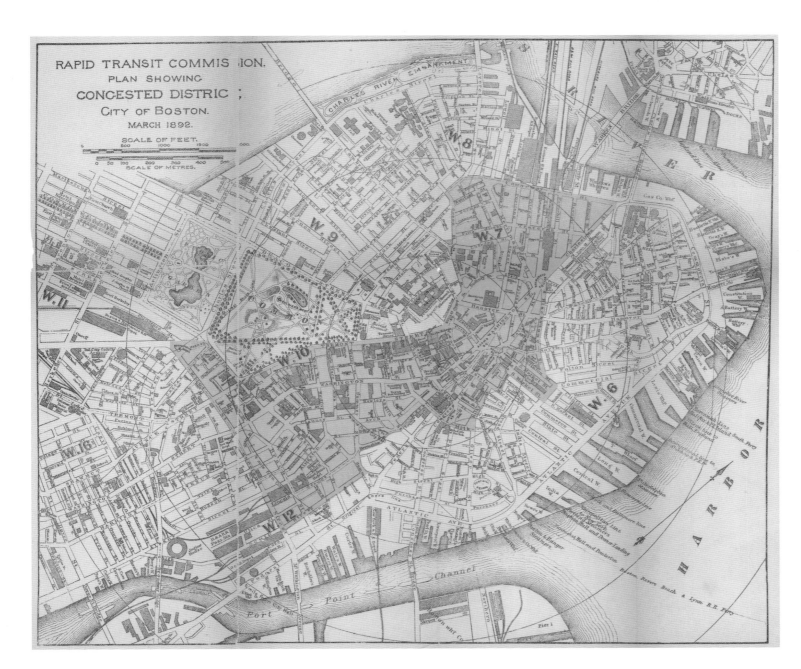

Figure 3.8 The "Congested District" of Boston, March 1892
The Rapid Transit Commission of 1891–92 highlighted in pink the area of most congested street traffic in Boston.

Massachusetts Governor William E. Russell and Boston Mayor Nathan Matthews established "A Commission to Promote Rapid Transit for the City of Boston and its Suburbs." In 1891 the General Court formalized the "Rapid Transit Commission," charging it with analyzing Boston's existing steam railroad, street railway, and road networks, and recommending improvements for each. The commissioners, including John Quincy Adams and Mayor Matthews, held over fifty public hearings and consulted with numerous engineers and experts. Delivered to the General Court on April 5, 1892, the

Rapid Transit Commission's final report included a map defining downtown Boston's "Congested District" (Figure 3.8). At the middle of the area, which spanned from Causeway Street to Kneeland Street and from Boston Common to the North End, sat Scollay Square.

Beyond identification of areas of traffic, the Rapid Transit Commission's 1892 report contained specific proposals for improving the flow of street traffic and maximizing efficiencies in the configuration of steam railroads and street railways. Some suggestions were straightforward, while others were quite ambitious. Among the recommendations were the widening and realignment of various streets to improve traffic flow, the reworking of street railways to address streetcar congestion, the construction of a streetcar subway, the erection of elevated railways for rapid transit trains, and the consolidation of Boston's seven steam railroad passenger terminals into two new stations, North Union Station and South Union Station. By recommending both a subway and elevated rapid transit trains, the commission put forth an unprecedented vision for public transportation for Boston, one that saw beyond steam railroad lines and surface streetcar tracks.

The commission mapped locations not only for both proposed union stations, but a proposed elevated steam railroad line linking the two stations together (Figure 3.9). A significant map from the report anticipated not only a massive expansion of steam railroad freight and harbor port terminal facilities in East Boston and South

Boston, but a network of elevated railroad lines crossing through and radiating from downtown. On the map (Figure 3.10), lines reach out to Harvard Square in Cambridge, Dudley Square in Roxbury, Sullivan Square in Charlestown, and across the harbor to South Boston. The lines to Cambridge and Roxbury meet at Cambridge Street, Scollay Square, and Tremont Street. The Charlestown and South Boston lines connect via two routes running through the North End. The rapid transit lines shown became a road map for subsequent decades of new public transit projects, including elevated railways, subways, and tunnels.

A special state committee reviewed the findings of the 1891–92 Rapid Transit Commission in 1893. After holding no fewer than forty public hearings, the special committee established two new and short lived commissions, the Metropolitan Transit Commission and the Board of Subway Commissioners. The latter was charged with constructing subways between Scollay Square and Pleasant

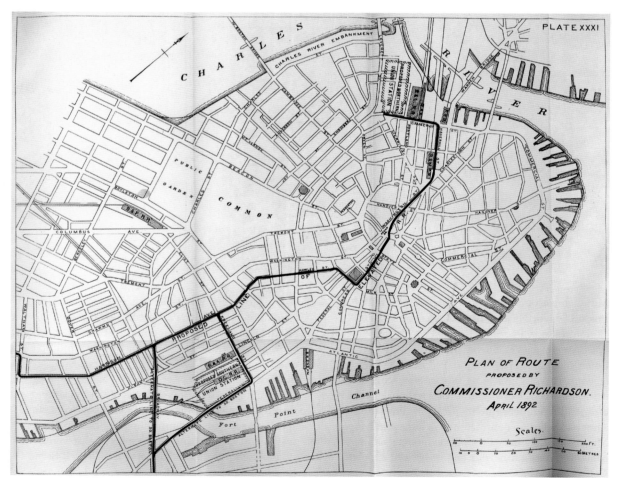

Figure 3.9 Proposed Elevated Railroad for Boston, 1892
With this map, the Rapid Transit Commission of 1891–92 proposed a new elevated steam railroad (thick black lines) connecting a "Proposed Northern Union Station" (top) with a "Proposed Southern Union Station" (bottom). The two stations were eventually realized, though not in the precise locations shown. The elevated steam railroad never came into being. In its place, a subway for streetcars arrived in 1897–98, elevated railways for rapid transit trains opened in 1901, and a tunnel for rapid transit trains opened in 1908.

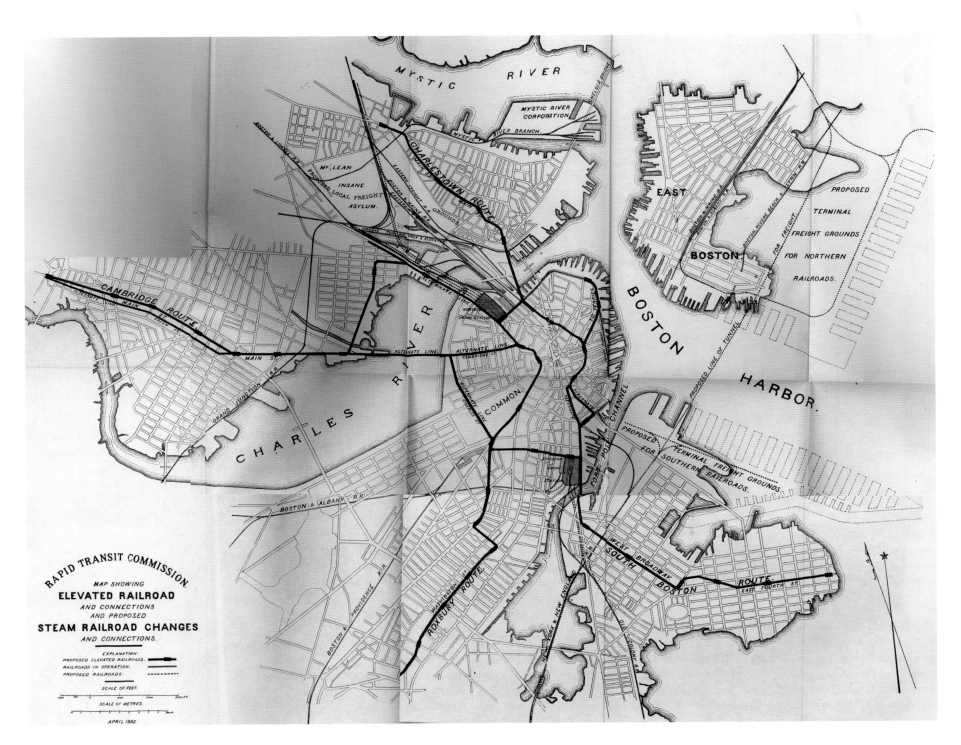

Figure 3.10 Proposed Transit Improvements, 1892
On this Rapid Transit Commission map, expanded port and steam railroad facilities are laid out. Dark black lines represent proposed elevated railroads for steam trains.

Street in Boston, through the heart of the congested district. Though the Board of Subway Commissioners did not exist long enough to oversee work on new transit tunnels, the task of constructing a subway was taken up by subsequent entities.

The work of the transit commissions of 1891–93 culminated in a report issued by the Board of

Subway Commissioners on February 12, 1894. The General Court followed the report with its July 2 passage of Chapter 548, establishing the Boston Transit Commission (BTC) and the Boston Elevated Railway Company (BERy). The Commonwealth charged the BTC and the BERy with implementing the recommendations of the previous

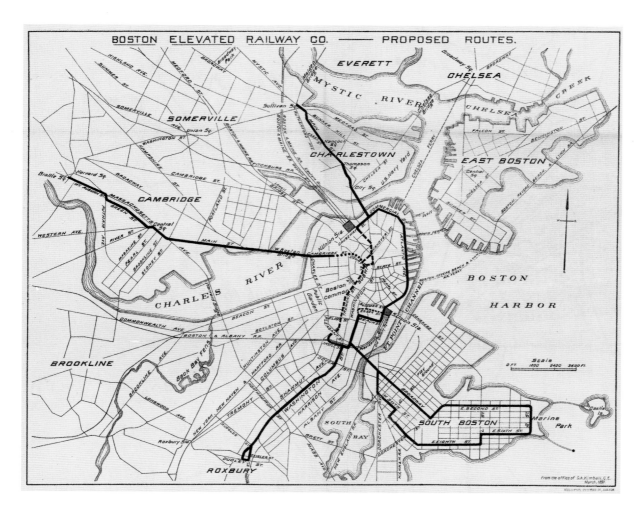

BOSTON ELEVATED RAILWAY CO. ———— PROPOSED ROUTES.

Figure 3.11 Proposed Rapid Transit Routes for Boston, 1897
A map prepared by civil engineer G.A. Kimball lays out rapid transit lines and subways proposed by the BERy. All of the railed lines became realized, either as elevated railways or as subways, except for the loop proposed for South Boston.

transit commissions. Together, these two entities dominated the planning, construction, oversight, and operation of Boston's public transportation system for decades.

The Boston Elevated Railway Company

In 1894, the Commonwealth established the BERy as a for-profit company with a mandate to construct and operate an elevated railway through downtown Boston. The BERy built upon the proposals of the 1891–92 Rapid Transit Commission, mapping a proposed network of rapid transit lines and subways for Boston (Figure 3.11). Subsequently, the BERy evolved to become the operator of virtually all aspects of non-steam railroad and non-ferry public transportation in Boston.

The BERy branded some of its publications with the phrase "Boston Elevated Railway • Reaches All Points" wrapping around a compass rose (Figure 3.12). Company stock certificates featured

a view of a rapid transit train speeding along an elevated railway, high above an electric streetcar, horse carriages, and pedestrians (Figure 3.13). Until the image became a reality in 1901, the BERy operated rapid transit trains underground, years before taking them to tracks supported above the streets.

The Boston Transit Commission

The BTC came into being overseen by six commissioners, three appointed by the governor and three appointed by Boston's mayor. Unlike the privately controlled BERy, the BTC was a public entity, an official seal resembling that of its namesake city (Figure 3.14). For each year of its existence, the BTC issued an annual report, each filled with detailed financial data, descriptions of work yet to be undertaken, summations of work completed, and analysis of precedent transit projects from around the world. The reports and their maps, drawings, and photographs of projects overseen by the BTC,

Figure 3.12 Boston Elevated Railway Company Graphics
A seal of the BERy (left) was featured on company letterhead. A "Reaches All Points" compass graphic (right) was featured on BERy paper maps.

No. 47

INCORPORATED UNDER THE LAWS OF THE · COMMONWEALTH OF MASSACHUSETTS.

BOSTON ELEVATED RAILWAY COMPANY.

This Certifies that Henrietta R. Ruggles is the owner of Two fully paid shares of the capital stock of the Boston Elevated Railway Company, transferable only by a conveyance in writing recorded on the books of the Company upon surrender of this certificate. This certificate will not be valid until countersigned by the Old Colony Trust Company, Transfer Agent, and the American Loan and Trust Company, Registrar.

In Witness Whereof, the Boston Elevated Railway Company has caused its corporate seal to be hereto affixed and this certificate to be signed by its President and Treasurer.

COUNTERSIGNED
OLD COLONY TRUST COMPANY,
TRANSFER AGENT.

By _____
ASSISTANT SECRETARY

_____
TRANSFER CLERK.

_____
PRESIDENT.

_____
TREASURER.

AMERICAN BANK NOTE COMPANY, NEW YORK & BOSTON.

Figure 3.13 BERy Stock Certificate, 1900
A rendering of an elevated railway graces a certificate for two shares of Boston Elevated Railway Company capital stock.

Figure 3.14 Seal of the Boston Transit Commission

including America's first subway, are vital windows into the planning and construction of public transit infrastructure improvements in Boston from 1894 to 1918.

The General Court authorized the BTC to oversee the design and construction of a subway for streetcars through the area of heaviest streetcar traffic in the city, along upper Tremont Street and beneath Scollay Square. In addition to the streetcar subway, which became known as the Tremont Street Subway, the Legislature tasked the BTC with also overseeing the creation of a transit tunnel under Beacon Hill, a transit tunnel from Scollay Square to East Boston, and a new bridge between Boston and Charlestown.

Planning a Subway for Boston

The world's first railed, public transit subway arrived in 1863, when the Metropolitan Railway opened a tunnel for passenger steam trains under London. The Metropolitan Railway's steam locomotives created a nasty atmosphere, leaving smoke, ciders, sparks, and grease in their wake. The second and third railed public transit subways appeared on the European continent. In 1896, a nearly four-mile-long subway opened in Budapest, Hungary with electric cars serving nine stations beneath busy Andrassy Avenue. The Budapest subway was the world's first public transit subway to transport riders in cars propelled by electricity. On December 14, 1896, a subway through which cars were pulled via cables opened in Glasgow, Scotland. In both Budapest and Glasgow, subway designers intelligently left steam locomotives and their smoke and grime out of the tunnels.

During its planning of the Tremont Street Subway, the BTC consulted with the West End Street Railway Company (West End) to make its plans a reality. No other entity had a better handle on the traffic problems facing streetcars in the streets of Boston than the West End. West End streetcars would make up the majority of cars to use the new subway, so advance coordination between the BTC and the West End was critical.

The BTC published is final proposed routing for the subway in 1895 (Figure 3.15). At its northern end, the subway commenced just south of Causeway Street. From there, it passed beneath Haymarket, Scollay, and Adams Squares, before running under Tremont Street and the eastern edge of Boston Common. At the intersection of Tremont and Boylston Streets, the subway split into two branches, with one running westward to the Public Garden, and the other, running southward to Pleasant Street. The routing mostly followed existing public streets and parkland. This would minimize the need for public land takings. The BTC proposed five underground stations, one each at Haymarket Square, Scollay Square, Adams Square,

Park Street, and Boylston Street, as well as three surface stops, one at the top of each of the subway's inclines. The inclines were ramps needed to carry streetcar tracks between street level and the tunnels of the subway. At the bottom of each incline was a portal, a threshold through which street-cars entered and exited the subway tunnels. The incline at the northern end of the subway was the Haymarket Incline. The incline at the western end was the Public Garden Incline. The incline at the southern end was the Pleasant Street Incline.

As the goal of the subway was to reduce street congestion, the route of the Tremont Street Subway traversed the "congested district" identified by the 1892 Rapid Transit Commission. Further quanti-fying the "congested district," the BTC made counts of streetcar traffic along its proposed route for the subway. The tabulated data (Figure 3.16 and Figure 3.17) confirmed what was visible to anyone standing on Tremont Street at the time, there were too many streetcars.

Boston's subway project made headlines outside of the city. The front page of the August, 31, 1895 edition of *Scientific American* was dedicated to Boston's subway project (Figure 3.1). At the time, *Scientific American* was a respected journal of

Figure 3.15 Proposed Route of Subway, August 1895
Solid black lines trace the proposed routing of the Tremont Street Subway, from Travers Street (right) to the Public Garden (upper left) and Pleasant Street (left). The routing branches at the corner of Tremont and Boylston Streets (middle left).

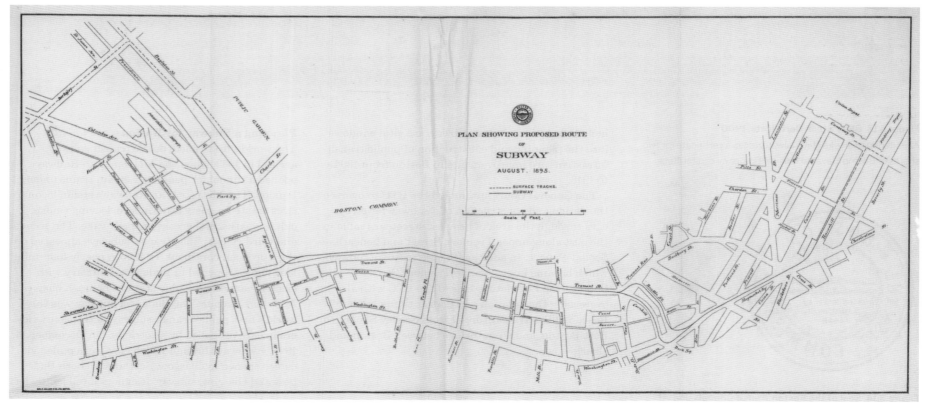

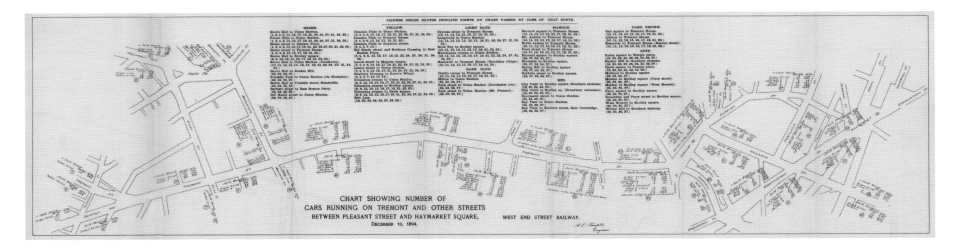

CHART SHOWING NUMBER OF
CARS RUNNING ON TREMONT AND OTHER STREETS
BETWEEN PLEASANT STREET AND HAYMARKET SQUARE,
DECEMBER 10, 1894.   WEST END STREET RAILWAY.

Figure 3.16 Streetcar Counts, December 10, 1894

On December 10, 1894, the BTC made counts of streetcar passings and destinations around the area of downtown to be served by the subway, from Haymarket Square (far right) to Park Square (top left) and Pleasant Street (bottom left). The tabulations are presented in list form (top) and at thirty-nine numbered points on the map. Counts in the list are arranged under headings, each of which denotes a specific streetcar color. An enlargement of the tabulations along Tremont Street, between Scollay Square and Park Street, is shown in Figure 3.17.

Figure 3.17 Streetcar Counts, December 10, 1894 (Detail)

An enlargement of Figure 3.16 shows four numbered locations (21, 22, 23, and 24) at which the Boston Transit Commission counted passing streetcars. The car counts are broken down by car color. On December 10, 1894, locations 21 and 22 witnessed over 2,100 southbound and over 2,600 northbound streetcars, the highest car counts of all of the locations mapped. Locations 21 and 22 are depicted in an 1895 photograph of a streetcar blockade (Figure 3.7).

scientific, technological, and industrial developments. Its publisher, Alfred Ely Beach, prior to overseeing *Scientific American*, designed, constructed, and operated an experimental subway in New York City in the early 1870s. Beach's private venture featured a short tunnel under Broadway in Manhattan, through which a small car carried passengers back and forth along approximately three hundred feet of track. The car was propelled by differences in air pressure created by a massive electric fan. Beach built his project as part of a failed attempt to obtain the contract to construct the first public subway for New York City. Had Beach's project not succumbed to the politics of the time, a large scale pneumatic subway in New York City might have informed the BTC and affected plans for Boston's subway. The only pneumatic tubes ever installed under the streets of New York City, or Boston for that mater, were pressurized pipes

that shuttled mail and documents in small canisters between buildings.

Constructing the Tremont Street Subway

On March 28, 1895, while members of the BTC and Massachusetts Governor Frederick Greenhalge looked on, work formally commenced on the Tremont Street Subway. Construction lasted just over three years and four and a half months. During that time, nearly 370,000 cubic yards of earth were moved, over 75,000 cubic yards of concrete were poured, over 11,000 cubic yards of brick were installed, over 8,100 pounds of steel were erected, over 88,100 square yards of plaster were spread, over 2,200 square yards of enamelled brick were installed, and over 2,800 square yards of enamelled tile were hung. Tragically, five workers lost their lives during construction. Upon its completion, the

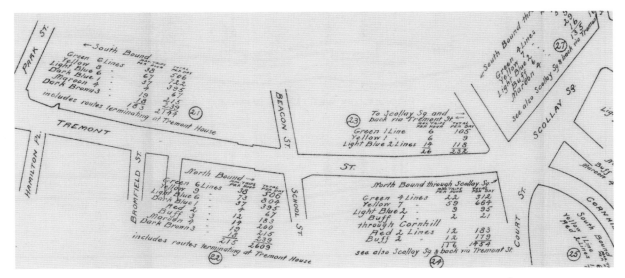

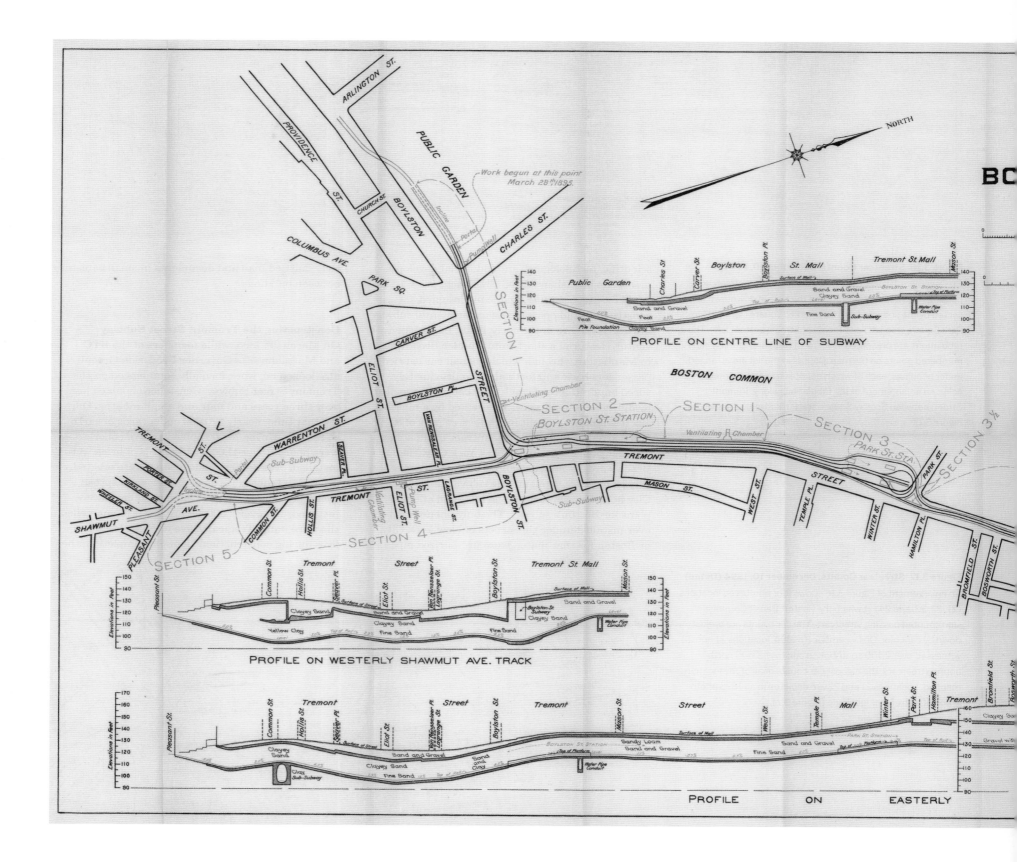

PROFILE ON CENTRE LINE OF SUBWAY

PROFILE ON WESTERLY SHAWMUT AVE. TRACK

PROFILE ON EASTERLY

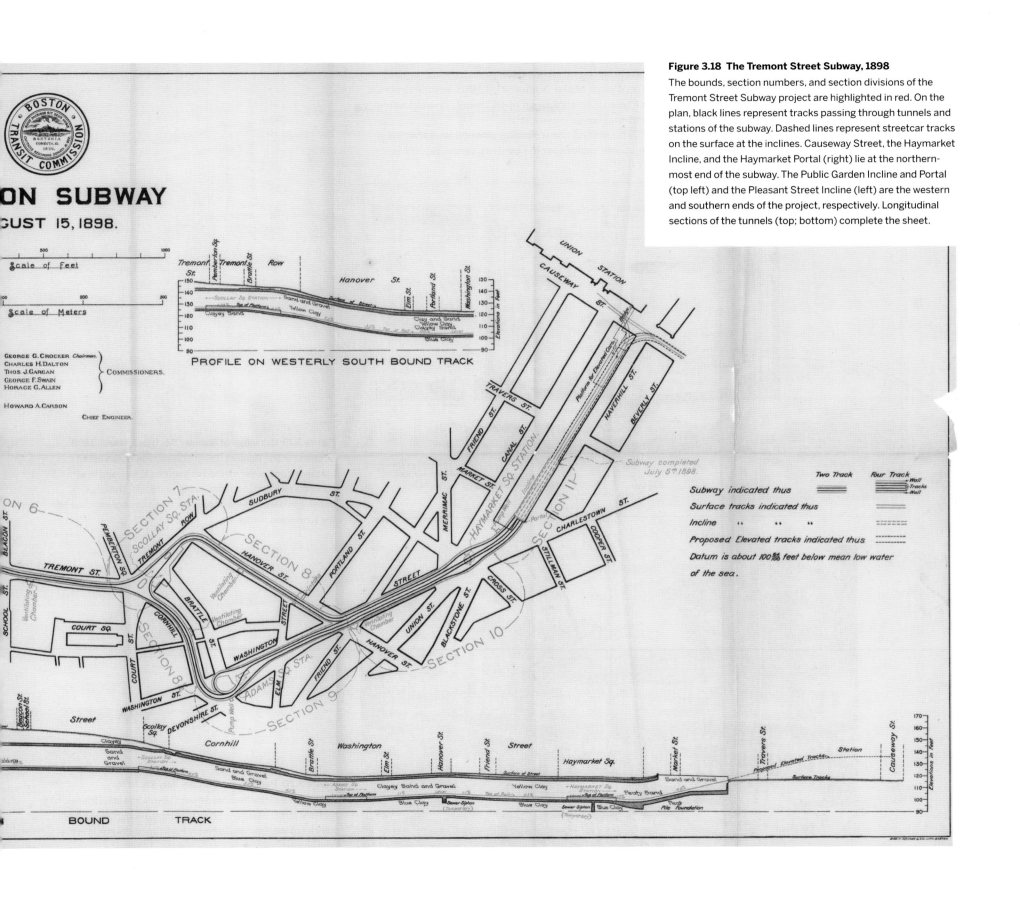

Figure 3.18 The Tremont Street Subway, 1898

The bounds, section numbers, and section divisions of the Tremont Street Subway project are highlighted in red. On the plan, black lines represent tracks passing through tunnels and stations of the subway. Dashed lines represent streetcar tracks on the surface at the inclines. Causeway Street, the Haymarket Incline, and the Haymarket Portal (right) lie at the northernmost end of the subway. The Public Garden Incline and Portal (top left) and the Pleasant Street Incline (left) are the western and southern ends of the project, respectively. Longitudinal sections of the tunnels (top; bottom) complete the sheet.

Tremont Street Subway, including its western and southern branches, measured approximately one and a quarter miles long.

The tunnels and stations of the Tremont Street Subway were generally built using variations of one of three construction methods. The first method was "cut and cover," by which workers excavated a large open trench and constructed the subway superstructure within. Builders then covered the works with earth, atop which they installed finished landscaping or street paving. A drawing on the front page of the August 31, 1895 *Scientific America* (Figure 3.1) depicts an open trench created using cut and cover construction.

The second construction method was the "slice method" accompanied by drift tunneling. This

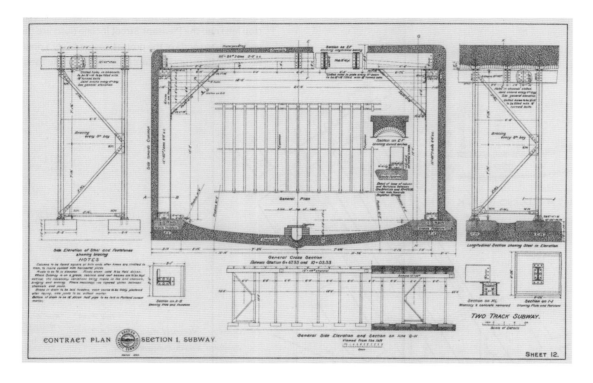

Figure 3.19 Drawings of Subway Section 1, March 1895
Section 1 of the Tremont Street Subway was constructed via the cut and cover method. It featured steel framing with concrete foundations, floors, walls, and roofs. The large drawing in the middle is a cross-section, cut perpendicular to the tunnel and tracks.

Figure 3.20 Park Street Station, July 28, 1896
At Section 3 of the Tremont Street Subway, the steel frame for Park Street Station is being assembled within a massive trench cut into Boston Common. Park Street Church is in the background.

Figure 3.21 Construction at Boylston Street Station, 1896
A massive, bespoke steam-powered lifting machine (middle) sits over a partially completed Boylston Street Station. Tremont Street (right) runs alongside the work site.

Figure 3.22 Under Boston Common, April 24, 1896
The four-track portion of the Tremont Street Subway between Park Street and Boylston Street Stations is under construction. The tunnel ceiling, composed of brick barrel vaults, is supported by steel cross beams. The beams are supported by the tunnel walls and columns supporting main beams running down the center of the tunnel. The image reveals the sloped concrete floor of the tunnel with a trench running down the middle. Trenches, typical throughout the subway, collected water and directed it to pumps for removal from underground.

method commenced with the digging of drifts, small tunnels just big enough for a worker to move through. Builders then constructed small increments of tunnel, or slices, from above. These slices were typically twelve feet wide. Workers excavated drifts between slices to construct portions of tunnel between slices. Unlike the cut and cover, which overtook an entire area to be excavated, the slice method offered minimal disturbances at street level. After one slice was completed, it was covered over, that part of the street was opened to the public, and construction moved onto to the next slice.

The third construction method was the "shield method," which featured a movable steel arch, or shield, that supported unexcavated earth over an area of work occurring entirely underground. Workers pushed the shield along as they dug, typically a few feet per day. As the shield advanced, workers installed a permanent tunnel roof behind it. The shield method allowed construction to creep along beneath the shield and without any disturbance of the street above. The shield method, pioneered by Marc Brunel in the 1820s, was first used successfully in the construction of the Thames Tunnel in London. The Thames Tunnel opened in March 1843 and is now part of London's railed public transit network.

Section by Section
The BTC divided the Tremont Street Subway into sections, numbered 1 through 11, and in a few cases, half-sections, 3 1/2, 8 1/2, and 11 1/2 (Figure 3.18). Generally, section numbers ascended across the project from the south to the north. Section 2, an exception to the pattern, was located in the middle of Section 1. Numeric segmentation allowed the project to be bid, constructed, and managed as a series of smaller and more manageable projects. Different contractors, some hailing from Chicago, Providence, and Boston, each worked on respective sections. Work on portions of Sections 9, 10, and 11 were undertaken directly by the BTC.

Construction techniques varied by section. Sections 1, 2, 3, 5, 11, and 11 1/2 were built using cut and cover. These sections featured steel frames with foundations, floors, walls, and roofs of reinforced concrete. A sheet of drawings published by the BTC in 1895 details the subway's structure at Section 1 (Figure 3.19). Figure 3.20 and Figure 3.21 show work underway at Section 3 and Section 2, respectively. A photograph taken between Park Street and Boylston Street Stations (Figure 3.22) shows the interior of Section 1, before the installation of trackage.

Section 6 included tunnel roofs of steel reinforced masonry arches. The arches spanned between reinforced concrete side walls and over concrete floors. Section 6, constructed by tunneling and some use of the shield method, saw the first documented use of a roof shield accompanied by the installation of a masonry arch tunnel roof in tunnel construction (Figure 3.23). Previous tunnel roofs installed using the shield method, including the roof of the Thames Tunnel in London, were made of cast iron and prefabricated off-site. At Section 6, workers typically advanced the roof shield in three foot increments, three times during a twenty-four hour period. When the shield was no longer needed, workers left it in place between the subway super-structure and Tremont Street above (Figure 3.24).

Sections 7, 8, and 9 of the Tremont Street Subway featured steel framing and steel reinforced concrete

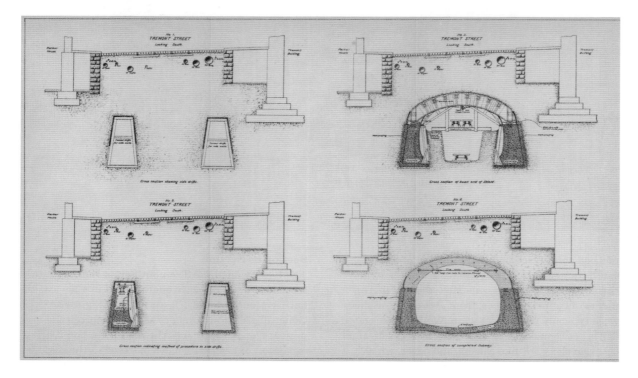

Figure 3.23 Construction Sequence at Tremont Street, 1897

Four cross-section drawings articulate the sequence of construction at Section 6 of the Tremont Street Subway under Tremont Street, between Boston Common and Scollay Square. The first cross-section (upper left) shows parallel side drift tunnels excavated. The second drawing (bottom left) shows reinforced concrete being installed within the drifts. The third drawing (upper right) depicts excavation between the former drifts, now filled and acting as the tunnel side walls, and use of the arched roof shield. The fourth cross-section (bottom right) shows the completed tunnel prior to installation of ballast and tracks.

Figure 3.24 Tremont Street, June 2, 1896

A photograph of Tremont Street looking towards Scollay Square was taken fourteen months after subway construc-tion began. A cacophony of streetcars and carriages jam the roadway. The wooden structure running along the right side of the street supports a steam-powered conveyor belt. The belt carried earth excavated from the subway to where it was loaded into wagons for transport away.

Figure 3.25 Scollay Square, July 15, 1897
Streetcar traffic swarms the statue of John Winthrop (bottom right) and a fenced-in area of work for the subway (right).

Figure 3.26 Construction Sequence at Scollay Square, 1897
Four cross-sections explain the construction of Section 7 of the Tremont Street Subway. The first (top left) depicts trenches dug and reinforced from above. The second drawing (bottom left) shows vertical structural steel supports and concrete installed in the trenches. The third cross-section (top right) shows steel roof girders added. The fourth drawing (bottom right) shows the completed tunnel shell, encased in concrete and waterproofing layers. The incremental means of construction was implemented to minimize closures and restrictions on the crowded streets of Scollay Square.

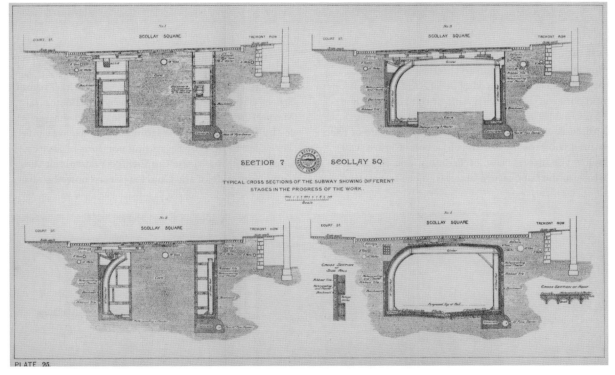

Figure 3.27 Under Hanover Street, December 31, 1896
Beneath Hanover Street near Scollay Square, a worker stands between the subway's roof and yet-to-be-excavated earth.

construction. At those sections, workers dug trenches across streets, then installed tunnel sidewalls and roofs within each trench. After covering up each partially completed portion of tunnel, they excavated under the tunnel roof and between the sidewalls to install the floors and finish the interiors of that segment. Figure 3.25 shows street traffic passing through Scollay Square while subway work continues below (Figure 3.26 and Figure 3.27). Section 10 featured steel framing and reinforced concrete construction. It was built using methods similar to those at sections 7, 8, and 9, with some use of the slice method.

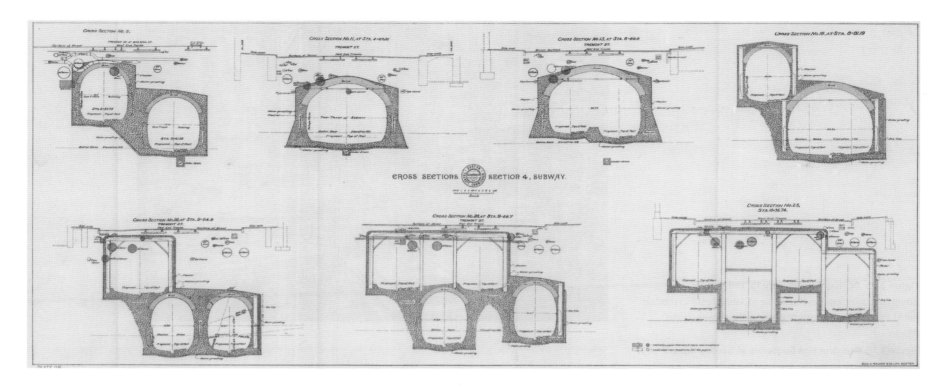

Section 4, which followed Tremont Street from Boylston Street Station to the Pleasant Street Incline, was constructed of steel reinforced masonry and concrete along with a bit of the slice method (Figure 3.28). A portion of Section 4 was nicknamed the "bell mouths" because the profile of each tunnel tube resembled that of a bell (Figure 3.29). Below the intersection of Tremont and Boylston Streets, the tubes were inserted close to existing underground utilities and next to the foundations of existing buildings (Figure 3.30).

A majority of the earth excavated for the Tremont Street Subway was hauled away by the Boston & Maine Railroad (Boston & Maine) at no charge to the BTC. Some spoils from subway excavations were distributed for regrading portions of Boston Common, filling in the Cambridge Flats along the Cambridge side of the Charles River (now the site

Figure 3.28 Section 4 of the Tremont Street Subway, 1896
Cross-sections are each "cut" through the tunnels of the subway under Tremont Street, between Boylston Street Station and the Pleasant Street Incline and Portal. As a series, the drawings reveal a progression from all reinforced concrete construction (top left) to steel frame with a concrete envelope (bottom right). The cross-sections break down the transition from two, single track tunnels (top left), one for inbound and one for outbound cars, to a four-track tunnel (bottom right), two tracks for inbound cars and two tracks for outbound cars.

Figure 3.29 The "Bell Mouths" at Section 4, 1898
Brightly whitewashed tunnels reflect bright electric light where the subway's tracks head south, towards the Pleasant Street Incline. The tube on the right was for southbound streetcars. The tube on the left was for cars heading northbound (towards the photographer) into Boylston Street Station. In the distance (right), two streetcars pause where the southbound tube splits again.

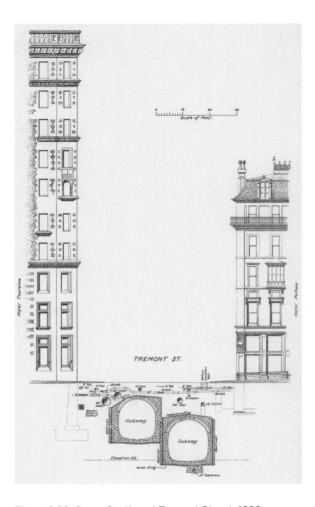

Figure 3.30 Cross-Section at Tremont Street, 1898
A drawing "cut" through the subway and Tremont Street where it crosses Boylston Street reveals two tunnel tubes (bottom), each carrying one set of subway tracks between the Pleasant Street Portal and Boylston Street Station.

of the Massachusetts Institute of Technology), reclaiming a small portion of the harbor at Russia Wharf (now Atlantic Wharf), and filling in along the Fort Point Channel at the future site of South Station.

Fresh air was brought into and stale air was expelled from the subway through ventilation structures that punctured Boston Common. Subway station head houses and streetcar portals exchanged the majority of air from the subway. Though the exterior of the tunnel and station envelopes were waterproofed with primitive, bituminous systems, water did enter the subway. It was collected in a series of drains, channels, and sumps. Electric pumps transferred the collected water out of the subway and into the city storm water system.

During construction of the Tremont Street Subway, the General Court required that Tremont Street and other streets along the project, including the busiest streetcar tracks in the city, remain open from 8:00 a.m. to 6:00 p.m. The BTC and its contractors employed various solutions, ranging from short street detours to the complete diversion of streetcar traffic around larger areas of work (Figure 3.31). Subway construction sites of the 1890s might have looked familiar to a Bostonian of a full century later, when another tunnel was constructed through downtown. The Central Artery / Third Harbor Tunnel Project, more commonly known as "The Big Dig," brought new highway tunnels through the city in the 1990s. The Big Dig work took place while many existing streets as well as an existing elevated highway, the Central Artery,

Figure 3.31 Park Street Station Site, November 27, 1896
A large trench open in Tremont Street (middle) precipitates the need for a pair of temporary tracks to carry streetcars over a portion of Boston Common (left).

remained in use. The construction of the Tremont Street Subway, while smaller in scale than The Big Dig, was a relatively ambitious and disruptive infrastructure undertaking in Boston. Unlike The Big Dig, the Tremont Street Subway came in under budget. After completion of the Tremont Street Subway, the chief engineer of the BTC recorded a total project cost of approximately $4.4 million.

Exhumation and Explosion

Eight months after construction of the subway commenced, the *Boston Daily Globe* published a series of cartoons under the headline: "When the Subway's Done!" (Figure 3.32). Accompanying each cartoon is a stanza of a poem, with one mentioning: "The street where once [electric streetcars] ran will be a shaded lane. No sound of traffic's swelling roar will there be heard gain." Another imagines a scene where a chaperone will "stay near lovers" to provide illumination and "stop all fun" within a darkened streetcar moving through the subway. A final cartoon presents a future where winged streetcars fly over Boston's skyline.

The construction of the Tremont Street Subway had its share of surprises and tragedies. While excavating for Park Street Station (Figure 3.33), workers unexpectedly unearthed one skeleton and

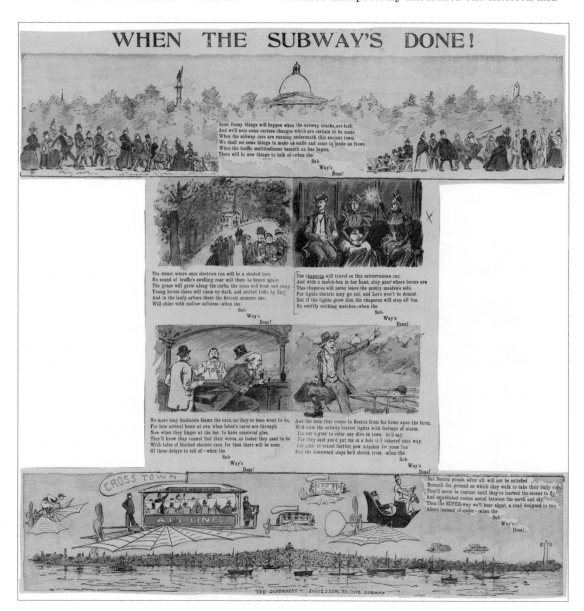

Figure 3.32 "When the Subway's Done!" 1895
Cartoons published in the November 17, 1895 edition of the *Boston Sunday Globe* present hypothetical scenarios for life in Boston before and after the Tremont Street Subway.

Figure 3.33 Under Boston Common, October 28, 1895

the remnants of twelve headstones. The construction of Boylston Street Station and the Boylston Street portion of the subway required the widening of Boylston Street and the removal of a portion of the Boston Common Burial Ground. The BTC hired Dr. Samuel Green, a former mayor of Boston, to oversee the sensitive exhumation and reinternment of the remains of 910 people buried between the 1780s and the 1830s.

Shortly before noon on March 4, 1897, a natural gas explosion devastated the area around the intersection of Tremont and Boylston Streets. The gas leaked from mains into voids between the roof of a nearly completed Boylston Street Subway Station and temporary wooden structures carrying streetcars over the subway works. The blast obliterated one electric streetcar, severely damaged another, and decimated a horsecar, killing its horses (Figure 3.34). The March 5, 1897 edition of the *Boston Daily Globe* recorded:

> The hands of the clocks pointed at 11:47 when there was a rumble and a roar at the intersection of Tremont and Boylston…which sound was heard in the state house on Beacon Hill, and even the farther banks of the river Charles.… Then came the shock. Timbers rose in the air. The ground trembled. Smoke floated upward, followed quickly by flashes of fire. The glass in a

thousand windows fell outward or inward with a crash.

The *Globe* continued: "Five men and one woman dead, and nearly three score persons…more or less seriously maimed." As a result of their injuries, four persons died soon after the event. Two of those who lost their lives were the conductor and driver of the destroyed horsecar. Though the blast shattered the glass out of hundreds of windows in surrounding buildings, it did not significantly damage the subway below. The area was mostly repaired by the time the subway opened a few months after the blast.

Opening of the Tremont Street Subway

Just short of a year before it opened the Tremont Street Subway, in August 1896, the BTC advertised to street railway companies the opportunity to run streetcars through the subway. The BTC sought to negotiate leases with the companies who would pay for the right to use the subway. Monies from lease payments would then be used to pay down bonds issued to finance subway construction. The BTC received three responses to their solicitations, but only two from entities with operational street railways, the West End and the Lynn & Boston Railroad Company (Lynn & Boston).

Figure 3.34 Explosion at Boylston Street, March 9, 1897
A photograph taken at the corner of Tremont and Boylston Streets shows the immediate aftermath of a natural gas explosion that destroyed streetcars, blew out windows, killed two horses, and caused the deaths of ten people. Horsecar #391 sits shattered on Tremont Street (center). In front of car #391 lies part of the frame of a decimated streetcar (left). The wooden beams and planks are the remnants of a temporary platform that carried streetcars over the site of Boylston Street Station.

In late 1896, the BTC and the West End entered into a contract allowing the West End use of the subway south of Park Street. A month later, the Massachusetts Board of Railroad Commissioners expanded the scope of the contract to permit the West End to use the entire subway. The BTC leased the Tremont Street Subway to the West End. The West End was required to make payments to the BTC in an amount no less than the sum of five cents per passenger traveling through the subway. Terms permitted the West End to use the Tremont Street Subway for its own streetcars, while also allowing the West End to permit other companies to operate cars within the subway. With a lease of the West End formalized on December 7, 1896, the BERy took control of not only Boston's largest streetcar operator, but also the Tremont Street Subway. The West End continued to exist as a corporate entity, but leased to the BERy.

After the BTC completed construction of the superstructures of the subway, the BERy installed ballast, tracks, trolley wires, signals, and other streetcar infrastructure. The BERy then became responsible for repairs, maintenance, and operations of the subway. On the last two days of August 1897, motormen and conductors practiced operating streetcars through the subway's soon-to-be-opened tunnels and stations.

The Tremont Street Subway opened to the public on September 1, 1897 with electric streetcars serving Boylston Street and Park Street Stations. The front page of the *Boston Daily Globe* celebrated the opening with the headline "Now for Speed." The same front page featured a collage of subway scenes under the headline "Cars Now Running in the Subway" (Figure 3.35). A newspaper article published on the second day of subway service included cartoons of unprecedented situations for Boston at the time, including an attendant cleaning an underground streetcar station, passengers holding on while their trolley takes a tight turn in a tunnel, and gentlemen waiting for ladies to pass

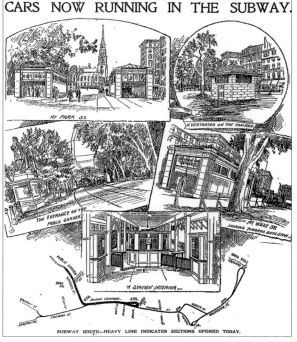

Figure 3.35 Boston Globe Front Page, September 1, 1897
Views of new subway station head houses, a ticket booth (bottom), and the surface streetcar stop at the Public Garden Incline (left) are accompanied by a map of the Tremont Street Subway (bottom).

Figure 3.36 "Odd Sights in the Subway," September 2, 1897
Newspaper renderings reveal unprecedented happenings in Boston after the opening of the Tremont Street Subway.

Figure 3.37 Top of the Public Garden Incline, 1898
Streetcars leaving the subway serve an open-air streetcar stop at the top of the Public Garden incline.

without being able to be escorted through exit gates (Figure 3.36).

The first streetcar to transport paying passengers through the Tremont Street Subway was West End electric streetcar number 1752, operating out of Allston Car House. On the morning of September 1, 1897, car 1752 turned off Boylston Street, passed the Public Garden surface stop, and travelled down the Public Garden Incline. It entered the subway at 6:02 a.m. This "First Car Off The Earth," as the headline of the *Boston Daily Globe Extra Evening Edition* described, carried over 100 passengers, despite only having a capacity of approximately forty. The paper recalled that passengers "yelled themselves to the verge of apoplexy" as they descended the incline from the Public Garden and into the new subway. At the bottom of the incline, car 1752

entered the subway to traverse freshly whitewashed tunnels, brightly lit by incandescent electric lights. After a pause to exchange passengers at Boylston Street Station, motorman James Reed piloted his car towards Park Street Station. The open-type streetcar arrived under the electric arc lights of Park Street Station and completed the first revenue service run between subway stations by a public transit vehicle in America.

Beyond newspaper headlines the opening of the Tremont Street Subway was memorialized in a variety of commemorative products. Novel scenes for Boston, including streetcars serving the surface stop at the top of the Public Garden Incline (Figure 3.37), were featured on silver spoons (Figure 3.38). A view of the four-track subway between Boylston and Park Street Stations was

Figure 3.38 Tremont Street Subway Spoons, Circa 1898
Silver spoons produced to commemorate the opening of the Tremont Street Subway included two versions of full-size table spoons (top and middle) and a smaller demitasse spoon (bottom). The bowls of the spoons feature a streetcar approaching the stop at the top of the Public Garden Incline. Along the necks and handles are representations of iconic Boston imagery, including the Massachusetts State House, Paul Revere on his ride, and the Bunker Hill Monument.

printed onto playing cards (Figure 3.39) and post-cards (Figure 3.40 and Figure 3.41). A photograph looking down the Public Garden Incline appeared on the cover of a "Subway Souvenir" booklet published in 1899 (Figure 3.42). Sheet music for "The Boston Subway March" was published in 1895 (Figure 3.43).

The same year that the first segment of the Tremont Street Subway opened, 1897, saw the Massachusetts legislature pass "An Act To Promote Rapid Transit For the City of Boston and Vicinity." The Act, which amended the 1894 legislation establishing the BTC and the BERy, brought many important transit infrastructure projects to Boston. The 1897 Act required the BTC to build a new subway under Cambridge Street and Bowdoin Square to connect with the Tremont Street Subway near Court Street. It also required that the Charlestown Bridge be constructed with a high level route for rapid transit trains and that the BTC construct a tunnel to East Boston. The Rapid Transit Act of 1897 set the fares throughout the entire streetcar

system of the BERy, including the subway, at five cents. Boston's standard five cent streetcar fare remained in place until 1918.

Initially, streetcars ran through the Tremont Street Subway from 6:00 a.m. to midnight. Between midnight and 6:00 a.m., streetcars operated on surface streets. Upon entry to a station on the subway, a patron approached the ticket booth, paid the nickel fare, and in return, received a paper ticket. The patron surrendered the ticket upon boarding a streetcar. Tickets sold in subway stations were good only for use boarding a streetcar within the subway that day and were void if carried from the subway without being used (Figure 3.44). Free transfer tickets were obtainable from trolley conductors or subway station fare collectors.

The Pleasant Street Incline
At the southernmost end of the Tremont Street Subway was the incline and portal at Pleasant

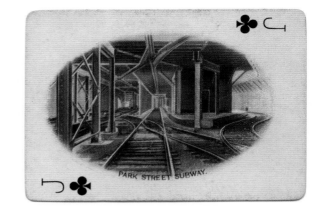

Figure 3.39 Tremont Street Subway Playing Card, 1899
A jack of clubs adorned with a photograph of the four-track section of subway was included with a deck of cards. Each card in the deck depicted an iconic building or place in Boston.

Figure 3.40 Four-track Portion of the Subway, Circa 1900
A view of the four track subway between Park Street and Boylston Street Stations looks towards the later. Raceways along the ceilings prevent trolley wires from making contact with the roof of the tunnel.

Figure 3.41 Park Street Station Head Houses, Circa 1900
Park Street Church stands tall beyond the glass-roofed head houses of Park Street Station. Signage above each entrance designates stairways for entrance and exit within each head house.

Figure 3.42 Subway Souvenir Booklet Cover, 1899
A photograph of the Public Garden Incline graces the cover of a multi-page, pocket-sized booklet packed with subway photos, construction data, and statistics.

Figure 3.43 Sheet Music Cover, 1895
The Cover of "The Boston Subway March" shows the Public Garden Incline of the Tremont Street Subway with the Massachusetts State House and Boston skyline in the background.

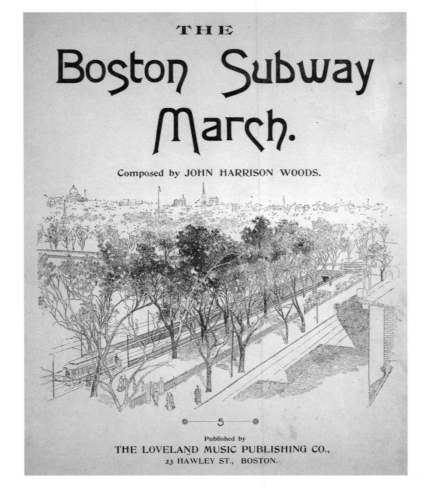

Figure 3.44 BERy Streetcar Subway Ticket, Circa 1890

Figure 3.45 Pleasant Street Incline, 1897
Taken from Pleasant Street, a photograph shows the southern end of the Tremont Street Subway. Two pairs of tracks run down the Pleasant Street Incline and into the Pleasant Street Portal. Along the right track in each pair, streetcars entered the subway. Along the left track in each pair, trolleys exited the subway.

Figure 3.46 Pleasant Street Incline, March 3, 1903
A photograph looks down upon the four tracks of the Pleasant Street Incline disappearing into the Tremont Street Subway.

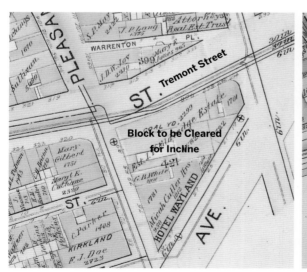
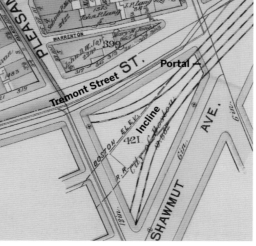

Figure 3.47 Pleasant Street Incline Site
Portions of two real estate maps depict the site of the Pleasant Street Incline in 1895 (left), before construction of the Tremont Street Subway, and in 1898 (right), after opening of the subway.

PLATE 33.

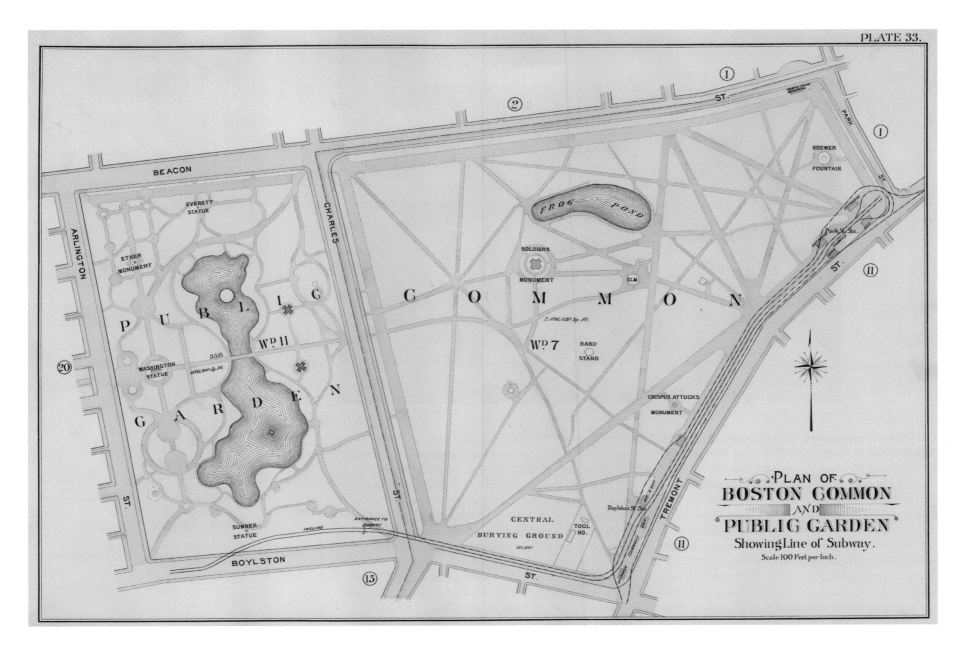

PLAN OF
BOSTON COMMON
AND
PUBLIC GARDEN
Showing Line of Subway.
Scale 100 Feet per Inch.

Figure 3.48 Mapping the Tremont Street Subway, 1898
A map shows the southern portion of the Tremont Street Subway that opened on September 1, 1897. Streetcar tracks (black and white lines) run from the Public Garden Incline (bottom left) into the Public Garden Portal (labeled "Entrance to Subway"). The tracks continue under the Public Garden, through Boylston Street Station (bottom right), and into Park Street Station (top right).

Street (Figure 3.45 and Figure 3.46). The tunnels connecting Boylston Street Station with the Pleasant Street Portal opened for service by the end of September 1897. The portal and incline at Pleasant Street were built upon a triangular piece of land bounded by Shawmut Avenue and Tremont, Warrenton, and Pleasant Streets (Figure 3.47). During spring 1896, no fewer than four buildings were removed for construction of the Pleasant Street Incline. The land takings made by the BTC for the Tremont Street Subway pale in comparison to those made later by the Commonwealth for construction of the Central Artery and Massachusetts

Turnpike Extension in the middle of the twentieth century.

When the southern portion of the Tremont Street Subway opened in 1897, G. W. Bromley & Company (Bromley) had been publishing atlases of real estate maps of Boston for nearly two decades. Bromley recognized the historical significance of the new subway by adding a map of Boston Common and the Public Garden to the 1898 edition of their *Atlas of Boston Proper*. The map (Figure 3.48), never before featured in one of their atlases of Boston, depicts the portion of the Tremont Street Subway that opened for service on September 1.

Figure 3.49 Boylston Street Station Head Houses, 1897
Signage above the entrance to each head house designated it as either a point of entry or exit to the station below.

Boylston Street & Park Street Stations

The first two stations of the Tremont Street Subway to open, Boylston Street and Park Street Stations, were each named for a street that intersected with the route of the subway at their location. The interiors of the two stations, like those of all stations of the Tremont Street Subway, featured ceilings and columns painted white and walls covered with glossy white tiles. Tunnels and stations were illuminated by electric lighting. The whiteness of the interiors maximized brightness within the subterranean spaces of the subway, helping to counteract centuries of negative associations people brought to the underground, a place historically reserved for tombs, mines, and sewers. In the event that a neophyte subway traveller became overwhelmed by their subterranean experience, or worse, injured while moving through the subway, the BTC was prepared. Tremont Street Subway stations opened with small "accident rooms," as they were labeled on plans of the stations, each equipped with a cot.

Boylston Street Station opened with two platforms, one for southbound cars and one for northbound cars. The platforms were separated from each other by the middle pair of tracks. A narrow underground passage allowed people to move between the platforms, one story below. Each platform had two stairway connections to the surface, where four head houses marked the station at the corner of Tremont and Boylston Streets (Figure 3.49). Today, only two of the four head houses remain and the underground pedestrian passage between the platforms is no longer open.

Form followed function at Boylston Street Station, where four tracks served passengers boarding streetcars bound for one of three directions (Figure 3.50). Two outer tracks carried cars between the Pleasant Street Portal and Park Street Station. Two inner tracks carried cars between the Public Garden Incline and Park Street Station. The outer track running along the eastern edge of the station was reserved for cars bound for the Pleasant Street Portal. The track descended into a "sub-subway" (Figure 3.51) that carried it under the tracks linking the station with the Public Garden Incline. The multi-level configuration of trackage at Boylston Street Station allowed cars bound for Pleasant Street to proceed through the station without having to cross the tracks of cars heading to the Public Garden Incline. Likewise, cars running to and from the Public Garden arrived and departed the station without crossing paths with other cars. The outermost tracks that once served the Pleasant Street Portal have been removed, though the

Figure 3.50 Boylston Street Station, 1898
Cross-sections (top) and a detailed plan explain the most complicated station on the Tremont Street Subway. A four-track portion of the subway (right) brought streetcars between Boylston Street and Park Street Stations. A pair of tracks (top left) brought cars between Boylston Street Station and the Public Garden Incline. Another pair (left) carried cars between the station and the Pleasant Street Incline.

Figure 3.51 Inside Boylston Street Station, 1897

This photograph was taken upon the station's westernmost track. Streetcars followed the track into the sub-subway towards the Pleasant Street Portal. Station name signs within Boylston Street Station feature white letters over a dark background. Black on white lettering, directing people to the Public Garden, is painted onto a roof beam.

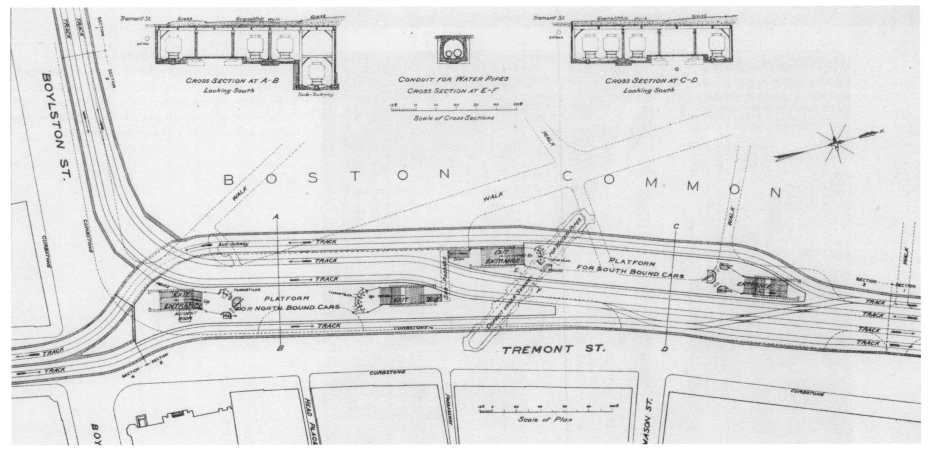

Figure 3.52 Park Street Station Head Houses, 1897
Designed by architects Wheelwright & Haven, the four head houses at Park Street Station wore copper and glass roofs and granite-lined exterior walls. Beyond the head houses stand the trees of Boston Common.

Figure 3.53 Inside Park Street Station, 1897
The station's western platform (left) was served by streetcars travelling southbound and westbound, towards Boylston Street Station. Signage lists destinations of southbound and westbound cars. The eastern platform (far right) was served by northbound cars. The view is toward the Northeast.

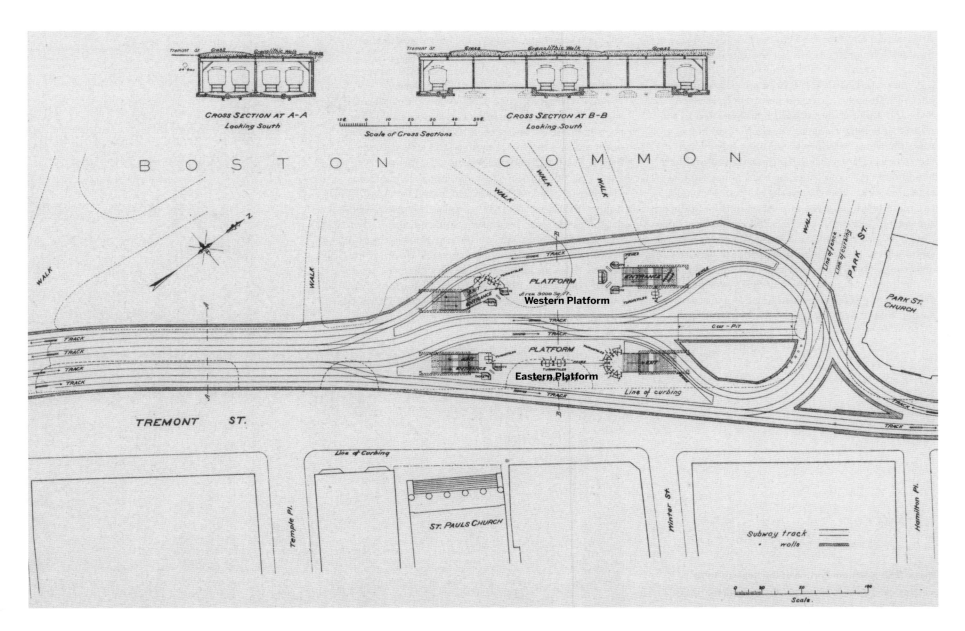

CROSS SECTION AT A-A
Looking South

CROSS SECTION AT B-B
Looking South

Scale of Cross Sections

B O S T O N   C O M M O N

Western Platform

Eastern Platform

TREMONT   ST.

ST. PAULS CHURCH

Subway track
walls

Scale.

Figure 3.54 Park Street Station 1898

Cross-sections (top) and a plan reveal the workings of Park Street Station. A four-track subway (left), consisting of two northbound and two southbound tracks, connects Park Street Station with Boylston Street Station. A two-track tunnel (right) contains one northbound and one southbound track running between Park Street and Scollay Square Stations. Park Street Station's western platform was served by southbound and westbound streetcars. Its eastern platform was served by northbound cars. Within the station, loop tracks allowed cars arriving from Boylston Street Station to turn at Park Street and head back west and south.

tunnels through which they passed under Tremont Street remain partially intact.

Park Street Station was similar in scope to Boylston Street Station, with four head houses (Figure 3.52) and four tracks serving two platforms (Figure 3.53 and Figure 3.54). Two tracks, both for southbound and westbound cars, ran alongside the western platform. Two tracks for northbound cars ran alongside the eastern platform. Park Street Station opened with loops tracks at its northern end. The loops allowed cars arriving from Boylston Street Station to turn around, pass back through Park Street Station, and then return southbound to Boylston Street Station. From there, cars

proceed towards an exit from the subway at either the Public Garden Incline or the Pleasant Street Incline. From early fall 1897 until the northern portion of the subway was complete in August 1898, all streetcars carrying passengers turned at Park Street Station.

Scollay Square Station and The Brattle Loop

The second and final segment of the Tremont Street Subway opened to the public on August 19, 1898. For the first time, streetcars began transporting people in the subway north of Park Street Station, serving newly opened stations at Scollay,

Adams, and Haymarket Squares (Figure 3.55). The first station north of Park Street was at Scollay Square, Boston's historic nexus of streetcar traffic.

A main stair, with segregated entrance and exit portions, linked the central platform to street level and a monumental head house erected in the middle of Scollay Square. The main head house was an elegant masonry structure topped with four clocks (Figure 3.56). To the north of the main head house, a second, smaller head house capped an exit-only stairway from the station. Ironically, the main head house was installed in the middle of the very intersection where Scollay's Building once hindered street traffic, and later, Winthrop's statue stood watch. During planning of the subway, the city objected to the BTC's placement of the head house in the middle of the street. The BTC prevailed after arguing that a freestanding covering was less susceptible to fire and that there was inadequate room on existing sidewalks for entrances to the station.

Below ground, Scollay Square Station's three tracks bracketed a main, central platform (Figure 3.57 and Figure 3.59). A second platform, separate from the central one, was accessible from the surface at Brattle Street. This second platform operated as a distinctly named stop, called Brattle Street Station. The track serving the Brattle Street platform received streetcars arriving from Haymarket Square Station and bound for Adams Square Station. Cars that travelled the grand loop southbound from Haymarket Square Station, then through Brattle Street and Adams Square Stations, and finally, back northbound through Haymarket Square Stations, followed a circuit called the Brattle Loop. The Brattle Street platform no longer exists, however a bit of the Brattle Loop lives on within the upper level of today's Government Center Station.

Figure 3.55 Northern Portion of the Subway, 1898
A real estate map of downtown Boston lays out the tracks of Tremont Street Subway as black and white lines, each representing a single track. Subway tracks run across the map, from Park Street Station (left) to Haymarket Square Station (far right). Between the stations, two subway tracks follow Tremont Street. Between Scollay Square Station (middle) and Haymarket Square Station, the subway diverges. One tunnel with two tracks follows Hanover Street. Another, with two tracks, runs under Cornhill to Adams Square Station (bottom), with its loop track. The divergent tunnels recombine under the intersection of Hanover and Washington Streets (right). From there, a four-track tunnel runs beneath Haymarket Square Station. In general, streetcar traffic ran counterclockwise around the grand loop formed by the tunnels under Cornhill and Washington, Hanover, and Court Streets. One exception was where streetcars could run from Haymarket Square Station and directly into the Adams Square Station loop.

Figure 3.56 Scollay Square Station Main Head House, 1898

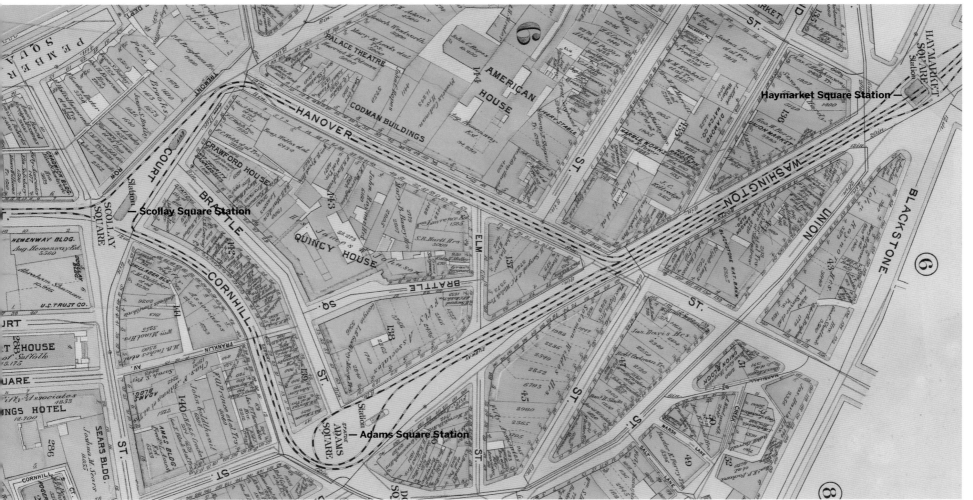

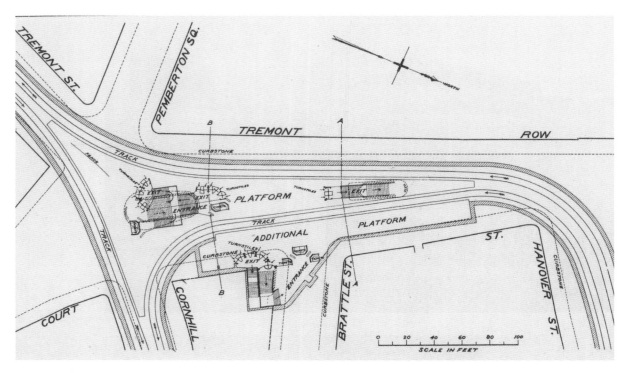

Figure 3.57 Scollay Square Station, 1898
Scollay Square Station opened being served by both northbound and southbound streetcars. Cars arrived from Haymarket Square Station along one of two tracks carried in a tunnel beneath Hanover Street (right). Streetcars arrived from Park Street Station in a tunnel sheltering one northbound and one southbound track (upper left). Northbound cars from Scollay Square Station departed along a pair of tracks into a tunnel under Cornhill (bottom left). The "Additional Platform" (center) is Brattle Street Station.

Adams Square and Haymarket Square Stations

At Adams Square Station, streetcars departed exclusively northbound (Figure 3.58 and Figure 3.60), in the direction of Haymarket Square Station. A loop track allowed southbound cars arriving from Haymarket Square Station to make an initial pass through Adams Square Station, then turn around, before passing back through Adams Square Station to pick up passengers and return northbound to Haymarket Square Station. The Adams Square Loop allowed streetcars to short circuit the longer Brattle Loop. The Adams Square Loop may have been intended for use by the Lynn & Boston (historians debate the amount of regular traffic the loop actually saw). The BERy terminated the utility of Adams Square Loop in 1901, when the

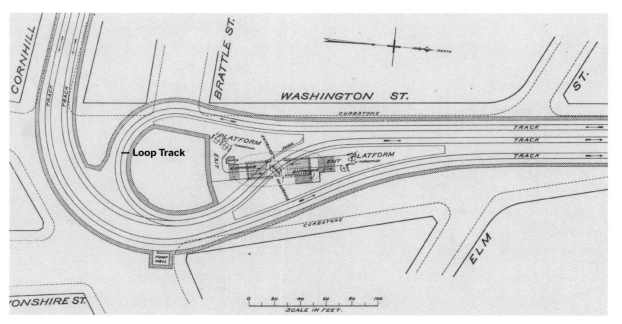

Loop Track

Figure 3.58 Adams Square Station, 1898
Streetcars arrived at Adams Square Station travelling either northbound or southbound, but only departed northbound. A tunnel under Cornhill (top left) brought cars from Scollay Square Station on a pair of northbound tracks. The pair of tracks continued through Adams Square Station, into a tunnel under Washington Street (right), and onward, to Haymarket Square Station. A single southbound track (right) brought streetcars from Haymarket Square Station into the Adams Square Station loop. There, cars turned to return northbound.

Figure 3.59 Inside Scollay Square Station, 1898
The track for northbound cars (right) passes alongside the central platform. Marked by an "Exit to Scollay Square" sign (left), stairs lead up to the station's main head house.

Figure 3.60 Inside Adams Square Station, 1898
An open-type streetcar is posed at Adams Square Station. The tracks on the left and the middle are for northbound cars. The track on the right brings southbound cars into the Adams Square Station loop, located behind the posed streetcar.

Figure 3.61 Adams Square Station Head House, 1898

Tremont Street Subway underwent a conversion from streetcar to rapid transit train service. The Adams Square Loop was gone by 1915.

Adams Square Station took its name from the intersection above it, the location of a statue of Samuel Adams. During construction of the subway, the BTC relocated Adams out of the way. The Adams statue stands today in front of Fanueil Hall. In place of the statue, Adams Square Station occupied its namesake square with a single head house (Figure 3.61), similar in design to the main head house at Scollay Square Station. By the 1930s, most of the head house structure was removed, except for low walls protecting stairways leading down to the station.

After World War II, use of Adams Square Station declined. The MTA provided only weekday and Saturday service to the station in 1954. During late night and on Sundays, cars did not even stop at Adams Square Station. The MTA permanently closed the station in 1963. Afterwards, it was abandoned in place during the construction of City Hall Plaza and the conversion of Scollay Square Station to Government Center Station. A portion of Adams Square Station survived, repurposed into storage

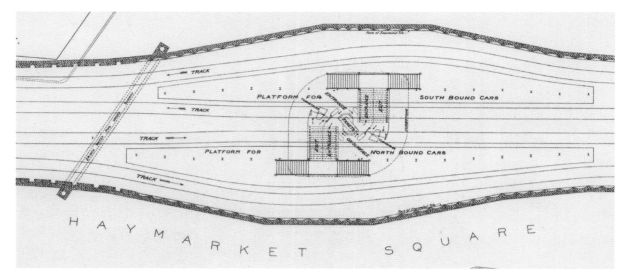

Figure 3.62 Haymarket Square Station, 1898
Haymarket Square Station opened with two platforms, each served exclusively by either northbound or southbound streetcars.

Figure 3.63 Inside Haymarket Square Station, 1898
Running down the middle of the station, an iron fence separates the northbound track and platform (right) from the southbound track and platform (left). Stairs lead up to a head house in the middle of Haymarket Square (Figure 3.64).

Figure 3.64 Haymarket Square Station Head House, 1898
Like an overturned satellite dish, a standing-seam copper roof caps the head house of Haymarket Station.

areas connected to subterranean levels of Boston City Hall.

Haymarket Square Station took its name from the historic site where farmers once brought hay and other commodities into Boston for sale. The two-platform station featured a western platform served by southbound streetcars, and an eastern platform served by northbound cars (Figure 3.62). Each platform sat between two tracks, one each for cars travelling in the same direction. The station's interior was functional, with its super-structure exposed (Figure 3.63). The platforms

were connected via stairs with a ticket mezzanine and a head house that squatted in the middle of Haymarket Square (Figure 3.64).

The Haymarket Incline

When planning the Tremont Street Subway, the BTC anticipated that a northern terminus for the project should be located north of the downtown "congested district" and close to the steam railroad depots at Causeway Street. After exploring various locations for the subway's northern portal and

Figure 3.65 Haymarket Square, February 8, 1897
The Boston & Maine Railroad's Haymarket Depot (background), with its pediment-capped facade, bears witness to subway construction in Haymarket Square (foreground).

incline, the BTC settled on the site of the Boston & Maine's passenger depot at Haymarket Square (Figure 3.65). The Boston & Maine vacated its depot in late 1894. In the following year, the BTC agreed to purchase the depot and associated lands. The BTC then demolished the depot and all structures on the blocks bounded by Causeway, Canal, Haverhill, and Charlestown Streets. Everything was replaced with the northernmost portion of the Tremont Street Subway, the Haymarket Incline (Figure 3.66).

The last portion of the Tremont Street Subway to be completed, the Haymarket Incline, opened on

August 19, 1898. The incline was installed between Haverhill and Canal Streets, with its top at Travers Street. There, streetcars entered and exited subway trackage through a portal at the bottom of the slope (Figure 3.67 and Figure 3.68). At the top of the incline, tracks from the subway connected with two loop tracks that served a surface streetcar stop and offered a means for streetcars to turn and head back into the subway (Figure 3.69). The loop tracks connected with streetcar tracks on Causeway and Haverhill Streets.

After conducting multiple studies for a streetcar station at the northern end of the subway, the

Figure 3.66 The Northern End of the Subway, 1898
Streetcar subway tracks (black and white lines) pass under Haymarket Square (right), along the Haymarket Incline (middle), into surface loops between Canal and Haverhill Streets (left), and connect with street-level tracks on Causeway Street (far left).

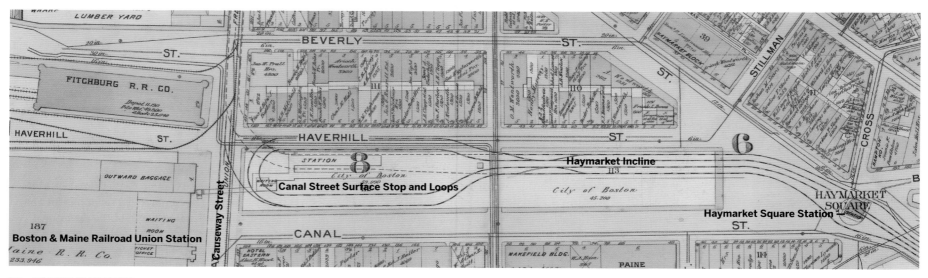

Figure 3.67 Northern End of the Subway, September 9, 1898
In the distance, daylight shines down the Haymarket Incline and into the Tremont Street Subway.

Figure 3.68 Steelwork at Haymarket Portal, May 23, 1898
The northernmost roof support beam for the subway is emblazoned with "1897," the year the southern portion of the subway opened to the public.

Figure 3.69 Canal Street Area, December 19, 1898
A photograph taken a few months after the opening of the northern half of the Tremont Street Subway shows streetcar tracks connecting the Haymarket Incline (far distance) with loop tracks serving the Canal Street streetcar stop (foreground).

BTC established a surface stop just beyond the Haymarket Incline, at the corner of Canal and Causeway Streets. Soon after the subway opened, the BTC erected a temporary covering over the trolley stop. Various structures sheltered the Canal Street streetcar stop until the structure of Boston's first elevated railways cast shadows over the entire area in 1901.

Workers excavating for the Haymarket Incline uncovered remnant layers of historic transportation infrastructure. In addition to foundations and piers that previously supported the Boston &

Maine's Haymarket Depot, a portion of wall that once bounded the Middlesex Canal extension, opened in 1813, was revealed. Canal Street, which bordered the incline work site, took its name from the southernmost portion of the canal, a segment that terminated alongside the street until 1843. After the opening of the Tremont Street Subway, additional layers of transportation infrastructure appeared along Canal Street; an elevated railway for rapid transit trains appeared in 1899, a streetcar elevated railway arrived in 1910, and an elevated highway appeared in the middle of the twentieth century. The site of the Haymarket Incline is now occupied by private development above ground and the MBTA's North Station rapid transit station below ground. Elevated railways and highways haves disappeared from the site.

Brimstone Corner After the Subway

After the opening of the Tremont Street Subway, as was required by statute, the BTC and BERy saw to the removal of streetcar tracks from Tremont and Boylston Streets, along the route of the subway. Streetcar tracks on Tremont Street, from Scollay Square to Boylston Street, and on Boylston Street, from Tremont Street to Park Square, were gone by the end of 1898. A postcard published shortly after the removal of streetcar tracks shows "Brimstone

Corner," so named for the abolitionists and their fiery sermons given there at the time of the Civil War, lacking the infrastructure that facilitated so many streetcar blockades (Figure 3.70). Karl Baedeker's 1899 guide to the United States agreed: "the construction of the subway…has done much to relieve the congestion of cars in the main business-streets of Boston."

The Tremont Street Subway allowed more streetcars, and thereby more people, to move with greater speed through downtown Boston. Before the opening of the subway, the maximum capacity of the Tremont Street streetcar tracks along Boston Common was approximately 200 streetcars, each way, per hour. Streetcar blockades regularly occurred as track capacity was reached. After one year of running streetcars beneath the same length of street, the BTC counted just over 280 streetcars running each way per hour while capacity along the route increased by forty percent. Before the subway, travel between Park Street to the far side of the Public Garden, via Tremont and Boylston Streets, regularly took ten to twenty minutes, especially during times of peak traffic. Blockades extended the duration significantly. In the Tremont Street Subway, the same trip took approximately seven to eight minutes.

TREMONT STREET AND PARK STREET. (BRIMSTONE CORNER). BOSTON. MASS.

Figure 3.70 Tremont Street After the Subway, Circa 1900
After the removal of surface streetcar tracks, the intersection of Tremont and Park Streets lost the possibility for streetcar blockades, like one photographed in 1895 (Figure 3.7).

Figure 3.71 Destination Indicator Boards, Circa 1899
Streetcar destination indicator boards hang above the western platform, served by southbound streetcars, at Park Street Station. The electric operated boards indicated the berth of arrival, numbered 1, 2, 3, 4 or 5, of trolleys bound for Boylston Street Station and beyond.

Park Street Station Gets Busy

The BTC recorded that 27.4 million passengers utilized Park Street Station during the station's first year of use. That number included both passengers entering the station from Boston Common and riders transferring between streetcars within. By 1899, the BTC described Park Street Station as the fourth busiest train station in the world, with a yearly passenger count larger than the fourteen million recorded at Grand Central Terminal in New York City. The BTC wrote in an annual report that the only train stations handling more passengers per year were St. Lazare Station in Paris (43.1 million), Liverpool Street Station in London (44.4 million), and Waterloo Station in London (28.7 million).

Within months of opening, Park Street Station was so heavily patronized that it became overcrowded, especially along its western platform. There, people constantly amassed to wait for southbound streetcars. On the busiest days, when three to five streetcars arrived for boarding at the same time, the trolleys showed up in no particular order

nor with any consistency as to where they stopped. In these situations, people waiting on the western platform were forced to make quick dashes through the waiting throngs to seek out their trolley, which may have arrived as far as one hundred feet away from where they were waiting. The BTC worked quickly to address the situation. In order to provide passengers with advance notification of where each southbound streetcar would arrive, the BTC painted berth numbers along the western platform. The BTC also installed car arrival indicator boards above the busy platform. The first indicator boards were hand operated. The BTC replaced the manual boards with two, double-sided, and electrically-operated car arrival indicator boards by 1899. On each board (Figure 3.71), berth numbers illuminated next to a list of destinations indicating where arriving streetcars would stop and for what destination they were bound for. In the 1890s, the BTC established five berths at the western platform in Park Street Station. Today, the MBTA maintains four berth designations along the same platform, now served by southbound light rail vehicles. Each berth corresponds to one of the four lettered branches of the Green Line.

Recognizing America's First Subway

The completion of the Tremont Street Subway, the first public transit subway in America, was an historic achievement. Immediately upon completion of the project, the BTC installed a bronze plaque commemorating the creation and opening date of the initial portion of the subway. The Tremont Street Subway was significant enough that the board of managers of the 1900 Exposition Universelle in Paris requested that the BTC prepare and submit an exhibit on Boston's subway. In response, the BTC sent to Paris a small exhibit on the Tremont Street Subway. The exhibit was awarded a diploma of "Grand Prix." In Paris, the BTC's subway exhibit was joined by an exhibit on South Station Terminal, prepared by the Boston Terminal Company, the builder of South Station. After Paris, the BTC's subway exhibit made the rounds. It was displayed at the 1904 Louisiana Purchase Exposition, the 1905 Lewis and Clark Exposition in St. Louis (where it was awarded a gold medal), the 1907 Jamestown Exposition, and the "Boston 1915" Exposition.

The Tremont Street Subway remained celebrated throughout the twentieth century. It was declared a National Historic Landmark by the National Park Service in 1964 and designated a National Historic Civil Engineering Landmark by the American Society of Civil Engineers in 1978. In the late 1990s, the MBTA celebrated the subway's centennial with the design of a "Celebrating 100 Years of Service"

graphic, printed onto car cards, posters, and stickers (Figure 3.72).

On March 28, 1995 the MBTA marked a century since the first ceremonial ground-breaking for the Tremont Street Subway with a ceremony on Boston Common. There, MBTA General Manager John Haley Jr., Boston Mayor Thomas Menino, State Secretary of Transportation James Kerasiotes, and state Senate President William Bulger reenacted the ground-breaking of March 28, 1895. The VIPs then descended into Park Street Station, where they ceremoniously turned on new lighting for the 1978-installed, 110-foot-long wall mural by Lilli Ann Rosenberg of Newton.

Throughout 1995, 1996, and 1997, various subway history events, exhibits, and publications were produced by the MBTA, the Society for the Preservation of New England Antiquities (now Historic New England), the Bostonian Society, the Boston Street Railway Association (BSRA), and others. Subway celebrations culminated on Monday, October 20 and Tuesday, October 21, coordinating with bicentennial celebrations for the U.S.S. Constitution, the world's oldest, operational commissioned warship. On Monday night, approximately two hundred VIPs attended a celebration at South Station. The following morning, a horse drawn carriage brought Acting Governor Paul Cellucci from the State House down to Park Street Station. After descending into the historic subway station, Cellucci joined Boston Mayor Thomas Menino and others for a ride on a four-car parade of trolleys to Boylston Street Station. The mixed train featured Type 5 streetcar number 5706, PCC car number 3295, light rail vehicle number 3495, wrapped with

Figure 3.72 Subway Centenary Graphic, 1997
The MBTA produced a graphic to celebrate one hundred years of operation of the Tremont Street Subway. An open-type streetcar and a light rail vehicle are joined by an MBTA token.

Figure 3.73 Subway Centennial Trolley Graphics, 1997
MBTA light rail vehicle number 3495 wears graphics commemorating a century of service by the Tremont Street Subway.

Figure 3.74 Boston's Streetcar Network, January 1, 1898
A map, produced by the Boston Elevated Railway Company in 1910 represents the extents of streetcar trackage of the West End (wholly owned by the BERy) on January 1, 1898. Solid and dashed lines represent surface tracks. A line of circles (center) represents the Tremont Street Subway.

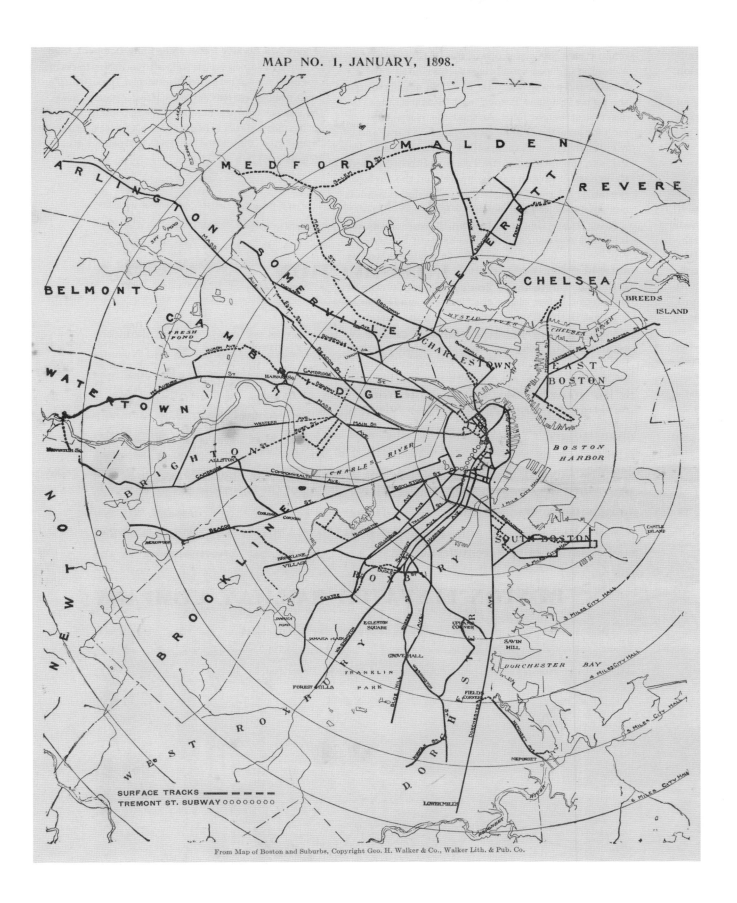

MAP NO. 1, JANUARY, 1898.

SURFACE TRACKS ———— — — —
TREMONT ST. SUBWAY OOOOOOOO

From Map of Boston and Suburbs, Copyright Geo. H. Walker & Co., Walker Lith. & Pub. Co.

centennial graphics (Figure 3.73), and light rail vehicle number 3719. At Boylston Street Station, the VIPs emerged onto the Tremont Street mall to a live band, festive tents, and a 1957 GMC-built bus number 2600 rendered in an MTA-era paint scheme. Banners hung from the head houses at both Park Street and Boylston Street Station.

Mapping the BERy After the Subway

Through its lease of the West End in 1897, the BERy became the largest, single public transit company in New England and one of the largest on earth. In 1898, the BERy operated more aspects of Boston's public transportation system than any other company. Looking back on this period from 1910, the BERy published a series of maps in Boston newspapers to tout its history, announce projects under construction, and share proposed expansion plans. One of the maps in the series depicts existing "Surface Tracks" and the "Tremont Street Subway" as they were on January 1, 1898 (Figure 3.74). In October 1898, the BERy prepared a detailed map of the "Surface Lines" of its empire (Figure 3.75 and Figure 3.76). The Tremont Street Subway, being sub-surface, was not represented. The 1898

map reveals the vast scope of the BERy's network, including the location of its streetcar lines, car houses, and power stations. The 1898 maps utilized the terms "Surface Tracks" and "Surface Lines" to describe streetcar lines. At the time, it was common for streetcars to be called "surface cars" and rapid transit trains to be called "elevated trains." Prior to the opening of the Tremont Street Subway, streetcars in Boston ran exclusively on the surface. Boston's first rapid transit trains ran not in tunnels, but upon elevated railways.

After completing the Tremont Street Subway, the BTC followed its mandates and brought to Boston a replacement for the Charles River Bridge as well as a streetcar tunnel from downtown to East Boston. Although it brought the Tremont Street Subway to completion before either the Charlestown Bridge or the East Boston Tunnel, the BTC simultaneously planned and developed designs for all three projects during the 1890s. In the next few decades, the BTC's streetcar subway, harbor tunnel, and river bridge were utilized not only by streetcars, but also by Boston's newest mode of public transit, electric rapid transit trains.

Figure 3.75 Surface Tracks of the BERy, October 1, 1898
A publicly sold map depicts surface street railway tracks of the BERy, highlighted in a terra-cotta color. Throughout the map, numbers call out car houses, transfer stations, power houses, and termini of BERy lines. The composition and scale of this map is similar to that of Chase's 1865 regional transit map (Figure 1.69) and the West End's 1891 network map (Figure 2.45).

Figure 3.76 Enlarged Portion of Figure 3.75

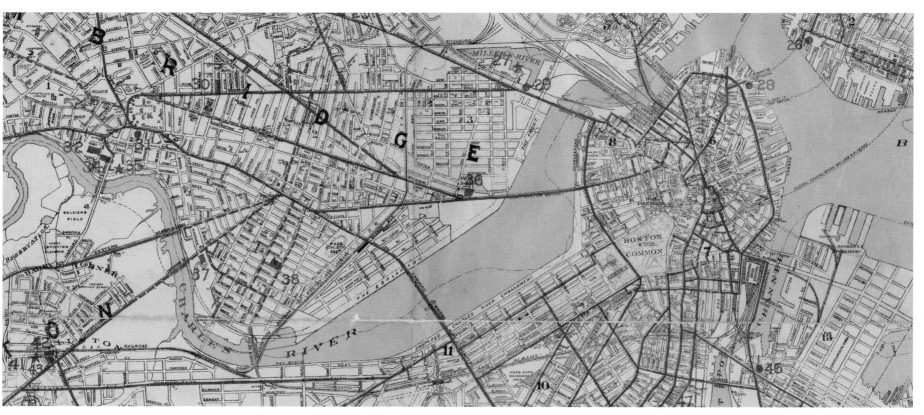

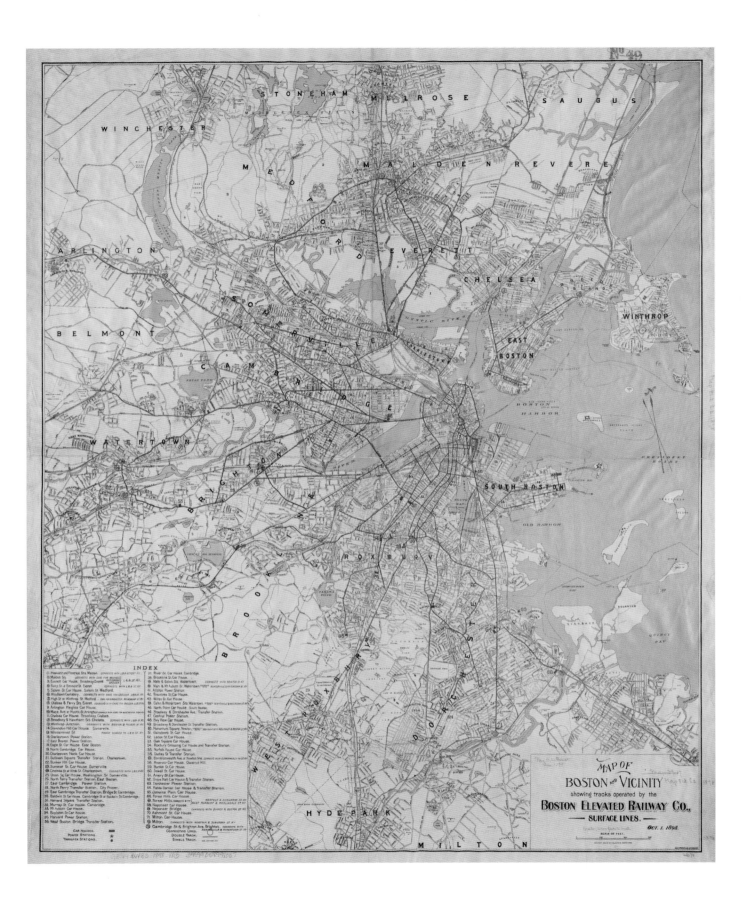

— Fitchburg Railroad

— Eastern Railroad

Boston & Lowell Railroad —

Boston & Maine Railroad —

Scollay Square —

— Boston & New York Central Railroad

— Boston & Providence Railroad

Boston & Worcester Railroad

— Old Colony Railroad

CHAPTER 4
Grand Terminals for Commuters

The Iron Horse Enters The Hub

Steam railroads arrived in Boston in the 1830s, some twenty-five years before the arrival of horse railroads. Steam railroads were started by private companies, each chartered by the Commonwealth to establish its own lines, passenger stations, and freight depots. In smaller towns, a single structure often served as both passenger and freight depot. In larger towns and cities, railroads erected distinct passenger and freight facilities. Stations at the terminus of a railroad line were terminal stations, or simply, terminals. While a terminal station was a public facility served by passenger trains, a different kind of terminal existed behind the scenes, a place for the storage, service, and inspection of locomotives and cars they pulled. The Boston & Maine

Figure 4.1 (Opp.) Boston's Steam Railroad Terminals, 1865
The terminal passenger stations of Boston's eight steam railroad companies are highlighted in red on a portion of Chase's 1865 railroad map of Boston (Figure 1.70).

Figure 4.2 (Right) Boston's Passenger Terminals, 1856
The front page of the March 8, 1856 *Ballou's Pictorial* catalogs the passenger terminals of seven of the eight steam railroads serving Boston. Clockwise from the bottom left are the depots of the Boston & Maine, Eastern, Boston & Lowell, Old Colony, Boston & Providence, and Boston & Worcester Railroads. In the center is the Fitchburg Railroad's "castle" depot.

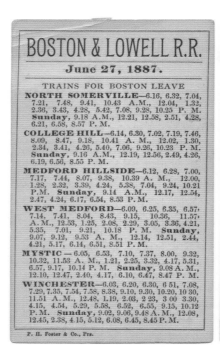
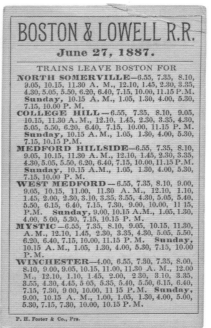

Figure 4.3 Boston & Lowell Commuter Schedule Card, 1887
One face of an 1887 schedule card (left) lists departure times from Boston for Boston & Lowell trains stopping at six stations along the railroad's main line. The other face (right) lists departure times for trains running inbound from the same stations.

Railroad's (Boston & Maine's) Boston Terminal, which sprawled across the intersection of Cambridge, Somerville, and Charlestown, was a prime example of a back-of-the-house type of terminal.

In the latter half of the nineteenth and first half of the twentieth centuries, railroads erected passenger terminals in major cities that were larger and more architecturally impressive than stations in minor towns. The physical grandeur of city passenger terminals was one part functional—multiple tracks and large waiting rooms were needed—and one part flamboyance—marketing through architectural edifice. In Boston, the Boston & Maine's Union Station was an impressive example of a railroad's grandiose city terminal.

By the middle of the 1850s, Boston was served by eight different steam railroad companies. These were the Boston & Lowell Railroad (Boston & Lowell), the Eastern Railroad (Eastern), the Fitchburg Railroad (Fitchburg), the Boston & Maine, the Boston & Worcester Railroad (Boston & Worcester), the Boston & Providence Railroad (Boston & Providence), the Old Colony Railroad (Old Colony), and the Boston & New York Central. Each company established a passenger terminal in Boston (Figure 4.1). Views of Boston's earliest steam railroad passenger terminals were reproduced on the cover of the March 8, 1856 issue of *Ballou's Pictorial* (Figure 4.2).

Through leases and mergers, and sometimes after bankruptcies and outright purchases, the eight steam railroads serving Boston in the mid-1850s were effectively consolidated into three by 1900. Correspondingly, Boston's steam railroad passenger stations became consolidated. The evolution of Boston's eight passenger terminals of the nineteenth century into the two terminals in use today, North Station and South Station, was the result of the consolidation of not only railroad companies, but also planning by the Commonwealth and Boston to improve transportation for the city.

After completing an initial main line, each railroad serving Boston continued to expand, adding branch lines to serve communities not served by a main line but that were demanding service. After two decades of development, Boston's steam railroads operated trains between the city and scores of stations on both main and branch lines. Towns nearest the city often saw more than one train per day. In their book *Boston's Commuter Rail: The First 150 Years*, Thomas J. Humphrey and Norton D. Clark recounted that "by 1870, Massachusetts had more miles of railroad per square mile than any other state or any foreign country...." They continued: "In 1871, 73% of riders on the eight Boston [steam] rail systems travelled to or from Boston, excluding trips entirely outside of the state." By the 1870s, the frequency of local trains travelling to and from Boston was highest during mornings

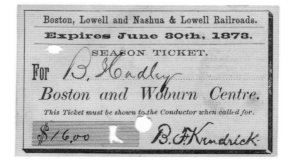

Figure 4.4 Steam Railroad Season Ticket, 1873
A season ticket was valid for travel on regularly scheduled trains, except Sundays, once daily in each direction between Boston and Woburn Center.

Figure 4.5 New York & New England Season Pass, 1877
A season pass valid for the last three months of 1877 was good for thirty-one trips on the New York & New England, between Boston and Hyde Park.

Figure 4.6 Boston & Maine Commutation Ticket, 1919
Issued on February 11, 1919, a Boston & Maine monthly commutation ticket was valid for thirty days. After the first ride, and during each subsequent trip, the bearer presented the ticket to a Boston & Maine conductor who punched out the next highest number on the ticket. On the bearer's sixtieth trip, all fifty-nine numbers were punched and the bearer surrendered the ticket back to the railroad. The ticket's sixty day allotment of trips accommodated two rides a day during a thirty day period, ideal for a weekday railroad commuter. A season pass valid for the last three months of 1877 was good for thirty-one trips on the New York & New England, between Boston and Hyde Park.

Figure 4.7 Boston & Maine Twelve-ride Ticket, 1921
Issued by the U.S. Railroad Administration, which oversaw American steam railroad operations during World War I, a ticket was good for twelve rides between Boston and Wake-field. Each ride was to be recorded by a conductor punching out one of the numbers, from 11 through 2. The conductor took the ticket after its twelfth and final use.

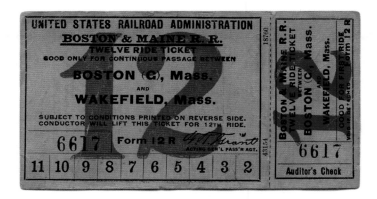

Figure 4.8 Fitchburg Railroad Twelve-ride Ticket, 1895
A ticket good for twelve rides between Boston and Cambridge, has been punched for trips two and three.

and evenings. To facilitate regular riders on local trains, railroads issued pocket-sized schedule cards listing inbound and outbound trains serving local stations (Figure 4.3).

To accommodate and retain frequent riders of their lines, steam railroads pre-sold multiple trips at discounted, or "commuted," rates. "Season tickets" (Figure 4.4 and Figure 4.5) allowed unlimited travel between two stations during a set time period, often a specific number of days or months. "Commutation tickets" were typically valid for a limited number of rides between two designated stations. Railroads required most season passes and

commutation tickets be signed by their bearers. The practice remained common with railroad passes, including MBTA commuter rail passes, throughout the twentieth century. Commutation tickets were available with a varying quantity of days each was valid for. Thirty-day, commonly called monthly tickets (Figure 4.6), and sixty-day tickets were designed for the daily railroad commuter. Twelve-ride (Figure 4.7 and Figure 4.8) and five-ride (Figure 4.18) tickets were intended for a business traveller, tourist, or person not needing an entire month of rides. Other advance-purchase tickets offered by steam railroads included booklets of tickets, each for a particular distance of travel. These "mileage tickets" were more often used for long distance rail travel, as opposed to short daily hops into and out of Boston.

Users of railroad commutation tickets became known as "commuters." The term commuter continues to apply to one travelling between home and work, often between suburb and city, on work days. But unlike today, where the automobile dominates the commute of many, throughout the majority of the nineteenth century, most of Boston's commuters rode the rails.

Boston's Four Northern Railroads

Of the eight steam railroads serving Boston in 1855, four provided service to points north of the city's latitude. Boston's northern railroads were the Boston & Lowell, Eastern, Fitchburg, and Boston & Maine. Each established their first Boston passenger terminal along the northern edge of Boston Proper, near Causeway Street. The June 1860 *Appleton's Railway and Steam Navigation Guide* broke down the daily quantities of passenger trains departing from Boston's northern steam railroad terminals as approximately one dozen each on the

Boston & Lowell and Eastern, a half dozen on the Fitchburg, and approximately two dozen on the Boston & Maine. Fares from Boston recorded in the guide were $.75 to Lowell on the Boston & Lowell, $.35 to Lynn and $1.10 to Newburyport on the Eastern, $1.55 to Fitchburg on the Fitchburg, and $.99 to Haverhill on the Boston & Maine.

The Boston & Lowell Railroad

The Boston & Lowell was chartered by the Commonwealth on June 5, 1830. Though it was established before the Boston & Worcester, operator of Boston's first passenger trains, the Boston & Lowell was the second company to provide steam passenger train service for Boston. The Boston & Lowell hired Irish laborers to lay its first main line, built partially with granite cross ties, and later, entirely rebuilt with more-forgiving wood ties. Early iron rails, with their "fish belly" profiles, were the first rails to link Boston with Lowell.

The Boston & Lowell's main line roughly followed the route of the Middlesex Canal (Figure 4.9 and Figure 4.10). The canal opened in 1804, connecting the city of Lowell and its textile mills with the port of Boston, where raw wool arrived and finished

Figure 4.9 (Opp.) Boston & Lowell Railroad Map, 1847
Published in the *Boston Almanac*, a miniature map plots the course of the southern end of the Boston & Lowell Railroad's main line. Other maps in the book covered the rest of the line.

Figure 4.10 (Below) Boston & Lowell Railroad Survey, 1836
Mapped a year after opening, Boston's second steam railroad line to carry paying passengers runs from Boston (far right) to Lowell (far left). Paralleling much of the railroad's route, the Middlesex Canal, opened twenty-six years before the railroad, runs from Boston to a point a bit west of Lowell (bottom left).

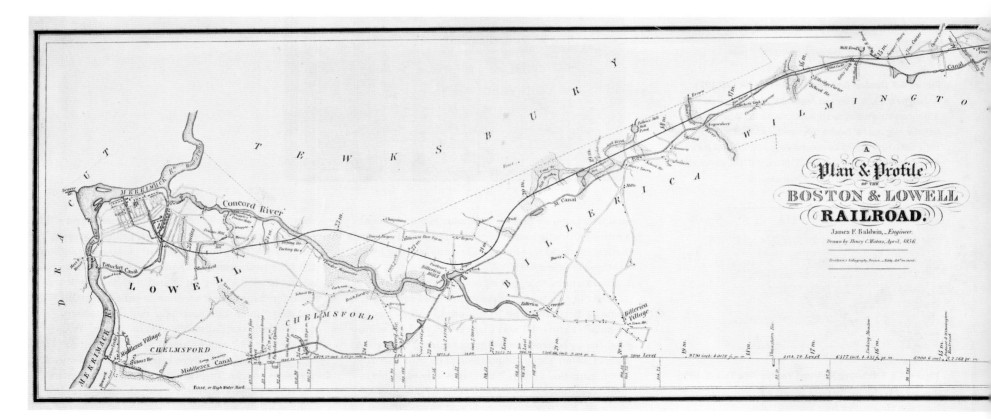

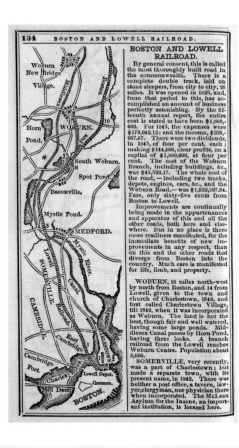

textiles shipped out. Nearing Lowell, the route of the railroad deviated from that of the canal nearer to Lowell. Whereas the railroad pushed right into the center of the industrial center, the canal's northern terminus was not in Lowell at all, but in the neighboring town of Chelmsford. At the northern end of the canal, boats utilized the Merrimack River to move between the Middlesex Canal and the mills of Lowell. The opening of the Boston & Lowell, with its downtown depots, faster service, and lower freight rates than the canal, directly contributed to the demise of the Middlesex Canal. The canal ceased regular operation in 1851 and was defunct by the end of 1852.

The Boston & Lowell's first steam locomotive was named for and constructed in England by George Stephenson, designer of the famed "Rocket" locomotive (see Chapter 1). The George Stephenson arrived in the Port of Boston before being barged along the Middlesex Canal to Lowell. There, railroad company employees assembled the machine in preparation for its inaugural run to Boston. The locomotive weighed seven tons, sat on four wheels, and was rated to provide thirty horsepower.

Stephenson's locomotive for the Boston & Lowell was designed to operate on early English railroads with a gauge of four feet, eight and one half inches. The gauge of a railroad is the distance between the inside edges of a track's pair of rails. After other American railroads ordered Stephenson-designed locomotives built to the same gauge of rails, additional railroads in America were built to what became known as Stephenson gauge or "standard gauge." The standard gauge for American railroads remains four feet, eight and one half inches, the most widely adhered to railroad gauge in the world.

The Boston & Lowell established its first Boston passenger terminal on Leverett Street, on the northeastern edge of Boston's West End (Figure 4.2). The depot sat near the Charles River and was a short walk from Causeway Street. The first train to traverse the entire Boston & Lowell main line carried a load of VIPs from Lowell to Boston on May 27, 1835. The inaugural run took approximately an hour and fifteen minutes. In the afternoon, the train travelled back to the mill city, where it arrived to fireworks, cheering throngs, and a celebratory banquet for those involved in the venture. Later that year, on June 24, the Boston & Lowell commenced regular passenger service between its namesake cities. Initially, the main line lacked intermediate stations. The one-way fare

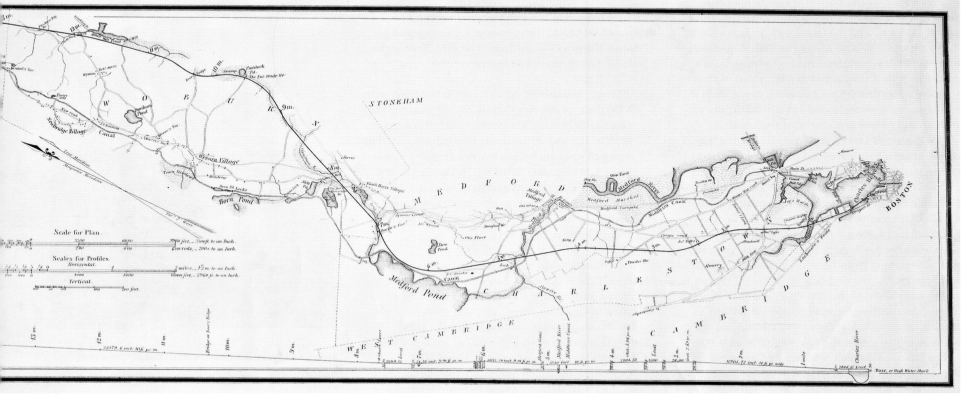

was $1.00. By the end of June, the *Boston Mercantile Journal* reported the Boston & Lowell operating two trips each way per day. Trains departed from Lowell at 6 a.m. and 2:30 p.m., and from Boston at 9:30 a.m. and 5:30 p.m. Along the line, stagecoach and omnibus companies coordinated schedules and routes to collect people and deposit them in time to make departing trains. Likewise, horse-drawn conveyances were stationed at railroad depots to pick up rail passengers alighting from trains.

The Boston & Lowell grew quickly. By the late 1840s, branch lines extended into the downtowns of communities like Woburn. Connections at Lowell allowed the railroad to market service north of the Commonwealth and into New Hampshire. Within a decade of commencing operations, the Boston & Lowell increased service ten-fold. A company schedule effective June 2, 1856 listed nearly twenty trains departing from Leverett Street daily. During summer 1857, a growing Boston & Lowell relocated its Boston passenger terminal to Causeway Street. There, the company opened its second Boston station on July 31. The depot was two stories tall and resembled a modest town hall (Figure 4.11).

The Boston & Lowell replaced its Causeway Street depot in place in the early 1870s. The railroad's third Boston passenger terminal opened on

November 24, 1873 with a four-story head house and a layout significantly larger than its previous station. (Figure 4.12) The terminal's seven-story tower stood tall at the corner of Causeway and Nashua Streets (Figure 4.13). The 1881 *Stranger's Guide to Boston* described the structure:

> The very handsome depot…is 700 feet long, with a frontage of 205 feet, but its main feature is the great arch of the train house, which has a clear span of 120 feet without any central support. The accommodations for passengers are very convenient and elegantly fitted up. In the center of the depot is a magnificent and lofty marble paved hall, finished in hard wood; out of these opens the ladies' and gents' rooms, restaurants, barber shop, bundle room, etc.

The terminal's train hall opened with four tracks. Natural light flooded the hall's interior through skylights punctuating a clear-span arched roof (Figure 4.14).

The Massachusetts Central Railroad (Mass Central) began to operate its trains from the Boston & Lowell's Boston depot to the town of Hudson on October 1, 1881. The Mass Central was technically the ninth steam railroad to serve Boston, but

Figure 4.13 Boston & Lowell Passenger Depot, Circa 1880
The Boston & Lowell's third Boston passenger terminal heroically marks the corner of Causeway Street (right) and Nashua Street (left), dwarfing the Eastern's second Boston passenger terminal (far right). Horse-drawn coaches and carriages access a covered carriageway at the base of the tower.

Figure 4.14 Boston & Lowell Terminal Train Hall, Circa 1880
The train hall of the third depot of the Boston & Lowell is occupied by two trains of passenger coaches. In the distance, large round windows and giant doors mark the end of the space.

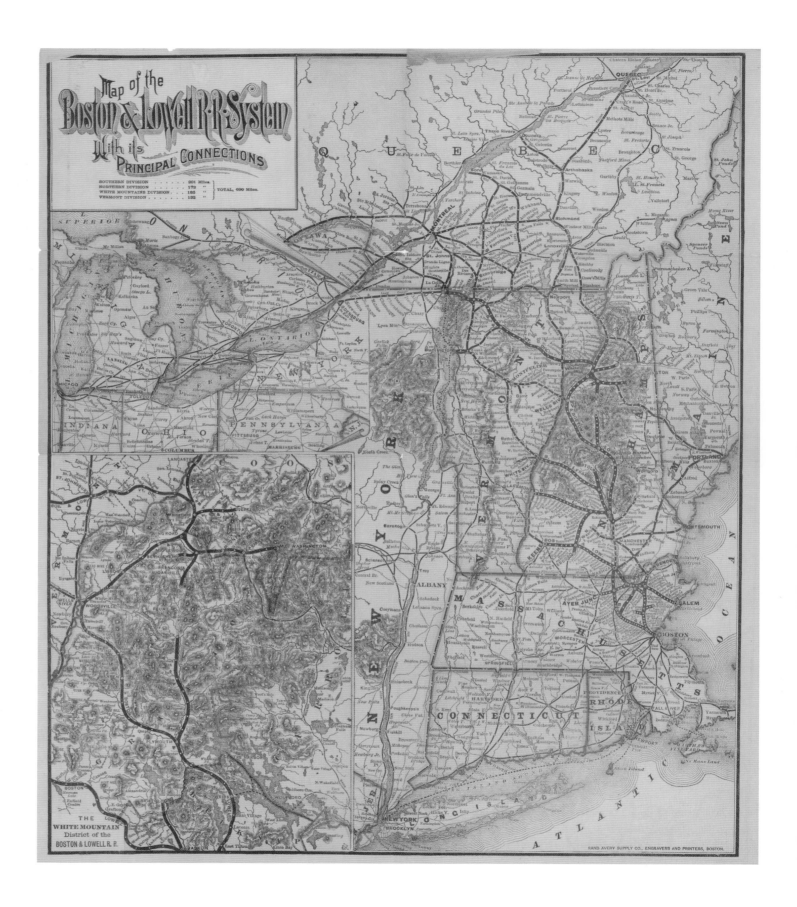

Figure 4.15 Mapping the Boston & Lowell, 1886

Stretching from Boston to the northern tip of Lake Champlain, thick black lines represent the lines of the Boston & Lowell. This map was likely one of the last public maps published by the Boston & Lowell. The company was leased to the Boston & Maine in the year following that of the map's publication.

it never opened a Boston passenger terminal of its own. The Mass Central was not long for this world; the railroad operated from Boston for just over two years. At the end of 1883, after being sold at a foreclosure auction earlier in the year, the company became the Central Massachusetts Railroad (Central Mass). The new company commenced operations in September 1885, but like its predecessor, the railroad did not last long. Under a lease agreement, the Central Mass disappeared into the fold of the Boston & Lowell during the later half of 1886.

As was common of steam railroad companies, the Boston & Lowell produced guide books and maps to attract new riders and benefit existing customers. A map of the Boston & Lowell's network that accompanied the 1886 edition of the company's *Summer Saunterings* guide (Figure 4.15) shows the company's lines and connections extending from Boston into Maine, New Hampshire, Vermont, and Canada. The year after the map was published, the Boston & Lowell was leased to the Boston & Maine. After the takeover, the Central Mass became a branch line of the Boston & Maine. The new owner continued to operate the Boston & Lowell as a distinct division for years after the takeover. The Boston & Lowell's main line from Causeway Street to Lowell remains in service, traversed by MBTA Lowell Line commuter rail trains.

The Eastern Railroad

The Eastern kicked off passenger service between Salem and East Boston's Lewis Wharf on August 27, 1838. The day before, a VIP-special carrying the railroad's directors departed Boston at noon. The fare from Boston to Salem was fifty cents (Figure 4.16). During its first few years of operation, the Eastern extended its main line northward from Salem to Newburyport (Figure 4.18), then to

EASTERN
RAIL ROAD.

THE EASTERN RAIL ROAD IS NOW OPEN BETWEEN
BOSTON & SALEM.

FOR THE PRESENT THE FOLLOWING ARRANGEMENT IS ADOPTED.

From Boston.

Passengers and Baggage will be taken from the Company's Depot, on Lewis's wharf, at the following hours, viz:

7 o'clock, A. M.	2½ o'clock, P. M.
9 " A. M.	3½ " P. M.
12¼ " P. M.	6 " P. M.

From Salem.

Trains will start from the Depot, foot of Washington-street, at the following hours, viz:

8 o'clock, A. M.	1½ o'clock, P. M.
10 " A. M.	4½ " P. M.
11 " A. M.	7 " P. M.

RATES OF FARE.

Between LEWIS's WHARF and SALEM DEPOTS,	50 Cents.
Between BOSTON and LYNN,	31 Cents.
Between BOSTON and MARBLEHEAD DEPOT,	31 Cents.
Between SALEM and LYNN,	25 Cents.

☞ All the Trains will stop at the *Lynn Depot* and the Trains leaving Boston at 9 A. M. and 3½ P. M., and Salem at 8 A. M. and 1½ P. M. will stop at the *Marblehead Depot*, to take and leave passengers.

The Coaches of the late Eastern Stage Company will be at the Depot in Salem to take passengers to the Eastward on the arrival of the 7, 9, 12¼ and 3½ Trains from Boston.

Passengers for Portsmouth and Dover, who take the 7 o'clock Train from Boston, can dine at either place.

Passengers by the 9 o'clock Train will arrive at Newburyport at 1 o'clock, and at Portsmouth at 4, P. M.

Passengers by the 12¼ Train can dine at Salem, and then proceed to Portsmouth and Portland the same evening in the Mail Stage.

Passengers by the 3½ Train will be taken as far as Newburyport.

Passengers by either of the above Trains will be taken to intermediate places, as usual.

ALL BAGGAGE WILL BE AT THE RISK OF ITS OWNERS.

September 7, 1838. STEPHEN A. CHASE, *Superintendent.*

Figure 4.16 The Eastern's First Timetable, 1838

A newspaper ad published during the Eastern's first months of service lists train times and fares for travel between Salem and East Boston's Lewis Wharf.

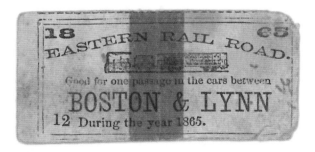

Figure 4.17 Eastern Railroad Commutation Ticket, 1865

A ticket features the image of a primitive steam train.

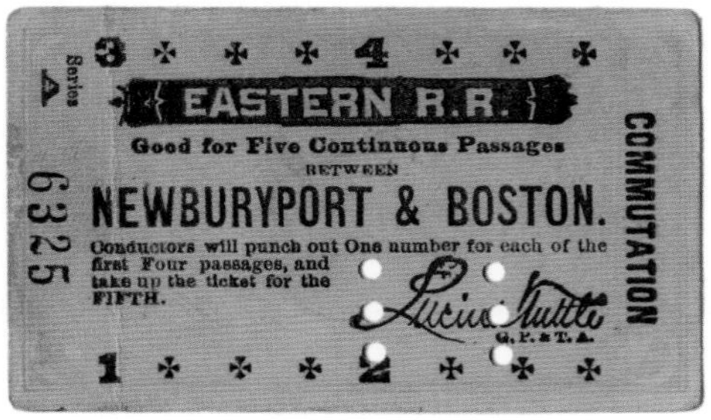

Figure 4.18 Eastern Railroad Five-ride Ticket, Circa 1880

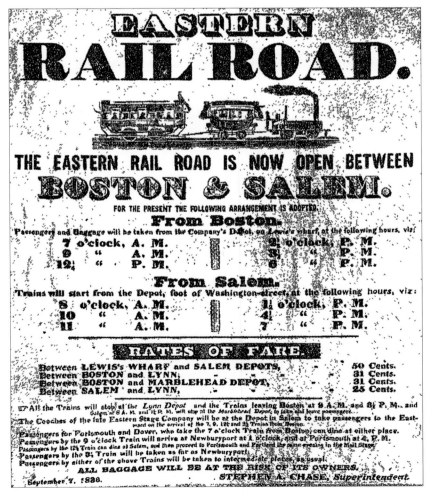

Portland, Maine. The company later opened branch lines to Marblehead and Gloucester (Figure 4.19).

The Eastern did not operate its trains into Boston proper until 1854. From 1838 to 1843, the company dispatched ferries to transport its patrons between Lewis Wharf and the North End waterfront. After 1843, Lewis Wharf was taken over and operated by two successive private companies. From 1843 to 1854, the Eastern operated ferries between the North End and a dedicated terminal on the East Boston waterfront.

The Eastern opened its first passenger terminal in Boston Proper in April 1854. The station, located on Minot Street at the head of Nashua Street, allowed the Eastern to jettison its cross-harbor ferry service and provide riders a single ride from Boston to Portland. The head house of the Eastern's Minot Street depot, complete with an omnibus arriving out front, is depicted on the left side of Figure 4.2. Elegant locomotives arrived at Minot Street like the Eastern's "Cape Ann," finely crafted and ornately detailed equipment typical of what powered American steam railroading in the 1850s and 1860s (Figure 4.20).

The Eastern's Minot Street depot burned on June 21, 1862. The Eastern established a replacement passenger terminal a few blocks to the south of Minot Street, on Causeway Street. Figure 4.11 shows the head house of the new depot erected next to the second Boston passenger terminal of the Boston & Lowell. Of the interior of the Eastern's Causeway Street depot, the 1881 *King's Handbook of Boston* recorded: "[it] is small and crowded. What space it affords is, however, well utilized; and the waiting-rooms are convenient and well arranged." Behind the terminal's head house was a train shed that sheltered two tracks and platforms. The shed measured 330 feet in length.

In addition to playing an important role in early steam railroading for Boston, the Eastern was the stage for a historic moment in the history of electric communication. On March 10, 1875, after Alexander Graham Bell successfully spoke over wire at Exeter Street in Boston, Thomas A. Watson, the receiver of Bell's landmark message, transmitted the first long-distance voice communication via a telegraph wire. Watson did so in December 1876, over telegraph wires of the Eastern, from North Conway, in the White Mountains of New Hampshire, back to Bell in Boston.

For approximately twenty-five years, the Eastern transported people along Boston's North Shore,

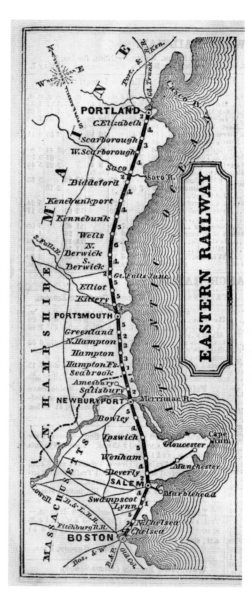

Figure 4.19 Map of the Eastern Railroad, 1860

Figure 4.20 The Eastern's "Cape Ann," October 20, 1860
Constructed in Taunton, an Eastern locomotive and tender poses at Cunard Dock in East Boston.

Figure 4.21 Fitchburg Railroad Ticket to Porter's
Porter's, named after the hotel of the same name, evolved to become today's Porter Station on the MBTA commuter rail.

Figure 4.22 The Fitchburg's Castle Terminal, Circa 1870
Carriages for hire (left) await alongside the Fitchburg's castle depot on Causeway Street (foreground).

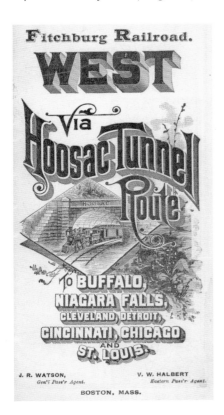

Figure 4.23 Fitchburg Railroad Timetable Cover, 1895
An image of a steam train emerging from the Hoosac Tunnel celebrates the Fitchburg's route westward from Boston.

between Causeway Street and Southern Maine. An Eastern timetable effective June 26, 1881 listed just over fifty passenger trains departing each weekday from Boston. The Eastern ceased to be an independent operation on December 2, 1884, when the company was leased to the juggernaut that was the Boston & Maine. Until 1910, the Boston & Maine operated the former Eastern as a distinct division, its Eastern Division.

The Fitchburg Railroad
The Fitchburg opened on December 20, 1843 with service linking Waltham with a point near City Square, Charlestown. The Fitchburg opened the full length of its Boston to Fitchburg Main Line on March 5, 1845. The Fitchburg's main line passed through North Cambridge, where it served "Porter's," a station named after a nearby hotel (Figure 4.21). Per the 1852 *Boston Directory*, fares from Boston to Porter's and Fitchburg were $.15 and $1.30, respectively. Thirteen years after the Fitchburg began serving Porter's, the stop became the northern terminus of the Cambridge Railroad's first horsecar line north of Harvard Square (See Chapter 1). The Porter Hotel lasted until 1909. Before expiring, the inn gave its name to the porterhouse cut of steak, a specialty made famous in its dining room.

The Fitchburg opened its first passenger terminal to serve Boston Proper on August 9, 1848. Located on Causeway Street, the terminal resembled a small castle, with a medieval-like stone exterior and crenelated towers standing tall at each corner (Figure 4.22). The castle's exterior was sheathed in granite quarried in Fitchburg. The 1881 *Stranger's Guide to Boston* described the Fitchburg's castle as:

> …a large massive building of undressed granite, of curious and ancient design. The interior of the station is roomy, having large and convenient waiting rooms, restaurant, new stand, baggage and parcel rooms.…

The first floor of the castle housed a two-track train hall, nearly 100 feet wide and approximately 320 feet long. Above the train hall was Depot Hall, for a time the largest auditorium in New England.

The cover of an 1895 railroad timetable advertises Fitchburg trains running west from Boston and into eastern upstate New York via the Hoosac Tunnel (Figure 4.23). After the tunnel was heroically drilled and dynamited through the Berkshire Hills in western Massachusetts, it became a vital connection between New England and the Midwest. The Fitchburg's first passenger train passed through the Hoosac Tunnel on October 13, 1875. Fitchburg trains were linking Boston with

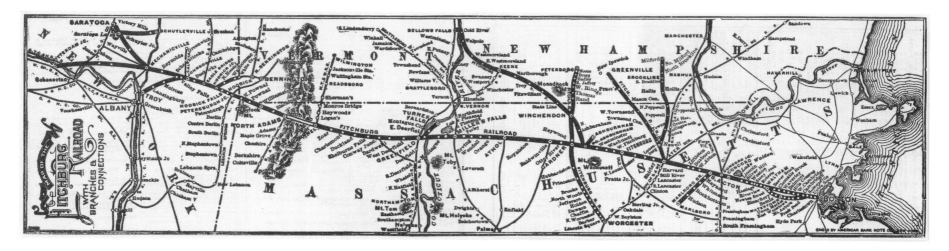

Saratoga Springs, New York, by 1898 (Figure 4.24). The Fitchburg was leased to the Boston & Maine in 1900. Nineteen years later, in 1919, the Fitchburg was formally merged into its lessor. The Fitchburg's main line from Causeway Street remains in use as the MBTA's Fitchburg commuter rail line, now with a terminus at Wachusett Station.

The Boston & Maine Railroad

The Boston & Maine evolved out of the Andover & Wilmington Railroad (Andover & Wilmington), a company which opened to the northwest of Boston in the later half of the 1830s, along with various corporations focused on establishing a railroad from Portland, Maine to Boston. The Andover & Wilmington became the Boston & Portland in the early 1840s, at which point the Boston & Portland was incorporated into the Boston & Maine. The Boston & Maine grew to consolidate not only all of Boston's northern steam railroads, but to consume a plethora of railroads throughout northern New England. The Boston & Maine's first trains to serve Boston travelled the tracks of the Boston & Lowell between Boston and Wilmington. North of North Wilmington, Boston & Maine trains traversed company-owned rails into New Hampshire and Maine (Figure 4.25).

The Boston & Maine opened its first Boston passenger terminal on July 1845. Located at Canal Street, the structure was temporary, used only for a few months while a larger terminal was completed. The temporary depot was erected on land "created" by the city a year earlier. Along Canal Street, the city filled in the southernmost extension of the defunct Middlesex Canal in preparation for the arrival of the Boston & Maine. From the Charles

River to Haymarket Square, tracks and trains of the Boston & Maine replaced boats of the canal with steam trains and their tracks.

The Boston & Maine opened its first permanent Boston passenger terminal on October 20, 1845. The graceful structure fronted Haymarket Square (Figure 4.26 and Figure 4.28). An 1852 print ad mentioned: "A large dining hall is located in the station, where excellent meals, at reasonable prices, will be served at short notice." After dining, travelers headed downstairs to board a train from one of three tracks within a long train hall. From Haymarket Square, the nascent Boston & Maine network carried trains departing to Lowell, Lake Winnipesaukee (NH), and Portland (Figure 4.27). Within fifty years of opening its Haymarket Depot, the Boston & Maine grew to become the largest railroad in Northern New England.

Between Haymarket Terminal and the Charles River, Boston & Maine trains crossed Causeway Street using one of two street-level tracks. At the often dangerously congested crossing, pedestrian, wagon, coach, omnibus, horsecar, and pedestrian traffic made way for Boston & Maine steam locomotives (Figure 4.29). In part to eliminate the dangerous crossing, the Boston & Maine relocated its terminal facilities from Haymarket Square to the north side of Causeway Street in the early 1890s. The vacated Haymarket Terminal was torn down and replaced by the Haymarket Incline segment of the Tremont Street Subway (See Chapter 3). By 1893, Boston & Maine trains no longer crossed Causeway Street. Instead, they served a massive new passenger terminal, Union Station.

Figure 4.24 Fitchburg Railroad Timetable Map, 1898
Along its main line and through the Hoosac Tunnel, the Fitchburg operated long distance trains from Boston (far right) into eastern New York state (far left). Commuter trains served cities and towns closer to Boston. Along the Fitchburg's Watertown Branch (right), trains connected Boston with stops in Watertown and Waltham. Additional branch lines served Marlborough, Worcester, and communities in southern New Hampshire.

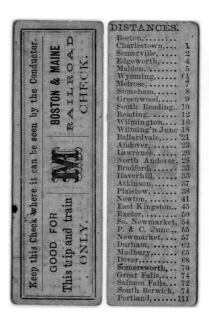

Figure 4.25 Boston & Maine Railroad Check
An early railroad check features vintage letterpress typography on one face (top) and distances from Boston to stations along the line to Portland, Maine on the other (bottom).

Figure 4.26 (Left) Boston & Maine Railroad Ad, 1852

The Boston & Maine's passenger terminal at Haymarket Square graces an advertisement from the 1852 *Boston Almanac*. Destinations touted include towns around Lake Winnipesaukee in New Hampshire

Figure 4.27 (Right) Boston & Maine Railroad Map, 1852

Before growing into one of the largest railroads in New England, the Boston & Maine hosted a single main line, linking Boston and Portland, Maine, and a few branch lines.

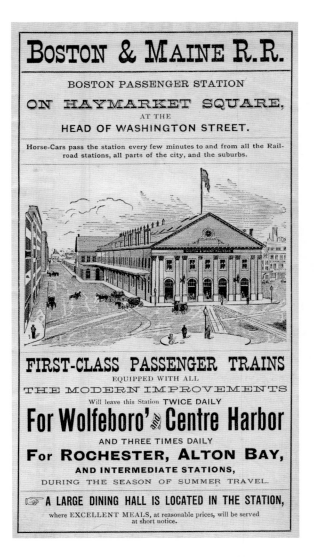

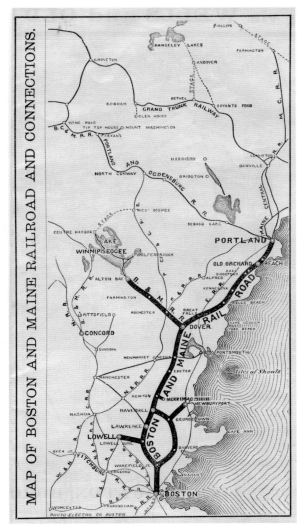

Figure 4.28 Haymarket Square, 1890

The Boston & Maine's Haymarket Passenger Terminal (center) fronts Haymarket Square, where electric streetcars and horse-drawn wagons share the streets with pedestrians.

Figure 4.29 Causeway Street, August 12, 1884

A cacophony of transportation modes tangle at the Boston & Maine Railroad crossing on Causeway Street. Behind the protection of movable gates, two steam locomotives cross the path of an omnibus (far left), horsecars, and thick street traffic. The Fitchburg Railroad's "castle" depot stands watch over the scene. The wood framework running along the side of the street is a temporary structure associated with city sewer work. Boston & Maine trains ceased crossing Causeway Street in the early 1890s.

Cadastral Maps at Causeway Street

Cadastral maps are a specific type of real estate maps. They represent data about property, buildings, and infrastructure. Constructed from land surveys, cadastral maps depict property boundaries, land owners, and building names. The golden age of cadastral map publishing in America was the 1870s through the 1930s. During that period, cadastral maps were published in large, bound atlases. Along with fire insurance map atlases, cadastral map atlases were used by real estate agencies, surveyors, land courts, municipalities, railroads, and other entities who sought to know who owned, and what structures existed, upon land. In the last decades of the nineteenth century, two publishers became dominant in the American cadastral map atlas business. G. M. Hopkins & Company (Hopkins) and G. W. Bromley & Company (Bromley) produced maps that are cartographic time capsules of public transportation infrastructure in Greater Boston. In 1874–75, Hopkins published a multi-volume set of cadastral map atlases of Suffolk County, Massachusetts. The first volume covered Boston's downtown, Beacon Hill, North End, South End, and Back Bay neighborhoods. A composite of Plates C, E, and H (Figure 4.30) from the atlas details the steam railroad depots and infrastructure around Causeway Street.

Union Station

During the last quarter of the nineteenth and early part of the twentieth centuries, competing and complementing railroads worked together to establish union stations in cities across America. The high price of land in urban centers was a common catalyst for the collaborative efforts. Hence, Union Stations typically appeared in places where expanses of affordable land were at a premium.

Union Stations for Boston were conceptualized by the Rapid Transit Commission of 1891–92. In its 1892 report, the commission proposed consolidating the passenger depots of the Boston & Lowell, Boston & Maine, Eastern, and Fitchburg into a single, massive terminal, to be located at Causeway Street. The scope of the commission's "North Union Station" was unprecedented for Boston. Plans laid out an expansive twenty-two-track train hall, capped by a head house packed with waiting rooms, dining rooms, ticket counters, and a main hall (Figure 4.31). Thinking of multi-modal connectivity, the commission proposed that North Union Station be fronted by an elevated railway with a station served by an "elevated circuit train."

When the Boston & Maine leased the Boston & Lowell in 1885, it gained possession of the Boston & Lowell's Causeway Street passenger terminal. Two years later, with its leasing of the Eastern in 1887, the Boston & Maine gained control of the majority

Figure 4.30 Boston's Northern Railroad Depots, 1874

The passenger terminals of Boston's four northern steam railroad companies lie clustered between the Charles River (far left) and Haymarket Square (far right). Horse railroad tracks (solid black lines) trace many streets. Steam railroad lines (solid black lines with tick marks) serve the depots along Causeway Street and at Haymarket Square. The largest building footprint is that of the passenger terminal of the Boston & Lowell (left). Located at the corner of Causeway and Nashua Streets, the depot opened one year prior to the map being published. Next door to the Boston & Lowell's terminal is the second Boston passenger terminal of the Eastern, opened in 1863. At the corner of Causeway and Beverly Streets is the Fitchburg's "castle" (left). The Boston & Maine's Haymarket Terminal sits south of Causeway Street, fronting Haymarket Square (right).

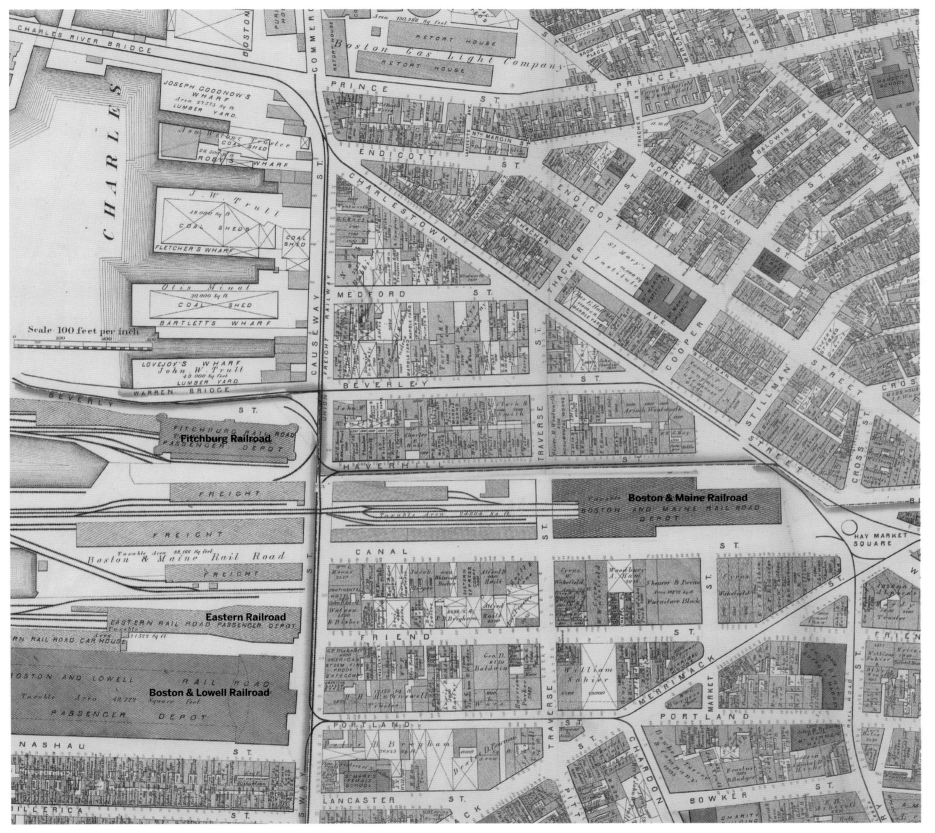

Fitchburg Railroad

Eastern Railroad

Boston & Lowell Railroad

Boston & Maine Railroad

ELEVATION ON CAUSEWAY STREET SHOWING
ELEVATED RAILWAY.

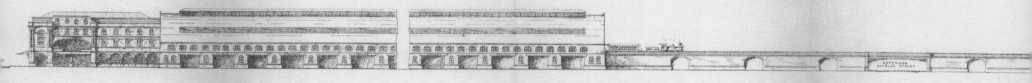

SIDE ELEVATION ON NASHUA STREET

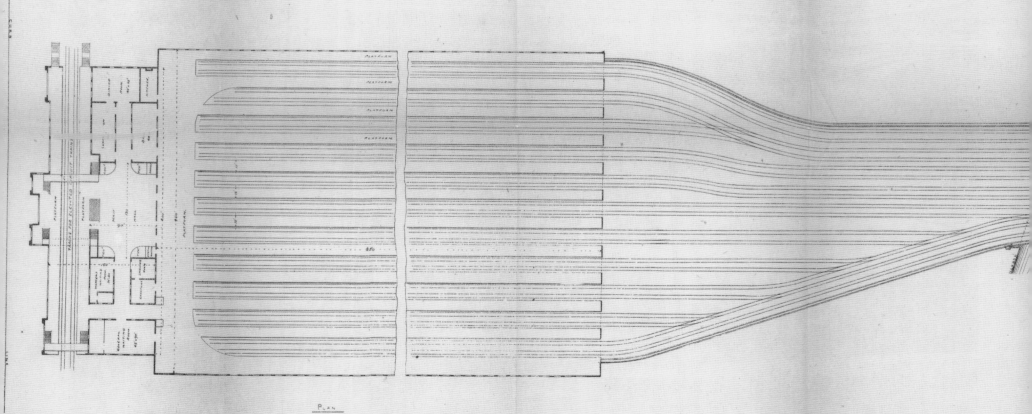

PLAN

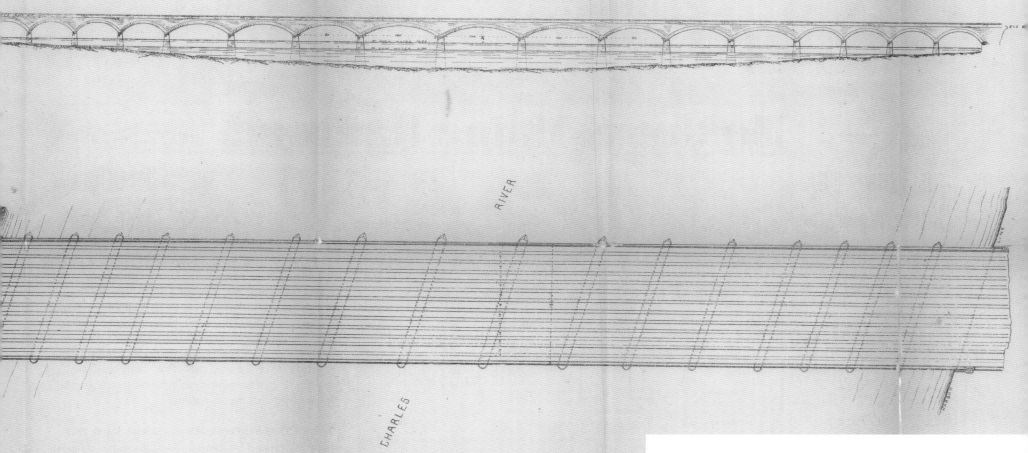

RAPID TRANSIT COMMISSION.
BOSTON.

PROPOSED UNION PASSENGER STATION
ON CAUSEWAY STREET, BOSTON
FOR
NORTHERN RAILROADS

SCALE OF FEET

SCALE OF METRES.

RIVER

CHARLES

Figure 4.31 Proposed North Union Station, 1892
The Rapid Transit Commission of 1891–92 proposed a North
Union Station to replace the steam railroad depots around
Causeway Street. Their designs included an elevation of the
building facing Causeway Street (top), a longitudinal section
of the complex (middle), and a plan of the terminal stretching
from the Charles River (right) to Causeway Street (left).

BOSTON PASSENGER TERMINAL OF THE

TRAIN HOUSE
CONTAINS 23 TRACKS.

Boston & Maine Railroad

AVERAGE NUMBER OF
PASSENGERS USING STATION.
100,000 DAILY.

THE TRUNK LINE
FROM
Boston, Worcester
and
Springfield

THE VACATION ROUTE
TO THE
Sea Coast, Lake
and

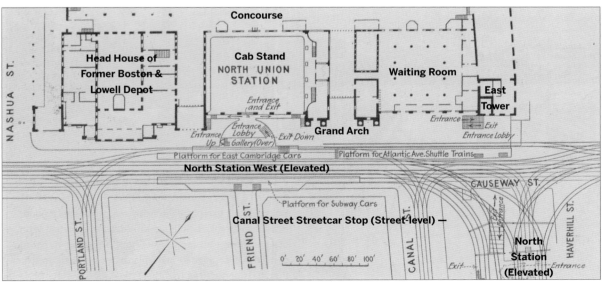

Figure 4.32 The Boston & Maine's Union Station, 1894
From left to right along Causeway Street are the former Boston passenger terminal of the Boston & Lowell (erected in 1873 and made part of Union Station in 1893–94) and the portion of Union Station constructed new by the Boston & Maine in 1894 (fronted by the grand arch). Behind the head houses, train sheds cover platforms and tracks. In the distance, Boston & Maine tracks cross the Charles River.

Figure 4.33 Public Transit at Union Station, March 1913
North Station West (middle) is an elevated streetcar station on the East Cambridge Extension. North Station (bottom right) is an elevated station for rapid transit trains. Surface streetcar tracks run beneath elevated tracks and stations. At the corner of Causeway and Nashua Streets are spaces within the former Boston & Lowell depot (left). The cab stand (center) measured one hundred feet square. Between the cab stand and the waiting room lie a newsstand, lunch counter and ticket office.

Figure 4.34 Main Entrance of Union Station, Circa 1895
To the left of the grand arch, portals lead to the carriage stand. To the right, a portion of the facade conceals the main waiting room. Above the main entrance, words carved into the arch's frieze read "Boston & Maine," "Union Station," and "Fitchburg."

Figure 4.35 Eastern Tower of Union Station, Circa 1910
A covered pedestrian bridge over Causeway Street (left) links the Boston & Maine's Union Station (center) with the BERy's North Station (left and out of view) on the Main Line Elevated. Tracks of the el (bottom) curve over Causeway Street.

of steam railroad infrastructure along Causeway Street. As it continued to consume railroads far beyond Boston and expand its tracks throughout New England, the Boston & Maine's assemblage of Causeway Street depots, each of a different vintage and size, became inadequate. As early as 1892, when the idea of a North Union Station was first formalized by the Rapid Transit Commission, the Boston & Maine began planning a new Boston passenger terminal, one large enough to accommodate its growing quantity of trains. The result was Union Station, a terminal erected not by a consortium of railroads, but by a single company, the Boston & Maine.

Throughout 1893 and 1894, the Boston & Maine constructed and opened Union Station in phases. To make room for the largest and only entirely new portion of the project, the Boston & Maine demolished its own freight houses and the former Eastern passenger depot on Causeway Street. During demolition, the railroad deployed its own steam locomotives to pull down taller portions of the shuttered Eastern depot. In place of the structures it leveled along Causeway Street, the Boston & Maine erected a new head house and train shed. The new

structure was essentially a large addition to the Boston & Lowell's 1873 passenger terminal. The completed Union Station stretched along Causeway Street, from Nashua Street to the Fitchburg's castle (Figure 4.32 and Figure 4.33).

Union Station was fronted by an impressive multi-story arch that dwarfed pedestrians on Causeway Street (Figure 4.34). The neoclassical facade of Union Station echoed that rendered in the 1892 drawings of the Rapid Transit Commission. The eastern corner of Union Station was capped by a four story tower. In 1901 the Boston Elevated Railway Company (BERy) erected a covered pedestrian bridge to connect the tower with North Station, the rapid transit station on the BERy's Main Line Elevated (Figure 4.35). The elevated railway, pedestrian, and elevated station were the actualization of the "elevated circuit train" proposed for North Union Station by the 1891–92 Rapid Transit Commission.

When completed in 1894, Union Station featured twenty-three numbered platforms with tracks capable of holding nearly 190 passenger coaches. The tracks and platforms occupied a train hall measuring 500 feet wide and 550 feet long, all sheltered by a soaring structure supported by over 120 slender columns (Figure 4.36). The main concourse was lit by skylights from above (Figure 4.37 and Figure 4.38). Train departure boards capped the ends of platforms and faced the concourse (Figure 4.39). Terminal staff manually updated the boards to display the time of departure and station stops of the next train to depart from corresponding tracks.

In designing Union Station, the Boston & Maine anticipated accommodating over 560 trains and serving 80,000 passengers each day. The railroad hit those targets almost as soon as it completed the project. The February 15, 1894 edition of *Baby Path-finder Railway Guide* listed no fewer than 250 Boston & Maine trains departing each weekday from Union Station. The guide listed an additional sixty-five or so weekly trains departing from the Fitchburg's

Figure 4.36 Union Station Train Hall, November 23, 1902
Boston & Maine passenger coaches lie within a forest of steel. The view is taken from the eastern end of the concourse, looking out to the terminal's tracks and platforms.

Figure 4.37 Union Station Concourse, Circa 1910s
Light streams down into the concourse in this easterly view.

Figure 4.38 Union Station Concourse, February 1, 1927
A gentlemen pauses at a service window (left) on the main concourse of the Boston & Maine's Union Station. Iron fencing and gates (right) protect the tracks and platforms. Train departure boards (Figure 4.39) punctuate the fencing. In the distance, under the billboards, the concourse extends into the portion of the complex opened in 1873 by the Boston & Lowell.

Figure 4.39 Union Station Track 13 Departure Boards, 1914
A pair of information boards display the time of departure and station stops for upcoming trains departing from track 13.

castle, next door to Union Station and by then owned by the Boston & Maine. In time, the Boston & Maine repurposed the former Fitchburg castle into office space, until the structure was heavily damaged by a fire in 1925. In the following year, the Boston & Maine demolished the castle in preparation for yet another expansion of its passenger terminal operations at Causeway Street.

As the 1800s became the 1900s, Union Station's sprawling train shed regularly sheltered scores of wood passenger coaches with open vestibules (Figure 4.40). But the days of wood coaches were numbered. After scores of deadly accidents involving coaches with wood shells in the nineteenth century, by the turn of the century, many railroads had already outfitted themselves with fleets of heavy-weight steel coaches.

The first half of the twentieth century saw railroads again upgrade their fleets of coaches, replacing heavy-weight coaches with newer, lightweight steel and aluminum models. In 1935, the Boston & Maine received a series of new,

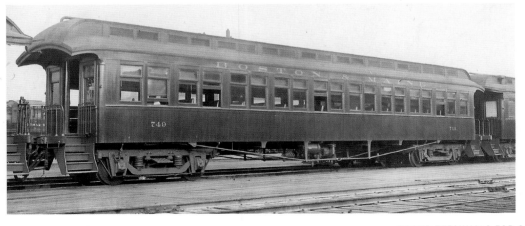

Figure 4.40 Boston & Maine Coach #749, 1912
A typical open-vestibule-type railroad passenger coach of the 1890s, Boston & Maine coach number 749 was constructed by the railroad. The coach was a "smoker," designated for those wishing to smoke en route. Operable window sashes and a roof monitor provided natural ventilation.

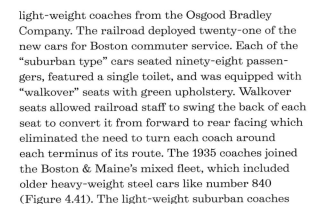

Figure 4.41 Boston & Maine Coach #840, Circa 1940
In 1940, the Boston & Maine purchased coaches, including number 840, second hand from the Pennsylvania Railroad. The car, constructed circa 1910–13 by the Pressed Steel Car Company, seated seventy-two riders. The Boston & Maine put 840 into use for commuter service from North Station.

light-weight coaches from the Osgood Bradley Company. The railroad deployed twenty-one of the new cars for Boston commuter service. Each of the "suburban type" cars seated ninety-eight passengers, featured a single toilet, and was equipped with "walkover" seats with green upholstery. Walkover seats allowed railroad staff to swing the back of each seat to convert it from forward to rear facing which eliminated the need to turn each coach around each terminus of its route. The 1935 coaches joined the Boston & Maine's mixed fleet, which included older heavy-weight steel cars like number 840 (Figure 4.41). The light-weight suburban coaches were numbered in the 2200-series. In the mid-1970s the cars were inherited by the MBTA, which scrapped the cars in 1980.

North Station
After completing Union Station and consolidating the Boston & Lowell, Eastern, and Fitchburg Railroads, the Boston & Maine entered the twentieth

century with a near monopoly on passenger and commuter rail service from Boston to points north. Boston & Maine lines sprawled throughout the northern half of New England, reaching into New York State as well as Canada (Figure 4.43). As the railroad reached its largest extent in the 1910s, the Boston & Maine outgrew Union Station. To improve its Boston passenger terminal facilities from 1926 to 1928, the railroad redeveloped just about all of the land along the north side of Causeway Street. Union Station and the Fitchburg's castle were demolished and replaced with a new multi-building complex, North Station.

The Boston & Maine formally opened North Station with a ceremony on November 14, 1928. Earlier that year, the railroad's "Timetable No. 1" listed scores of trains serving the new terminal, an interconnected assemblage of structures. It was composed of a twenty-three-track intercity and commuter rail terminal, a twenty-story hotel, a massive office building, and an enclosed arena (Figure 4.42). The Boston & Maine utilized

Figure 4.42 (Right) North Station, Circa 1930
A circa 1930 postcard view idealizes the architecture of North Station through the omission of surrounding buildings, pedestrian bridges, and elevated railways that cluttered Causeway Street.

Figure 4.43 (Opp.) The Boston & Maine Railroad, 1901
A portion of a map that folded out from Boston & Maine traveler's guide books, schedules, and other promotional publications shows, highlighted in red, the dense network of lines controlled by the Boston & Maine.

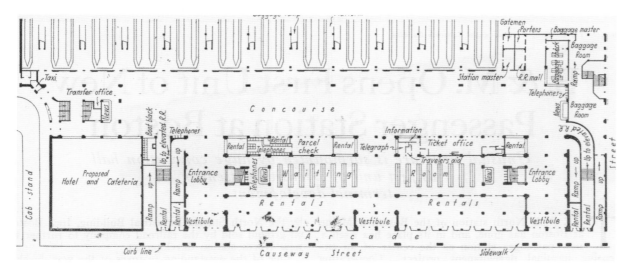

Figure 4.44 Plan of North Station Terminal, 1928

A street-level floor plan of North Station reveals the ends of the terminal's tracks and platforms (top), the broad concourse, the long waiting room (middle), and retail spaces and the arcade along Causeway Street (bottom). The yet to be completed hotel and the cab stand anchor the western end of the complex (far left). Ramps throughout the terminal communicate with the sports arena above.

the former Boston & Lowell depot as a temporary terminal during its construction of North Station's passenger terminal and office building. After opening the passenger terminal, the Boston & Maine demolished the 1873 Boston & Lowell depot, replacing it with additional tracks, platforms, and the hotel portion of North Station. As the last of the nineteenth century depots along Causeway Street disappeared, so did regular use of "North Union

Station" and "Union Station" to describe the grand terminal at Causeway Street.

A 1928 ground floor plan of North Station (Figure 4.44) reveals the wide concourse and ends of the terminal's twenty-three platforms. Across the concourse from the platforms were a ticket office, parcel check, retail kiosks, and information booth. The largest ground-level space, besides the concourse, was the main waiting room, measuring

Figure 4.45 Boston & Maine Timetable Cover, 1943

Published during World War II, a timetable presents a view of the North Station waiting room. The mezzanine, one level above, featured a barber shop, retail spaces, and railroad offices.

Figure 4.46 Boston & Maine Single-ride Ticket, 1945

The rear face (left) of a Boston-Cambridge ticket shows the date and location of its sale, July 29, 1945, at North Station.

Figure 4.47 North Station from Above, 1930
North Station stands like a small city, with its hotel (left), sports arena and passenger terminal (middle), and office building (right). Behind the hotel and terminal, platform shelters and tracks extend towards the Charles River (top). In front of North Station, elevated railways carry streetcars to North Station West and North Station on the el.

forty feet by 275 feet. Its sixteen massive wooden benches were capable of seating over 500 people (Figure 4.45). The waiting room was a sanctuary for many a traveller, as the September 1948 issue of *Trains* confirmed:

> During the war, weary servicemen who found it necessary to wait between trains in North Station blessed the terminal's designers for their thoughtfulness in providing waiting-room benches that guaranteed that travellers not miss their trains because they took a cat nap. Signs along the back of the benches designated waiting space for individual trains, and when departure time came for a particular train a station employee would wake all sleepers on the proper bench.

At the center of North Station was the arena for indoor sporting events and large-scale performances (Figure 4.47). Boston Madison Square Garden, as the arena was initially known, was the vision of the same developer of the third iteration of Madison Square Garden in Manhattan. Shortly after its opening, Boston's arena had its name shortened to Boston Garden. The Boston Garden became the home venue for Boston's professional basketball and ice hockey teams, the Celtics and Bruins, respectively. Behind North Station, circus trains unloaded and wild animals, clowns, and acrobats marched up North Station's ramps into Boston Garden to perform. Thousands of concerts were held in the arena while countless commuters caught trains in the terminal below.

A 1928 cadastral map (Figure 4.49) shows the configuration of North Station and the layering of public transit infrastructure fronting the complex. Published by Bromley, the 1928 map covers the same area as Hopkins' 1874 map (Figure 4.30).

Unlike Hopkins' map, Bromley's wears colors differentiating the material of buildings and structures; yellow signifies wood frame construction, pink represents brick masonry construction, and blue calls out iron construction. Before launching his own cadastral map publishing house in the 1880s, George Washington Bromley was on the team of surveyors who contributed to the set of Suffolk County atlases published by Hopkins in the 1870s.

World War II brought increased rail traffic across America. During the war, and for years afterwards, North Station remained a busy place. The Boston & Maine recorded in an 1955 educational brochure that "230 passenger trains arrive and depart each working day, with 9 million commuters passing through its gate every year." Referring to the completeness of North Station, the railroad observed: "Here... one could live comfortably from birth to death without having to leave [the station's] shelter and its services."

RDCs for Commuters
After World War II, the Boston & Maine joined railroads across the country replacing their steam locomotives with diesel-powered vehicles. A last hoorah for steam locomotives in regular service on the Boston & Maine was marked by a "Farewell to Steam" trip in 1956 (Figure 4.48). By the 1960s, steam disappeared from the head end of Boston & Maine commuter trains serving Boston; commuter rail service exclusively operated with Rail Diesel Cars (RDCs). Each RDC had its own diesel engine and did not require a separate locomotive to propel it. RDCs allowed the Boston & Maine to provide service on a shoe-string budget, meaningful to a company that went bankrupt multiple times in the twentieth century.

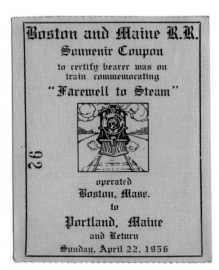

Figure 4.48 "Farewell to Steam" Ticket, 1956
Souvenir coupons were issued to riders of the Boston & Maine's "Farewell to Steam" train that ran on Sunday April 22, 1956 from Boston to Portland, Maine, and back.

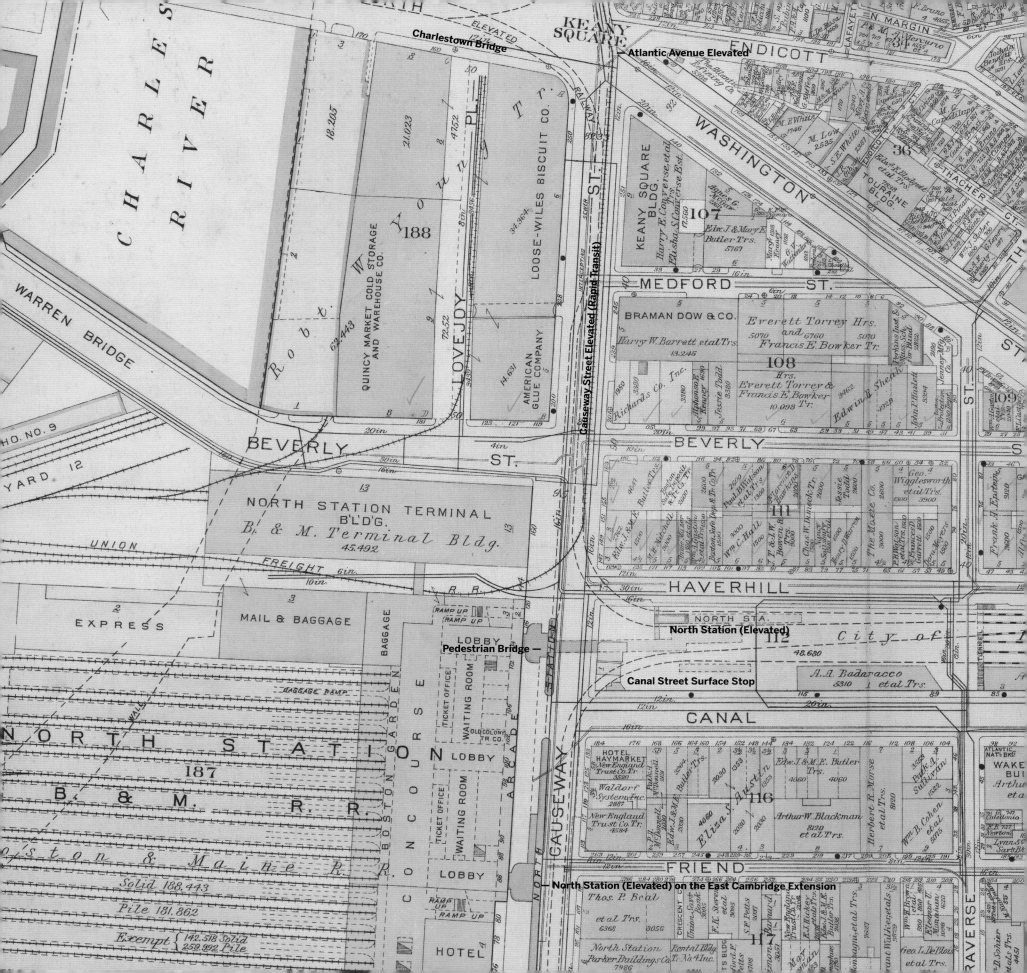

Charlestown Bridge

KEANY SQUARE

ELEVATED

Atlantic Avenue Elevated

N. MARGIN

ENDICOT

WASHINGTON

CHARLES RIVER

Roby W. PL

LOVEJOY

18.205

21.023

4752

50

188

QUINCY MARKET COLD STORAGE AND WAREHOUSE CO.

62.443

72.52

LOOSE-WILES BISCUIT CO.

34.364

14.631

AMERICAN GLUE COMPANY

KEANY SQUARE BLDG.

Harry E. Converse, etal

Elisha S. Converse Est.

107

Edw. J. & Mary E. Butler Trs.

5767

Causeway Street Elevated (Rapid Transit)

MEDFORD ST.

BRAMAN DOW & CO.

Harry W. Barrett etal Trs.

13.245

Richards Co. Inc.

Everett Torrey Hrs. and Francis E. Bowker Tr.

5070   6760   5070

108

Hrs. Everett Torrey & Francis E. Bowker 10.098 Tr.

WARREN BRIDGE

HO. NO. 9

YARD 12

BEVERLY   ST.

20in

4in

30in

16in

NORTH STATION TERMINAL BL'D'G.
B. & M. Terminal Bldg.
45.492

13

13

UNION

FREIGHT 6in

10in

16in

12in

BEVERLY

HAVERHILL

30in
6in
12in

The Mabie Co.

Geo. Wigglesworth etal Trs.

111

North Station (Elevated)

NORTH STA.

112

48.680

City of

EXPRESS

MAIL & BAGGAGE

BAGGAGE

RAMP UP
RAMP UP

Pedestrian Bridge —

Canal Street Surface Stop

A. A. Badaracco
5310 1 etal Trs.

115

CANAL

12in

20in

CONCOURSE

BOSTON GARDEN

WALL

TICKET OFFICE
WAITING ROOM

OLD COLONY TR. CO.

LOBBY

ARCADE

WAITING ROOM

LOBBY

NORTH STATION

CAUSEWAY

16in

HOTEL HAYMARKET
New England Trust Co. Tr. 3520

Waldorf System Inc. 2887

New England Trust Co. Tr. 4584

Edw. J. & M. E. Butler Trs.

2030

Eliza S. Austin

116

Arthur W. Blackman 8120 etal Trs.

Herbert R. Morse etal Trs. 8120

NORTH STATION

187

B. & M. R. R.

Boston & Maine R. R.

Solid 188.443

Pile 181.862

Exempt { 142.518 Solid
259.992 Pile

LOBBY

RAMP UP
RAMP UP

— North Station (Elevated) on the East Cambridge Extension

FRIEND

Thos. P. Beal et al Trs. 6368

North Station Parker Buildings Co.

117

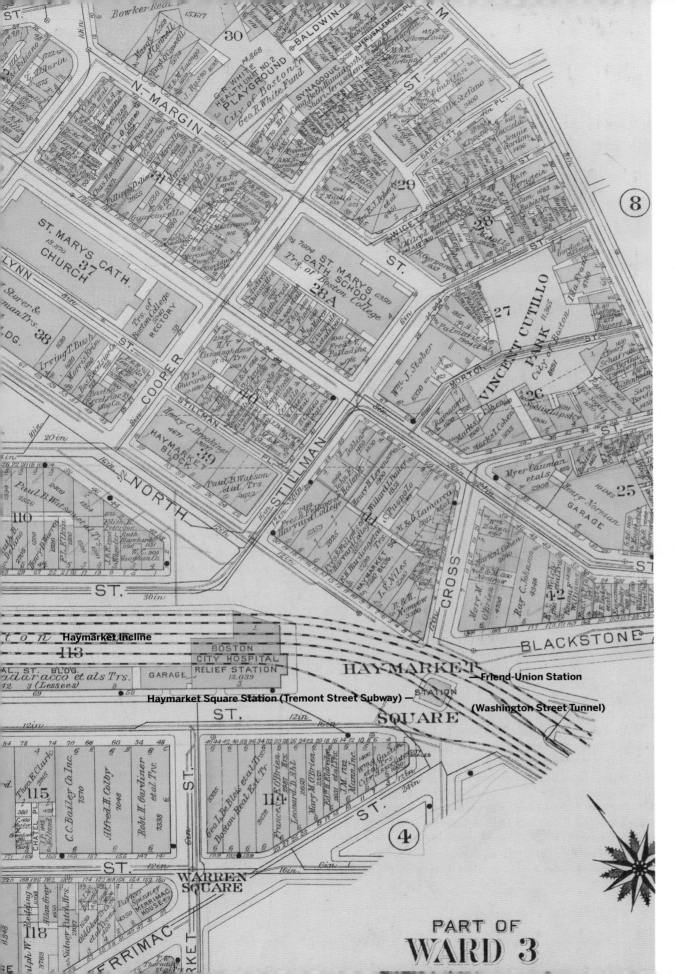

Figure 4.49 Mapping Transit at North Station, 1928

The Boston & Maine's North Station complex occupies the bottom left quadrant of a 1928 cadastral map. Extending like corn rows from behind the passenger terminal concourse are the station's tracks and platform coverings (colored in yellow). On the opposite side of the head house, elevated railways (shown dashed) trace Causeway Street. From the bottom of the map, the East Cambridge Extension for streetcars follows Causeway Street past North Station, before turning eastward and running between Canal and Haverhill Streets. There, the line follows the Haymarket Incline into Haymarket Square Station of the Tremont Street Subway. From the top left corner of the map, the Charlestown Elevated crosses the Charles River via the Charlestown Bridge. At "Keany Square," the rapid transit branches into the Atlantic Avenue Elevated (running off the top of the map) and the el for rapid transit trains over Causeway Street. The rapid transit el follows Causeway Street southward, before turning eastward, away from North Station at Haverhill Street. The rapid transit line runs through the North Station rapid transit elevated station, before descending into the Washington Street Tunnel via the Haymarket Incline.

Figure 4.50 Boston & Maine RDC-1 #6100, 1952
The first RDC built for the Boston & Maine poses for a glamour shot. The interior of car 6100 is shown in Figure 4.51.

Figure 4.51 Interior of Boston & Maine RDC-1 #6100, 1952
"Passengers" pose within the Boston & Maine's first RDC. The exterior of the car is shown in Figure 4.50.

The Boston & Maine's RDCs were constructed by the Edward G. Budd Manufacturing Company (Budd), the same company that constructed Amtrak's Amfleet I and Amfleet II coaches. Budd-built RDCs, or "Budd Cars," came in one of five types. An RDC-1 was fully dedicated to passenger travel and seated ninety passengers. Each RDC-2 featured a baggage compartment and a passenger compartment that seated seventy-one. An RDC-3 seated forty-nine passengers and had distinct compartments for both baggage and a Railway Post Office (RPO). RDC-4s were exclusively dedicated to baggage and RPO service. RDC-9s were non-controller-equipped versions of RDC-1s. They were essentially trailers that required an RDC-1 to act as its locomotive.

The first Budd Car built specifically for the Boston & Maine arrived in 1952 and received number 6100.

The unit, an RDC-1, was staged for official Boston & Maine promotional photographs (Figure 4.50 and Figure 4.51). At the end of 1959, the Boston & Maine recorded 108 Budd Cars in inventory. Boston & Maine RDCs wore the railroad's minuteman logo (Figure 4.52) and later, the modern interwoven blue and white "B" and "M" logo (Figure 4.54) of the railroad's later years..

During the 1960s, Boston & Maine RDCs carried rail fans on excursion trips and final run specials. Rail fan photos document Budd Cars making various last passenger service and fan trips around Massachusetts, including, Peabody to Boston on May 16, 1958, Marblehead to Boston on June 12, 1959, along the Amesbury Branch on May 27, 1967, and to Topsfield in April 1969. A special RDC run closed out Boston & Maine passenger service through the Hoosac Tunnel on November 30, 1959.

Figure 4.52 Boston & Maine RDC-2 #6201

A typical RDC-2 with a baggage compartment (left with the large door and lack of windows) and passenger compartment (right with row of windows). Boston & Maine minuteman logos brand the front of the car (far left).

Figure 4.53 Boston & Maine "Form A" Duplex Check, 1963

Sold on board a train, a duplex check is composed of two identical pieces of paper, each listing destination, date, and other fare information. Both pieces were punched simultaneously and separated by the conductor. The conductor retained one copy and provided the other as a "ticket" to its purchaser. The check shown is punched for an inbound trip from Newburyport to Lynn on January 26.

Figure 4.54 Boston & Maine RDCs at North Station, 1961

One Boston & Maine RDC, number 6211, lives on in static display. The RDC-2 resides at Bedford Depot Park, alongside the former Boston & Maine Lexington Branch (now the Minuteman Commuter Bikeway). Just after the turn of the twenty-first century, a group of volunteers extensively rehabilitated the car inside and out.

Replacing North Station

No buildings remain of the Boston & Maine's 1928 North Station complex. After the twentieth century financial demise of the Boston & Maine, portions of North Station were replaced incrementally. The hotel closed in 1976. Eight years later, the structure was brought down by a spectacular controlled demolition, televised live in May 1983. The hotel

was replaced by the Thomas P. "Tip" O'Neill, Jr. Federal Building, opened in 1986. The North Station office building was demolished in advance of the Central Artery / Third Harbor Tunnel Project (The Big Dig) and was replaced with another landmark named after "Tip." O'Neill was a congressman in Massachusetts' General Court during the 1940s–50s and represented the Commonwealth in Congress during the 1950s–80s. The northern portal of the Thomas P. O'Neill, Jr. Tunnel, where I-93 meets the Leonard P. Zakim Bunker Hill Memorial Bridge, occupy the former site of the North Station office building. The North Station passenger terminal and Boston Garden came down in 1998.

During 1993–95, a new arena rose over the tracks behind a soon-to-be-demolished Boston Garden. Sequenced work allowed for the demolition of the

Boston Garden after the new building, initially named the Shawmut Center, was complete. Under the Shawmut Center (now TD Garden) the MBTA opened its North Station commuter rail terminal, a replacement for the worn terminal lost with the demolition of the Boston Garden. An expansion of the MBTA commuter rail concourse at North Station opened in 2007, doubling the size of commuter rail public spaces. While the projects provided commuters with much needed additional waiting area, improved signage, and additional food options, the architectural experience for rail passengers in North Station remains a far cry from that of a century ago. Recently, an improvement harkening back to the grand arch of Union Station has been made. A grand entrance for North Station has returned somewhat to Causeway Street, with the completion of the "The Hub on Causeway Street" on the former site of the Boston Garden.

Boston's Four Southern Railroads

Of the eight steam railroads providing passenger service to Boston in 1855, four connected the city with points to the south and west. Boston's four southern railroads were the Boston & Worcester, Boston & Providence, Old Colony, and Boston & New York Central. Each of the four established a Boston passenger terminal at the southwestern edge of downtown (Figure 4.1).

Appleton's Railway and Steam Navigation Guide for June 1860 tallied daily numbers of trains departing from Boston on the southern railroads: twenty-seven on the Boston & Worcester; fourteen on the Boston & Providence; and fifteen on the Old Colony. A ride on the Boston & Worcester cost eight cents per mile. The one-way fare from Boston to Worcester was $1.16. The one-way fare to Providence on the Boston & Providence was $1.50. On the Old Colony, the fare was twenty-five cents to Mattapan, thirty cents to Quincy (now Quincy Center), and thirty-five cents to Braintree.

The Boston & Providence Railroad

The Boston & Providence's charter from the Commonwealth was issued on June 22, 1831. Immediately, the company proceeded to lay out a main line of admirable directness, with limited changes of grade and minimal twists of track. As *Steelways of New England* tells it:

> The final survey is almost an air line; in fact, there was one stretch of 16 miles absolutely straight, and no curve sharper than a 6000-foot radius. From Boston, for nearly 15 miles the track is almost continuously level, and no grade on the road exceeds 37 feet to the mile.

To maintain its straight-line route, the Boston & Providence relocated a portion of a church cemetery in Attleboro rather than adjust its "air line." The raceway established by the Boston & Providence lives on, providing one of the only places in America where high-speed train travel occurs, albeit briefly. Between Mansfield and northern Rhode Island, Amtrak's Acela Express, the fastest passenger train in regular service in America, regularly reaches speeds of up to 150 miles per hour.

Figure 4.55 Boston & Providence Depot, Circa 1860
The railroad's first Boston passenger terminal featured a clock tower on Pleasant Street.

Figure 4.56 Boston & Providence Ticket, Circa 1830s
An early ticket for travel between Boston and the city's Jamaica Plain neighborhood displays a primitive steam locomotive and stagecoach-type passenger cars.

Figure 4.57 Park Square Passenger Station, Circa 1880
A clock tower rises from the head house of the Boston & Providence Railroad's second Boston passenger terminal. Stretching from the back of the head house into the distance, the train shed covers the terminal's tracks and platforms. In front of the station, horsecars ply street railway tracks along Columbus Ave.

The Boston & Providence opened its first Boston passenger terminal on June 4, 1834. The modest two-story structure (Figure 4.55) was located on a portion of Pleasant Street, a road later renamed Broadway before being lost to urban redevelopment. The former site of the depot is currently marked by the Abraham Lincoln statue at Park Plaza. The exterior of the Boston & Providence terminal at Pleasant Street was rendered on the cover of the March 8, 1856 edition of *Ballou's Pictorial* (Figure 4.2).

On the same day it opened its Boston depot, the Boston & Providence ran its first train to carry passengers. A primitive steam locomotive departed from Pleasant Street pulling stagecoach-type passenger cars. The train achieved speeds of nearly thirty miles per hour and travelled approximately ten miles from downtown. An early Boston & Providence ticket (Figure 4.56) features the profile of a train similar to that which ran in June 1834. By the end of September, Boston & Providence trains were running between Boston and Canton, a town some fifteen miles south of downtown. The Boston & Providence opened as far as East Providence on June 11, 1835, and later, extended to downtown Providence in 1847.

Between its namesake cities, the Boston & Providence erected the Canton Viaduct, a stone masonry structure that provided a level crossing for Boston & Providence trains across a tributary of the Neponset River. During construction of the viaduct from September 1834 to July 1835, stagecoaches transferred Boston & Providence riders across the temporary gap in the railroad's main line. When opened on July 28, 1835, the 615-foot-long and seventy-foot-tall Canton Viaduct was the world's longest and tallest railroad viaduct. The Canton Viaduct remains a vital structure, carrying MBTA commuter rail trains and long distance trains serving Amtrak's Northeast Corridor. The structure, listed on the National Register of Historic Places, was designated a National Historic Civil Engineering Landmark in 1998.

In the middle of the 1870s, the Boston & Providence replaced its first Boston passenger terminal with a larger, more ornate facility. Located at Park Square and designed by prominent architects Peabody & Stearns, the Boston & Providence's second Boston passenger terminal opened on January 4, 1875. At the time, Grand Central Depot in New York City was America's only large railroad terminal. The Boston & Providence's Park Square terminal featured an elegant head house with an eighty-foot-tall tower crowned by a multi-face clock (Figure 4.57). The illuminated clock was visible from Boston Common, the Public Garden, and

many area streets (Figure 4.59). Within the head house, a two-and-a-half-story main hall with Gothic woodwork and rose windows was akin to a place of worship (Figure 4.58). The Boston & Providence's Park Square passenger terminal was described in the 1881 edition of *King's Handbook of Boston*:

The Boston station, situated on Columbus Avenue, is the most convenient and comfortable, as well as most beautiful, architecturally speaking, in the United States; and it is the longest in the world, being 850 feet from end to end. The portion assigned to the accommodation of passengers contains large and pleasant waiting-rooms,

Figure 4.58 Park Square Terminal Main Hall, Circa 1880
The ornate main hall was the centerpiece within the Boston & Providence's Park Square passenger terminal.

Figure 4.59 Park Square Terminal, Circa 1871
On a messy winter day, electric streetcars and horse-drawn conveyances traverse Eliot Street towards Park Square. The clock tower of the Boston & Providence's passenger terminal towers in the distance.

Figure 4.60 (Left) Park Square Train Shed, Circa 1880s
A train of passenger coaches (left) is parked alongside the train hall. In the distance, the clock tower marks the station's head house, facing Park Square.

Figure 4.61 (Right) Park Square Train Hall, Circa 1880s
Trains occupy two tracks in the Boston & Providence's Park Square passenger terminal.

Figure 4.62 (Left) Locomotive "Governor Bradford," 1845
The first steam locomotive employed by the Old Colony in passenger service was this 4-2-0 type.

Figure 4.63 (Right) Old Colony Locomotive #2
The former Governor Bradford (Figure 4.62) is posed after its conversion from a 4-2-0 to a 0-4-0 type.

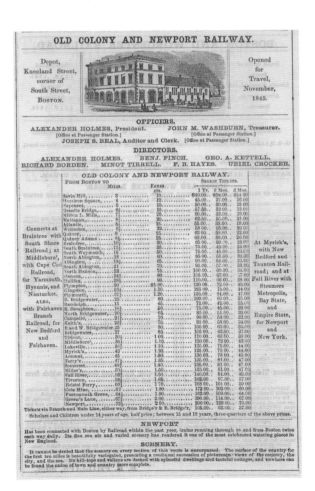

Figure 4.64 Old Colony List of Fares, Circa Late 1860s

dining, reading, billiard, and smoking rooms, a barber-shop, and wash-rooms, all finished and equipped in a style equalled only by our best hotels. Upon the walls of the passenger-rooms are painted an index of stations and distances, and maps of the country passed through by this road and its connections.

Behind the Park Square passenger terminal head house, trains arrived at and departed from a train shed that was 600 feet long and 130 feet wide (Figure 4.60). The shed was supported by massive iron trusses that spanned five tracks and three platforms (Figure 4.61). A freight depot sat alongside the passenger terminal.

The Boston & Providence was leased to the Old Colony in 1888. Five years later, in 1893, the Old Colony and Boston & Providence were both leased to the New York, New Haven & Hartford Railroad (New Haven). By the end of 1899, the New Haven vacated the Park Square passenger terminal for space within a recently completed South Station. After being ravaged by fire, the Park Square building was razed in 1909. The former sites of the Boston & Providence's passenger and freight depots at Park Square are currently occupied by the Statler Office Building and the Park Plaza Hotel, both opened in 1927.

The Old Colony Railroad

The Old Colony Railroad Corporation (Old Colony) came into being in March 1844. Three months later, the company began construction on its main line, from Boston to Plymouth. The Old Colony began operating trains between Boston and Plymouth on November 10, 1845. The Old Colony's first Boston passenger terminal was in South Boston, on what is now Dorchester Avenue. For its first decades of existence, as did Boston's other steam railroad

companies, the Old Colony named its locomotives. The Old Colony's first locomotive used to transport passengers was the "Governor Bradford" (Figure 4.62), a wood-burning locomotive sporting a flared stack to limit the release of flaming cinders. A massive, oil-fired head lamp was mounted at the front of the machine.

The Governor Bradford was a 4-2-0 type steam locomotive. The numeric designation explained that the locomotive had four leading wheels, two driving wheels, and zero trailing wheels. After the Old Colony converted the Governor Bradford to a more powerful 0-4-0 type, the railroad rechristened the locomotive number 2 (Figure 4.63). In time, Boston's steam locomotives grew in size and tractive power. Correspondingly, wheels grew in both quantity and diameter; 0-4-0s were replaced by 4-4-0s, 2-8-0s, 2-8-4s, 4-6-2s, etc., each type more powerful than previous configurations.

In 1846, the Old Colony relocated its Boston passenger terminal from South Boston to downtown, at the corner of Beach and Albany Streets. The site was owned by and contiguous with the passenger terminal of the Boston & Worcester. The Old Colony's second Boston passenger terminal opened on March 2, 1846. The front page of *Ballou's Pictorial* for March 6, 1856 (Figure 4.2) reveals the neighboring depots used by the Old Colony and Boston & Worcester terminals. By the time that the issue of *Ballou's* came out, the Old Colony had vacated Beach Street and the Boston & Worcester was utilizing both depots.

On May 19, 1847, the Old Colony opened its third Boston passenger terminal three blocks to the south and one block to the west of its former Beach Street depot. The Old Colony's Kneeland Street terminal, before it was renovated and augmented, is depicted on a list of fares published during the 1862–72 decade when the Old Colony did business as the Old Colony & Newport Railway (Figure 4.64). The third

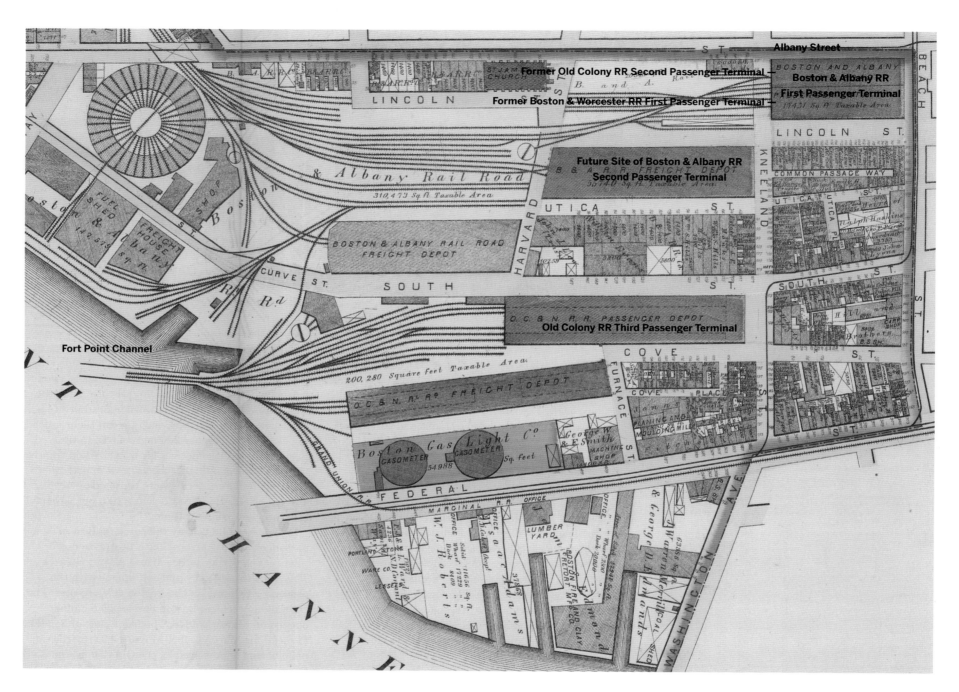

On the map:

Albany Street

Former Old Colony RR Second Passenger Terminal

BOSTON AND ALBANY
Boston & Albany RR
First Passenger Terminal

Former Boston & Worcester RR First Passenger Terminal

LINCOLN

LINCOLN ST.

COMMON PASSAGE WAY

Future Site of Boston & Albany RR
Second Passenger Terminal

B. & A. R. R. FREIGHT DEPOT
35,140 Sq. Ft. Taxable Area.

& Albany Rail Road
310,473 Sq Ft Taxable Area.

UTICA

UTICA ST.

BOSTON & ALBANY RAIL ROAD
FREIGHT DEPOT

CURVE ST.

SOUTH

SOUTH ST.

O. C. & N. R. R. PASSENGER DEPOT
Old Colony RR Third Passenger Terminal

COVE

Fort Point Channel

200,280 Square feet Taxable Area.

FURNACE ST.

COVE PLACE

O. C. & N. R. Rd. FREIGHT DEPOT

Boston Gas Light Co.
GASOMETER   GASOMETER
54,988   Sq. feet

George W. & E. Smith
PLANING AND
MOULDING MILL

FEDERAL

MARGINAL R.R. OFFICE

LUMBER YARD

Fort Point Channel

terminal faced Kneeland Street and was backed by South and Cove Streets (Figure 4.65). A view of the terminal's head house is shown in Figure 4.2. On the day of the station's opening, the *Boston Transcript* listed daily Old Colony trains departing from Kneeland Street to: Plymouth at 8:30 a.m., 2:30 p.m. and 5:30 p.m., except Sundays; South Braintree at 10:30 a.m. and 7:00 p.m.; and a connection with the Fall River Railroad at 7:00 a.m. and 4 p.m. As the nineteenth century progressed, the Old Colony

enlarged its Kneeland Street terminal (Figure 4.66). Behind the depot's head house, trains arrived at and departed from a long train hall (Figure 4.68). From Kneeland Street, Old Colony Trains served towns along the South Shore of Massachusetts Bay (Figure 4.70).

The Old Colony was more than a steam railroad. The company coordinated schedules with the Old Colony Steamship Company, a separate but closely related company that operated a fleet of steamships.

Figure 4.65 Passenger Terminals at Kneeland Street, 1874
A cadastral map shows the first passenger terminal of the Boston & Albany Railroad, at the corner of Beach and Albany Streets (top right), and the third Boston passenger terminal of the Old Colony Railroad, occupying the block bounded by South, Kneeland, and Cove Streets (middle). Behind the terminals (left) are the tracks, freight depots, and round houses of the two companies. Today, while some railroad infrastructure remains, much of the area has been consumed by the tunnels and ramps of Interstates 93 and 90.

Figure 4.66 Old Colony's Kneeland Street Terminal, 1890
The Old Colony's third Boston passenger terminal gained its external clock during an 1867 expansion and renovation. Behind the head house, the station's train hall extends into the distance (right). In front of the depot, a horsecar passes along Kneeland Street.

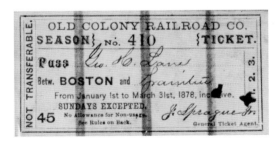

Figure 4.67 Old Colony Season Ticket, 1878
A commutation pass for the first quarter of 1878 was valid for travel between Boston and Braintree, except on Sundays.

Figure 4.68 Old Colony Terminal Train Hall, Circa 1889
Clocks set to the times of upcoming train departures top platform gates.

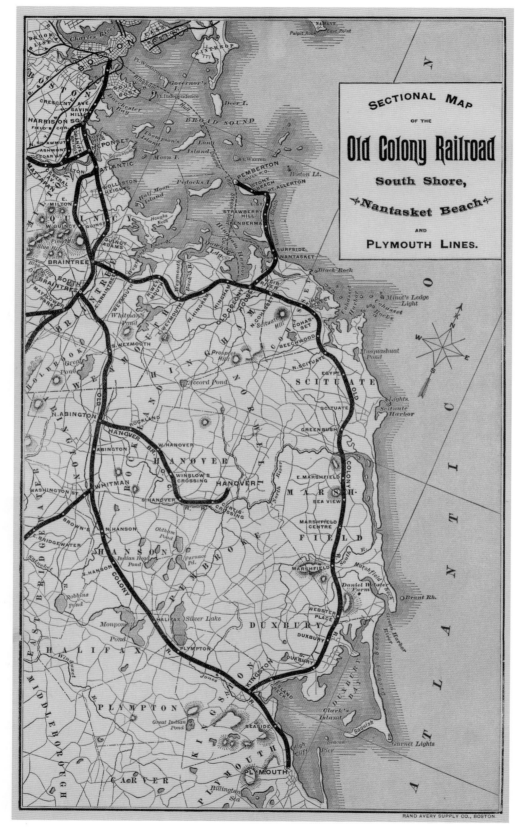

Figure 4.69 Old Colony Railroad Timetable Cover, 1881

Figure 4.70 Old Colony Railroad South Shore Map, 1888
The lines of the Old Colony stretch from Boston (top) and across Plymouth County.

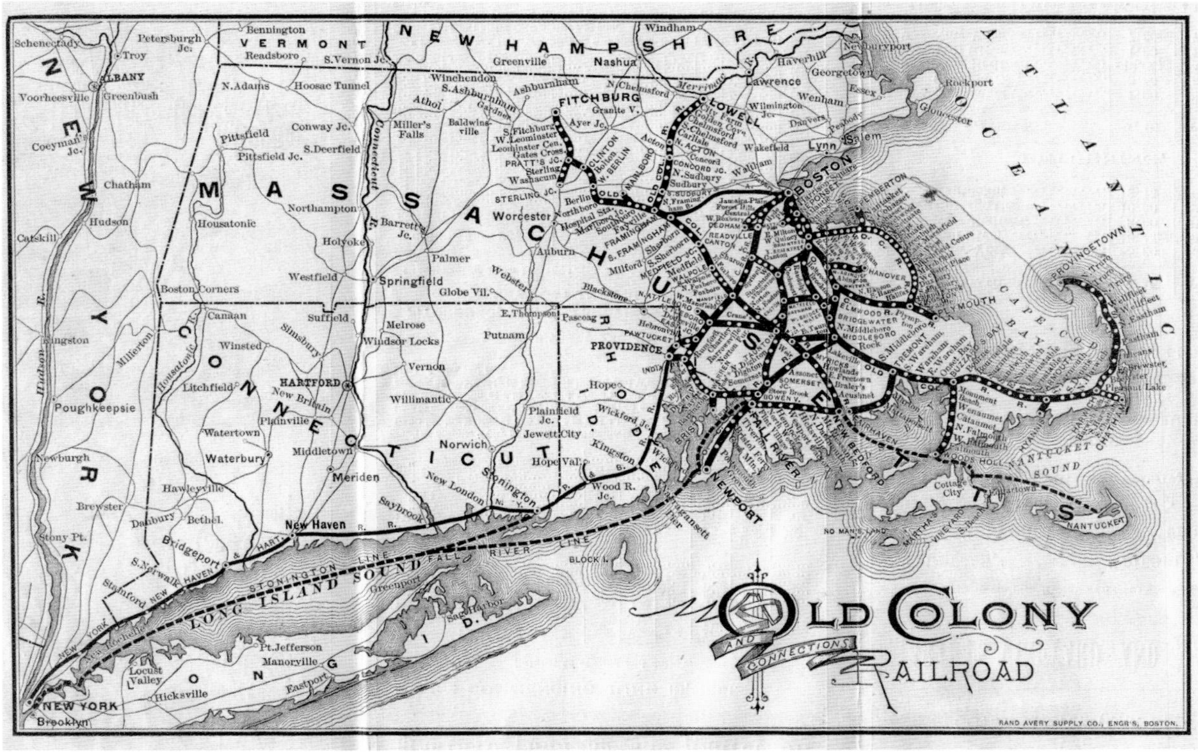

Figure 4.71 Old Colony Railroad Timetable Map, 1891

Thick black lines represent the railed network of the Old Colony Railroad. Represented by dashed lines, steamship routes traverse Long Island Sound, linking New York City with Old Colony rails in southeastern Massachusetts.

Figure 4.72 Boston & Albany Kneeland Street Depot, 1889

Old Colony timetables advertised the "Fall River Line" as the "Great Route Between Boston & New York" (Figure 4.69). The Great Route began in Boston, where passengers boarded Old Colony trains that ran to, and terminated at, a depot in the waterfront city of Fall River. There riders transferred to Old Colony Steamship Company boats for the balance of their journey to New York City. An 1881 timetable cover mentions "colossal steamships" named "Bristol" and "Providence." At its peak, the coordinated Old Colony system included over 600 miles of railroad lines and 400 miles of steamship routes (Figure 4.71). The Old Colony was leased to the New Haven in 1893. The MBTA refers to its commuter rail lines tracing routes first established by the Old Colony as its "Old Colony Lines."

The Boston & Albany Railroad

The Boston & Albany Railroad (Boston & Albany) grew out of the consolidation of Massachusetts' Western Railroad (Western) with the Boston & Worcester and various short lines in the Berkshires and Hudson River Valley. The combined main lines of the Western and the Boston & Worcester formed a continuous route across the Commonwealth, from Massachusetts Bay to New York state. After various mergers and lease arrangements, the Boston & Albany formally came into being in 1867. The Boston & Albany's first Boston passenger terminal was the pair of depots formerly inhabited by the Boston & Worcester and the Old Colony. The recycled depots occupied the block bounded by Beach, Kneeland, Albany, and Lincoln Streets.

In 1881, the Boston & Albany constructed its second Boston passenger terminal on the block bounded by Kneeland, Harvard, Lincoln, and Utica Streets. The site was previously occupied by a Boston & Albany freight depot. The Boston & Albany's second Boston passenger terminal was an elegant three story structure (Figure 4.72). The head house of the Boston & Albany's 1881 Kneeland Street terminal included the requisite ladies' and gentlemen's waiting rooms, a newsstand, and a restaurant. The ladies' waiting room was tailored for female travellers, as described in the 1883 *King's Dictionary of Boston*:

> …The ladies waiting room, 35 by 75 feet,…with three large fireplaces….The ticket office has a window opening into [the ladies' waiting room] with a counter at which ladies can buy tickets without inconvenience or suffering the jostling of the crowd always pressing at the main window.

Figure 4.73 Boston & Albany Terminal, June 9, 1898
A 4-4-0 type steam locomotive with tender (left) pauses, while, in the distance, a train (center) is partially sheltered by the shed of the Boston & Albany's second Boston passenger terminal. Tracks sprawl from the shed and around a Boston & Albany freight depot (far right).

Figure 4.74 Boston & Albany Terminal, June 9, 1898
Tracks and wood platforms extend from behind the Boston & Albany's depot (behind the photographer). Semaphore signals stand high on signal masters. In the distance is a 4-4-0 steam locomotive with tender (center).

Figure 4.75 Boston & Albany Timetable Cover, 1904

Behind the head house of the Kneeland Street depot, six tracks and platforms were flanked by inward and outward baggage rooms and covered by a barn-like train shed. Sheltering six numbered tracks, the shed measured nearly 450 feet long and approximately 120 feet wide. Each track was capable of holding four to seven passenger cars. Behind the train shed, a web of tracks served the Boston & Albany passenger station and freight houses (Figure 4.73 and Figure 4.74).

From Kneeland Street, the Boston & Albany's main line formed an iron spine across the length of Massachusetts. The line was a physical manifestation of the trans-state routes explored and proposed by the Commonwealth's canal and railroad commissions of the 1820s (see Chapter 1). The Boston & Albany celebrated its vital route westward on the cover of a 1904 schedule (Figure 4.75).

The New England Railroad
The Boston & New York Central Railroad (B&NYC) opened its first Boston passenger terminal on New Year's Day 1855. The station, located at the intersection of Summer Street and Atlantic Avenue, sat directly on the downtown waterfront. The terminal's opening followed years of the B&NYC and predecessor companies utilizing the Boston depots of other railroads. After various reorganizations, in 1863, the B&NYC became part of the Boston, Hartford & Erie Railroad (BH&E). Nearly a decade later, the BH&E's passenger and freight depots at Summer Street were destroyed in the Great Boston Fire of 1872.

A year after the fire, a new company, the New York & New England Railroad (New York & New England), formed and took control of the lines initiated by the Boston & New York Central Railroad. Replacing structures lost in the fire, the New York

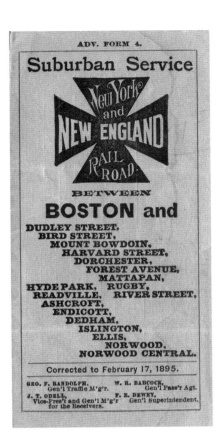

Suburban Service

New York and NEW ENGLAND RAIL ROAD.

BETWEEN

BOSTON and

DUDLEY STREET,
BIRD STREET,
MOUNT BOWDOIN,
HARVARD STREET,
DORCHESTER,
FOREST AVENUE,
MATTAPAN,
HYDE PARK, RUGBY,
READVILLE, RIVER STREET,
ASHCROFT,
ENDICOTT,
DEDHAM,
ISLINGTON,
ELLIS,
NORWOOD,
NORWOOD CENTRAL.

Corrected to February 17, 1895.

GEO. F. RANDOLPH, W. R. BABCOCK,
Gen'l Traffic M'g'r. Gen'l Pass'r Agt.
J. T. ODELL, F. E. DEWEY,
Vice-Pres't and Gen'l M'g'r Gen'l Superintendent.
for the Receivers.

Figure 4.76 New York & New England Timetable Cover, 1895

Figure 4.77 New York & New England Depot, Circa Late 1880s
A rare photograph shows the head house of the New York & New England's Boston passenger terminal facing the intersection of Summer Street and Atlantic Avenue. Trolley wires for electric streetcars are suspended over the intersection.

Figure 4.78 New York & New England Boston Depot, 1881
A plan of the New York & New England's Boston passenger terminal represents the configuration of the building before later renovations. The head house (left) encloses waiting rooms, a dining room, and ticket offices. The long train hall (right) encloses a pair of tracks, each with its own platform. A platform reserved for the movement of baggage runs between the tracks.

& New England established freight and passenger depots facing the intersection of Federal Street and Atlantic Avenue. The New York & New England's Boston passenger terminal was fronted by a single-story, wood-framed head house (Figure 4.77). Behind the head house was a narrow train shed enclosing two tracks and platforms (Figure 4.78). For approximately twenty years, trains of the New York & New England arrived and departed at the foot of Summer Street. In 1895, a bankrupt New York & New England became the New England Railroad.

On August 22, 1896 the New England Railroad vacated its waterfront depots, moving its passenger operations to the Old Colony's Kneeland Street depot. The change was made to allow for demolition of the New England Railroad's waterside depots in advance of the construction of South Station. The New England Railroad was leased to the New Haven on July 1, 1898. Ten years later, when it was merged into the New Haven on April 1, 1908, none of its depots remained.

Back Bay Station

In addition to erecting terminal stations serving downtown, Boston's southern railroads established depots in the city's other neighborhoods, including

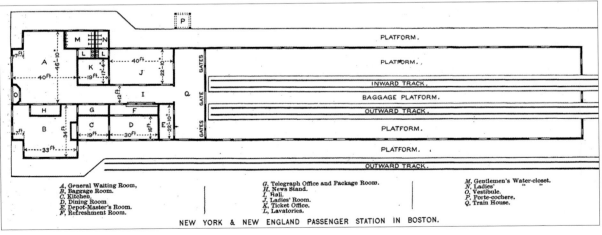

A, General Waiting Room.
B, Baggage Room.
C, Kitchen.
D, Dining Room.
E, Depot-Master's Room.
F, Refreshment Room.

G, Telegraph Office and Package Room.
H, News Stand.
I, Hall.
J, Ladies' Room.
K, Ticket Office.
L, Lavatories.

M, Gentlemen's Water-closet.
N, Ladies' " "
O, Vestibule.
P, Porte-cochere.
Q, Train House.

NEW YORK & NEW ENGLAND PASSENGER STATION IN BOSTON.

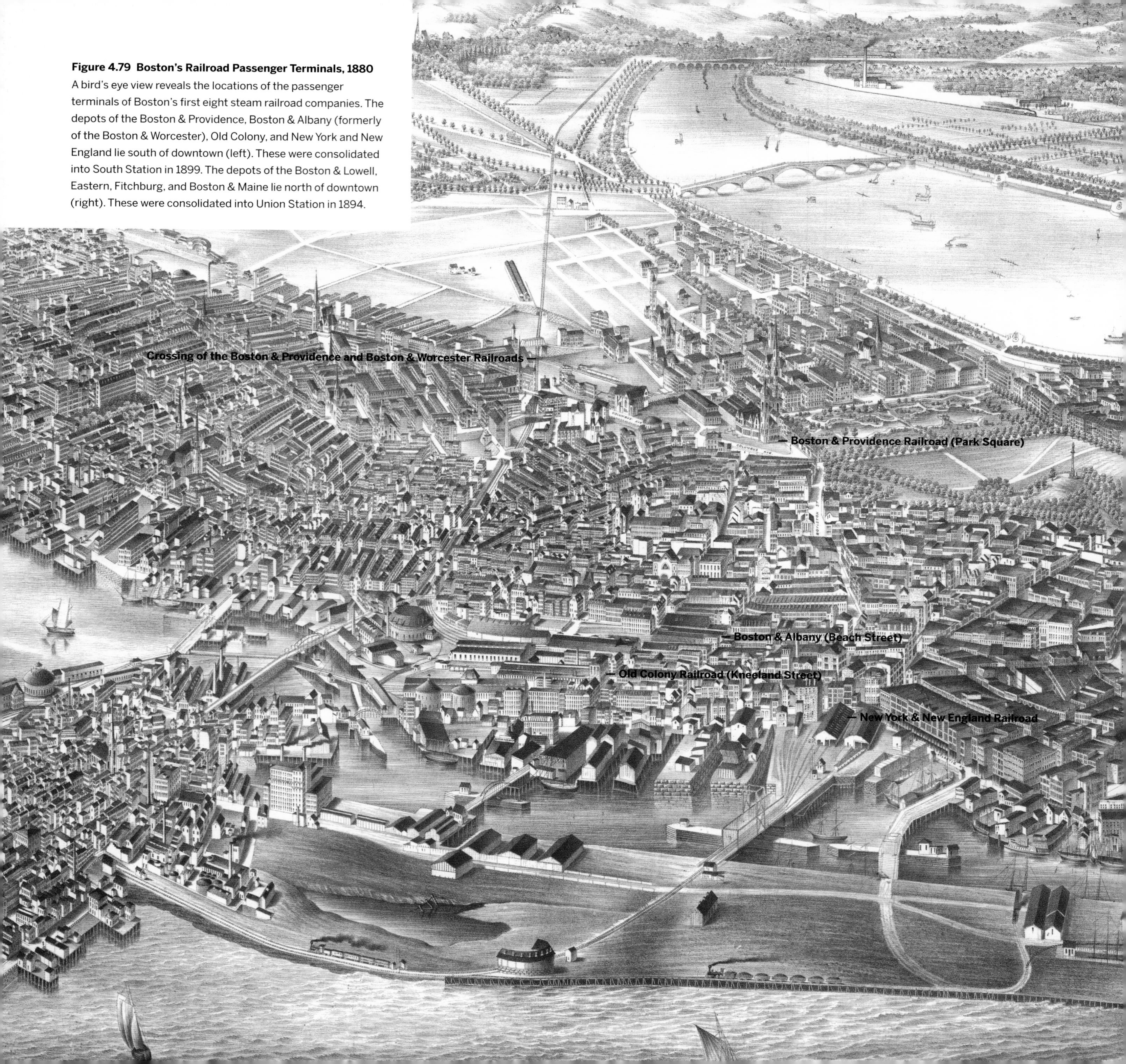

Figure 4.79 Boston's Railroad Passenger Terminals, 1880
A bird's eye view reveals the locations of the passenger terminals of Boston's first eight steam railroad companies. The depots of the Boston & Providence, Boston & Albany (formerly of the Boston & Worcester), Old Colony, and New York and New England lie south of downtown (left). These were consolidated into South Station in 1899. The depots of the Boston & Lowell, Eastern, Fitchburg, and Boston & Maine lie north of downtown (right). These were consolidated into Union Station in 1894.

Crossing of the Boston & Providence and Boston & Worcester Railroads —

— Boston & Providence Railroad (Park Square)

— Boston & Albany (Beach Street)

— Old Colony Railroad (Kneeland Street)

— New York & New England Railroad

Boston & Lowell Railroad —

Eastern Railroad —

— Fitchburg Railroad

Boston & Maine Railroad (Haymarket)—

Winnisimmet Ferry —

North Ferry —

— South Ferry

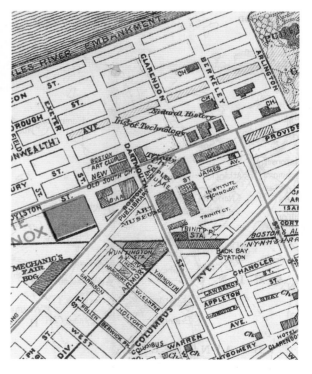

Figure 4.80 Huntington Avenue Station
An easterly view from the Huntington Avenue bridge over the tracks of the Boston & Albany reveals a train paused at the railroad's second depot to serve the location. The station was served by trains heading inbound to South Station.

Figure 4.81 Trinity Place Station, Circa 1950
Trinity Place Station was the Boston & Albany's second Back Bay depot for trains running outbound from South Station. The view is westerly from the Clarendon Street bridge.

Figure 4.82 Back Bay Railroad Stations, 1900
A pocket folding map by Walker highlights Huntington Avenue and Trinity Place Stations, both of the Boston & Albany, and Back Bay Station of the New Haven.

the Back Bay. The site of today's Back Bay Station has seen passenger train service since the mid-1830s. From 1834 until the late 1890s, the site was the crossing of the steam railroad lines of the Boston & Providence and Boston & Worcester. The crossing was captured in an 1835 view (Figure 1.41), long before the location was subsumed by urban development. The trackage extending from the crossing to Park Square was removed by the New Haven after its 1899 cessation of service to Park Square Terminal, a station erected by the Boston & Providence in 1875.

As early as the late 1880s, Boston & Albany passenger trains serviced two stations located in the Back Bay, one for inbound trains and the other for outbound trains. The first pair of stations were Columbus Avenue and Huntington Avenue Stations. Both were located near the avenues of

their respective names. Huntington Avenue was for inbound trains and Columbus Avenue Station was for outbound service. Coordinated with its involvement with the 1898 completion of South Station, the Boston & Albany replaced its two Back Bay stations with new depots, both designed by architect A. W. Longfellow. The second Huntington Avenue Station (Figure 4.80) and Trinity Place Station (Figure 4.81), a replacement for Columbus Avenue Station, opened in 1900. Both of the Boston & Albany's stations and the New Haven's first Back Bay Station were within walking distance of each other (Figure 4.82).

At the site of the former crossing of the Boston & Providence and Boston & Worcester, the New Haven constructed its first Back Bay Station during 1898–99. The depot provided replacement of service to the Back Bay lost when the railroad closed its

Figure 4.83 The New Haven's First Back Bay Station, 1898

A design drawing lays out the neoclassical facade of the New Haven's first Back Bay Station. Large arches on Dartmouth Street (left) allowed carriages and pedestrians into and out of the station. The long facade along Buckingham Street (center; right) is punctuated by large windows.

Park Square Terminal. Opened in 1899, the New Haven's first Back Bay station was a long, narrow structure, stretching from Dartmouth Street to Clarendon Street (Figure 4.83). The station was wrapped in limestone with large archways facing Dartmouth Street. Within the building, a central, covered carriageway was bracketed by waiting rooms, baggage rooms, a restaurant, a barber shop, and station offices (Figure 4.84). Large skylights brought natural light into the carriageway and waiting rooms (Figure 4.85).

The New Haven's first Back Bay station burned on April 15, 1928. Following demolition of the ruins, the railroad opened its second Back Bay station in

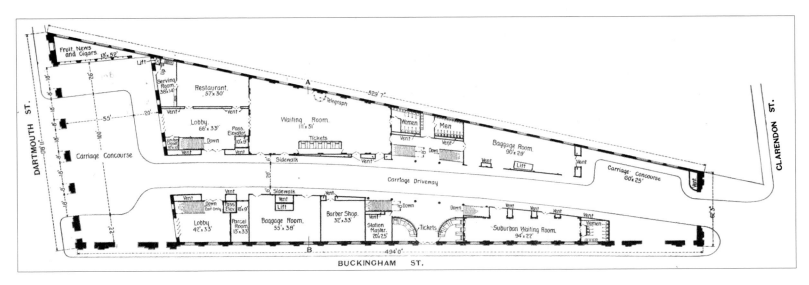

Figure 4.84 Plan of Back Bay Station, 1898

A central carriageway forms the spine of the New Haven's first Back Bay Station. Sprinkled throughout the station, stairways connect lobbies and waiting rooms to platforms, one story below street-level.

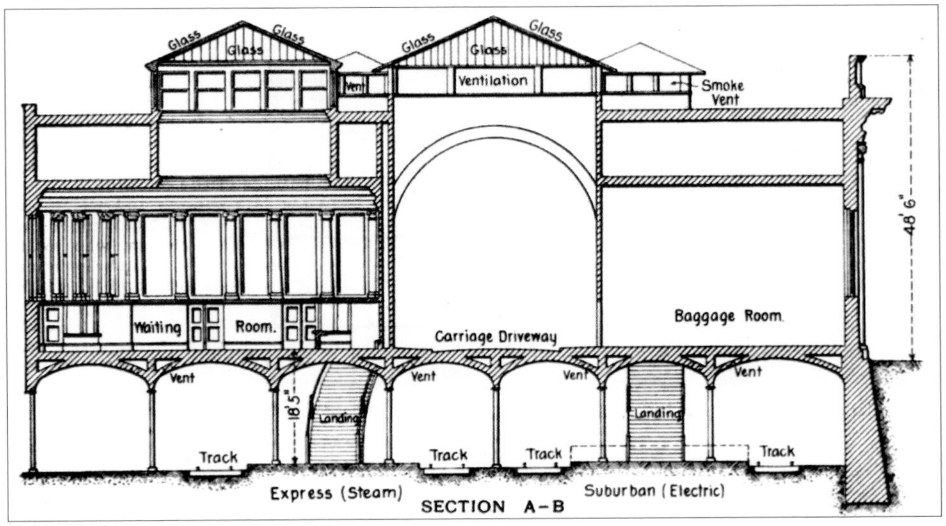

Figure 4.85 Cross-section of Back Bay Station, 1898

From left to right, a waiting room, carriageway, and baggage room are supported by an arched superstructure over four tracks and two platforms (bottom) of the New Haven's depot. Pyramidal skylights cap the waiting room and carriageway.

1929 (Figure 4.86). It was significantly smaller than the previous station, just a vessel for the requisite waiting and baggage rooms (Figure 4.87). Gone was the long, sky lit carriageway. Coordinated with the opening of the New Haven's station, the Boston & Albany renovated its stations in the Back Bay to connect them not only with each other via lengthened platforms and pedestrian passageways, but with Back Bay Station as well (Figure 4.88).

The MBTA inherited the New Haven's 1929 Back Bay Station in 1973. Prior to it being demolished for construction of the Southwest Corridor Project,

Figure 4.86 New Haven's Second Back Bay Station, 1929
Taxis line up along the Buckingham Street side of Back Bay Station. A large glass canopy protects the station's main entrance, facing Dartmouth Street.

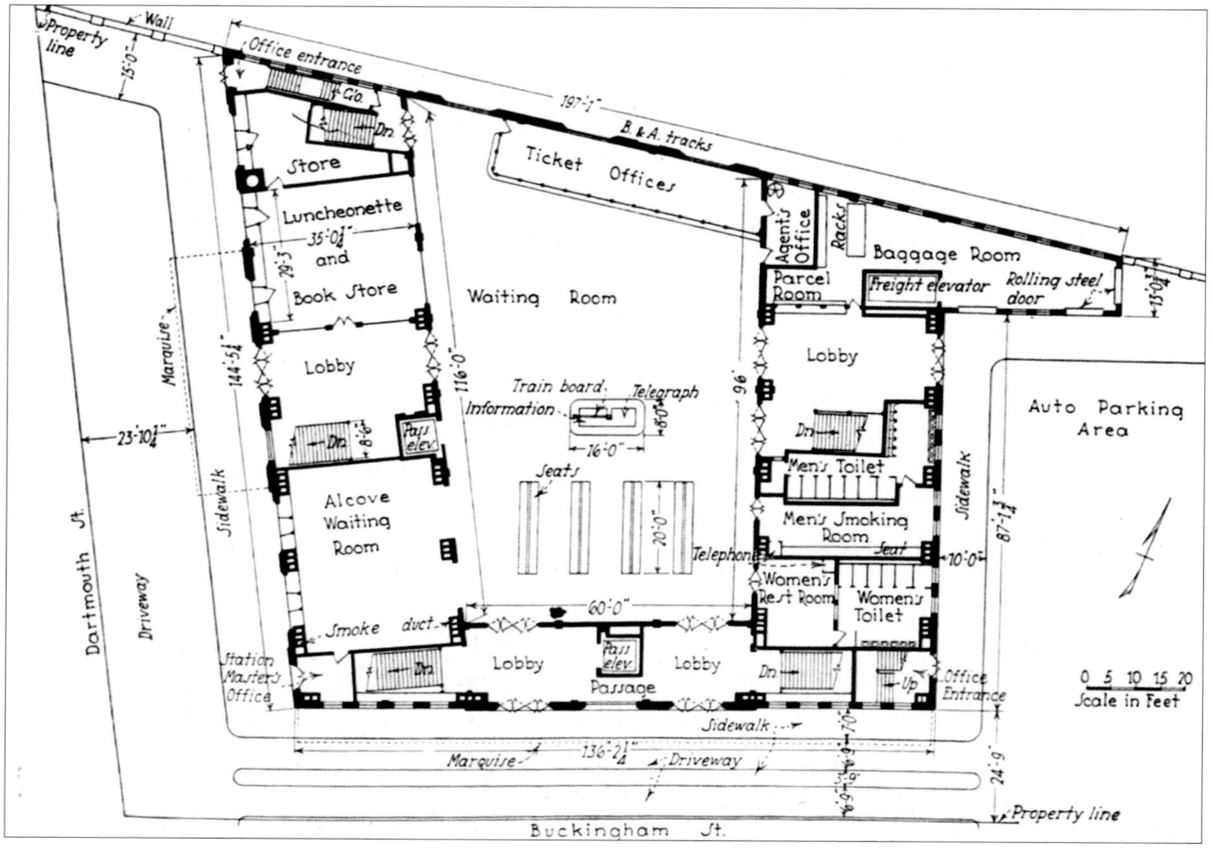

Figure 4.87 New Haven's Second Back Bay Station, 1929
A central waiting room is surrounded by a luncheonette, book store, lobbies, rest rooms, baggage room, and ticket offices. The station is approximately one half the length of the depot it replaced. The extra street-level space was designated for the parking of cars (right).

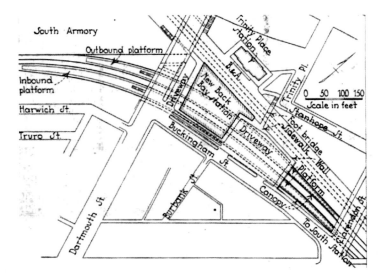

Figure 4.88 Back Bay Railroad Stations, 1929

which brought Orange Line rapid transit service to the station, the federal government funded a photographic survey of Back Bay Station at the end of the 1970s (Figure 4.89). The MBTA replaced the New Haven's depot with a new station, opened in 1987.

The Back Bay Station in place today is slated for renovation as part of a large public-private redevelopment of its site.

Figure 4.89 Back Bay Station, October 1979

In the late 1970s, behind the station's Dartmouth Street facade (top), departure boards (bottom) list some of the final trains to depart before the MBTA replaced the station in the mid-1980s. A notice in the Track 3 departure board case reads: "Station will close Nov. 3." The photographs were taken within months of the station's closure for demolition.

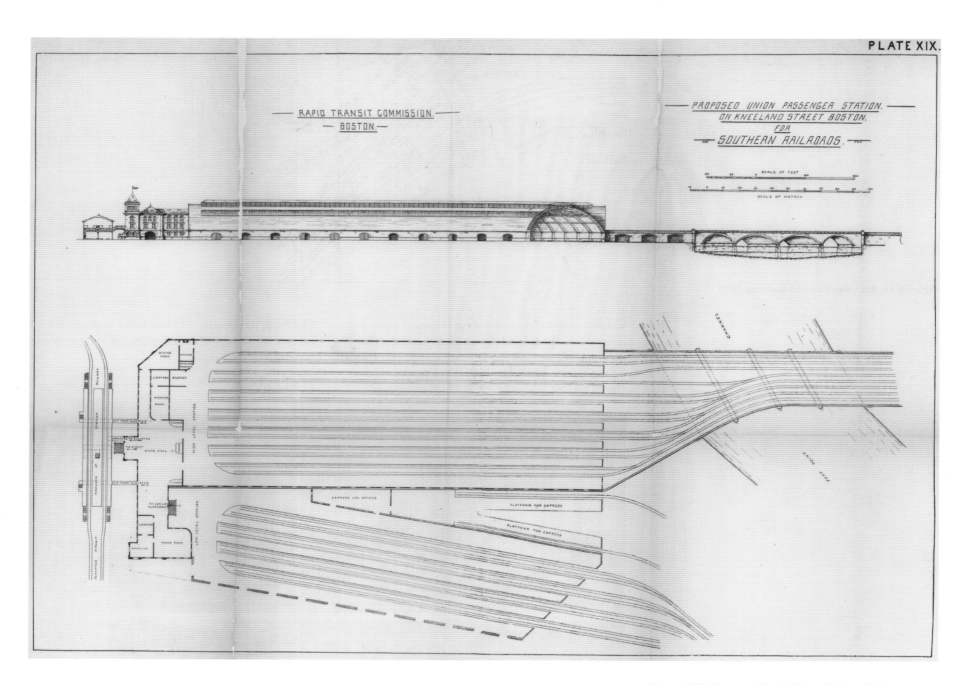

PLATE XIX.

Figure 4.90 Proposed South Union Station, 1892

South Station

South Station was the realization of the "South Union Station" (Figure 4.90) proposed by the Rapid Transit Commission of 1891–92. After encouragement from the Commonwealth, the Boston & Albany, New Haven, and New England Railroads collaborated to establish the Boston Terminal Company, charted in June 1896 to design, build, and operate South Station. Ownership of the company was divided amongst its founding railroad companies. The Boston Terminal Company sold bonds

(Figure 4.91) to fund construction of South Station, the largest railroad passenger terminal ever constructed in New England, and one of the largest in the world. Ground was broken for South Station in 1897. A vast site for the new terminal sprawled along the Fort Point Channel, from the intersection of Summer Street and Atlantic Avenue to the Broadway Bridge. The entirety of South Station rose where no dry land existed when Boston was established in 1630 (Figure 4.92). South Station replaced three centuries of wharves and maritime

Figure 4.91 (Right) Boston Terminal Co. Bond Certificate, 1897

Figure 4.92 (Below) Layers at South Station Site, Dec. 1899
On a composite drawing, layers of land development, each from a specific time, are overlaid, including: the original shoreline of the Shawmut Peninsula (hatched; top right); the lines of wharves in 1795, 1850, and 1896; various areas of solid and pile infilling of former tidal waters; and the building foundations and sewer lines of 1896. The foundation plan of South Station is rendered in a pale gray.

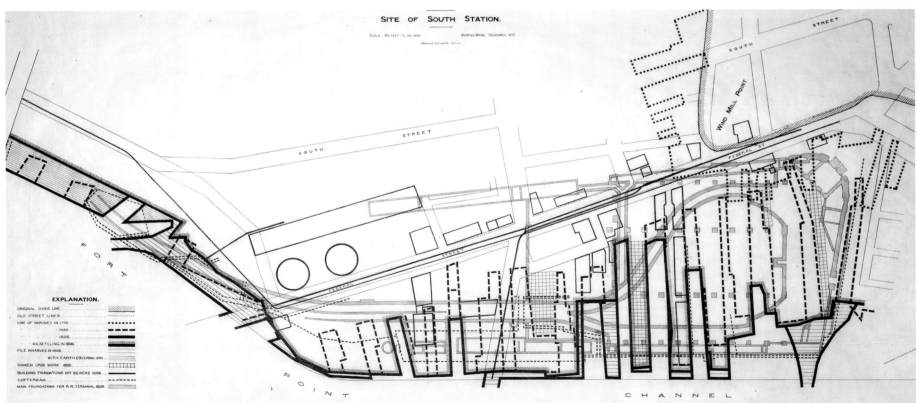

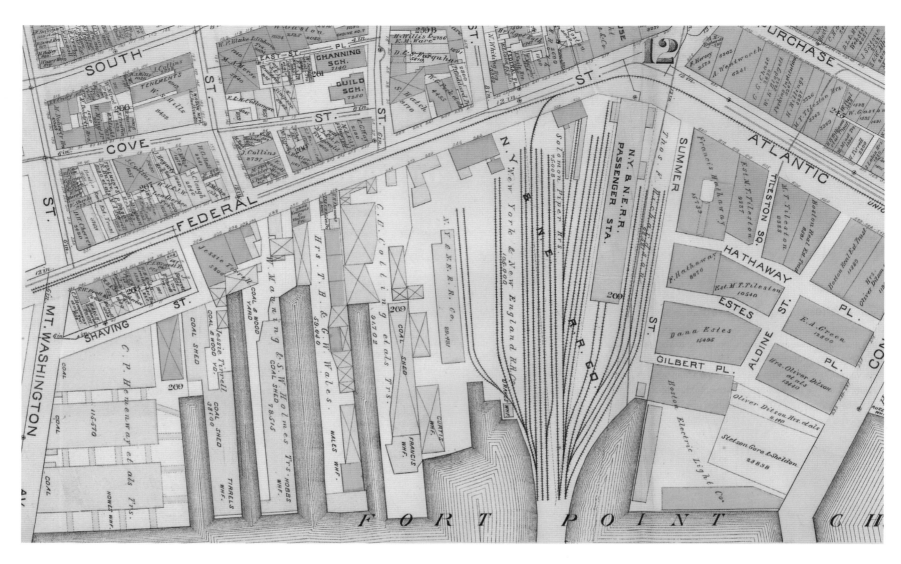

facilities along the Fort Point Channel with a grand terminal for passenger railroad service.

The Boston Terminal Company oversaw construction of South Station during 1897 and 1898. Simultaneously, Boston reconstructed the streets and a portion of the Fort Point Channel seawall around the railroad terminal. The city extended Atlantic Avenue south of Summer Street and widened and realigned the western end of Federal Street. Boston replaced the New England Railroad depots with an extension of Summer Street. The Summer Street extension ran from Atlantic Avenue, crossed in front of South Station, traversed a new bridge over the Fort Point Channel, and ran into South Boston. The Summer Street extension traced the former trajectory of the New England Railroad's tracks to the South Boston Flats, themselves rapidly being filled in for industrial and railroad uses. Along the

Southern periphery of the South Station site, the city oversaw the construction of a new seawall to serve as a new northern edge of the Fort Point Channel. The city extended Dorchester Avenue northward from South Boston, along the new seawall to a new intersection with Summer Street. The site of South Station is depicted on two cadastral maps, one from 1890 (Figure 4.93), prepared before construction began, and another from 1902 (Figure 4.94), published three years after completion of the terminal. As part of the development of South Station, the city established Dewey Square at the intersection of Federal Street and Atlantic Avenue. The square was named after Civil War and Spanish-American War hero George Dewey.

Boston Mayor Josiah P. Quincy and New Haven President Charles P. Clark dedicated South Station on December 30, 1898. In front of a crowd of 5,000

Figure 4.93 South Station Site Before, 1890
Tracks serve the freight and passenger depots of the New York & New England Railroad (right). All of the New York & New England's infrastructure, along with no fewer than five parallel wharves along Federal Street, were replaced by South Station (Figure 4.94).

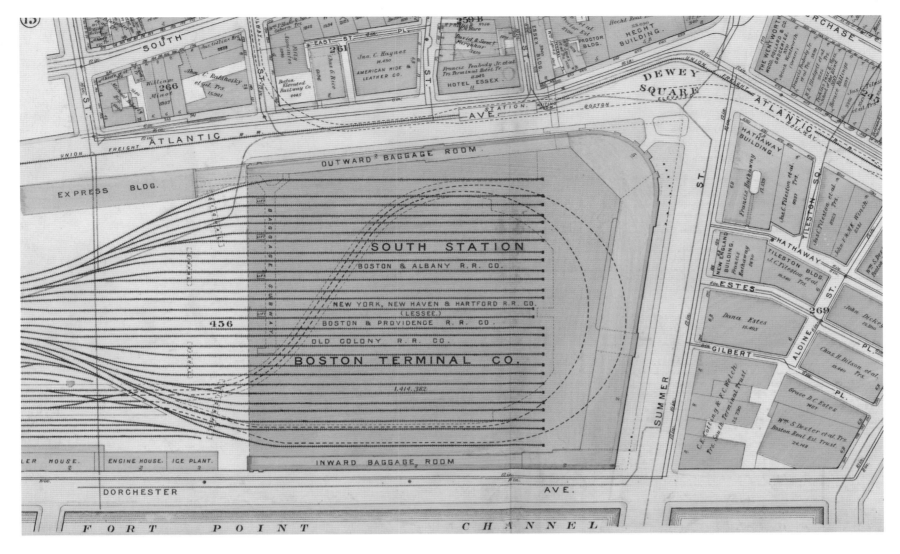

Figure 4.94 South Station Site After, 1902

Dominating the map highlighted in blue, the terminal's massive train hall covers platforms and stub-end tracks at street level. Dashed lines trace the tunnels, and run-through tracks of the station's lower level.

Figure 4.95 South Station and Dewey Square, Circa 1901

The steel trusses of the Atlantic Avenue Elevated rapid transit line cross Dewey Square in front of South Station.

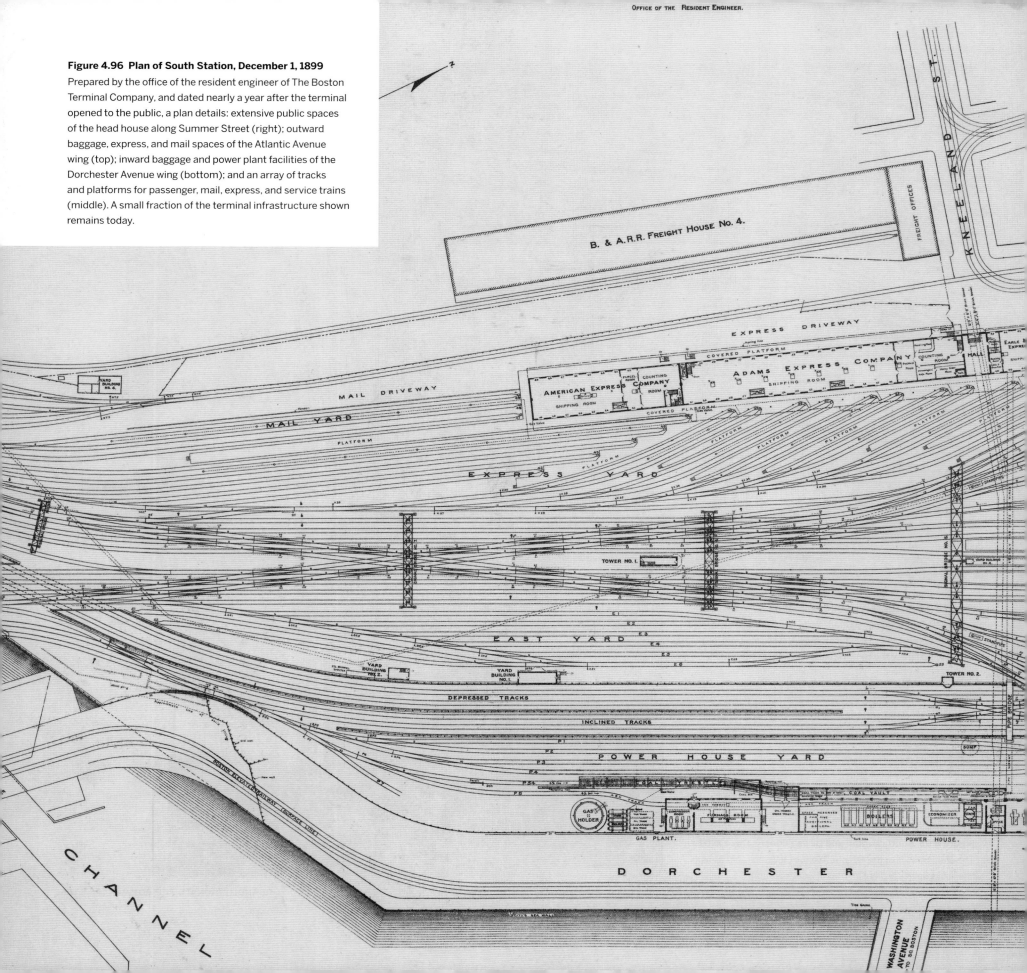

Figure 4.96 Plan of South Station, December 1, 1899
Prepared by the office of the resident engineer of The Boston Terminal Company, and dated nearly a year after the terminal opened to the public, a plan details: extensive public spaces of the head house along Summer Street (right); outward baggage, express, and mail spaces of the Atlantic Avenue wing (top); inward baggage and power plant facilities of the Dorchester Avenue wing (bottom); and an array of tracks and platforms for passenger, mail, express, and service trains (middle). A small fraction of the terminal infrastructure shown remains today.

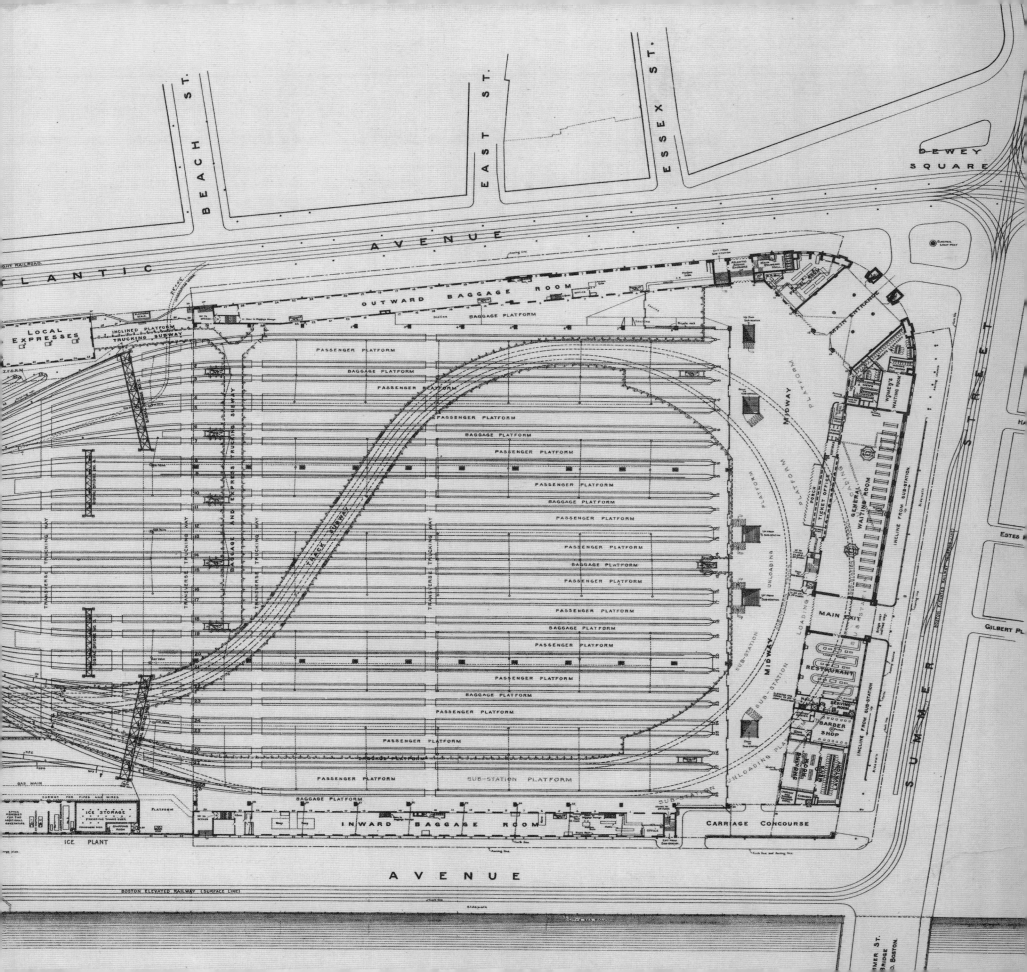

THE BOSTON
LONGITUDINAL SECTION
SCALE: 8 FEET TO AN INCH.

Figure 4.97 South Station Section, January 9, 1900

An architectural drawing cuts through the terminal along its longitudinal axis. From left to right are train shed, midway, waiting room, head house, and Summer Street. Beneath the train shed, a seven-car passenger train is fronted by a 4-4-0 type steam locomotive. Underneath the midway and head house are platforms and tracks intended for run-through, suburban commuter trains. Along the bottom of the drawing, hundreds of wooden piles extend like bundled tree roots to support the station's massive granite piers and foundations.

Figure 4.98 South Station Midway, August 27, 1899

Ticket windows and passages to waiting rooms (left) line the midway opposite platform gates and departure boards for the station's tracks (right). Above, a web of steel trusses support the midway's roof and skylights. The view is towards Fort Point Channel. A long exposure time caused people in motion to be captured as slight blurs, if at all.

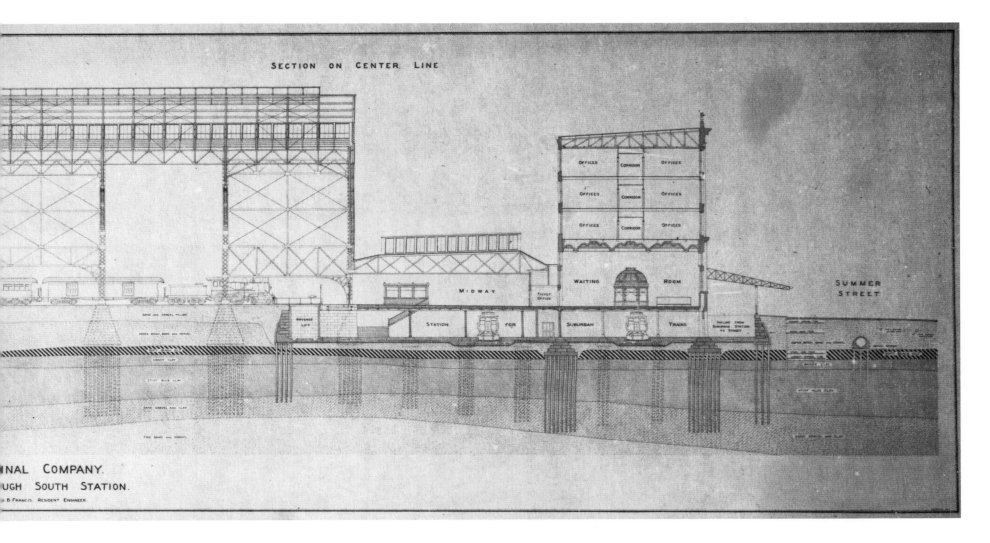

SECTION ON CENTER LINE

NAL COMPANY.
UGH SOUTH STATION.

invited VIPs, members of the press, and curious Bostonians, the dignitaries celebrated the completion of the public-private collaboration that established South Station. On New Year's Eve 1898, the public was welcomed into South Station, a finely engineered masterpiece on par with grand urban railroad stations of the world. Under the watchful eyes of a forty-ton granite eagle with an eight foot wingspan and poised upon a massive clock built by the Edward Howard Clock Company of Roxbury, the citizens entered Boston's largest passenger terminal. The station's front door faced Dewey Square and downtown Boston (Figure 4.95).

The architecture of South Station was magnificently designed to facilitate the efficient movement of massive crowds of people, hundreds of daily trains, and countless quantities of baggage and parcels (Figure 4.96 and Figure 4.97). From Dewey Square, the public passed below the eagle

and clock to enter South Station's main entrance hall. Correspondingly, a main exit hall communicated with Summer Street to facilitate people existing the station. All of the public street-level entrance and exit points were organized around and connected with a grand concourse, initially called the "midway" (Figure 4.98). Between the midway and Summer Street, was an expansive general waiting room outfitted with wood benches, concession stands, mosaic tile floors, and walls of polished stone and enameled bricks (Figure 4.99). In addition to massive windows along its Summer Street side, the waiting room was illuminated by over a thousand electric lights shining down from an ornate coffered ceiling. A small portion of the waiting room's coffered ceiling remains visible today in South Station's Amtrak Acela lounge.

Adjoining the terminal's general waiting room was a separate women's waiting room, outfitted

Figure 4.99 South Station General Waiting Room, 1899

Figure 4.100 Union News Shop at South Station, 1924
The Union News Company sold maps and guide books to visitors and Bostonians. Some maps featured in *Boston in Transit* were produced by the Union News Company and sold from their shop.

Figure 4.101 Track 20 Departure Board, January 3, 1900
South Station opened with manually operated departure boards at each track. The board in the photograph indicates that the next train to leave from Track 20 will be the 3:00 p.m. departure of a New Haven train bound for Fall River. Dozens of intermediate stops are listed.

with rocking chairs and baby cribs. The main ticket offices had windows facing both the general waiting room and the midway. Between the waiting rooms and Dorchester Avenue was a restaurant capable of seating 200 patrons at marble counters. The restaurant had private and rentable dining rooms on the second floor. Between the concourse and Summer Street was a smoking room, a barber shop, ample lavatories, and a covered carriage concourse. South Station also housed a variety of retail spaces, including one for the Union News Company (Figure 4.100).

Directly across the midway from the waiting rooms were tracks numbered one through twenty-eight. The stub-end tracks were separated by long platforms from which passengers boarded trains departing on both commuter and long distance runs. Train departure boards capped each platform and informed travellers of upcoming departures (Figure 4.101). South Station's tracks were arranged in pairs. Between each pair was a baggage platform dedicated for the movement of passenger luggage to and from trains. The arrangement kept the passenger platforms clear of baggage carts.

Figure 4.102 Under the Great Shed, November 28, 1898
A fresh layer of snow covers the platforms, tracks, and work cars underneath the soaring arches of the South Station train shed. The terminal opened just over a month after this photograph was taken.

South Station's platforms and tracks were flanked by extensive outward and inward baggage rooms extending along Atlantic Avenue and Dorchester Avenue, respectively. Beyond the baggage rooms were the terminal's power plant, spaces for the United States Postal Service, and rooms for express companies, the parcel shippers of the day. Tracks numbered twenty-nine through forty-two made up a yard for the express companies and featured platforms for use by the shippers. Next to the express yard, tracks numbered forty-seven through forty-nine were designated for United States mail service. Secure driveways connected the express and mail yards with the Atlantic Avenue extension.

The largest space at South Station was that covered by the great train shed. The steel and glass roof of the shed was supported by an intricate web of three-story tall steel trusses, themselves supported two stories over the street-level platforms by a forest of riveted columns (Figure 4.102 and Figure 4.103). Thousands of glass panes in both the roof and end walls of the shed allowed light to

Figure 4.103 Coaches Under the Great Shed, Circa 1930
Taken on a cold winter day, an atmospheric photograph documents New Haven passenger coaches in repose at South Station. An interior fog of steam mingles with the matrix of steel of one of the largest train sheds erected.

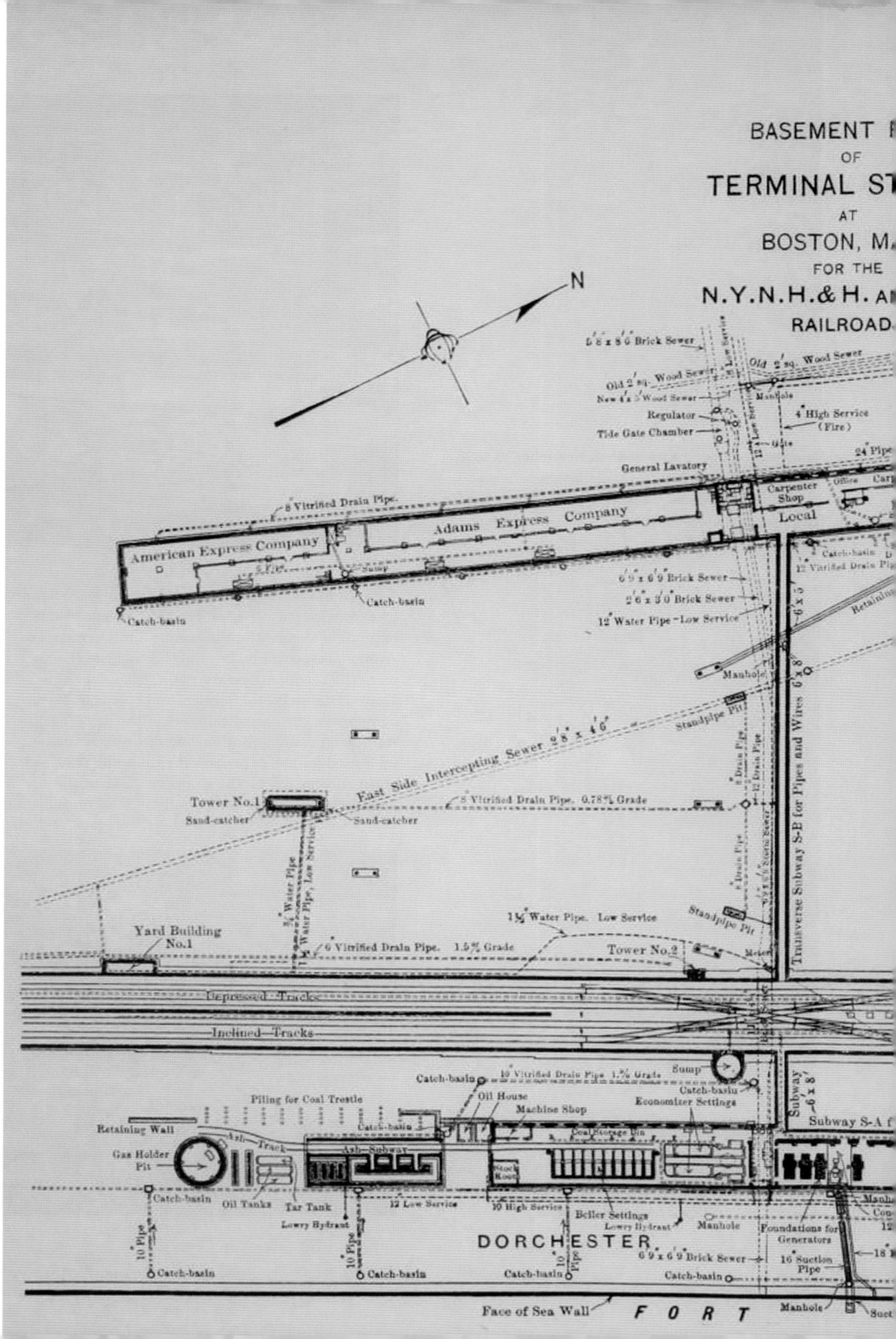

Figure 4.104 Basement Plan of South Station, Circa 1900
Basement spaces for the express companies and outward baggage areas line the Atlantic Avenue side of the terminal (top). Sub-grade spaces for the terminal's power plant and inward baggage department are arranged along Dorchester Avenue (bottom). The centerpiece of the lower level is a massive platform intended for run-through commuter trains (right). The subterranean platform is served by a pair of tracks that loop from and back to a four-track incline (left). The suburban platform is served by pedestrian ramps that ascend up to Summer Street (right). The suburban platform never saw regular service and has been lost to multiple renovations and demolitions on the site.

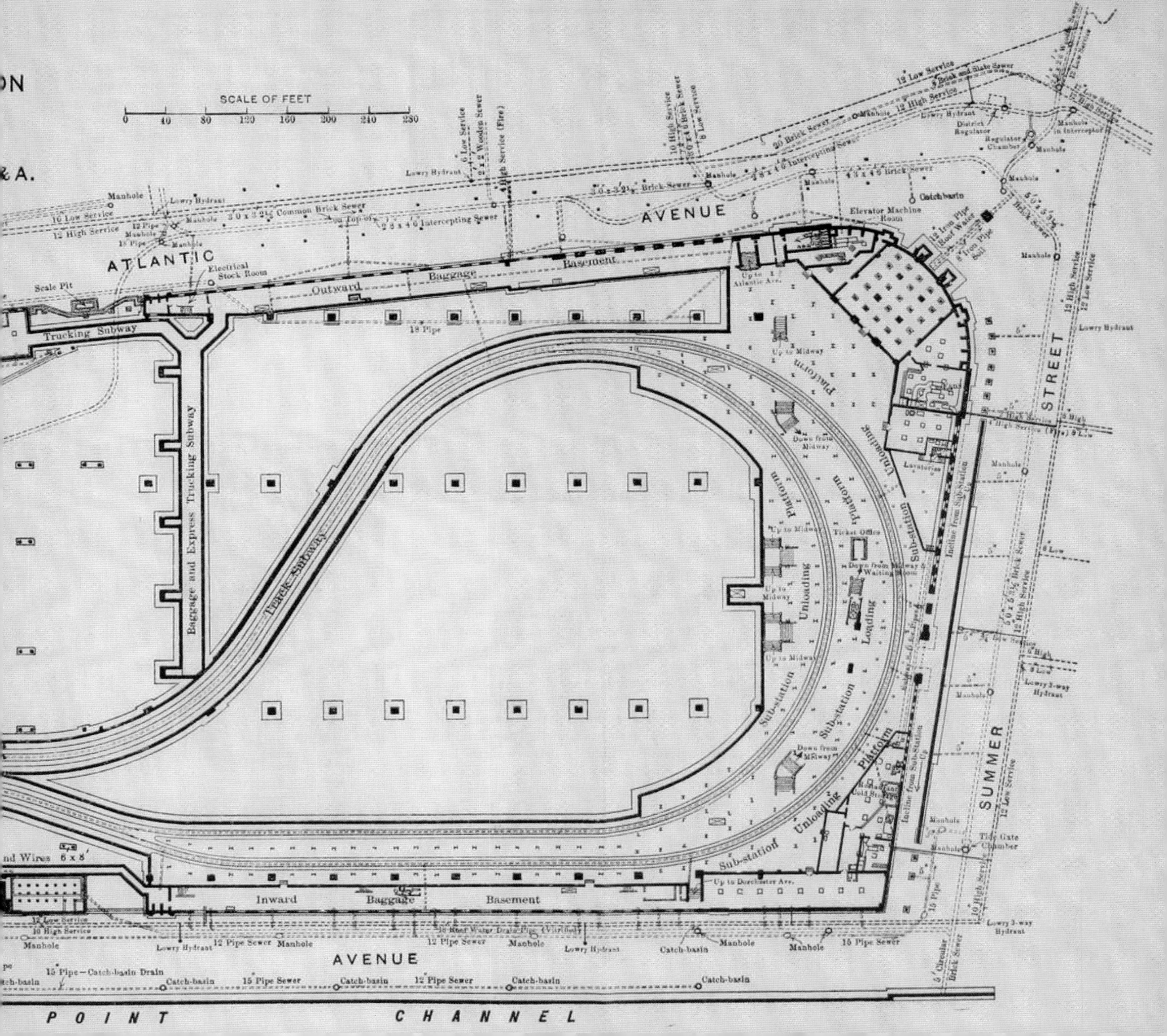

SCALE OF FEET

0   40   80   120   160   200   240   280

ON

& A.

ATLANTIC   AVENUE

Manhole
Lowry Hydrant
10 Low Service
12 High Service
12 Pipe
15 Pipe
Scale Pit
Electrical Stock Room
Trucking Subway

Outward   Baggage   Basement

Baggage and Express Trucking Subway

Trucking Subway

POINT   CHANNEL

AVENUE

Inward   Baggage   Basement

and Wires 6 x 8'

5' Low Service
10 High Service
Manhole
Lowry Hydrant
12 Pipe Sewer   Manhole
12 Pipe Sewer   Manhole
Lowry Hydrant
15 Pipe—Catch-basin Drain
Catch-basin   15 Pipe Sewer   Catch-basin   12 Pipe Sewer   Catch-basin   Catch-basin
18 Roof Water Drain Pipe (Vitrified)
Catch-basin   Manhole   15 Pipe Sewer
Lowry Hydrant

Platform   Unloading   Platform   Unloading   Substation   Substation   Substation
Up to Midway
Up to Midway
Down from Midway
Up to Midway
Ticket Office
Down from Midway & Waiting Room
Loading
Down from M'dway
Up
Cold Sto
Up to Dorchester Ave.
Sub-station
Incline from Sub-Station

SUMMER   STREET

Up to Atlantic Ave.
Elevator Machine Room
Lavatories
Manhole

12 Low Service
12 High Service
6 Low Service
5 Woodup Sewer
High Service (Fire)
10 High Service
8 Low Service
4' 6" Brick Sewer
8 Low Service
20 Brick Sewer
Brick and Slate Sewer
Lowry Hydrant
District Regulator
Regulator Chamber
Manhole
Manhole in Intercepter
4' 8" x 4' 6" Intercepting Sewer
4' 3" x 4' 6" Brick Sewer
3' 0" x 3' 2½" Brick Sewer
Manhole
Catch-basin
12 Iron Pipe Roof Water
6 Iron Pipe Boil
Manhole
5' 0" x 5' 0" Brick Sewer
12 High Service
12 Low Service
Lowry Hydrant
High Service (Fire)
Manhole
Lowry 3-way Hydrant
6 Low
4 High Service
5' 0" x 3' 8½" Brick Sewer
Manhole
15 Pipe
Tide Gate Chamber
Manhole
12 Low Service
12 High Service
Lowry 3-way Hydrant

30 x 3 2½ Common Brick Sewer
Top of
2' 8" x 4' 6" Intercepting Sewer

Figure 4.105 South Station from Above, 1929

South Station's masonry-clad head house is topped by an eagle and clock. Behind the head house is the great train shed, sheltering platforms and trains. Atop the shed, rows of clearstories provide natural light and ventilation for the train hall beneath. In front of the terminal, a northbound BERy rapid transit train rattles over Dewey Square, having just departed from South Station on the Atlantic Avenue Elevated (right).

reach the platforms far below (Figure 4.105). South Station's train shed endured until 1930, when it was removed due to degradation caused by salt air present at the terminal's harbor-side location. The rest of the terminal received renovations during 1929–31.

South Station was designed to handle passenger trains on two levels. Directly below the street-level platforms and midway was a double-track loop with broad platforms intended for pass-through commuter trains. The basement tracks were connected to the surface via a four-track incline, with two tracks intended for arriving and two for departing trains. The underground run-through configuration for commuter trains was unprecedented in Boston and remains to this day the only underground loop track for heavy railroad passenger trains ever installed in Boston. South Station's loop tracks were never fully utilized. The terminal opened with its basement level tracks and platforms incomplete, awaiting the Boston Terminal Company's final decision on what type of non-steam propulsion would be used for suburban trains. The

operation of steam trains, with their oil, smoke, and steam, was not a viable prospect along the underground tracks.

After the Boston Terminal Company confirmed that all train service at South Station would remain above ground, the lower level tracks and platforms were converted to other uses, including a fabled bowling alley for railroad employees. Lower level spaces at South Station that did see significant use as intended included tunnels for the movement of baggage and express shipments out of the way of public circulation paths above. A "Basement Plan of Terminal Station" (Figure 4.104) reveals the labyrinth of service spaces as well as the inclines, loop track tunnels, and platforms intended for suburban trains.

By the 1930s, a movie theater was operating inside South Station adjacent to track twenty-eight. The theater displayed neon signs reading "Theater: Continuous Latest News Reels—Featurettes." Admission to the 400-seat venue was twenty cents. At one point, a chapel at South Station offered "the fastest mass in Boston" for railroad commuters.

Figure 4.106 New Haven Eastern District Timetable, 1899
Effective January 1, 1899, and coordinating with opening day of South Station, a timetable lists New Haven passenger trains operating within the railroad's Eastern District.

South Station was designed by architects Shepley, Rutan and Coolidge. The architects wrapped the terminal in finely cut stone, a material of permanence and strength. Facing Dewey Square, a curved facade with three-story ionic columns supported a detailed frieze and parapet. The classical columns sat upon a two-story base, punctuated by doors leading to the main entrance hall. Engraved in the granite frieze, high above the main entrance and still legible today, is the phrase "ERECTED BOSTON TERMINAL COMPANY MDCCCXC-VIII." Behind the frieze, South Station's head house sheltered three floors of offices. The second floor was occupied by Boston Terminal Company offices and areas for trainmen and conductors. The third and fourth floors housed offices of the Boston & Albany and New Haven.

The New Haven commenced operation of the first scheduled trains to serve South Station on New Year's Day 1899. The first train, carrying Boston newspapers, departed at 4:38 a.m., bound for Newport, Rhode Island. Coordinating with the opening of South Station, the New Haven issued a new timetable (Figure 4.106). Over sixty trains departed from the terminal on the first day of regular service. Prior to the opening of South Station, and during the period of consolidation of the Old Colony, Boston & Providence, and New England Railroads under the New Haven umbrella, the New Haven continued to operate passenger trains to more than one Boston terminal. The railroad served two terminals from 1893–99 and three during 1898–99. The Boston & Albany commenced running trains to and from South Station in July 1899 (Figure 4.107). By fall of that year, over 700 trains operated daily at South Station daily.

In 1917, South Station handled over thirty-eight million passengers, twice the number as served by Grand Central Terminal in New York City during the same year. As the 1910s rolled into the 1920s, South Station saw even more patrons. The Boston Terminal Company reported serving over forty-five million passengers in 1920. The highest daily count of trains at South Station was on June 16, 1907, when there were 867 regular train movements and 1,711 individual train movements recorded.

Figure 4.107 Boston & Albany's First Train, July 19, 1899
A rare and ghostly cyanotype image captures the Boston & Albany's first scheduled passenger train to enter South Station. The train, led by a 4-4-0-type steam locomotive (left), sits on Track 14.

Figure 4.108 New Haven South Station Ticket
An undated ticket allowed travel between South Station (Terminal Station) and Back Bay Station.

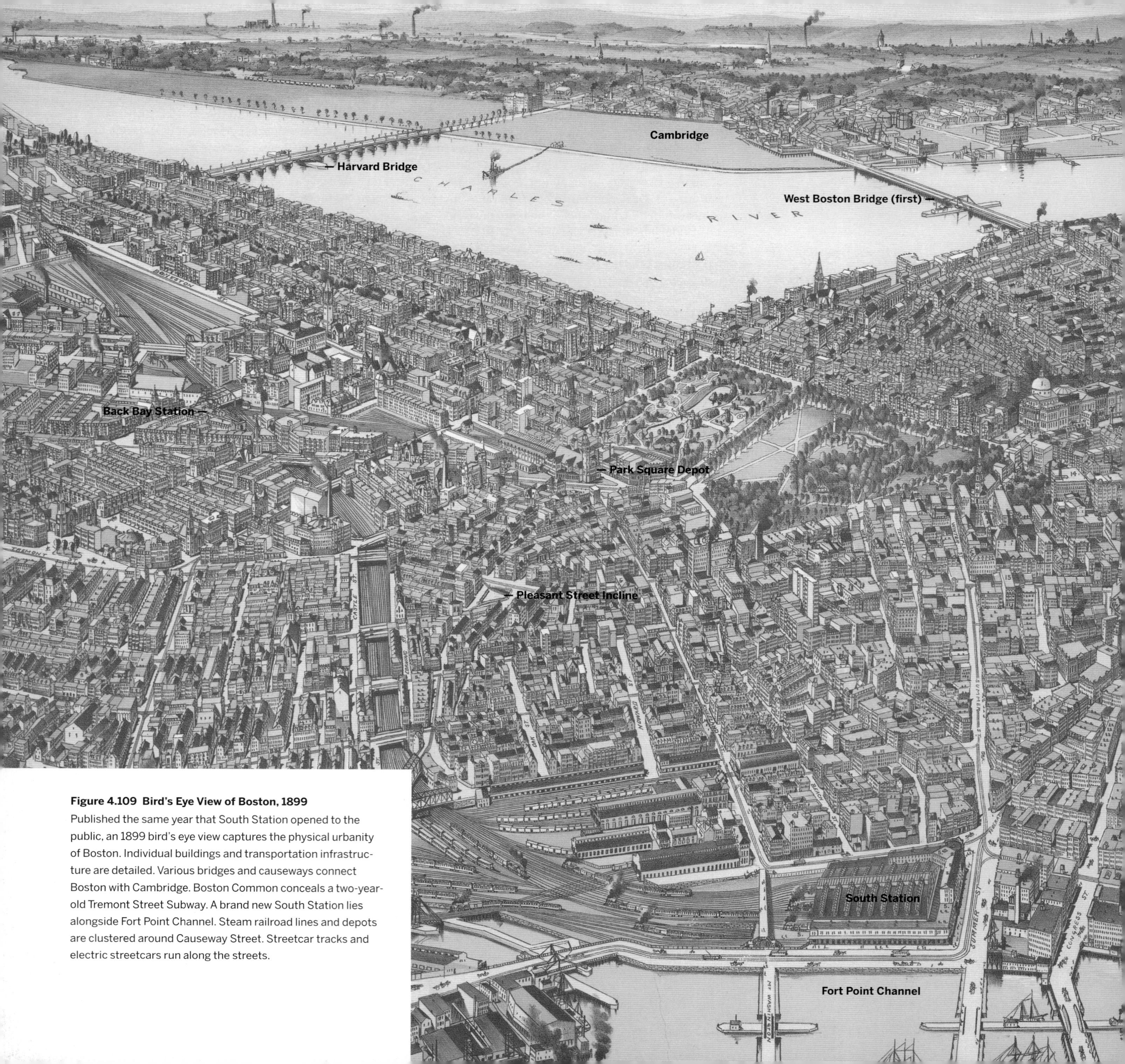

Labels on image:
Cambridge
← Harvard Bridge
West Boston Bridge (first) →
CHARLES RIVER
Back Bay Station —
— Park Square Depot
— Pleasant Street Incline
South Station
Fort Point Channel

Figure 4.109 Bird's Eye View of Boston, 1899

Published the same year that South Station opened to the public, an 1899 bird's eye view captures the physical urbanity of Boston. Individual buildings and transportation infrastructure are detailed. Various bridges and causeways connect Boston with Cambridge. Boston Common conceals a two-year-old Tremont Street Subway. A brand new South Station lies alongside Fort Point Channel. Steam railroad lines and depots are clustered around Causeway Street. Streetcar tracks and electric streetcars run along the streets.

Craigie's Bridge —

Union Station

Warren Bridge

Charles River Bridge

Charlestown

— Haymarket Incline

— Winnisimmet Ferry

— North Ferry

North Ferry —

— South Ferry

— Boston, Revere Beach & Lynn Railroad Ferry

South Ferry —

East Boston

A circa 1904 photograph (Figure 4.110) lays out the awesome infrastructure of South Station. Mail and express tracks are on the far left. The power plant, with coal cars on a raised track, is on the far right. A sprawling array of tracks are shown, including platform tracks emerging from under the great shed, incline tracks serving the lower level commuter platforms, and mail, express, and power plant tracks. Spanning the tracks are trussed signal bridges, upon which sit semaphore signals. The position and light color of a particular signal indicated how a train was permitted to proceed, or not, upon a track associated with that signal. Most of the infrastructure in the 1904 photograph no longer exists. Everything in the right half of the image is gone. The southern half of the terminal, including fifteen of the platforms and tracks, the wing along Dorchester Avenue, and the power plant, were replaced by a monolithic United States Postal Service facility and an office building for Stone & Webster at 245 Summer Street. The express and mail wing along Atlantic Avenue no longer stands. The street-level portion of the South Station Bus Terminal occupies some of the former site of the mail and express wing. While the granite eagle still watches over Dewey Square, South Station is a ghost of its former self.

The Boston & Albany was leased to the New York Central & Hudson River Railroad (New York Central) in 1900. The New York Central continued

Figure 4.110 South Station, Circa 1904

A photograph captures the sprawling grandeur of the tracks, switches, towers, and signal bridges that facilitated the movement of trains at South Station Terminal. Inclines (right) brought trains into and out of lower level commuter loops. The great train shed looms in the distance. The terminal's head house, with its midway and waiting rooms, lies beyond.

to operate the Boston & Albany under its distinct name. After 1900, and until the MBTA took the helm of Boston's commuter rail operations in the second half of the twentieth century, the New Haven, the New York Central (initially via its lease of the Boston & Albany, and later, as Penn Central Railroad), and their subsidiary companies dominated commuter rail service to and from South Station.

The construction of North Station and South Station as grand terminals for steam railroads established Boston's two-terminal configuration that remains in place today. Though now publicly owned and operated, Boston's commuter rail network remains bifurcated, with lines radiating from, but not linking, North Station and South Station. Boston continues to lack direct passenger train service between the northern and southern portions of its commuter rail network.

In 2017 the Massachusetts Department of Transportation (MassDOT) approved the study of the construction of a tunnel to link the northern and southern portions of Boston's commuter rail network. The idea for a tunnel to connect North Station and South Station, known as the North-South Rail Link, has been around longer than the terminals themselves. Meanwhile, the MBTA, the current owner of South Station, is exploring plans to restore additional tracks and platforms for the at-capacity terminal by reclaiming land occupied by the United States Postal Service facility.

Boston's Other Commuter Railroad

The Boston, Revere Beach & Lynn Railroad (BRB&L) was Boston's other commuter railroad, arriving decades after Boston's four northern and four southern steam railroads established themselves in the city. The BRB&L was charted on May 23, 1874 to build and operate a line connecting the city of Lynn with East Boston. The BRB&L commenced construction of its narrow gauge main line on May 22, 1875. With a track gauge measuring less than the standard gauge used by all of Boston's other steam railroads, the BRB&L was the only narrow gauge steam railroad to serve the city.

Figure 4.111 BRB&L Timetable Cover, Summer 1892
A summer timetable is covered with seaside scenes and places served by the Boston, Revere Beach & Lynn Railroad.

Figure 4.112 BRB&L Locomotive #2 with Coach, 1875
An engineer and fireman stand on their locomotive while a conductor holds onto the coach.

Figure 4.113 BRB&L Ferry "Dartmouth," Undated Image

Opening day on the BRB&L was July 22, 1875. On that day, no fare was charged. The first train left Lynn at 9:00 a.m. carrying a brass band. As it headed towards East Boston, the celebration train paused at seaside hotels along Revere Beach. At the East Boston waterfront, the train deposited its riders at the BRB&L's depot. There passengers transferred to the railroad's ferry "Union." The Union ferried passengers approximately three quarters of a mile across Boston Harbor. At 11:00 a.m., the inaugural train departed East Boston for a return trip to the BRB&L passenger terminal in Lynn.

The BRB&L commenced operations with three steam locomotives, seven first class coaches, two baggage cars, and two open cars. The railroad's open cars became popular with people who used the railroad not just for commuting, but to take in ocean air during a trip through the marshes of East Boston and along the dunes of Revere Beach. In time, closed coaches were also pulled by the railroad's steam locomotives (Figure 4.112).

Revenue service on the BRB&L was in full swing by the end of July 1875. Initially, the BRB&L charged twenty cents for travel from East Boston to Lynn, one dollar for seven tickets from East Boston to Lynn, thirty-five cents for a round trip ticket, and eighteen cents for travel from Lynn to East Boston. The latter was a special fare reserved for Lynn residents. After a year of service, the BRB&L expanded its inventory of vehicles. Documents from the October 19, 1876 annual meeting of the BRB&L Railroad Corporation record that the company expanded its fleet to include six steam locomotives, eleven passenger cars, two passenger cars for smokers, twenty-six freight cars, and two ferries.

During its sixty-five year existence the BRB&L owned and operated eight named ferries. Initially, the railroad provided service with the "City of Lynn," "Swampscott," "Oriole," and "Union." These four boats were eventually replaced by the "Ashburnham," "Brewster," "Dartmouth" (Figure 4.113), and "Newtown." All of the vessels were steam-powered. Typical operations saw two boats in active service, with one scheduled to pass the other as one moved west and the other moved east. The railroad added a third ferry as needed during rush hours and often kept a fourth in reserve.

As listed on a BRB&L timetable for spring 1892, the stations along the railroad's main line, from north to south, were Lynn, West Lynn, Ocean House, Revere Beach, Revere House, Atlantic, Revere, Orient, Winthrop, Wood Island, and Jeffries Point. The latter was the site of the BRB&L's East Boston depot. The timetable lists thirty-five weekday trains departing East Boston, with approximately two thirds of the trains terminating in Lynn and one third terminating at either Orient Heights or headed to Winthrop. Eight years after the 1892 timetable was published, a November 20, 1898 timetable listed thirty weekday trains running from East Boston to Lynn, thirty-one trains operating from Lynn to East Boston, twenty-six weekday trains running from East Boston and terminating at Orient Heights, and twenty-seven trains initiating at Orient Heights and terminating at East Boston. The number of trains on a Sunday was approximately half that of any given weekday. Trains operated from approximately 6 a.m. to 11 p.m. Over time, the locations and names of stations along the BRB&L's main line changed. The final

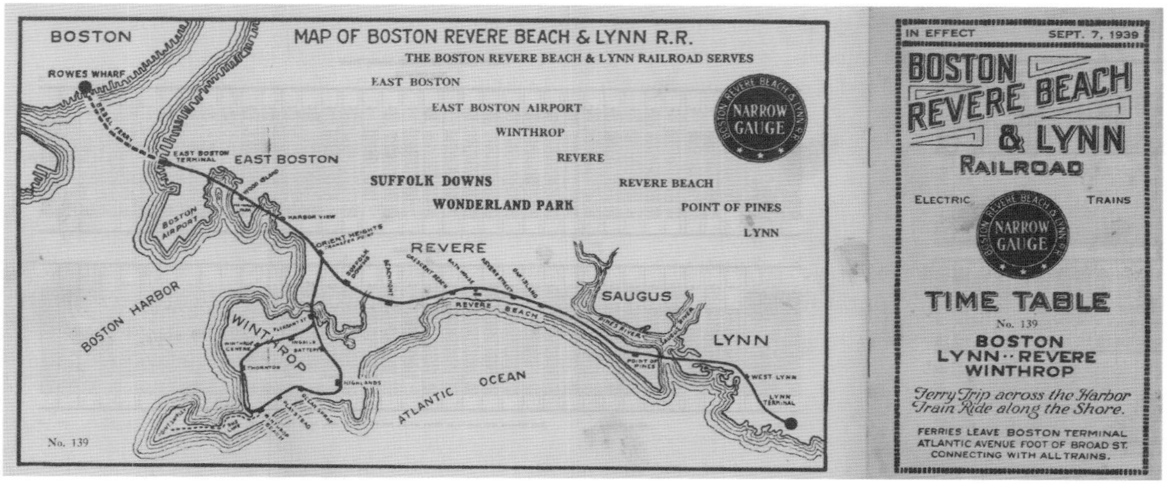

Figure 4.114 BRB&L Timetable Number 139, 1939

A time table map lays out the BRB&L's system, from Rowe's Wharf (left) to Lynn (right). A branch serving Winthrop (bottom) was gained by the BRB&L after its 1886 leasing of the Boston, Winthrop and Shore Railroad.

extents of the railroad's system, along with its final set of station names, were recorded on a 1939 timetable map (Figure 4.114).

Unlike the other and significantly larger steam railroad companies that provided passenger service in Boston, the BRB&L did not erect a downtown railroad terminal. Instead, the railroad established a ferry terminal at Rowe's Wharf with a front door on Atlantic Avenue. In 1901 the BERy opened Rowe's Wharf Station on the Atlantic Avenue Elevated and directly in front of the BRB&L's ferry terminal (Figure 4.115). BRB&L patrons exiting

Figure 4.115 BRB&L Rowe's Wharf Ferry Terminal, Circa 1910

The railroad's downtown ferry terminal wears billboards advertising service to Lynn, Winthrop, and Revere. Stairs connect the sidewalk to the BERy's Rowe's Wharf Station on the Atlantic Avenue Elevated. A portion of the elevated station occupies the left side of the image.

the ferry terminal at Atlantic Avenue would find: "Elevated trains from Rowe's Wharf…every 8 minutes. Buses to the shopping district…every five minutes."

On the East Boston side of the harbor, BRB&L ferries arrived at one of two slips that were in place by the 1920s (Figure 4.116 and Figure 4.117). The slips backed up to a large, wood-framed depot that sheltered platforms served by BRB&L trains bound for Lynn and Winthrop (Figure 4.118 and Figure 4.119). Within the depot, customers

transferred conveniently between harbor ferries and narrow gauge trains (Figure 4.120).

In 1928 the BRB&L shifted from employing steam locomotives pulling non-powered coaches to the use of electric coaches in multiple-unit (MU) operation. Of the earliest electric cars operated by the BRB&L, some were ex-Eastern Massachusetts Street Railway Company (Eastern Mass) semi-convertible type streetcars. The first BRB&L electric cars (Figure 4.121) were similar in scale and capacity to open-vestibule steam railroad coaches of the time. The BRB&L powered its electric trains

Figure 4.116 BRB&L Ferry at East Boston, 1922

Figure 4.117 BRB&L East Boston Ferry Slips, Circa Late 1930s
The ferry "Brewster" (right) serves one of the railroad's two ferry slips in East Boston.

Figure 4.118 BRB&L East Boston Facilities, Circa 1930s
The BRB&L packed a lot of railroading into a small area at Jeffries Point in East Boston. Multiple tracks serve two train sheds and multiple wharves. Each shed was a transfer point, where passengers transferred between trains and ferries operated by the railroad. Beyond the sheds, BRB&L ferries crossed the harbor between East Boston and Rowe's Wharf. Railroad workers man the tower (left) and track switches (right).

Figure 4.119 BRB&L East Boston Terminal, Circa 1930s
A view towards East Boston captures a train of coaches (left), the railroad's East Boston terminal sheds (background), and the railroad's ferry "Newtown" (right).

Figure 4.120 BRB&L East Boston Train Sheds, Circa 1940
A photograph taken on or shortly before the final day of service on the BRB&L shows two trains ready to depart (for either Lynn or Winthrop) inside the railroad's East Boston train sheds.

Figure 4.121 BRB&L Electric Train, 1929
A six-car train of BRB&L electric coaches runs under wire near Lynn, the northern terminus of the railroad's line.

Figure 4.122 BRB&L East Boston Tunnel Portals, 1939
A BRB&L train of electric cars in multiple-unit operation passes through the tunnel at Jeffries Point.

via overhead wire. Taken one year before the demise of the BRB&L, a 1939 photograph shows a train of BRB&L cars in MU operation moving through the railroad's Jeffries Point tunnel in East Boston (Figure 4.122). The short tunnel allowed the BRB&L to operate trains on a near-level route between the East Boston waterfront and Lynn.

During its last decade of operations, the BRB&L endured increasing financial difficulties, exacerbated after the opening of the Sumner Tunnel in 1934. The Sumner Tunnel, the construction of which was overseen by the Boston Transportation Department, was the city's first under-harbor tunnel built expressly for rubber-tired road vehicles. For the first time, automobiles, trucks, and buses had a direct non-ferry route of travel between East Boston and downtown. In 1940, the BRB&L abruptly ceased operations and abandoned its

infrastructure in place. At the end of the last day of service, rail fans took whatever they could carry off from the railroad's trains and stations.

The Commonwealth took over the BRB&L's properties after their abandonment. In the last half of the twentieth century and early portions of the twenty-first century, segments of the former narrow gauge rights-of-way were reused for public transit projects. The Metropolitan Transit Authority (MTA) put a long stretch of former BRB&L right-of-way to use for rapid transit service, including the Revere Extension. A significant portion of the MBTA's Blue Line currently operates along former BRB&L rights-of-way.

Figure 5.1 The Meigs Elevated Railway, 1886

The front page of the July 10, 1886 issue of *Scientific American* depicts the Meigs Elevated Railway, a short-lived experiment with elevated rapid transit infrastructure. In a fantastical view (bottom), a Meigs train steams over a landscape crowded with startled horses and curious people. A rendering (top left) imagines a plush interior of a Meigs passenger car.

CHAPTER 5

Rapid Transit Takes Shape

Defining Rapid Transit

In the context of public transportation, rapid transit is a mode characterized by trains of high capacity passenger cars operating along dedicated rights-of-way and making limited stops at fixed stations. Rapid transit lines are typically railed and most often found in densely populated areas. Rapid transit trains commonly run on elevated structures or in tunnels, out of the street traffic that often hinders buses and street railways. A typical car in a rapid transit train can transport hundreds of passengers, significantly more than the largest streetcar or bus. In the last quarter of the nineteenth century, in cities where growing urban populations increasingly needed to be moved more efficiently and where the capacity of existing streetcar networks was maxing out, rapid transit arrived.

Early rapid transit lines in the United States were synonymous with elevated railways, or "els" for short. America's first els supported steam locomotives pulling passenger cars in intracity service. By the end of the 1870s, America's largest network of els was in New York City, where steam trains rattled above Second, Third, Sixth, and Ninth Avenues. The Ninth Avenue line, opened by the New York Elevated Railway Company in 1871, was the first significant elevated railway in America. After a failed attempt to run cable cars along a line in the 1860s, the New York Elevated Railway Company deployed steam locomotives to pull cars high above the streets of Manhattan.

Rapid transit train design and operations improved as the late nineteenth and early twentieth centuries unfolded. Configurations of rapid transit car doors and seating evolved to maximize rider capacity and movement into and out of cars. The source of motive power shifted from locomotives with steam boilers, to cars with their own electric traction motors. Similar to electric streetcars, electric rapid transit cars were propelled by motors integrated into their trucks, the structures containing the cars' axles and wheels. Multiple electric rapid transit cars ran together in trains without a locomotive. Multiple-unit (MU) operation of rapid transit cars is now the norm. Rapid transit cars in MU operation are controlled by a driver located within a small cab at the front, or "head end" of the train. The first generations of MU rapid transit cars were powered by direct current (DC) traction motors. Newer MU cars are likely to be powered by alternating current (AC) motors.

The East Boston Suspension Railroad

Boston's first experiments with rapid transit were modest and short lived elevated railways. Before modern els arrived in the city, the "Suspension Carriage Road at East Boston" was advertised in the *Boston Advertiser* from August 27 to September 2, 1834. At the time, Noddle's Island, the genesis of East Boston, was sparsely settled. It and surrounding islands composed the fiefdom of the East Boston Company. The company, seeking to promote the sales of parcels of its land, allowed the construction of a primitive monorail from the ferry slip at the foot of Hotel Square (now Maverick Square) into the marshes of East Boston towards the city of Lynn. A sheet of drawings on file in the State Library of Massachusetts (Figure 5.2) depict the proposed route of the East Boston Suspension Railway. The line was never completed to Lynn, but at least one half mile of it, starting at the ferry slip (now Lewis Street), was erected.

PROPOSED ROUTE and DETAILS for a

FROM

EAST BOSTON   TO

By Robert H. Eddy, Civil Engineer. Jan.ʸ 27. 1856.

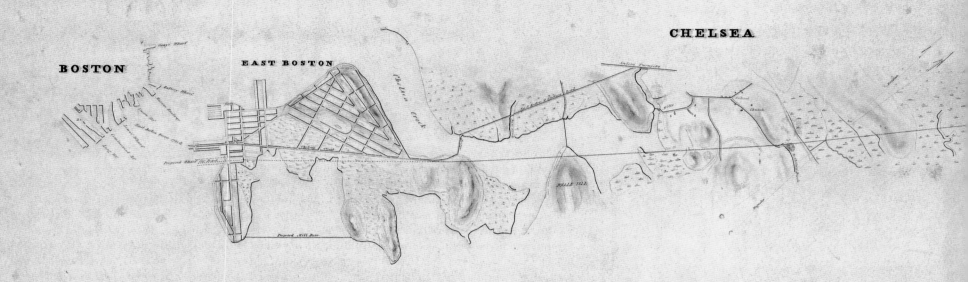

BOSTON   EAST BOSTON   CHELSEA

PROFILE OF THE ROUTE

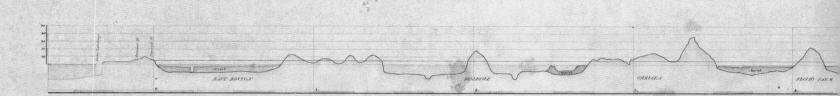

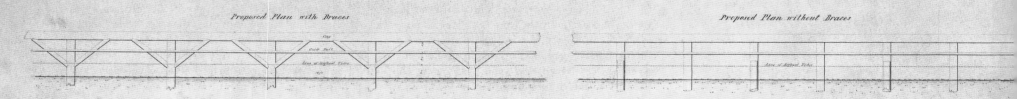

Proposed Plan with Braces   *Proposed Plan without Braces*

Plan for renewal of Posts over Marsh   *Cross Section of Bridge*   *Longitudinal Section of Bridge*

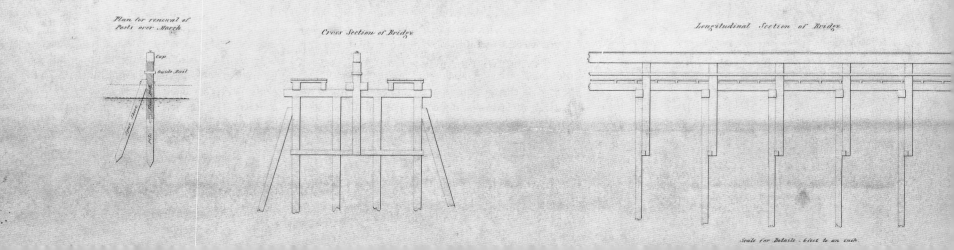

Scale for Details - 6 feet to an inch.

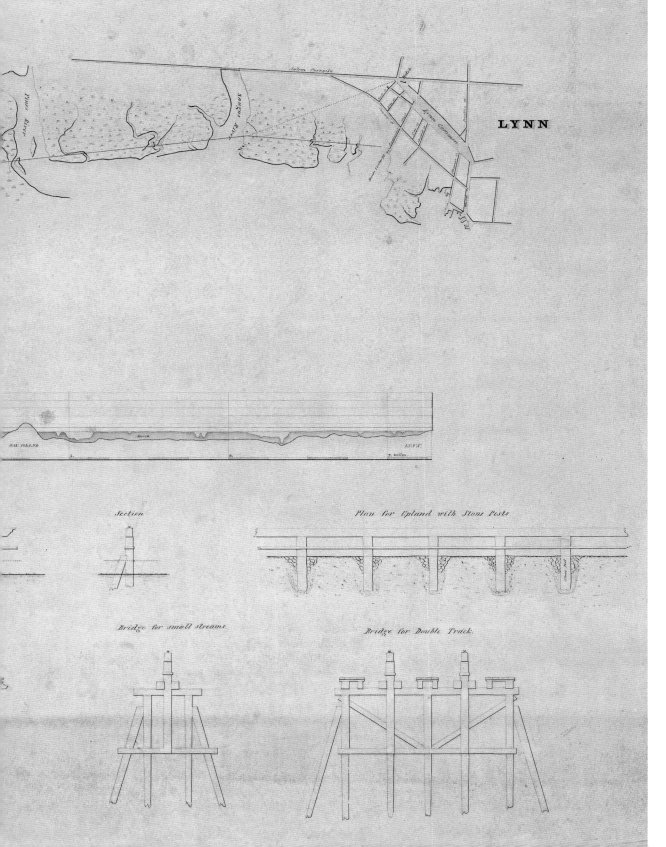

Figure 5.2 The East Boston Suspension Railway, 1835

A map (top), route profile (middle), and construction details (bottom) explain the "Suspension Railway from East Boston to Lynn."

While the 1835 drawings call out timber construction for single and double-track portions of the East Boston Suspension Railway, they do not depict the railway's steam-powered engine or passenger cars. Written descriptions recorded that the railway featured the most unique passenger cars ever to be used in Boston. Each car featured two side-by-side compartments, together capable of transporting a total of six people. Each compartment had a capacity of three persons. Within each car, the compartments were separated from each other by the monorail. Just like packs slung over the backs of horses, each car hung over the monorail, suspending passengers on either side of the el structure.

The East Boston Suspension Railway operated commercially for nine summer days in 1834. Shortly before the line opened, an advertisement in the *Boston Advertiser* announced that trains would run into the East Boston marshes and back, from 10:00 a.m. until sundown. The newspaper advertised train fare of four pence and one half penny per person. The monorail quickly closed due to a lack of operating funds, low ridership, and at its eastern end, the lack of a destination. Meaningful railed transit service did not arrive in East Boston until four years after the closing of the Suspension Railway.

The Eastern Railroad connected East Boston with Salem in 1838, and later, East Boston with downtown in 1854.

The Meigs Elevated Railway

In 1884 Massachusetts assigned the Meigs Elevated Railway Company (Meigs) the right to construct an elevated railway from Cambridge to Boston's Bowdoin Square. Meigs' el was a uniquely-designed monorail. In order for Meigs to receive final approval from the Commonwealth, the company, under the direction of its master engineer Josiah Meigs, constructed a full-size prototype train and short test track in East Cambridge. Unlike the wooden structure of the East Boston Suspension Railway, the Meigs superstructure was made from riveted iron. The site of the test track (Figure 5.3) occupied land used by the Bay State Glass Works, makers of transom glass for horsecars, from the late 1840s until the 1870s. The prototype train consisted of a steam-powered locomotive, a tender that carried water and coal, and an elegantly appointed passenger car. The train crawled along the test track like an oversized steam-punk centipede (Figure 5.4 and Figure 5.5).

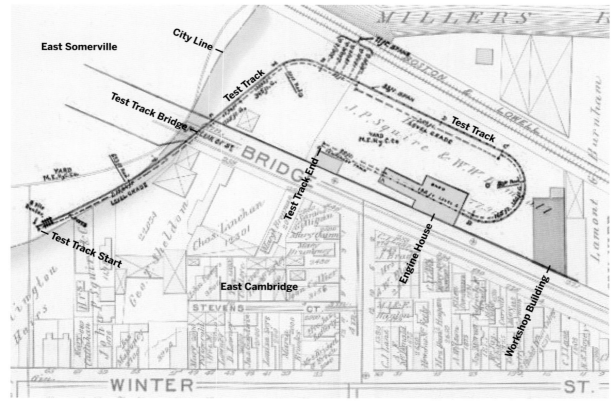

Figure 5.3 Mapping the Meigs Elevated Railway, 1887
An overlay of an 1887 plan of the Meigs Elevated Railway upon an 1894 map of East Cambridge shows Meigs' test track starting at the Cambridge-Somerville city line (left). A bridge carries the track over Bridge Street. At the top of the map, the track turns and runs parallel with the tracks of the Boston & Lowell Railroad before entering a one hundred and eighty degree turn. The track terminates alongside Bridge Street after passing through an engine house (highlighted in yellow).

Figure 5.4 The Meigs Elevated Railway, Circa 1886
On display in East Cambridge, Meigs' three-car experimental rapid transit train consists of a steam-powered locomotive (left), a tender (middle), and a passenger car with open vestibules (right).

Figure 5.5 Team Meigs and Their Train, Circa 1886
The Meigs train is posed on its test track, in front of the company's workshop building. Angled wheels kept the train on the monorail track. Horizontal wheels under the locomotive provided the tractive effort.

In order to put the test train and track through their paces, Meigs configured the monorail not unlike a roller coaster, with inclines of different slopes and curves of varying radii. During rigorous testing, and seeking to prove the inherent safety of its designs, Meigs removed a wheel from the train. Even sans-wheel, the train moved along the test track and did not derail. In fact, the train was not hindered from safely moving. The prototype train and test track of the Meigs Elevated Railway operated on an experimental basis as early as 1886. It opened for public demonstration soon thereafter. The project made the cover of the July 10, 1886 edition of *Scientific American* (Figure 5.1).

A detailed study of the performance and engineering of both the train and monorail was prepared by Meigs and submitted to the Commonwealth for review in 1886. In the following year, the study was featured in a report published by the Massachusetts Board of Railroad Commissioners. Meigs' designs, engineering, and data resulting from thorough testing were received positively. Despite the praise from the Railroad Commissioners, Meigs' designs never appeared in large scale nor as an integrated part of Boston's public transportation system. One reason was city prohibitions on the operation of steam trains through downtown. Another, and perhaps more powerful reason, was years of successful operation of non-experimental multi-track elevated railways and trains, like those operating in New York City since the 1870s.

Marketing to prospective investors, state regulators, and its anticipated rail-riding public in 1887, Meigs produced a brochure detailing the designs and testing of their train and monorail (Figure 5.6). In newspaper format, the publication espoused the benefits of the Meigs rapid transit system over others. Furthering its mission to establish a safe and viable operation, the company reprinted letters of support from structural engineers and documentation of tests conducted on the train and monorail.

In the same year that Meigs' project was under review by the Railroad Commissioners, a suspicious early morning fire severely damaged the Meigs train and the building in which it was stored. The company never recovered and its track and train were scrapped. The Meigs Elevated Railway Company was formally dissolved in 1893.

THE MEIGS ELEVATED RAILWAY.

It does not disturb light and air.   It is the only absolutely safe railway.   It is officially proved to be safer and more stable than any railway hitherto.

A Broken Wheel is Not Dangerous.   A Broken Rail is Not Dangerous.   A Broken Engine is Harmless.   Broken Rods Injure No One.
Collision is Impossible.   Derailment is Impossible.   Curves Hitherto Impossible are Easily Made.
Grades Hitherto Impractical are Perfectly Possible.

The roadbed does not lie on the surface; it is so securely fastened into the earth that a washout or torrent of water would not dislodge it.   The tracks are the strongest yet built, bearing loads and resisting winds which would wreck any other railway; tested officially by the State of Massachusetts in a way which no other railway could for an instant have withstood.   ITS ENGINES ARE THE MOST POWERFUL EVER BUILT, capable of greater speed than hitherto.   ITS ROLLING STOCK IS THE MOST COMFORTABLE.   Its engine is the least noisy.   All of these things, save the statement about collision, have been officially reported.   You can see them for yourself at East Cambridge.   Then why not place my railway at the service of the people of the whole Commonwealth, if they want it, under the same laws that apply to all other railways which happen to have the legal gauge.   I could not build it anywhere without special legislation if I chose.
IS THIS RIGHT?   IS IT POLITIC?   OUGHT IT TO EXIST?   PRAY HELP TO PLACE IT ON THE SAME FOOTING WITH ALL OTHER RAILWAYS.

READER, YOU CAN SEE FOR YOURSELF WHY THE MEIGS RAILWAY IS ABSOLUTELY SAFE.

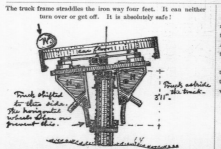

The truck frame straddles the iron way four feet.   It can neither turn over or get off.   It is absolutely safe!

The ordinary wheel flange is all that holds the train on the track, hence speed is dangerous. A broken wheel will derail the train.

The Meigs Railway obviates these things — then why not let the people build them if they wish.

The Meigs truck is astride of the track four feet.   Its wheels are merely rolling braces and are always at right angles to the load and keep the truck just clear of the track so that if a wheel were broken no plunge could occur.   The wheel-pressures are inward and a broken or rotten rail is harmless. Its turntable attaches the car bottom and truck five thousand times stronger than does the kingpin.   The load rests lower down, and the track-way is more stable than that of any road ever built. Are these things reasons why it ought not to be lawful to build it, like other railways?

YOU CAN SEE FOR YOURSELF THAT THE MEIGS RAILWAY RESISTS LOADS THAT WOULD DESTROY OTHER RAILWAYS.
OUGHT IT THEREFORE TO BE REFUSED THE SAME LAWS THAT OTHER RAILWAYS HAVE?

The Meigs way and its post as pulled sideways, by General Stark, by a force equivalent to a hurricane wind, plus 20 per cent.   No other railway could withstand such a test as this did—ought it therefore to be placed under special and onerous provisions not applicable to other roads?   Surely not!

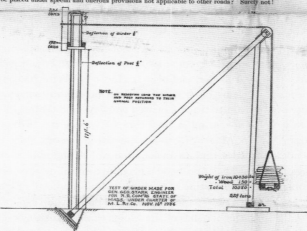

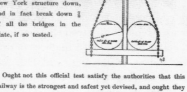

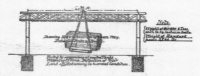

The Meigs way supports a load which would pull the New York structure down, and in fact break down ⅞ of all the bridges in the State, if so tested.

Ought not this official test satisfy the authorities that this railway is the strongest and safest yet devised, and ought they not to place it on the same footing with all other railways, so that the people of the whole State can use it?   It is absolutely safe against any possible load, or against any wind.

THE MEIGS RAILWAY DOES NOT OBSTRUCT LIGHT AND AIR, AND IS, BY REASON OF THE CYLINDRICAL FORM OF ITS CARS, FREE FROM SIDE STRAINS BORNE BY OTHER ROADS.

This railway as variously placed in the streets.   Its remarkable freedom from obstruction to light and air is readily seen.   Might it not therefore have all damages arising from its use settled by the courts, as they are now settled for all other railways?

End views of the Meigs way, with the engine.   The car outside.   The car inside.   They show little obstruction, great comfort, absolute freedom from derailment, and great stability.

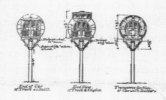

Figure 5.6 Meigs Elevated Railway Paper, 1887
A multi-page publication, sized and formatted like a newspaper, was produced by the Meigs Company to not only explain their radical designs, but to disseminate the positive results of exhaustive testing to convince people that their unique designs were safe.

Figure 5.7 Old and New Spans Over the Charles, 1900
In the foreground, the Charles River Bridge sits on wood piles alongside its replacement, the Charlestown Bridge.

Figure 5.8 The Charlestown Bridge Draw Turntable, 1899
Scores of wheels allowed the turning of the rotating draw portion of the Charlestown Bridge.

Figure 5.9 The Charlestown Bridge, June 3, 1901
Horse-drawn conveyances and a streetcar (far right) utilize the Charlestown Bridge's broad main deck. Above, rapid transit trains of the Boston Elevated Railway Company travel along the upper level. The large truss structure in the middle of the bridge is the rotating draw portion.

The Charlestown Bridge

In the last quarter of the nineteenth century, Boston began working towards replacing the Charles River Bridge. After exploring the digging of a tunnel beneath the Charles in the early 1870s, the city decided to replace the venerable wooden bridge with a new steel span. Property takings for the project began in 1896. The Boston Transit Commission (BTC) awarded the first construction contract for the Charlestown Bridge in July. By the end of 1897, massive concrete and granite piers were installed in the Charles River and the new bridge's design was revised to include an elevated railway for electric rapid transit trains. The Charles River Bridge remained alongside its replacement until the new bridge was completed (Figure 5.7).

The Charlestown Bridge was Boston's first bridge constructed with transit modes segregated on multiple levels. The main deck featured two streetcar tracks and four lanes for general road traffic. The upper level, one story above the main deck, featured a pair of elevated railway tracks for rapid transit trains. At the middle of the bridge was a movable portion, called a "revolving draw." To allow tall boats to pass beneath the bridge, and between Boston Harbor and the Charles River Basin, the movable draw could be rotated perpendicular to the bridge's span. The draw measured 240 feet wide and 100 feet long. It rotated on wheels supported by a massive, fifty-four-foot-diameter foundation set into the middle of the Charles River (Figure 5.8).

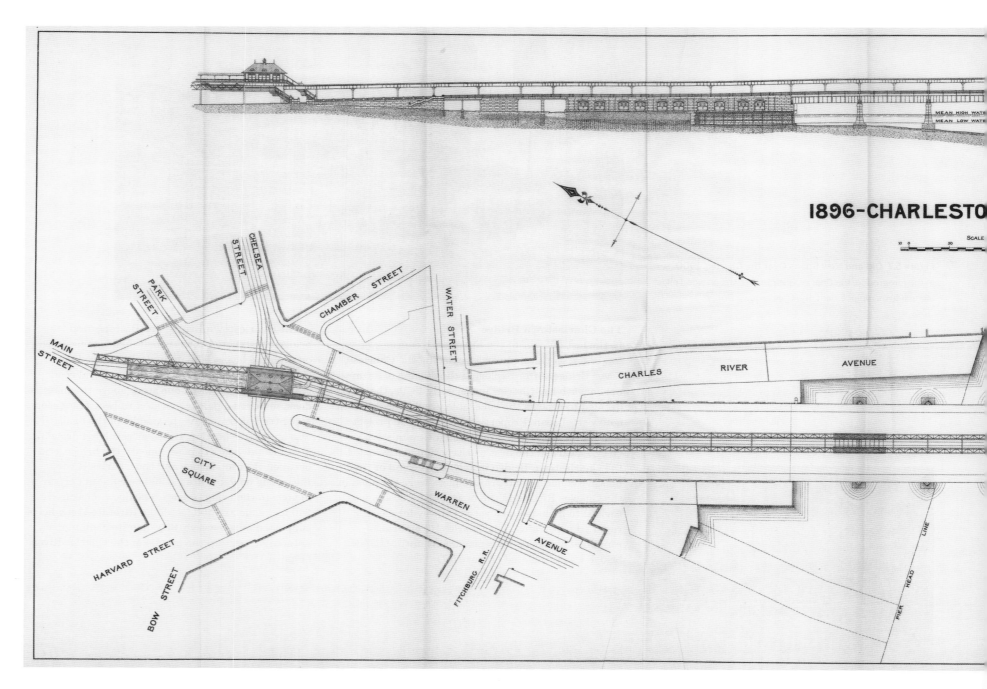

The Charlestown Bridge was 1,900 feet long. 1,090 feet of the bridge's length was composed of ten, fixed steel spans, each eighty-five feet in length (Figure 5.10). The bridge officially opened to street traffic on November 27, 1899. Soon afterwards, the 1786 Charles River Bridge was removed. After elevated railways were connected to both ends of the new bridge, rapid transit trains began traversing the upper level (Figure 5.9).

Well into the twentieth century, the Charlestown Bridge was an essential connection for streetcars, rapid transit trains, and general street traffic traveling between Boston, Charlestown, and points north of the city. Streetcars disappeared from the main deck by the 1960s. In the mid-1970s, most of the upper level was removed after the Massachusetts Bay Transportation Authority (MBTA) re-routed rapid transit trains off of the Charlestown Elevated and onto the Haymarket North

Figure 5.10 The Charlestown Bridge, 1899

The nearly 2,000 foot long Charlestown Bridge is shown in both side elevation (top) and plan (bottom). At the middle of the span is the trussed, revolving draw, which rotated to allow marine traffic to pass. At the northern end of the bridge (far left) are City Square and its el station. At the southern end of the span (far right) is the intersection of Washington, Causeway, and Commercial Streets.

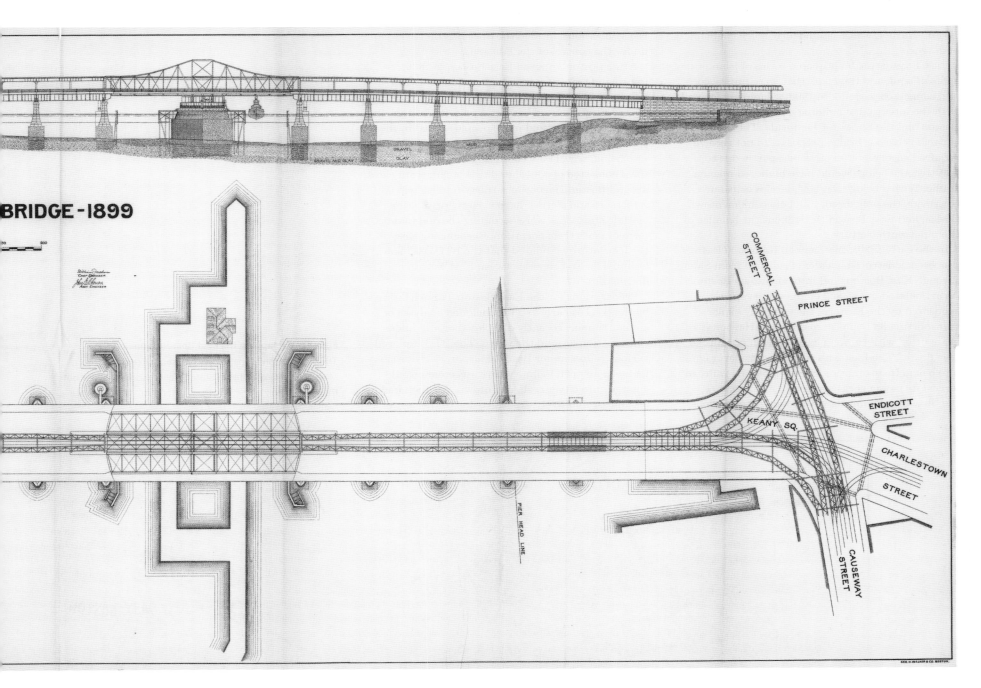

BRIDGE - 1899

COMMERCIAL STREET

PRINCE STREET

ENDICOTT STREET

KEANY SQ.

CHARLESTOWN STREET

CAUSEWAY STREET

PIER HEAD LINE

Extension (See Chapter 9). The Charlestown Bridge is still used by street traffic and pedestrians, though the parallel Leonard P. Zakim Bunker Hill Memorial Bridge and Interstate 93 carry far more rubber-tired vehicles across the Charles River. Until recently, at the center of the aging bridge, a small portion of the upper level remained in place atop the long-closed draw. After 120 years of use, the Charlestown Bridge is currently being replaced. While the new span will lack transit tracks, it will feature more space for the inclusion of bike lanes, bus lanes, and broader sidewalks.

The East Boston Tunnel

Erecting a new bridge over the Charles River was a relatively straightforward project for the BTC. Establishing a new railed transit connection between the Shawmut Peninsula and East Boston, places separated by the busy waters of

Boston Harbor, was a significantly more challenging endeavor.

East Boston was built upon a series of islands, dry splits of land, and tidal flats that were improved and connected with fill. In 1808, a company formed with the intention of building a bridge between East Boston and the Shawmut Peninsula. The company's audacious harbor bridge proposal did not receive required governmental blessings, partly due to the fact that the bridge would have hindered marine traffic. With a bridge scuttled, ferries continued to provide the only direct link between downtown Boston and East Boston throughout the balance of the nineteenth century.

In the early 1830s, the Eastern Railroad (Eastern) proposed constructing a steam railroad from Salem, through East Boston, and into downtown Boston. As articulated in an 1832 engineering report sponsored by the Eastern, the company explored transporting its trains across Boston Harbor via boats fitted with rails, an early version of railroad "car floats." The Eastern's special boats never came into being. Instead, from 1838 to 1854, the railroad ferried its passengers between East Boston and the Shawmut Peninsula with boats. After various

reorganizations, in 1836 the East Boston Ferry came under the control of the Eastern.

After Boston annexed East Boston in 1836, improving transportation connections between downtown and its most geographically disconnected neighborhood became a priority for the city, especially as more and more people settled in the enclave. In 1894, the same year that the BTC came into being, travel between East Boston and downtown consisted of convoluted ride steam train rides around Boston Harbor or a thirty minute trip on streetcars and a cross-harbor ferry. At the time, electric streetcars were becoming the dominant form of mass transportation. Recognizing this, the legislature mandated that the BTC establish a tunnel for streetcars between East Boston and downtown.

Preparations for the East Boston Tunnel, begun by the BTC as early as 1895, included analyses of similar tunnels recently completed or still under construction around the world. The BTC explored various routes under Boston Harbor. Early designs featured an open incline where streetcars would emerge onto city streets downtown. An open incline became prohibitively expensive due to the cost of

Figure 5.11 Mapping the East Boston Tunnel, 1901
The East Boston Tunnel in plan and section (bottom), from Maverick Square (right) to State Street (middle). In plan, both the East Boston Tunnel and the Tremont Street Subway are highlighted in gray.

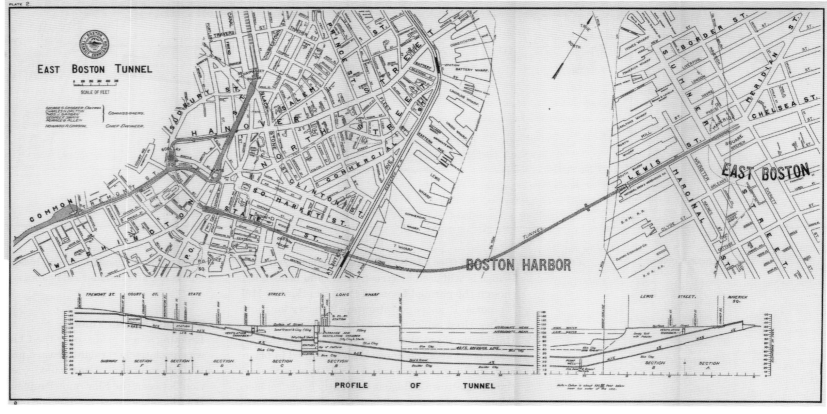

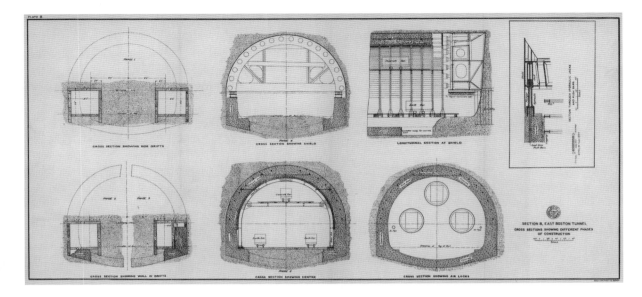

Figure 5.12 Constructing the East Boston Tunnel, 1901
A series of drawings articulates the sequence of construction of the portion of the East Boston Tunnel dug beneath Boston Harbor. First, small drift tunnels were dug. Then, tunnel sidewalls were constructed within each drift. Next, an iron roof shield was slid incrementally along rails running atop the side walls. Installation of the tunnel's reinforced concrete lining was the final step.

land takings it would have required. With an open incline in downtown Boston out of the picture, the BTC explored, as an alternative, an underground connection between the yet-to-be-constructed East Boston Tunnel and the Tremont Street Subway at Scollay Square. A connection between the new tunnel and the existing subway would have hindered traffic flow in the existing subway, so the BTC did not proceed with the link. The BTC did not finalize the location of the downtown portion of the East Boston Tunnel until after construction was well under way at the East Boston end of the project (Figure 5.11).

Working Under Pressure
Construction on the East Boston Tunnel commenced in May 1900. The BTC, as it had done with the Tremont Street Subway, divided contract work on the project into segments. At Section A, which included all of the work on the East Boston side, the cut and cover method was employed. Builders constructed a portal for the new tunnel at Maverick Square along with a short section of tunnel under Lewis Street.

Section B, the most technically challenging portion of the project, was the under-harbor portion (Figure 5.12). At this section, earth was excavated by man and horse from under the protection of the roof shield (Figure 5.13). Within Section B, pumps maintained air at a higher pressure within the excavation than the outside atmosphere. The higher pressure air, in combination with the protection of the massive roof shield, prevented millions of tons of soft under-harbor sediments from collapsing in on tunnel excavations. The increased air pressure

Figure 5.13 East Boston Tunnel Roof Shield, Nov. 22, 1900
A BTC official inspects the roof shield to be used to protect workers digging the East Boston Tunnel through the soft mud under Boston Harbor.

Figure 5.14 Tunnel Air Locks, March 17, 1903
A pair of air locks protected the high-pressure area of tunnel excavation from the East Boston side of the project. A second level of air locks existed above the ones shown.

Figure 5.15 Digging the East Boston Tunnel, 1901
Tunnel diggers pause inside of the pressurized portion of the dig. The roof shield, the top of which is concealed behind roof beams, shelters the workers at the cutting face.

was maintained until the entire under-harbor portion of the tunnel was lined with reinforced concrete. Workers accessed their pressurized work area through air locks on the East Boston side of the tunnel (Figure 5.14). Horses used for moving materials with the sealed work site were stabled inside the pressurized tunnel. Feed and water was brought in and manure was brought out. Within the pressured area, and under the protection of the roof shield men excavated by hand (Figure 5.15). Of construction of the East Boston Tunnel, the June 9, 1901 *Boston Daily Globe* recorded: "About 100 men are employed days, and the same number nights. Last week 36 feet of tunnel was completed, but the average is five feet a day." The article stated that

the men enjoyed working in the tunnel and air locks because "[the contractors] pay good wages, there is no loss of time owing to the weather, and the digging is easy and dry.

According to the BTC, the use of the roof shield in combination with the construction of an arched, steel-reinforced concrete roof was a world first. Similar tunnels were built using the shield method in the 1880s and 1890s, but they featured cast iron tunnel enclosure sections. Concrete with steel reinforcing installed after the excavation of drifts and the use of a sliding roof shield was used under Boston Harbor because it was less expensive than an iron lining.

Figure 5.16 East Boston Tunnel Portal, Circa 1905

A streetcar descends from Maverick Square towards downtown Boston via the East Boston Tunnel.

Today, modern transportation tunnels are often constructed with giant Tunnel Boring Machines (TBMs). TBMs simultaneously excavate, protect workers, eject spoils, and install a permanent tunnel lining. Prefabricated, steel-reinforced concrete tunnel linings installed with TBMs are now common. TBM construction techniques evolved directly from the roof shield construction method, behind which riveted iron sections were installed (pioneered by Marc Brunel in Europe) or which steel reinforced arch work was installed (pioneered by the BTC in Boston).

Stations of the East Boston Tunnel Line

The eastern terminus of the East Boston Tunnel Line was at Maverick Square. There, streetcars entered and exited the double-track tunnel along an incline and through a portal (Figure 5.16). At the top of the incline, streetcars stopped to drop off and pick up passengers (Figure 5.17 and Figure 5.18). From Maverick Square, the East Boston Tunnel ran westward, under Lewis Street, and deep below the East Boston slip of the "South Ferry." Beyond the ferry slip, the tunnel continued westward under Boston Harbor, before turning to align with and run the length of State Street.

In downtown Boston, the East Boston Tunnel Line served three streetcar subway stations, all situated along State Street. The closest station to the waterfront was Atlantic Avenue Station, constructed with the shield method and opened to the public on April 5, 1906. Atlantic Avenue Station opened approximately a year and a half after the other two stations on State Street. Passengers accessed Atlantic Avenue Station, the deepest

Figure 5.17 Maverick Square, East Boston, Circa 1905

A streetcar arrives from downtown out of the portal of the East Boston Tunnel into Maverick Square.

Figure 5.18 Streetcars at Maverick Square, Circa 1905

Streetcars are about to descend from Maverick Square into the East Boston Tunnel.

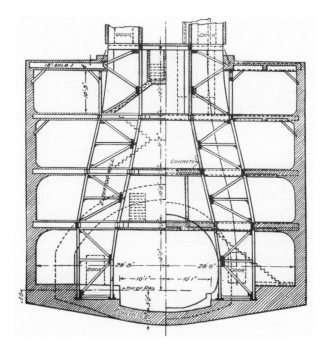

Figure 5.19 Cross-Section of Atlantic Avenue Station, 1924
A unique steel framework supported the incline elevators at Atlantic Avenue Station.

Figure 5.20 Atlantic Avenue Station, November 16, 1908

transit station in Boston when it opened, with elevators that descended over fifty feet beneath the surface while simultaneously running over six feet horizontally (Figure 5.19). The station's interior was a long cavern sheathed in glossy white tiles (Figure 5.20). At street-level, the station was capped by a head house wrapped in eclectic stonemasonry (Figure 5.21). The head house was lost to a fire in 1950. The station it once topped is now

named Aquarium Station and is served by trains of the MBTA's Blue Line.

The second East Boston Tunnel station along State Street was Devonshire Street Station. The BTC wove the new station into the existing foundations of one of Boston's most historic buildings, the Old State House, erected in 1713. When Devonshire Street Station opened on December 30, 1904, it had the most historically significant head house of any

Figure 5.21 Atlantic Avenue and State Street Stations, 1905

The head house of Atlantic Avenue Station on the East Boston Tunnel Line is connected by a pedestrian bridge to State Station on the Atlantic Avenue Elevated.

subway station in America. In chronological order, the 1713-built structure served as a meeting house for English colonists, the seat for the English royal government, home of the Massachusetts' colonial legislature, and the first capital building of the state of Massachusetts. The Old State House replaced Boston's Town House, which stood on the same site from the late 1650s until 1711, when it was destroyed by fire. Devonshire Street Station featured white tiled walls, white plaster ceilings, and painted

columns at platform level (Figure 5.22). The interior finishes of Devonshire Street Station were typical of most BTC subway and tunnel stations. Devonshire Street Station is now part of the MBTA's State Station and is served by Blue Line rapid transit trains.

Court Street Station was the third station, and original downtown terminus, of the East Boston Tunnel Line. At Court Street Station, streetcars arrived from East Boston to exchange passengers

Figure 5.22 Devonshire Street Station, May 14, 1905

Taken four months after the opening of the East Boston Tunnel Line, a photograph shows the platforms served by streetcars from 1904 until 1924. Devonshire Street Station is now the Blue Line portion of the MBTA's State Station.

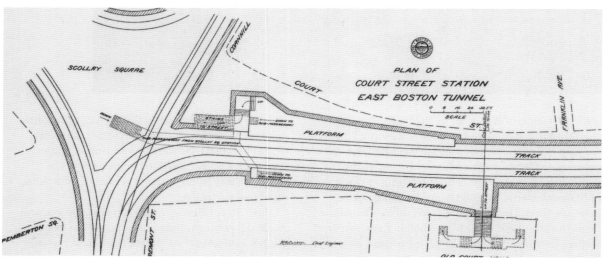

Figure 5.23 Court Street Station, Circa 1905

Figure 5.23 Court Street Station, Circa 1905

Figure 5.24 Proposed Plan of Court Street Station, 1903
Court Street Station was the initial Boston terminus for street-cars travelling into downtown from East Boston via the East Boston Tunnel. As built, Court Street Station did not include trackage connecting it with the Tremont Street Subway (left).

Figure 5.25 Court Street Station Head House, 1904
A glass-roofed pavilion was one of two street-level entrances to Court Street Station. The other was inside the old court house for which Court Street was named.

(Figure 5.23). Trolleys then reversed direction and returned under the harbor to East Boston.

Court Street Station was constructed at the same elevation as, and up against the eastern side of, Scollay Square Station of the Tremont Street Subway. In early designs for the station, the BTC anticipated that trackage at Court Street Station might connect with that of neighboring Scollay Square Station (Figure 5.24). In the end, Court Street Station's tracks never directly connected with those of Scollay Square Station or the Tremont Street Subway; an underground pedestrian passageway connected the neighboring streetcar stations for over a decade.

Court Street Station saw streetcar service from December 30, 1904 until November 15, 1914, when it was closed to allow for the East Boston Tunnel Extension. Today, only portions of the station's shell remain, some enclosing ventilation and other back-of-house equipment of the MBTA.

The East Boston Tunnel Extension
Costing $3.1 million in 1904, the nearly mile-and-a-half long East Boston Tunnel Line opened from Maverick Square to Court Street Station on December 30. Eight years later, work authorized by the General Court in 1911, and commenced on November 29, 1912, extended the East Boston Tunnel Line just shy of a mile and a half further into downtown. The East Boston Tunnel Extension ran from the site of Court Street Station to Bowdoin Square. Between Scollay and Bowdoin Squares, the extension traced Court Street (Figure 5.29).

The East Boston Tunnel Extension saw the reconstruction of some 350 feet of the existing streetcar tunnel beneath State Street and the closure of Court Street Station. The floor of Court Street Station was removed and earth excavated from below it, allowing the East Boston Tunnel Line to pass under Scollay Square Station. The pedestrian passageway between Court Street and Scollay

Figure 5.26 Scollay Under Station, January 31, 1916
The track for southbound streetcars at Scollay Under Station on the East Boston Tunnel Extension (shown) is now found at the lower level of the MBTA's Government Center Station. Having been upgraded, it is served by Blue Line rapid transit trains bound for East Boston.

Figure 5.27 Bowdoin Station, January 31, 1916
Tracks of the East Boston Tunnel Extension bracket the platforms at the terminal station on the East Boston Tunnel Line.

Square Stations closed. In 1916, the BTC recorded the total cost of the approximately two-mile-long East Boston Tunnel Line and Extension as $5.59 million.

The East Boston Tunnel Extension's two stations opened to the public in 1916. On March 18, Scollay Under Station opened directly beneath Scollay Square Station of the Tremont Street Subway. Scollay Under featured an island platform bracketed by two tracks, one for northbound streetcars and one for southbound cars. The extension's other station was located at Bowdoin Square. When it opened to the public, Bowdoin Station became the downtown terminus for the entire East Boston Tunnel Line.

The interiors of both Scollay Under and Bowdoin Stations featured terrazzo wainscot with borders of colored tiles on the lower portions of the walls. The upper portions of walls as well as the ceiling were sheathed in cement plaster painted white. The stations' painted columns, tiled walls, and white ceilings were illuminated by electric lighting (Figure 5.26 and Figure 5.27). Cleanliness of the new stations was a priority for the BTC.

Figure 5.28 Cambridge Street Incline, 1915
A double-track incline allowed streetcars, and later, rapid transit cars, to travel between the East Boston Tunnel and surface tracks on Cambridge Street (right).

Floors were of the "sanitary type," meaning they lacked hard corners, especially where floors met walls and columns. Hospital corners aided station maintenance crews when they hosed down, or "flushed," the platforms with water.

Each station's name was installed alongside the station's platforms in contrasting black and white tile. During the conversion of Scollay Square and Scollay Under Stations into Government Center Station in the early 1960s, the Metropolitan Transit Authority (MTA) covered over most of Scollay Under's 1916 mosaics. Recently, during a 2014–16 renovation of Government Center Station, the MBTA uncovered, exposed, and restored many original mosaics at the station formerly known as Scollay Under.

At the downtown end of the East Boston Tunnel Line, Bowdoin Station featured a long central platform and a loop track. Streetcars arrived at Bowdoin Station from Scollay Under Station. They then dropped off passengers before moving into the loop. Trolleys returned from the loop, passed back through the station and picked up passengers before heading back towards Scollay Square and East Boston. The Bowdoin Station loop eliminated the need for streetcars to reverse direction at the Boston end of the East Boston Tunnel Line, as they were forced to do at Court Street Station.

West of Bowdoin Square, the BTC established an open incline and portal connecting tracks of the East Boston Tunnel Extension with tracks on Cambridge Street (Figure 5.28). The incline paralleled Cambridge Street, between Chambers and North Russell Streets (Figure 5.29). The Cambridge Street Incline allowed for the first time a direct connection between the streetcar tracks of the East Boston Tunnel Line and surface streetcar tracks in downtown. The incline offered a straight shot into the East Boston Tunnel Line for trolleys arriving from Cambridge via the West Boston Bridge. For a time, streetcars carried paying passengers between Central Square in Cambridge and Orient Heights in East Boston via the Cambridge Street Incline. The service was discontinued by the Boston Elevated Railway Company (BERy) by the end of April 1924.

When a public transit vehicle operates to pick up and drop off paying riders, the vehicle is in "revenue service" and is making a "revenue movement." When a public transit vehicle moves for service, maintenance, storage, or any way that prohibits the transportation of fare-paying passengers, the vehicle is making a "non-revenue movement." The Cambridge Street Incline, used only briefly for revenue service, remained critical for non-revenue movement of transit vehicles between East Boston and Cambridge until its closure in the mid-twentieth century. Though the incline and portal have disappeared, a segment that connected them with the Bowdoin Loop remains. This tunnel may one day see use as part of a long-planned extension of the Blue Line from Bowdoin Station to Charles Station on the Red Line.

Rapid Transit via the East Boston Tunnel

The opening of the East Boston Tunnel Extension caused ridership to more than double on the East Boston Tunnel Line. Consistent heavy ridership was the impetus for BTC successor, the Boston Transit Department (BTD), to transform the East Boston

Figure 5.29 The East Boston Tunnel Extension, 1917
Black and white lines represent streetcar subway tracks. The East Boston Tunnel Line and Extension run from Washington Street (far right), through Scollay Under Station (right), to Bowdoin Station (top), and to the Cambridge Street Incline (left). At Scollay Square, East Boston Tunnel Extension tracks pass under those of the Tremont Street Subway.

Figure 5.30 East Boston Tunnel Type 1 Car, Circa 1923
Car number 0501, featuring three doors on each side, was amongst the first rapid transit cars to operate along the East Boston Tunnel Line.

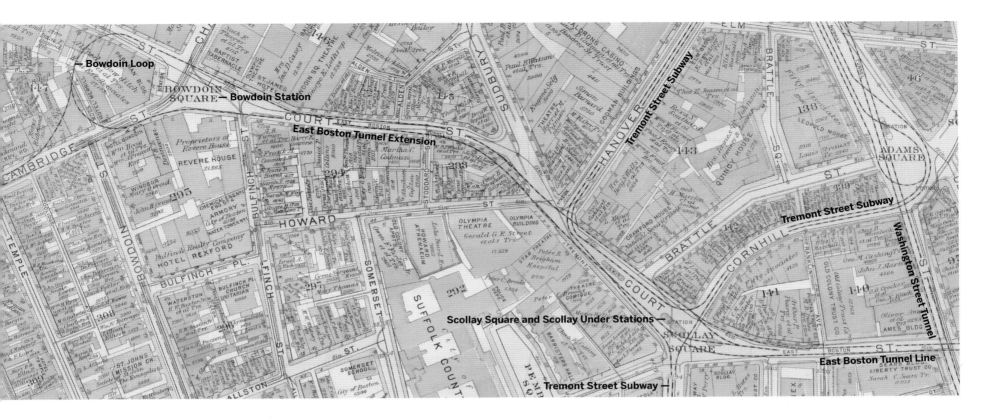

Tunnel Line from the domain of jam-packed street-cars to that of higher capacity rapid transit trains. After mere months of work to convert the line, on April 21, 1924 BERy rapid transit trains began to transport passengers through the East Boston Tunnel Line and Extension.

To provide service along the converted line, the BERy commissioned new rapid transit cars. Forty East Boston Tunnel Type 1 (Figure 5.30) and eight East Boston Tunnel Type 2 (Figure 5.31) rapid transit cars, all built by the Pullman Company, were put into service during 1923 and 1924. Unlike the sixty-nine-foot-long behemoths already plying the BERy's Cambridge-Dorchester rapid transit line, the East Boston Tunnel rapid transit cars measured only forty-eight feet in length. The shorter cars were compact by necessity. They needed to operate through the tight radius of the Bowdoin Loop,

Figure 5.31 East Boston Tunnel Type 2 Cars, Circa 1951
Car number 0541, with number 0540 behind, poses for the camera. Car 0540's pantograph is extended to reach the overhead power wire. 0541 wears a massive light atop its head end.

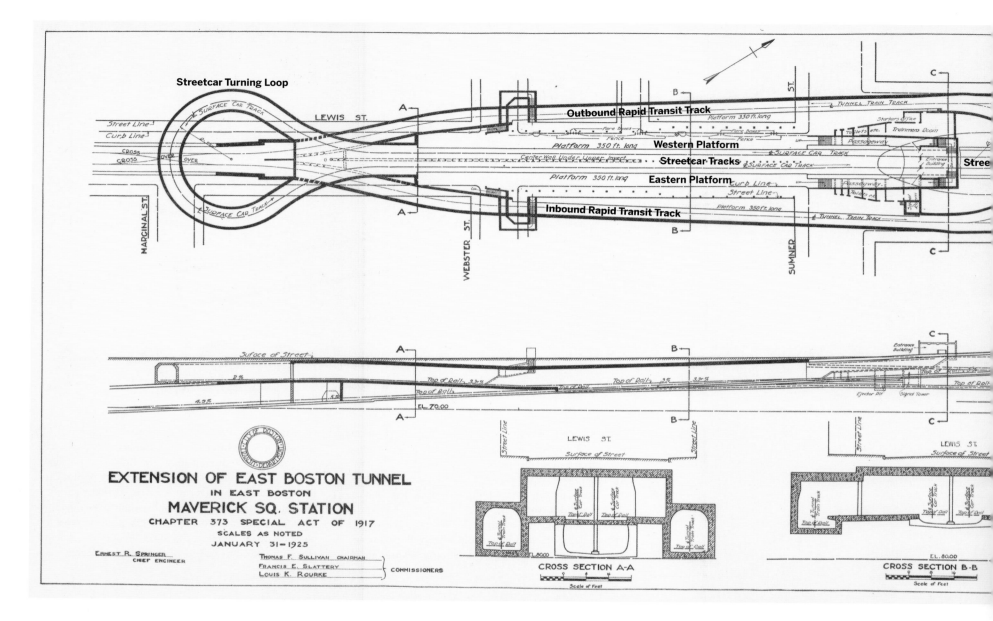

Within the drawing:

Streetcar Turning Loop

LEWIS ST.

Outbound Rapid Transit Track

Western Platform

Streetcar Tracks

Eastern Platform

Inbound Rapid Transit Track

EXTENSION OF EAST BOSTON TUNNEL
IN EAST BOSTON
MAVERICK SQ. STATION
CHAPTER 373 SPECIAL ACT OF 1917
SCALES AS NOTED
JANUARY 31–1925

ERNEST R. SPRINGER
CHIEF ENGINEER

THOMAS F. SULLIVAN CHAIRMAN
FRANCIS E. SLATTERY   COMMISSIONERS
LOUIS K. ROURKE

CROSS SECTION A-A

CROSS SECTION B-B

constructed for nimble streetcars. To accommodate the new rapid transit cars, with their door thresholds many feet off the ground than those of streetcars, the BERy raised station platforms all along the East Boston Tunnel Line. The BERy also installed electrified third rails. Unlike streetcars, which drew power from overhead trolley wire, rapid transit cars drew power from third rails through small paddles extending from their trucks. All of the BERy's efforts to improve service along the East Boston Tunnel Line were successful. Trains of rapid transit cars in MU operation more than doubled the capacity of the former streetcar subway.

As part of the conversion of the East Boston Tunnel Line from streetcar to rapid transit service, the BTD added a new station at the eastern end of the line, beneath Maverick Square. Maverick Station was East Boston's first rapid transit subway station. At tunnel level, Maverick Station allowed transit patrons to transfer between rapid transit trains, running to and from Boston, and streetcars, serving East Boston and surrounding locales (Figure 5.32). At street level, a main head house was the primary public entry and egress point (Figure 5.33). Within the head house, the BTC's familiar white aesthetics were complimented by

Figure 5.32 Maverick Square Station, January 31, 1925
Drawings represents Maverick Station in plan (top), longitudinal section (middle), and a series of cross-sections (bottom). A pair of streetcar tracks forms the station's spine. Streetcars entered and exited the station along an incline in Maverick Square. After entering the station and dropping off riders, cars proceeded into a loop at the station's western end. There, they turned around before returning back through the station to pick up passengers and head for the surface. Rapid transit trains arrived and departed along the station's southern and northern peripheries, respectively. Both of the station's platforms offered simple, cross-platform transfers. At the station's eastern end, a loop track allowed trains from Boston to turn around between dropping off and picking up passengers.

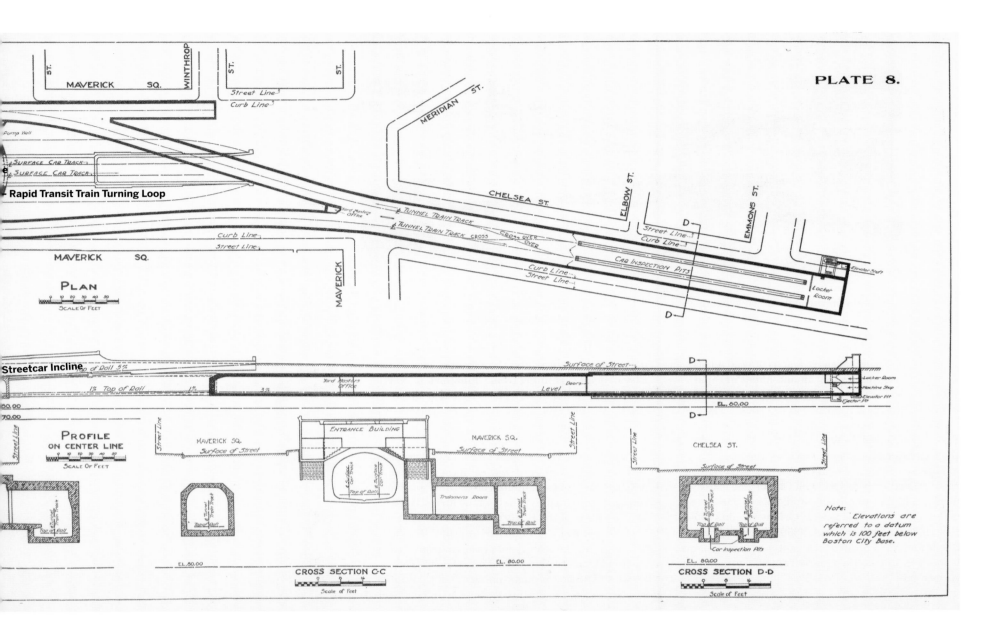

PLATE 8.

MAVERICK SQ.

Rapid Transit Train Turning Loop

Streetcar Incline

PLAN
Scale of Feet

MAVERICK SQ.

MERIDIAN ST.

CHELSEA ST.

ELBOW ST.

EMMONS ST.

Car Inspection Pits

Locker Room

Elevator Shaft

PROFILE
ON CENTER LINE
Scale of Feet

Note:
Elevations are
referred to a datum
which is 100 feet below
Boston City Base.

CROSS SECTION C-C
Scale of Feet

CROSS SECTION D-D
Scale of Feet

Figure 5.33 Maverick Station Head House, 1925

Figure 5.34 Maverick Station Head House Interior, 1925

natural light flooding in through multiple windows (Figure 5.34).

Along with Maverick Station, and just beyond the rapid transit loop, the BTD created a short tunnel. There, several short tracks offered a location for storage and minor maintenance of rapid transit cars. East Boston Tunnel rapid transit cars in need of significant service were brought via the East Boston Tunnel Extension, the Cambridge Street Incline, the New West Boston Bridge, and the Cambridge Subway to the Eliot Square Shops in Harvard Square. The movement of East Boston rapid transit cars to and from Cambridge lasted until the MTA established rapid transit car storage and maintenance facilities at Orient Heights in East Boston. Opened in the early 1950s, Orient Heights Shops and Yard remains the center of maintenance, inspection, and storage for MBTA Blue Line rapid transit cars.

The BERy's Elevated Division

While the BTC was overseeing the design and construction of the Tremont Street Subway, the Charlestown Bridge, and the East Boston Tunnel in the late 1890s, the BERy orchestrated the construction of Boston's first rapid transit lines, many of which followed routes similar to those proposed by the Rapid Transit Commission in 1892 (Figure 3.10). The BERy's first rapid transit line ran through downtown Boston, from Charlestown to Roxbury. This line formed the foundation of the BERy's Elevated Division.

The Elevated Division was initially composed of four major segments (Figure 5.35): the Charlestown Elevated, an el extending northward from downtown to Sullivan Square; the Washington Street Elevated, an el extending southward from downtown into Roxbury; a tunnel running through the middle of downtown; and the Atlantic Avenue Elevated, an el running from Chinatown to North Station along the waterfront. These four major segments were tied together by short sections of el, one at Causeway Street north of downtown, and one at Castle Street south of downtown.

The Elevated Division epitomized rapid transit, with dedicated rights-of-way composed of elevated railways and tunnels, limited stops, and stations spaced approximately a half a mile apart. Rapid transit trains of the BERy's Elevated Division transported people from Charlestown to Roxbury and back in significantly less time than streetcars plodding along traffic-choked city streets. The Elevated Division brought hundreds of thousands of residents closer to downtown Boston and connected Boston's two steam railroad terminals by a single, seven-minute ride.

The BERy operated much of its Elevated Division as the "Main Line Elevated," the genesis of the MBTA's Orange Line. The Main Line Elevated consisted of the Charlestown Elevated, the downtown tunnel, and the Washington Street Elevated. It was essentially the entire Elevated Division minus the Atlantic Avenue Elevated. At both the Charlestown and Roxbury ends of the Main Line Elevated, the BERy constructed significant terminal stations for the interchange of passengers between rapid transit trains and streetcars.

Construction of the BERy's elevated railways, along with associated back-of-house storage and

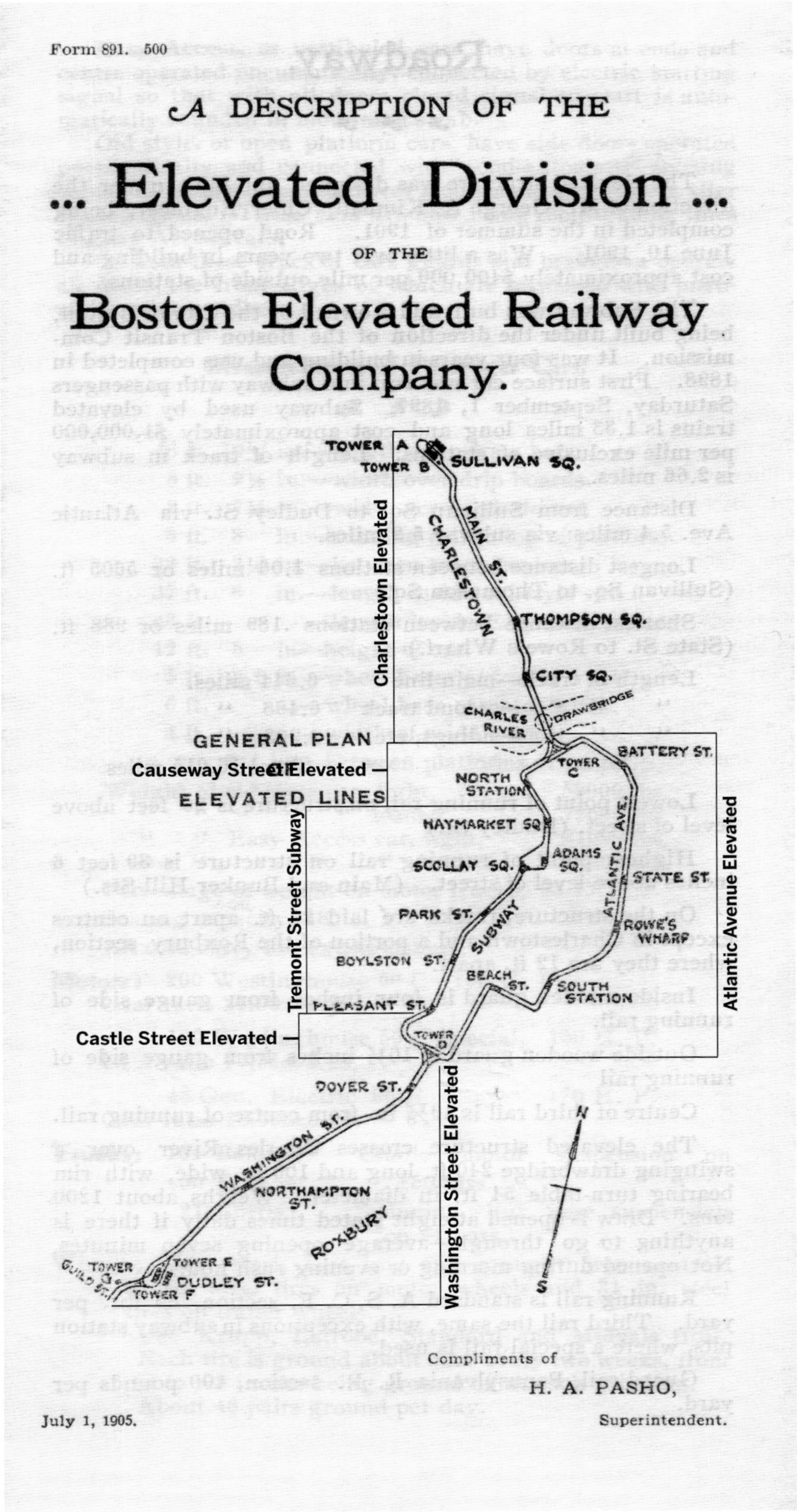

Figure 5.35 Mapping the BERy's Elevated Division, 1905

In conjunction with the opening of its rapid transit lines, the BERy began issuance of an informational brochure describing the infrastructure, operation, cars, and equipment of its Elevated Division. The cover of the July 1, 1905 edition features an elegantly minimal map of the Boston's rapid transit lines.

maintenance facilities for rapid transit cars, commenced in late summer 1899 and wrapped up during summer 1901. Within two years' time the Charlestown, Washington Street, and Atlantic Avenue Elevateds, with a combined length of six and a half miles, rose to form a steely spine through the heart of Boston. The Main Line Elevated opened for rapid transit service on June 10, 1901. The Atlantic Avenue Elevated opened shortly thereafter, on August 22.

BERy Elevated Type 1 Rapid Transit Cars

The tracks of the BERy's Elevated Division were constructed for electric rapid transit trains. Unlike the elevated railroads of the 1870s in New York City, with their steam locomotives pulling trains of non-powered passenger coaches, the BERy's Elevated Division opened with electric rapid transit cars in MU operation. The BERy designated the first rapid transit cars to operate on its Elevated Division as Elevated Type 1 cars. These were numbered 01 through 0150 and constructed by three different manufacturers. BERy Elevated Type 1 car number 01 was built by the Wason Manufacturing Company (Wason) (Figure 5.36). Cars 01, 02, and 03, prototypes which the BERy used for testing, arrived in

Boston in late 1899. Over time, BERy Elevated Type 1 cars were joined or replaced by newer car types, each numbered sequentially higher than the previous type.

BERy Elevated Type 1 rapid transit cars closely resembled steam railroad coaches of the same time period, but with doors located at the middle of each side, in addition to each end. An enclosed motorman's cab occupied one third of each vestibule (Figure 5.37). The BERy described its Type 1 cars as being "of the easy access type...having doors at ends and middle operated pneumatically." The doors were operated by guards and brakemen. Only after all doors were closed on all cars did a signal ring in the motorman's cab, indicating that it was safe for him to proceed. Initially, riders were encouraged to enter each car through the end vestibules and depart via the side doors.

Type 1 cars seated forty-eight passengers. Including standing room, the cars easily carried over 100 riders each. Cars were elegant, with interiors featuring polished brass fittings and exteriors adorned in deep red paint with gold lettering. Type 1 cars were powered by electric motors of approximately 160–170 horsepower and traveled at forty miles per hour. In 1910 the BERy reported an average speed for its Type 1 cars travelling between

Figure 5.36 Elevated Type 1 Rapid Transit Car #01, 1900
Paused near Canal Street, car number 01 was one of the first electric rapid transit cars to operate in Boston.

Figure 5.37 Elevated Type 1 Car #0103, June 26, 1902

From his cab, a motorman pauses his train on the el, alongside a semaphore signal (left). The position of the semaphore's arm and configuration of its lights indicated to the driver how, if at all, to proceed. To the right of the cab is an open vestibule. A ceiling-mounted sign within the car requests riders to "leave by side door."

Charleston and Roxbury of sixteen and a half miles per hour.

Rapid Transit via the Tremont Street Subway

Early on during its planning of Boston's first rapid transit lines, the BERy sought to construct elevated railways through downtown Boston, where land was limited and highly valued. Reacting to the risk posed by the loud, unsightly, and dirty structures to private property, the city banned the construction of elevated railways through the center of downtown. With its action, Boston protected a historic and vibrant portion of the city from partial demolition. Ironically, in the middle of the twentieth century, the same city, drunk on federal urban renewal and highway dollars in the 1950s and 1960s, failed to protect its historic core and lost hundreds of properties it once saved from demolition for elevated railways. Boston's mid-twentieth century sanctioning of the destruction of large parts of downtown allowed the erection of an elevated transportation infrastructure, not for rapid transit trains, but for automobiles and trucks. The Central Artery has come and gone, but the scars remain.

After Boston prohibited elevated railways from the center of downtown, the BERy looked to weave rapid transit beneath and around the area of prohibition. A rapid transit tunnel through downtown, complemented by elevated railways outside of the area from which elevated railways were banned, became the BERy's solutions. Since it would take time to design and construct a new rapid transit tunnel, the BTC and the BERy decided that the Tremont Street Subway would be temporarily utilized as the downtown tunnel portion of the Elevated Division.

Preparations begin in 1900 to alter the Tremont Street Subway to accommodate rapid transit trains. At the northern and southern ends of the subway, new sections of elevated railway were constructed. One section started at the Haymarket Incline and ran along Causeway Street. The other ran along Castle Street and linked to the Pleasant Street Incline. New inclines allowed rapid transit trains to ascend and descend between the new els and the existing subway inclines. Work at the Haymarket and Pleasant Street Inclines took place during a blitz that started at 8:15 p.m. on Friday June 7, 1901 and ended at 5:00 a.m. on Saturday June 8. On Saturday and Sunday, the BERy ran test trains and instruction trains for its motormen. Rapid transit service within the Tremont Street Subway commenced on Monday morning, June 10.

Within the subway, significant changes were made to accommodate rapid transit trains. Parts of tunnels, originally designed for streetcars, were enlarged to allow passage of larger and longer

Figure 5.38 Park Street Station, August 5, 1901
From 1901 to 1908, rapid transit trains ran along the outermost tracks at Park Street Station. The wooden platform (left) on the southbound platform allowed passengers to walk up to and board southbound rapid transit cars. The lower portion of the platform remained as is served by streetcars just on the other side of the information booth (right).

rapid transit trains. Third rail power was installed along the two outer tracks at Boylston Street, Park Street, and Haymarket Square Stations, as well as through Scollay Square Station and along the northbound track at Adams Square Station. Portions of platforms at subway stations were raised to allow passengers to board rapid transit trains, with their higher floors than streetcars. At stations that saw both streetcar and rapid transit service, wood stairs were installed as transitions between high-level rapid transit platforms and low-level streetcar platforms (Figure 5.38 and Figure 5.39).

From June 10, 1901 to November 30, 1908, both rapid transit trains and streetcars operated within the Tremont Street Subway (Figure 5.40). Streetcars that previously traversed the entire length of the subway were rerouted to serve rapid transit stations along the Main Line Elevated. Free transfers were possible for riders between rapid transit trains and streetcars at Park Street and Boylston Street Stations. Streetcars continued to access the western end of the Tremont Street Subway at the Public Garden Incline, using the two innermost tracks between Boylston and Park Street Stations.

Figure 5.39 Boylston Street Station, November 12, 1908
Short stairways connect the streetcar side "Surface Platform" with the rapid transit side "Elevated Platform" of the northbound platform at Boylston Street Station. The configuration existed from 1901 to 1908, when the station was served by both streetcars and rapid transit trains.

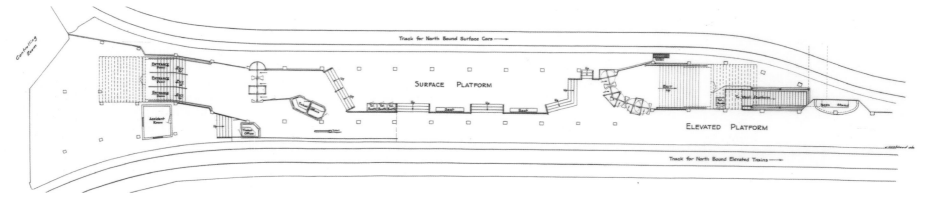

Figure 5.40 Park Street Station, Circa 1901
A vintage composite image reveals rapid transit trains on the outer tracks and streetcars on the inner tracks, a configuration in place from 1901 to 1908.

Northbound streetcars turned around via the inner loop at Park Street Station. Rapid transit trains utilized only two tracks to run between Park Street and Scollay Square Stations. This precluded streetcars from doing the same. At Haymarket Square Station, streetcars ran along the inner two tracks and rapid transit trains ran along the outer two.

At the northern end of the subway, streetcars entered and exited the underground along the central pair of the four tracks of the Haymarket Incline (Figure 5.41). The outer two tracks were reserved for rapid transit trains running between the Tremont Street Subway and the el over Causeway Street. Streetcars that entered the

Figure 5.41 The Haymarket Incline, July 19, 1901
From 1901 to 1908, the Haymarket Incline was configured to allow rapid transit trains to utilize the Tremont Street Subway. During that time period, streetcars were relegated to the inner pair of tracks and rapid transit trains used the outermost tracks.

Pleasant Street Portal

SB Platform

NB Platform

Station Entrance

Pleasant Street

— Southbound Train

Figure 5.42 Pleasant Street Station, July 2, 1901
On level below the street, the open air station was served by rapid transit trains running into and out of the Tremont Street Subway through the Pleasant Street Portal (top). The central two of the portal's four openings, used by streetcars from 1897 to 1901, and again after 1908, are blocked by the station's platforms. A southbound train has just departed the station and is passing beneath the Pleasant Street Bridge.

Figure 5.43 Downtown Boston Rapid Transit Lines, 1902
A Boston Transit Commission map highlights: elevated rapid transit lines as solid dark blue lines; the Tremont Street Subway as solid red lines; and the incomplete East Boston Tunnel (right) as solid and dashed red lines. A proposed rapid transit line from Cambridge (top) is represented as a dark blue dashed line, where it runs over the surface and the Charles River, and as a red dashed line, where it runs underground into Scollay Square. Circles denote public transit stations.

subway at the Haymarket Incline could not proceed beyond Scollay Square and serve Park Street Station. Instead, they utilized the Brattle Loop, serving only Scollay Square and Adams Square Stations before returning to Haymarket Square Station and the Haymarket Incline.

The tunnels connecting the Pleasant Street Portal and Boylston Street Station were entirely turned over to rapid transit service and withdrawn from use by streetcars. Boston formally protested the loss of streetcar access, citing the expense and time it had spent to previously install the complicated infrastructure for streetcars at the Pleasant Street end of the subway. As part of the conversion of the subway to rapid transit service, a new, open-air rapid transit station was built at the Pleasant

Street Portal. Pleasant Street Station (Figure 5.42) was in use from June 10, 1901 to November 29, 1908.

The BTC highlighted downtown Boston's elevated railways, subways, and tunnel on a 1902 map (Figure 5.43). The map showed short elevated railways, one at Causeway Street, where the Charlestown and Atlantic Avenue Elevated met, and one at Castle Street, where the Washington Street and Atlantic Avenue Elevateds linked up. The BERy removed the elevated railway over Castle Street in 1936.

The Charlestown Elevated
On the Boston side of the Charlestown Bridge, the BERy's Elevated Division branched between the Charlestown Elevated, the Atlantic

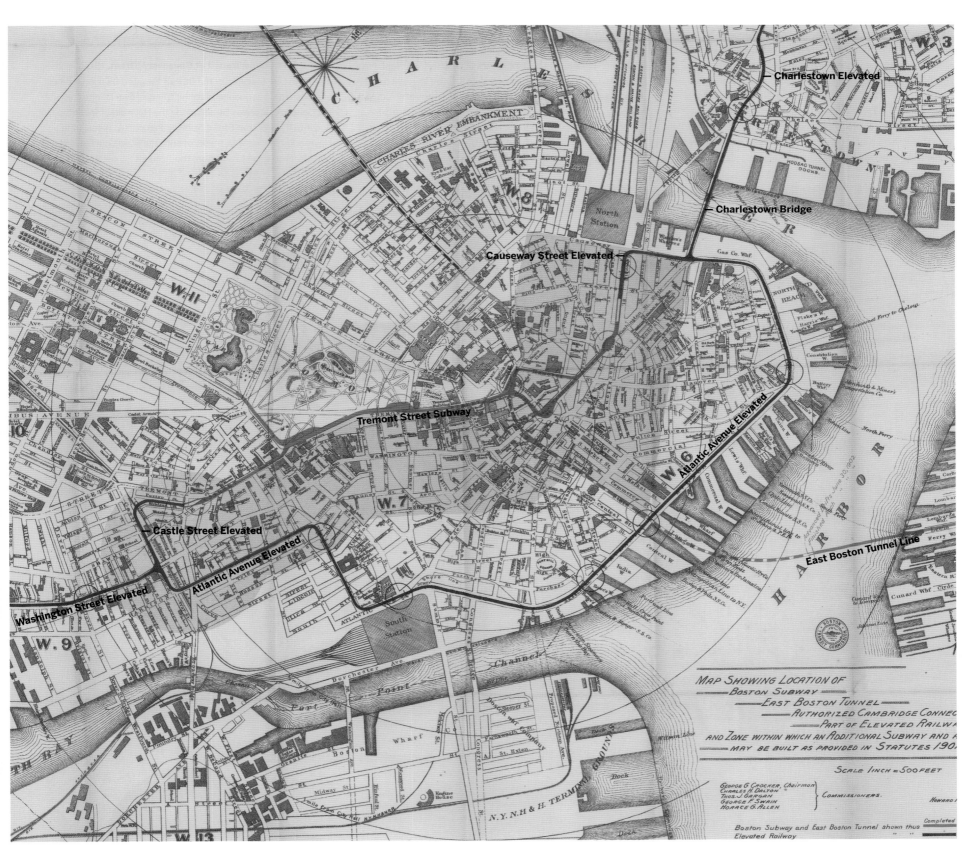

Charlestown Elevated

Charlestown Bridge

Causeway Street Elevated

Tremont Street Subway

Atlantic Avenue Elevated

Castle Street Elevated

Atlantic Avenue Elevated

East Boston Tunnel Line

Washington Street Elevated

MAP SHOWING LOCATION OF
BOSTON SUBWAY
EAST BOSTON TUNNEL
AUTHORIZED CAMBRIDGE CONNEC
PART OF ELEVATED RAILWA
AND ZONE WITHIN WHICH AN ADDITIONAL SUBWAY AND
MAY BE BUILT AS PROVIDED IN STATUTES 190

SCALE 1 INCH = 500 FEET

GEORGE G CROCKER, Chairman
CHARLES H. DALTON
THOS. J. GARGAN } COMMISSIONERS.
GEORGE F. SWAIN
HORACE G. ALLEN

Boston Subway and East Boston Tunnel shown thus
Elevated Railway

Avenue Elevated, and the el over Causeway Street (Figure 5.44). Just past where the Causeway Street el turned ninety degrees towards the Haymarket Incline, at the corner of Haverhill and Causeway Streets, was an el station named North Station (Figure 5.45). Below the station, at street level, an open-sided shelter protected patrons at the streetcar stop at the corner of Canal and Causeway Streets (Figure 5.46).

Running north from Causeway Street, the double-track Charlestown Elevated crossed the Charles River on the upper level of the Charlestown Bridge. On the Charlestown side of the river, the el continued north along Main Street, following very closely the "Charlestown Route" from the Rapid Transit Commission's 1892 map (Figure 3.10). Between the Charlestown Bridge and Sullivan Square, the Charlestown Elevated was punctuated

Figure 5.44 Rapid Transit at Causeway Street, 1902

The Main Line Elevated of the BERy's Elevated Division follows els (dashed) in sequence from the Charlestown Bridge (top left), above Causeway Street, along the Haymarket Incline, and into the Tremont Street Subway. Figure 5.41 reveals the Haymarket Incline with tracks of both the Main Line Elevated and streetcars run to and from the Tremont Street Subway.

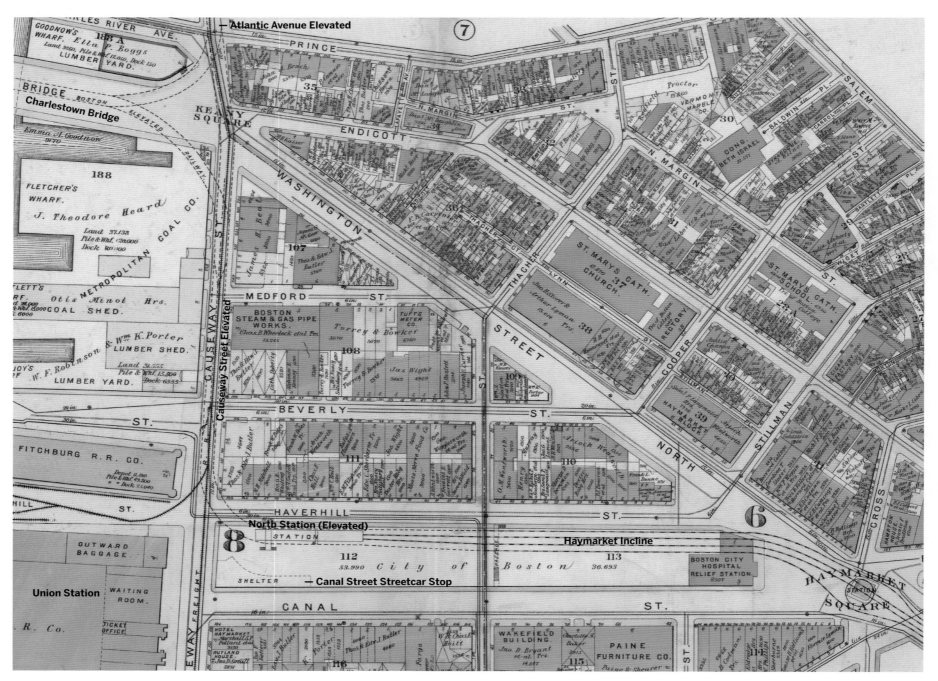

Figure 5.45 North Station on the El, December 2, 1907

North Station on the el exhibits the typical configuration of a BERy elevated station. A head house (left) encloses a ticket office, waiting room, and toilets. A central platform is served by southbound trains on one side (shown) and northbound trains on the other. The platform is accessorized (from center to right) by a penny scale, a Schrafft's Candy dispenser, a framed map of the BERy's system, and advertisements. The map (center) was also published as one side of a two-sided folding map.

Figure 5.46 View from Causeway Street, June 13, 1901

From left to right are the Main Line Elevated, North Station on the el, and the street-level Canal Street streetcar shelter. The Haymarket Incline is in the distance. A three-car rapid transit train pauses at North Station before descending the incline into the Tremont Street Subway.

Figure 5.47 Thompson Square Station, April 1, 1902
Workers put the finishing touches on the last station to open along the Charlestown Elevated.

Figure 5.48 City Square Station, September 20, 1898
Architectural drawings represent the near-final design for City Square Station. A plan (top) and elevation (bottom) lay out the station's overall design, including its amenities, platforms, and entrance and exit stairways.

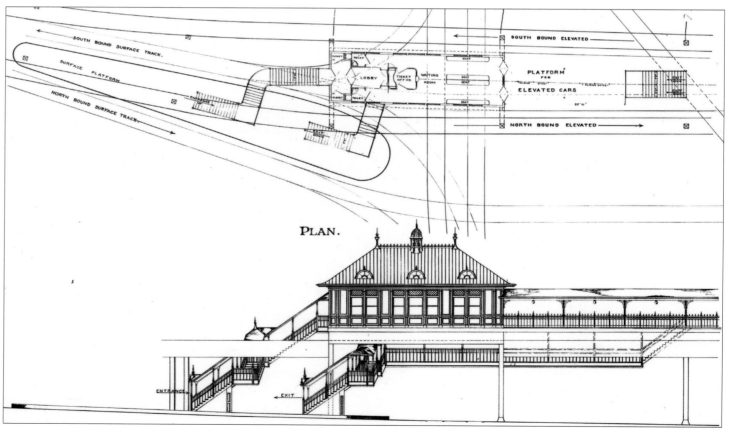

by two intermediate stations, Thompson Square Station (Figure 5.47) and City Square Station (Figure 5.48 and Figure 5.49). Each station featured a track-level head house enclosing a ticket lobby, toilets, and small waiting area. Outside of each cupola-topped head house was a center-island platform sheltered by a standing-seam metal roof. Thompson Square Station opened a year after the rest of the Charlestown Elevated.

Sullivan Square Terminal

The northern terminus of the Charlestown Elevated was at Sullivan Square, in the extreme northwest corner of Boston. There, the BERy erected a temple to public transportation, Sullivan Square Terminal (Figure 5.50). Initially served by streetcars and rapid transit trains, and later by buses and trackless trolleys, Sullivan Square Terminal was a multi-level, multi-modal transit hub.

Figure 5.49 City Square Station, May 31, 1901

A two-car rapid transit train (right) has just departed from City Square Station on the Charlestown Elevated. The train is bound for the Charlestown Bridge and downtown Boston.

Figure 5.50 Sullivan Square Terminal, May 25, 1908

At the level of the Charlestown Elevated, rapid transit tracks split. To the left, a pair of tracks continue above Main Street and around the backside of the terminal. To the right, a single track extends into the second level of the station. The terminal's arched shed roof serves as a backdrop to a large clock. Below the clock, and above the portal through with rapid transit trains entered the terminal, "Boston Elevated Railway" is carved into the station's facade. Nothing shown remains today.

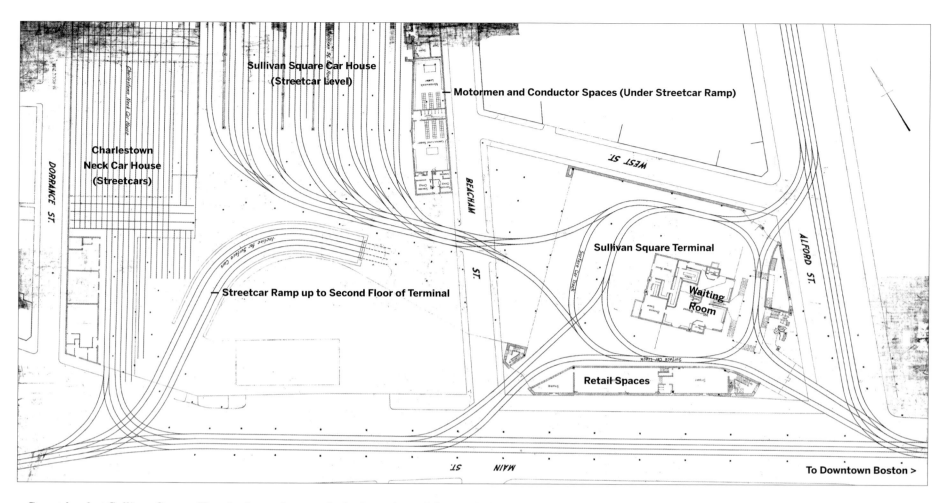

Labels on figure:
Sullivan Square Car House (Streetcar Level)
Motormen and Conductor Spaces (Under Streetcar Ramp)
Charlestown Neck Car House (Streetcars)
Streetcar Ramp up to Second Floor of Terminal
Sullivan Square Terminal
Waiting Room
Retail Spaces
DORRANCE ST.
BEACHAM ST.
WEST ST.
ALFORD ST.
MAIN ST.
To Downtown Boston >

Street level at Sullivan Square Terminal was the domain of streetcars (Figure 5.51). Loop tracks allowed streetcars to parade through boarding areas sheltered by the station's second level. At the center of the loops was an enclosure (Figure 5.52), sheltering a waiting room, ticket office, lunch counter, and barber shop. While streetcars paraded around the enclosure on loops of tracks, inside, customers looked out through large windows upon a carousel of streetcars arriving and departing. Retail space lined the Main Street side of the terminal.

The upper level of Sullivan Square Terminal was served by both streetcars and rapid transit trains (Figure 5.53 and Figure 5.54). It opened with two broad transfer platforms, each served by five dead-end streetcar tracks and a single run-through

Figure 5.51 Sullivan Square Street-level Plan, June 1906
Streetcar tracks (pairs of solid lines) weave around and through the street-level of Sullivan Square Terminal. The tracks connect with those within the Sullivan Square Car House. Black dots represent vertical supports for elevated railway structures.

Figure 5.52 Street-level at the Terminal, June 24, 1901
Streetcar tracks run in front of the lower level waiting room.

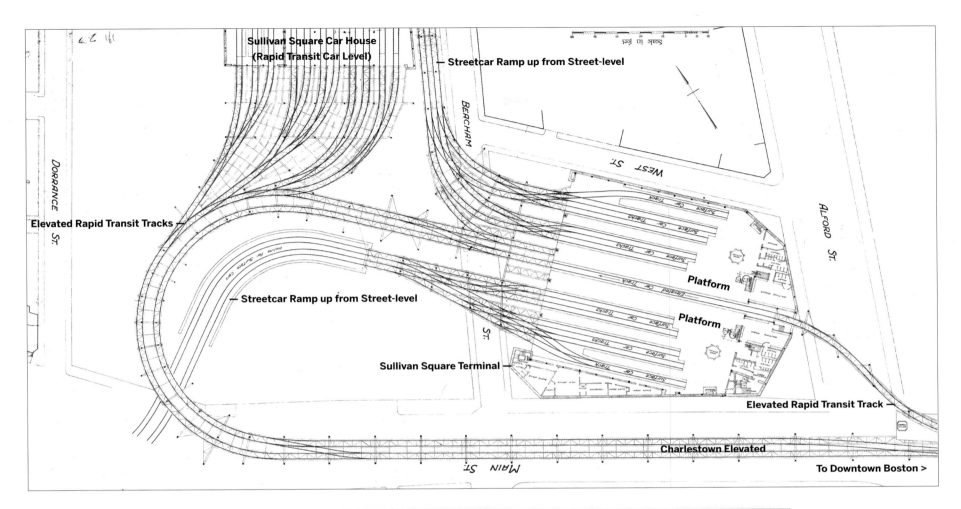

Sullivan Square Car House
(Rapid Transit Car Level)

Streetcar Ramp up from Street-level

BEACHAM

DORRANCE ST.

Elevated Rapid Transit Tracks

WEST ST.

ALFORD ST.

Platform

Streetcar Ramp up from Street-level

Platform

Sullivan Square Terminal

Elevated Rapid Transit Track

Charlestown Elevated

MAIN ST.

To Downtown Boston >

Figure 5.53 Sullivan Square Second Floor Plan, June 1902
Elevated rapid transit tracks run along Main Street, through
the terminal, and into the upper level of the Sullivan Square
Car House. Ramps, one at Main Street and one at Beacham
Street, carry a pair of streetcar tracks each between street-
level and the second level of the terminal. There, five stub-end
streetcar tracks on the Main Street side were generally served
by cars from Arlington, Medford, and Somerville. Five stub-end
tracks on the West Street side were generally served by cars
from Malden and Everett.

Figure 5.54 Transferring at Sullivan Square, July 26, 1901
On the station's second level, transit patrons transfer between
a rapid transit train (center) and streetcars serving points in
Medford (left).

Figure 5.55 Sullivan Square Second Floor, July 26, 1901
A rapid transit train pauses on the central track on the terminal's second level. Open-type streetcars occupy the eastern streetcar tracks (left). The terminal's third floor, occupied by offices of the BERy (top), spans the portal through which rapid transit trains entered the station from the Charlestown Elevated. The direction of the view is opposite of that shown in Figure 5.56.

Figure 5.56 Under the Terminal's Shed, August 13, 1901
Taken from the station's third story directly over the central rapid transit track, a photograph shows transit patrons waiting on the transfer platforms on either side of the central rapid transit track. Streetcar tracks lie to the left and right.

Figure 5.57 Newsstands on the Second Level, 1901
Two ornate newsstands serve as information hubs and places to purchase a cigar. A man in a bowler hat reads his paper as he leans casually against the newsstand in the foreground.

rapid transit track (Figure 5.55). The platforms, each punctuated by five streetcar tracks, mirrored each other across the central rapid transit track (Figure 5.56). Each transfer platform had its own rest rooms, newsstand (Figure 5.57), soda fountain, and stairway leading down to the lower, street-level trolley boarding area. The upper level platforms and their eleven tracks were covered by an arched train shed, over three stories tall at its apex. Steel and glass enclosed the ends of the shed (Figure 5.58).

Beneath the soaring shed was a spacious train hall, akin to a grand steam railroad terminal then found in London or Paris.

Rapid transit trains entered the train hall through a portal punctuating the south side of the terminal (Figure 5.59). Trains roared out of the portal and into the expanse of the train hall as passengers lined up to board the arriving train. Rapid transit trains departed from the terminal via an elevated railway that looped back to Main Street

Figure 5.58 Rear of Sullivan Square Terminal, Circa 1910

A rapid transit train (left) and streetcars (middle) operate on elevated tracks and ramps serving the station's upper level.

Figure 5.59 Sullivan Square Terminal, Circa 1901

A rapid transit train (center) moves from the Charlestown Elevated into the second level of Sullivan Square Terminal. Underneath the el (left), streetcars run along Main Street.

and the Charlestown Elevated. The loop configuration allowed trains to pass into the terminal, pause to exchange passengers, and then exit in the same direction of movement to head back downtown.

Behind Sullivan Square Terminal, the BERy erected a layered web of tracks, ramps, and elevated railways (Figure 5.60). Beyond lay the Charlestown Neck and Sullivan Square Car Houses. The bi-level Sullivan Square Car House, constructed by the BERy concurrently with the terminal, featured a dozen streetcar tracks at street-level. Directly above, on a second level, the car house featured no fewer than eleven tracks for rapid transit trains. There, the BERy maintained and stored its fleet of Elevated Division rapid transit cars, which, by spring 1910, consisted of 219 cars. Charlestown Neck

Figure 5.60 Behind Sullivan Square Terminal, May 9, 1901

A north-facing photograph taken from the back of the station shows a sprawling landscape of elevated railways. Tracks in the foreground serve the upper level of the terminal (out of view, below and to the right). Rapid transit cars sit in front of the Sullivan Square Car House (middle). The roof of the Charlestown Neck Car House squats in the background (left). Far beyond is the smoke stack of the BERy's Charlestown Power Station. Almost nothing shown exists today.

Car House, which predated Sullivan Square Car House, was utilized for streetcar operations by the BERy.

In late summer 1912, the BERy significantly altered Sullivan Square Terminal to improve service (Figure 5.61). Rapid transit platforms were extended to accommodate eight-car trains. The stub-end streetcar tracks on the west side of the upper level were replaced with run-through tracks connected to a new loop. Along Main Street, the BERy added a large platform dedicated for the boarding of rapid transit trains bound for Boston. The original rapid transit platforms were converted to unloading only. Outside of the terminal the BERy installed connections for a proposed extension of the Main Line Elevated towards Malden. An expanded footprint of Sullivan Square Terminal, along with acres of surrounding public transit

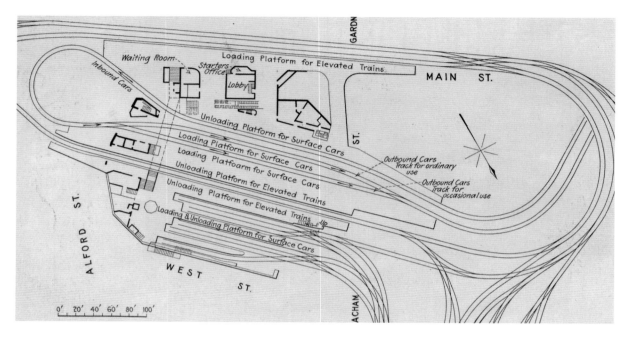

Figure 5.61 A Renovated Second Level, March 1, 1913
A rapid transit train loading platform (top) and streetcar loop (left) were added to the second level of Sullivan Square Terminal in 1912. The loop expedited movement of street-cars through the upper level. Instead of pulling into one of the stub-end tracks on the east side and then reversing out, streetcars entered the reconfigured west side tracks, stopped once to discharge passengers, turned around via the loop, and returned to pick up passengers before exiting the terminal.

Figure 5.62 Streetcar Departure Boards, July 16, 1913
In the train hall, large signs list routes and destinations of streetcars departing from numbered tracks. Track numbers illuminated to the right of each route and destination.

infrastructure, is depicted on a 1912 real estate map (Figure 5.63). By summer 1913, the BERy hung illuminated destination signs within the terminal's upper level (Figure 5.62). The electrically controlled signs indicated the numbered berth location of an arriving streetcar.

The Everett Extension

After serving nearly eighteen years as the northern terminus of the Charlestown Elevated, Sullivan Square Terminal became Sullivan Square Station on March 15 1919. On that date, the BERy inaugurated rapid transit service beyond Sullivan Square,

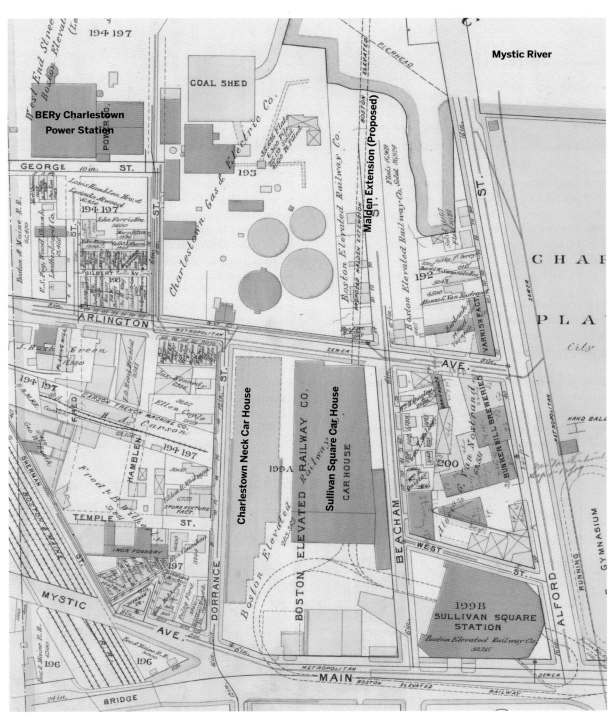

Figure 5.63 Transit Infrastructure at Sullivan Square, 1912

A real estate map, covering the far northwest portion of Charlestown, depicts the BERy's Charlestown Power Station (top left), proposed Malden Extension of the Charlestown Elevated (top), Charlestown Neck Car House (middle), Sullivan Square Car House (middle), and Sullivan Square Terminal, with its 1912 additions (bottom right).

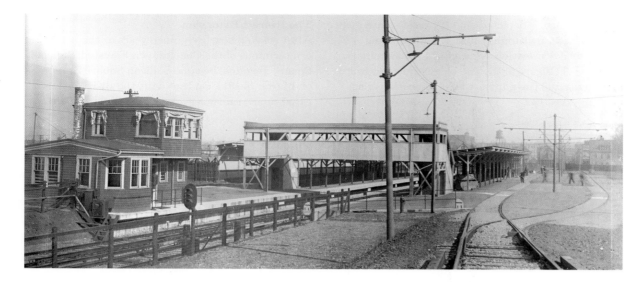

northward across the Mystic River, and into a terminal in the city of Everett. Initially proposed by the BERy to extend beyond Everett and into Malden, the one mile long Everett Extension brought rapid transit service north of Boston for the first time.

Like Sullivan Square Terminal, Everett Terminal opened as a transfer station served by rapid transit trains and streetcars. Unlike Sullivan Square Terminal, Everett Terminal was not a monumental structure. Everett Terminal was a functional assemblage of wood and steel frame structures with simple concrete platforms (Figure 5.64). Over forty years after its opening, Everett Terminal remained a modest affair (Figure 5.65).

Contiguous with Everett Terminal, the BERy constructed a sprawling complex of maintenance, repair, and inspection facilities for its rapid transit

vehicles. Everett Shops underwent many expansions and alterations. Initially used by the BERy as a centralized repair facility for rapid transit cars of its Elevated Division, the shops were subsequently used by the MTA and the MBTA.

Today, the BERy's Everett Terminal, Sullivan Square Station, and the Charlestown Elevated no longer exist. Despite the absence of the el and its stations, much of the land and some of the support buildings once occupied by the BERy and MTA, both in Charlestown and in Everett, remain in use by the MBTA. Between Sullivan Square and the Mystic River, near former sites of the Charlestown Neck and Sullivan Square Car Houses, the MBTA operates acres of back-of-house facilities including, offices, shops, its central stores, and the Charlestown Bus Garage. The site of Sullivan Square Station is currently an empty lot. Across the river

Figure 5.66 Erecting the Elevated, November 1, 1899
Construction of the Washington Street Elevated is underway in front of the Cathedral of the Holy Cross in Boston's South End. The derricks perched upon the superstructure of the el are being used to hoist additional parts into place. Piles of pre-fabricated pieces lie in the foreground. Crews moved the mantis-like derricks forward onto newly erected portions of the el to erect the next section.

in Everett, in the shadow of the Encore Casino, the MBTA operates Everett shops for the maintenance, repair, and rebuilding of vehicles and their components.

The Washington Street Elevated
The portion of the BERy's Elevated Division that extended from downtown into Roxbury was the Washington Street Elevated. It followed much of the "Roxbury Route" laid out on the Rapid Transit Commission's 1892 map (Figure 3.10). Initially, the Washington Street Elevated ran from an elevated incline at the Pleasant Street Portal of the Tremont Street Subway, over Castle Street, along Washington Street, to a terminus at Dudley Street. South of Dudley Street, the BERy established a modest

inspection, layover, and repair facility for rapid transit trains at Guild Street. The distance from Guild Street to Sullivan Square Terminal, via the Main Line Elevated, was approximately six and a half miles.

During 1899–1901, the Washington Street Elevated was constructed simultaneously with the Charlestown and Atlantic Avenue Elevateds. The superstructures of all els of the BERy's Elevated Division were assembled like full-scale erector sets from thousands of riveted steel pieces, many pre-fabricated off-site (Figure 5.66).

Between Pleasant and Dudley Streets, the Washington Street Elevated featured two intermediate stations, one at Dover Street (now East Berkeley Street), and another, at Northampton Street (Figure 5.67). Dover and Northampton

Figure 5.67 Northampton Station, May 3, 1901
A northbound two-car train serves Northampton Station, one of two Washington Street elevated stations erected in Boston's South End.

Stations, along with other intermediate stations of the BERy's Elevated Division, were designed by architect Alexander Wadsworth Longfellow. Jr. The designer was the nephew of Henry Wadsworth Longfellow, author of poems incorporating elements of Boston's transit infrastructure, including "The Bridge." A. W. Longfellow Jr. won a design competition held by the BERy with his designs for functional but finely fenestrated stations. The exteriors of Longfellow's stations were marked by copper sheathing, cupolas, clearstory windows, and hipped gable roofs with generous overhangs. At street level, streetcars served stops beneath each station.

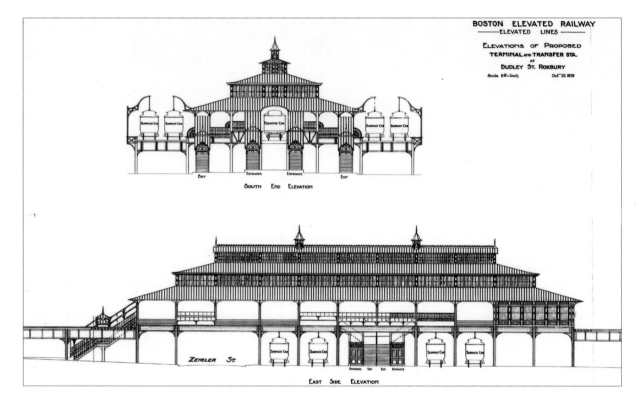

Figure 5.68 Designing Dudley Street, October 25, 1898
Architectural elevations represent a late design iteration for Dudley Street Terminal. A south elevation (top) shows streetcars flanking the station on elevated tracks and a rapid transit car occupying a single, central track. An east elevation (bottom) shows streetcars at ground-level running perpendicular to the rapid transit track, one story above. The terminal was essentially erected as designed above.

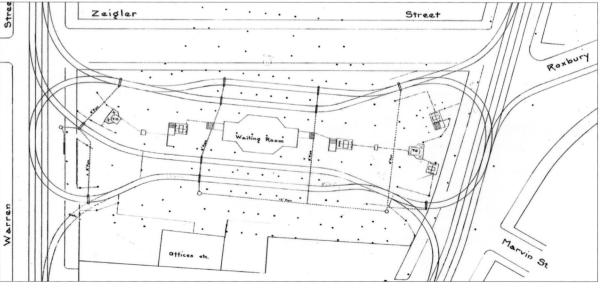

Figure 5.69 Street-level at Dudley Street, April 29, 1910
At ground level, streetcar tracks (paired lines) run though a forest of columns and around a central waiting room.

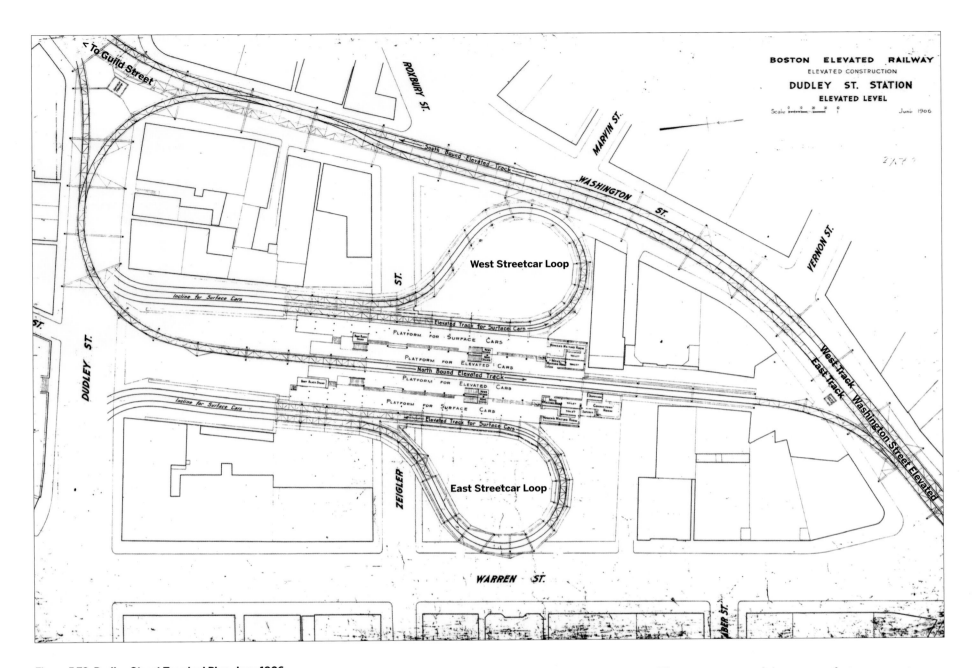

Within the image:
BOSTON ELEVATED RAILWAY
ELEVATED CONSTRUCTION
DUDLEY ST. STATION
ELEVATED LEVEL
Scale   June 1906

ROXBURY ST.
MARVIN ST.
WASHINGTON ST.
VERNON ST.
< To Guild Street
South Bound Elevated Track
West Streetcar Loop
Incline for Surface Cars
Elevated Track for Surface Cars
PLATFORM FOR SURFACE CARS
PLATFORM FOR ELEVATED CARS
North Bound Elevated Track
PLATFORM FOR ELEVATED CARS
PLATFORM FOR SURFACE CARS
Elevated Track for Surface Cars
Incline for Surface Cars
East Streetcar Loop
DUDLEY ST.
ST.
ZEIGLER
WARREN ST.
West Track Washington Street Elevated
East Track

Figure 5.70 Dudley Street Terminal Plan, June 1906

On a plan of Dudley Street Terminal, the double-track Washington Street Elevated runs from the bottom right to the top left. Southbound trains arriving from downtown followed the eastern track of the el. Above the intersection of Washington and Dudley Streets (top left), the el diverged into two single-track els. One ran to a rapid transit car service area at Guild Street. The other ran into the station. Trains headed northbound via the western track of the Washington Street Elevated. Ramps and loops, mirroring each across the terminal, brought streetcars between street level and the upper level transfer platforms.

Dudley Street Terminal

The initial southern terminus of the Washington Street Elevated was at Roxbury's Dudley Street. There, the BERy established Dudley Street Terminal, a counterpoint to Sullivan Square Terminal. Dudley Street Terminal was a prime example of architect Longfellow's designs and, like Sullivan Square Terminal, was a bi-level place of transfer between rapid transit trains and streetcars (Figure 5.68).

The lower level of Dudley Street Terminal was a street-level streetcar transfer area (Figure 5.69).

There, streetcars plying routes that ran crosstown and typically did not terminate at Dudley Street travelled through loops sheltered by the terminal's upper level. The loops encircled an enclosed waiting room.

The upper level of Dudley Street Terminal, like that at Sullivan Square Terminal, featured a single run-through rapid transit track bracketed by transfer platforms served by elevated streetcar tracks (Figure 5.70). Within the upper level, rapid transit trains passed through a cathedral-like

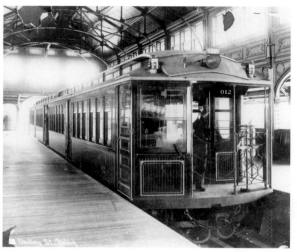

Figure 5.71 Rapid Transit Train Hall, May 3, 1901
The rapid transit track (center) and transfer platforms are enclosed in a structure resembling a cast-iron church. Stairs on each side of the platforms lead down to streetcar boarding areas and station exits.

interior roofed by iron trusses and lit from above by clearstory windows (Figure 5.71 and Figure 5.72).

Streetcars with routes that generally began or terminated at Dudley Street Terminal arrived at one of the two, upper level transfer platforms, one each on the east and west sides of the station. Each transfer platform had a lower section, served by streetcars, and a slightly higher section, served by rapid transit trains. Short flights of stairs connected the platform sections (Figure 5.73). To access their upper level platforms, streetcars moved up and down from street level via two looping ramps. Streetcars arriving from and departing to Forest Hills, Jamaica Plain, and Roxbury Crossing stopped

Figure 5.72 Rapid Transit at Dudley Terminal, May 3, 1901
A test train of BERy Elevated Type 1 rapid transit cars pauses at the upper level of Dudley Terminal.

Figure 5.73 Upper Level Newsstand, November 5, 1902
To the side (left) of a newsstand stocked with cigars and monthly magazines, stairs lead down from the rapid transit platform (foreground) to the eastern streetcar platform.

at the western platform. Streetcars arriving from and departing to points throughout Dorchester stopped at the eastern platform (Figure 5.74).

Dudley Street and Sullivan Square Terminals, along with the rest of the Main Line Elevated, opened for service on June 10, 1901. On that day, the *Boston Daily Globe* reported:

…[A]ll trains moved with click-like regularity, making the north bound trip [from Dudley Terminal to Sullivan Square Terminal] in the scheduled time, 19 minutes, and the south bound trip in 21 minutes.

Figure 5.74 Boarding a Trolley At Dudley Street, 1920
On the station's upper level west-side streetcar platform, patrons wait to board a trolley signed for "Egleston Square."

Figure 5.75 Dudley Street Terminal, Circa 1902

A postcard view depicts a rapid transit train and streetcars serving the upper level of Dudley Street Terminal. A streetcar departs from the west side of the station (left). A streetcar moves up the ramp and into the loop towards the eastern streetcar platform (right). The last car of a rapid transit train pokes out of the center of the terminal (middle).

Figure 5.76 Dudley Street Station, September 20, 1910

Renovations of 1909–10 brought lengthened platforms, additional covered walkways, and more complexity to the station.

Figure 5.77 Upper Level Trolley Platform, 1920

Safety signage and advertising posters decorate one of the upper level streetcar platforms at Dudley Street Station.

Transit patrons arriving at Dudley Street Terminal to board streetcars or rapid transit trains first purchased a ticket from a street-level booth. They then approached a "chopper," a primitive turnstile that shredded their ticket. On the other side of the choppers, patrons either boarded a crosstown streetcar at ground level or alighted to the upper level and boarded an inbound rapid transit train or departing streetcar.

The BERy significantly reconfigured Dudley Street Terminal in 1909–10. The work was coordinated with the BERy's construction of the Forest Hills Extension and the rebuilding of Elevated Division stations to accommodate longer rapid transit trains. In the renovation, the station gained a complex network of elevated walkways (Figure 5.76) and additional signage (Figure 5.77).

Rapid transit trains rumbled through Dudley Street Station until the 1980s, when the MBTA relocated Orange Line rapid transit service from the Washington Street Elevated to a former right-of-way of the New York, New Haven & Hartford Railroad (New Haven). After it relocated rapid transit service out of Dudley Square in 1987, the MBTA dismantled Dudley Street Station and the Washington Street Elevated. Remnants of the terminal building remain in Dudley Square, recycled into a shelter for bus stops. Today's bus transfer station at Dudley Square, which also serves as the southern terminus for the MBTA's Silver Line, is named Dudley Station.

Opening Day on the El

On Monday, June 10, 1901, the BERy opened the Main Line Elevated and rapid transit trains commenced carrying paying passengers between Sullivan Square and Dudley Street Terminals. Each train of BERy Type 1 rapid transit cars was operated by a motorman and crew. The lead car of every train was reserved for passengers wishing to smoke en route. Each terminal and intermediate station was staffed with BERy employees who sold tickets and assisted with the operation of train doors.

The first day of service on the el was marked by overcrowding and operational hiccups. The BERy planned to limit the duration of stops for each train to: thirty seconds at Park Street Station; twenty seconds at Pleasant Street Station; fifteen seconds at City Square, Scollay Square, and Boylston Street

Stations; and ten seconds at Haymarket Square, Dover Street, and Northampton Street Stations. The BERy's careful scheduling went out the window almost immediately. A perfect swarm of regular transit riders, new patrons curious about the el, and riders who quickly realized they could ride the newfangled rapid transit trains all day for a nickel, caused monster crowds and delayed smooth operation of trains along the entire Main Line Elevated. At Sullivan Square, crowds were so intense that people threw nickels in the general direction of BERy employees selling tickets. In return, staff threw tickets back, hoping for a complete reception.

A day after the commencement of service, on June 11, 1901, *The Boston Post* lambasted the BERy:

> There was a seemingly utter inability to handle the vast crowd that wanted to ride, and there was certainly inability to run trains regularly or to make anything like schedule time.

Within the Tremont Street Subway, the overcrowding became dangerous. Per the June 11, 1901 *Boston Post*:

> [At Park Street Station, b]etween 4 and 5 o'clock in the afternoon the mass of humanity whirled and swayed back and forth....It resembled in many respects an incipient riot. As the gates of each train swung open the crowd seeking to leave the [rapid transit] cars, and a second more numerous crowd wishing to board the cars, met with a crush. Guards and station men were pushed aside. It was a football game, 'mass play,' with hundreds of players on each side.

At no station on the road was the situation any worse than at Adams Square between...5 and 6:30 last evening. Between these hours...this station was packed with a hustling, bustling crowd, which defied the efforts of the solitary "L" guard, fighting and swearing for a chance to board the over-crowded trains....

It was utterly impossible to open the gates [of the cars] at either Adams or Haymarket Squares, or the Union Station, as the press from the platform surged in upon the cars, completely preventing egress....men climbed over the locked gates and frequently through the windows, jostling and trampling upon the seats.

Subway stations initially designed for streetcar service became packed with hoards of newbie rapid transit riders. Customers asked the BERy for refunds after being unable to board trains already filled to capacity.

The Boston Post recorded that during "the crush" on the first day of service, the average travel time from Sullivan Square to Dudley Street was one hour. The BERy intended to have its trains make a one-way trip between Sullivan Square and Dudley Street in approximately twenty-five minutes. *The Boston Post* noted that on the first day of service, cars rated for 120 seated passengers and a combined 300 seated and standing, carried 500 riders during rush hours. The paper estimated that half a million people rode the trains on the first day of service. The BERy itself recorded collecting over 200,000 fares during the first tumultuous day on the el. Missing from their count were the many

Figure 5.78 Early BERy Ticket for El Travel, Undated

Figure 5.79 Egleston Square Station, October 23, 1908
Construction continues at the station on the Forest Hills Extension.

consecutive round-trips made by persons who paid only once but took multiple trips to experience Boston's first rapid transit line.

General Bancroft, president of the BERy, was quoted in the June 11, 1901 *Boston Post*: "There are delays, hitches, there was the circus on the surface, and there was an accident to the first north-bound train this morning." The accident was fairly minor. Early in the morning on the first day of service, a loaded train heading out of the Tremont Street Subway towards Charlestown stopped while ascending the Haymarket Incline. Unable to get the fully-loaded train moving up the incline, the motorman backed his train down the slope towards Haymarket Square Station. Inadvertently, he backed his train smack into the front of a train just departing from the station. The incident was not severe enough to cause significant damage or injuries and service resumed shortly afterwards.

Wherever a new elevated railway appeared in Boston, riders and residents partook in a new urban experience, that of looking out from rapid transit trains rattling by second and third story windows of city buildings. In the first weeks after the opening of the Washington Street Elevated, newspapers printed imagined views into private spaces that one might see from the train. In reality, building occupants alongside the el not only had to accept a fresh load of unintentional voyeurs every few minutes, they also had to endure the incredible noise made by each passing train. The August 26, 1901 edition of the *Boston Daily Globe* featured an article titled "Bostonians Developing the L Voice" providing the following account: "[When a train passes,] the speakers have to raise their voices, with the result that they grow loud, and worse still, strident."

The Forest Hills Extension

In 1903 the BERy acquired additional streetcar routes in Boston's West Roxbury neighborhood. To improve connections between those surface routes and its recently opened rapid transit line to Roxbury, the BERy extended the Washington Street Elevated from Dudley Street to Forest Hills, in the Jamaica Plain neighborhood of Boston. The two-and-a-half-mile-long Forest Hills Extension opened for service on November 11, 1909 with two stations, one at Egleston Square, and another at Forest Hills. Egleston Square Station (Figure 5.79) featured a ticket lobby sandwiched one story above the street and one level below the superstructure of the el. Green Street Station, opened on November 11, 1912, was of similar configuration.

With the opening of the Forest Hills extension, Dudley Square Terminal became Dudley Square Station and Forest Hills Terminal became the southern terminus of the BERy's Elevated Division lines. Unlike older rapid transit terminals at Sullivan Square or Dudley Street, Forest Hills Terminal lacked ramps to bring streetcars from street-level up to the level of the el. At Forest Hills, rapid transit tracks and platforms were stacked directly over the portion of the terminal served by streetcars. Figure 5.80 shows the BERy's Forest Hills Terminal in context with the adjacent

Figure 5.80 Forest Hills, August 5, 1910
A train of BERy Elevated Type 1 rapid transit cars occupies an upper level track at the BERy's Forest Hills Terminal (left). The New Haven Railroad's Forest Hills Station sits alongside the railroad's steam railroad line (right).

Forest Hills Station of the New Haven. The lower, streetcar level of the BERy's reinforced concrete terminal featured large openings, framed by piers and arches. The rapid transit level was wrapped in standing seam copper with operable windows. Just south of Forest Hills Terminal, the BERy completed a modest shop and yard for rapid transit cars on March 31, 1923. Shortly thereafter, the BERy closed its Guild Street facility near Dudley Square.

The Washington Street Tunnel

Although the BERy and the BTC orchestrated significant alteration of the Tremont Street Subway to accommodate rapid transit trains, neither intended rapid transit service through the subway to be permanent. As early as 1898, the BTC and the BERy worked towards construction of a new tunnel through downtown that would be a permanent underground connection between the northern and southern portions of the Main Line Elevated. The General Court passed Chapter 534 in 1902, granting the BTC permission to construct a new tunnel

with two tracks for rapid transit trains and two tracks for streetcars under downtown Boston. After exploring various routes for the four-track tunnel, the BTC selected a route that ran mostly beneath Washington Street, between Haymarket Square and Oak Street (Figure 5.81).

At its southern end, the Washington Street Tunnel began at an incline and portal at Ash Street. The incline linked tunnel tracks with those of the elevated railway over Castle Street, the same el that intersected with the Washington Street and Atlantic Avenue Elevateds. From the portal at Nassau Street, the Washington Street Tunnel followed Washington Street northward and passed beneath Haymarket Square.

At its northern end, the tunnel ended at a new portal and incline installed next to the existing Haymarket Incline and Portal of the Tremont Street Subway. From there, a new rapid transit incline connected the tracks of the Washington Street Tunnel with tracks of the el over Causeway Street. The Haymarket Incline was reworked to accommodate parallel pairs of tracks, one for

Figure 5.81 Rapid Transit Through Downtown Boston, 1904
Colored lines highlight the BERy's streetcar subway and rapid transit lines. Tunnels of the Tremont Street Subway are orange. Elevated railways on the Charlestown Bridge, Causeway Street, Atlantic Avenue, and Castle Street are blue. The Washington Street Tunnel is red. The dark black line is a proposed but unbuilt routing of the Washington Street Tunnel.

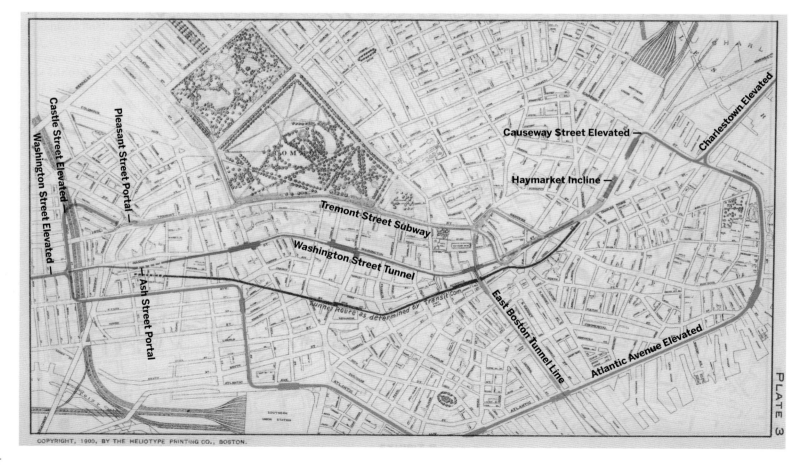

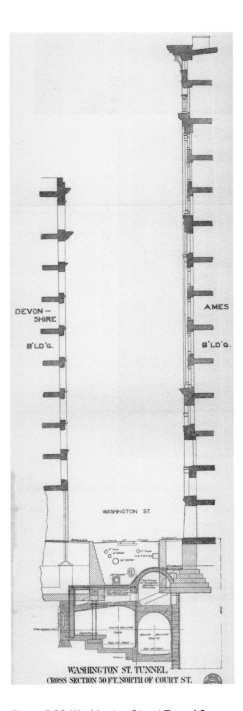

Figure 5.82 Washington Street Tunnel Cross-section, 1906
Intricate engineering was required to thread the Washington Street Tunnel (bottom) between the Devonshire Building (left) and the Ames Building (right).

Figure 5.83 Washington Street Tunnel Cross-section, 1905
A drawing "cuts" through Essex Station. The station's platform (left) slopes down towards the northbound side of the tunnel. The southbound tube (right) is set lower than northbound.

streetcars of the Tremont Street Subway, and another for rapid transit trains of the Washington Street Tunnel (Figure 5.103).

The BTC began construction of the Washington Street Tunnel on October 6, 1904. The project took approximately four years to complete. Due to narrow confines along the route, the tunnel was constructed with only two of the four tracks approved by the Legislature. The final route was not wide enough to accommodate a pair of streetcar tracks in addition to a pair of rapid transit tracks. A cross-section through Washington Street (Figure 5.82) shows the new tunnel squeezed between and inserted partially beneath the foundations of existing buildings. The tight installation was typical along much of the tunnel's route. Careful engineering and expensive underpinning of existing buildings was required along both sides of the tunnel. In its twenty-fourth annual report, the BTC stated that "the cost per mile of track of the tunnel is probably the greatest of any tunnel ever constructed for traffic in a city."

The BTC opened the two-and-a-half-mile-long Washington Street Tunnel on November 30, 1908. As it had with the Tremont Street Subway, the BTC leased the tunnel to the BERy for fit out and transit operations. After the opening of the Washington Street Tunnel, the Tremont Street Subway reverted to the exclusive domain of streetcars.

Before the Washington Street Tunnel came online, spatial constrictions of the Tremont Street Subway limited Main Line Elevated trains to five cars in length. Washington Street Tunnel stations were able to accommodate eight-car rapid transit trains, allowing the BERy to carry more people with a single train through the city.

The double-track Washington Street Tunnel opened with eight rapid transit stations, four on each side of the line. Hemmed in by the foundations of buildings along both sides, the stations were unable to be installed directly opposite and across the tracks from each other. Offset stations, in combination with the BTC naming each for streets intersecting the tunnel's route, led to stations along the northbound tunnel track having distinct names from those along the southbound tunnel track. Along the tunnel, the BTC omitted the word "Street" from official station signage, breaking from the precedent it set at the Tremont Street Subway, where "Street" or "Square" was incorporated into station names and signage. Connecting the Washington Street Tunnel's stations with city streets above were twenty-two stairways, most carved into existing buildings. With one exception, the stations of the Washington Street Tunnel lacked distinctive head houses.

To assist passengers navigating along the Main Line Elevated after the opening of the Washington

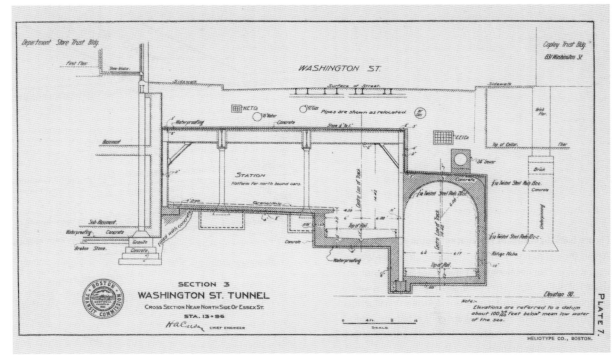

Street Tunnel, the BERy installed pairs of signs in rapid transit cars that travelled between Everett and Forest Hills via the Washington Street Tunnel (Figure 5.84). The larger of the two signs listed all of the stations of the Main Line Elevated, including the Washington Street Tunnel's pairs of offset stations. A separate smaller sign instructed transit users how to make use of the larger sign, the one with the list of station names. The larger sign was designed to be read from top to bottom, or from bottom to top, depending on which direction the reader was traveling. "Order of Main Line Stations" signs were found in rapid transit cars of the Main Line Elevated as early as 1919, after the opening of Everett Terminal. The sign format was retired from use when the MBTA replaced later versions with maps in the late 1960s.

Following down the Order of Main Line Stations sign shown in Figure 5.84, the first offset station pair of the Washington Street Tunnel was Friend-Union. Friend and Union Stations sat immediately to the southeast of Haymarket Square Station of the Tremont Street Subway (Figure 5.85). Friend-Union was connected to Haymarket Square Station via a pedestrian underpass. Though Friend and Union Stations just about mirrored each other across the tracks of the Washington Street Tunnel, each platform still bore a unique name.

The next station pairing south of Friend-Union was Milk-State, where platforms were offset

vertically. At Milk-State, not only were the platforms constructed above one another, the tunnel itself was separated into two tubes, each accommodating a single-track. The tube for southbound trains ran above the tube for northbound trains. Pedestrian passageways and stairs connected Milk and State Stations with each other as well as Devonshire Street Station on the East Boston Tunnel Line. Located at a higher elevation than State Station and its northbound trains, Milk Station was served by southbound trains only (Figure 5.86). State Station featured the earliest escalators installed in a transit station in Boston (Figure 5.87). Today, the platforms of Milk and State Stations of the Washington Street Tunnel, along with Devonshire Street Station of the East Boston Tunnel Line, remain interconnected. Together, the complex forms the MBTA's State Station.

South of Milk-State, the next station pairing along the tunnel was Winter-Summer. The names of Winter and Summer Stations were each derived from that of a street intersecting with the Washington Street Tunnel. At Winter-Summer, there was adequate width for both stations to be constructed at the same vertical elevation, despite being offset horizontally. Winter Station extended south from its namesake street and was served by southbound trains. Summer Station extended north from Summer Street and was served by northbound

Figure 5.84 Order of Main Line Stations Signs, Circa 1920

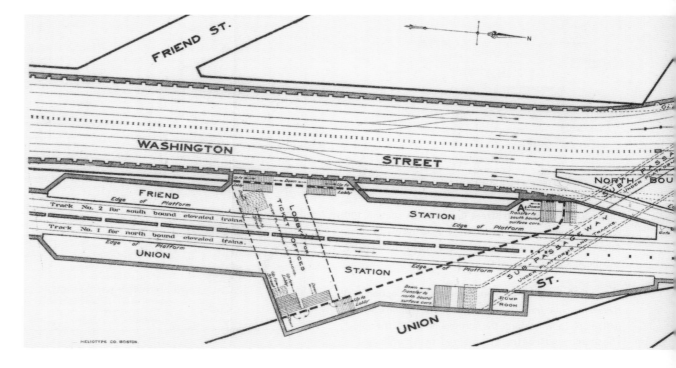

Figure 5.85 Stations at Haymarket Square, 1909

A plan shows Friend and Union Stations (left) of the Washington Street Tunnel alongside Haymarket Square Station (right) of the Tremont Street Subway. Friend Station was for southbound rapid transit trains. Union Station was for northbound trains. The three stations are connected via underground, pedestrian passageways. Today, the entire complex is named Haymarket Station.

Figure 5.86 Milk Station, 1909

The station's platform was served by southbound trains. The offset and stacked nature of Milk and State Stations precluded the need for columns along the platform's edge.

Figure 5.87 State Station, Circa 1910

Citizens promenade along the platform at State Station, a northbound-only rapid transit station on the Washington Street Tunnel. The station opened with primitive escalators.

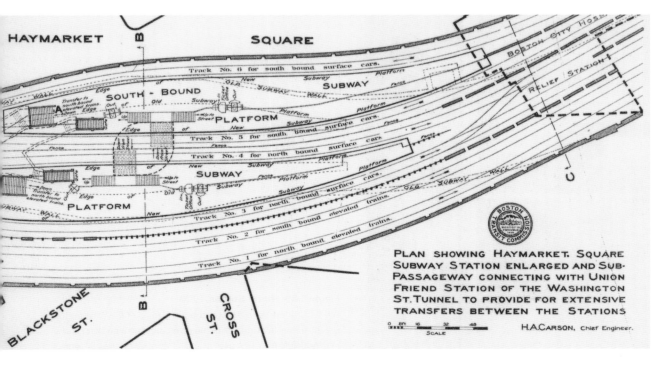

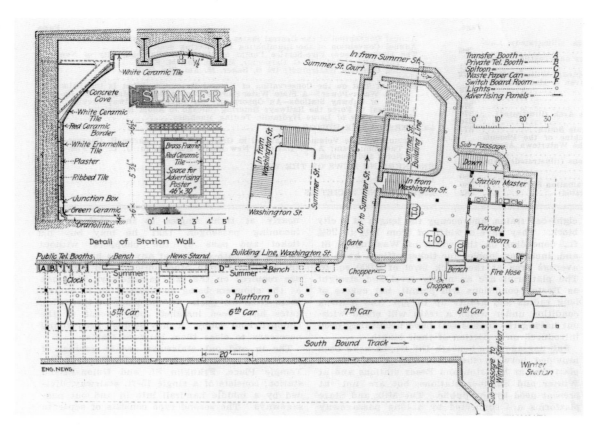

Figure 5.88 The Architecture of Summer Station, 1907
Architectural details (top left) and a floor plan explain the layout, finishes, and signage at Summer Station. The details were typical for all stations of the Washington Street Tunnel.

Figure 5.89 Winter Station, 1909
Winter Station, served by southbound trains of the Washington Street Tunnel, features its name on a porcelain sign (left) and in mosaic tile (right). A newsstand sits closed on the platform.

Figure 5.90 Essex Station, 1909

Train destination boards, a clock, and porcelain signage hang from the ceiling within Essex Station. The electrically controlled and back-lit destination boards displayed the destinations of arriving northbound trains.

Figure 5.91 Milk Station Sign, Photographed in 2019

Long ago removed from Milk Station on the Washington Street Tunnel, a porcelain enamel sign has not lost its original white on green color scheme.

trains. Both stations featured a ticket booth, employee office, parcel room, fixed benches, phone booths, built-in trash cans, wall-mounted spittoons, and mosaic tile station names (Figure 5.88). The signage styles, finishes, and programmatic elements were typical of Washington Street Tunnel stations (Figure 5.89). Today, the platforms of Winter and Summer Stations are served respectively by southbound and northbound trains of the MBTA's Orange Line. They form the upper level of the MBTA's Downtown Crossing Station.

The southernmost station pairing of the Washington Street Tunnel was Boylston-Essex, where each station was offset horizontally as well as vertically from the other. Boylston Station was on the southbound side and lower than Essex Station, on the northbound side. A 1909 photograph (Figure 5.90) reveals a newly completed Essex Station. Hanging from the ceiling are train destination boards where lines of text call out the destination of the next train. The boards were illuminated by electric light. Today, Boylston and Essex Stations make up Chinatown Station on the MBTA's Orange Line.

Washington Street Tunnel stations, just like the stations of the Tremont Street Subway and East Boston Tunnel Line opened before them, announced

that cleanliness, or at least the appearance of it, was important to the BTC. Washington Street Tunnel stations opened with hospital corners. Station walls wore white tiled wainscot and thirty-inch-wide by forty-six-inch-tall advertising panels, each with a mosaic tile border. Over the course of a year's time, tile setters installed approximately 22.5 million tiles within the tunnel stations. Ceilings, coves, and tops of columns were finished with smooth plaster, painted white. Coves smoothed the transitions between ceilings and the tops of columns and walls.

To provide identifying characteristics beyond station signage at each tunnel station, the BTC painted the bottom three quarters of platform columns a particular color: gray at Boylston and Essex Stations; terra-cotta at Winter and Summer Stations; dark green at Milk and State Stations; and blue at Friend and Union Stations. The colors of porcelain station signs mounted within a particular station were coordinated with the color of columns in that station (Figure 5.91).

The Atlantic Avenue Elevated

The Washington Street Tunnel replaced the Tremont Street Subway as the most direct route through downtown Boston for rapid transit trains of the

Figure 5.92 Rapid Transit in Downtown, June 30, 1909

On a portion of a BTC report map, the Atlantic Avenue Elevated runs along Harrison Avenue and Beach Street (bottom), then Atlantic Avenue and Commercial Street (right), before turning towards North Station (top). The Washington Street Tunnel crosses the map from the portal at Ash Street (bottom left) to the Haymarket Portal (top right). Surface streetcar lines (pairs of blue lines) run throughout the streets. The unbuilt Riverbank Subway for streetcars (top left) runs along the edge of the Back Bay and the Charles River.

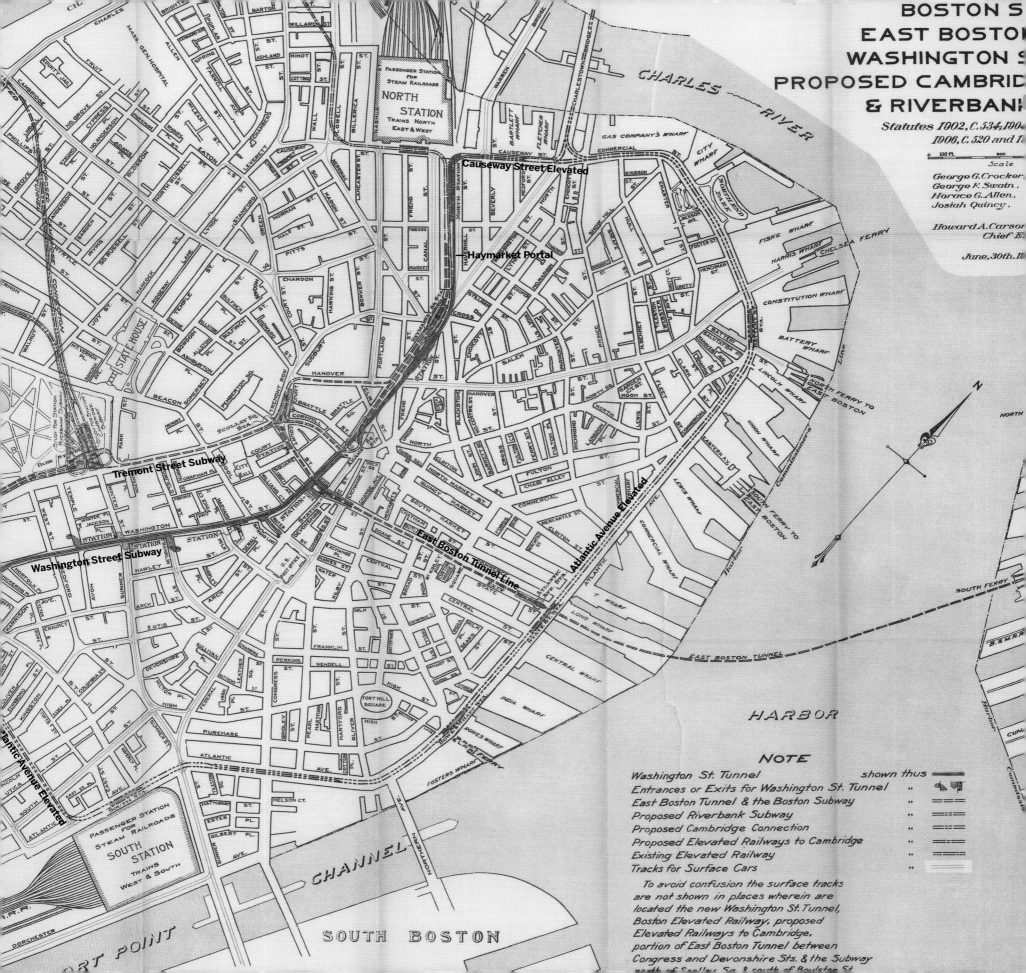

BOSTON S
EAST BOSTON
WASHINGTON S
PROPOSED CAMBRID
& RIVERBANK

Statutes 1902, C.534,190
1906, C.520 and 1

Scale

George G. Crocker
George F. Swain
Horace G. Allen
Josiah Quincy.

Howard A. Carson
Chief E.

June, 30th. 18

CHARLES RIVER

PASSENGER STATION
For
STEAM RAILROADS
NORTH STATION
TRAINS NORTH
EAST & WEST

Causeway Street Elevated

Haymarket Portal

Tremont Street Subway

Washington Street Subway

East Boston Tunnel Line

Atlantic Avenue Elevated

Atlantic Avenue Elevated

PASSENGER STATION
For
STEAM RAILROADS
SOUTH STATION
TRAINS
WEST & SOUTH

EAST BOSTON TUNNEL

HARBOR

NOTE

Washington St. Tunnel .... shown thus
Entrances or Exits for Washington St. Tunnel "
East Boston Tunnel & the Boston Subway "
Proposed Riverbank Subway "
Proposed Cambridge Connection "
Proposed Elevated Railways to Cambridge "
Existing Elevated Railway "
Tracks for Surface Cars "

To avoid confusion the surface tracks
are not shown in places wherein are
located the new Washington St. Tunnel,
Boston Elevated Railway, proposed
Elevated Railways to Cambridge,
portion of East Boston Tunnel between
Congress and Devonshire Sts. & the Subway

CHANNEL

SOUTH BOSTON

PORT POINT

Main Line Elevated. A second link, the Atlantic Avenue Elevated, skirted downtown by passing along the waterfront (Figure 5.92). At its northern end, the Atlantic Avenue Elevated began over the intersection of Commercial and North Washington Streets, where the elevated railways running over the Charlestown Bridge and Causeway Street intersected with each other as well as the Atlantic Avenue Elevated. At its southern end, the Atlantic Avenue Elevated linked up with the Washington Street Elevated above the intersection of Castle and Washington Streets. There, rapid transit tracks branched off towards the Washington Street Tunnel. The Atlantic Avenue Elevated was constructed contemporaneously with the Charlestown and Washington Street Elevateds.

After over a decade of low ridership along the Atlantic Avenue Elevated, the BERy stopped running Main Line Elevated trains along it. The BERy replaced through service on the Atlantic Avenue Elevated with shuttle service between North Station and South Station. The el at Castle Street that carried elevated trains between the Pleasant Street Portal of the Tremont Street Subway was removed by the BERy in 1936.

Between Causeway Street and Castle Street were five intermediate stations along the Atlantic Avenue Elevated. The stations were Battery Street (Figure 5.93), State Street (Figure 5.94), Rowe's Wharf (Figure 5.95), South Station (Figure 5.96), and Beach Street (Figure 5.97). Each station featured a single center platform served by northbound and southbound trains. Beach Street Station, the southernmost station on the Atlantic Avenue Elevated, was the only el station to lack a head house. Its platform was covered by a simple, peaked-roof structure. The stations, designed by Longfellow, wore their architect's signature copper sheathing, domed cupolas, and ornate ironwork for gates, stairways, and railings. Station interiors were outfitted with stained wood. The August 21, 1901 *Boston Daily Globe* raved about the new stations:

Figure 5.93 Battery Street Station, 1901
The BERy's Lincoln Wharf Power Station looms behind Battery Street Station on the Atlantic Avenue Elevated.

Figure 5.94 State Street Station on the El, November 7, 1901
The view is towards the north, looking down the southbound track and into State Street Station of the Atlantic Avenue Elevated. The bridge (right) connects the mezzanine level of State Station with the street below.

Figure 5.95 Atlantic Avenue at Rowe's Wharf, April 17, 1901
The downtown terminal of the Boston, Revere Beach & Lynn Railroad sports first floor arches and a clock above its second story (right). In the distance, stairs extend to the street from Rowe's Wharf Station on the Atlantic Avenue Elevated, running above the street.

Figure 5.96 South Station on the El, September 14, 1939
In the distance, a pedestrian bridge (left) connects the second floor of South Station Terminal (left) with the mezzanine level of South Station on the el (right).

Figure 5.97 Beach Street El Station, February 18, 1909
Snow and ice cover the southbound platform and tracks at the station above Beach Street.

Figure 5.98 The Atlantic Avenue Elevated, 1932
The Atlantic Avenue Elevated follows its namesake street. Rowe's Wharf Station is in the foreground. State Street Station is in the distance.

While the stations of the new line are not as expensively finished as are those on the line first opened, they are models of station building, contain every convenience necessary for the comfort of passengers and are way ahead of anything in New York or Chicago.

The BERy located the stations of the Atlantic Avenue Elevated to afford el riders convenient interchange with other modes of transit. State Street Station was established adjacent to Atlantic Avenue Station of the East Boston Tunnel Line. Rowe's Wharf Station was erected in front of the Boston, Revere Beach & Lynn Railroad's (BRB&L's) ferry terminal. South Station on the el was constructed next to the steam railroad terminal of the same name. A mezzanine-level bridge offered a direct connection between the el station and the steam railroad terminal.

The Atlantic Avenue Elevated opened to the public on August 22, 1901. Service was limited to trains running back and forth between North Station and Pleasant Street Station. Trains from Charlestown or Roxbury did not run along the Atlantic Avenue Elevated until the BERy received additional rapid transit cars to support the service.

The Great Molasses Flood
In Boston's North End, the Atlantic Avenue Elevated ran along Commercial Street, past the wharves, warehouses, and storage tanks of an industrial waterfront (Figure 5.99). One of those tanks, filled with millions of gallons of molasses, was located on property owned by the BERy. The BERy, definitively not in the molasses business, was merely the lessor of the land upon which the tank sat.

On January 15, 1919, the multi-story molasses tank catastrophically failed, unleashing a wave of 2.3 million gallons of molasses that spread in all directions. The event killed nineteen people and injured hundreds more. Horses became terminally stuck and were shot in place. The wave of molasses and the debris which it carried slammed

Figure 5.99 Mapping the Molasses Tank and the El, 1917
On a real estate map of the North End, the Atlantic Avenue Elevated, represented by a pair of parallel dashed lines, follows the grand arc of Commercial Street. Tracks of the Union Freight Railroad, represented by dark lines with cross ticks, trace Commercial Street and the el. To the west of "North End Beach" is a waterfront parcel of land with "Boston Elevated Railway Co." indicated as its owner (top left). On the parcel is a blue circle representing the infamous molasses tank that burst on January 15, 1919.

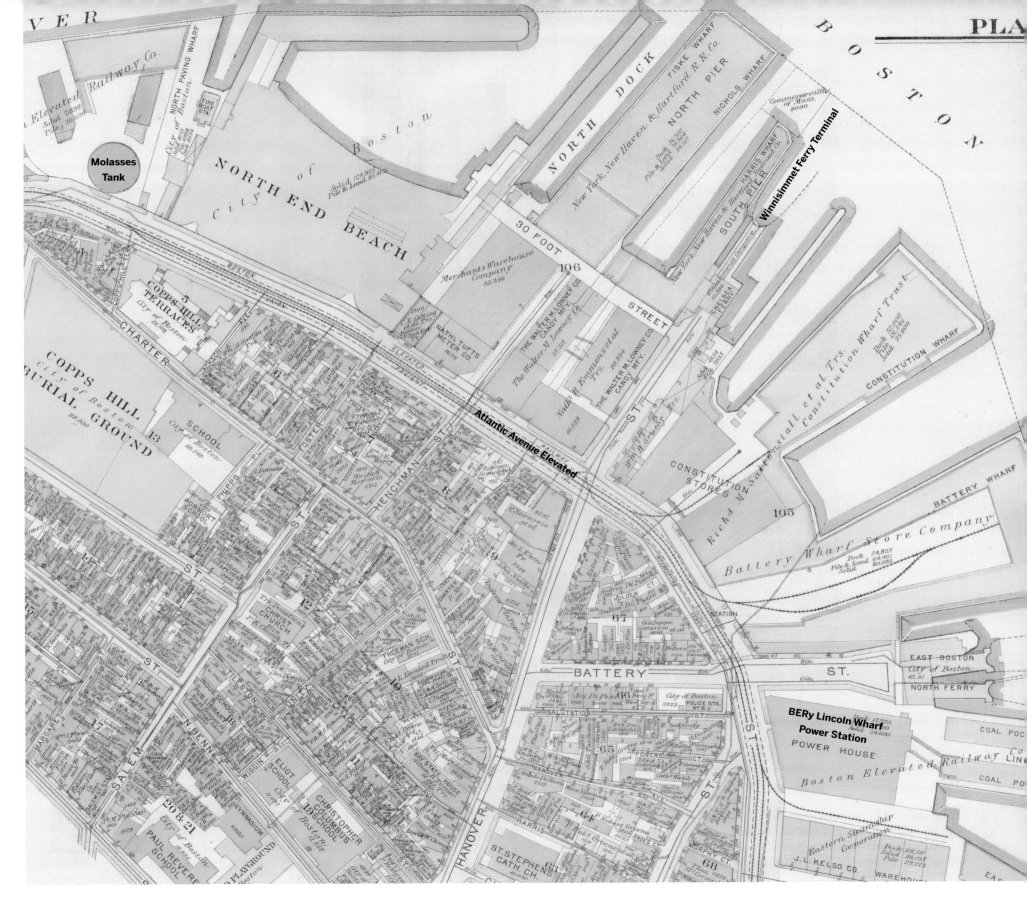

Molasses
Tank

Winnisimmet Ferry Terminal

Atlantic Avenue Elevated

BERy Lincoln Wharf
Power Station

Figure 5.100 Damage to the El, January 15, 1919
Soon after a tsunami of molasses erupted from a failed storage tank in Boston's North End, men search through debris around the crippled Atlantic Avenue Elevated.

Figure 5.101 Aftermath of The Flood, January 15, 1919
A massive piece of the failed molasses tank and residual molasses lie in front of the damaged el. The twin stacks of the BERy's Lincoln Wharf Power Station lurk in the distance.

into the legs of the Atlantic Avenue Elevated, severely damaging the structure (Figure 5.100 and Figure 5.101). After two months of rebuilding, the BERy reopened the Atlantic Avenue Elevated to trains.

All service on the Atlantic Avenue Elevated came to an end in 1938. From a profit and loss basis, closing the line was not a difficult decision for the BERy to make. The line never brought in the revenue anticipated by the BERy. Between March and June 1942, the superstructure and stations of

the Atlantic Avenue Elevated between Castle and Causeway Streets were torn down and scrapped for the war effort. Much of the el was cut apart in place and lowered into gondolas waiting below on the tracks of the Union Freight Railway (Figure 5.102), a line that linked North and South Station along Commercial Street and Atlantic Avenue. Because the Union Freight Railway typically ran its trains at night, when streets were devoid of traffic, the operation was nicknamed "the railroad that only came out at night."

Figure 5.102 Scrapping the Atlantic Avenue Elevated, 1942

Union Station

East Cambridge Extension

Causeway Street

Canal Street

Streetcar Stop

Fitchburg Station

North Station

Southbound Streetcar Track

Southbound Rapid Transit Track

Northbound Rapid Transit Track

Northbound Streetcar Track

Streetcar Track from Subway

Figure 5.103 Haymarket Incline, January 27, 1922
The Haymarket Incline was significantly reconfigured to accommodate the East Cambridge Extension. Immediately to the right of the streetcar incline is the two-track incline for rapid transit trains of the Main Line Elevated. At the top of the rapid transit incline is North Station on the el. In the distance, are the Boston & Maine's Union Station and the Fitchburg's "castle" depot. At street level, streetcars continue to run into and out of the subway as well as serve the Canal Street streetcar stop.

The East Cambridge Extension
After removing rapid transit trains from the Tremont Street Subway in 1909, the BERy worked to improve connections for streetcars using the subway and serving destinations northwest of downtown Boston. One improvement, opened on June 1, 1912 by the BERy, was the East Cambridge Extension, the first elevated railway in Boston constructed for the exclusive use of streetcars. The nearly two-mile-long extension expedited streetcars running between the Tremont Street Subway and East Cambridge. Before the East Cambridge Extension, streetcars were forced to navigate along traffic-choked Causeway Street and the narrow streets of Boston's West End. Frequent openings of a

street-level drawbridge spanning the Charles River further hindered streetcar movement between the West End and East Cambridge.

When complete, the East Cambridge Extension was a double-track, elevated streetcar line. It not only removed streetcars from the streets of the West End, it also allowed trolleys to cross high above the Charles River. At its southern end, the extension began at the Haymarket Portal of the Tremont Street Subway. Just outside of the portal, an inclined elevated railway structure carried a pair of streetcar tracks between the subway and the East Cambridge Extension. The streetcar incline paralleled the incline for rapid transit trains of the Main Line Elevated (Figure 5.103). At the top of

Figure 5.104 North Station West, June 6, 1912
A streetcar pauses at the southbound platform of North Station West, a station located above Causeway Street on the East Cambridge Extension. On the far left is a portion of the grand arch of the Boston & Maine's Union Station.

the streetcar incline the East Cambridge Extension became an elevated railway that followed Causeway Street in front of the grand arch of Union Station. There, North Station West opened to streetcars on the East Cambridge Extension (Figure 5.104). Around the corner from, and one story below, North Station West, the existing streetcar stop at the corner of Canal and Causeway Streets was reworked and formally named Canal Street.

Northwest of Causeway Street, the East Cambridge Extension wound through Boston's West End as an elevated railway, before crossing the Charles River along a reinforced concrete viaduct (Figure 5.105). The viaduct was 1,700 feet long, with long arches that carried streetcars two stories above the river. Alongside the East Cambridge Viaduct remained Craigie's Bridge, with its water-level draw that long hindered streetcar traffic. Though an operable draw existed on the new viaduct, its high elevation meant fewer openings for marine traffic than required on the older bridge.

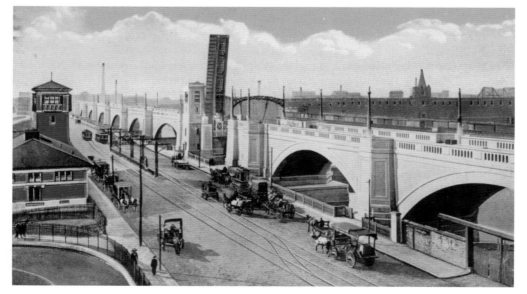

Figure 5.105 East Cambridge Viaduct, Circa 1912
An iconic portion of the East Cambridge Extension was its viaduct. The draw portion of the viaduct is in the open position (center). On Craigie's Bridge, streetcars and surface traffic cross the Charles River alongside the viaduct (foreground). The control room for the Craigie's Bridge draw is located in the tower (left).

Figure 5.106 Lechmere Terminal, June 7, 1922
Streetcar transfer areas and simple shelters bracket the terminal's loop tracks (center). Broadway is on the far left. Bridge Street is on the far right. The image, taken one month before the terminal's opening, is from the northern end of the East Cambridge Extension.

On the Cambridge side of the river, the tracks of the East Cambridge Extension returned to street level at the intersection of Bridge Street (now Monsignor O'Brien Highway) and Cambridge Street. There, streetcars moved between tracks in the street and tracks of the East Cambridge Extension.

Lechmere Terminal and Science Park Station

Ten years after opening the East Cambridge Extension, the BERy established a terminal station at the Cambridge end of the line. Sited just off of Lechmere Square, Lechmere Terminal occupied a site where streetcars previously moved between Cambridge's streets and the East Cambridge Extension. At the center of the terminal, loop tracks allowed streetcars to arrive from the viaduct crossing the Charles River, pass through the terminal to exchange passengers, and depart back onto the viaduct towards the Tremont Street Subway. On either side of the loop tracks were platforms, beyond which local streetcars arrived from, and departed back onto, surface streets. The BERy opened Lechmere Terminal to the public on July 10, 1922 (Figure 5.106). A busway structure opened at Lechmere Terminal in the early 1930s. Buses have long replaced streetcars exchanging passengers outside of the streetcar loops.

Today, Lechmere Terminal is the northern terminus of the MBTA's Green Line light rail line, but not for long. The Green Line Extension Project (GLX), currently in construction, is extending the Green Line to the northwest, beyond Lechmere Terminal. As part of its GLX project, the MBTA will replace Lechmere Terminal with a new station to be constructed on the eastern side of Monsignor O'Brien Highway.

The MTA added a second intermediate station to the East Cambridge Extension in 1955. Located between Boston's West End Elevated and the Charles River, the station was named Science Park, after the neighboring park on the Charles River Dam. The park has since been consumed by buildings of the Museum of Science. The MBTA renamed Science Park Station to Science Park / West End Station in early 2009. By that time, the vast majority of the historic fabric of the West End neighborhood had not existed for decades, having been wiped out by urban renewal in the middle of the twentieth century. During the late 1950s and into the 1960s, Boston's West End disappeared into the profits of developers who replaced the neighborhood's narrow streets and dense blocks with placeless apartment towers, parking garages, and incoherent green spaces. Today, between Science Park / West End Station and Lechmere Terminal, the arches of the East Cambridge Extension's viaduct remain. The elevated railways over Causeway Street and the West End were demolished after the MBTA redirected trolleys through its underground North Station "super station" and a tunnel beneath the Fleet Center (now TD Garden).

The Cambridge-Dorchester Rapid Transit Line

With its completion of both its Elevated Division and East Cambridge Extension, the BERy established rapid transit lines and elevated railways radiating from downtown Boston to Charlestown, Roxbury, and East Cambridge. These realized three of the rapid transit lines proposed on the Rapid Transit Commission's 1892 map (Figure 3.10). During the 1910s, the two other radial rapid transit lines proposed in 1892, one to Cambridge and another to South Boston, came into existence. The line from Boston across Cambridge mostly followed the route to Harvard Square proposed on the 1892 map. The line to South Boston did not become the loop line proposed in 1892. Instead, the line skirted the western edge of South Boston before continuing deep into Boston's largest neighborhood, Dorchester. Boston's rapid transit lines from downtown into Cambridge and Dorchester were constructed as a series of distinct projects, over the course of years, with some overseen by the BERy and others by the BTC. The projects were generally constructed from north to south, starting in Cambridge. The project that brought rapid transit trains from Cambridge, through downtown Boston, and into Dorchester was the Cambridge-Dorchester rapid transit line, the core for the MBTA's Red Line.

The first segments of the Cambridge-Dorchester rapid transit line were constructed as three distinct projects. These were the Cambridge Subway, a new bridge over the Charles River, and the Beacon Hill Tunnel. Much of the three-and-three-quarter-mile-long grouping of projects followed the same streets upon which the Cambridge Railroad operated Boston's first horse railroad in 1856 (Figure 5.107).

The Cambridge Subway

During planning for the Cambridge Subway, constituents to be served by the new line debated the number of stations to be constructed within Cambridge. Arguments for as few as one or two stops between Harvard Square and Boston were championed to benefit passengers connecting to streetcars and points farther afield at each end of the proposed line. A differing argument, supported by locals seeking a stop in their own neighborhood, was made for as many as five intermediate stations. A compromise solution balanced the needs of both long distance and local passengers; the Cambridge Subway would be constructed with two intermediate stops in Cambridge and a terminal station at Harvard Square. The intermediate stops were located at Central and Kendall Squares.

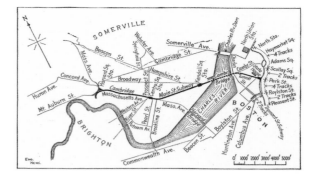

Figure 5.107 Mapping the Cambridge Subway, 1912
The Cambridge Subway (dark line) runs from Harvard Square (left), through Central and Kendall Squares (middle), to a terminus at Park Street Station of the Tremont Street Subway (right).

Figure 5.108 Above Central Station, Cambridge, June 1912
Capped by "Out" and "To Park Street" signs, stairways connect the sidewalk to the southbound platform of Central Station on the Cambridge Subway. An open-type streetcar (right) and railway post office streetcar (far right) traverse Massachusetts Avenue through Central Square.

The construction of the Cambridge Subway was overseen by the BERy with work commencing in July 1909. The subway tunnels and stations were constructed of steel reinforced concrete, mostly via the cut and cover method. Construction progressed in short segments, each typically forty feet long. A small section of tunnel between Harvard and Central Squares was constructed using a roof shield.

The Cambridge Subway opened to the public on March 23, 1912, when rapid transit trains began carrying riders between Harvard Square and the Boston terminus of the line at Park Street. The March 24, 1912 *Boston Daily Globe* ran with the headline "Eight Minutes to Harvard Sq." Below the headline, an article detailed the first day of service: "The first train left Harvard Station at 5:24 a.m.... and arrived seven minutes and 45 seconds later at Park st, Boston" (sic). The *Globe* continued: "That train of four cars brought about 1,000 people from Cambridge to Boston....Trains ran until 12:45

o'clock this morning." For comparison, the newspaper noted that travel between Harvard Square and Park Street by streetcar often took a half an hour. The March 24 newspaper captured the excitement exhibited by the Cambridge Subway's first passengers:

The opening of the new Subway at Harvard sq was something of an event. People remained up all night in the waiting room and around the circular station anxious to get a ride on that first historic train.

When the gates were opened there was more than 1,000 in front of the first woman and man to buy tickets, including many Harvard students who furnished "rah-rahs" and cheers for the crowd on the square and for the passengers in the train all the way in to Park st and all the way back again on the same train...(sic).

Figure 5.109 Harvard Station, 1912

Drawings expose the rabbit warren that was Harvard Station. Tunnels for streetcars and tunnels for rapid transit trains come together to form a "Y" in plan, before running parallel to each other beneath Brattle Street (bottom left). In the middle of the "Y," a knot of passageways connects platforms and stairways communicating with the surface. Crossing the plan at various points are lines bracketed by pairs of letters. Each line corresponds to a cross-section shown. The maze of underground passageways is gone, replaced by a new station in the 1980s.

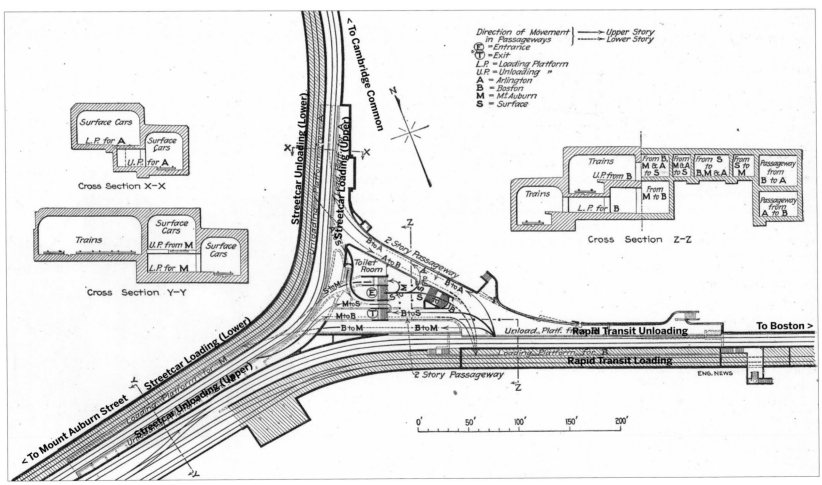

In 1918, the BERy sold the Cambridge Subway to the Commonwealth, which in turn leased it back to the BERy for operation.

At Kendall and Central Stations, narrow stairways, each protected by low walls sheathed in polished stone, offered pedestrian connections between sidewalks and station platforms below (Figure 5.108). Signage at street level designated each stairway leading down as either an entrance or exit. The platforms at both Central and Kendall Stations mirrored each other across the double-track subway. Within each station, one track and platform was dedicated to either northbound or southbound service. The platforms of both stations were not connected by transfer mezzanines nor sub-passageways. To move between the northbound and southbound side of either station, people had to leave one side, cross the street above, and enter the opposite side of the station. This disconnected configuration remains in place today.

The stations of the Cambridge Subway were outfitted with benches, clocks, public bathrooms, newsstands, and telephone booths. The stations featured white tiles on the walls, hospital corners at the platforms, white painted plaster on the ceilings, and mosaic tile accents throughout. The finishes were similar to the BTC-built Washington Street Tunnel stations. The names of each Cambridge Subway station, "Harvard," "Central," and "Kendall," were set in contrasting mosaic tiles, high upon the walls, and along their respective platforms. Following the convention of station naming used by the BTC along the Washington Street Tunnel, the BERy omitted the word "Square" from the Cambridge Subway station name mosaics.

The Cambridge Subway brought unprecedented public transportation infrastructure to Harvard Square. A multi-level, subterranean transfer station was served by streetcars and rapid transit trains. A massive rapid transit car maintenance and storage facility arose between the square and the Charles River. A power station provided DC power for the growing BERy network. At the center of it all was Harvard Station, the northern terminus of the Cambridge-Dorchester rapid transit line.

Underground, Harvard Station was a maze. Multiple tunnels, platforms, and passageways, some reserved for one way pedestrian or transit vehicle traffic, were tightly packed beneath Harvard Square and surrounding streets. The February 1, 1912 issue of *Engineering News* featured architectural drawings explaining the interwoven, subterranean spaces of Harvard Station (Figure 5.109). At the surface, Harvard Station was marked by a head house clad in neoclassical masonry (Figure 5.110). The 1912 head house was replaced by a new structure in 1929 (Figure 5.111).

Rapid transit trains arrived at Harvard Station to unload passengers at a dedicated platform (Figure 5.112). After disgorging riders, trains continued west into a tunnel under Brattle Street. There, trains utilized a crossover to move between the northbound and southbound tracks. After crossing over to the southbound track, trains reversed direction and proceeded back into the station, where, alongside the lower level boarding platform, they picked up riders bound for Boston. The unloading and loading platforms were offset from each other vertically as well as horizontally.

Harvard Station featured a second pair of tunnels, reserved for streetcars. The streetcar tunnels

Figure 5.111 Harvard Station Head House, Circa Late 1950s

Figure 5.112 Rapid Transit Train Unloading Platform, 1912

Natural light floods down onto the platform where trains from Boston unloaded their passengers. "Harvard" is set in mosaic tile on the wall.

and their platforms were stacked, one atop the other. Streetcars ran from north to south in the lower tunnel, and from south to north in the upper tunnel. Each of the two streetcar tunnels featured one platform divided into dedicated unloading and loading areas (Figure 5.113 and Figure 5.114). The streetcar tunnel tracks linked with street-running tracks at two portals. The southern portal was located between Brattle and Mount Auburn Streets. The northern portal occupied a small park at the confluence of Harvard Street and Massachusetts Avenue. By the fall of 1925, the northern portal saw 1,900 streetcars pass through it daily. Great care was taken by the BERy to coordinate the aesthetics of the walls surrounding the incline leading to the northern portal, as it was located just steps from historic Harvard Yard. Architect Robert Peabody,

of Peabody & Stearns, provided designs for ornamental stone and brick masonry that the BERy described in 1925 as "the most ornamental and pleasing of those forming parts of the subways and tunnels in the Boston Elevated System."

With its elaborate design for Harvard Station, the BERy attempted to establish Greater Boston's most efficient underground, multi-modal, public transit station. Unlike the spacious Elevated Division terminals at Sullivan Square and Dudley Street, Harvard Station was a warren of corridors, ramps, and stairways woven together with the platforms, entry, and egress points. Lacking the space of an above-ground site and being hemmed in on all sides by development, some dating back the seventeenth century, Harvard Station was the result of a highly constricted site. Harvard Station held down the

Figure 5.113 Upper Streetcar Platform, March 20, 1913

An iron fence (middle) separates the platform into two sections, one (background) where northbound streetcars unloaded passengers, and another (foreground), where cars picked up passengers. Overhead signage directs patrons where to proceed "Out To Harvard Sq." On the far side of the fence, a sign directs arriving streetcar riders to rapid transit trains heading to Park Street in Boston.

Figure 5.114 Lower Streetcar Platform, March 5, 1912

As it was one level above, the lower streetcar platform was divided by a gate (left) into areas for unloading and loading.

northern end of the Cambridge-Dorchester rapid transit line from 1912 until the mid-1980s, when the Northwest Extension to Alewife Station was opened by the MBTA.

Beyond Harvard Station

Published four years after the opening of the Cambridge Subway, a 1916 real estate map of Harvard Square documents the plethora of public transportation infrastructure supporting both rapid transit trains and streetcars at Harvard Square (Figure 5.115). The BERy's major facilities at Harvard Square were Harvard Station, Eliot Square Shops and Yard, Bennett Street Car House and Yard, and the BERy's Cambridge Power Station (Figure 5.116).

The BERy constructed Eliot Square Shops and Yard in conjunction with the Cambridge Subway. The complex served as the main repair, inspection, and storage locations for cars of the Cambridge-Dorchester rapid transit line. The shops also served rapid transit cars of the East Boston Tunnel Line until the opening of dedicated facilities for those vehicles at Orient Heights. At Eliot Square Shops, BERy staff serviced rapid transit cars inside of a building accommodating six-car trains and many single cars. Next to the shops, the BERy stored rapid transit cars in a large yard of parallel and mostly stub-end tracks. Utilizing a rapid transit track that looped around the entire Eliot Square complex, trains could exit the Cambridge Subway at the Eliot Square Portal, travel around the shops,

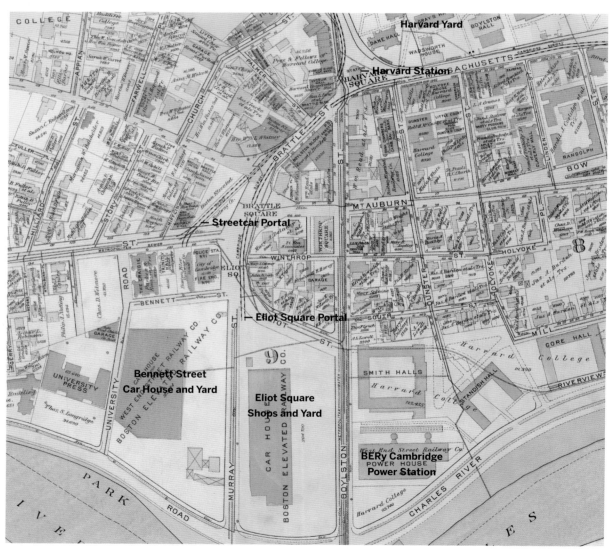

Figure 5.115 Transit Facilities at Harvard Square, 1916
Streetcar tunnel tracks run from the northern streetcar portal, through Harvard Station, and to the southern portal, at Mount Auburn Street. Rapid transit tracks of the Cambridge Subway pass beneath the oval footprint of the Harvard Station head house. West of the station, the subway turns south before following Brattle Street to the far side of Eliot Square. There, the subway tracks passed through a portal and into daylight.

Figure 5.116 The BERy at Harvard Square, December 1930
From left to right are the Boston Elevated Railway Company's: Bennett Street Car House and Yard, both for streetcars; Eliot Square Shops and Yard, both for rapid transit cars; Stadium Station, served by trains of the Cambridge Subway; Boylston Street (now JFK Street); and Cambridge Power Station.

and then head back into the subway without reversing direction.

Along the eastern edge of Eliot Square Yard, the BERy established an open-air station for the use of patrons attending games at Harvard Stadium. Stadium Station was an open-air platform installed between the loop track and perimeter wall along the eastern edge of the Eliot Square Yard (Figure 5.117). A concrete wall punctuated by gates separated the platform from the sidewalk of Boylston Street (now JFK Street). The platform opened on October 26, 1912 with accommodations for twenty-four ticket sellers and eight points of entry and exit. A large ramp served as the main access point for

Figure 5.117 Stadium Station, Circa 1920s–30s
Harvard dormitories and Stadium Station form a backdrop for trains and tracks of Eliot Square Yards. The station is an open platform running along the perimeter wall of the yard. Gates in the wall were opened only when the station was open, typically only on game days at nearby Harvard Stadium.

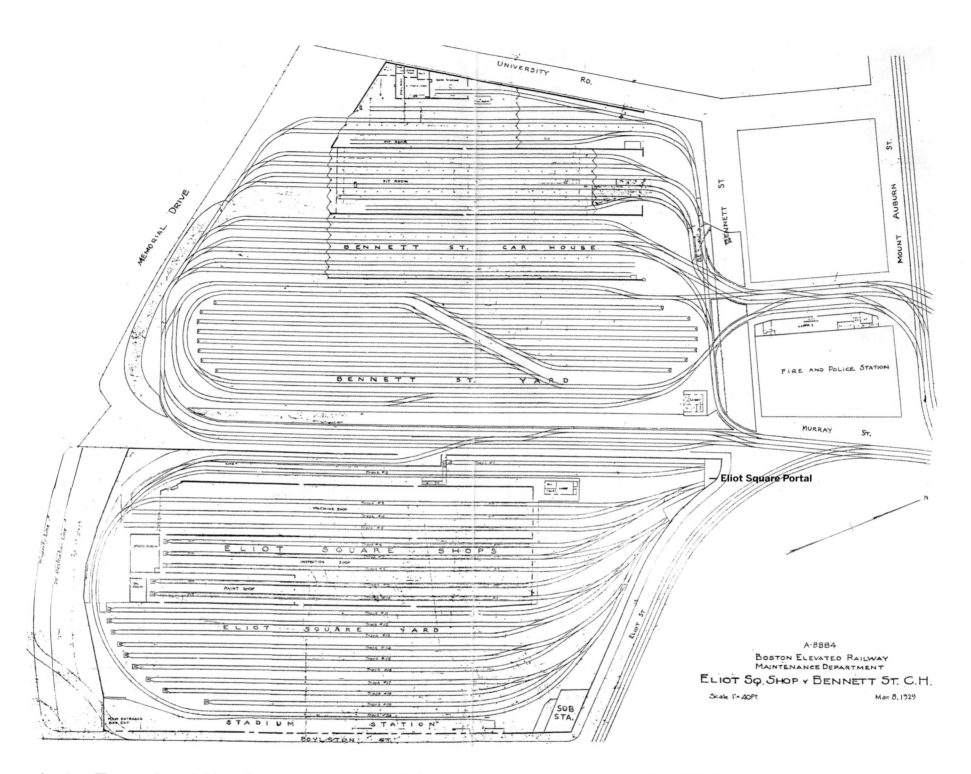

University Rd.

Memorial Drive

PIT ROOM

PIT ROOM

BENNETT ST. CAR HOUSE

BENNETT ST. YARD

BENNETT ST.

MOUNT AUBURN ST.

FIRE AND POLICE STATION

MURRAY ST.

— Eliot Square Portal

N

Track #1

Track #2

MACHINE SHOP

Track #3

Track #4

Track #5

ELIOT SQUARE SHOPS

STOCK ROOM

INSPECTION SHOP

Track #6

OIL ROOM

PAINT SHOP

Track #11

ELIOT SQUARE YARD

Track #12

Track #14

Track #15

Track #17

Track #18

Track #19

ELIOT ST.

A-8884
BOSTON ELEVATED RAILWAY
MAINTENANCE DEPARTMENT
ELIOT SQ. SHOP & BENNETT ST. C.H.
Scale 1"=40ft.   Mar. 8, 1929

SUB STA.

MAIN ENTRANCE

STADIUM STATION

BOYLSTON ST.

pedestrians. The ramp descended from the station towards Harvard Stadium, a ten minute walk away. Four car trains were typical on game days, with special service between Park Street and Stadium Stations taking ten minutes. During the 1912–13 football season, the BERy recorded serving 26,000

passengers during a single forty-five-minute period. Since it was used irregularly, Stadium Station seldom appeared on publicly available transit maps. The platform disappeared with the rest of Eliot Square Yard and Shops in the 1970s.

Figure 5.118 Mapping Bennett-Eliot Facilities, 1929
The BERy's maintenance department mapped the extensive trackage of Bennett Street Car House and Yard as well as Eliot Square Shops and Yard. Bennett was the domain of streetcars; Eliot, that of rapid transit cars. Stadium Station runs along the edge of Eliot Square Yard (bottom).

Immediately to the west of Eliot Square Shops was Bennett Street Car House and Yard, opened on March 30, 1911. Whereas Eliot Square was the territory of rapid transit cars, Bennett Street was the domain of streetcars. The facilities at Bennett Street were contiguous with those at Eliot Square. Bennett Street Car House had no fewer than 15 tracks upon which streetcars were inspected, repaired, and stored. Outside, Bennett Street Yard featured multiple loop tracks and fifteen stub-end tracks for the storage of streetcars (Figure 5.118).

Decades before rapid transit trains arrived in Harvard Square, streetcars called the area around Bennett Street home as early as 1871. In the 1870s, the Union Horse Railroad Company, operator of the Cambridge Railroad, oversaw land along the southern side of Bennett Street. During its consolidation of Boston's horse railroad companies in 1887, the West End Street Railway Company (West End) took over horsecar infrastructure at Bennett Street. By the time the BERy leased the West End, the horsecar barns at Bennett Street had been replaced by a large car house and yard for electric streetcars. During its tenure, the BERy improved and expanded the facilities at Bennett Street. Trackless trolleys arrived and joined streetcars on the site in April 1936. By the end of 1958, the BERy's successor, the MTA, ceased regular operation of streetcars at Bennett Street.

The Eliot Square Shops and Yard were sold off by the MBTA in February 1968. After nearly becoming the site of the presidential library for John F. Kennedy, the Eliot Square facilities were replaced by Harvard University with a building housing its John F. Kennedy School of Government. The site of Bennett Street Car House and Yard is now occupied by a mixed-use complex composed of the Charles Hotel and 975 Memorial Drive. A right-of-way, perhaps for a future transit tunnel connecting Cambridge and Allston, remains between the Kennedy School and the Charles Hotel. Across JFK Street from the Kennedy School, Harvard's Eliot House occupies the former site of the BERy's Cambridge Power Station.

The New West Boston Bridge

The eastern end of the Cambridge Subway emerged into daylight in the middle of Cambridge's Main Street. From there, the double-track rapid transit line crossed the Charles River on the New West Boston Bridge (now the Longfellow Bridge). The span, constructed by an Act of the General Court, replaced the venerable first West Boston Bridge, opened in 1793. The older bridge, upon which horse-drawn coaches, omnibuses, horsecars once crossed the Charles, remained in place during construction of the new bridge (Figure 5.119). Demolition of the

Figure 5.119 Old and New Bridges to Cambridge, 1907
The New West Boston Bridge (now Longfellow Bridge) spans the Charles River alongside a temporary replacement (background) for the demolished West Boston Bridge. On the new bridge, a central reservation and abutment (center) await the installation of rapid transit tracks of the Cambridge-Dorchester rapid transit line. On the bridge, electric streetcars run under trolley wire between Boston and Cambridge.

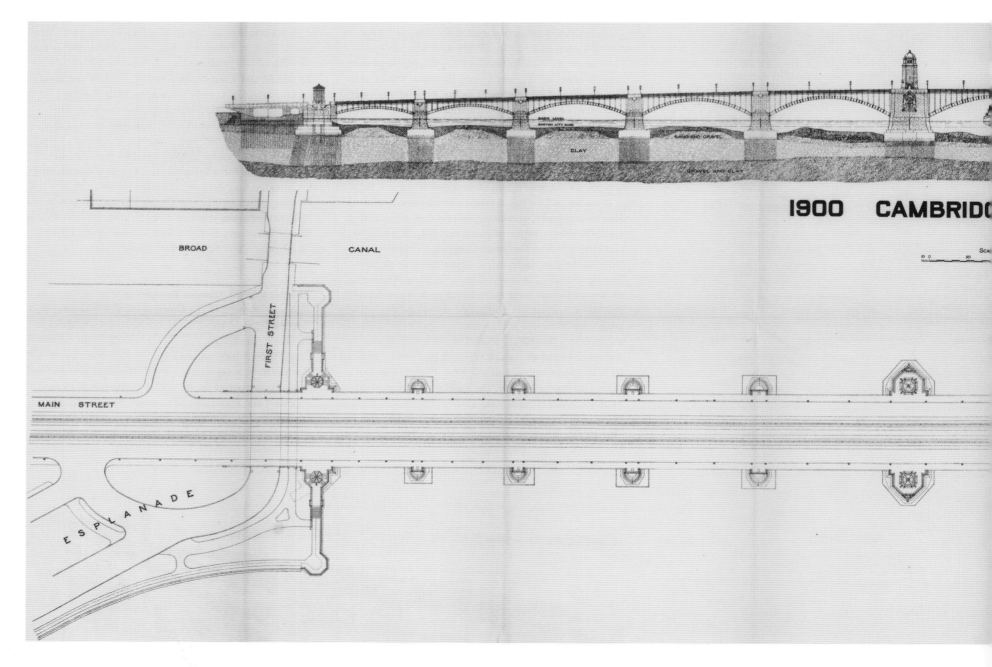

BROAD

CANAL

1900 CAMBRIDG

FIRST STREET

MAIN STREET

ESPLANADE

first West Boston Bridge commenced shortly after the August 3, 1906, opening of its replacement.

The New West Boston Bridge was just over one half of a mile long (Figure 5.120). Eleven steel arches spanned between ten massive piers of structural masonry and concrete. Bracketing the middle of the bridge, four towers stood three stories taller than the bridge's deck. Four shorter towers marked the bridge's landed ends. The profiles of the bridge's tallest towers led to the bridge gaining the nickname "salt and pepper bridge." The towers and most

of the bridge were dressed in granite from Rockport, a community at the extreme northern reach of Massachusetts Bay and famed for its stone.

Within five years of it opening, the New West Boston Bridge received a pair of rapid transit tracks with third rail along its central reservation. In 1927, the New West Boston Bridge was renamed the Longfellow Bridge. The name honored poet Henry Wadsworth Longfellow, who, in 1845, penned "The Bridge," a poem in which the narrator speaks while standing on the first West Boston Bridge.

Figure 5.120 Elevation (top) and Plan (bottom) of the New West Boston Bridge (now Longfellow Bridge), 1907

The Cambridge Bridge Commission published an elevation and plan of the 105-foot-wide bridge supporting sidewalks and two, double-lane roadways. Each roadway opened with tracks and trolley wire for electric streetcars. Separating the roadways and running the length of the bridge was a central reservation, reserved for the future installation of a double-track rapid transit line.

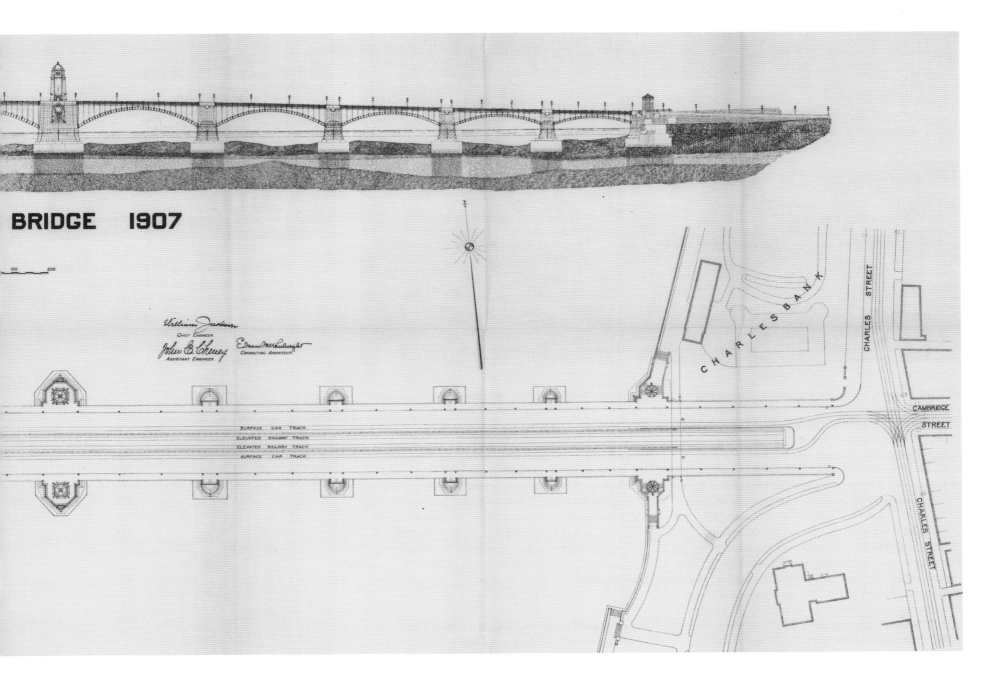

BRIDGE 1907

William Jackson
CHIEF ENGINEER.

John B. Cheney
ASSISTANT ENGINEER.

Edmund M. Wheelwright
CONSULTING ARCHITECT.

SURFACE CAR TRACK
ELEVATED RAILWAY TRACK
ELEVATED RAILWAY TRACK
SURFACE CAR TRACK

CHARLESBANK

CHARLES STREET

CAMBRIDGE STREET

CHARLES STREET

The Beacon Hill Tunnel and Park Street Under

Between the New West Boston Bridge and Park Street, the Cambridge-Dorchester rapid transit line passed through a tunnel beneath Beacon Hill. Construction of the Beacon Hill Tunnel was overseen by the BTC. It was among the last legislatively-mandated projects brought to completion by the BTC. On its western end, the tunnel began at Lindall Place, at the foot of Beacon Hill. A short stretch of elevated railway carried the double-track rapid transit line from the Boston end of the New

West Boston Bridge to the portal of the Beacon Hill Tunnel. From there, a tunnel 2,500 feet long was constructed in an easterly direction. Under the protection of a roof shield, work progressed at an average rate of as much as fifty feet per week (Figure 5.121).

At its eastern end, the Beacon Hill Tunnel terminated at a new rapid transit station inserted beneath Park Street Station of the Tremont Street Subway. Despite being signed Park Street in mosaic tiles on its walls, the new station was referred to

Figure 5.121 Excavating the Beacon Hill Tunnel, June 29, 1910
Under protection of a roof shield, a worker wields a pick to excavate a portion of the Cambridge-Dorchester line.

Figure 5.122 Park Street Under, 1912
Park Street Under opened with three platforms, two for unloading (far left; right) and one for loading (middle).

as Park Street Under, distinguishing it from the older and upper portion of the station served by streetcars. Park Street Under featured two parallel tracks that stub-ended under Tremont Street (Figure 5.122). Each track was flanked by a platform along the station's perimeter. Between the pair of tracks was a single, central platform. Initially, the central platform was reserved for patrons waiting to board an outbound train to Cambridge; the two outer platforms were designated for detraining passengers. The central platform was punctuated by columns supporting flattened arches, which in turn, supported the roof of the station. The arches were a signature element of Park Street Under and the two intermediate stations of the Cambridge Subway.

Park Street Under brought with it a new ticket lobby at the level of the Tremont Street Subway, sandwiched above the rapid transit station and below Tremont Street. The lobby was connected by stairs and passageways to not only Park Street and Park Street Under, but also to the east side of Tremont Street. The new stairs allowed patrons arriving from downtown Boston to access Park Street Station without needing to cross busy Tremont Street.

After the opening of Park Street Under, Park Street Station became busier than ever. In response, the BTC increased capacity of the streetcar platforms at Park Street Station with work starting in August 1914 and completed in March 1915. The eastbound and westbound platforms were extended and tracks leading to and from Boylston Street Station were straightened.

On February 27, 1932, the BERy opened Charles Station along the short section of el that connected the Longfellow Bridge with the portal of the Beacon Hill Tunnel. The station was accessed via a lobby located beneath the el, in the middle of Charles Circle. In the early 1930s, Charles Station almost became the first transit station in Boston to see trains passing through the base of a skyscraper (Figure 5.123). The tower was scuttled by The Great Depression.

Cambridge-Dorchester Rapid Transit Cars

To transport riders along the Cambridge-Dorchester rapid transit line, the BERy commissioned the largest rapid transit cars yet to roll in Boston. When they commenced operation between Harvard Square and Park Street Under in 1912, the BERy's Cambridge-Dorchester Type 1 cars were the largest rapid transit cars in MU operation (Figure 5.124). The sixty-nine-foot-long cars were nearly twenty feet longer than their contemporaries in New York City. On their interiors, the cars displayed Order of Stations signs (Figure 5.125). Between 1911 and 1928, the BERy placed 154 Cambridge-Dorchester rapid transit cars into service. The cars, identified as Type 1s, Type 2s, Type 3s, and Type 4s, were

Figure 5.123 Charles Station Design Proposal, Circa 1930
A rendering of a tower and station proposed for the Cambridge-Dorchester rapid transit line in Charles Circle, at the Boston end of the Longfellow Bridge. The tower was never built, but the station, distinguished by the copper cladding it still retains, opened to the public in 1932.

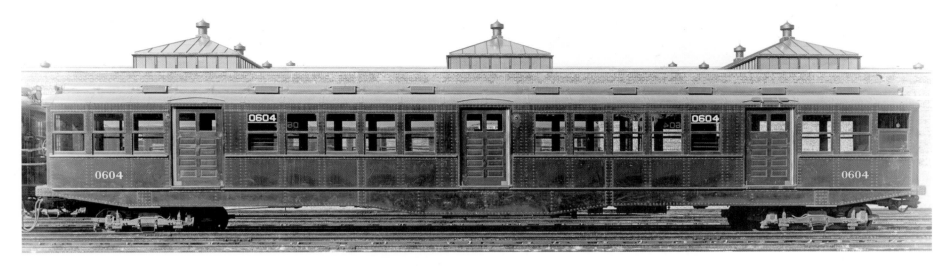

Figure 5.124 Cambridge-Dorchester Type 1 Car, 1911
Cambridge-Dorchester Type 1 Rapid Transit Car #0604 sits
outside Eliot Square Shops.

Figure 5.125 Cambridge-Dorchester Type 1 Car, 1911
The interior of car #607, the same type of car shown in
Figure 5.124, bears "Order of Stations" signs above its end
door (left) and next to the side door (right). The signs list the
stations served by the car as "Harvard," "Central," "Kendall,"
and "Park." As the Cambridge-Dorchester line was extended
beyond Park Street Under, the BERy replaced the signs with
updated versions (Figure 5.151).

numbered 0600–0754. Cambridge-Dorchester Type 5 rapid transit cars did not arrive until the 1960s.

The Dorchester Tunnel

A month after regular rapid transit service commenced between Harvard Station and Park Street Under, the BTC began work on the Dorchester Tunnel, an extension of the Cambridge-Dorchester line through downtown Boston into South Boston and Dorchester (Figure 5.137).The Dorchester Tunnel featured four stations, South Station Under, Broadway, and Andrew Square Stations. Between 1912 and 1918, the BTC opened the stations from

North to South at the approximate rate of one per year.

The first station to open along the Dorchester Tunnel was Washington Station, located where the Cambridge-Dorchester line passed beneath the Washington Street Tunnel of the Main Line Elevated. Construction began on May 30, 1912, with cut and cover work along Winter and Summer Streets, through the heart of Boston's downtown shopping district (Figure 5.126). Washington Station opened two stories below the busy streets on April 4, 1915, with familiar BTC interiors, including plaster-enclosed columns and ceilings, mosaic tile station names, and minimalist white finishes

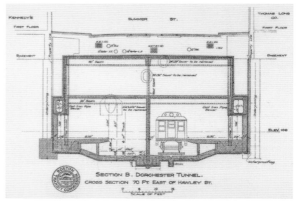

Figure 5.126 Summer Street Above Washington Station, 1913
A busy street scene takes place above the Dorchester Tunnel and Washington Station. The view is towards South Station.

Figure 5.127 Cross-section of Washington Station, 1913
A cross-section of Washington Station shows the stacked arrangement of Summer Street (top), the station's concourse (middle), and the station's tracks and platforms (bottom).

Figure 5.128 Washington Station, 1915
The interior of Washington Station of the Cambridge-Dorchester rapid transit line is now the southbound platform for MBTA Red Line trains at Downtown Crossing Station.

Figure 5.129 Entrance to South Station Under, 1917
A sign calls attention to a pedestrian entrance for South Station Under, a station on the Dorchester Tunnel segment of the Cambridge-Dorchester rapid transit line. On the other side of Summer Street (right), signs mark other entrances to the tunnel station. South Station, the grand steam train terminal, stands in the background.

(Figure 5.128). The BTC applied these features throughout all the stations of the Dorchester Tunnel.

Between the roof of Washington Station and Winter Street was an underground concourse designed to protect people from the elements as they walked between Washington Station on the Dorchester Tunnel and Winter and Summer Stations on the Washington Street Tunnel. In time, the concourse became populated with spaces for retailers and entrances into the lower levels of department stores flanking the tunnel. On August 13, 2012, the MBTA opened a ticketing and customer service center, branded its "CharlieCard Store," within the concourse.

The BTC extended the Dorchester Tunnel east from Washington Station using the roof shield method. The work followed Summer Street to a new tunnel station located beneath Dewey Square and the Atlantic Avenue Elevated, South Station Under. The name not only indicated the tunnel station's proximity to Boston's grand steam train terminal, it differentiated the underground station from the other South Station, high upon the Atlantic Avenue Elevated. South Station Under was constructed using the cut and cover method and opened to the public on December 3, 1916. It was accessed from street level stairways sprinkled around Dewey Square (Figure 5.129). Within the station, transit patrons enjoyed a lofty, two-story-high lobby (Figure 5.130), atypical for tunnel station in Boston. The spaciousness of the 1916 lobby was lost during the construction of late twentieth century tunnels of The Big Dig and the MBTA's Silver Line.

Figure 5.130 South Station Under Concourse, 1917
South Station under featured the most expansive lobby on the Dorchester Tunnel. Two-story tall columns support the roof and Dewey Square above. Stairs lead down to the platforms, one level below.

East of South Station Under, the BTC pushed the Dorchester Tunnel further along Summer Street, past South Station. At Dorchester Avenue, the tunnel turned ninety degrees towards the south to run under the bed of Fort Port Channel. In the soft mud beneath the waterway, workers constructed two separate, parallel, reinforced concrete tunnel tubes. Each tube accommodated a single rapid transit track, one for northbound trains, and another, for southbound trains. The unstable ground conditions beneath the channel required that the tubes be constructed with the full shield method, a first in Boston transit tunnel construction. Instead of advancing a roof shield along freshly constructed tunnel side walls, as had been done for portions of the Tremont Street Subway, the East Boston Tunnel, and the Beacon Hill Tunnel, workers under the Fort Point Channel utilized a full shield. Each shield protected the entire circumference of the working face for one tunnel tube. A drawing of one of the full shields, referred to by the BTC as a "plant" (Figure 5.131), reveals a contraption resembling an early Tunnel Boring Machine

(TBM). Modern TBMs, with their automatic cutting mechanisms, are common in modern tunnel construction. In 1916, men scratched out mud by hand at the face of the "plant" under the Fort Point Channel.

South of the Fort Point Channel, the Dorchester Tunnel continued into South Boston. There, under the intersection of Dorchester Avenue and Broadway, the BTC established South Boston's first station on the Cambridge-Dorchester rapid transit line. Broadway Station was a multi-level, multi-modal station arranged like a layer cake, with three levels tied together by a vertical spines of stairways (Figure 5.132). The uppermost of the three levels was an open-air streetcar platform that sat in the middle of Broadway, at the approach to the West Broadway Bridge (Figure 5.133). Streetcars running on surface tracks, mostly serving South Boston, stopped at the street-level platform.

Underground at Broadway was served by both streetcars and rapid transit trains. One story below the street, streetcars served both sides of a single platform that followed

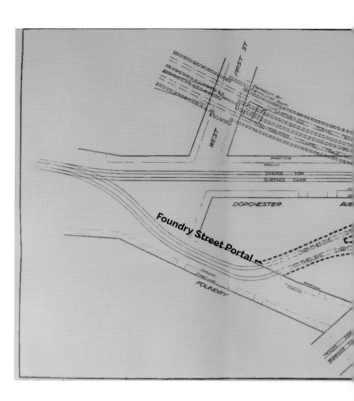

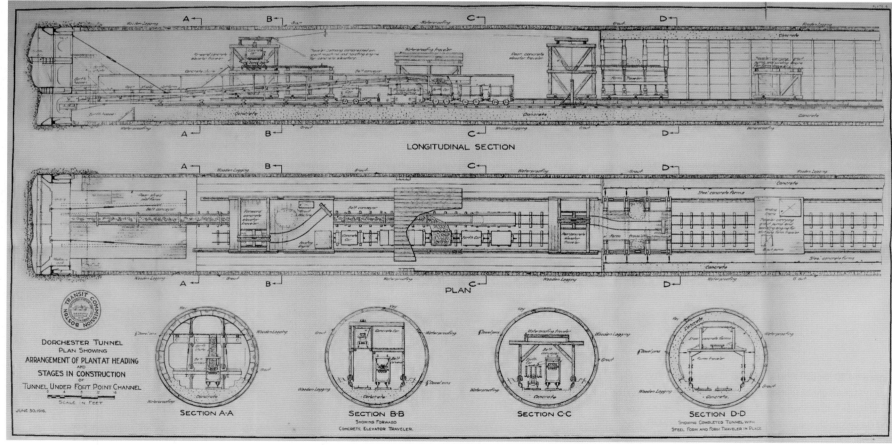

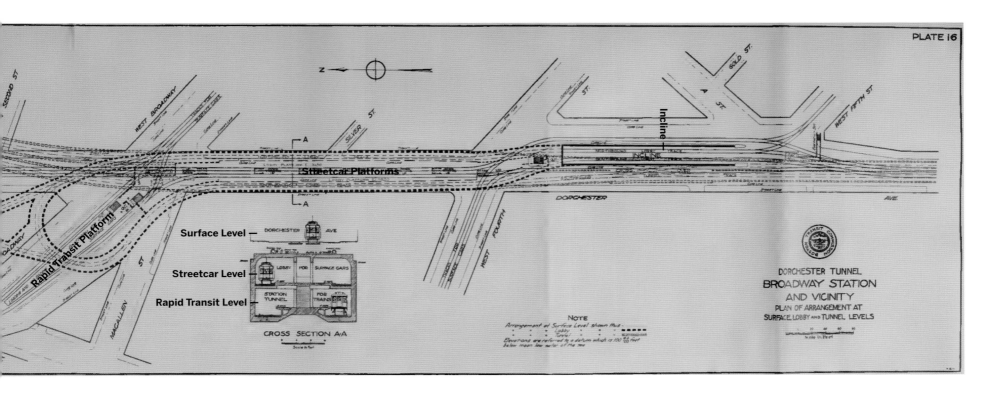

PLATE 16

Surface Level —

Streetcar Level —

Rapid Transit Level —

CROSS SECTION A-A

NOTE

DORCHESTER TUNNEL
BROADWAY STATION
AND VICINITY
PLAN OF ARRANGEMENT AT
SURFACE, LOBBY AND TUNNEL LEVELS

Figure 5.131 (Opp.) Digging Beneath the Channel, 1916
Drawings depict the "plant" used in the construction of the two Dorchester Tunnel tubes under Fort Point Channel. A longitudinal section (top), plan (middle), and cross-sections (bottom) reveal a primitive Tunnel Boring Machine.

Figure 5.132 (Above) Broadway Station Plan, 1916
A plan lays out the multi-level Broadway Station, served by rapid transit trains underground, and streetcars both underground and at street-level. A cross-section (bottom) reveals the layers of service provided.

Figure 5.133 (Right) Street-level at Broadway Station, 1917
At the foot of the approach to the West Broadway Bridge, a shelter protects the surface streetcar stop at Broadway Station.

Figure 5.134 Broadway Station, December 15, 1917
The mid-level portion of Broadway Station was served by streetcars. A stairway (left) leads down to the rapid transit platform, located on the station's lowermost level.

Dorchester Avenue (Figure 5.134). Streetcars, generally from Dorchester and points south of Boston, entered and exited the subterranean streetcar level through an incline and portal on Dorchester Avenue as well as a portal on Foundry Street. A streetcar loop track at the far northern end of the mid-level allowed cars to enter Broadway Station from, and return back to, the incline on Dorchester Avenue.

On the lowest level of Broadway Station, rapid transit trains of the Cambridge-Dorchester line served a central platform aligned beneath the mid-level streetcar platform. Rapid transit trains began running between Harvard and Broadway Stations on December 15, 1917. Streetcars served Broadway Station's mid-level.

Streetcar service came to an end within the mid-level of Broadway Station on October 14, 1919. Since June 2013, the former mid-level streetcar station has been occupied by an anti-terrorism and emergency preparedness training center. The federally-funded center contains decommissioned transit vehicles installed in simulated transit station environments. The station opened with retired MBTA vehicles, including a Type 8 light rail vehicle, a Blue Line rapid transit car, a Silver Line bus, and a typical city bus. Broadway's former mid-level now mimics modern transit stations and tunnels. It is equipped with smoke machines and audio systems to simulate real world scenarios. The training

center is used by various agencies, authorities, and first responders.

The final portion of the Dorchester Tunnel to be constructed was a cut and cover segment that followed Dorchester Avenue south, from Broadway Station to Andrew Square in Dorchester. At Andrew Square, the BTC established a terminal station for the Cambridge-Dorchester line (Figure 5.135). To make room for Andrew Square Station, the BTC relocated multiple buildings and homes. At street level, three streetcar platforms were served by two, run-through streetcar tracks, all protected by a large roof structure (Figure 5.136). Beneath the eastern end of the streetcar transfer area was the rapid transit portion of the station. Andrew Square Station opened for rapid transit service on June 29, 1918. For approximately a decade, it remained the southern terminus of the Cambridge-Dorchester rapid transit line.

After Andrew Square Station and the Dorchester Tunnel were completed in 1918, the term of the BTC expired on July 1. A day later, the Boston Transit Commission reconstituted itself as the Boston Transit Department (BTD). The BTD continued to oversee the planning and construction of transportation projects, but unlike the BTC, the BTD did not focus exclusively on public transit. In addition to orchestrating extensions and improvements to transit lines, the BTD oversaw completion of

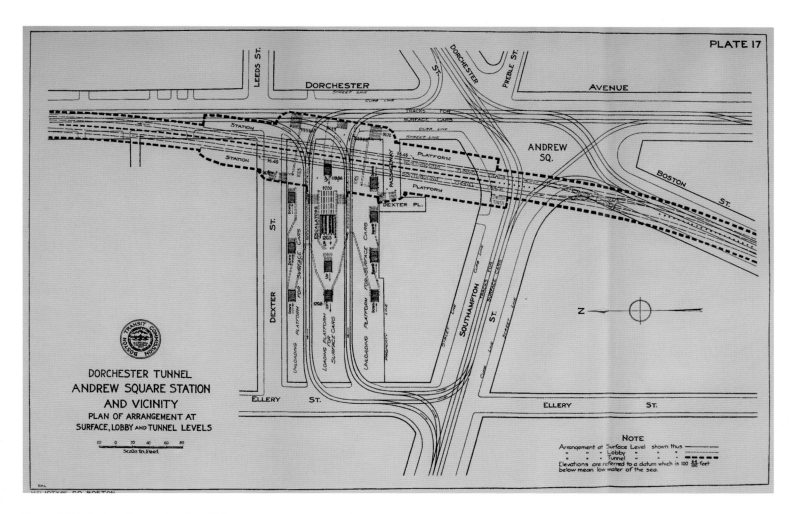

Figure 5.135 Andrew Square Station, 1916

Extensive surface streetcar tracks run around and through the station. Thick dashed lines denote the rapid transit tunnel and station running underground and perpendicular to the streetcar platforms.

Figure 5.136 Erecting Andrew Square, November 24, 1917

Steel framing rises for the above-ground streetcar transfer portion of Andrew Square Station.

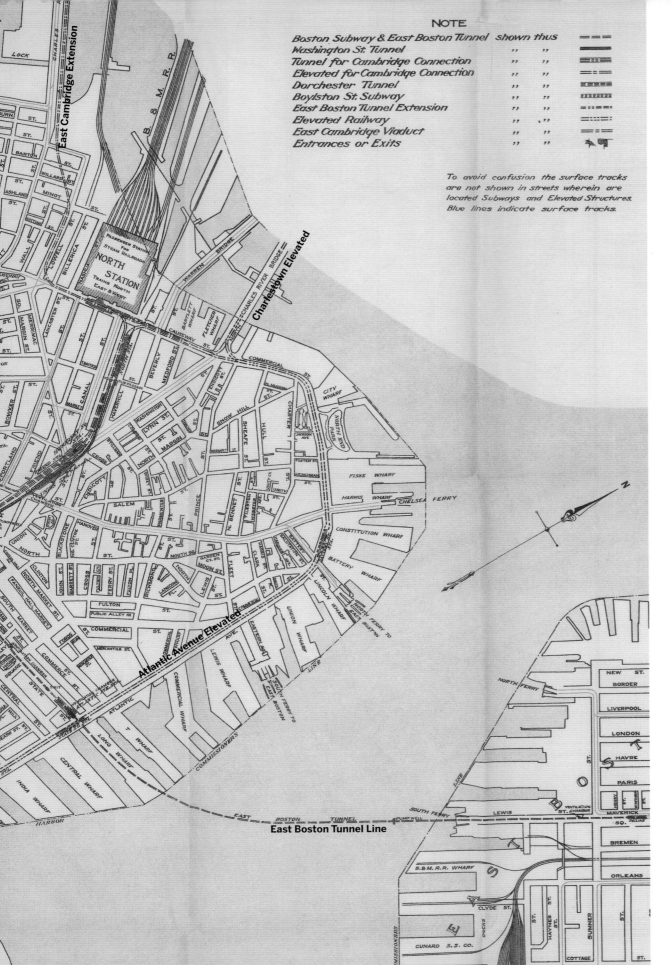

Figure 5.137 Boston Transit Commission Map, 1917
Dated one year before the Boston Transit Commission became
the Boston Transit Department, a map depicts major public
transit infrastructure projects brought to life by the BTC and
the BERy.

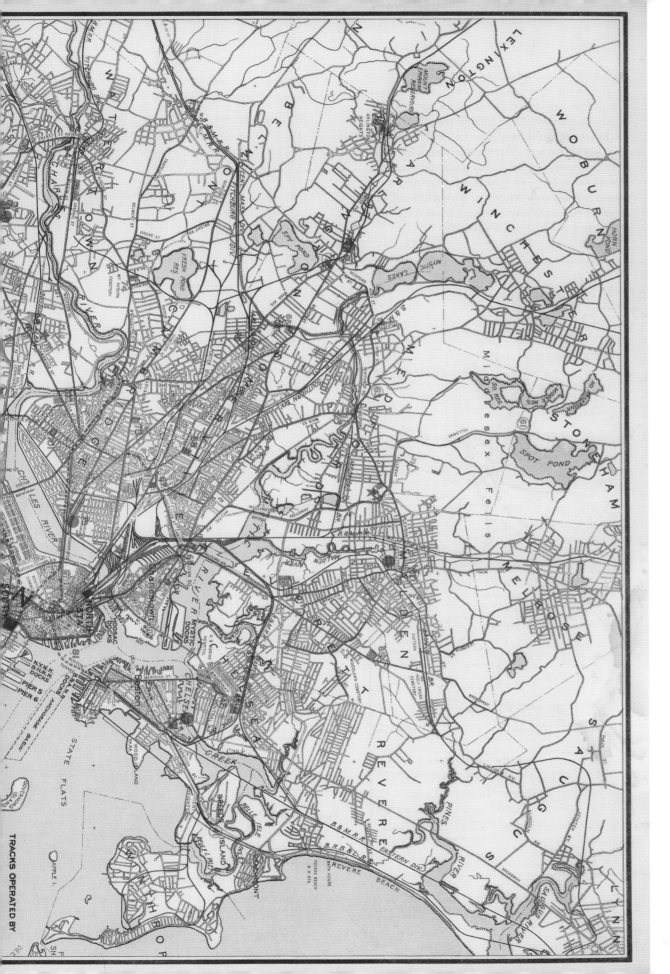

Figure 5.138 Mapping the BERy's System, January 1916

A map shows car houses as red rectangles, power stations as green stars, sub-power stations as green circles, double elevated railway tracks as green lines, subway and tunnel tracks as dashed green lines, surface tracks as red lines, single surface tracks as dashed red lines, and non-BERy tracks in yellow.

automobile-centric projects, including the Sumner Tunnel under Boston Harbor. The BTD was absorbed by the MTA in 1949.

At the end of the BTC era, Boston was outfitted with a modern network of radiating rapid transit lines that efficiently transported passengers between regional points (Figure 5.138 and Figure 5.139). An article, titled "Improvements on Boston Elevated System" in the March 1, 1913 edition of *Electric Railway Journal*, celebrated Boston's rapid transit system at the time:

Each new rapid transit line has added free transfer points where it has been articulated with the rest of the system and has from its opening day of service shortened the time of transit between the heart of the city and the outlying districts to an extent little less than revolutionary. Probably no other system in the world gives the possessor of a nickel so large an opportunity to enjoy a varied journey over interconnecting lines of such diverse character, often without even the effort of asking for a free transfer check.

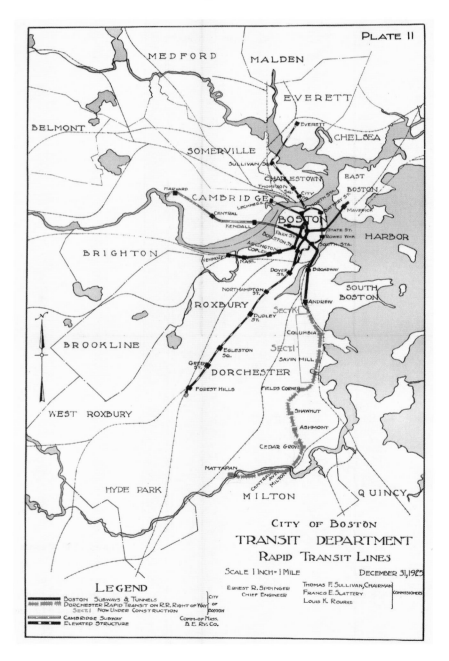

Figure 5.139 Rapid Transit Lines, December 31, 1925
Solid and dashed black lines represent the BERy's elevated railways, streetcar subways, and rapid transit tunnels. A dashed red line highlights the proposed Dorchester Tunnel Extension and Mattapan High Speed Line.

Figure 5.140 New Haven Railroad Ticket, Undated
A ticket for travel between Boston and Jamaica Plain, Ashmont, Dorchester, and Neponset indicates a fare of five cents.

The Dorchester Tunnel Extension

In the mid-1920s, the Cambridge-Dorchester rapid transit line was extended south, from Andrew Square Station, to serve Dorchester's growing population. Various routes were explored for the Dorchester Extension, including a never-realized tunnel that would have followed much of Dorchester Avenue, the traditional spine of the neighborhood. The finalized route followed existing steam railroad rights-of-way, making the line more economical to build and less disruptive to the community than tunneling beneath the length of busy Dorchester Avenue. The conversion of a steam railroad right-of-way into a rapid transit line was unprecedented in Boston, though the concept was proposed as early as 1926, by the Commonwealth's Division of Metropolitan Planning.

The double-track Dorchester Tunnel Extension wove its way from Andrew Square to Dorchester's Ashmont section (Figure 5.139). From Andrew Square Station, the extension first ran towards Boston Harbor. It then followed alongside a portion of the New Haven Railroad trackage, once the main line of the Old Colony Railroad (Old Colony). A New Haven ticket, good for travel along the lines that became the foundation of the Dorchester Tunnel Extension, is shown in Figure 5.140. South of Andrew Square, the first two stations along the Dorchester Tunnel Extension were Columbia (now JFK/UMass) and Savin Hill Stations. Both were center-platform type and sat at grade. Each station had a head house attached to the side of a road bridge spanning the parallel tracks of the Cambridge-Dorchester line and the New Haven (Figure 5.141 and Figure 5.142).

Beyond Savin Hill Station, at Harrison Square, the Dorchester Tunnel Extension diverged from the former Old Colony main line to the follow the right-of-way of the New Haven's Shawmut Branch, and then, a portion of a New Haven branch to

Figure 5.141 Columbia Station, 1927
Beneath the sign "Columbia," doors are designated as for moving "in" or "out" of the station. The station's covered platform lies below (right).

Figure 5.142 Savin Hill Station, 1927
The station's head house sits at street-level, while its platform lies below (right).

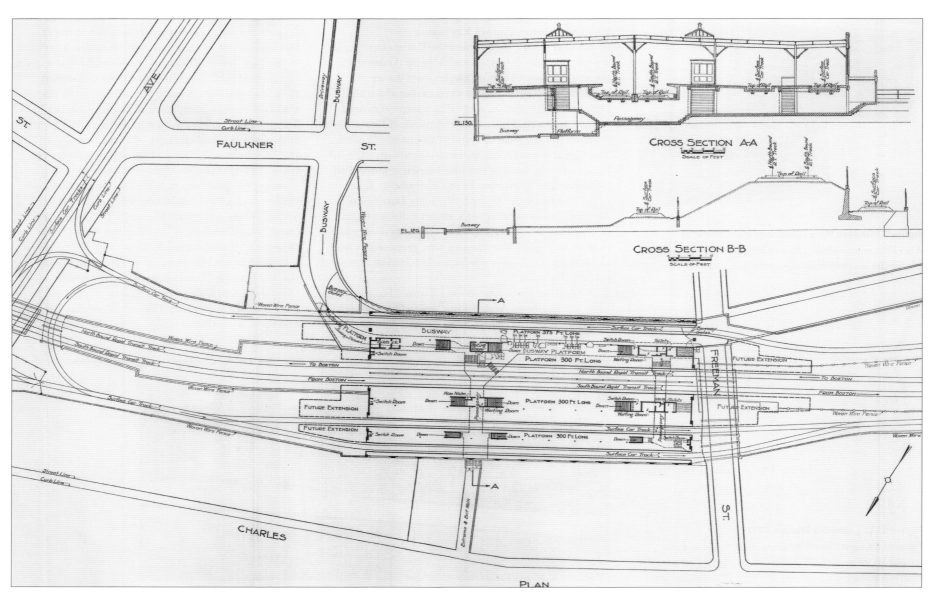

CROSS SECTION A-A

CROSS SECTION B-B

PLAN

Mattapan. As was the case with all former Old Colony lines, the Shawmut Branch was taken over by the New Haven in 1893. The New Haven's 1926 arrangement with the BTD to discontinue passenger service along the Shawmut Branch allowed the BTD to convert the Shawmut Branch, as far south as Ashmont, into the southernmost portion of the Dorchester Tunnel Extension. Between Savin Hill Station and Ashmont, the BTD established two intermediate stations, Fields Corner and Shawmut Stations.

Fields Corner Station, located next to the neighborhood commercial center of the same name, was a transfer station, with three streetcar tracks and a pair of rapid transit tracks (Figure 5.143).

A covered busway and pedestrian passageway occupied a lower level. Various ramps brought streetcars into an upper level, where rapid transit trains passed through the center of the station (Figure 5.144). Transit patrons transferred between streetcars and rapid transit trains by crossing platforms (Figure 5.145) or utilizing the lower level transfer passageway.

The site of the BTD's Shawmut Station was previously used by the Old Colony, and later, the New Haven, for a depot on the Shawmut Branch. As part of its conversion of the former steam railroad line, the BTD replaced the railroad depot with an underground station and short stretch of tunnel (Figure 5.146). Shawmut Station became the only

Figure 5.143 Fields Corner Station, 1927

The double-track Cambridge-Dorchester rapid transit line passes through the middle of the upper level of Fields Corner Station. Alongside the southbound rapid transit track are two platforms and two streetcar tracks. Alongside the northbound rapid transit track are one platform and one streetcar track. The station's busway (shown dashed) lies beneath the northbound platform. On the station's lower level, passageways connect entrances with stairways leading up to the platforms. Cross-sections (top) reveal one of the passageways and the relative elevations of the station's busway, streetcar tracks, and rapid transit tracks.

Figure 5.144 Fields Corner Station, 1927
Of the four large portals on the eastern side of the station, the single portal on the left and the two portals on the right are for streetcars. The two portals in the middle are for rapid transit trains of the Cambridge-Dorchester line.

Figure 5.145 Fields Corner Station Interior, 1927
The platform between the southbound rapid transit track (left) and pair of streetcar tracks running through the northern portion of the station (right) is connected via stairs (center) to an underground passageway. The view faces the same direction as Figure 5.144.

Figure 5.146 Shawmut Station, May 26, 1927
Construction of Shawmut Station and tunnel for trains of the Cambridge-Dorchester rapid transit line is underway alongside the shuttered former New Haven steam railroad depot.

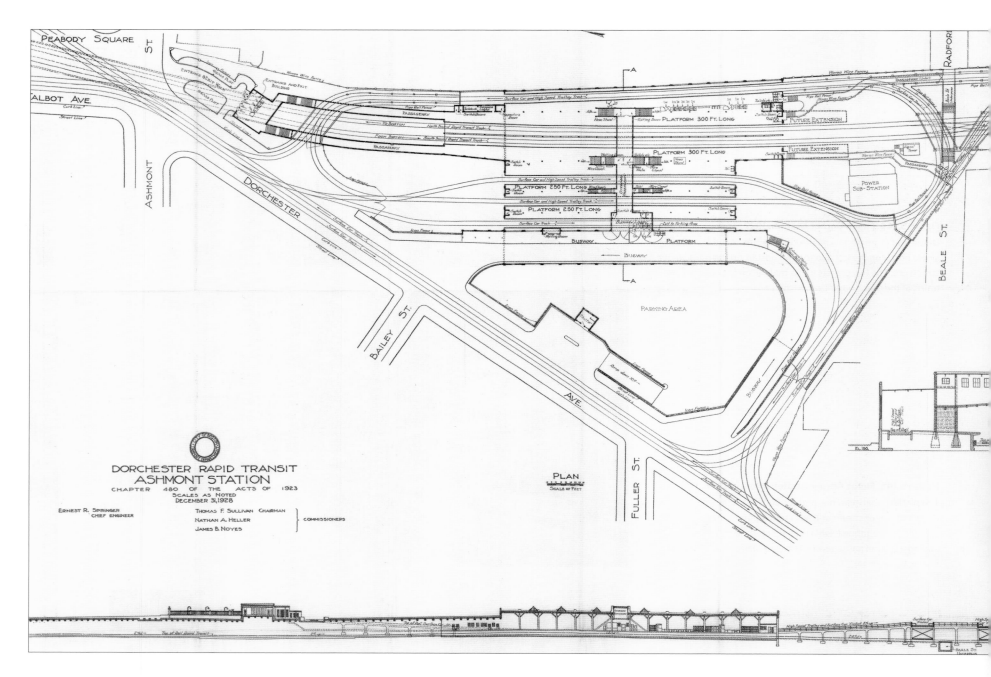

DORCHESTER RAPID TRANSIT
ASHMONT STATION
CHAPTER 480 OF THE ACTS OF 1923
SCALES AS NOTED
DECEMBER 31, 1928

ERNEST R. SPRINGER
CHIEF ENGINEER

THOMAS F. SULLIVAN CHAIRMAN
NATHAN A. HELLER
JAMES B. NOYES

COMMISSIONERS

PLAN
Scale of Feet

tunnel station between Andrew and Ashmont Stations. The names of the BTD's Savin Hill, Fields Corner, Shawmut, and Ashmont Stations were all recycled names of former New Haven depots.

The southern terminus of the Dorchester Tunnel Extension, along with the entire Cambridge-Dorchester rapid transit line, was Ashmont Station (Figure 5.147 and Figure 5.148). At Ashmont, the Cambridge-Dorchester line passed under Peabody Square, through the center of Ashmont Station, and into a rapid transit car storage yard at Codman

Street. A pair of covered passageways one level below the street linked the station's Peabody Square head house with the station's rapid transit platforms. The passageways, which were essentially windowless tunnels, remained in use until December 1975, when the MBTA, citing safety concerns, closed them and the Peabody Square head house.

Within the station, the streetcar and rapid transit tracks and platforms were at the same grade, one level below Peabody Square (Figure 5.149).

Figure 5.147 (Above) Ashmont Station, December 31, 1928
Drawings depict the southern terminus of the Cambridge-Dorchester rapid transit line at Ashmont. A plan of the two-level, multi-modal station (middle) dominates the sheet. A cross-section (right) exposes the configuration of spaces within. Streetcar tracks wind around and through the station. Rapid transit tracks form the station's spine.

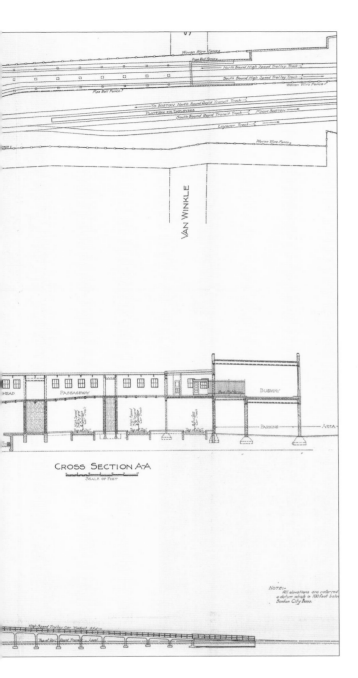

CROSS SECTION A-A

Figure 5.148 (Top) Ashmont Station, 1928
The station lies behind and below its head house (left) and
Dorchester Avenue (right). Rapid transit tracks and pedestrian passageways lie concealed within the roofed enclosure
(middle) connecting the head house and the station. The four
lower portals are for streetcars. The busway is on the right.

Figure 5.149 (Right) Inside Ashmont Station, 1928
The southbound rapid transit platform (far left) and northbound rapid transit platform (middle) are protected by the
turnstiles (right) from the eastern streetcar boarding area.

Figure 5.150 Ashmont Parking Lot and Busway, 1928

An upper level walkway was a feeder from the station's street-level busway to all of the train and streetcar platforms below. West of the busway, and located at the same grade of the rapid transit tracks and platforms, was an open parking area (Figure 5.150). A ramp linked the parking area with Dorchester Avenue. Buses and streetcars ran to and from Dorchester Avenue, through the station, and around the parking area.

After multiple renovations, the configuration of Ashmont Station, as it is for Fields Corner Station, is significantly different today. A major renovation kicked off in December 1975 and another was completed in the late 2000s. Today, Ashmont Station is essentially a long building enclosing the two rapid transit tracks and platforms with an open busway along one side. The parking lot was lost to private development. All of the streetcar tracks and platforms at Ashmont have been eliminated, save for a single loop and exterior platform at the extreme southern end of the station. The loop carries MBTA streetcars between Ashmont and Dorchester's Mattapan neighborhood. Transit riders continue to transfer between rapid transit trains, streetcars, and buses at Ashmont Station, one of the few places remaining in the United States where all three modes never ceased regular revenue operation.

On November 5, 1927, the Dorchester Tunnel Extension opened to the public as far south as Fields Corner Station. The BERy operated four-car trains during rush hours and two-car trains at other times. Regular service between Harvard Square and Ashmont commenced on September 1, 1928. Coinciding with the opening of service between Cambridge and Ashmont, the BERy fitted Cambridge-Dorchester rapid transit cars, including its Cambridge-Dorchester Type 3 cars (Figure 5.152 and Figure 5.153) with new Order of Stations signs (Figure 5.151).

Figure 5.151 Cambridge-Dorchester Order of Stations Sign
As early as 1928, Cambridge-Dorchester rapid transit cars wore Order of Stations signs listing stations from Harvard to Ashmont. As the sign instructs, riders heading "To Dorchester" "read down" the list for upcoming stops. Conversely, riders "read up" if they were travelling "To Cambridge."

Figure 5.152 Cambridge-Dorchester Type 3 Car, 1937

Interior of Cambridge-Dorchester Type 3 car number 0688 is outfitted with wooden benches, rigid hangers, and Order of Stations signs (far right). Figure 5.153 shows the exterior of a typical Cambridge-Dorchester Type 3 car.

Figure 5.153 Cambridge-Dorchester Type 3 Car, 1922

Cambridge-Dorchester Type 3 car number 0671 sits parked next to Eliot Square Shops in Cambridge. The interior of another Type 3 car is shown in Figure 5.152.

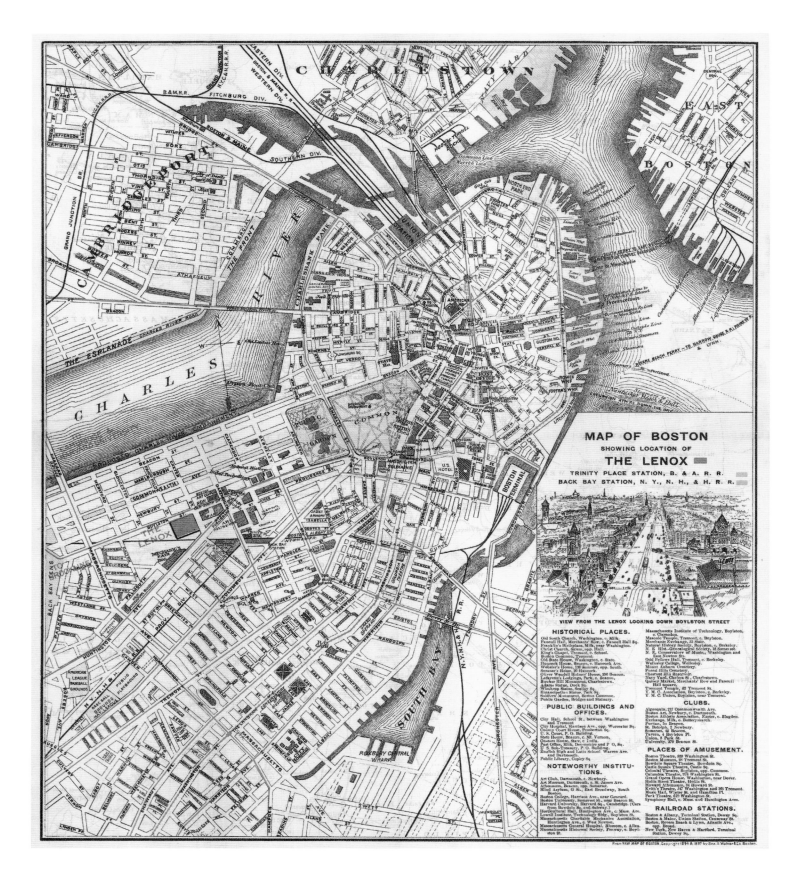

MAP OF BOSTON

SHOWING LOCATION OF

THE LENOX

TRINITY PLACE STATION, B. & A. R. R.

BACK BAY STATION, N. Y., N. H., & H. R. R.

VIEW FROM THE LENOX LOOKING DOWN BOYLSTON STREET

HISTORICAL PLACES.

Old South Church, Washington, c. Milk.
Faneuil Hall, Merchants' Row, c. Faneuil Hall Sq.
Franklin's Birthplace, Milk, near Washington.
Christ Church, Salem, opp. Hull.
King's Chapel, Tremont, c. School.
Boston Common, Tremont.
Old State House, Washington, c. State.
Hancock House, Beacon, c. Hancock Ave.
Webster's House, 10 Summer, opp. South.
Sumner's House, 37 Hancock.
Oliver Wendell Holmes' House, 296 Beacon.
Lafayette's Lodgings, Park, c. Beacon.
Bunker Hill Monument, Charlestown.
Adams Statue, Dock St.
Winthrop Statue, Scollay Sq.
Emancipation Statue, Park Sq.
Soldiers' Monument, Boston Common.
Public Garden, Bridge and Statuary.

PUBLIC BUILDINGS AND OFFICES.

City Hall, School St., between Washington and Tremont.
City Hospital, Harrison Ave., opp. Worcester Sq.
County Court House, Pemberton Sq.
U. S. Court, P. O. Building.
State House, Beacon, c. Mt. Vernon.
Custom House, State, c. India.
Post Office, Milk, Devonshire and P. O. Sq.
U. S. Sub-Treasury, P. O. Building.
English High and Latin School, Warren Ave. and Dartmouth.
Public Library, Copley Sq.

NOTEWORTHY INSTITUTIONS.

Art Club, Dartmouth, c. Newbury.
Art Museum, Dartmouth, c. St. James Ave.
Athenaeum, Beacon, opp. Somerset.
Blind Asylum, G St., East Broadway, South Boston.
Boston College, Harrison Ave., near Concord.
Boston University, Somerset St., near Beacon St.
Harvard University, Harvard sq., Cambridge. (Cars from Bowdoin Sq. and Subway.)
Horticultural Hall, Huntington Ave., c. Mass. Ave.
Lowell Institute, Technology Bldg., Boylston St.
Massachusetts Charitable Mechanics Association, Huntington Ave., c. West Newton.
Massachusetts General Hospital, Blossom, c. Allen.
Massachusetts Historical Society, Fenway, c. Boylston St.

Massachusetts Institute of Technology, Boylston, c. Clarendon.
Masonic Temple, Tremont, c. Boylston.
Merchants Exchange, 53 State.
Natural History Society, Boylston, c. Berkeley.
N. E. Hist.-Genealogical Society, 18 Somerset.
N. E. Conservatory of Music, Washington and East Newton Sts.
Odd Fellows Hall, Tremont, c. Berkeley.
Wellesley College, Wellesley.
Mount Auburn Cemetery.
Forest Hills Cemetery.
Charter Hill Reservoir.
Navy Yard, Chelsea St., Charlestown.
Quincy Market, Merchants' Row and Faneuil Hall square.
Tremont Temple, 88 Tremont St.
Y. M. C. Association, Boylston, c. Berkeley.
Y. M. C. Union, Boylston, near Tremont.

CLUBS.

Algonquin, 217 Commonwealth Ave.
Boston Art, Newbury, c. Dartmouth.
Boston Athletic Association, Exeter, c. Blagden.
Exchange, Milk, c. Batterymarch.
Puritan, 30 Beacon.
B. Botolph, 2 Newbury.
Somerset, 42 Beacon.
Tavern, 4 Boylston Pl.
Union, 8 Park St.
University, 270 Beacon St.

PLACES OF AMUSEMENT.

Boston Theatre, 539 Washington St.
Boston Museum, 29 Tremont St.
Bowdoin Square Theatre, Bowdoin Sq.
Castle Square Theatre, Castle Sq.
Colonial Theatre, Boylston, opp. Common.
Columbia Theatre, 978 Washington St.
Grand Opera House, Washington, near Dover.
Hollis Street Theatre, Hollis St.
Howard Athenaeum, 34 Howard St.
Keith's Theatre, 547 Washington and Mt Tremont.
Music Hall, Winter St. and Hamilton Pl.
Park Theatre, 619 Washington St.
Symphony Hall, c. Mass. and Huntington Aves.

RAILROAD STATIONS.

Boston & Albany, Terminal Station, Dewey Sq.
Boston & Maine, Union Station, Causeway St.
Boston, Revere Beach & Lynn, Atlantic Ave., opp. Rowe's.
New York, New Haven & Hartford, Terminal Station, Dewey Sq.

CHAPTER 6

Pocket Maps and Transit Improvements In the Early Twentieth Century

Walker's Vest Pocket Maps

Today, pocket-sized public transit maps, some printed onto paper and others accessed with mobile devices, are ubiquitous. Long before public control of public transportation in Greater Boston, transit riders relied on commercially available maps, often produced by third-party companies instead of transit operators themselves. During the late nineteenth and early twentieth centuries, a prolific Boston-based maker of maps, including portable maps showing Boston's transit lines, was George H. Walker. By the time South Station opened in 1899, George H. Walker & Company (Walker) was one of the largest cartographic publishing houses in New England. From facilities on High Street, and later on Newbury Street, Walker designed, printed, and published maps covering all parts of the American northeast. The Boston Transit Commission (BTC) commissioned Walker to print maps for its publications and reports. The West End Street Railway Company (West End) and Boston Elevated Railway Company (BERy) mapped their systems over base maps prepared by Walker.

One of Walker's most popular products was its "Vest Pocket Map of Boston," produced from the 1890s through the 1930s (Figure 6.1). The Vest Pocket Map was printed onto thin paper and folded out from a protective, card-stock cover featuring a map highlighting Walker's place of business (Figure 6.2). Walker's Vest Pocket Maps detailed not only Boston' streets and important buildings, but also the city's streetcar lines, subway tunnels,

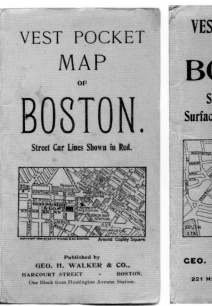
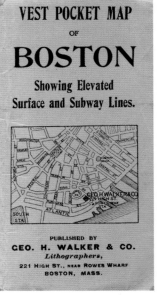

Figure 6.1 (Opposite) Vest Pocket Map of Boston, 1900
Red lines highlight railed transit lines tracing Boston's streets. Dashed lines represent tracks in streetcar subways. Solid lines with cross-ticks show elevated railways. Black lines highlight steam railroad lines.

Figure 6.2 Vest Pocket Map Covers, 1899; 1905
Covers of Walker's "Vest Pocket Map of Boston" feature a small map guiding users to Walker's establishment, on Harcourt Street in 1899 (left), and on High Street in 1905 (right).

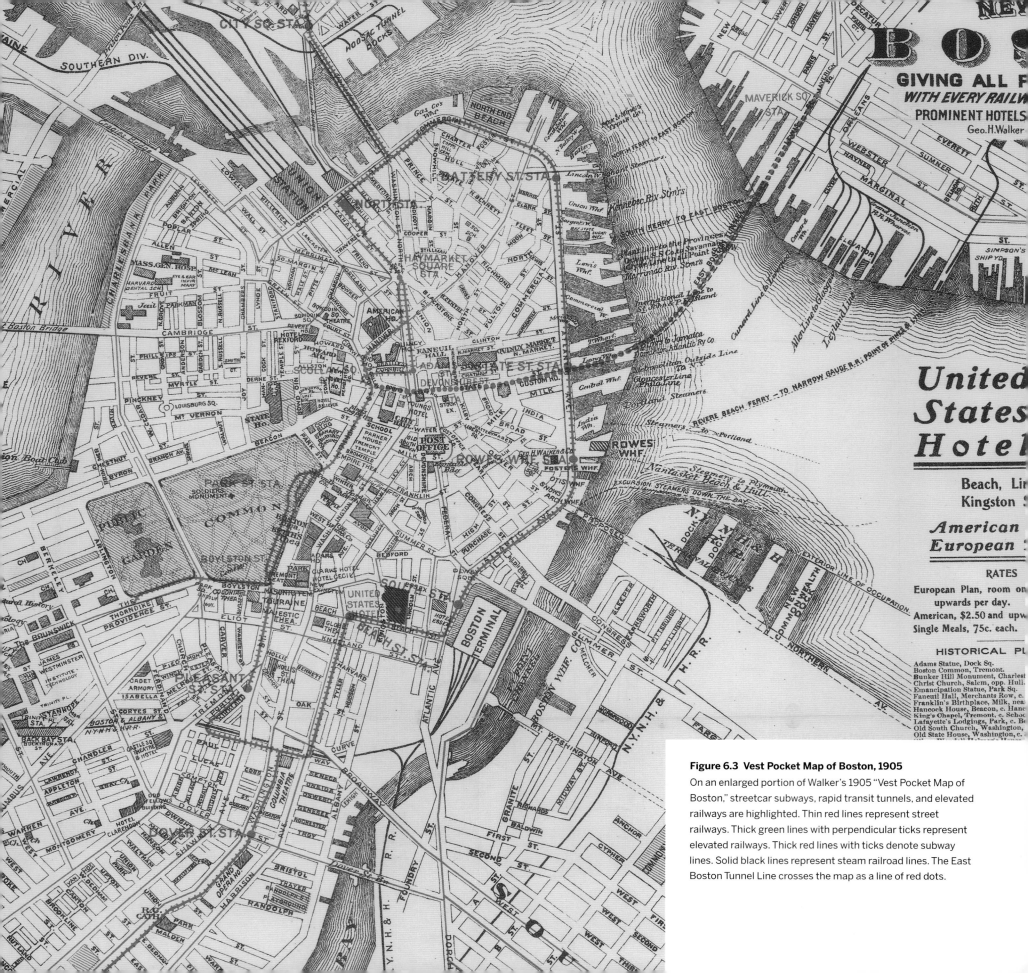

Figure 6.3 Vest Pocket Map of Boston, 1905

On an enlarged portion of Walker's 1905 "Vest Pocket Map of Boston," streetcar subways, rapid transit tunnels, and elevated railways are highlighted. Thin red lines represent street railways. Thick green lines with perpendicular ticks represent elevated railways. Thick red lines with ticks denote subway lines. Solid black lines represent steam railroad lines. The East Boston Tunnel Line crosses the map as a line of red dots.

Figure 6.4 Newman the Shoeman Map of Boston, 1899

A map produced by George H. Walker & Company highlights in red the newly opened Tremont Street Subway as well as locations of a retailer for whom the map was produced, "Newman The Shoeman."

transit stations, elevated railways, ferry routes, and ferry terminals (Figure 6.2). Walker's maps were available at newsstands throughout Boston.

Initially as George H. Walker & Company, and later as Walker Lithograph & Publishing Company, Walker produced maps branded for particular businesses, including a 1905 Vest Pocket Map was branded for the United States Hotel (Figure 6.3). The landmark hotel sat across the street from the Boston & Albany Railroad (Boston & Albany)

station, strategically poised to receive travellers arriving on trains from the interior of America. Another branded Walker map, the "Map of Boston Published for Newman the Shoeman" (Figure 6.4), elegantly maps the recently completed Tremont Street Subway. Thirteen years after publishing the Shoeman map, Walker again updated maps for Boston, this time to include the first extension of the Tremont Street Subway, the Boylston Street Subway.

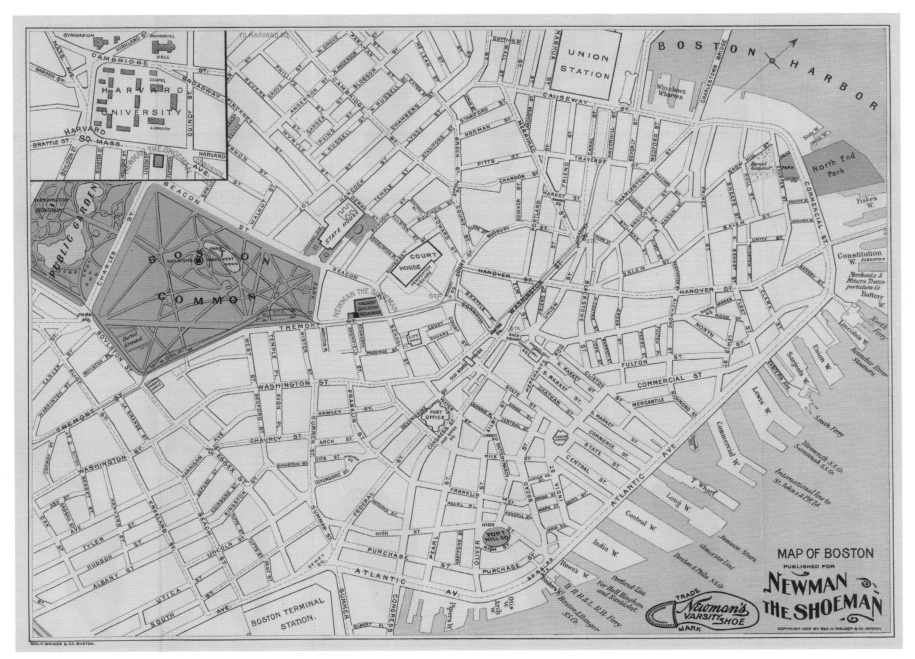

The Boylston Street Subway

Construction of the Boylston Street Subway, approved by the General Court in 1911, was overseen by the BTC. The Boylston Street Subway extended the 1897–98 Tremont Street Subway to the west, beyond the Public Garden, and across the length of Boston's Back Bay neighborhood. Work commenced on the double-track subway and its two stations on March 18, 1912. The Boylston Street Subway was constructed through land claimed from tidal waters during the last half of the nineteenth century. As such, much of the project was constructed beneath the level of ground water. Portions of the subway and its two stations were supported by thousands of wooden piles, all driven into the same mud encapsulating piles supporting the Boston Public Library, Trinity Church, and many other Back Bay buildings.

A plan published by the BTC in 1912 (Figure 6.5) lays out the route and stations of the Boylston Street Subway. From its connection with the Tremont Street Subway under Charles Street, the subway followed beneath its namesake street. After passing alongside the Public Garden Incline, it crossed the alphabetized streets of the Back Bay. West of Copley Square, the subway turned to parallel the tracks of the Boston & Albany, before passing beneath Massachusetts Avenue. West of the avenue, the subway followed a portion of Newbury Street, where it passed alongside the headquarters of the Walker Lithograph & Publishing Co. The subway then headed towards the intersection of Beacon Street and Commonwealth Avenue. In the central reservation of Commonwealth Avenue, the Boylston Street Subway's pair of tracks emerged into daylight along an incline, the top of which

Figure 6.5 The Boylston Street Subway, June 30, 1912
A plan (top) covers the area from Park Street (far right) to what is now Kenmore Square (far left). The Boylston Street Subway runs east to west (right to left): from the Public Garden Incline of the Tremont Street Subway (right); under Boylston Street, from Arlington to Hereford Streets (middle); alongside the Boston & Albany Railroad tracks (left); and under the Back Bay Fens to a portal and incline at Kenmore Street (far left). Below the plan is a longitudinal section of the subway tunnel. The plan does not show the Boylston Street Incline. The location of the incline had yet to be finalized.

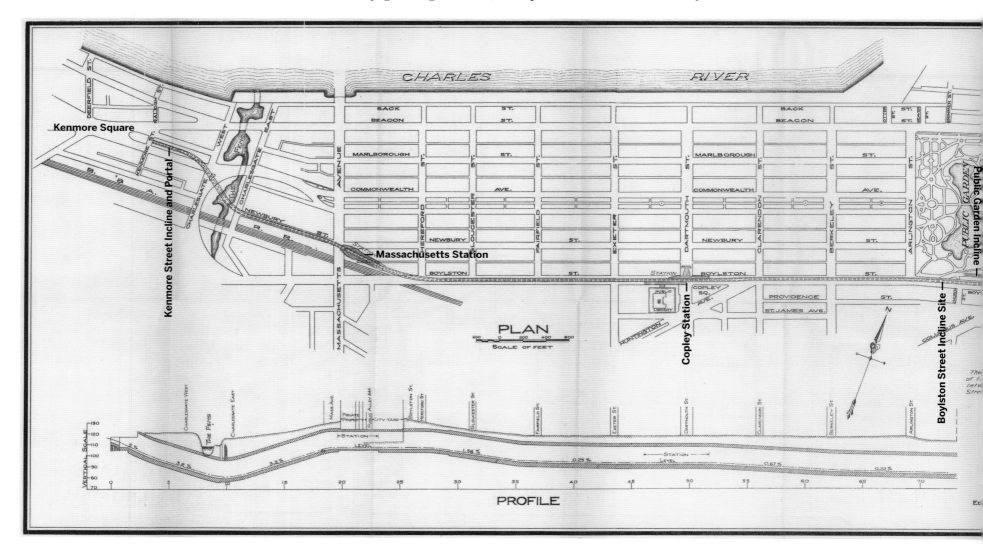

Figure 6.6 The Incline at Kenmore Street, October 2, 1914
Taken the day before the public opening of the Boylston Street Subway, a photograph shows a brand new incline and portal at Kenmore Street, the western end of the subway.

Figure 6.7 (Bottom) The Boylston Street Incline, 1915

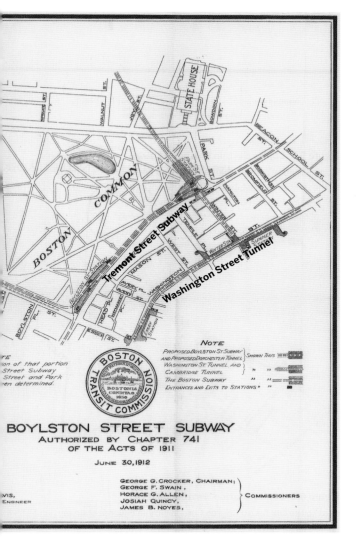

NOTE

PROPOSED BOYLSTON ST. SUBWAY
AND PROPOSED DORCHESTER TUNNEL } SHOWN THUS ═══
WASHINGTON ST. TUNNEL AND
CAMBRIDGE TUNNEL } ″ ″ ═══
THE BOSTON SUBWAY ″ ″ ═══
ENTRANCES AND EXITS TO STATIONS ″ ″ ■

BOYLSTON STREET SUBWAY
AUTHORIZED BY CHAPTER 741
OF THE ACTS OF 1911

JUNE 30, 1912

GEORGE G. CROCKER, CHAIRMAN;
GEORGE F. SWAIN,
HORACE G. ALLEN, } COMMISSIONERS
JOSIAH QUINCY,
JAMES B. NOYES,

aligned with Kenmore Street. There, tracks of the subway connected with surface tracks (Figure 6.6).

Omitted from the 1912 BTC map, but part of the final scope of the Boylston Street Subway, was a second incline, situated in the middle of Boylston Street alongside the Public Garden. The Boylston Street Incline replaced the Public Garden Incline, the Tremont Street Subway's western entrance for streetcars since 1897. Using the Boylston Street Incline streetcars made the transition between subway and surface tracks (Figure 6.7). The Boylston Street Incline remained in use until

1941, when it was covered over at street-level. Underground, the lowermost portion of the incline remains visible from the windows of Massachusetts Bay Transportation Authority (MBTA) Green Line trolleys moving between Boylston and Arlington Stations.

When completed, the Boylston Street Subway reduced average travel time for streetcars travelling between Park Street Station and Governor Square (now Kenmore Square) from sixteen to nine minutes. The subway extension eliminated a mile

and a half of surface travel through busy Back Bay streets for streetcars. The project, including its two stations cost just shy of $5 million.

The Boylston Street Subway opened on October 3, 1914 with two streetcar subway stations, Copley and Massachusetts Stations. Copley was named for the square that it served while Massachusetts was named for the avenue at which it was located. Copley Station opened with three head houses, one for its eastbound and two for its westbound platform. Copley's eastbound head house sat only a few

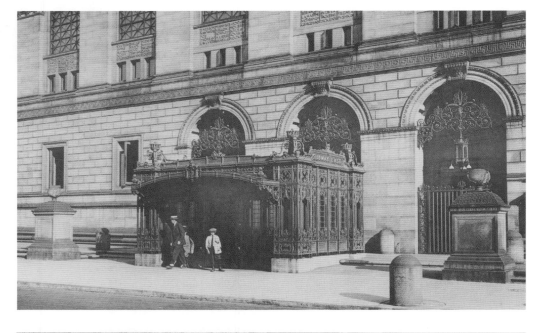

Figure 6.8 Copley Station Eastbound, 1915
Copley Station's ornate eastbound head house stands in front of the Boston Public Library. The ironwork of the head house was inspired by that of the library behind it.

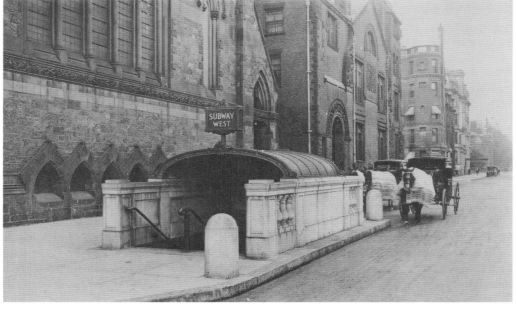

Figure 6.9 Copley Station Westbound, 1915
Next to the Old South Church (left), a simple covered stairway served as an entrance to the westbound side of Copley Station.

feet from the Boylston Street facade of the Boston Public Library. The architecturally-significant temple to knowledge was designed by architects McKim, Mead and White. Due to the closeness of the head house and the library, the BTC engaged an architect to design a special head house, one architecturally sensitive to the library. Copley's eastbound head house became an enclosure of ornate iron-work with details echoing the ornamental iron-work of the library (Figure 6.8). Across the street, one of Copley's westbound head houses, located at the corner of Boylston and Dartmouth Streets, was essentially a stairway surrounded by granite-faced half-walls and capped by a vaulted roof. Crowning

the structure was an electrically illuminated sign that read "Subway West" (Figure 6.9).

The Boylston Street Subway's other station, Massachusetts Station, was located at the corner of Newbury Street and Massachusetts Avenue. Unlike Copley Station, Massachusetts Station opened with a transfer mezzanine one level below the street and one level above its platforms. The mezzanine allowed pedestrians to cross between the westbound and eastbound platforms without having to leave the paid area of the station.

When Massachusetts Station opened in 1914, it immediately became a busy transfer point for people moving between trolleys running in the

Figure 6.10 Massachusetts Station, November 28, 1919
The streetcar transfer portion of Massachusetts Station spans the tracks of the Boston & Albany Railroad (bottom), from Boylston Street (far left) to Newbury Street (out of view, to the right). The interior of the space is revealed in Figure 6.11.

Figure 6.11 Streetcar Transfer Area, November 28, 1919
At street-level within Massachusetts Station, streetcars dropped off and picked up passengers from one of two tracks. Ceiling-hung signs clarify which trolleys will arrive along which track. Between the tracks, stairs lead down to the streetcar subway portion of the station. Streetcars entered and exited the transfer area via portals on Newbury Street (shown in the distance) and Boylston Street (behind the photographer).

Figure 6.12 Massachusetts Station, November 28, 1919
A pair of portals on Boylston Street, along with a corresponding pair on Newbury Street (Figure 6.13), allowed streetcars to move through the street-level portion of Massachusetts Station.

subway and streetcars travelling above ground. In order to make transfers easier at Massachusetts Station, the successor to the BTC, the Boston Transit Department (BTD), added a streetcar transfer station atop the streetcar subway station in 1919. The street-level addition spanned the block from Boylston Street to Newbury Street (Figure 6.10). Stairs linked the streetcar transfer station with the mezzanine and platforms of the subway station. The transfer station eliminated the need for people to exit onto the street to locate a trolley and coordinate a transfer. Instead, subway travelers simply walked upstairs and waited within the covered transfer area (Figure 6.11). Streetcars entered and exited the transfer area via portals on both the Boylston Street (Figure 6.12) and Newbury Street sides (Figure 6.13). Much of the upper level, including the entire portion along Boylston Street, was lost to construction of the Massachusetts Turnpike in the mid-twentieth century. Today, the portals on the Newbury Street side, though long sealed to streetcars, remain visible, concealing MBTA electrical equipment that powers the subway.

The 1914 interiors of Copley and Massachusetts Stations featured colored terrazzo, inlaid mosaic tiles, tiled walls, and cement-covered painted columns. Both stations opened with newsstands,

Figure 6.13 Newbury Street Entrance, Circa 1920s
From Newbury Street (right), pedestrians entered Massachusetts Station through a small portal (center) between two larger portals, reserved for streetcars, and in time, buses. Just inside of the pedestrian portal is a ticket booth and turnstile.

Figure 6.14 Mezzanine Level at Arlington Station, 1921
Low walls covered in tile protect stairways leading down to the station's platforms.

Figure 6.15 Platform Level at Arlington Station, 1921
A porcelain station name sign (left) hangs on concrete-covered steel posts that divide the eastbound tracks and platform from the westbound side of the station.

telephone booths, and public bathrooms. Copley Station retains its given name, while Massachusetts Station was renamed to Auditorium Station in 1965, then Hynes/ICA Station in 1990. Later, the MBTA shortened the station's name to simply Hynes. Most recently, MBTA maps have depicted the station as Hynes Convention Center. Massachusetts Station is unique in Boston for having been renamed more times than any in-service MBTA subway, tunnel, or elevated station.

The BTD added a third station along the Boylston Street Subway in 1921. Located under the intersection of Arlington and Boylston Streets, the station received the name Arlington. With the Back Bay neighborhood experiencing unprecedented commercial growth in the 1910s and early 1920s, Arlington

Station provided an additional subway access point for the burgeoning neighborhood.

Arlington Station opened to the public on November 13, 1921. Entrance and exit stairways connected the surface with a mezzanine level spanning beneath the intersection of Boylston and Arlington Streets. The mezzanine level featured a ticket lobby and stairs down to westbound and eastbound streetcar subway platforms (Figure 6.14). One level below the mezzanine were two platforms, one for eastbound and another for westbound cars. Each platform wore porcelain enamel station signs typical of the Boylston Street Subway (Figure 6.15).

Over the years, multiple renovations significantly upgraded the interiors of Arlington Station. In the late 1960s, the MBTA kicked off its re-branding of public transportation for Greater Boston with work at Arlington Station (see Chapter 9). A recent renovation was completed in 2014.

Subways That Never Were

Before the Boylston Street Subway, streetcars clogged Boylston and other Back Bay streets as they moved between points west of the Back Bay and the Public Garden Incline of the Tremont Street Subway. To mitigate the situation, as early as 1906, the BTC identified three potential routes for a "Back Bay Subway:" one, along the south bank of the Charles River; a second, running beneath the length of the Commonwealth Avenue Mall; and a third, following Boylston Street. The route along the Charles River was the Riverbank Subway. The General Court authorized construction of the Riverbank Subway in 1907, but after protests from the BERy and landowners along the route, the Riverbank Subway was cancelled in 1911. In place of the scuttled Riverbank Subway, the Boylston Street Subway received the go ahead from the Commonwealth.

During planning and construction of the Boylston Street Subway, the BTC explored extending the project east of the Tremont Street Subway, into Boston's central business district (Figure 6.16). The extension of the Boylston Street Subway to Post Office Square was cost prohibitive for the BTC to construct and never came into being.

Beyond the Riverbank and Post Office Square Subways, other projects that were planned but never constructed include a rapid transit subway to Brighton and a connection between the East Boston Tunnel Line and the Tremont Street Subway at Park Street Station.

Type 5 Streetcars

In the 1920s, at the same time the BTC worked to expand the Tremont Street Subway, the BERy brought to Boston a new streetcar, its Type 5 (Figure 6.17 and Figure 6.18). The BERy commissioned the new trolleys to replace the oldest cars in its fleet. Between 1922 and 1927, the BERy purchased over 470 Type 5s from manufacturers Brill Corporation (Brill), Laconia Car Company (Laconia), and Wason Manufacturing Company (Wason). Wason was a subsidiary of Brill and only produced a handful of the cars. Prior to constructing Type 5s, back in 1899, Wason constructed the first rapid transit cars for the BERy. By the time Brill received its first contract to produce Type 5s, the company had already consumed not only Wason, but also G. C. Kuhlman Car Company and the John Stephenson Company.

Figure 6.16 A Proposed Subway to Post Office Square, 1913
A planned extension of the Boylston Street Subway runs from Boylston Street Station (top left) to Post Office Square (right). On the map, the unbuilt line follows Boylston, Kingston, Otis, and Devonshire Streets. Three stations are laid out. One, at Boylston Street (top left), connects with Boylston Street Station of the Tremont Subway. A second, at the intersection of Washington, Kingston, and Otis Streets (middle), features passageways linking it with Washington Station of the Cambridge-Dorchester line. A third station (right) consists of a pair of platforms, one for unloading and one for loading, located on opposite sides of the basement of Boston's Post Office on Post Office Square (right).

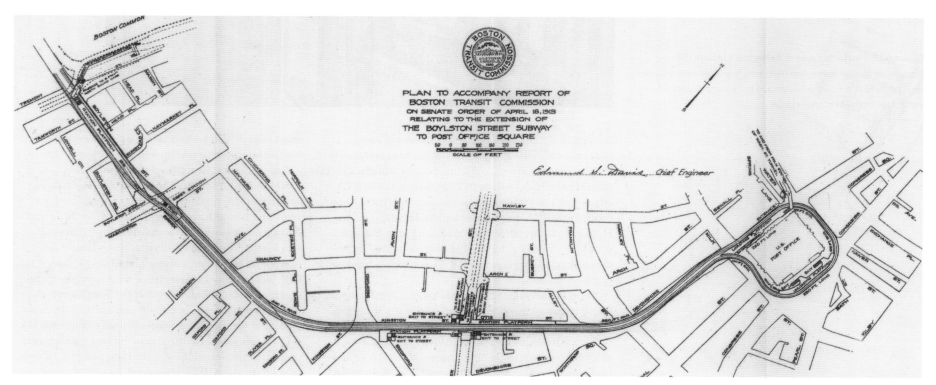

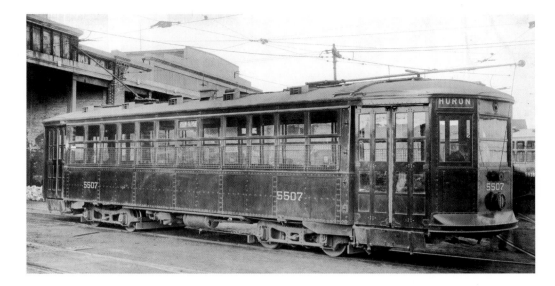

Figure 6.17 Type 5 Streetcar #5507, November 23, 1922

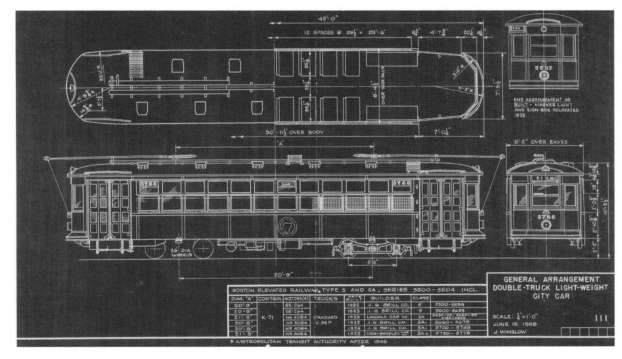

Figure 6.18 MTA Type 5 Streetcar Specifications, 1948

Boston's Type 5 streetcars were operated from 1922 to 1959, initially by the BERy, and later, by the Metropolitan Transit Authority (MTA). Though most Type 5s went to scrap by the end of the 1950s, BERy Type 5 number 5374 lives on in the collection of the Seashore Trolley Museum of Maine. For years, it has sat on display within Boylston Street Station.

The BERy assigned the Type 5 trolleys 5500-series to 5900-series numbers. By the end of the 1920s, Type 5s were the workhorse of the BERy's streetcar system, seeing system-wide deployment and heavy usage. BERy Type 5s numbered 5961–5970 were the final streetcars to be built by Laconia, a company established in the 1840s to build carriages and stagecoaches. Laconia, based in the New Hampshire city of the same name, closed its doors in 1928.

Despite minor variants in mechanics and structure between Type 5s from each of sixteen batches ordered by the BERy, overall, Type 5s were similar. Each measured approximately forty-five feet long and approximately eight and a half feet wide. Each car had two sets of pneumatically operated folding doors, sat forty-eight passengers, and had a total capacity, including standees, of 137 persons. Early models arrived from manufacturers with four, twenty-five horsepower traction motors. Later models arrived with four, thirty-five horsepower

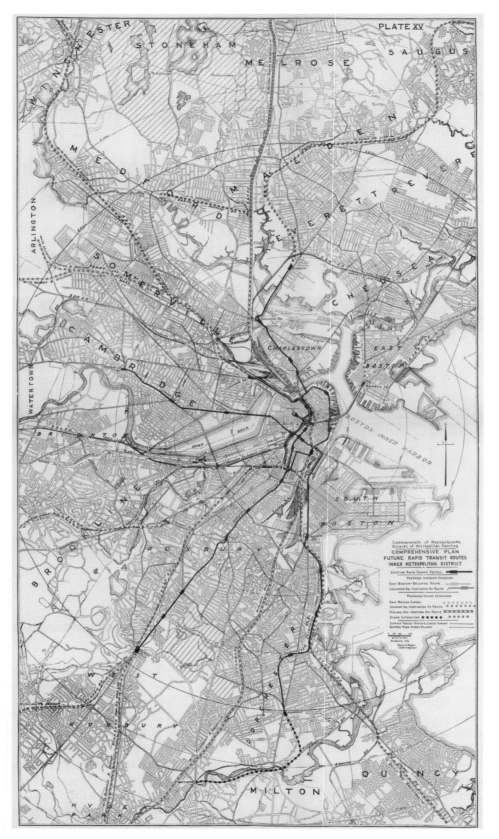

Figure 6.19 Future Rapid Transit Routes for Boston, 1926

Mapped are existing (solid black lines) and proposed (dashed) rapid transit lines for Greater Boston. Many of the proposed lines follow steam railroad rights-of-way. The map was issued with a complimenting map of existing and proposed rapid transit lines in central Boston (Figure 6.20).

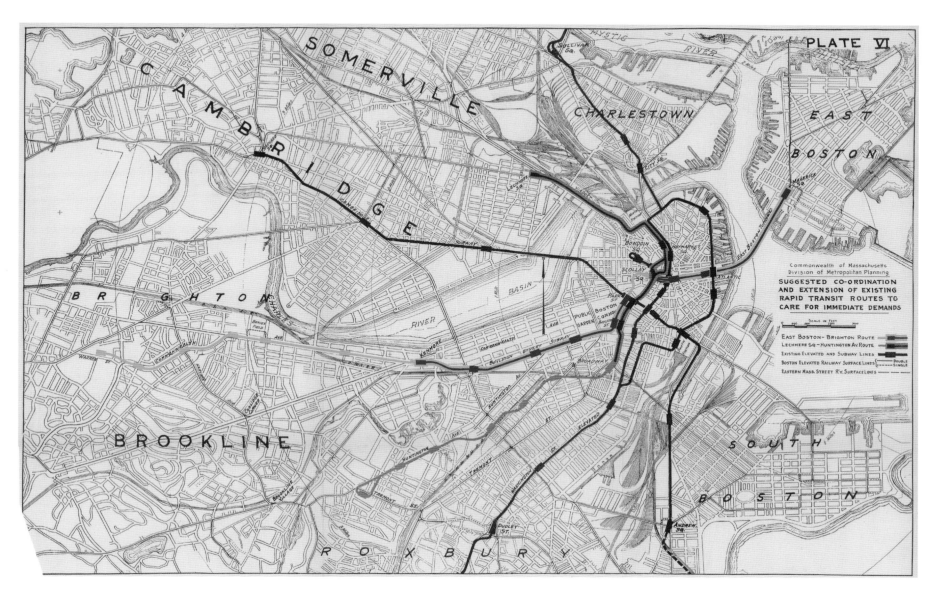

Figure 6.20 Proposed Rapid Transit Improvements, 1926
Issued by the Commonwealth's Division of Metropolitan
Planning in their *Report on Improved Transportation
Facilities in the Metropolitan District*, a map shows existing
subway, tunnel, and elevated railway lines as dark lines.
Stations are dark boxes along each. Highlighted in yellow,
is a proposed conversion and extension of the East Boston
Tunnel and Boylston Street Subway into a single rapid transit
line connecting Maverick Square in East Boston (right) with
Warren Street in Brighton (left). Highlighted in pink is a
proposed extension of the Tremont Street Subway and East
Cambridge Extension from Lechmere Terminal to Brigham
Circle (bottom).

motors. A typical Type 5 had a maximum speed
rating of twenty-five miles per hour. All Type 5s
used in revenue service featured illuminated sign
boxes containing roll sign curtains mounted at each
car end and side. Initially Type 5s wore the BERy's
green livery. Later, both new models arriving from
manufacturers and existing models in operation
received an orange paint scheme. The bright color
increased the visibility of the streetcars in city
traffic.

Ambitious Expansion Plans: The 1926 Report
Since the nineteenth century, public agencies and
commissions established by the Commonwealth
have prepared reports and recommendations

for improvements to transportation for Greater
Boston. With one report, completed in 1926, the
Massachusetts Division of Metropolitan Planning
(MDMP) proposed aggressive augmentations of
Boston's transit lines, tunnels, and stations. A map
from the report articulates no fewer than a dozen
major extensions of rapid transit and streetcar
lines (Figure 6.19). On the map, the Main Line
Elevated rapid transit line extends northward, from
Everett, through Malden, and into Saugus. From
its southern terminus in Dorchester, the Cam-
bridge-Dorchester line reaches into Milton, passes
through Quincy, and continues towards South
Shore communities. The map confirms that the
Commonwealth was interested in utilizing Greater
Boston's web of railroad rights-of-way as paths for

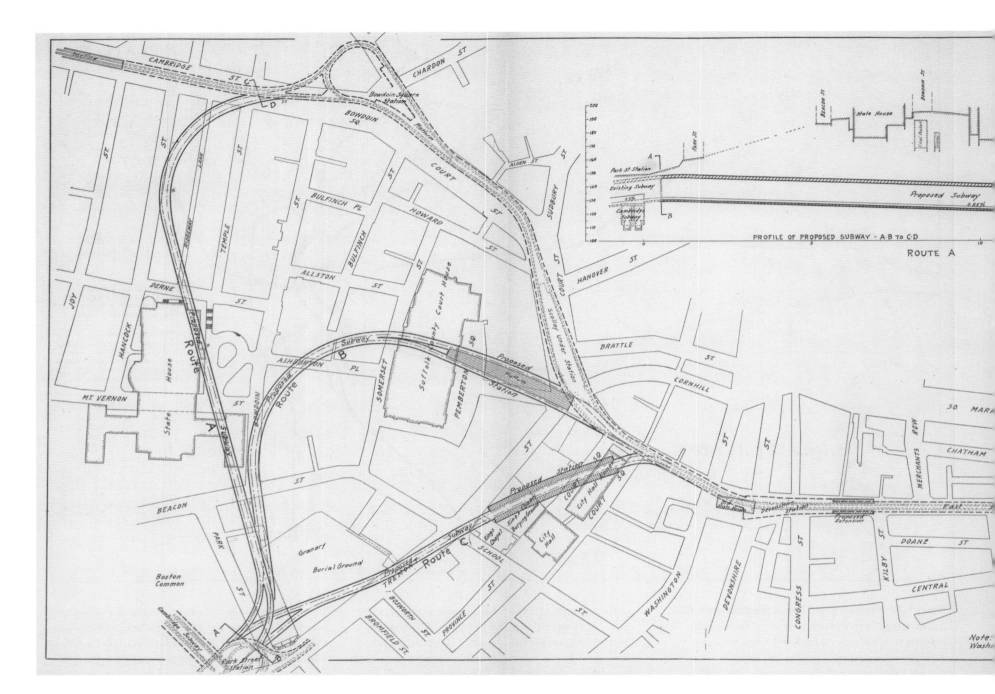

extensions of rapid transit lines. Had the complete web of new lines and extensions proposed by the MDMP come to fruition, Boston's public transit system, and most certainly the urban form of Greater Boston, would be quite different today.

A different map from the 1926 report, titled "Suggested Coordinated and Extension of Existing Rapid Transit Routes to Care for Immediate Demands," focuses in on the central portion of the BERy's system (Figure 6.20). Proposed improvements are highlighted on the map. An extension of the Tremont Street Subway runs into western Roxbury. A proposed "East Boston – Brighton Route" makes use of the East Boston Tunnel Line from Maverick Square to Court Street. From there, a tunnel beneath Beacon Hill (Figure 6.21) connects the East Boston Tunnel Line with the Tremont Street Subway at Park Street Station. West of Park Street, the Tremont Street and Boylston Street Subways are converted from

Figure 6.21 From East Boston to Brighton, 1926

A map lays out three potential routes for a tunnel under Beacon Hill, connecting the East Boston Tunnel Line (right) with the Tremont Street Subway (bottom left). A tunnel was part of a plan to convert the East Boston Tunnel Line and much of the Tremont Street Subway, including the Boylston Street Subway, to rapid transit service, with the line having termini at East Boston and Brighton. Neither the tunnel or the conversion were made.

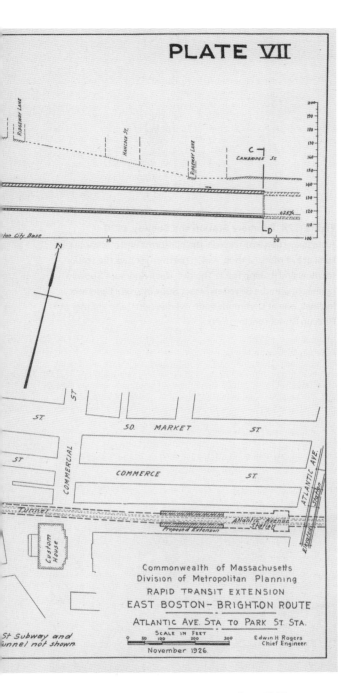

Commonwealth of Massachusetts
Division of Metropolitan Planning
RAPID TRANSIT EXTENSION
EAST BOSTON – BRIGHTON ROUTE
ATLANTIC AVE. STA TO PARK ST. STA.

SCALE IN FEET
0   50   100   200   300

Edwin H Rogers
Chief Engineer

November 1926

streetcar to rapid transit service. The proposed rapid transit line runs west of Kenmore Square, follows Commonwealth Avenue, and ends at Warren Street in Brighton. The MDMP designated its proposed "East Boston – Brighton Route," along with another proposed improvement, a "Lechmere Square – Huntington Avenue Route," as being for immediate implementation. Neither project came into being.

The Kenmore Square Subway

From 1913 to 1932 the western end of the Boylston Street Subway remained the portal and incline at Kenmore Street. At the top of the incline, streetcars paused at a surface stop to exchange passengers. A few steps to the west was Governor Square, where automobiles, trucks, and buses tangled with track-bound trolleys (Figure 6.22). The BTD saw to the liberation of streetcars from general street traffic at Governor Square by creating a new subway beneath the busy intersection.

Figure 6.22 (Above) Kenmore Square, Circa 1930
Streetcars traverse Kenmore Square (bottom) to and from the Kenmore Street surface stop and subway incline in the middle of Commonwealth Avenue (center).

Figure 6.23 (Right) Kenmore Square, Circa 1940
The central reservation of Commonwealth Avenue is restored after the replacement of the incline at Kenmore Street with the Kenmore Square Subway. The flattened arch of the mostly concealed Kenmore Street portal remains visible (center).

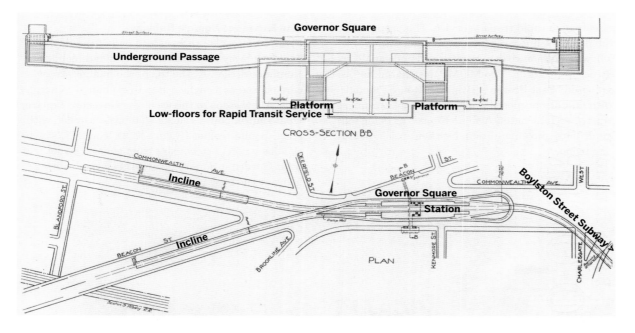

Construction of the Kenmore Square Subway began in July 1930. As they had done since first collaborating on the Tremont Street Subway in the 1890s, Boston funded construction of the subway's superstructure and the BERy provided the streetcar tracks, power system, signals, and other operational infrastructure. A "General Plan of Governor Square Improvement" (Figure 6.24) reveals the two-track Kenmore Square Subway and its four-track streetcar subway station. To the east of the station the Kenmore Square Subway connected with the western end of the Boylston Street Subway. To the west of the station, the Kenmore Square Subway branched into two, short tunnels, each leading to an incline constructed as part of the project. One incline was situated in the central reservation of Commonwealth Avenue. The other was located in the middle of Beacon Street. Streetcars travelling between points west of Governor Square utilized the inclines to access the Kenmore Square Subway, serve the subway's station, and pass unhindered by surface traffic into the Boylston and Tremont Street Subways.

The Kenmore Square Subway opened with one station with two platforms, each centered between a pair of westbound or eastbound streetcar tracks. The station's mezzanine, one level above the platforms and one level below the street, offered pedestrians a safe means of crossing busy Governor Square and accessing the station. A loop at the eastern end of the station allowed streetcars to arrive from and depart back to the Beacon Street

incline without interrupting the flow of streetcars on the station's two innermost tracks, one reserved for eastbound and one for westbound cars. The inner pair of tracks formed a straight shot from the western end of the Boylston Street Subway and the Commonwealth Avenue incline. The configuration anticipated potential conversion of the Kenmore and Boylston Street Subways to rapid transit service, as proposed in 1926 for the unrealized "East Boston – Brighton Route." A conversion to rapid transit service never took place beneath Kenmore Square.

The Kenmore Square Subway and Kenmore Station (Figure 6.25) opened to the public on October 23, 1932. A pair of cadastral maps depict Kenmore Square before (Figure 6.26) and after (Figure 6.27) the subway. After decades of Bostonians referring to the Kenmore Street trolley stop at Governor Square as being at Kenmore Square, the square became better known as Kenmore Square. The opening of the Kenmore Square Subway and Kenmore Station reaffirmed the name.

During construction of the Kenmore Square Subway, the surface stop and incline at Kenmore Street disappeared. Where the incline previously existed, the BTD restored the central reservation of Commonwealth Avenue. To allow ventilation for the Kenmore Square Subway, the BTD left open a portion of the portal that marked the bottom of the incline. The ventilation opening can still be visited today, in the middle of the Commonwealth Avenue Mall.

Figure 6.25 Kenmore Station, Circa 1933

A view from the outbound platform looking east, reveals, in the distance, where tracks diverge between the station's turning loop and the subway's main line.

Figure 6.26 (Right) Governor Square, 1928

A pair of streetcar tacks (black and white lines) within the Boylston Street Subway curves beneath Charlesgate West (far right), under the square, and out into daylight at the surface streetcar stop "Kenmore Station" (middle). The area was mapped a decade later (Figure 6.27), after the completion of the Kenmore Square Subway.

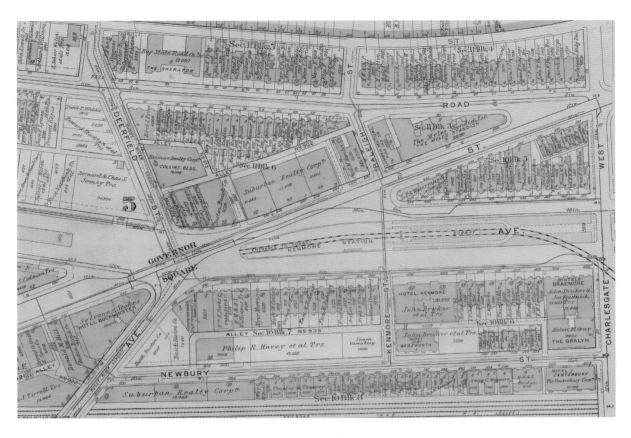

Figure 6.27 (Below) Kenmore Square, 1938

After completion of the Kenmore Square Subway, streetcar subway tracks (black and white lines) link the Boylston Street Subway under Charlesgate West (far right) with the underground Kenmore Station (center) and subway tracks leading to inclines and surface trackage on Commonwealth Avenue and Beacon Street (left).

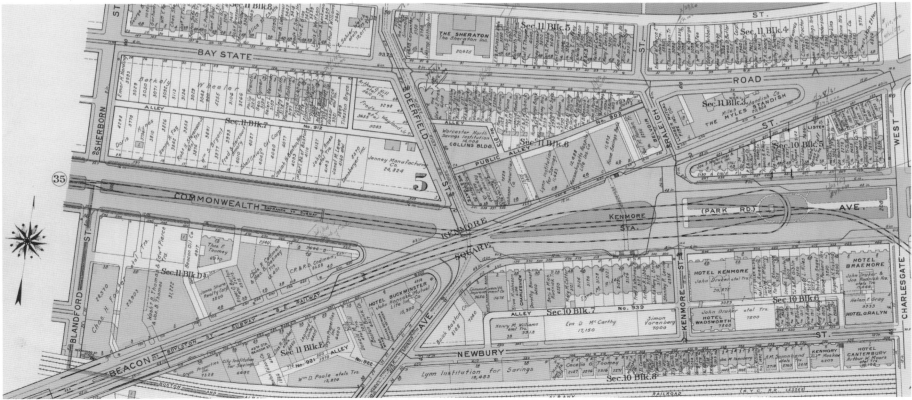

Park Street Station Gets Some Upgrades

After the opening of the Boylston Street Subway, the BERy improved signage at Park Street Station's platform served by westbound streetcars. In 1925, the platform's berth indicator boards instructed, that unless otherwise indicated, streetcars bound for the Boylston Street Subway stopped at berths numbered one, two, or three; cars headed for Huntington Avenue stopped at berths four, five, or six. The board hung over the platform located between Park Street's two westbound tracks (Figure 6.28). Today, the same platform has four designated boarding areas, one each for trolleys serving one of the four branches of the Green Line. By 1930, massive illuminated "Points of Interest" boards replaced the 1920s-era berth indicator

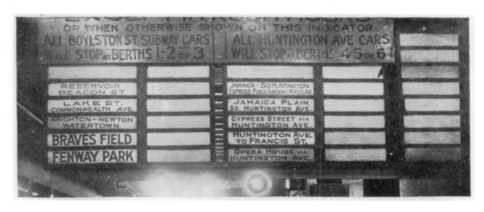

Figure 6.28 Indicator Board at Park Street Station, 1925
From above the westbound streetcar platform an electric board displays from which of six numbered berths the next car will depart, bound for the illuminated destination. The sign displays both Braves Field and Fenway Park, Boston's major league baseball parks.

Figure 6.29 Park Street Station, Circa 1930
A large board lists "Points of Interest Reached by the 'EL' System." The board's upper row of panels list points south and west of Park Street Station. Its lower row of panels list points north of the station. The board replaced the electronic indicator boards of the 1920s (Figure 6.28).

Figure 6.30 Huntington Avenue Subway Site, May 16, 1940
Surface work along Huntington Avenue is marked by a sign celebrating WPA funding for the project.

boards. The boards suggested particular cars and connections for transit riders to use when traveling to a listed destination (Figure 6.29). One suggestion read: "Take North Station and Lechmere Cars for Fanueil Hall, Quincy Market, Boston Garden."

Beyond signage improvements made in the early 1930s, physical improvements increased the capacity and usability of Park Street Station. In the mid-1930s, the successor to the BTC, the Boston Transportation Department (BTD), installed a new platform along the eastern side of the station's northbound track. Completed with the platform work, new underground pedestrian passageways linked the westbound and northbound streetcar platforms. As well, new stairs and sidewalk entrances served the east side of Tremont Street. The renovations brought Park Street Station into the configuration in use today.

Coinciding with the BTD's work at Park Street Station, the BERy installed large signs at no fewer than nineteen places throughout the rapid transit system. Each sign displayed the speed of transit service from a particular point to Park Street, Winter, or Summer Stations.

The Huntington Avenue Subway

The BTD oversaw the addition of a branch to the Boylston Street Subway beginning in late 1937. The Huntington Avenue Subway was built to expedite streetcars traveling between Huntington Avenue and the Boylston Street Incline. As it had done at Kenmore Square, the BTD's relocation of streetcar traffic to the underground was a solution to surface traffic congestion.

The Huntington Avenue Subway was built with federal Works Progress Administration (WPA) funds (Figure 6.30). The WPA funding was one of the earliest examples of federal funding being used for a local public transit infrastructure project. The WPA was the largest of the "New Deal" agencies set up to counteract the massive unemployment of Americans caused by The Great Depression.

The Huntington Avenue Subway branched off of the Boylston Street Subway immediately to the west of Copley Station. From there, it ran under Exeter Street to Huntington Avenue, before turning to the west and tracing its namesake street to the west side of Massachusetts Avenue. West of Massachusetts Avenue, an incline in the middle of Huntington Avenue brought the subway's eastbound and westbound tracks to the surface.

The Huntington Avenue Subway opened with two streetcar subway stations. Mechanics Station (Figure 6.31) was located in front of Mechanics Hall, the site of which is now occupied by part of the Prudential Center complex. Mechanics Station became Prudential Station in 1964 (Figure 6.32). The subway's second station was Symphony Station, located at the intersection of Huntington and

Figure 6.31 Mechanics Station, December 29, 1943
A two-car train of center-entrance streetcars destined for the Tremont Street Subway pauses at the inbound platform of Mechanics Station, on the Huntington Avenue Subway.

Figure 6.32 Renaming Mechanics Station, December 3, 1964

Massachusetts Avenues, in front of Symphony Hall. At Symphony Station the eastbound track, platform, and associated entrances were separated from their westbound counterparts by the wide expanse of Huntington Avenue. Between the eastbound and westbound streetcar tunnels an underpass, constructed concurrently with the subway, allowed Huntington Avenue street traffic to pass beneath Massachusetts Avenue.

Unlike the majority of Boston's transit stations to open before them, Mechanics and Symphony Stations received names for landmarks, as opposed to streets, proximate to each. Mechanics and Symphony Stations opened with their names set with black tile, contrasting against white tiled walls (Figure 6.33). Opening day for the Huntington Avenue Subway was February 16, 1941.

The Mattapan High Speed Line

One augmentation of rapid transit service proposed by the MDMP in 1926 did come to life, an extension of the Cambridge-Dorchester line from Ashmont to Mattapan. Inspired by the MDMP's and earlier proposals, the BTD tackled the extension. South of Ashmont Terminal, the BTD converted the southern half of the Shawmut Branch steam railroad line, along with much of a steam railroad line following the Neponset River, to use by streetcars. The New Haven surveyed and mapped its rights-of-way to be utilized for both the High Speed Line and Dorchester Tunnel Extension in 1924 (Figure 6.38).

The Mattapan High Speed Line opened on December 21, 1929, a little more than a year after rapid transit trains began serving Ashmont Station. Between Ashmont and Mattapan, streetcars operated at significantly higher speeds than along city streets. The high speeds of the trolleys gave the High Speed Line its name.

The Mattapan High Speed Line opened with five surface stops, Cedar Grove, Milton, Central Avenue, Valley Road, and Capen Street. Some replaced steam railroad stations. In Milton, a former New Haven station (Figure 6.34) was replaced with open streetcar platforms and a parking lot for BERy patrons (Figure 6.35). At Central Avenue, a former New Haven depot (Figure 6.36) was replaced with a surface streetcar stop (Figure 6.37).

Figure 6.33 Symphony Station, Circa 1941
Passengers line up to board a BERy Type 4 semi-convertible streetcar amidst glossy tile walls, tile-framed wall advertisements, and ceiling-mounted signage.

Figure 6.34 Milton Railroad Depot, December 27, 1927
The Milton depot was erected by the Old Colony Railroad. In 1928, the building was demolished by the Boston Transportation Department and replaced by a parking lot and platforms for a stop along the Mattapan High Speed Line (Figure 6.35).

Figure 6.35 Milton Streetcar Stop, April 21, 1930
A streetcar pauses at the Milton stop along the Mattapan High Speed Line. The parking lot occupies the former site of a steam railroad depot erected by the Old Colony (Figure 6.34).

Figure 6.36 Central Avenue Railroad Depot, January 19, 1928
New Haven passenger trains stopped serving the cottage-like depot (center) at Central Avenue in Milton by the end of 1929. The railroad trackage heads into the distance, towards Mattapan. Less than two years after this photograph was taken, the tracks of the Mattapan High Speed Line and a new streetcar stop replaced the New Haven's depot (Figure 6.37).

Figure 6.37 Central Avenue Streetcar Station, 1932
At Central Avenue, the BTD replaced a New Haven depot (Figure 6.36) with a new stop along the Mattapan High Speed Line. In the photograph, a BERy center-entrance type streetcar pauses at the station. Three tracks are shown. The left and middle tracks are, respectively, the eastbound and westbound tracks of the High Speed Line. The right most track is the New Haven's, then in use for limited freight service.

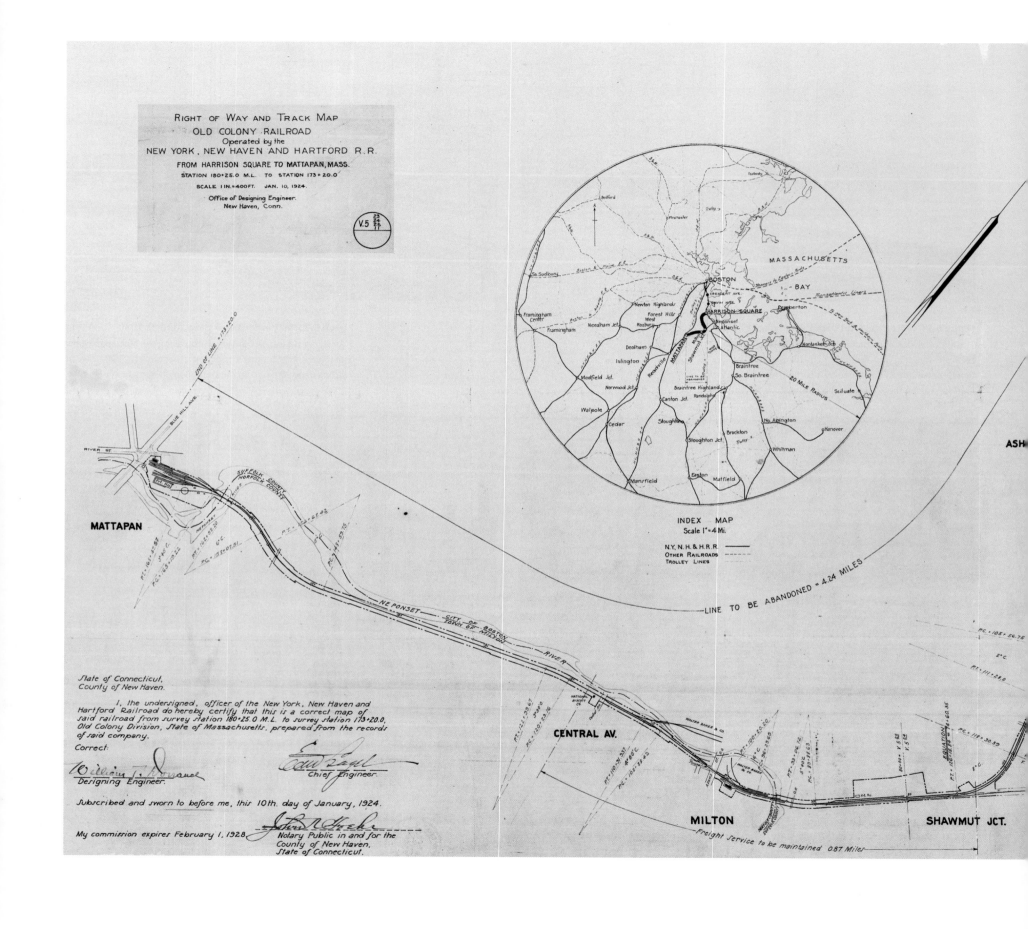

RIGHT OF WAY AND TRACK MAP
OLD COLONY RAILROAD
Operated by the
NEW YORK, NEW HAVEN AND HARTFORD R.R.
FROM HARRISON SQUARE TO MATTAPAN, MASS.
STATION 180+25.0 M.L. TO STATION 173+20.0
SCALE 1 IN.=400FT.   JAN. 10, 1924.
Office of Designing Engineer,
New Haven, Conn.

V.5

INDEX MAP
Scale 1"=4 Mi.

N.Y., N.H. & H.R.R. ————
OTHER RAILROADS --------
TROLLEY LINES ———————

MASSACHUSETTS BAY

LINE TO BE ABANDONED = 4.24 MILES

MATTAPAN

CENTRAL AV.

MILTON

SHAWMUT JCT.

ASH

NEPONSET RIVER

Freight Service to be maintained 0.87 Miles

State of Connecticut.
County of New Haven.

I, the undersigned, officer of the New York, New Haven and
Hartford Railroad do hereby certify that this is a correct map of
said railroad from survey station 180+25.0 M.L. to survey station 173+20.0,
Old Colony Division, State of Massachusetts, prepared from the records
of said company.

Correct:

William T. Dowance
Designing Engineer.

Edw. Page
Chief Engineer.

Subscribed and sworn to before me, this 10th day of January, 1924.

John R. Stocker

My commission expires February 1, 1928.   Notary Public in and for the
County of New Haven,
State of Connecticut.

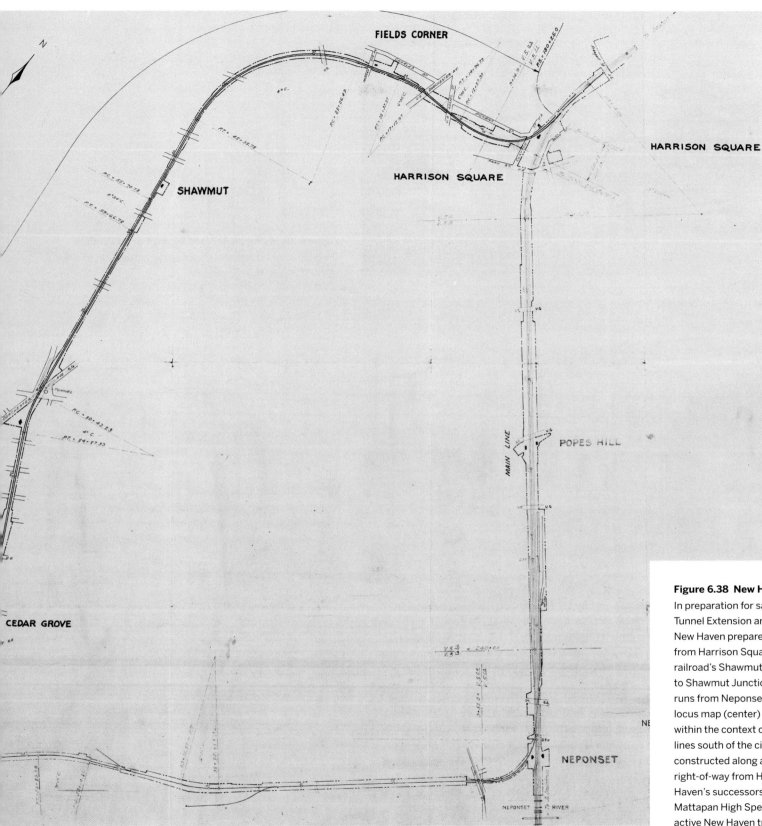

Figure 6.38 New Haven Railroad in Dorchester, 1924
In preparation for sale of its properties for the Dorchester
Tunnel Extension and Mattapan High Speed Line projects, the
New Haven prepared a detailed survey of its rights-of-way,
from Harrison Square (top right) to Mattapan (far left). The
railroad's Shawmut Branch (right) runs from Harrison Square
to Shawmut Junction (bottom). Another New Haven branch
runs from Neponset (bottom right) to Shawmut Junction. A
locus map (center) highlights the area covered by the survey
within the context of Greater Boston and other New Haven
lines south of the city. The Dorchester Tunnel Extension was
constructed along and occupied the entire former railroad
right-of-way from Harrison Square to Ashmont. Until the New
Haven's successors completely ceased service 1982, the
Mattapan High Speed Line shared some rights-of-way with
active New Haven tracks.

Figure 6.39 Mattapan Railroad Depot, August 29, 1929
Deconstruction of platform structures is underway in advance of the Mattapan High Speed Line.

Figure 6.40 Mattapan Terminal, 1930
A photograph taken a year after that shown in Figure 6.39 shows the former railroad depot (left) joined by Mattapan Terminal (right). A busway (middle) has replaced the depot's platform and shelter.

The far terminus of the Mattapan High Speed Line was located on the southeastern edge of Mattapan Square. There, the BTD established a major streetcar terminal where the Old Colony, and later the New Haven, previously operated a passenger depot. Unlike in Milton and at other intermediate stops along the Mattapan High Speed Line, at Mattapan Terminal, the existing railroad depot was not entirely demolished, though its platform and canopy were removed to make room for a new busway (Figure 6.39 and Figure 6.40). Mattapan Terminal opened with a covered boarding area, reversing loops, and streetcar storage tracks (Figure 6.41). The boarding area was served by four tracks protected by a boxy, reinforced concrete structure (Figure 6.42). Between the streetcar

terminal and the former railroad depot, a busway was served by BERy motor coaches. Streetcar tracks at Mattapan Terminal connected with those on Blue Hill Avenue.

The Mattapan High Speed Line remains a rare example of a pre-World War II American streetcar line that never ceased revenue operation. Today, historic Presidents' Conference Committee Cars (PCC cars), originally built in the mid-1940s and completely rebuilt by the MBTA since, convey riders in vintage style between Ashmont and Mattapan. The standardized design of PCC cars came out of a design collaboration amongst transit company representatives and streetcar manufacturers from across America that took place in the late 1920s and early 1930s. Boston's first PCC car was received by

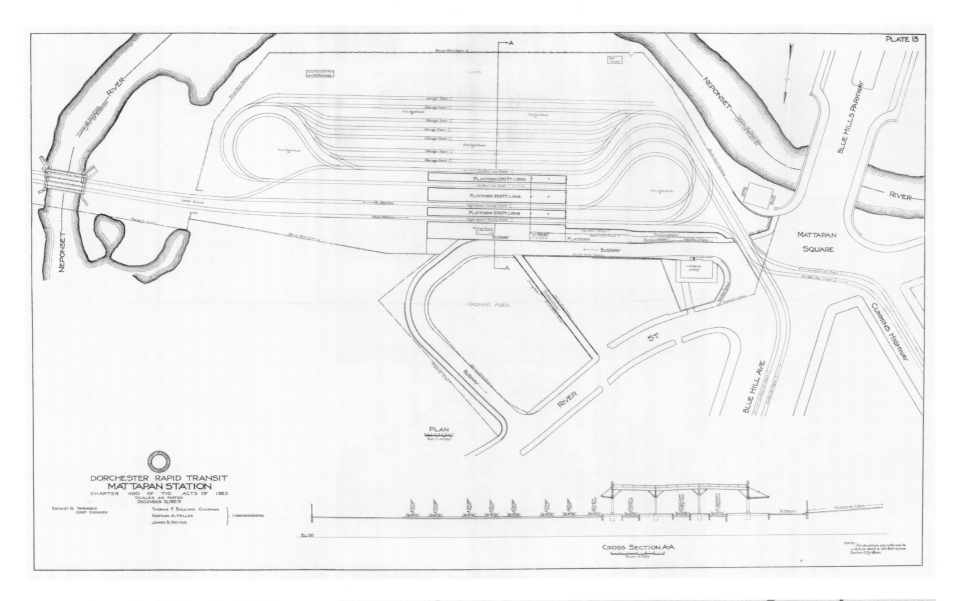

Figure 6.41 Mattapan Terminal, December 31, 1929

Mattapan Terminal ran along the banks of the Neponset River (right). Seven storage tracks and four platform tracks are connected by loops at either end of the terminal. Four parallel, grade-level platforms sit alongside the platform tracks (middle). The northernmost platform was separated from the busway by turnstiles. The former New Haven railroad depot (bottom) was repurposed and is labeled "Carmen's Lobby."

Figure 6.42 Mattapan Terminal Building, 1929

A reinforced concrete structure shelters the station's streetcar platforms (center) and a portion of the busway platform (far left).

Figure 6.43 BERy PCC Car #3190, 1945

The trolley pole is extended on freshly completed Presidents' Conference Committee car number 3190, built for the BERy by Pullman-Standard in 1945.

Figure 6.44 Inside BERy PCC Car #3190, 1945

Most PCC cars had some combination of side-facing (left) and forward-facing (right) benches. Grab bars facilitated standees.

Figure 6.45 Front End of PCC Car #3190, 1945

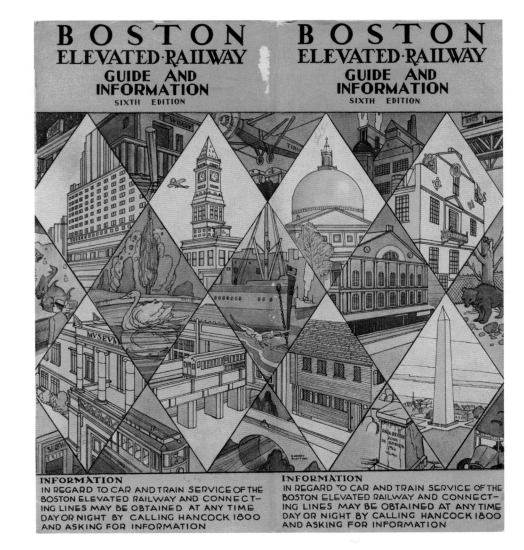

Figure 6.46 BERy Guide And Information Cover, 1930
The sixth edition of the guide wears a collage of images of landmarks of Boston, transit vehicles of the BERy, and a nod to early aviation for the city. Images of the Old State House, renderings of a streetcar, and an early airplane celebrate Boston's history, present, and future.

the BERy in 1937. An additional twenty, constructed by Pullman-Standard, arrived in 1941. During 1944–46, 225 "wartime" PCC cars brought multiple-unit (MU) operation to Boston's PCC car fleet. One wartime PCC, was number 3190 (Figure 6.43, Figure 6.44, and Figure 6.45). After the war, an additional twenty-five PCCs arrived in 1946. The last PCCs to arrive in Boston were procured by the MTA in the 1950s.

The MBTA inherited the MTA's fleet of PCC cars. Under its PCC Reconstruction Program of the early 1980s, the MBTA rebuilt over four dozen of its PCC cars. After December 1985, when the MBTA retired the last PCCs from regular service on the Green Line, approximately a dozen of the rebuilt PCCs retired to Mattapan, and the Mattapan High Speed Line became the last bastion of MBTA PCC car operation. In the late 1990s, the MBTA's Mattapan

PCC fleet of eleven cars built by Pullman-Standard in the mid-1940s began to enter an in-house overhaul and restoration program. Spending approximately $500,000 per car, the MBTA fabricated parts no longer available and painted each car to vintage BERy orange. The MBTA recorded six PCC cars in active service at the end of 2018. Four others remained on hand but sidelined due to damage and mechanical issues.

BERy Maps at Boston's Tercentenary
Amidst celebrations of Boston's tercentenary in 1930, the BERy issued the sixth edition of its *Guide And Information* brochure. The commemorative edition featured fresh cover art (Figure 6.46). Within the 1930 brochure were three maps. The smallest of the three, a diagrammatic map of the BERy's rapid

transit lines, occupied the back cover (Figure 6.47). A second map lays out all of the BERy's transit lines and routes, with each mode of transit assigned a particular color (Figure 6.48). On these maps, the colors differentiating lines and modes are not the same as those used by the MBTA today. Nonetheless, the two maps are early examples of the use of colors to distinguish transit lines on a public transit map for Boston.

The third map in the 1930 edition of *Guide And Information* was a unique production, a large map issued neatly folded within the brochure. A reader unfolded the map to a color piece of cartographic splendor expanding to thirty inches wide by twenty-two-and-a-half inches tall (Figure 6.49). A bit too large for regular use inside a crowded bus or streetcar, the map was wall art, memorializing public transit at the time of Boston's tercentenary. The fold-out map focused on downtown Boston and the Back Bay. Rapid transit lines, streetcar lines, bus routes, and subways prominently crisscross the composition.

As Boston celebrated its tercentenary, it was falling under the grip of the unemployment and

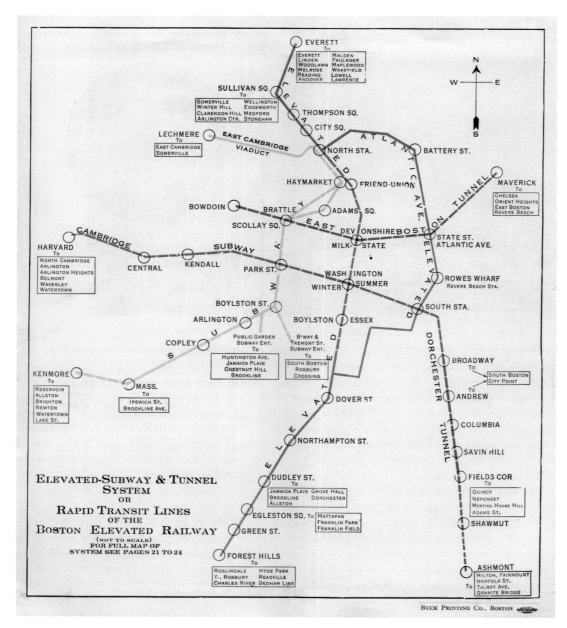

Figure 6.47 Rapid Transit Lines of the BERy, 1930

A colored map of Boston's subway, tunnel, and elevated lines was featured in the sixth edition of the BERy's *Guide And Information* brochure. The Tremont Street Subway, East Cambridge Extension, Boylston Street Subway and Kenmore Square Subway are highlighted yellow. The East Boston Tunnel Line and Extension are blue. The els and tunnels of the Elevated Division are red. The Cambridge-Dorchester rapid transit line is blue.

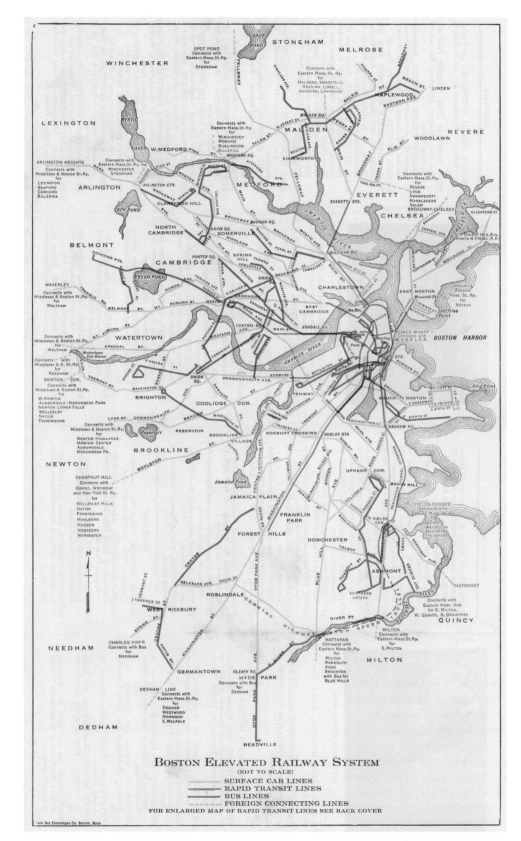

Figure 6.48 BERy Guide and Information Map, 1930

The centerfold map of the 1930 edition of the BERy's *Guide and Information* brochure lays out the rapid transit lines, streetcar lines, and bus lines serving Boston at the time of the city's tercentenary.

BOSTON ELEVATED RAILWAY SYSTEM
(NOT TO SCALE)
SURFACE CAR LINES
RAPID TRANSIT LINES
BUS LINES
FOREIGN CONNECTING LINES
FOR ENLARGED MAP OF RAPID TRANSIT LINES SEE BACK COVER

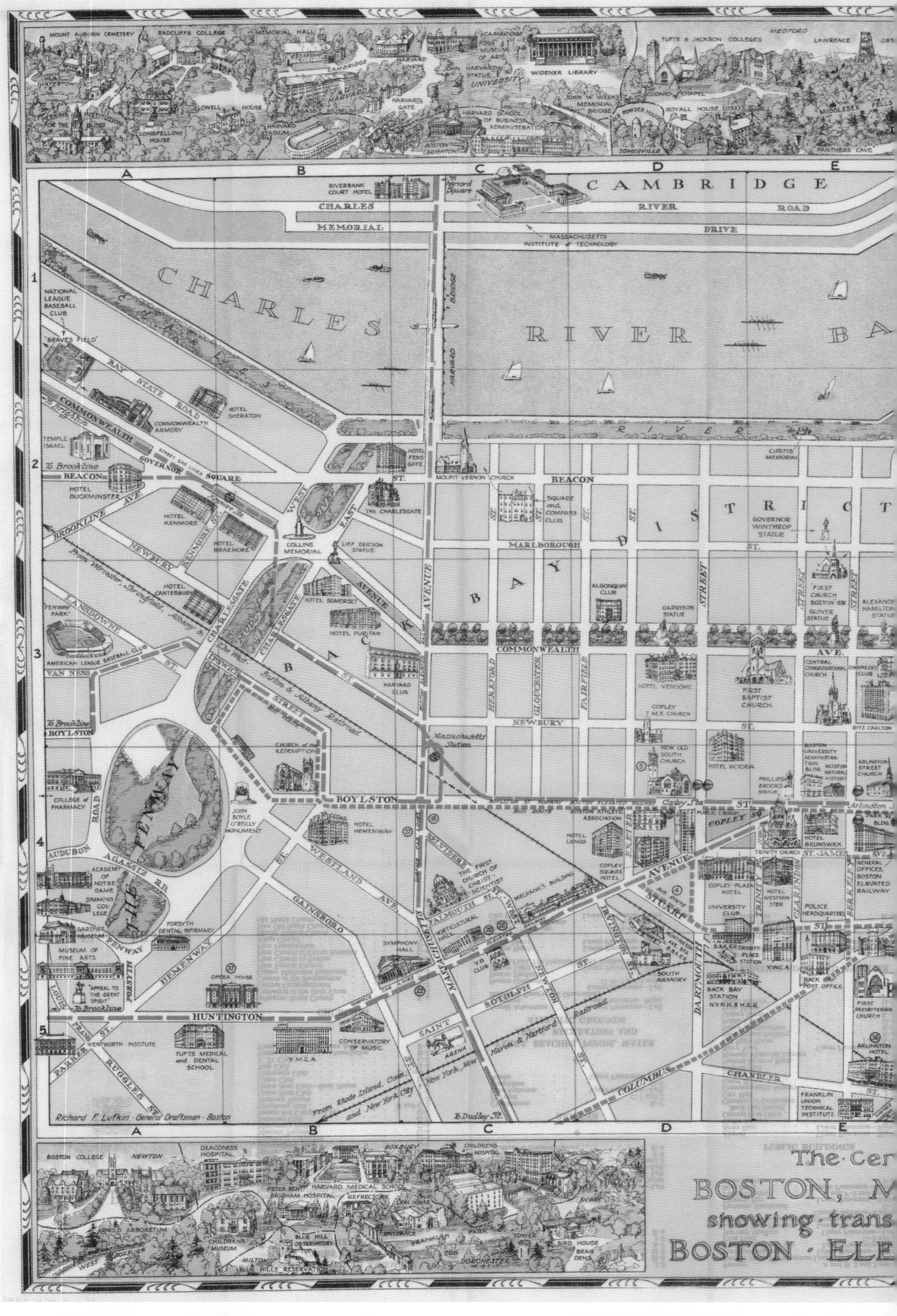

Figure 6.49 BERy Transit Map for Central Boston, 1930
On a large-format map from the 1930 edition of the BERy's
Guide and Information brochure, bus caricatures follow
bus routes; significant buildings and landmarks are depicted
by miniature perspective drawings. Along the top, a strip of
whimsical vignettes depicts places of significance north of
downtown Boston, including Harvard University and Charlestown (top). Boston's "Municipal Airport," still in its infancy,
is shown (top right). Along the bottom, vignettes represent
scenes south of downtown, including Franklin Park Zoo.

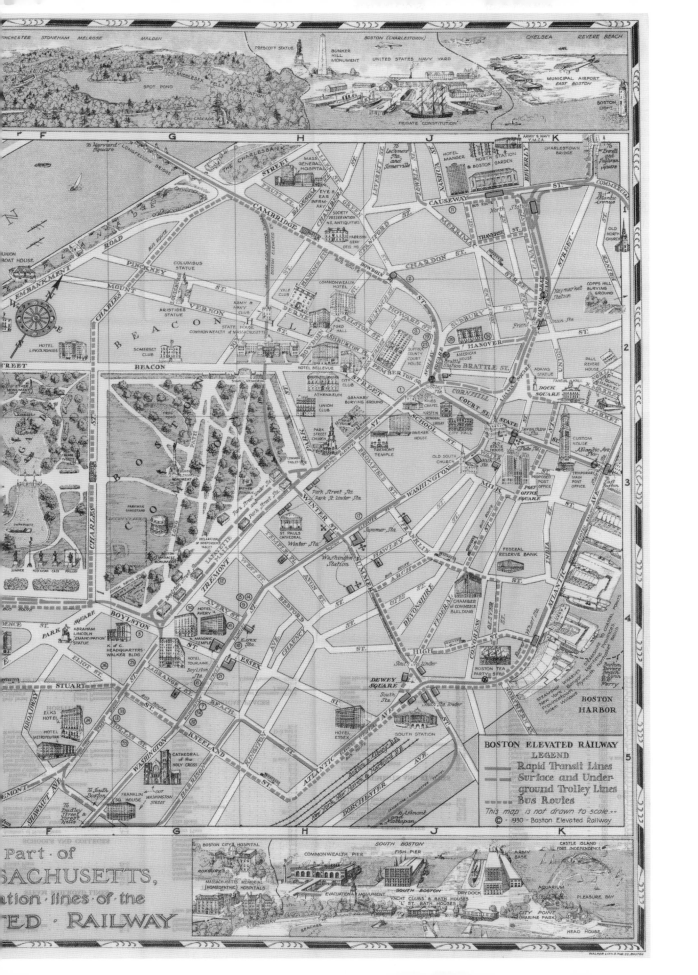

BOSTON ELEVATED RAILWAY
LEGEND
Rapid Transit Lines
Surface and Underground Trolley Lines
Bus Routes

This map is not drawn to scale

© · 1930 · Boston Elevated Railway

Part of
SACHUSETTS,
ation lines of the
ED · RAILWAY

economic devastation of the Great Depression. Meanwhile, a shock wave emanating from London forever recalibrated how public transit maps were designed. The blast came not from the machines of war but from the mind of a designer.

A Bit About Beck

From 1902 to 1933, the Underground Electric Railways of London (UERL), a holding company created by companies operating underground railways in England's capital, produced transit maps of its consortium's lines. The UERL branded its network "The Underground." On the 1911 edition of the UERL's "Underground Map of London," the lines of each railway company are coded with a unique color. The lines are overlaid upon a base map showing major streets, parks, landmarks, and the River Thames (Figure 6.50).

In 1933, the UERL released a pocket-sized folding map representing a sea-change in public transit mapping. Titled "Map of London's Underground Railways," it was designed by Henry Charles Beck (Beck). The composition was a refinement of a design Beck developed as early as 1931. Before the debut of Beck's 1933 map, the vast majority of public transportation system maps, especially pocket-sized examples produced by the UERL in London and the BERy in Boston, represented transit lines over a base map tied to local geography. Beck did away with those base maps, letting geometric rules form the skeleton of his map. Beck constructed his map upon an invisible grid, complimented by calculated placement of textual elements. All maps of the London Underground published after 1933 built upon Beck's work (Figure 6.51).

Beck's maps have informed generations of public transit map designers around the world. His great leap was mapping a rapid transit system as an elegant network diagram subject to geometric and typographic rules. Graphic clarity for the map reader and usefulness for the transit rider was

Figure 6.50 UERL London Underground Map, 1911

On a pre-Beck London Underground map, lines of different railways, distinguished from each other by differing colors, follow a base map showing major streets, parks, and water features. A key explains which color represents the lines of a particular company.

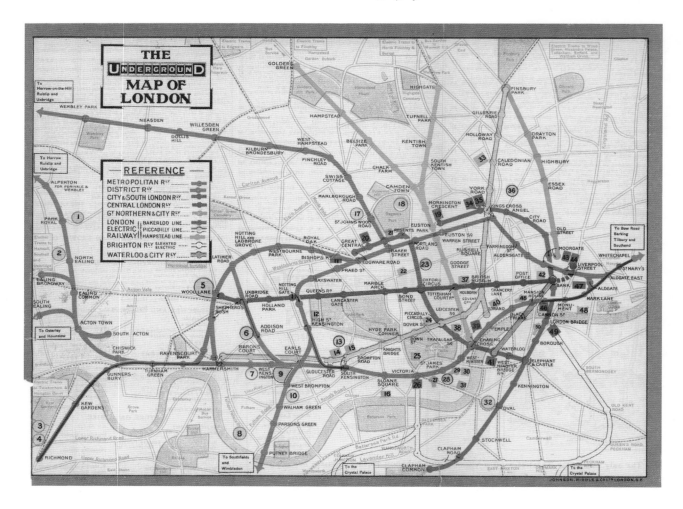

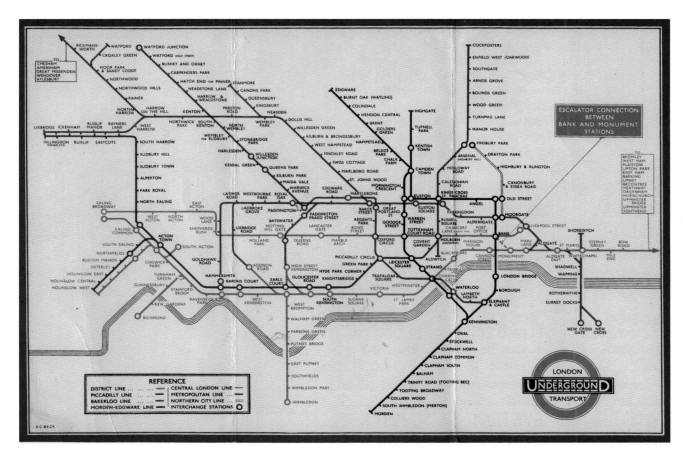

Figure 6.51 London Underground Railway Map Number 1, 1935

Unlike the UERL's 1911 London Underground map (Figure 6.50), Beck's compositions, including the one shown above, lack a geographic base map, instead, relying on an invisible geometric grid. Only the River Themes provides some geographic context in the map above.

paramount. Beck's maps, along with subsequent maps that followed his rules, allowed users to quickly identify a desired transit line and note how many stations until they transferred or arrived at their destination. Though Beck's work was echoed somewhat in the BERy's maps of the 1930s and 1940s, a refined Beck-type transit map for Boston did not appear until the late 1960s. Until then, a majority of the BERy's, and later the MTA's, public transit maps featured geographically-accurate base maps at their core.

The BERy's System Route Map Number 1

Though the BERy opened operations within America's first subway in 1897, the company did not issue a folding paper transit map, its "System Map Number 1," until 1936. Previously, the BERy released portable maps within brochures and guides, but rarely, if ever, as a dedicated pocket-sized instrument. As did the BERy, other major transit operators waited decades after their systems came online to begin issuing folding paper system maps. Shortly after the opening of the Paris Metropolitan (Metro)

in 1900, private companies began to produce portable paper maps of the Metro. Portable public maps were not produced by the operators of the Metro until the early 1920s, over twenty years after the Metro's opening. In New York City before 1940, banks and department stores regularly produced folding subway maps. In 1940, the New York City Board of Transportation (NYCBOT) took over the Interborough Rapid Transit Company (IRT) and the Brooklyn-Manhattan Transit Corporation (BMT). The NYCBOT consolidated the IRT and the BMT with its own, city-owned, Independent Subway System (IND), and began to issue pocket-sized maps. The New York City Transit Authority, which succeeded the NYCBOT in 1953, published public subway maps as early as 1958.

In Boston, the BERy's "System Map Number 1" was first released in fall 1936. The map was available at the BERy's information desk in the lobby of the Park Square Building, at the information booth on the streetcar level of Park Street Station, and at other select stations. System Map Number 1 was issued pre-folded. When closed, it measured just six and one quarter inches tall by three inches wide, perfectly sized for most pockets. On the cover of all BERy editions of the system route map, a compass logo implied that the map was a serious cartographic tool, and like a compass would provide unfaltering clarity of direction for the user (Figure 6.52). The cover merely hinted at what it concealed. Nine folds opened to reveal an eighteen-inch-wide by thirty-inch-tall piece of paper, information-rich on two sides.

One side of System Map Number 1 was dominated by a map of the entire BERy network at a scale of one and one half inches to the mile (Figure 6.53 and Figure 6.54). The reverse side of System Map Number 1 featured a comprehensive list of the BERy's lines and routes (Figure 6.55).

The BERy credited the cartography of System Map Number 1 to Richard F. Lufkin, a Boston map maker who advertised himself as cartographer,

Figure 6.52 System Route Map Covers, 1936–64
The first seven editions of the Lufkin Format folding system map were published by the Boston Elevated Railway Company. The subsequent eight editions were issued by the Metropolitan Transit Authority.

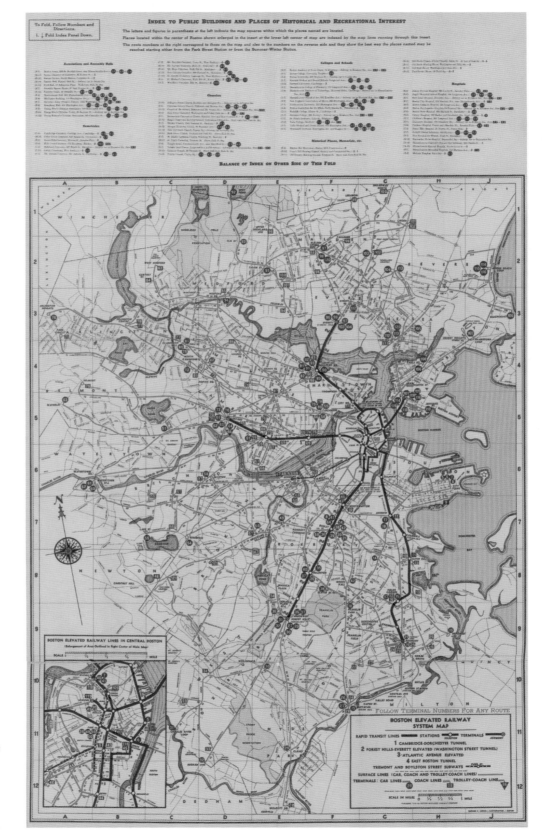

Figure 6.53 BERy System Route Map Number 1, 1936

A key (bottom right) explains the syntax of the map: rapid transit lines are thick, solid blue lines; the Tremont Street Subway is a series of narrow blue lines with white ticks; rapid transit and subway stations are paper-colored circles; and rapid transit terminal stations are differentiated from intermediate stations by their having an "X" inside the circle representing each. Examples of terminal stations marked by the X include those at Everett, Harvard Square, Forest Hills, and Ashmont. Each of the four rapid transit lines are assigned a number, from one through four. The key directs the reader to "Follow Terminal Numbers For Any Route." The thick blue line of the Cambridge-Dorchester rapid transit line, with its accompanying number "1s," can be followed across the map. Throughout the map, "Surface Lines" (streetcar, bus, and trackless trolley lines) are represented with red lines. Routes numbered five through 121 are assigned to each of the surface lines. The number of each route is printed in white inside of the terminal flags for that route. The terminal flags denote the end points of each route. An inset map (bottom left) represents downtown Boston at twice the scale of the larger map. Above both maps (top) is an index to public buildings that can be located on the map by a number and letter coordinate system.

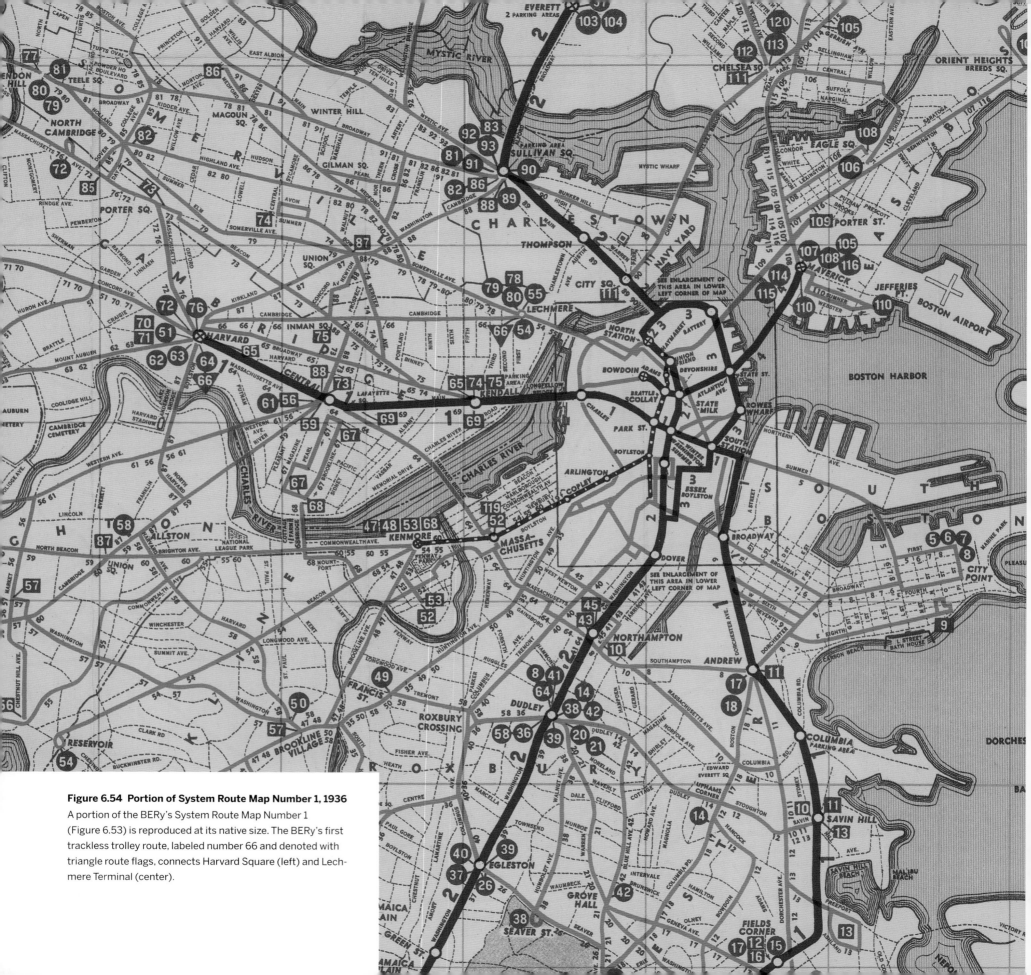

Figure 6.54 Portion of System Route Map Number 1, 1936

A portion of the BERy's System Route Map Number 1 (Figure 6.53) is reproduced at its native size. The BERy's first trackless trolley route, labeled number 66 and denoted with triangle route flags, connects Harvard Square (left) and Lechmere Terminal (center).

1

(D-5) HARVARD STATION—ASHMONT STATION (G-9)

VIA CAMBRIDGE—DORCHESTER TUNNEL

WEEKDAYS				SUNDAY	
FIRST	LAST			FIRST	LAST
5:24	1:02	HARVARD STA. TO ASHMONT STA.		5:54	1:02
5:17	12:54	ASHMONT STA. TO HARVARD STA.		5:51	12:54

2

(F-3) EVERETT STATION—FOREST HILLS STATION (E-9)

VIA MAIN LINE ELEVATED—WASHINGTON ST. TUNNEL

WEEKDAYS				SUNDAY	
FIRST	LAST			FIRST	LAST
5:20	12:56	EVERETT STA. TO FOREST HILLS STA.		5:51	12:56
5:16	12:54	FOREST HILLS STA. TO EVERETT STA.		5:47	12:54

3

(B-10) NORTH STATION—SOUTH STATION (B-11)

VIA ATLANTIC AVE. ELEVATED

WEEKDAYS				SUNDAY	
FIRST	LAST			FIRST	LAST
5:34	12:30	NORTH STATION TO SOUTH STATION		6:04	12:30
5:36	12:32	SOUTH STATION TO NORTH STATION		6:14	12:32

SERVICE BETWEEN NORTH STATION AND DUDLEY STA. IN RUSH HOURS

4

(G-5) MAVERICK STATION—BOWDOIN STATION (A-10)

VIA EAST BOSTON TUNNEL

WEEKDAYS				SUNDAY	
FIRST	LAST			FIRST	LAST
5:08	{12:36 / 1:08*	MAVERICK STA. TO BOWDOIN STA.		5:42	{12:36 / 1:08*
5:17	{12:46 / 1:18†	BOWDOIN STA. TO MAVERICK STA.		5:55	{12:46 / 1:18†

*TO SCOLLAY STA.
†FROM SCOLLAY STA.

TRAIN SERVICE IS OPERATED IN EAST BOSTON TUNNEL BETWEEN MAVERICK AND SCOLLAY STATIONS THROUGHOUT EARLY MORNING HOURS ON HALF-HOURLY SCHEDULE.

5

(H-6) CITY POINT—ROWES WHARF (B-11)

VIA P, 4TH, L, SUMMER, ATLANTIC AVE.

WEEKDAYS				SUNDAY	
FIRST	LAST			FIRST	LAST
5:15	12:15	CITY POINT TO ROWES WHARF		6:15	12:15
5:35	12:35	ROWES WHARF TO CITY POINT		6:35	12:35

ADDITIONAL SERVICE WEEKDAY RUSH HOURS BETWEEN CITY POINT AND SOUTH STATION

66

(D-5) HARVARD SQUARE—LECHMERE STATION (F-5)

VIA CAMBRIDGE

WEEKDAYS				SUNDAY	
FIRST	LAST			FIRST	LAST
4:35	1:18	HARVARD SQ. TO LECHMERE STA.		5:25	1:18
4:48	1:36	LECHMERE STA. TO HARVARD SQ.		5:38	1:36

67

(E-6) BROOKLINE & GRANITE—GREEN & PEARL (E-8)

VIA BROOKLINE, GREEN. RETURN VIA PEARL, PUTNAM, MAGAZINE, GRANITE

WEEKDAYS				SUNDAY	
FIRST	LAST			FIRST	LAST
5:23	12:59	BROOKLINE & GRANITE TO GREEN & PEARL . .		6:52	12:59
5:17	12:53	GREEN & PEARL TO BROOKLINE & GRANITE . .		6:45	12:53

Figure 6.55 BERy System Route List, 1936

The opposite side of System Route Map Number 1 (Figure 6.53) was a list of all rapid transit, streetcar, trackless trolley, and bus routes operated by the BERy. Two portions of the list are enlarged above.

industrial engineer, and draftsman. He produced maps for the BERy, the Boston Chamber of Commerce, and others. The orientation, scale, proportion, and general language of representation of Lufkin's System Map Number 1 was a refinement of earlier transit maps for Boston, including Chase's 1865 regional map (Figure 1.69), the West End's 1891 system map (Figure 2.45), and the BERy's 1898 system map (Figure 3.75). As a testament to its usefulness, the "Lufkin Format" map was reissued, with revisions made only for content, first by the BERy, then the MTA, and finally by the MBTA. By referencing the list of routes along with the maps on the other side of the sheet, a user of System Route Map Number 1 could locate any desired route, discover its operating times, plot connections

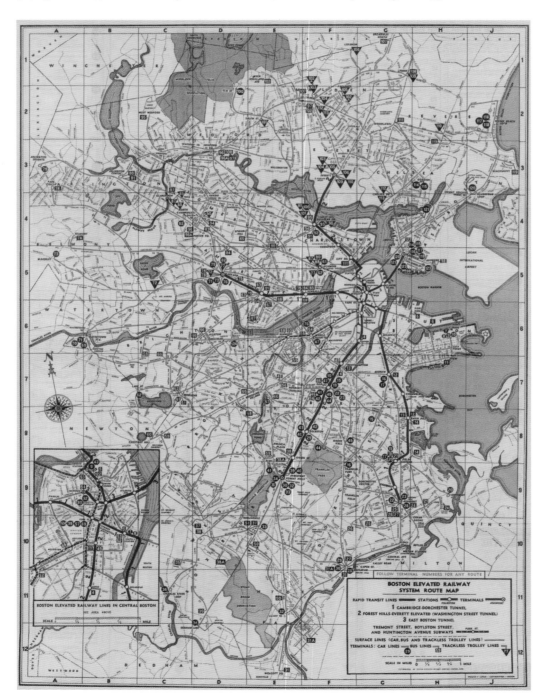

Figure 6.56 BERy System Route Map Seventh Ed., 1946

This is the last edition of the folding system route map published by the Boston Elevated Railway Company. Lufkin Format details are present, including an inset map of downtown Boston (bottom left) and circles, squares, and triangles representing termini of streetcar, bus, and trackless trolley routes, respectively. A comparison of the number of surface route flags shown on the map with those depicted on the BERy's first edition (Figure 6.53) reveals that many routes served by streetcars in 1936 were replaced with buses and trackless trolleys by 1946. The number of streetcar lines on the 1946 map is forty-eight, down from the sixty-three on the 1936 map. Bus routes increased from fifty-two in 1936 to sixty in 1946. Trackless trolley routes multiplied from only one in 1936 to sixteen in 1946.

between routes, and navigate all modes of the BERy's network.

World War II brought rationing and shortages of materials and labor in the 1940s. The war put a damper on the BERy making significant expansions of its system. During the war, the BERy hunkered down to focus on operations. After the war, the BERy published its final edition of the Lufkin Format folding system map, in 1946 (Figure 6.56).

After taking over the BERy in 1947, the MTA issued editions of the Lufkin Format folding system map eight times. Appearing in 1949, the "First M.T.A. Edition" (Figure 6.57) reflected changes to public transit in Greater Boston since 1946.

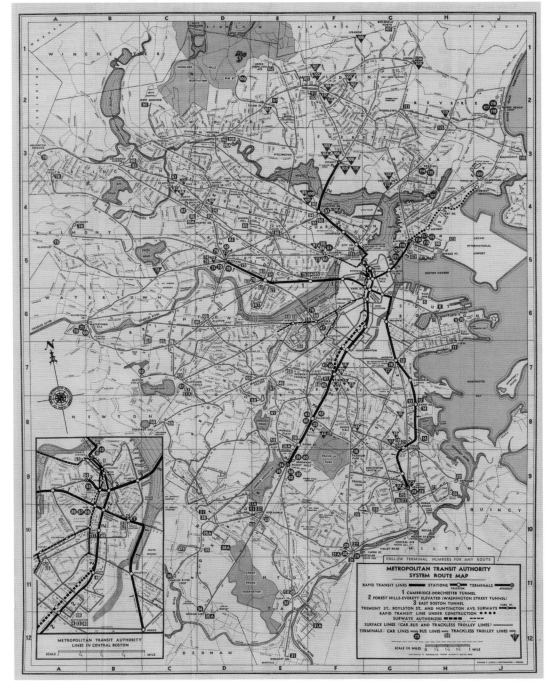

Figure 6.57 MTA's System Route Map First Ed., 1949

This is the "First M.T.A. Edition" of the Lufkin Format folding system map. MTA branding replaces that of the BERy present in earlier editions. The map depicts projects on the boards of the MTA, including the Revere Extension. It also features an oddity—a dashed blue line runs parallel to the Washington Street Elevated, from north of Dover Station to Dudley Station. The never-built rapid transit tunnel was authorized by the Commonwealth to replace existing elevated railways.

Figure 6.58 BERy Newspaper Ads, Circa 1930s

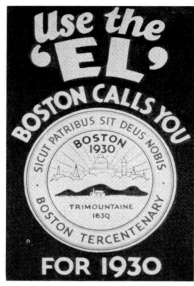

Figure 6.59 BERy "Use The EL" Print Ad, 1930

A print ad encourages people to "Use The EL" and visit Boston during the city's tercentenary. The graphic shows two skylines of Boston, a modern one, with the statehouse and church steeples, and a historic one, with a profile of the Trimount as it may have looked in 1630. The modern skyline is labeled Boston 1930. The historic profile, labeled "Trimountaine 1630," recalls an early seventeenth century view of the city (Figure 1.2).

Figure 6.60 "Park Where the 'EL' Begins" Print Ad, 1930

Figure 6.61 BERy Bus Charter Print Advertisement, 1931

Figure 6.62 BERy "Ride the EL" Print Ads, 1930

Ads for the El

The BERy consistently marketed itself in various types of media, including radio and print (Figure 6.58). In the mid-1920s, the company took to the airwaves with radio addresses given by its general manager, Edward Dana. The BERy expanded its marketing efforts in the 1930s with improved signage, newspaper inserts, and posters. The slogan "Use The "EL" appeared in many BERy print advertisements, including one that tied into Boston's tercentenary (Figure 6.59).

Many of the BERy's print ads were designed to woo automobile commuters. The request to "Park Where the 'EL' Begins for Speed Safety Convenience" beckoned from many (Figure 6.60). "Charter a Bus! For Conventions - Outings - Tours" screamed ads for BERy charter bus service (Figure 6.61). A set of graphically-striking ads attempted to convince automobile drivers that taking public transportation is "less worrisome," "less troublesome," and "more convenient" then driving into and parking in the city (Figure 6.62). After World War II, the BERy launched a fresh series of print ads, the first of which was dominated by an elevated rapid transit train cruising unhindered over roadways chocked with automobile traffic (Figure 6.63).

An elaborate series of print advertisements, titled "Where the "EL" Begins," explained how motorists might integrate a particular BERy rapid transit or elevated streetcar line into their automobile commute (Figure 6.64). Each ad included a map of a BERy line and the "highways" leading to it. Each listed running times between a particular outlying BERy stop and a downtown station.

Figure 6.63 "Ride the 'EL'" Print Ad, 1946

Figure 6.64 "Where the El Begins" Print Ads, Circa 1930s

Travel Information Guides

Five years before issuing its first folding system map, in 1931 the BERy commenced issuance of a pocket guide titled *Travel Information*. The BERy revised and reissued the multi-page *Travel Information* until 1947, after which time the MTA continued to reissue editions into the 1950s. Early editions of *Travel Information* had simple covers, the hue of which varied from issue to issue (Figure 6.65 and Figure 6.66). By the end of the 1930s, advertisements for BERy charter bus service appeared on the back cover (Figure 6.67). Editions published during World War II featured faces of armed service members and a welcome message for troops visiting

Boston (Figure 6.68). After the war, information for service members was replaced with pictograms of Boston buildings "Easily Reached by The Boston EL" (Figure 6.69). *Travel Information* brochures of the late 1940s and early 1950s featured images of Boston landmarks "Easily Reached by the El" (Figure 6.69) and cartoons of a woman and a man calling on citizens to "Ride the MTA to Work and Play" (Figure 6.70). Between pages listing destinations and calling out transit lines serving each, *Travel Information* contained a centerfold map of Boston's subway, tunnel, and elevated railway lines (Figure 6.71).

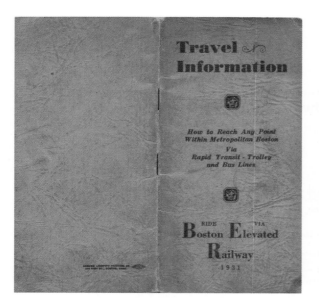

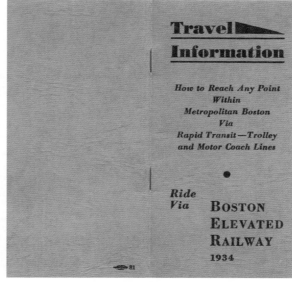

Figure 6.65 (Left) BERy Travel Information Cover, 1931

Figure 6.66 (Right) BERy Travel Information Cover, 1934

Figure 6.67 (Left) BERy Travel Information Cover, April 1940

Figure 6.68 (Right) BERy Travel Information Cover, Aug. 1943

Figure 6.69 (Left) MTA Travel Information Cover, May 1947

Figure 6.70 (Right) MTA Travel Information Cover, Mar. 1952

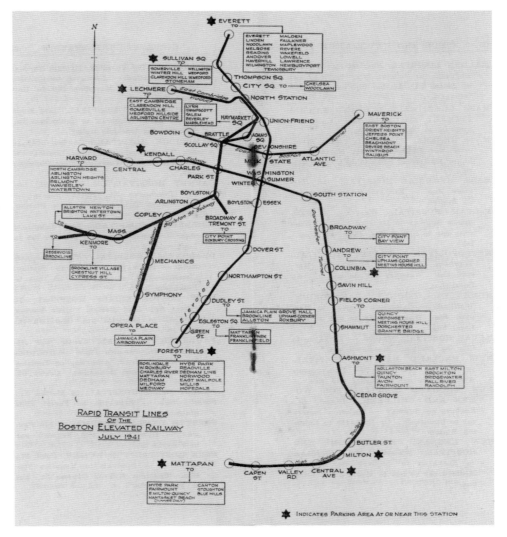

Figure 6.71 BERy Travel Information Map, July 1941

Concurrent with its issuance of *Travel Information*, the BERy continued to produce its *Guide and Information* brochures. The cover of the 1929 and fifth edition (Figure 6.72) bears a bird's eye perspective of Boston covered with colorful pictographs of landmarks, activities, and transportation infrastructure.

While the BTD was working on the Huntington Avenue Subway in 1939, the BERy issued a revised edition of its *Rapid Transit Lines* brochure (Figure 6.73). Every edition of the brochure, including the 1905 first edition (Figure 5.35), was packed with data and statistics on BERy routes, lines, and infrastructure. The BERy revised and reissued its *Rapid Transit Lines* brochure until 1947, when it was taken over by the MTA. The MTA continued to revise and reissue the publication into the late 1950s (Figure 8.20). Beyond transit maps, guides, and brochures, the BERy also published unique informational handouts. A "Special Air Raid

Issue" of "El News" instructed transit riders what to do during an air raid or blackout, should they be caught in such an event while riding in a BERy vehicle (Figure 6.74). The 1942 pamphlet directed riders to stay calm and follow the direction of BERy employees.

Ambitious Expansion Plans: The MTRC Report

In 1943, the Commonwealth established the Metropolitan Transit Recess Commission (MTRC), tasking it with exploring potential improvements for public transportation in Greater Boston. After issuing initial findings in 1945, the MTRC issued a final report in 1947. The MTRC put forth two significant concepts: one, that the limited geographic reach of the BERy was a problem; and two, that a wholly public entity should replace the BERy and could provide improved public transportation for Greater Boston. In its report, the MTRC wrote:

Figure 6.72 BERy Brochure Cover, 1929

Figure 6.73 BERy Rapid Transit Lines Pamphlet, 1939

Behind a cover with an image of Sullivan Square State (left), was a map of Boston's elevated railways, subways, and rapid transit tunnels (right).

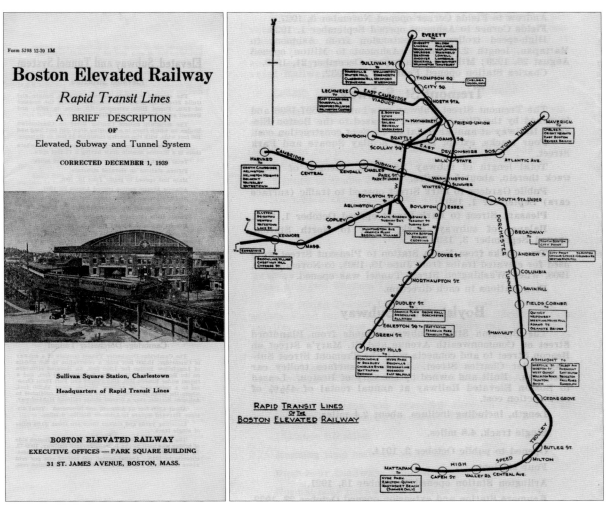

Figure 6.74 BERy Preparedness Brochure, June 1942

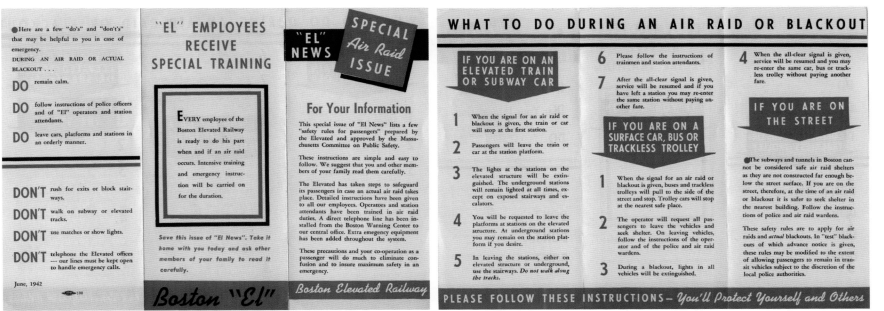

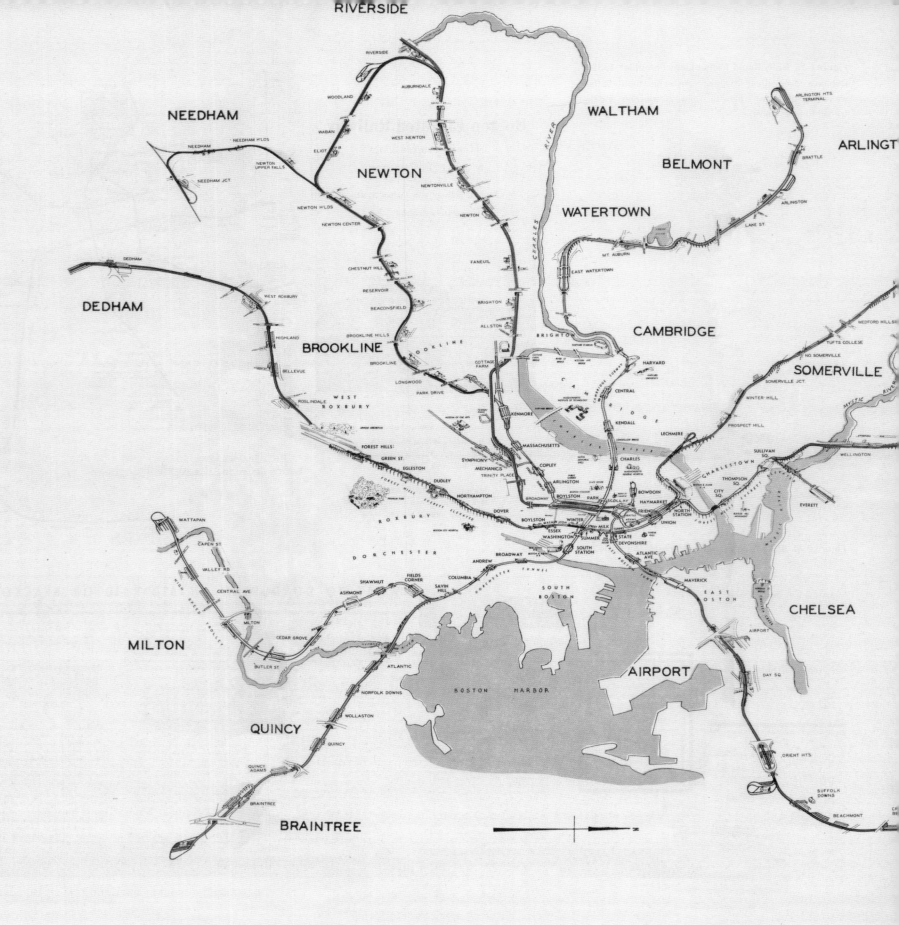

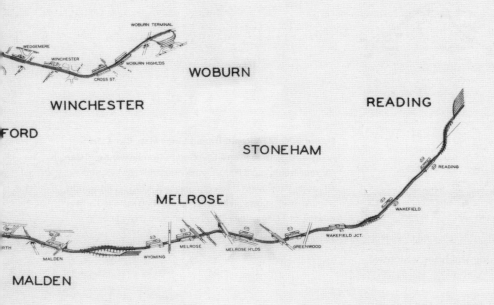

WEDGEMERE
WOBURN TERMINAL
WINCHESTER
WOBURN HIGHLDS
CROSS ST.

WOBURN

WINCHESTER

FORD

READING

STONEHAM

READING

MELROSE

WAKEFIELD

MALDEN
WYOMING
MELROSE
MELROSE HLDS
GREENWOOD
WAKEFIELD JCT.

MALDEN

METROPOLITAN TRANSIT RECESS COMMISSION

A I R   V I E W

PRESENT RAPID TRANSIT SYSTEM – BOSTON ELEVATED RAILWAY
AND
PROPOSED EXTENSIONS OF RAPID TRANSIT
INTO SUBURBAN BOSTON

APRIL 1945

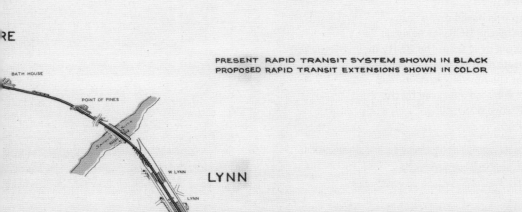

RE

BATH HOUSE

POINT OF PINES

PRESENT RAPID TRANSIT SYSTEM SHOWN IN BLACK
PROPOSED RAPID TRANSIT EXTENSIONS SHOWN IN COLOR

W. LYNN

LYNN

LYNN

Figure 6.75 MTRC Air View Map, 1945
A map prepared by the Metropolitan Transit Recess Commission (MTRC) lays out existing and proposed streetcar and rapid transit lines and stations. The map accompanied the MTRC's report of 1945. The basis of the map was created by the BERy and installed in rapid transit cars by the mid-1940s (Figure 6.77).

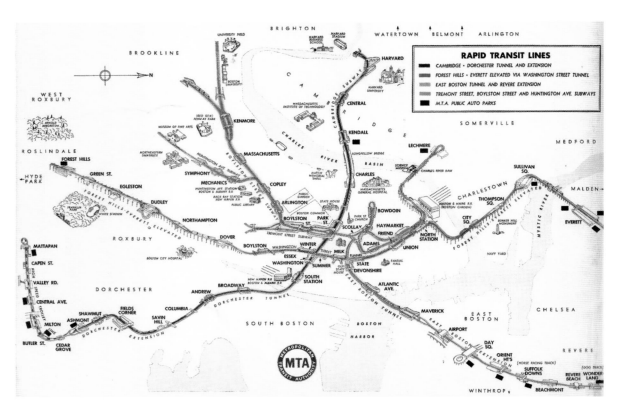

RAPID TRANSIT LINES

- ■ CAMBRIDGE · DORCHESTER TUNNEL AND EXTENSION
- ■ FOREST HILLS · EVERETT ELEVATED VIA WASHINGTON STREET TUNNEL
- ■ EAST BOSTON TUNNEL AND REVERE EXTENSION
- ■ TREMONT STREET, BOYLSTON STREET AND HUNTINGTON AVE. SUBWAYS
- ■ M.T.A. PUBLIC AUTO PARKS

Figure 6.76 MTA Rapid Transit Lines Map, Circa 1955

An in-window map from a Cambridge-Dorchester rapid transit car represents rapid transit lines, elevated railways, and streetcar subways in three-dimensions. A 1952 photograph (Figure 6.77), shows an iteration of the map installed on a window of a Cambridge-Dorchester rapid transit car.

Our efforts and investigations make it perfectly clear that rapid transit must be extended out to the areas of population which have developed in the last twenty years. Otherwise, the population will continue to use the buses and automobiles, the results of which will be the worsening of the already intolerable traffic conditions and increasing deficits for the [BERy].

The commission continued: "Only those cities and towns which will be served by rapid transit will assume any obligation whatever towards it." The MTRC recommended that the Commonwealth create an entity that could expand the BERy's service area and liberate public transportation from the financial drain of private ownership (under the BERy). Despite decades of public oversight, in the 1940s the BERy remained financially accountable to stock and bond holders. The MTRC stated bluntly:

We cannot too strongly urge those in authority who are responsible for a solution of the transportation problem of the metropolitan area to set up at once the MTA which we have recommended; that public ownership of the Boston Elevated Railway be completed now and that the Authority be directed to proceed to establish the system of rapid transit along the lines which we have offered as a guide.

The system of rapid transit to which the commission referred was represented on maps accompanying its 1945 (Figure 6.75) and 1947 reports. The 1945 map is visually engaging to both the layman and the planner. It is covered with three-dimensional vignettes of stations, existing and proposed. Beyond the central portion of the BERy's system, the map lays out ambitious expansions of rapid transit service for Greater Boston. Extensions of existing lines radiate from downtown Boston to Braintree, Dedham, Needham, Arlington, Woburn, Reading, and Lynn. Some of the proposed extensions follow steam railroad rights-of-way, echoing routes laid out on the 1926 "Comprehensive Plan [of] Future Rapid Transit Routes [for the] Metropolitan District" (Figure 6.19).

The MTRC's 1945 map was based on an "air view" system map in use by the BERy as early as the mid-1940s. After taking over from the BERy in 1947, the MTA produced its own versions of the map (Figure 6.76). Versions of the air view system map were installed in transit vehicles operated by the MTA (Figure 6.77 and Figure 6.78).

Figure 6.77 Order of Stations Sign and Map, 1952
An MTA-owned Cambridge-Dorchester rapid transit car wears both an Order of Stations sign (left) and a window decal map (center), similar to that shown in Figure 6.76.

Figure 6.78 Cambridge-Dorchester Car #0670, July 25, 1961
The well-worn interior of an 0600-series Cambridge-Dorchester car wears an "air view" map on one of its windows (far left). Across the car, an "Order of Stations" sign is mounted on the wall, next to the door (far right). The car went into service in the early 1920s and is ready for retirement.

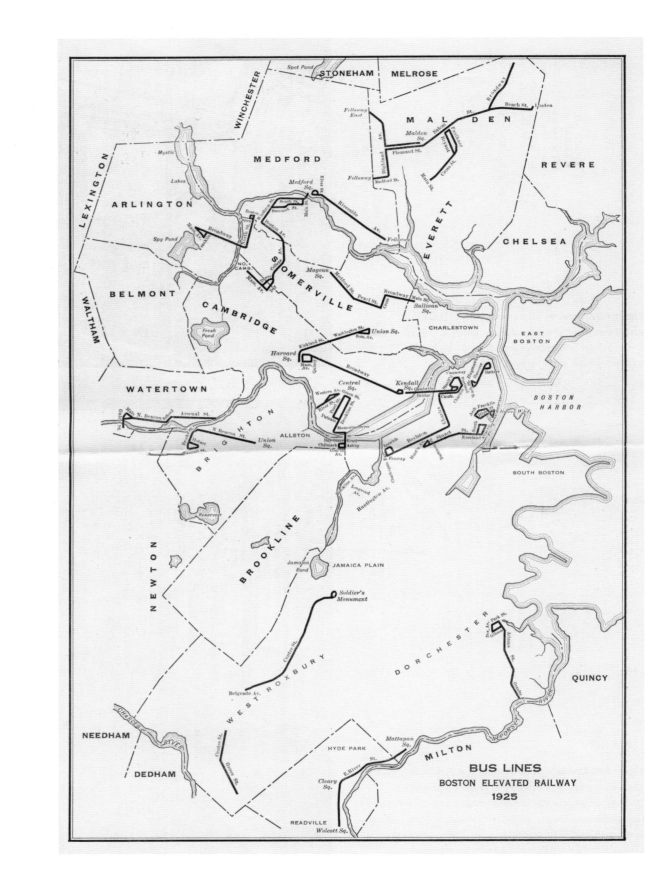

BUS LINES
BOSTON ELEVATED RAILWAY
1925

CHAPTER 7

Catching the Bus

Dawn of Public Bus Transit in Boston

At the beginning of 1920, the foundation of public transportation throughout Greater Boston consisted of hundreds of miles of steel rails. Thousands of streetcars and scores of rapid transit trains carried passengers through, above, and beneath the streets. Steam railroads and street railway companies transported people between Boston and outlying towns. At the end of 1920, the largest public transportation company by ridership in New England, the Boston Elevated Railway Company (BERy), reported using its combined fleets of 2,229 streetcars and 420 rapid transit cars to transport nearly 336 million paying passengers. The BERy's vehicles travelled fifty-one million revenue miles of combined surface and rapid transit rails in 1920. A dense network of railed transit lines stitched together Boston's neighborhoods and eleven other municipalities. Complementing and sprawling to the north and south of the BERy's network was that of the Bay State Street Railway Company (Bay State). In 1920, the Bay State operated hundreds of miles of track and served dozens of cities and towns in eastern Massachusetts. After the BERy, the Bay State was the second largest public transportation company in the Commonwealth.

As the 1920s progressed, combustion engine vehicles increasingly challenged the supremacy of streetcars. America's burgeoning automobile industries continuously improved production methods, materials, technology, and vehicle designs to provide increasingly affordable and reliable automobiles, trucks, and buses. The first few decades of the twentieth century saw the personal automobile foster freedom from railed public transportation for the individual, and the truck offer liberation from steam railroads for the shipper of goods. On the

public transportation front, early buses, also known as "motor coaches" and "motor buses," allowed public transportation providers to economically carry passengers along city streets without fixed rails. The word "bus" is a shortened version of the older word, "omnibus." The moniker "motor coach" features the attachment of "motor" to the name for the centuries-old mode of transportation, the horse-drawn "coach."

Boston's first public transit motor buses arrived in the 1920s. The vehicles had a capacity similar to larger omnibuses, but they were propelled by combustion engines instead of literal horsepower. A bus of the 1920s did not have the passenger capacity of its streetcar or rapid transit car contemporaries. Early buses featured an enclosed cab for the driver and a modest passenger compartment, both set onto a primitive truck chassis. They were less than thirty feet long and typically seated no more than two dozen passengers. The vehicle was propelled by a combustion engine powertrain. Early motor coaches rolled on solid tires and were subject to the jerky motions of standard transmissions. In time, balloon tires, automatic transmissions, more reliable engines, and better interiors contributed to smoother operation of, and more comfortable rides within, buses.

The cost of establishing and maintaining a route for a bus was markedly less than that for a streetcar or rapid transit train. Streetcars, in addition to having higher individual purchase prices than buses, required fixed steel rails, overhead wire, and power stations. Rapid transit cars required expensive elevated railways, tunnels, and third rail power systems. Buses lacked a need for tracks, trolley wire, third rail, or power plants. Wherever there was a reasonable road and a gas pump nearby, buses

Figure 7.1 Mapping the BERy's Earliest Bus Routes, 1925
Three years after the BERy launched its first bus service, many of the company's routes were geographically isolated (black lines) from one another but connected with existing streetcar and rapid transit service (not shown).

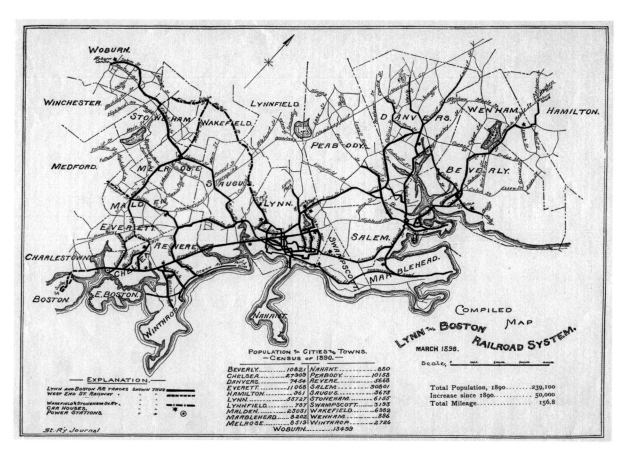

Figure 7.2 The Lynn & Boston Railroad, March 1896
The Lynn & Boston operated streetcars from as far south as Boston's Scollay Square (far left) to as far north as the town of Hamilton (far right).

could run. The "go anywhere" capability of buses coupled with lower capital costs than railed-transit made the rubber-tired vehicles attractive to transit companies. Buses were deployed by transit operators looking to provide service on routes where the expense or infrastructure for either street-cars or rapid transit trains was not desired or cost-prohibitive.

The operators of Eastern Massachusetts' two largest streetcar networks, the BERy and the Bay State's successor, were leaders in the early adoption of buses and the conversion of their streetcar lines to bus routes. Today's MBTA bus network has its roots in those of the BERy and Bay State.

The Bay State Street Railway Company

In the last quarter of the nineteenth century, decades of consolidations lead to a few companies dominating street railway service in eastern Massachusetts. After the BERy, the two largest companies became the Boston & Northern Street Railway Company (Boston & Northern) and the Old Colony Street Railway Company (Old Colony St Ry).

The Boston & Northern resulted over the course of 1899–1901 from the consolidation of fifteen street railway companies, all entities providing service north of Boston. The largest of these was the Lynn & Boston Railroad (Lynn & Boston), established in 1854. It was the only street railway company serving downtown Boston not absorbed by the West End Street Railway Company (West End) during its consolidation of Boston's horse railroads in 1887. A map from *The Street Railway Journal* captures the Lynn & Boston's network in March 1896 (Figure 7.2). The Lynn & Boston renamed itself the Boston & Northern in July 1901. By the end of the decade, Boston & Northern lines radiated from Boston to the Merrimack Valley and Cape Ann.

While the Boston & Northern connected Boston with points north, the Old Colony St Ry, itself the result of the consolidation of sixteen street railway companies between 1899 and 1901, linked points south of the city. By 1909, Old Colony St Ry lines extended from Boston's southern periphery into Norfolk and Bristol Counties, and even as far south as Newport, Rhode Island (Figure 2.58). The Boston & Northern formally absorbed the

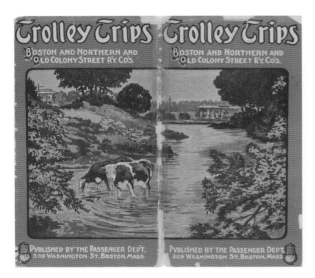

Figure 7.3 Trolley Trips Brochure, Circa 1910

Figure 7.4 The Bay State's Trolley Trips Brochure, 1911

The 1911 edition of *Trolley Trips* was sent to press with both "Boston & Northern" and "Old Colony St Ry" printed on its cover. Prior to distribution, "Bay State Street Railway Co." was stamped over the two legacy names (above).

Old Colony St Ry in July 1911. The merger occurred after years of both companies being operated under common management. A month after the takeover, the newly expanded company renamed itself the Bay State Street Railway Company (Bay State).

Trolley Trips

The Bay State released its latest edition of *Trolley Trips*, a brochure previously published jointly by the Boston & Northern and Old Colony St Ry, in 1911 (Figure 7.3). *Trolley Trips* advertised journeys by electric streetcar that could be taken on the lines of the Boston & Northern and Old Colony St Ry, and subsequently, the Bay State.

The 1911 edition of the Bay State's *Trolley Trips* featured a centerfold regional streetcar map, titled "Aero View Map," and a cover with a streetcar wheel "flying" with outstretched wings along a steel rail (Figure 7.4). Within the guide, a page or two dedicated to a particular trip featured descriptive text, photographs of the destination, and color maps of the route (Figure 7.5).

The centerfold map from the Bay State's 1912 edition of *Trolley Trips* featured a drawing of a biplane in the map's title block (Figure 7.6). The inclusion of a biplane on a street railway map reflected America's excitement over powered flight, which began with the Wright Brothers' take off in 1903. On the Bay State's 1911 and 1916 (Figure 7.7) maps, the Bay State's streetcar lines are abstracted to minimize their actual twists and turns. With smoothed out route lines, and an accompanying flying trolley wheel or biplane graphic, the *Trolley Trips* brochures and their maps implied that electric

streetcars might provide the speed and as-the-crow-flies directness of powered flight.

The masthead for multiple editions of *Trolley Trips* (Figure 7.7) featured two contrasting photos, one of a horse-drawn streetcar accompanied by a subtitle "the old way," and another, of an electric streetcar subtitled "the new way." With this masthead, the Bay State announced that it was utilizing the latest transportation technology, the electric streetcar, and confirming that the horsecar was a relic of the past.

The Bay State's *Trolley Trips* were not the only streetcar guides published with similar titles (See Chapter 2). Among many variants was the BERy's August 1931 first edition of *Trolley Trips* (Figure 7.8). Odd for a trolley guide, its cover lacked any representation of a streetcar.

The Eastern Massachusetts Street Railway Company

At the time of America's entry into World War I in 1917, the financial situation of the Bay State was dire. The street railway company lost almost $600,000 in fiscal 1916 alone. Responding to the crisis, the Bay State raised its standard fare from a nickel to six cents, effective July 15, 1917. Despite the fare change, sharp increases in the costs of materials, rising labor expenses, and the growing popularity of private automobiles became insurmountable obstacles in the eyes of many of the Bay State's investors. Attempting to protect their investments, creditors pushed the money-losing Bay State into a court-ordered receivership. In June 1918 the General Court stepped in to assist, passing the "Public Control Act," part of which permitted the reconstitution of the Bay State into a new company, the

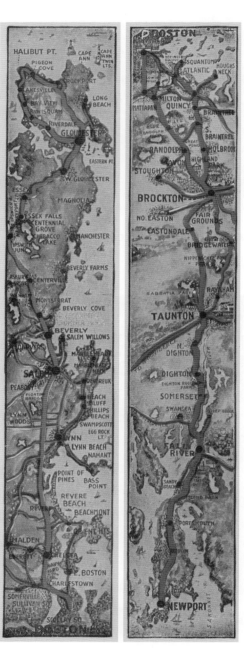

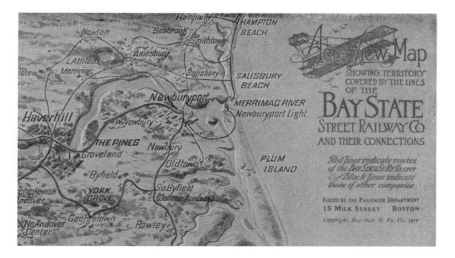

Figure 7.5 Maps from Bay State's Trolley Trips, 1916
Maps accompanying descriptions of trips "Along the Famous North Shore" (left) and to "Newport, The Queen City of The Sea" (right) and were featured in editions of the Bay State's *Trolley Trips* during the 1910s.

Figure 7.6 Bay State Trolley Trips Map Title Block, 1912

TRIPS BY TROLLEY
ALONG
BAY STATE STREET RAILWAY CO.
LINES AND CONNECTIONS

Figure 7.7 Bay State's Trolley Trips Masthead and Map, 1916

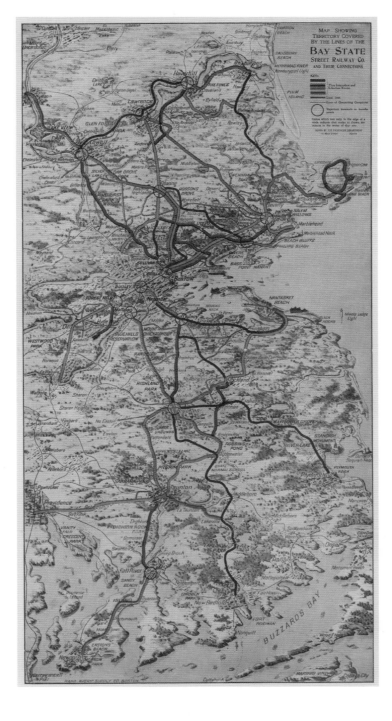

Figure 7.8 Cover of the BERy's Trolley Trips, 1931

Eastern Massachusetts Street Railway Company (Eastern Mass).

The Eastern Mass was incorporated in January 1919. After taking control of the assets of the Bay State in April, the Eastern Mass formally began operations on June 1. The Eastern Mass immediately implemented a new fare structure, one that the Bay State had in the works during its final months as a corporate entity. The new fares included a city fare, costing ten cents for one ride, or thirty-five cents for five. Interurban fares were broken down into a seven cent fare for travel within one zone, and a ten cent fare for travel between one or two zones. The fare for travel beyond two zones was five cents for each additional zone. A combined city and interurban fare cost fifteen cents or a seven-cent ticket plus a nickel. The Eastern Mass also sold pre-paid tickets in packages of twenty.

At the end of 1930, the Eastern Mass's fleet of 114 buses accounted for fourteen percent of its total revenue mileage. The company continued to jettison trolleys and add buses. By the end of 1932, the Eastern Mass had 202 active buses and its streetcar revenue had decreased by over twenty-five percent; bus revenue had increased by over thirty percent. The replacement of streetcars with buses continued, ramping up as America became involved in World War II. Ninety-seven percent of the Eastern Mass's routes were served by buses in 1941. In its annual report for that year, the company recorded:

> The marked increase in riding brought about by defense employment and restrictions limiting the use of personal automobiles required the delivery of seventy-six motor coaches during the year.

In the same report, the Eastern Mass listed 910 motor coaches in inventory without any mention of active streetcars. A two-page spread from the report featured renderings of a horsecar and a bus, both underscored by the slogan "80 Years of Progress" (Figure 7.9). In its annual report for 1946, the Eastern Mass mentioned: "The only remaining service now rendered by electric cars is the double tracked line running between the Shipyard in Quincy and Neponset." At the end of the 1940s the Eastern Mass became, in all matter of fact except by name, a bus company.

Jitneys

A decade before the Eastern Mass and the BERy began to replace their streetcars with motor coaches, in the mid-1910s, motorized jitneys

Figure 7.9 Eighty Years of Progress on the Eastern Mass, 1941
A two-page spread from the 1941 annual report of the Eastern Massachusetts Street Railway Company shows a horsecar posed before nineteenth century buildings (left), recalling the origins of the company in horse railroad operations, and a motor coach shining against a modern skyline (right).

appeared throughout Greater Boston. Jitneys were typically motor buses or large automobiles that were privately owned, and operated to pick up paying passengers on established, but flexible, routes. The word Jitney is slang for a five cent piece that riders gave as payment to drivers of private automobiles as early as the 1910s. Jitneys were unregulated and served routes that often duplicated those of the regulated transit companies. When jitneys picked up passengers along established transit routes, they poached riders from the transit companies,

including the BERy. Jitneys operated outside of the tightly regulated transit industry, much like ride-sharing companies operate outside of most hackney regulations today.

In the 1910s, public transit providers, including the Eastern Mass and the BERy, began working with Boston and the Commonwealth to tame or even eliminate competition from jitneys. A 1919 hand-drawn map (Figure 7.10) depicts jitney routes and the companies operating them within the service area of the BERy. The map, attributed to

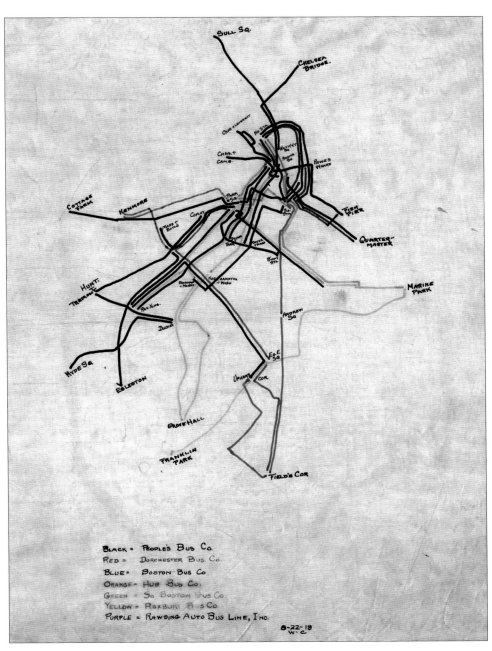

Figure 7.10 Boston's Jitney Routes, August 22, 1919
A hand-drawn map documents where unlicensed jitneys operated within the service area of the BERy. Seven companies are listed in the key. The lines of each company, and the routes they follow, are represented in a unique color.

the BERy's engineering staff, was prepared as the BERy worked to identify and subvert jitney operations that were in direct competition with its own lines. In Boston, as a result of the efforts of the BERy, the city regulated jitneys out of business. By 1930 the Hackney Carriage Unit of the Boston Police Department was in place to issue licenses to automobiles driven as taxis in the city. The state's Department of Public Utilities took on the regulation of intrastate bus services throughout the Commonwealth, a role it continues to play today.

Ride All Day for $1

The Eastern Mass issued a plethora of printed guides to advertise its services. By the 1930s, colorful Eastern Mass brochures wore the slogan "Ride All Day for $1" (Figure 7.11). As the company converted its streetcar lines to bus service the Eastern Mass often gave buses equal billing with streetcars on its guides, as exemplified by pocket-sized "Ride All Day" guides of the 1930s (Figure 7.11). Typically, each of the depression-era guides contained a connect-the-dots-style, Eastern Mass system map (Figure 7.12).

A brochure titled "Ride All Day for $1.00 Through Historic Eastern Massachusetts" (Figure 7.13),

Figure 7.11 "Ride All Day for $1" Brochure Covers, 1930s
Covers of pocket-sized guides published by the Eastern Massachusetts Street Railway Company beckon riders to "Ride All Day for $1.00."

Figure 7.12 Eastern Mass Guide Map, 1935

Looking more like a map of a celestial constellation, a map shows points linked by the lines of the Eastern Mass.

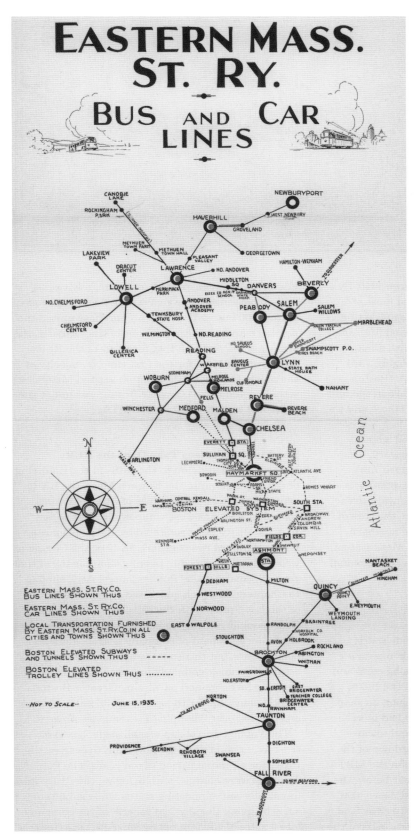

Figure 7.13 Eastern Mass Brochure, Circa 1940

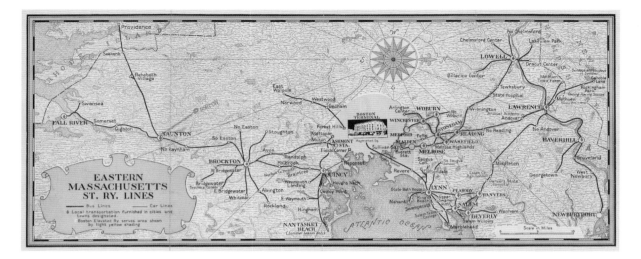

Figure 7.14 Eastern Mass Street Railway Co. Map, Circa 1940
An Eastern Mass brochure map bears an atypically formatted map of Boston—north is oriented to the right, not to the top, of the map. At the center of the map, a view of the Eastern Mass' Boston Terminal is superimposed over an area highlighted in yellow, representing the service area of the BERy. From the Boston Terminal, Eastern Mass bus lines radiate to the north and south of Boston.

was published by the Eastern Mass circa 1940. By that time, the company had eliminated most of its streetcar lines and was focusing its marketing efforts on bus riders. The brochure listed fifty-one towns served by the company along with a map of its network. The brochure's map (Figure 7.14) contained a view of the Eastern Mass's "Boston Terminal," opened in Haymarket Square in the mid-1930s. The terminal housed company offices and was a transfer station for bus travellers.

The maps of the Eastern Mass reveal a large gap in the middle of the company's network, a gap completely occupied by the BERy (Figure 7.15). The bifurcation of the Eastern Mass system was a result of the consolidation of street railways to the south and to the north, but not within, the core of Boston. In order to travel between the northern and southern portions of the Eastern Mass system, passengers transferred at the Haymarket Terminal and utilized the lines of the BERy.

Closing the Gap

The Eastern Mass operated for fifty-one years, until, like the Bay State before it, the company's financial health was jeopardized by rising costs and declines in ridership. By the middle of the 1960s, the Eastern Mass was considering closing up shop. For a decade, the company's ridership had increasingly turned away from public buses and towards personal automobiles. A potential shutdown of the Eastern Mass was averted in 1968, when the MBTA purchased the company whole. The year before the acquisition the Eastern Mass operated nearly 600 miles of bus routes and served sixty-two cities and towns. At the time of its takeover by the MBTA, the

Eastern Mass transported approximately twenty million passengers per year with a fleet of approximately 300 buses. The MBTA's purchase united the northern and southern portions of the former Eastern Mass system with that formerly of the BERy. By the end of 1968, for the first time, a majority of the public transportation system around Massachusetts Bay and across Greater Boston was under the control of a single entity, the MBTA.

The Public Trustees Take Over the BERy

In the years leading up to the 1918–19 restructuring of the Bay State into the Eastern Mass, the BERy experienced financial troubles of its own. Rising costs of operations were compounded by the fact that the BERy was prohibited by statue from raising its standard five cent fare. In 1918, the Commonwealth finally stepped in passing Chapter 159 of that year's Special Acts, a "Public Control Act," similar to Chapter 188 which addressed the restructuring of the Bay State. With the legislation, the General Court sought not only to keep the BERy solvent for the financial benefit of company shareholders and bondholders, but to also prevent the single largest public transit company in New England from shutting its doors and paralyzing Greater Boston. In 1917 alone, the BERy operated 532 miles of track and carried over 380 million revenue passengers.

The Public Control Act established a board of trustees, appointed by the governor, to oversee the BERy for an initial period of ten years. The Public Trustees were charged with bringing the BERy into financially self-supporting status while simultaneously bringing the physical aspects of the company into a state of efficient operation. After the General

Figure 7.15 Eastern Mass Marketing Mailer Map, 1945
The northern and southern portions of the Eastern Mass system bracket that of the BERy, highlighted in pink.

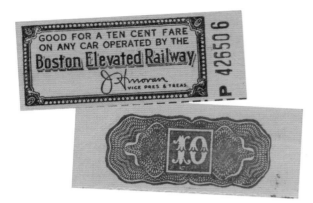

Figure 7.16 BERy Ten Cent Ticket, 1919

Court extended their term beyond the initial ten years, the Public Trustees remained in control of the BERy until the company was legislated out of existence in the 1940s, when it was replaced by the MTA. The takeover of the BERy by the Public Trustees preserved the continuity of public transit operations in Boston and was a step towards complete public control of public transportation for Greater Boston.

Fares on the BERy in the 1910s and 1920s

The Public Trustees took formal control of the BERy on July 1, 1918. One of their first actions was to increase the BERy's standard fare from five cents to seven cents, effective in August. A scant six months after establishing the seven cent fare, the Public Trustees deemed the higher fare inadequate to increase company revenue to keep pace with rising labor and operating costs. So they raised the regular fare again, this time to eight cents, effective December 1, 1918. Alas, the increase was not enough to allow the Public Trustees to fulfill their mandates. Hence, they raised the BERy's regular, fixed fare to ten cents on July 10, 1919 (Figure 7.16). In August, the BERy implemented a fare system consisting of five, ten, fifteen, and twenty cent fares. The incremental fare structure, in combination with assessments imposed by the BERy upon cities and towns which it served, did the trick. By the end of 1919, revenue finally exceeded expenditures; the company was back on sound financial footing, at least for the short term. The BERy sought to maintain the ten cent fare to combat perpetually rising costs and fund ongoing debt obligations throughout the early 1920s. At the same time, the company's riders sought to reduce the fare, hoping for a return to the previously long-standing five cent fare.

Beyond regular tickets, the BERy issued special pupils' tickets to be used exclusively by students commuting to and from school. After completing an application (Figure 7.17) a student was issued books of tickets. (Figure 7.18).

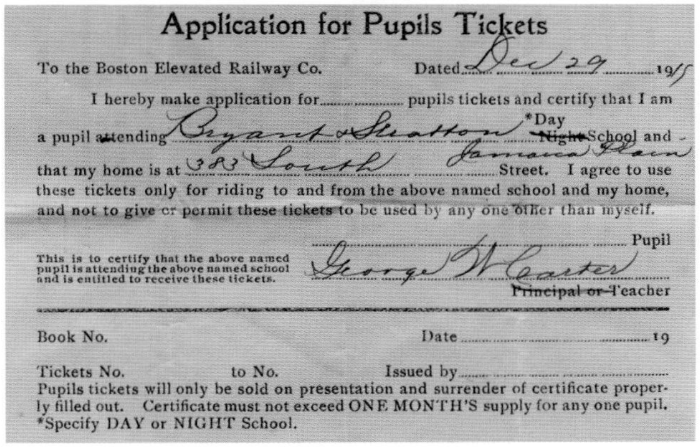

Application for Pupils Tickets

To the Boston Elevated Railway Co. Dated Dec 29 19

I hereby make application for .... pupils tickets and certify that I am a pupil attending Bryant & Stratton *Day ~~Night~~ School and that my home is at 383 South Jamaica Plain Street. I agree to use these tickets only for riding to and from the above named school and my home, and not to give or permit these tickets to be used by any one other than myself.

.... Pupil

This is to certify that the above named pupil is attending the above named school and is entitled to receive these tickets. George W. Carter Principal ~~or Teacher~~

Book No. Date 19

Tickets No. to No. Issued by ....

Pupils tickets will only be sold on presentation and surrender of certificate properly filled out. Certificate must not exceed ONE MONTH'S supply for any one pupil.
*Specify DAY or NIGHT School.

Figure 7.17 BERy Pupils Tickets Application, 1919

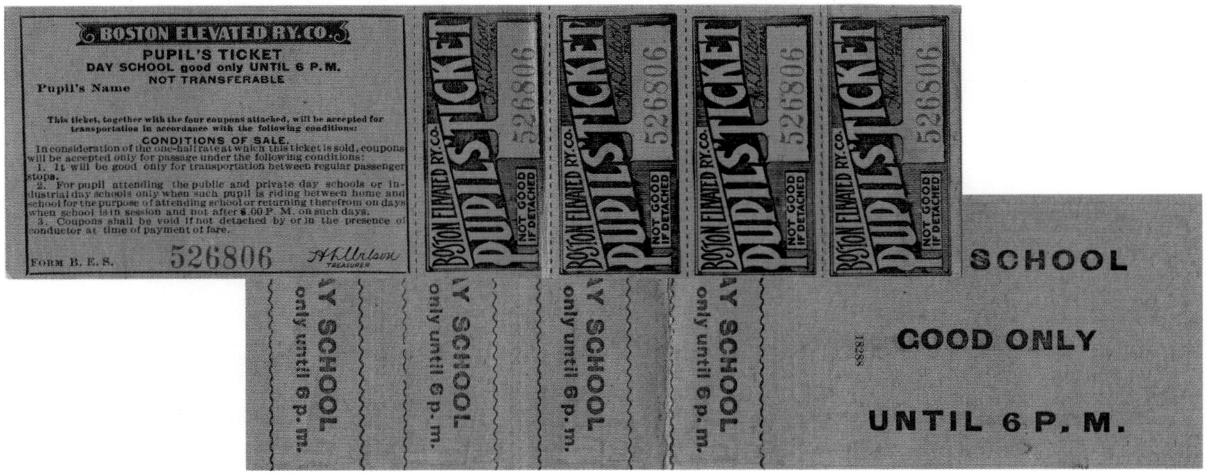

Figure 7.18 BERy Pupils' Ticket Book

On the front of Pupils' ticket book is space for the name of the student to whom the book was issued. Each day, travelling to or back from school, the student detached one "Pupil's Ticket" from the book and presented it to board a BERy vehicle.

Figure 7.19 The BERy's First Bus, 1922

Figure 7.20 (Left) Inside the BERy's First Bus, February 7, 1922
Simple, bench seats face towards the driver's area, with its manual shifter and parking brake. An early mechanical fare box is mounted near the front door.

Figure 7.21 (Right) Seating in the BERy's First Bus, 1922
The center portion of the rear-most bench concealed a door that opened at the back of the bus like that of an omnibus.

Figure 7.22 Bus at Union Square Car House, Somerville, 1926

BERy Buses for Boston

Three years after its takeover by the Public Trustees, the BERy applied to local regulators to transport passengers on motor buses along a mile and a half of North Beacon Street, between the Charles River and Union Square in Allston. What would become the BERy's first bus line was already served by BERy streetcars, but the North Beacon Street tracks were worn and in need of replacement. The BERy wanted to substitute buses for streetcars to save the significant expense of replacing and maintaining the aging streetcar infrastructure. Beyond saving the BERy money, conversion of the North Beacon Street line would set a precedent for it to build upon and replace other streetcar lines with bus service.

The BERy began providing bus service along Beacon Street on February 21, 1922. Three motor buses, two for regular service and one reserved for rush hour service, replaced streetcars along Beacon Street. The BERy's self-described "first bus used in Boston Elevated service" was essentially a large omnibus cab tacked onto a primitive truck chassis (Figure 7.19, Figure 7.20, and Figure 7.21). The four-speed bus featured primitive brakes and a self-starter.

The BERy launched a second bus route, again to replace existing streetcar service, on February 21, 1923. The route served Malden, a city due north of Boston. The BERy quickly added additional bus routes to its network. Of the company's twenty-five initial bus routes, a majority replaced existing streetcar service.

Less than two years after deploying buses along North Beacon Street, the BERy was operating thirty-five "motor buses." Spring 1926 saw an expanded fleet of 190 motor buses fan out to serve twenty-five routes. At the end of the year, the BERy tallied that its buses carried twenty-seven million passengers, over seven percent of the total it transported in 1926. At the time, the local fare for a trip on a BERy bus was six cents. Local fare with a transfer was ten cents. For a dime, a patron could traverse virtually the BERy's entire network. A typical bus of 1926 seated two dozen passengers (Figure 7.22).

In the first half of the twentieth century, the replacement of streetcars became increasingly common for the BERy, the Eastern Mass, and other American streetcar operators. The 1952 *Popular Mechanic's Picture History of American Transportation* confirmed that the BERy was ahead of the curve with its deployment of buses: "as late as 1920 there were only about 60 motor buses operated by electric railways in the entire country." Forty years later, the situation changed. By 1960, most American cities had eliminated their street railway networks and replaced them with fleets of rubber-tired buses. According to a list published by the Boston Street Railway Association in 1979, of major American cities, only Boston and a handful of other municipalities operated any vestiges of their once substantial streetcar systems in 1964. At that time, the only surface streetcar lines remaining in revenue service in Boston were the Mattapan High Speed Line and branches of the Tremont Street Subway.

Co-operation

In the same year that the BERy launched motor buses in Boston, the company began producing *Co-operation*, a multi-page, company newsletter. The title reflected the philosophy espoused by the BERy, that its thousands of employees working for the nation's largest public transit company cooperated "together to make the company safe, successful, and profitable." The main audience for *Co-operation* was an internal one. The BERy published monthly issues of *Co-operation* beginning in January 1922. Early issues were structured around motivational texts and poems with examples of cooperation. Within a few years of its launch, *Co-operation* was regularly packed with articles pertinent to BERy employees, including lists of customer praises and complaints, updates on the company's bowling league, and articles intended to improve the lives of workers, some with pithy titles like "Asbestos," "When Dynamite Explodes," "Watch Your Gas-Stove Flues," and "No Evidence of Co-operation Here." Later issues announced new developments in BERy operations, presented financial summaries, and looked back with detailed histories.

As it added rapid transit, and later buses, to its system, the BERy updated the *Co-operation* masthead. The first two years of *Co-operation* mastheads sported a simple diamond logo reading "Safe Sure Satisfactory Service For The Car Riders." By 1924, a rendering of an electric streetcar joined the diamond-shaped graphic (Figure 7.23). An electric streetcar remained the sole transit vehicle in the masthead until April 1928, when a motor bus and an entrance to the subway joined a streetcar (Figure 7.24).

The growth of the BERy's bus network was recorded in *Co-operation*. The November 1925 issue

Figure 7.23 Co-operation Masthead, 1925

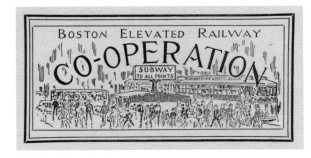

Figure 7.24 Co-operation Masthead, 1928–29

included a map of the BERy's nascent network of twenty-one bus routes (Figure 7.1). A mere four years later, the February 1929 issue of *Co-operation* described seventy-six miles of bus routes composed of thirty-three "basic" routes and twenty-one "rush hour" and "short" routes, all served by over 300 buses.

The Bus Garage

With the arrival of motor buses, the term garage, where buses were stored and repaired, was added to the BERy's infrastructure lexicon. The terms car barn and car house remained, generally reserved for streetcars and rapid transit cars, respectively. The earliest BERy bus garages were not company-owned buildings but structures owned by third parties from which the BERy leased space. In 1923 the BERy converted its own decommissioned Allston Power Station into its first company-owned bus

garage. The power station was constructed in 1889 by the West End to supply power to Boston's first electric streetcar line (see Chapter 2). By the mid-1920s, buses began to displace streetcars from BERy car houses.

The first bus garage constructed from the ground up by the BERy opened at Arborway on January 10, 1925. The brick-clad facility was accompanied by a large bus storage yard (Figure 7.25). A month after the opening of Arborway Garage, an article in *Co-operation* described the BERy's 20,000-square-foot Forest Hills Garage as "probably the largest unobstructed floor space for garage purposes… at least in New England states, if not east of the Mississippi." The fireproof building accommodated forty-two buses with areas for vehicle repair, inspection, and washing. In time, the BERy constructed additional bus garages. Bartlett Street Garage opened as a functional affair, with a low-slung wing sheltering scores of buses (Figure 7.26).

Figure 7.25 Arborway Garage, Circa Early to Mid-1930s
A cadre of Mack-built buses are parked in front of the BERy's first purpose-built bus garage. The opposite side of the building (Figure 7.27; top) housed BERy offices and driver facilities.

Figure 7.26 Bartlett Street Garage, Roxbury, 1936
Multiple, drive-through bays shelter BERy buses at Bartlett Street Garage. The facility was sited alongside the Forest Hills Extension of the Washington Street Elevated.

The BERy published photographs of its major bus garages in the September 1932 issue of *Co-operation* (Figure 7.27).

The BERy was on the forefront of developing bus transit operations and other cities looked to the company for guidance. The BERy shared its bus garage construction and operation expertise in various articles, including one published in the October 1929 issue of *Railway Age*. Penned by BERy Superintendant of Maintenance H. M. Steward,

BUS GARAGES OF THE BOSTON ELEVATED RAILWAY
1, Arborway; 2, Fellsway; 3, Somerville; 4, Dorchester; 5, Bartlett Street;
6, Fellsway Addition

Figure 7.27 BERy Bus Garages, September 1932

Figure 7.28 Cover of Boston Elevated Railway Guide and Information Book, 1926
The dome of the Massachusetts State House and steeple of Park Street Church punctuate a bright sky, below which street-cars operate within Park Street Station and the Tremont Street Subway. Two levels below, a train of the Cambridge-Dorchester rapid transit line pauses at Park Street Under.

the article recommended how to maximize natural light, minimize fire risk, and maintain safe levels of ventilation within bus garages. Steward provided recommended clearances for interior spaces as well as commentary about maintenance pits and ancillary shop spaces. Over the years, BERy management, staff, and even general manager Edward Dana penned a plethora of articles disseminating their collective expertise. Dana personally promoted the free exchange of know-how within the BERy and between the company and transit operators around the world.

The BERy Guide & Information Brochure
Two years after the BERy brought buses to Boston and began producing *Co-operation*, the company commenced publication of a new brochure. Initially titled *Boston Elevated Railway Guide and Information Book*, the multi-page publication was a mixture of promotional literature, explanations of transit

services, and navigational aid. The guide, which the BERy updated and reissued on a yearly basis, contained some of the earliest portable maps of the BERy's system. The first edition, published in 1924, listed 488 miles of track for "surface cars," forty-five miles of track for "third rail trains," 1,680 "surface cars," 461 "rapid transit cars," and 35 "motor buses" in operation by the BERy. The cover of the premiere edition featured a black and white cross-section drawing of Park Street Station. The graphic revealed streetcars and rapid transit trains plying the tunnels and serving the platforms at Park Street and Park Street Under Stations. The second edition of the guide, published in 1926, featured the same cover art, but in glorious color (Figure 7.28).

The second edition of the *Guide and Information Book* contained a BERy system map which represented "surface car lines," "rapid transit lines," "bus lines," and "foreign connecting lines," each in a distinct color (Figure 7.29). Though the colors were most likely arbitrary, their presence as a graphic

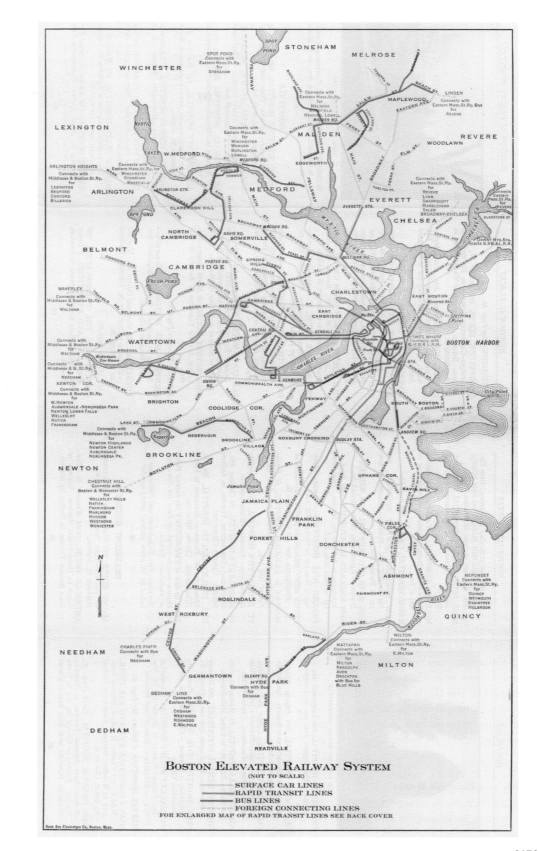

Figure 7.29 Portable Map of the BERy System, 1926

On a BERy brochure map, surface streetcar lines are yellow, rapid transit lines are pink, bus lines are blue, and other companies' lines are yellow and dashed.

Figure 7.30 BERy Double-deck Bus, March 1924
The BERy's only double-deck bus used in revenue service is signed for Bowdoin Square, Boston.

Figure 7.31 BERy Deluxe Service Bus, 1928

Figure 7.32 Interior of a BERy Deluxe Service Bus, 1928

device for differentiating transit lines on a map was relatively new for Boston. Complimenting the map was text with which the BERy described its buses as "the most modern and updated type." The BERy articulated how buses were being applied to routes with ridership too low or streets too constricted for financially viable use of streetcars.

Inside the sixth edition of the *Guide and Information Book*, released in 1930, the system map represented more bus routes than any previous version. Serving the routes were over 360 buses. The number of buses owned by the BERy continued to increase throughout the 1930s and 1940s. During the same period, the quantity of streetcars in company car barns correspondingly decreased.

BERy Deluxe, Charter, and Electric Buses
The BERy was a leader when it came to experimenting with new bus models, technologies, and services. The BERy tested progressive vehicles,

including a double-deck beast, purchased from manufacturer Safeway in 1926 (Figure 7.30). The BERy operated it in short-lived service between Boston's Fenway and North Station neighborhoods. The BERy's use of the double-deck bus came to end after the Commonwealth's Department of Public Utilities (DPU) denied the BERy permission to continue operation of the bi-level vehicle. The DPU was concerned about stability of the vehicle, with its tall and narrow profile. After the DPU's decision, the BERy converted the double-deck bus into a single-level vehicle and used it in regular service.

The BERy experimented with a higher level of motor bus service for customers willing to pay for it for two and a half years, during 1927–30. The BERy launched "extra fare" bus service between Beacon Street in Brookline and Scollay Square in Boston. For the service, the BERy commissioned the construction of what it described as a deluxe bus. Manufactured by White, the deluxe bus featured air-brakes, extra cushions, improved

Figure 7.33 Early BERy Mack-built Bus, Circa 1930

springs, better lighting, and wider aisles than standard BERy buses. The deluxe bus was an elegant cruiser (Figure 7.31 and Figure 7.32), similar to early luxury buses used in tourist service in Europe and the American west. BERy deluxe bus fare was twenty-five cents, more than double the regular ten cent fare.

The BERy introduced the first "transit type" buses to Boston in 1929. The vehicles, which seated forty passengers and were produced by Twin Coach, were soon joined by other transit type buses, including one built by Mack in 1931 (Figure 7.33). The Mack buses featured hydraulic steering, an industry first for a motor coach operator in Greater Boston. In March 1924, the BERy became the first company in the region to add buses with pneumatic

tires to its fleet. The BERy began to deploy buses with power steering in 1931.

As it had with its streetcars, the BERy offered its buses for rent. Fees from charter service brought extra cash into the company. Charter operations keep BERy buses earning, especially on evenings and weekends when ridership was light and not all of the vehicles were needed for revenue service. A circa 1930s brochure advertising the BERy's charter bus service listed "business firms," "schools and colleges," "clubs and veterans' organizations," and "churches and associations" as recommended clients (Figure 7.34). In 1946 alone, the BERy brought in over $110,000 from over 4,500 orders for rentals of its buses. The BERy's successor, the MTA, also rented out buses in charter service (Figure 7.34).

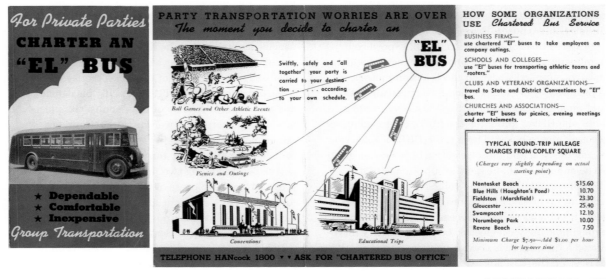

Figure 7.34 BERy Charter Bus Brochure, Circa 1930s

Figure 7.35 **BERy Gas-electric Bus #910, February 1929**

During World War II, the federal government restricted the production of new buses to a set of standardized models. Hence, government-approved vehicles were the only ones procured by the BERy during wartime. After the war, commercial bus production and development resumed, with mechanical, safety, and capacity improvements rapidly applied to new models by bus manufacturers.

In the second edition of the *Guide and Information Book*, the BERy wrote:

> The Boston Elevated Railway has been a pioneer in coordinating the motor bus with street railway service in the endeavor to furnish a complete and comprehensive transportation service.

Exemplifying its progressive philosophy, was the company's implementation of both gas-electric and diesel-electric buses. From 1928 to 1939, the BERy operated a fleet of buses with gasoline-powered combustion engines that turned generators which, in turn, supplied electricity to traction motors. A typical 1928 gas-electric model featured air brakes and pneumatic doors (Figure 7.35). From 1938 into 1949, the BERy, and later the MTA, operated diesel-electric motor buses. Though the BERy's collection of gas-electric and diesel-electric buses never grew large enough to challenge the supremacy of its fleet of combustion engine vehicles, the company's application of electric motors to power rubber-tired transit vehicles proved successful. After a decade of experimenting with electric buses, the BERy introduced a new, electric transit vehicle onto the streets of Boston, the "trackless trolley."

Trackless Trolleys

A trackless trolley, also known as a "trolley bus" or a "trolley coach," is an electrically powered bus that draws power from overhead wires via a pair of poles extending from its roof (Figure 7.36). Trackless trolley wire is energized by a remote power station. Lacking metal wheels or tracks to complete a circuit, trackless trolleys require two wires, both suspended above the street. One wire provides the current while the other completes the circuit.

In Boston, demonstrations of early trackless trolley technology first took place in the late 1880s. Later, in the first decade of the twentieth century, a start up company known as the American Trackless Trolley Company made various proposals to establish a trolley bus network in Massachusetts. The Commonwealth's first public trackless trolley service was most likely a short-lived line that connected the city of Fairhaven and town of Mattapoisett, both on Massachusetts' South Coast. Trial service started along the line in 1915 but was terminated at the end of the year. The General Court legalized the operation of trackless trolleys within the Commonwealth in 1916, formally blessing use of the technology. Outside of Massachusetts, successful trolley bus operations were up and running in American cities by the 1920s and early 1930s. The first permanent trolley bus service in Massachusetts operated along two lines in the city of Fitchburg. After the success of the Fitchburg lines and an analysis of a substantial network operating in Providence, Rhode Island, the BERy implemented trolley bus service for Boston.

Lacking steel wheels on steel tracks to complete a circuit with a power station or substation, trolley

Figure 7.36 Trackless Trolley in Harvard Square, June 1, 1936
One of the BERy's first trackless trolleys, number 8003, arrives in Harvard Square from Lechmere, after traversing Greater Boston's first trolley bus route. At the front of the vehicle, white text on the rollsign curtain above the driver reads "HARVARD." After exchanging passengers at Harvard Square, the driver will prepare the trackless trolley for the trip back to East Cambridge by turning the rollsign to display "LECHMERE." At the far right is a corner of Harvard Station's head house. To the right of the vehicle, a pedestrian waits to cross the street. Another waits under the overhang of the Harvard Station head house (far right).

buses tapped a pair of overhead wires to complete their power circuits. Though tethered to catenaries, trackless trolleys could operate on virtually any street over which wires could be strung. Without the need for rails, trackless trolleys were able to navigate more nimbly through street traffic than a streetcar confined to fixed rails.

Trackless trolleys arrived on the BERy in the mid-1930s. During the later half of 1935 and early 1936, the company converted its Harvard Square to Lechmere Terminal streetcar line to trackless trolley service. Along the line, which mostly followed Cambridge Street, the BERy replaced trolley wire with overhead paired wire. On April 11, 1936 the BERy re-opened its Cambridge Street line (Figure 7.36). A year after commencement of the Cambridge Street trolley bus service, an additional trackless trolley route opened to serve Everett and Malden. The BERy called out its nascent trackless trolley bus routes on company maps (Figure 7.38).

Figure 7.37 BERy Trackless Trolley #8113, Circa 1940
A driver poses with his trolley bus at the BERy's Bennett Street facility in Harvard Square.

Boston's first trolley buses had many advantages over both streetcars and early buses. Trackless trolleys rode smoother and quieter than streetcars. Their interiors were more spacious than those of early buses. Trolley buses, lacking the finicky engines of early motor buses, were more cost effective to maintain and operate. In short order, trackless trolleys became excellent fits for routes too busy for bus service and too lightly patronized for streetcar service. Trolley buses also provided the BERy with an extra bonus, they allowed the BERy to tap into an increasing amount of excess power generating capacity created as more streetcar lines saw conversion to bus service.

During the 1930s and 1940s, the BERy replaced more of its streetcar lines with trackless trolleys

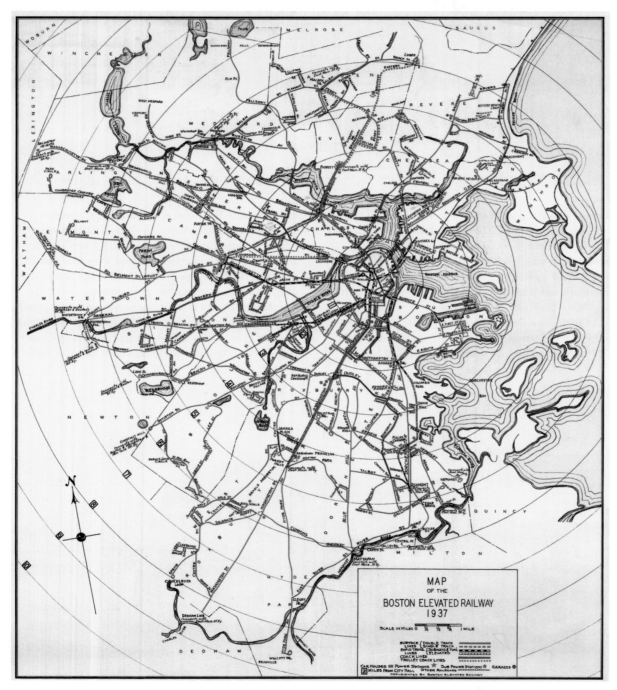

Figure 7.38 Mapping the BERy's Trolley Bus Routes, 1937
Red dotted lines call out Greater Boston's first trackless trolley lines.

Figure 7.39 Trackless Trolley at Harvard Station, May 4, 1938
BERy trolley bus number 8114 pauses at the lower busway inside Harvard Station. Beneath the vehicle, streetcar tracks remain, entombed in paving.

than with buses (Figure 7.37). As it converted more and more streetcar lines to bus or trackless trolley service, the BERy upgraded portions of larger terminals (Figure 7.39) and entirely remodeled smaller transfer stations. During 1930–31, the BERy altered the lower level of Sullivan Square Station to accommodate buses. The windowed waiting room was reduced in size and space previously occupied by a restaurant was procured to accommodate bus turning areas. Streetcar ramps were reworked to accommodate buses, and later, trackless trolleys (Figure 7.40).

Implementation of new trackless trolley and bus routes in Boston slowed during World War II. After the rationing and tight government restrictions of wartime were lifted, Boston's trolley bus system expanded exponentially. During the last half the 1940s, the BERy's successor, the MTA, purchased over 200 trackless trolleys from manufacturer Pullman. At the same time, and throughout much of the 1950s, the MTA expanded the network of trackless trolley lines and bus routes started by the BERy. The size of Boston's trackless trolley network peaked just before the middle of the 1950s, when

Figure 7.40 Sullivan Square Station, December 11, 1946
Descending along one of the ramps converted in the early 1930s for use by rubber-tired vehicles, BERy trackless trolley number 877 departs from the upper level of Sullivan Square Station.

forty-three trolley bus routes were serviced by a fleet that was the third largest in the nation. Only Chicago and Atlanta had larger trolley bus fleets.

After the departure of the MTA's progressive general manager Edward Dana in 1959, the tide at the MTA quickly turned against trackless trolleys. In its 1962 annual report, the MTA celebrated a recent order of 125 new diesel buses, writing: "buses are paving the way for the elimination of the trackless trolleys, the outmoded vehicle...." By 1963, the MTA trimmed its once robust network of trackless trolleys to less than five routes. Today, the MBTA operates three numbered trackless trolley lines, all radiating out of Harvard Square. The MBTA's trackless trolley routes cover only eleven revenue miles, a small remnant of the vast network in place in 1955.

Tokens for Transit
The first half of the twentieth century saw not only the arrival of bus and trackless trolley transit in Boston, it also witnessed the widespread use of metal public transit tokens. The Bay State issued two varieties of tokens for use in its District 1 service area, and one for use in its District 2. District 1 tokens featured "Bay State" in relief on one face and "District 1 City Zone Fare" on their other (Figure 7.41). A void in the shape of a star distinguished the token from those issued by other companies.

In 1947 the Eastern Mass began issuing white metal tokens, each twenty-three millimeters in diameter, a bit smaller than a modern quarter. The tokens featured a stylized "EM" on each face (Figure 7.42). In 1952, the Eastern Mass reissued

Figure 7.41 Bay State District 1 Token, Circa 1920
The 16mm white metal token features a die-cut star.

Figure 7.42 Eastern Mass Token, 1947
The first to be issued by the Eastern Massachusetts Street Railway Company was white metal and 23mm in diameter.

Figure 7.43 Eastern Mass Token, 1952
The 1952 reissue of the Eastern Mass Series-of-1947 token (Figure 7.42) is copper-plated and 23mm in diameter.

Figure 7.44 Eastern Mass 16mm Diameter Token, 1965

Figure 7.45 Middlesex & Boston Token, 1915

Figure 7.46 BERy 21mm Diameter Token, Circa 1919

Figure 7.47 BERy 23mm Diameter Token, Circa 1919

Figure 7.48 BERy Local Fare Token, Circa 1919

Figure 7.49 BERy Local Fare Token, Circa 1919

its 1947 token with copper plating that read "Good for One Fare" on one face and "Eastern Massachusetts St Ry Co" on the other (Figure 7.43). The Eastern Mass began issuing a smaller version of its "EM" token (Figure 7.44) in 1965. There are four known variations of the 1965 token. Neither the Bay State nor the Eastern Mass were the first transit companies in Massachusetts to issue metal tokens. Roxbury Coaches and Maverick Coaches issued metal tickets as early as 1837. In central Massachusetts, the Worcester Horse Railroad Company issued tokens, twenty for one dollar, as early as 1863.

Transit tokens were commonly branded with a transit company's name, symbol, or design related to a particular operator. A beautifully detailed token was issued by the Middlesex & Boston Street Railway Company (Middlesex & Boston) in 1915. The white metal token featured the image of a pocket watch at its center (Figure 7.45). The watch recalled the origins of the Middlesex & Boston in Waltham, Massachusetts, a town west of Boston

and an important early center for the mass production of timepieces.

After relying on paper tickets since the 1890s, in February 1919, the BERy began to issue metal tokens for pre-payment of the company's eight cent fare, established in 1918. There were at least four versions of BERy tokens issued during this time (Figure 7.46, Figure 7.47, Figure 7.48, and Figure 7.49). The BERy discontinued use of tokens in July 1919, when it raised its standard fare from eight cents to ten cents and a dime or paper ticket sufficed.

Night Lines

The operation of "night cars" on "night lines" was common practice for horse railroad companies, and later, for electric street railway companies. Typical BERy night time streetcar lines of the 1910s–30s operated between 1:00 a.m. and 5:00 a.m., a period when rapid transit service did not run. An

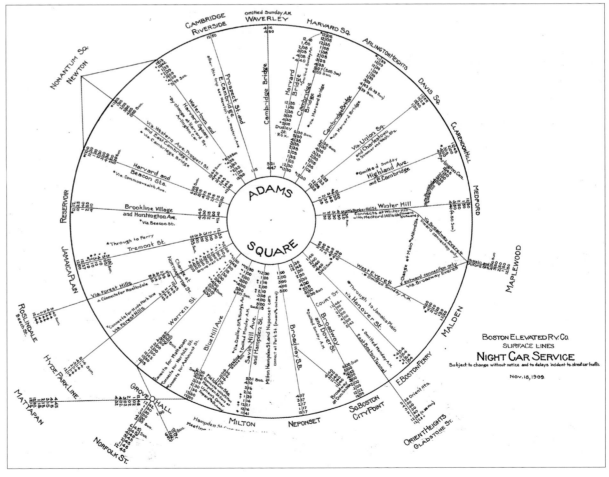

Figure 7.50 Night Car Service Diagram, November 18, 1909
A diagram articulates BERy streetcar service between Adams Square (center) and remote points (around the periphery) that operated between midnight and sunrise. The remote points lie at the end of radial lines, each representing a particular night car route. Major street names and route information are attached to each route. Departure times for outbound cars are strung along the radiating route lines. Departure times for inbound cars are stacked along the radial lines, close to each remote point.

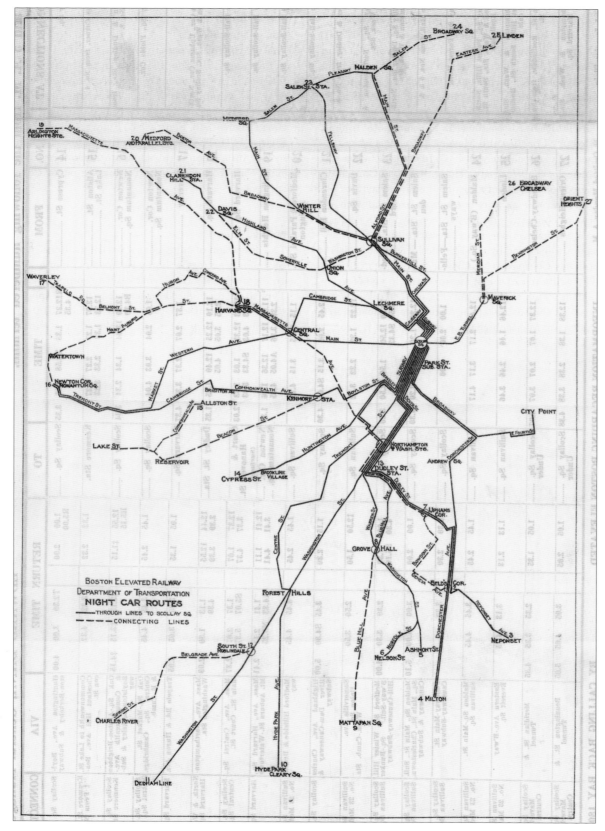

BOSTON ELEVATED RAILWAY
DEPARTMENT OF TRANSPORTATION
NIGHT CAR ROUTES

—— THROUGH LINES TO SCOLLAY SQ.
----- CONNECTING LINES

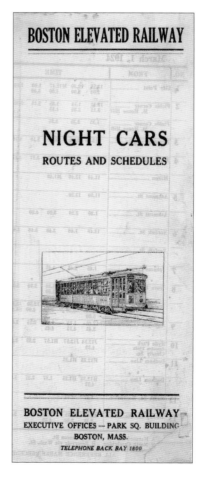

BOSTON ELEVATED RAILWAY

NIGHT CARS

ROUTES AND SCHEDULES

BOSTON ELEVATED RAILWAY
EXECUTIVE OFFICES — PARK SQ. BUILDING
BOSTON, MASS.
TELEPHONE BACK BAY 1800

Figure 7.51 BERy Night Cars Brochure, 1924

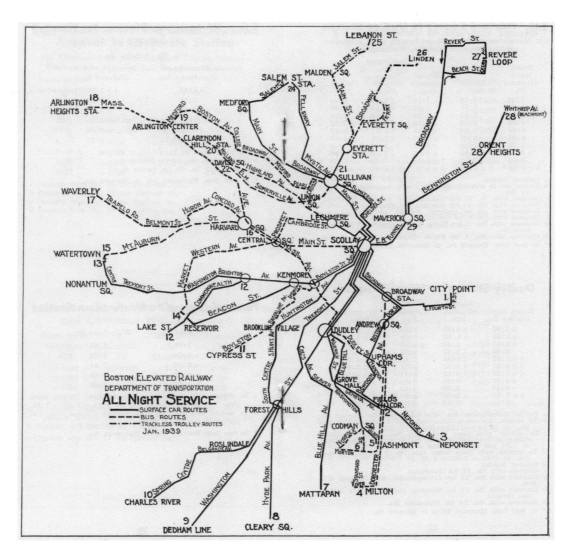

Figure 7.52 BERy Schedules of Night Service, January 1939
On the map (left) of the third edition of the BERy's *Schedule of Night Service*, streetcar routes are solid lines, bus routes are dashed lines, and trackless trolley routes are dashed-dot lines. Numbered routes are arranged in a counterclockwise manner, beginning with route 1 in South Boston and ending with route 29 (or 30, depending on the edition of the map) in East Boston.

intriguing schedule of BERy "Night Car Service" from Adams Square was prepared by the company at the end of 1909 (Figure 7.50). At the time, Adams Square was the epicenter for BERy night cars. During the 1920s and 1930s, the BERy issued *Night Cars* pamphlets, paper handouts that featured a map of night car routes and schedules of night car service. Later, the pamphlets described nighttime motor bus service. The BERy's 1924 *Night Cars* pamphlet (Figure 7.51) designates Scollay Square as the center of night car service.

On February 8, 1937, the BERy kicked off publication of a new guide, one tailored for passengers riding its nighttime surface lines. The premier edition, titled *Schedules of Night Service*, featured timetables for nearly thirty night lines and a map of nighttime routes. The BERy made the pocket-sized *Schedules of Night Service* guides available at the

Park Street Station information booth, rapid transit stations, and its office at Park Square. Within each, the BERy wrote that night service was coordinated to minimize waiting time to a maximum of fifteen minutes for customers transferring between lines. In the 1939 edition, the BERy shared: "[the fare on] night cars and buses is ten cents except that on trips operated over day routes the fare within local fare zones is five cents." Night fare remained ten cents through the issuance of the 1947 edition.

The maps in *Schedules of Night Service* show BERy night routes providing a reasonable blanket of coverage over the company's daytime service area. While major transfer points at selected subway and elevated stations are shown, the rapid transit tunnels and elevated railways are not. Rapid transit lines did not operate overnight. Maps from the January 1939 edition (Figure 7.52) and May 1947

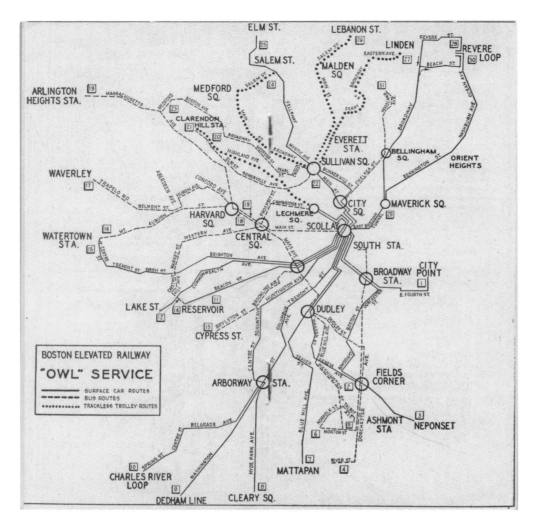

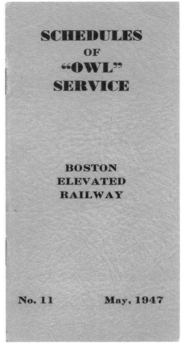

Figure 7.53 BERy Schedules of "Owl" Service, May 1947

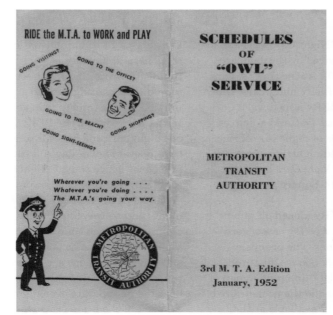

Figure 7.54 MTA "Owl" Service Brochure, January 1952

Figure 7.55 MTA Owl Service Check, Circa 1950s

A paper ticket was valid for travel on an MTA Owl Service route on September 5 of an unidentified year.

Figure 7.56 Boston & Maine Motor Coach Timetable, 1926

Figure 7.57 Boston & Maine Timetable, 1941

A Boston & Maine timetable advertises travel by airplane, a motor coach, and a streamlined locomotive.

edition (Figure 7.53) lay out all night lines. Mapped route numbers are keyed to timetables printed within each guide. For the seventh edition of the night service guide, dated December 1942, the BERy revised the title to *Schedules of "Owl' Service* (Figure 7.53).

After the 1947 handoff of public transit for Boston from the BERy to the MTA, the owl service titling was continued by the MTA. The 1952 *Schedules of "Owl" Service* included engaging MTA advertisements. One such ad features the smiling faces of a woman, a man, and a uniformed MTA employee, all accompanied by the rhyme "ride the M.T.A. to work and play" (Figure 7.54). The inside cover features an advertisement for MTA charter bus service (Figure 7.54). The MTA operated its Owl Service until June 25, 1960. 1950s-era tickets for MTA Owl Service indicated: "not good on day routes" (Figure 7.55).

Railroad Buses

The bus networks of the BERy, MTA, and Eastern Mass were not the only motor coach operations to provide local service within Eastern Massachusetts.

Smaller streetcar companies followed the lead of larger operators, replacing their trolleys with buses, and in the process became motor coach operators. Steam railroad companies established motor coach operations to increase their sphere of influences beyond their fixed rails. Railroads ran buses as feeder and distribution networks that were flexible and economical extensions of their tracks. In time, railroads also deployed buses to replace train service discontinued from lightly traveled rail lines.

The Boston & Maine, which dominated passenger and commuter rail service from Boston to points north for over a century, operated a network of motor coaches connecting Boston with Albany, New York, the White Mountains of New Hampshire, and coastal Maine. In the mid-1920s, Boston & Maine motor coaches were the long distance touring type, with large windows and broad seats (Figure 7.56).

After establishing its bus and truck subsidiary, the Boston & Maine Transportation Company, in 1925, the Boston & Maine asserted its intentions to operate as more than just a rail or bus company. By the 1930s, the Boston & Maine provided coordinated air, motor coach, and rail travel around New England (Figure 7.57). Colorful brochures depicted

travellers being whisked by motor coach through pastoral scenes (Figure 7.58).

Complementing the Boston & Maine's motor coach network linking Boston with northern New England, a larger railroad bus network sprawled west and south of the city. The New Haven Railroad's subsidiary, New England Transportation Company (NETC), operated bus routes that connected Boston with New York City and communities throughout southern New England. (Figure 7.59 and Figure 7.60). On a local level, some NETC routes supplemented Boston commuter rail service (Figure 7.61).

As horse railroad, trolley, and steam railroad guides did before them, motor coach guides came into being to assist riders. *The Motor Coach Guide* was published monthly in Boston as early as 1925. The majority of motor coach routes listed in the

August 1928 edition were intercity bus routes. Complementing long distance route information were schedules for local routes of the Eastern Mass and a list of thirty-one BERy bus lines. The BERy schedule was accompanied by the text: "The BERy operates motor buses in a coordinated transportation system of street cars, rapid transit trains and buses."

As the first half of the twentieth century unfolded, steam railroad companies were not only in the process of adding buses to their networks, they were also increasingly replacing their steam locomotives with diesel-electric locomotives. The switch was mostly an economic choice. Diesel-electric locomotives were less costly to operate and required less infrastructure than steam locomotives. During steam railroads' push to eliminate steam engines from their rosters, the word "steam" was no longer

Figure 7.58 Boston & Maine Transp. Co. Bus Schedule, 1932
A map (left) and cover (right) from a 1932 Boston & Maine bus schedule touts routes between Boston, the Mohawk Valley, and the White Mountains of New Hampshire.

Figure 7.59 New England Transportation Co. Brochure, 1927

needed to distinguish a steam railroad from a horse railroad. Horse railroads hadn't been seen in Boston since 1900.

The MTA's Rubber-Tired Fleet

Between the end of 1926 and the end 1946, the count of motor buses in garages of the BERy grew from less than a half dozen to over 600. During the same period, the BERy's stable of trackless trolleys grew to 2,365 vehicles. As the BERy's fleet of rubber-tired transit vehicles grew, its inventory of streetcars declined. The BERy recorded revenue miles for company streetcars at 25.1 million, down from a high point of 40.4 million in 1924. For the same year, revenue miles for buses was 12.2 million (up from zero in 1921) and revenue miles for trackless trolleys was 3.6 million (up from 0 in 1935).

Figure 7.60 New England Transportation Co. Schedule, 1934

Figure 7.61 Railroad Bus Pocket Schedule Card, 1928

Figure 7.62 MTA Bus #2148, May 21, 1956
An MTA 2100-series, diesel-powered bus poses in Franklin Park wearing an egg-shaped MTA logo on its side. The interior of another 2100-series bus is shown in Figure 7.63.

When the MTA took over from the BERy in 1947, it inherited a mixed fleet of transit vehicles. The first annual report of the MTA recorded 1,060 streetcars, 478 rapid transit cars, 582 buses, and 187 trackless trolleys on hand as of December 31, 1947. Of the buses listed, 456 were gasoline-powered with mechanical drive (no power steering), 115 were gasoline-powered with hydraulic drive, 10 were diesel-electric drive, and one was diesel-hydraulic drive.

Throughout the 1950s and into the early 1960s, the MTA purchased hundreds of new buses. Most of the models were marked by rounded, light-colored roofs and two tiers of side windows. Nearly 200 2100-series buses arrived from manufacturer GMC during 1953–56 (Figure 7.62 and Figure 7.63). 2200-series buses constructed by Mack came online in the mid-1950s (Figure 7.64). Towards the end of the decade, the MTA acquired additional GMC models, assigned 2300 and 2600-series numbers. At the end of 1959, the MTA stabled just shy of 600 buses in operating condition. Of those, 222 ran on gasoline and 377 were fueled by diesel. As the 1950s became the 1960s, the MTA worked towards the elimination of gasoline-powered buses and conversion of its entire fleet to diesel-powered models.

Figure 7.63 Interior of MTA Bus #2138, November 19, 1955
The exterior of a 2100-series bus is shown in Figure 7.62.

Figure 7.64 MTA Bus #2294, July 12, 1957
A Mack-built MTA 2200-series bus.

Figure 7.65 MTA "New Look" Bus, 1961
A new GMC-built bus poses for an MTA marketing photograph. The "arctic white" roof and "tangerine" body paint colors are complimented by anodized aluminum side panels.

Of the larger purchases of buses executed by the MTA, one made in 1961 was for 125 diesel "New Look" buses constructed by GMC. The vehicles indeed sported a new look for the MTA. Gone were the round-top, chunky-looking designs of the 1950s. Instead, large windows, an expansive windshield, and sleek aluminum side panels became standard aesthetics for MTA buses (Figure 7.65). During its last few years of existence, the MTA purchased additional New Look models. The MBTA inherited the vehicles and operated them alongside New Look buses that it purchased new. On the MBTA, the vehicles wore 5000-series (Figure 7.66), 6000-series, and 7000-series (Figure 7.67) numbers.

Surface Lines of the MTA
In order to assist passengers in navigating its evolving network of bus and trolley bus lines, in 1954 the MTA issued 50,000 copies of fold-out publications

Figure 7.66 MBTA "Fishbowl" Bus #5718, 1980

Figure 7.67 MBTA Bus #7516 at Lynn Garage, Circa 1980s

titled "Surface Lines Schedules." After 1954, the
pocket-sized, paper schedules were issued in pairs,
with one covering routes "North of Boston," and the
other, routes "South of Boston." The MBTA revised
and reissued the schedule pairs seasonally. The
summer 1955 schedules sported a bus and a streetcar on their covers (Figure 7.68). The covers of the
1958 and 1959 schedules (Figure 7.69) featured only
a single bus. The removal of the streetcar from the
cover art was a calculated move by the MTA, which
regarded buses as the future of surface transit
for Boston. Each *Surface Lines Schedules* unfolded
to reveal a comprehensive list of surface routes
arranged by route number with schedules of service
for each (Figure 7.70).

As the 1950s progressed, ridership and revenue
from many surface routes, including those of trackless trolleys, decreased for the MTA, mostly due to
increased use of personal automobiles. From the
late 1940s until the late 1950s, the attitude of the
MTA evolved from championing trolley buses to
promoting reasons why trackless trolley service
should be discontinued. The MTA began phasing
out trolley bus service in earnest in the early
1960s. By 1964, there were only four MTA trackless trolley routes in operation. The 1964 MTA
"System Route Map" shows the MTA's last trackless trolley routes radiating from Harvard Square,
to North Cambridge, West Cambridge, Waverley
Square (in Belmont), and Watertown Square. The
four routes were saved from extinction because of

Figure 7.69 MTA Surface Line Schedules Pairs, 1958–59

Figure 7.70 Surface Lines Schedules North, Spring 1958

the MTA's need to operate electric vehicles instead of combustion engine buses through the former streetcar tunnels under Harvard Square. The MTA also had difficulties procuring buses with doors on the left side, as was required for Harvard Square tunnel service at the time. As motor bus technology improved and larger and more reliable vehicles

became available, buses forever replaced the majority of Greater Boston's streetcars and trackless trolleys.

As the 1950s rolled into the 1960s, the financial situation of the MTA deteriorated due to exploding use of passenger cars by Boston-area commuters and increased costs of providing public transit

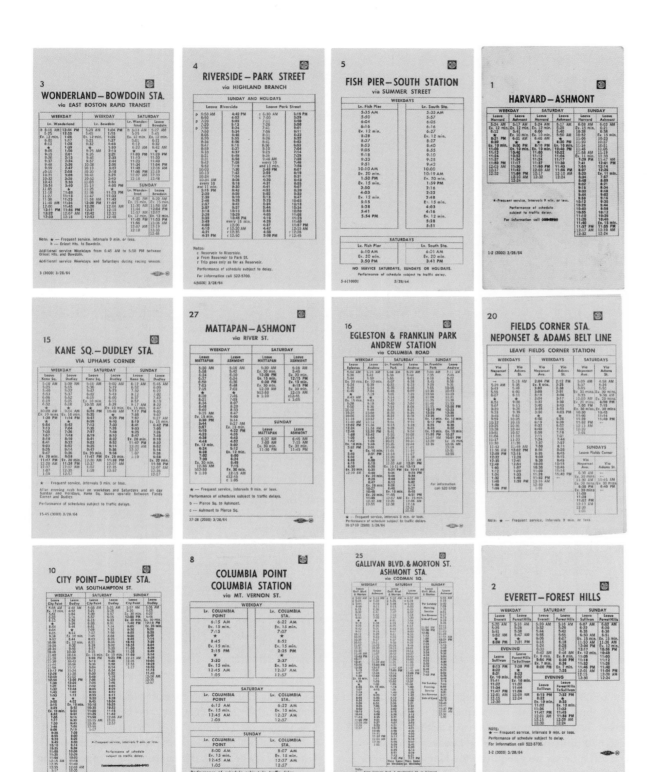

Figure 7.71 MTA Route Schedules Cards, Spring 1964

Selections from the first of only two schedule card sets issued by the MTA. The schedule cards replaced fold-out "Surface Lines Schedules" of the 1950s (Figure 7.70). After its summer 1964 takeover of the MTA, the MBTA issued subsequent sets of schedule cards.

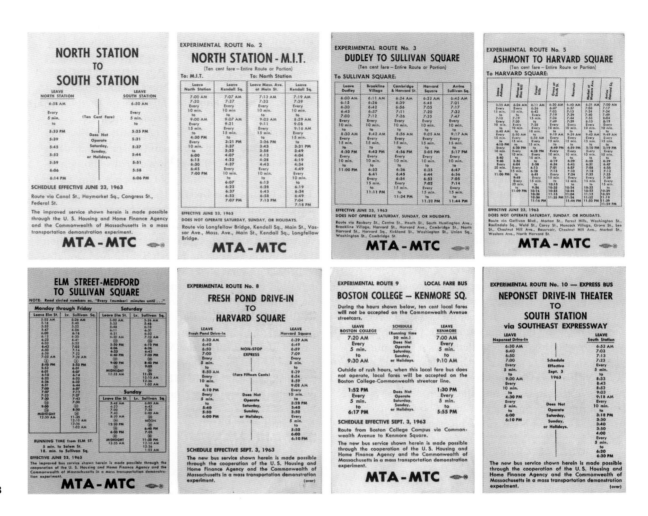

Figure 7.72 Schedule Cards for MTA-MTC Bus Routes, 1963

Figure 7.73 Experimental Bus Route #6 Signs, 1963
Each side of a card stock bus sign displays the destination of MTA-MTC Experimental Bus Route number 6. The sign was displayed by a bus assigned to the short-lived route.

service. In response, the MTA implemented cost-saving measures, including a new fare system and parking fees at MTA parking lots. Before the fees, free parking was the norm. Free transfers between surface modes and rapid transit lines were eliminated in 1961. As compensation for the loss of free transfers, and to increase ridership on rapid transit lines, surface routes that did not connect with rapid transit stations were extended or configured to do so. A cost saving measure tested by the MTA in 1961 was the cessation of printing surface route schedules. Ironically, the $10,000 or so in printing costs saved may have been largely offset by a loss in ridership likely caused by passengers not having printed schedules available. The MTA brought back printed pocket-sized schedules in 1963, though in a much condensed, card stock format (Figure 7.71); gone were the comprehensive folding schedules of the 1950s. The route numbers coordinated with those on the 1964 folding system route map, the last produced by the MTA. After taking over for the

MTA in mid-1964 the MBTA continued publishing pocket-sized schedule cards.

MTA Experimental Bus Routes

In late 1963 and early 1964, funding from the United States Housing and Home Finance Agency was made available to states for the operation of experimental bus routes. The federal funds were administered in Massachusetts through the Commonwealth's Mass Transportation Commission (MTC). The MTA, seeking new ways to increase ridership, applied the federal funds to test the feasibility, ridership, and routing of new bus routes. The MTA operated eleven MTA-MTC experimental bus routes, numbered E1 through E11, and reported analysis of the trial services back to the MTC. Schedules cards for MTA-MTC routes were issued to the public (Figure 7.72). Placards were displayed in the front of MTA buses serving Experimental Routes (Figure 7.73). The program came to an end when most of the experimental routes were discontinued by the end of 1964. Segments of the most successful of the new routes, including one connecting Ashmont Station in Dorchester with Harvard Station in Cambridge, were retained by the MTA.

Fishbowls, Express Buses, and a Century of Buses
The MBTA put into service the first buses purchased with 100% public (mostly federal) funds for public transit in Boston in 1966. The vehicles were the same models as the MTA's New Look buses (Figure 7.65) but became known on the MBTA as "fishbowls," because of their formed windshields (Figure 7.74). The Authority assigned the GMC-built buses 6000-series numbers.

The MBTA deployed its fishbowls along its first express bus routes to utilize interstate highways. In 1967, the Authority launched express bus service between downtown and both Newton and Watertown. Along the Massachusetts Turnpike, air-conditioned fishbowls with high-speed transmissions whisked riders between termini in seventeen minutes. Within three months, ridership grew from a first day count of just over 750 passengers to over 2,600. Turnpike express bus service expanded

to Saturdays in September 1968. On June 24, the MBTA launched "employment express" buses between Dudley Station in Roxbury and areas of employment along Massachusetts Route 128 in Boston's western suburbs. The fare on the employment express was fifty cents each way.

The MBTA inaugurated rush hour, express bus service between downtown and Riverside Station in Newton in 1969. The Riverside route launched in August with a seventy-five cent, one-way fare. The following year brought new express bus service between Burlington and Boston, improvement of express bus service between the North Shore and downtown, and experimental bus service between Logan Airport and the North Shore. Additional express bus service arrived in 1971, with routes between Riverside Station and Copley Square launching on March 29, and Central Square in Waltham and the intersection of Chauncy and Summer Streets in downtown Boston commencing on August 2. In 1973, the MBTA initiated express bus service between West Medford and Haymarket Square. Since 1967, the MBTA has added and revised approximately thirty express bus routes, some of which continue to leverage interstate highways.

Figure 7.74 MBTA Bus #6522 at Everett Shops, October 1966

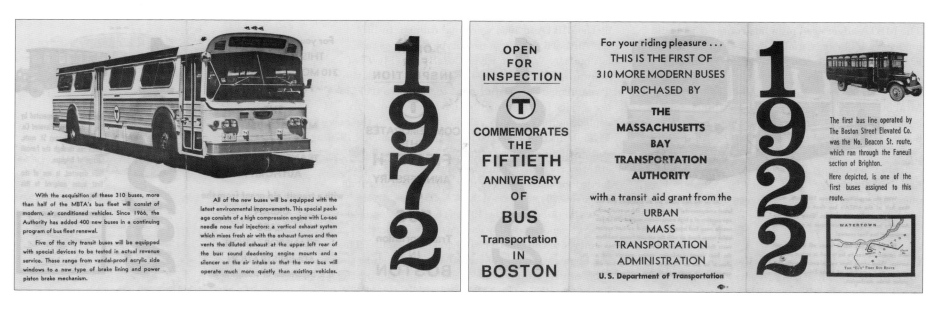

Figure 7.75 50 Years of Bus Transit in Boston, 1972
A paper handout commemorates fifty years of public transit buses in Boston and features an image of the first motor coach operated by the BERy as well as the latest bus to be operated by the MBTA, a Flxible-built model.

Figure 7.76 MBTA Mini Bus, Circa 1974

Decades before today's "zipper lane" movable HOV lane became a fixture along the Southeast Expressway, a counter-flow bus lane for express buses appeared along the busy highway. The state DPW set up and managed rush hour bus lanes on the Southeast Expressway in 1971 and 1972. From May through October 1971, each weekday morning, one southbound lane was reserved for northbound buses. In the evening, one northbound lane was reserved for southbound buses. Private carrier buses utilized the counter-flow lane to shave fifteen to twenty minutes from their inbound runs and approximately five minutes from their outbound trips. Some 3,500 commuters were transported daily.

In September 1971, the MBTA Board of Directors awarded a $11.36 million contract to the Flxible Company (Flxible) for 200 new buses, 150 of which were tailored for city transit, and fifty of which were designed for turnpike express service. The purchases were paid for with two-thirds federal funding and one-third MBTA capital. The Authority celebrated the new vehicles on February 24, 1972 by parking bus number 7200 in the middle of Boston's City Hall Plaza. Amidst snow and slush, a ceremony was presided over by MBTA General Manager Joseph Kelly and Edward Dana. Dana had been General Manager of the BERy when that company put its first bus into service. At the event, the MBTA provided handouts to announce the new buses and commemorate fifty years of public bus service in Boston (Figure 7.75).

The MBTA's Flxible buses were manufactured with rollsigns displaying bus route numbers with destination names. Though standard practice today, and despite the historic use of various internal route numbering systems by the West End, the BERy, the MTA, and the MBTA, the prominent and standardized display of route numbers on surface vehicles was a significant MBTA achievement. Before the MBTA, some streetcars and buses displayed route numbers alongside destination names on their rollsigns, but not with the consistency that the MBTA bought to the table. The MBTA intended to coordinate the system of route numbers displayed on the Flxible buses with existing, multi-digit numbering systems used internally and with route numbering historically used on system route maps. The Authority's 1968 takeover of the Eastern Mass expedited the MBTA's homogenization of bus route names and numbers. By the end of the early 1970s, route numbers displayed on MBTA surface vehicles were essentially the same numbers used by the Authority internally and remain the foundation of the numbering systems in use today.

Mini Buses
The early 1970s saw the MBTA experiment with novel public transit equipment, including mini buses. The Authority contracted Highway Products of Ohio to fabricate ten mini-buses, each capable of seating approximately two dozen passengers, in 1972 (Figure 7.76). A year later the MBTA deployed the compact vehicles to serve routes in Cambridge, Somerville, Brookline, Salem, Lynn, and Boston's Jamaica Plain, Allston, and Brighton neighborhoods.

The MBTA advertised mini bus routes with radio jingles, on billboards, and in print (Figure 7.77 and Figure 7.78). The Authority marketed mini bus service with the slogan "What has the MBTA done for [insert city name] lately? Mini bus is what." Mini buses ran along set routes, but unlike full size buses that stopped only at signed bus stops, mini buses picked up and dropped off riders at any street corner. Mini buses generally ran on weekdays, from morning to evening. Initially mini buses ran with half hour headways. The Cambridge mini bus were operating with one hour headways by 1975. They no longer circulate.

Committing to Trackless Trolleys

Most of the trackless trolley routes established by the BERy and the MTA were discontinued by the latter. The few remaining trolley bus lines inherited by the MBTA in 1964 were maintained. In 1971, the Authority tested a prototype trackless trolley, built by Western Flyer Coach Ltd. (Flyer) of Winnipeg, Canada. Three years later, in 1974, the T reaffirmed its commitment to trackless trolley service by ordering fifty new trolley buses to replace aging ex-MTA vehicles. The first of the new Flyer-built trackless trolleys debuted in spring 1976. Assigned 4000-series numbers, the trolley buses entered revenue service on April 29. Each seated forty-four passengers and was forty-one feet long (Figure 7.79).

At the tail end of the 1970s, the MBTA opened a new trackless trolley garage and yard on the former site the North Cambridge Car House. The car house was a hub of streetcar activity since the nineteenth century before passing into the portfolios of the BERy, the MTA, and finally, the MBTA. The MBTA's North Cambridge complex, which

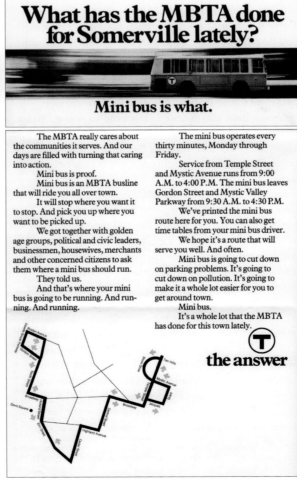

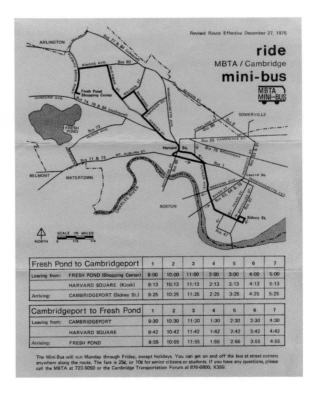

Figure 7.77 MBTA Cambridge Mini Bus Timetable, 1975

Figure 7.78 MBTA Mini Bus Brochures, 1973

Figure 7.79 MBTA 4000-series Trackless Trolley, Circa 1976
During a test run, a new MBTA trolley bus pauses at the southern portal to the Harvard Square bus tunnels.

replaced facilities lost with the Authority's sale of its Bennett/Eliot lands in Harvard Square, remains the center for the storage, inspection, and maintenance of the Authority's trackless trolley fleet.

MBTA Bus Improvements of the Late 1970s

The late 1970s saw the MBTA continue to add new bus models to its fleet. The Authority purchased ninety buses from AM General and twenty-five GM-built buses for use on routes along the Massachusetts Turnpike. The MBTA ordered an initial batch of 100 buses from General Motors in 1978. The first of the buses arrived in 1979, received 6400-series numbers, and commenced service out of the Authority's Albany Street Garage. Each forty-foot bus seated approximately fifty passengers.

In 1978, via its $10.6 million Transit Efficiency Program, the MBTA worked to address specific public-side issues, including the lack of priority for buses at controlled street intersections, excess traffic congestion along bus routes, and lack of

clearly defined bus shelter and stopping areas. A solution to the later problem was the installation of new bus stop signage at approximately 8,000 bus and trackless trolley stops (Figure 9.145). While the two-sided color format did not become a lasting standard, the tombstone shape and most of the front face information did.

The MBTA's Transit Efficiency Program dovetailed with the city of Boston's conversion of streets at the intersection of Washington and Summer Streets into a pedestrian-friendly district, Downtown Crossing. Commencing on September 5, 1978, private automobiles were restricted from the area. Delivery trucks were permitted in the morning only. Taxis were permitted at all times. The city renovated the sidewalks and streets by paving them in endless red brick. The MBTA coordinated its bus routes to serve the new district. Working together, the state DPW, the MBTA, the Boston Redevelopment Authority, and the city of Boston tapped over $3 million in federal funding to realize Downtown Crossing.

Figure 7.80 New MBTA Bus Stop Signage, 1980
The 1980 MBTA system map featured depictions and explanations of the Authority's newest bus stop signage, the front face of which (left) features an MBTA logo, a bus icon, and a "no parking" symbol. The rear face (right) includes a list of route numbers of buses and trackless trolleys serving a particular stop. Beneath each route number is a list of each route's starting point, significant intermediate stops, and final destination.

16th Annual Report

The M.T.A.

J. Schmidt

the wheels of the NEW Boston!

CHAPTER 8

The Rise and Fall of the MTA

Figure 8.1 MTA Sixteenth Annual Report Cover, 1962
Colorful graphics announce the arrival of "Blue Bird" cars for the Cambridge-Dorchester line and "New Look" buses for Boston.

The Metropolitan Transit Authority

Twenty-nine years of Public Trustees oversight of the Boston Elevated Railway Company (BERy) came to an end in 1947. Decades of management by the Trustees failed to keep the BERy solvent. Despite experiencing record-setting ridership of 433 million passengers in 1946, the BERy was in poor financial shape after years of expenditures exceeding revenues. Per the recommendation of the Metropolitan Transit Recess Commission of 1943–47 (MTRC), responding to declining ridership, acknowledging rising costs of operation of the BERy, and in order to protect Boston's public transit system for the public good, the General Court of the Commonwealth of Massachusetts passed Chapter 544 of the Acts of 1947, establishing the Metropolitan Transit Authority (MTA). By its own definition, the MTA was:

> …a body politic and corporate and a political subdivision of the Commonwealth,…composed of the territory within, and the inhabitants of, the 14 cities and towns served by this railway system: namely Arlington, Belmont, Boston, Brookline, Cambridge, Chelsea, Everett, Malden, Medford, Milton, Newton, Revere, Somerville, and Watertown.

By the 1940s, Boston's metropolitan area was expanding rapidly beyond the service area of the BERy. In creating the MTA, the Commonwealth anticipated that the fourteen municipality service area of the MTA would be large enough to allow the new entity to adequately serve the public transportation needs of Eastern Massachusetts, and not solely the immediate vicinity of Boston.

The MTA was the first public entity with complete ownership and control over public transportation (except for commuter rail service) in Boston, and only the third such entity in Massachusetts. Prior to its creation of the MTA, the Commonwealth formed the Greenfield Montague Transportation Area to take over streetcar operations in Greenfield and the Athol Transportation District to oversee streetcar lines in Orange. When the MTA came into being in 1947, steam railroads operating throughout Massachusetts remained private enterprises. Except for periods of federal control during World War I, commuter rail services provided by railroads did not come under complete public control until the second half of the twentieth century.

Upon its creation, the MTA was overseen by a five-member board of trustees. Appointed by the governor, the trustees appointed a general manager and other officers for the MTA. The first general manager of the MTA was Edward Dana, who, from 1937–47, had been the president of the BERy. On July 2, 1947, the trustees of the MTA began the process of taking over the infrastructure, real estate, and equipment of the BERy. By September 1, 1947, and after some legal wrangling over the valuation of the BERy's assets, the BERy was completely subsumed under the MTA.

The MTA announced its arrival with new branding for public transit in Boston. A textual logo (Figure 8.2) features the MTA's acronym wrapped by its name. A map logo (Figure 8.3) represents the MTA's fourteen-town service area tied together by transit lines radiating from downtown Boston. The MTA applied its map logo onto the exterior of its streetcars (Figure 8.4), buses, and trackless trolleys. A version of the map continues to be worn by

Presidents' Conference Committee (PCC) street-cars on the Mattapan High Speed Line of the Massachusetts Bay Transportation Authority (MBTA).

The MTA's Expansion Plans

In 1947 the MTA hit the ground running, increasing service on existing lines, launching new bus routes, and establishing a long term plan to upgrade existing transit stations with new lighting, painting, and signage. Many of Boston's transit stations had not seen significant physical improvement since being opened by the Boston Transit Commission (BTC), the Boston Transit Department (BTD), or the BERy. Complimenting public-side improvements, the MTA undertook back-of-the-house upgrades, including work at the thirty-seven-year-old South Boston Power Station and construction of a new office building in Charlestown.

By the end of 1947, the MTA proposed six major transit expansion and improvement projects. The first was a new double-track streetcar tunnel to run parallel with the Tremont Street Subway, between Scollay Square and Park Street Stations. The project proposed a joining of the platforms at Park Street and Boylston Street Stations. The super-station was intended to serve as Boston's hub for streetcar traffic as well as provide a second tunnel to relieve streetcar subway congestion downtown (Figure 8.5). Preliminary designs for the project were worked on into the early 1950s. Due to projected excessive project costs, neither the new tunnel nor the super-station were constructed.

When the General Court established the MTA, it mandated that the MTA prepare plans and estimates for extensions of rapid transit service to both Braintree, south of Boston, and to Revere, north of the city. Following these legislative mandates, the MTA proposed extending the

Figure 8.2 Metropolitan Transit Authority Logo, 1954

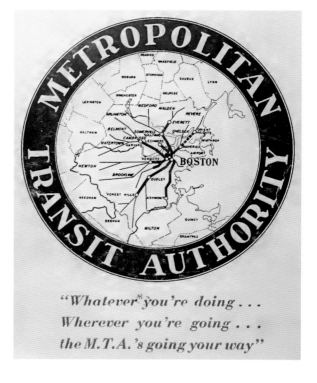

Figure 8.3 MTA Map Logo with Slogan, 1948
The text "Metropolitan Transit Authority" wraps around the map and embraces the communities within. A unified area for public transportation is reinforced by the lack of boundary lines between the cities of towns within the MTA's service area. The map logo was accompanied on the inside cover of the MTA's 1948 annual report by the slogan "Whatever you're doing... Wherever you're going... the M.T.A.'s going your way."

Figure 8.4 MTA Map Logo on PCC Streetcar, 1947
A motorman poses next to a map logo freshly applied to an MTA streetcar.

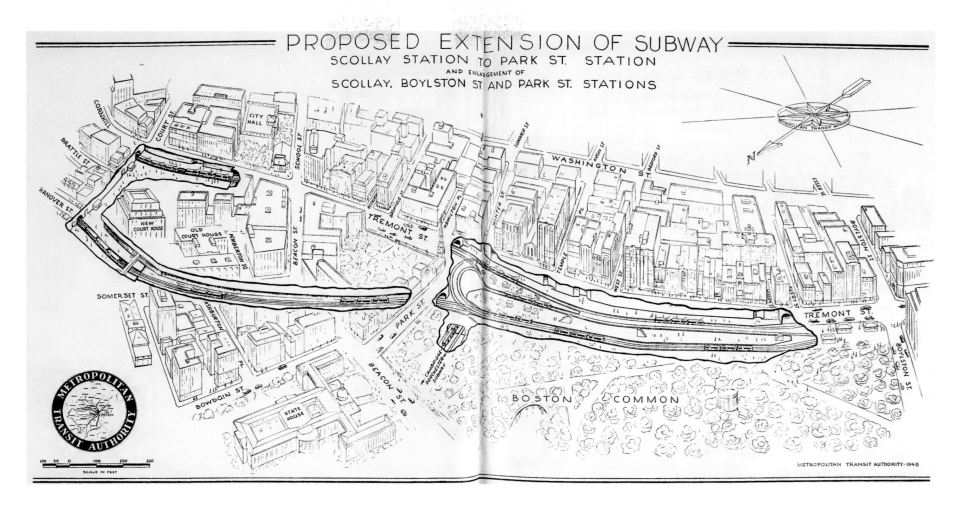

PROPOSED EXTENSION OF SUBWAY
SCOLLAY STATION TO PARK ST. STATION
AND ENLARGEMENT OF
SCOLLAY, BOYLSTON ST AND PARK ST. STATIONS

METROPOLITAN TRANSIT AUTHORITY-1948

Figure 8.5 Proposed Streetcar Subway Expansion, 1947
An MTA proposal for expanding the capacity of the Tremont Street Subway calls for a second streetcar tunnel (left) connecting Scollay Square and Park Street Stations, an expanded Scollay Square Station (far left), and a super-station created by combining Park Street and Boylston Street Stations (right). The project remains unbuilt.

Cambridge-Dorchester rapid transit line southward from Dorchester, through Quincy, and into Braintree. The MTA proposed that this southern extension utilize a right-of-way of the New York, New Haven & Hartford Railroad (New Haven). The viability of converting a railroad line to rapid transit service was proven in the late 1920s by the BERy, with its extension of the Cambridge-Dorchester rapid transit line to Ashmont.

A third large-scale project proposed by the MTA, and the first to reach completion, was a mandated extension of the East Boston Tunnel Line northward from Maverick Square, through East Boston, and into the city of Revere. The MTA recommended that much of the Revere Extension be constructed along the former right-of-way of the defunct Boston, Revere Beach & Lynn Railroad (BRB&L). The fourth large-scale project proposed by the MTA was an extension of the Cambridge Subway, from Harvard Square to the northwest. The project remained entirely on paper during the MTA's

tenure, only becoming realized by the MBTA in the 1980s.

Beyond constructing new rapid transit extensions, the Commonwealth mandated that the MTA also tackle replacing Boston's existing elevated railways, or "els." Hence, the fifth major project proposed by the MTA project was the removal of elevated railways and replacement of the els with rapid transit lines or subways. The sixth of the MTA's major proposals was the conversion of streetcar lines in Boston's Roxbury and Dorchester neighborhoods to trackless trolley operations. In time, the MTA established trackless trolley routes not only in Roxbury, but throughout much of its service area.

During and after the MTA's tenure, five of the MTA's six major projects were brought to life. Only the second tunnel and super-station proposed for the Tremont Street Subway remained unbuilt. Amidst the grand plans, the MTA commenced a myriad of modest, but quickly implemented, improvements. By January 1948, the MTA established regular bus service to connect South Station,

Figure 8.6 MTA Airport Bus Service Brochure, Circa 1948

North Station, and Logan International Airport (Figure 8.6).

The Revere Extension

Proposals for extending the East Boston Tunnel Line north of Maverick Square appeared as early as 1920, when the BERy suggested an extension to East Boston's Central Square. The Commonwealth of Massachusetts Division of Metropolitan Planning (MDMP), in its 1926 *Report on Improved Transportation Facilities In The Boston Metropolitan District*, recommended extending the line to a transfer station and connection with the BRB&L in the heart of East Boston. The transfer station was never built. When the BRB&L ceased operations on January 27, 1940, it abandoned its properties in place. After taking over the defunct railroad's lands, the Commonwealth recycled former BRB&L rights-of-way into foundations for various public transit projects, the first of which was the Revere Extension.

The Commonwealth approved construction of the Revere Extension from Maverick Square to Day Square as early as 1945. A year later, Massachusetts approved pushing the route farther north, to Orient Heights. Construction of the Revere Extension was initiated by the BTD in 1947. In that same year, the MTA took over from the BERy, and under its state-imposed mandate, oversaw completion of the extension to Revere.

The MTA opened the Revere Extension in phases throughout 1952, 1953, and 1954. During those years, the MTA issued its third (1952) and fourth (1954) editions of the Lufkin Format folding system map. A portion of the 1954 map depicts the entire East Boston Tunnel Line, including the Revere Extension (Figure 8.7). The Revere Extension began underground, at the northern end of Maverick Station. From there, the existing train storage tunnel was extended as a two-track subway to a new portal and incline to grade. The incline was situated at the approximate location of the transfer

Figure 8.7 Mapping the Revere Extension, 1954
The MTA's third system route map shows the East Boston Tunnel Line and Revere Extension as a thick blue line labeled "3." The extension runs from Maverick Square in East Boston (center) to Wonderland Station in Revere (top right).

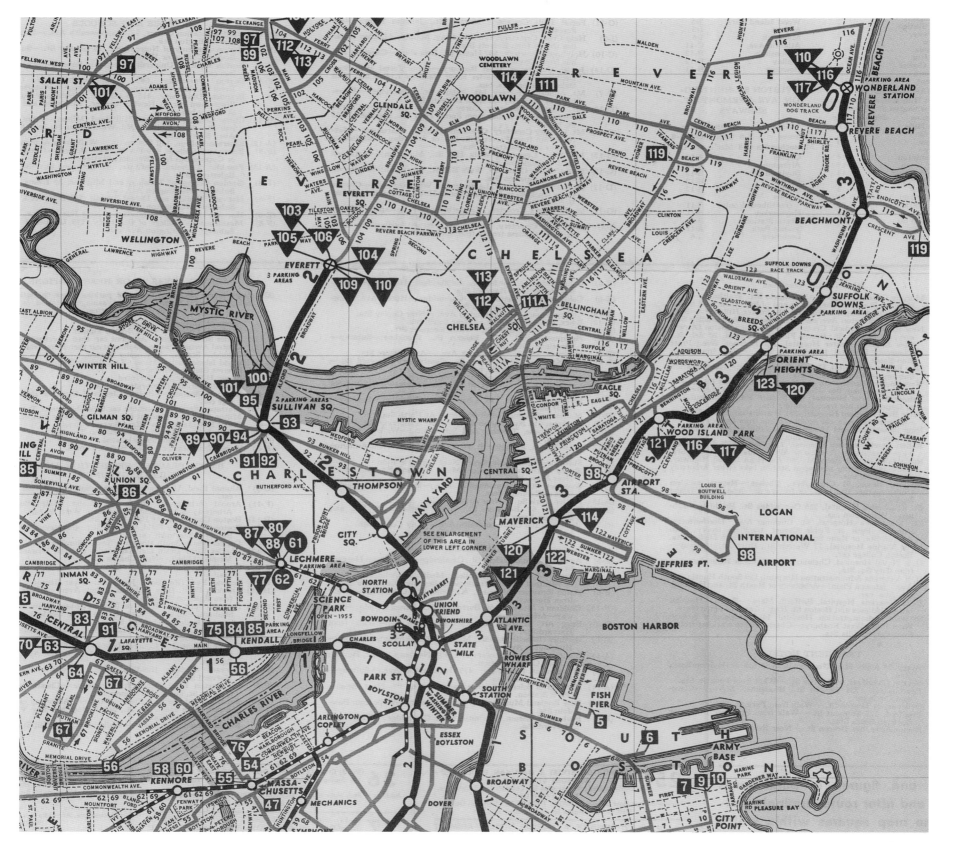

station proposed by the MDMP in 1926. Inside Maverick Station, the existing streetcar loop and transfer platforms were closed; streetcars never entered the station again.

The MTA purchased forty East Boston Tunnel Type 3 rapid transit cars for the Revere Extension in 1951 (Figure 8.8). The cars, numbered 0548–0587, were built by the Saint Louis Car Company and operated in married pairs. They remained in regular service until as late as 1980. All cars serving the East Boston Tunnel Line after the opening of the Revere Extension drew electrical power from both third rail and overhead wire. They were the only rapid transit vehicles in Boston to do so. From the Bowdoin loop in downtown Boston, to the 1951-built portal north of Maverick Station, trains made contact with third rail with small paddles. At Maverick Station, trains switched between third rail and overhead power wires, as they still do today. From Maverick Station, and extending along the line north of the station, trains utilized their pantographs to make contact with overhead wires. Beyond Maverick Square, the Revere Extension ran through East Boston, mostly outside, at grade, and

towards the northeast. The line's first station north of Maverick Station was Airport Station. From Airport Station buses served the terminals at Logan International Airport (Figure 8.9).

Beyond Airport Station, and after passing under a Boston & Albany Railroad (Boston & Albany) right-of-way, the double-track Revere Extension ran through Day Square Station. The station opened as a two-level transfer station. An enclosed upper level was dedicated to trackless trolleys and buses (Figure 8.10). A lower level featured platforms for northbound and southbound rapid transit trains (Figure 8.11). Day Square Station opened with parking for 340 private automobiles. On October 21, 1954, the MTA renamed Day Square Station to Wood Island Park Station, after the neighboring

Figure 8.10 Day Square Station Busway, January 8, 1952
Passengers at the upper level of the three-day-old station board an MTA trackless trolley signed for "Maverick Square." Above the platforms, signs designate numbered berths for buses and trackless trolleys. A stairwell (left) leads down to platforms served by trains of the East Boston Tunnel Line.

Figure 8.11 Day Square Station, January 8, 1952
Over a fresh layer of snow an East Boston Tunnel Line rapid transit train pauses at Day Square Station. One level above, large windows (top left) conceal the station's upper level busway.

Figure 8.12 Inside Orient Heights Shops, February 12, 1952
MTA employees pose with a married pair of East Boston Tunnel Type 3 cars raised for inspection.

seaside park of the same name. Wood Island Park was lost to expansions of Logan International Airport and "Park" was dropped from the station's name in 1967.

Outbound from Day Square, the next stop along the Revere Extension was Orient Heights Station, which took its name and location from that of a shuttered BRB&L depot. From 1875 to 1940, Orient Heights was a nexus of narrow-gauge BRB&L railroad operations, with a passenger depot, train yard, repair shops, and junction between the BRB&L's main line and its loop branch serving the city of Winthrop. In the 1950s, the MTA established rapid transit trackage, storage yards, repair shops, and a new rapid transit station at Orient Heights. The MTA used the shops at Orient Heights to maintain rapid transit cars of the East Boston Tunnel Line (Figure 8.12). The shops and yard facilities at Orient Heights, significantly upgraded since 1952, remain in use for the inspection, maintenance, and storage of rapid transit cars of the MBTA's Blue Line.

Figure 8.13 Orient Heights Eastern Busway, January 16, 1952

Figure 8.14 Orient Heights Station, January 11, 1952

A pair of East Boston Tunnel Type 1 rapid transit cars (right) has just departed from Orient Heights Station. The station's western busway (left) runs alongside the inbound side of the station.

Figure 8.15 Suffolk Downs Station, July 1952

A train of East Boston Tunnel Type 3 rapid transit cars (right) pauses across the platform from a fence bearing a porcelain station sign (left).

The MTA's Orient Heights Station was of simple design, with two covered platforms, one along each side of the double-track Revere Extension. Paralleling each platform was a busway, one along the western side and one along the eastern side of the station (Figure 8.13 and Figure 8.14). At the northern end of the station, a covered stair and pedestrian bridge linked the station's east and west sides. The MTA provided parking for 200 automobiles at Orient Heights.

The MTA opened rapid transit service between Bowdoin and Orient Heights Stations on January 5, 1952. Along the Revere Extension, the MTA reconfigured surface routes to coordinate with the new rapid transit service. During the first few years of service along the Revere Extension, Orient Heights Station served as the line's northern terminus; trains made intermediate stops at Airport and Day Square Stations.

North of Orient Heights, the Revere Extension continued to follow the former right-of-way of the BRB&L. In April 1952 the MTA opened a temporary station structure (Figure 8.15) at the old BRB&L stop near Suffolk Downs race track. During race days in 1952, the MTA operated special, four-car rapid transit trains with five

Figure 8.16 Wonderland Amusement Park, Circa 1910

A postcard image shows Boston, Revere Beach & Lynn Railroad steam trains serving Wonderland at Revere Beach. The park closed in 1906.

Figure 8.17 A New Order of Stations, January 3, 1952
MTA General Manager Edward Dana (left) reveals the names of Airport, Day Square, and Orient Heights Stations on a new Order of Stations sign inside an East Boston Tunnel car. A fabrication drawing for the sign is shown in Figure 8.18.

Figure 8.18 Order of Stations Sign Fabrication Drawing, 1951
A sign installed by the MTA in East Boston Tunnel rapid transit cars coincided with the 1952 opening of service between Bowdoin and Orient Heights Stations.

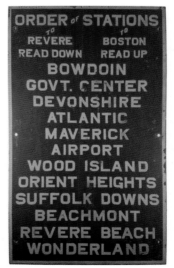

Figure 8.19 East Boston Tunnel Order of Stations, Circa 1963
The final iteration of an Order of Stations sign for East Boston Tunnel cars lists stations in use today on the MBTA's Blue Line, though Devonshire is now State and Atlantic is now Aquarium. The bright text of the sign was screen printed after the 1963 renaming of Scollay Under to Government Center.

minute travel times between Bowdoin and Suffolk Downs Stations. Outbound express trains ran in the morning. Inbound express trains ran back to Boston in the afternoon. Regular trains typically travelled between Bowdoin and Suffolk Downs Stations in thirteen minutes, including time for making intermediate stops. By the mid-1950s, the MTA opened a permanent station structure at Suffolk Downs.

North of Suffolk Downs Station, the MTA established rapid transit stations where the BRB&L previously operated depots at Beachmont and Crescent Beach, both located in Revere. The Beachmont name was reused by the MTA as its name for a station along the Revere Extension. The MTA retired Crescent Beach Station, replacing it with Revere Beach Station.

The northern terminus of the Revere Extension was Wonderland Station. The terminal station took its name from a nearby dog-racing track, which operated from 1935 to 2010. The dog track took its name from an even older amusement park, Wonderland, opened at Revere Beach in 1906

(Figure 8.16). At the time, Revere Beach was for Bostonians what Coney Island was for New Yorkers. The amusement park closed after going bankrupt in 1911. When naming Wonderland Station, the MTA did not recycle the name Bath House Station, the name of the BRB&L's depot near the amusement park. Beachmont, Revere Beach, and Wonderland Stations opened along the Revere Extension on June 19, 1954. Today, the East Boston Tunnel Line, East Boston Tunnel Extension, and Revere Extension make up the MBTA's Blue Line.

After opening the initial segment of the Revere Extension, from Maverick Station to Orient Heights Station in 1952, the MTA installed Order of Stations signs in East Boston Tunnel rapid transit cars (Figure 8.17 and Figure 8.18). After the opening of the final segment of the Revere Extension, to Wonderland Station in 1954, and the renaming of Scollay Under Station to Government Center Station in 1963, the MTA again revised East Boston Tunnel Order of Stations signs (Figure 8.19). Complementing the new signage were updated maps, including one in the brochure titled *Rapid Transit System of the Metropolitan Transit Authority* (Figure 8.20). Published in 1957, the brochure was an updated version of BERy editions of 1905 (Figure 5.35) and 1939 (Figure 6.73).

Tokens on the MTA

On January 29, 1950, the MTA confirmed the fare for its rapid transit service would soon increase from ten to fifteen cents. As advertised on signs installed in transit vehicles (a portion of one is captured in the top right of Figure 8.17), the new fares would go into effect on November 10, 1951. Between the time of the 1950 announcement and the moment when the fare increase became effective, the MTA was unable to convert its rapid transit station turnstiles, known as "passimeters," to accept more than one coin for payment of a single fare. The passimeters could only accept a single coin before letting a person pass. This configuration worked well when a dime was all that was required to pay

Figure 8.20 MTA Rapid Transit System Pamphlet, 1957
An MTA brochure features a photograph of East Boston Tunnel rapid transit cars (above) and map (right).

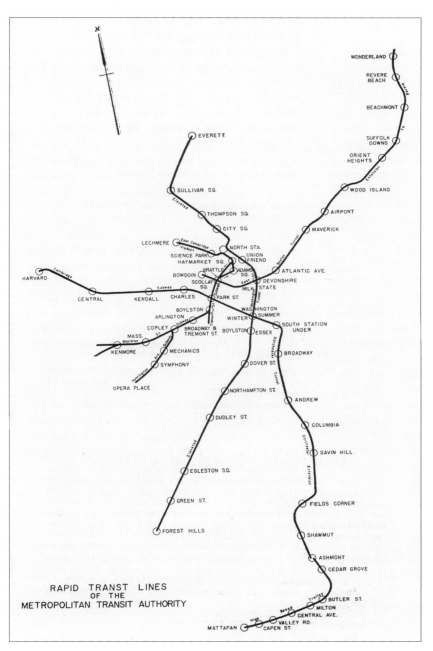

for entry, but the low-fi passimeters were never able to accept fifteen cents in the form of one dime plus one nickel or in the form of three nickels. The situation caused the MTA to issue its first tokens in 1951 (Figure 8.21). Prior to issuing tokens for the new fifteen cent fare, the MTA published an information card explaining when tokens would be needed for entry at rapid transit stations (Figure 8.22). MTA Series-of-1951 tokens were accepted, first by the MTA, and then by the MBTA, until electronic fare collection arrived in the mid-2000s.

No Exit

In 1949 the MTA began charging a supplemental fare to passengers who, after riding a streetcar within the subway, exited their car after it reached the surface outside of the subway. This "exit fare," paid at the end of a rider's journey, was in addition to any fare the patron may have paid previously on the same journey. In response to the establishment of exit fares, a campaign song was written for a local politician to use as he fought against exit fares. The song, "M.T.A.," told the tale of a fictional rider named "Charlie," who, lacking a five cent exit fare, was condemned to ride in perpetuity through Boston's subway tunnels. A 1959 rendition of the song was made famous by the Kingston Trio. A comprehensive "History of The Song Charlie on The M.T.A." was prepared by the MBTA (Figure 8.23).

For a time, the MBTA charged exit fares at certain stations, most notably at Quincy Adams and Braintree Stations on the Red Line. Though exit fares were abolished by the time electronic fare collection arrived, Charlie lives on as the name of today's MBTA electronic fare tickets and variable value cards, CharlieTickets and CharlieCards, respectively. In 2012 the MBTA opened its CharlieCard Store within the concourse under Summer Street and above the former Washington Station (now Downtown Crossing Station on the Red Line). The store is a customer service center for MBTA passes, tickets, and, of course, CharlieTickets and CharlieCards.

The Highland Branch

After successfully converting railroad lines into the Mattapan High Speed Line in the 1920s and the Revere Extension in the 1940s, the MTA completed a third conversion in the 1950s, the Highland Branch. Whereas the Mattapan High Speed Line and Revere Extension served communities to the

south and north of downtown, respectively, the Highland Branch served Boston's western suburbs.

The genesis of the Highland Branch was the Brookline Branch Railroad, constructed by the Boston & Worcester Railroad (Boston & Worcester) from Kenmore Square to Brookline Village. The line opened in 1848. Five years later, the Charles River Branch Railroad extended the line westward, to Newton Upper Falls. In 1867, the Boston & Worcester evolved into the Boston & Albany. After purchasing the portion of the line opened by the Charles River Branch Railroad in 1882, the Boston & Albany gained complete control over what the railroad called its Highland Branch.

In 1884, the Boston & Albany extended the Highland Branch to the edge of the Charles River. There, the railroad opened Riverside Station. West of the station, the Boston & Albany established a connection between the Highland Branch and its main line linking Boston with Albany. The connection allowed the Boston & Albany to operate commuter trains in a loop, from South Station, out to Riverside Station along either the Highland Branch or its main line, and back again. The loop commuter service was called the "Highland Circuit." A 1933 Boston & Albany ticket for travel between South Station and Reservoir Station on the Highland Branch is shown in Figure 8.24. A 1958 schedule for Boston & Albany service between Boston and Riverside features the New York Central & Hudson River Railroad (New York Central) logo on its cover (Figure 8.25). Though the Boston & Albany was leased to the New York Central in 1900, the New York Central continued to do business in Massachusetts under the Boston & Albany name.

During the first half of the twentieth century, expansion of streetcar and bus service, along with growing automobile use, increasingly chipped away at ridership of, and profitability for, the Highland Circuit. By the mid-1950s, unprecedented nationwide declines in the financial health of the railroads, including the Boston & Albany, were becoming critical. Many railroads sought to shed unprofitable passenger services and lines. Between 1900 and 1950, various entities, public and private, conducted studies and published articles recommending that the Highland Branch could better serve the public if converted into a rapid transit line. Rapid transit service could bring more frequent trains and potentially a direct connection to existing rapid transit lines downtown.

Amidst the nationwide railroad crisis, the Boston & Albany petitioned to terminate service along its

Figure 8.21 MTA Series-of-1951 Token
Both faces of the MTA's first token were identical.

Figure 8.22 MTA Token Information Card, 1951
The MTA circulated cards to inform riders that as of 5:00 am on November 10, 1951, MTA tokens would be the only form of payment accepted by turnstiles at rapid transit stations.

Charlie on the M.T.A.

In 1947, the Massachusetts Legislature created the Metropolitan Transit Authority (MTA), the predecessor to today's MBTA, to take over Boston's subway system from the financially troubled Boston Elevated Railway Company. Two years later, faced with its own financial shortfall, the MTA increased fares by as much as fifty percent on some lines and began to charge subway riders an extra nickel when they exited trolleys above ground. Walter A. O'Brien, Jr., the Progressive Party candidate for mayor of Boston in 1949, opposed the state's "bailout" of the private transit system and called for a rollback of the fare increase. In order to call attention to O'Brien's position, some of his supporters got together and wrote some campaign songs for him. That is how Charlie was born.

"Charlie on the MTA" (the actual title of the song is "M.T.A.") was written by Jackie Steiner and Bess Lomax Hawes, one of several written for O'Brien's campaign. It was recorded in the fall of 1949 by a group of O'Brien supporters who called them-

selves the Boston Peoples Artists. It was performed live by the group as well as played over a sound truck that drove around the streets of Boston. The song became immediately popular. But it didn't help O'Brien's campaign–he finished last in a field of five candidates.

Several years later, a former O'Brien campaign volunteer taught the song to a folk singer named Will Holt, who recorded the story of Charlie for Coral Records in 1957. The song seemed well on its way to becoming a hit, until it generated a deluge of protests from Boston because it made a hero out of a local "radical." During the McCarthy era of the 1950s, O'Brien and his wife, along with many other members of the Progressive Party had been charged with being "Communists or Communist Party sympathizers." Although it was a charge the O'Briens denied, neither of them could find work in Boston after that and they were forced to move back to Maine, where both had been born and raised.

As a result of the controversy, Holt's recording of "M.T.A." was withdrawn from the airwaves. But in 1959, The Kingston Trio released their own recording of the song. To avoid the problems that Holt experienced, they changed the name of the real-life Walter A. O'Brien to a fictional character named George O'Brien. The song became a hit, and in the years since has become a part of American folklore, sung around campfires and recorded by artists from all over the world in styles ranging from folk to funk and rock to reggae.

Walter O'Brien became a school librarian and a bookstore owner. He died in July 1998. Today, Jackie Steiner and Bess Lomax Hawes and the other surviving members of the Boston Peoples Artists have fond memories of him, and are proud of the progressive politics they shared and the role they played in creating the folk classic known as "Charlie on the MTA."

M.T.A.
by Jackie Steiner and Bess Lomax Hawes

Let me tell you the story of a man named Charlie
On a dark and fateful day
He put ten cents in his pocket and he kissed his loving family
And he went to ride the MTA.

Did he ever return? No, he never returned
And his fate is still unlearned
He may ride forever 'neath the streets of Boston
He's the man who never returned.

Charlie handed in his dime at the Kendall Square Station,
And he changed for Jamaica Plain
When he got there the conductor told him, 'One more nickel'
Charlie couldn't get off the train.

As his train rolled on through greater Boston
Charlie looked around and sighed
"Well, I'm sore and disgusted and I'm absolutely busted
I guess this is my last long ride."

Now all night long Charlie rode through the tunnels
Saying, "What will become of me?
Oh, how can I afford to see my sister in Chelsea
Or my brother in Roxbury?"

"I can't help," said the conductor
"I'm just working for a living but I sure agree with you
For the nickels and dimes you'll be spending in Boston
You'd be better off in Timbuktu."

Charlie's wife goes down to the Scollay Square Station
Every day at a quarter past two
And through the open window she hands Charlie a sandwich
As his train goes rumbling through.

Now, citizens of Boston, don't you think it is a scandal
That the people have to pay and pay?
Join Walter A. O'Brien and fight the fare increase
Get poor Charlie off that MTA!

Figure 8.23 "Charlie on the MTA," Prepared by the MBTA

Highland Branch. Responding in 1957, the General Court passed Chapter 450 of the Acts of that year, authorizing the MTA to purchase the Highland Branch from the New York Central and convert it to rapid transit service. With the running of a final train on May 31, 1958, the Boston & Albany wrapped up over a century of passenger service along the Highland Branch. On June 24, and after paying $600,000 to the Boston & Albany, the MTA received title to the Highland Branch.

The official ground breaking for the MTA's Highland Branch project took place on July 10, 1958. Due to a lack of funding from the Commonwealth, the MTA broke ground to convert the Highland Branch

not into a rapid transit line, but into a streetcar line instead. Streetcars cost considerably less and required far simpler infrastructure than rapid transit trains. To convert the railroad line to trolley service, the MTA strung trolley wire from steel poles along the route. After some minor improvements, much of the existing railroad trackage was reused in place. Even after realizing the savings from opting for streetcars over rapid transit trains, the MTA still lacked enough of a project budget to purchase new streetcars. Hence, the MTA reassigned existing streetcars from elsewhere within its system. The cars, all PCCs, were refurbished by the MTA for deployment on the Highland Branch.

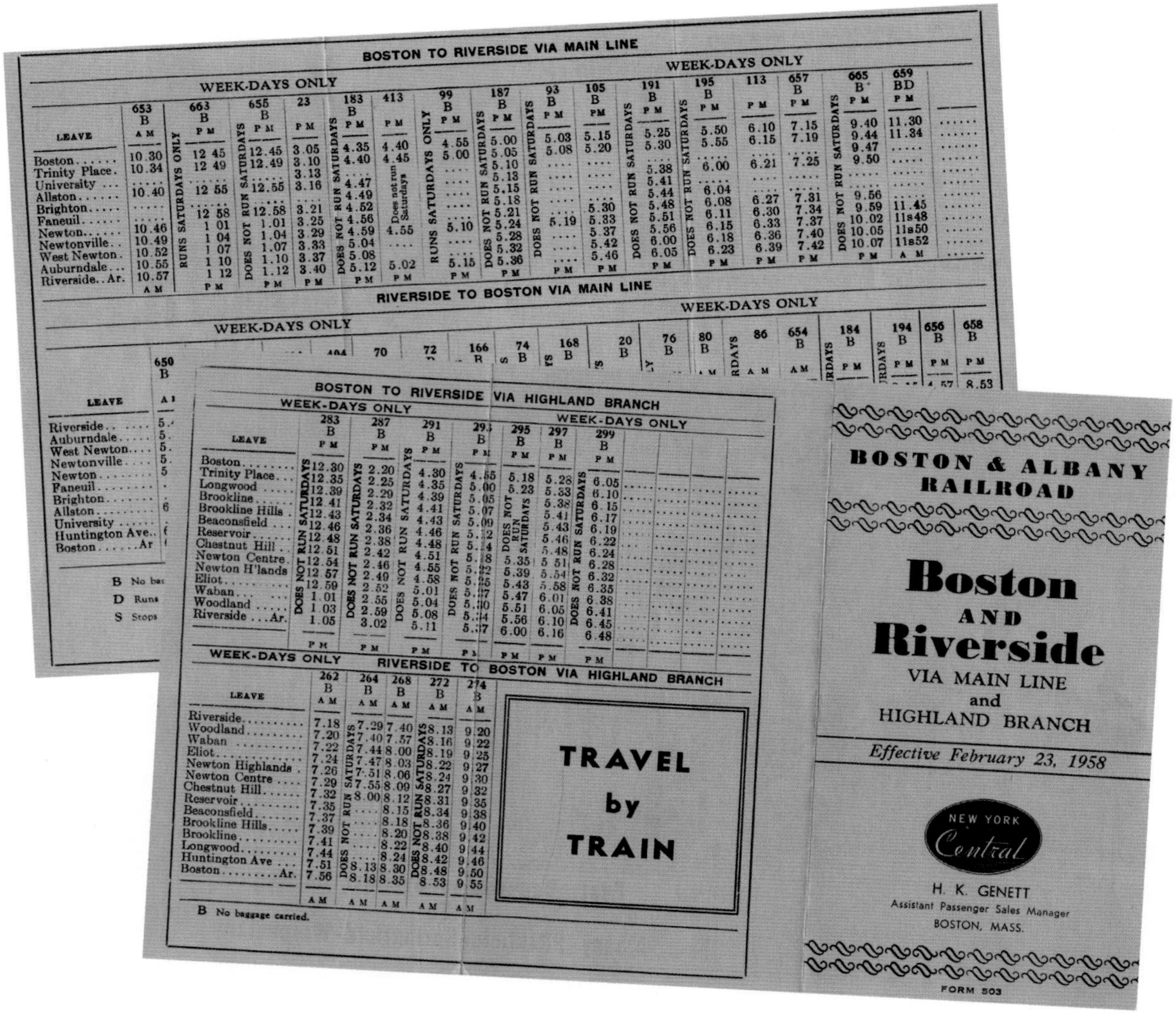

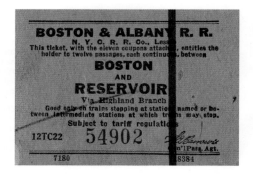

Figure 8.24 Boston & Albany Railroad Ticket, 1933
A ticket good for travel on the Boston & Albany's Highland Branch, between Boston's South Station and Newton's Reservoir Station, in Newton.

Figure 8.25 Boston & Albany Highland Circuit Schedule, 1958
A timetable lists station stops between South Station and Riverside Station, along the Boston & Albany's main line and Highland Branch. Just over a year after the schedule's effective date, February 23, 1958, MTA streetcars replaced Boston & Albany commuter trains along the Highland Branch.

The majority of the MTA's Highland Branch followed the existing railroad right-of-way. At the far eastern end of the line, the MTA established a new connection between the Highland Branch and the Kenmore Square Subway, and by extension, the Tremont Street Subway. West of Kenmore Square, a two-track streetcar subway was constructed using the cut and cover method. The new subway tied into the existing tunnels under Beacon Street. There, the subway split into a pair of two-track branches. One branch followed Beacon Street to an existing portal and incline west of Audubon Circle, where the streetcar tracks linked with surface tracks in the middle of Beacon Street. The other branch ran southwesterly to a new portal and incline east of Park Drive. At the top of the incline, where subway tracks linked with those of the Highland Branch, the MTA established a surface streetcar stop, Fenway Park Station. Later, the MBTA shortened the stop's name to Fenway Station.

West of Fenway Park Station, the MTA's Highland Branch traced the former Boston & Albany right-of-way. Between Fenway Park and Riverside Stations, the MTA established streetcar stops, typically where the Boston & Albany previously operated passenger depots. All of the Highland Branch station names listed on the Boston & Albany's 1958 schedule were recycled by the MTA except "Brookline," which the MTA replaced with "Brookline Village." The updated name distinguished the station from Brookline Hills Station.

Along the Highland Branch in 1958, most of the Boston & Albany's depots were sold by the railroad to the MTA. The MTA proceeded to raze some of the stations, replacing them with tiny, wooden streetcar shelters. In time, others were sold into private hands. The shelters, with their multiple roof peaks (Figure 8.26), were intended to recall the architecture of the lost stations. Instead, the three-sided shelters mocked the memory of the substantial station structures lost to the wrecking ball. Woodland Station, in addition to receiving three shelters from the MTA, one on each side of the tracks and a third at a busway area, opened with a significant parking lot for automobile commuters.

The MTA installed modest parking areas at other Highland Branch stops, working to draw automobile commuters from Boston's western suburbs to the Highland Branch.

The MTA announced the opening of the Highland Branch streetcar line with multiple promotional items. A printed brochure featured maps of the line, a list of its stations, and a friendly motorman greeting prospective riders (Figure 8.27). Another

Figure 8.26 Brookline Village Station, November 12, 1959
The MTA erected glorified bus shelters at Highland Branch stops, including this one, at Brookline Village.

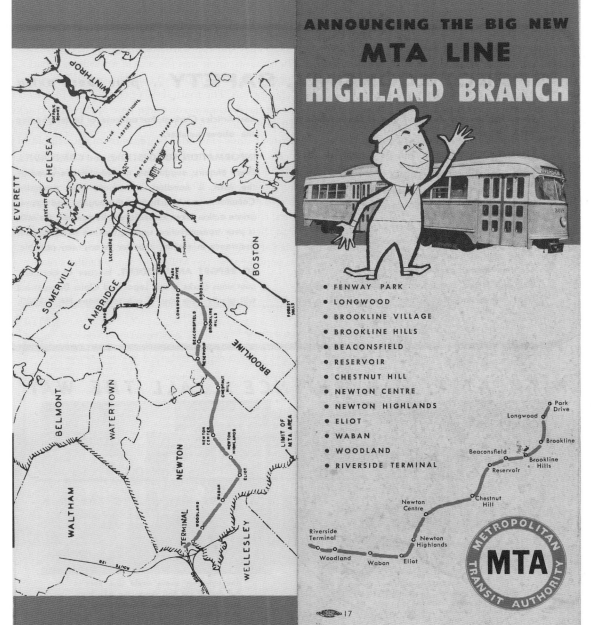

Figure 8.27 MTA Highland Branch Pamphlet, 1959
A grinning motorman waves from in front of a PCC streetcar and above a list of stations of the MTA's new Highland Branch. The pamphlet's map (left) depicts rapid transit and subway lines in black and the Highland Branch in red.

MTA print publication touted the "Speed, Economy, Safety" of the Highland Branch (Figure 8.28). A cardboard promotional sign featured images of stations and streetcars of the Highland Branch (Figure 8.29). On the sign, above a photograph of a woman emerging from an MTA subway station looking refreshed and ready to take on her day, text read: "Drive where driving is fun; Relax for the rest of the run! Ride your scenic Highland Branch."

The MTA's Highland Branch was officially dedicated on June 30, 1959. Regular service with MTA PCC streetcars commenced on Saturday, July 4. By the end of the first year of streetcar operations 26,000 commuters were riding the line and the MTA declared that its trolleys were carrying more commuters in one hour than the Boston & Albany had in one day. By the end of 1960, the Highland Branch was carrying 27,000 passengers daily, a significant increase over a single year's passenger count of the Boston & Albany. In that same year, forty percent of riders on the Highland Branch were from outside of the MTA's service area. The MTA achieved its goal of drawing automobile commuters off the roads west of Boston and into parking lots along its Highland Branch.

Coinciding with the summer opening of the Highland Branch, the MTA issued a double-sided paper pamphlet that listed specifications, schedules, and streetcar running times for the line. The MTA produced editions of the pamphlet for summer 1959 (Figure 8.30), fall 1959, winter 1959–60, and spring 1960 (Figure 8.31). Initially, the regular fare from Riverside Terminal and inbound to Boston was twenty cents. The MTA raised the fare to forty cents in 1961. Streetcars running outbound from Boston to Riverside Terminal displayed roll signs indicating "Riverside" as their destination. The Highland Branch is now the D branch of the MBTA's Green Line, but commonly referred to as the Riverside Line.

Reservoir and Riverside

Located at the approximate midpoint of the MTA's Highland Branch was the site of an 1888 railroad depot. The MTA replaced the depot with Reservoir Station. The main level of the station featured streetcar storage yards and a pair of through-tracks with outside platforms. On either side of the platforms, ramps carried streetcars from the Highland Branch up, into a return loop, and to connections with surface streetcar tracks at the level of Chestnut Hill Avenue. The loop allowed streetcars to arrive at Reservoir Station and exchange passengers, then run up, turn around, and head back down into the station, before returning to Boston. Streetcar service on the Highland Branch was initially so popular that the MTA ran many trolleys from

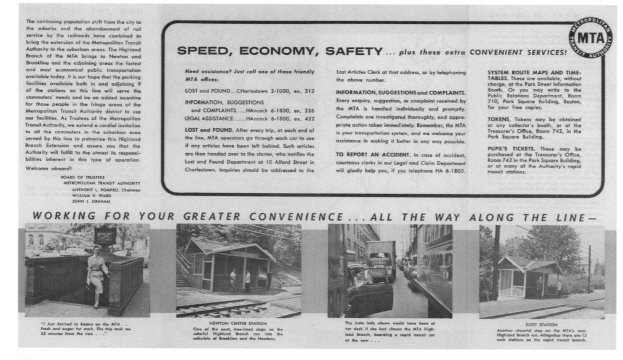

Figure 8.28 MTA Highland Branch Advertisement, Circa 1959
An MTA marketing publication trumpets the "Speed, Economy, Safety" of the new Highland Branch. Photographs and captions articulate how MTA riders have "arrived in Boston on the MTA…fresh and eager for work" and are enjoying "another cheerful stop on the MTA's new, Highland Branch run." Two images reveal MTA-built shelters along the line.

Figure 8.29 Highland Branch Advertisement, Circa 1959

A cardboard display, designed to stand up on an information counter, features renderings of stations and streetcars of the MTA's Highland Branch. The display targets automobile commuters, reading "Take Route 128, 9 or 16 to the station nearest your home" and "Travel the thrifty way—save wear and tear on your automobile."

Figure 8.30 MTA Highland Branch Schedule, Summer 1959

Figure 8.31 MTA Highland Branch Schedules, 1959–60

Boston through Reservoir, avoiding the loop, and all the way to the end of the line at Riverside.

At Reservoir, a streetcar storage yard at the level of Chestnut Hill Avenue became known as the "upper yard," distinguishing it from the neighboring "lower yard" at the level of Beacon Street. The lower yard pre-dated the MTA's conversion of the Highland Branch. The MBTA reconstructed Reservoir Station and yards in the 1980s. The ramps and loop track were removed and the through-track platforms were enlarged. The MBTA expanded the lower yard with maintenance facilities for light rail vehicles.

The western terminus of the MTA's Highland Branch was on a former Boston & Albany property,

along Newton's Grove Street. The Boston & Albany's Riverside Station was located a bit to the west of the MTA's streetcar terminal of the same name, established in 1959. The railroad station sat closer to the Boston & Albany main line (now the MBTA's Worcester commuter rail line). Upon opening for streetcar service in summer 1959, the MTA's Riverside Terminal featured a parking lot capable of holding hundreds of cars. It was larger than any other along the Highland Branch. Amidst a sea of asphalt, the MTA erected a simple, single story station building (Figure 8.32). Riverside Terminal opened with a streetcar loop, boarding platforms, and storage yard (Figure 8.33).

Figure 8.32 Riverside Terminal, June, 1959
A freshly paved parking lot surrounds the station's loop tracks, platform, and building. The station opened a few weeks after this photograph was taken.

Figure 8.33 Riverside Terminal, July 4, 1959
Patrons line up to board an MTA PCC streetcar on the first day of service on the Highland Branch.

Riverside Terminal was reconfigured by the MTA in 1960, and again, by the MBTA, in 1974, when a car house and additional yard tracks were constructed behind the station. The MBTA has since made multiple improvements to the cars houses, storage tracks, and station at Riverside. An entirely new Riverside Station opened in 1995, by which time the original station building had been turned over to use by interstate bus companies. Riverside Terminal continues to be a busy transfer station, served by light rail vehicles (LRVs) of the MBTA's Green Line D branch, MBTA buses, and intercity motor coaches. Riverside is the main repair and maintenance facility for MBTA LRVs, successors to the PCC streetcars for which the complex was initially established.

Edward Dana Retires

In addition to the opening of the MTA's Highland Branch, 1959 brought with it the retirement of the MTA's first general manager, Edward Dana. For years leading up to his retirement, Dana was "Mr. Transit" in Boston. He started his career on a BERy streetcar in 1907. Dana worked his way up through the BERy's ranks, becoming general manager of the company in 1919, and then president of the BERy in 1937. He was subsequently appointed the first general manager of the MTA. In its annual report of 1959, the Board of Trustees of the MTA wrote of Mr. Transit:

> A kind, introspective man, Edward Dana never lost the energy and enthusiasm that marked his long career in mass transportation....Last summer, he stood on a platform at Riverside Terminal in Newton and watched a long-cherished dream become a reality. The new Highland Branch run over the abandoned Boston and Albany roadbed sprung into life, bringing mass transportation in truth to the suburbs. Shortly thereafter, Edward Dana called it a day.

However celebratory the MTA was as it basked in the opening of its Highland Branch, Dana, always looking ahead and thinking of the best interest of transit riders, provided the following sobering statement upon his retirement:

> I shudder to think of what the future has in store for public transit in our great Boston Metropolitan area as time runs out on its proper solution.

The automobile, essential to the successful functioning of our economy, has proven that public transit essential to the salvation of a great core city can no longer be considered able to function only from the revenues of the fare box. A realistic, statesmanlike effort to apportion equitably the necessary subsidies must be forthcoming to lay the foundation for a substantial improvement in public transit that is sorely needed if we are to avoid the deterioration of values already created.

Dana articulately promoted that subsidized public transportation with an affordable fare, should coexist with automobile commuting, itself subsidized by federal highway dollars.

Edward Dana passed away March 27, 1981. Published in the *Boston Globe*, part of Dana's obituary read:

> His contributions to the transit industry throughout the world are considered monuments in the industry. They include the training of personnel, and efficiency and safety of operation and development of improved vehicles.

The MBTA dedicated its 1981 annual report to Mr. Transit, recording Dana, commenting on the creation of the MBTA in 1964, saying: "At long last the state has faced up to the fact that mass transportation is vital to the core city—the New Boston."

Ridership Drops and Costs Rise

After being swelled with wartime ridership in the 1940s, public transit use across Greater Boston declined during the late 1940s and throughout the 1950s. Public transit systems across America saw similar if not more significant drops. By 1950, counts of revenue passengers utilizing the MTA dropped a whopping nineteen percent from 1947 levels. Between 1952 and 1953 alone, there was a nine percent drop in revenue passengers carried. The downward spiral continued until bottoming out in 1960, when the MTA carried only 199 million revenue passengers, down from 389 million in 1947. As a direct result of the crash in ridership, the MTA recorded a record low of $36 million in revenue for 1960. Previously, revenue for its first full year of operations was $39.3 million.

Despite some slight revenue tick ups during the 1950s, overall decreases in ridership and lack of any sustained increase in revenue were compounded

Figure 8.34 Edward Dana, January 3, 1952
A pair of airline stewardesses flank Mr. Transit during a promotional ride along the Revere Extension.

by steady and marked increases in the cost of service. Total cost of service rose to $58.9 million by the end of 1962. All the while, the MTA had to draw upon a stagnant pool of financial resources as it attempted to improve and expand service. The Authority's finances were also strained from the burdens of maintaining aging legacy infrastructure, constantly increasing labor costs, and the legislatively required absorption of the BTD in 1949. Each year, as permitted by law, the MTA typically passed its deficit on to its fourteen constituent municipalities. Formulas determined the financial share borne by each city and town served by the MTA.

Nemesis: Automobile, Suburbia, and Weather

The MTA consistently identified the chief causes of its declining financial situation, specifically calling out debt costs, rising labor costs, perpetual maintenance expenses, and dwindling passenger counts. The MTA placed some blame, and often outright loathing, onto increasing use of personal automobiles, with operational subsidies that came in the form of public highways. After World War II, federal initiatives that encouraged single family home ownership in the suburbs put more and more people out of the reach of the MTA and into their automobiles to get around. By the mid-1950s, interstate highway construction, along with private suburban land development, were being undertaken with seemingly reckless abandon within and around the MTA's service area. As early as 1951, the MTA stated plainly in its annual report for that year that "the increased use of automobiles has been the greatest cause of decrease in riding of the authority's system." By 1959, the MTA widened its accusations beyond the automobile, acknowledging that with so much suburban development occurring beyond its limited service area, both the MTA and the regional populace would suffer without some rethinking of Greater Boston's public transportation system. Only a year prior, the Board of Trustees of the MTA penned in its 1958 annual report:

> We believe the system is destined to grow, expand its boundaries and thrive. We believe that the MTA MUST grow, expand and thrive if the community is to experience the same kind of growth, expansion and well-being.

A year later, the trustees got a bit more personal, addressing constituents in its 1960 annual report:

A thriving, heavily populated metropolitan area cannot exist without an efficient transportation system. The man behind the wheel of his automobile, at long last, must realize that his vehicle moves in luxury. The M.T.A. moves him when all else, including when his automobile fails.

Just weeks before those words were published, on Monday, December 12, 1960, a record-setting winter storm dropped multiple feet of snow onto Boston. The fresh snowfall arrived on the heels of an earlier storm that had delivered over a foot and a half of snow and brought the city to a standstill. While much of the city was paralyzed by the compound weather events, the MTA was not. The Authority brought this fact to the attention of the public, writing in its 1960 annual report:

> …the snowbound residents of the M.T.A. district flocked to the M.T.A. and no longer was there any talk of deficits, no longer any muttering about standees or rush hour traffic. The M.T.A. now was a shining, fast-moving and dependable servant.

As the 1950s became the 1960s, the voice of the MTA became more emphatic, reaching a feverous pitch in the Authority's final annual report. There, the MTA articulated the problems of the day for public transportation in Boston, emphasizing three main points, the continued abandonment of passenger service by the railroads, the increased use of the automobile, and harsh weather events. Laying out "the problem at hand," the Public Trustees of the MTA shouted in their "Declaration From The Board Of Trustees:"

> The Board of Trustees asks you to conjure up a transportation nightmare made up of a city of commuterless trains, resulting in an escalated traffic mishmash and the one equalizer that everyone understands and which the weather bureau, in the winter months, describes as 'eight to ten inches'! NOW YOU REALLY HAVE CRISIS. NOW YOU REALLY HAVE CHAOS. NOW SOMEONE MUST FACE THE NAGGING, GUILT-RIDDEN INQUIRY: 'WHY DIDN'T SOMEONE DO SOMETHING?

The MTA Fights the Good Fight

Having identified the increasing use of the automobile and the continued geographic decentralization

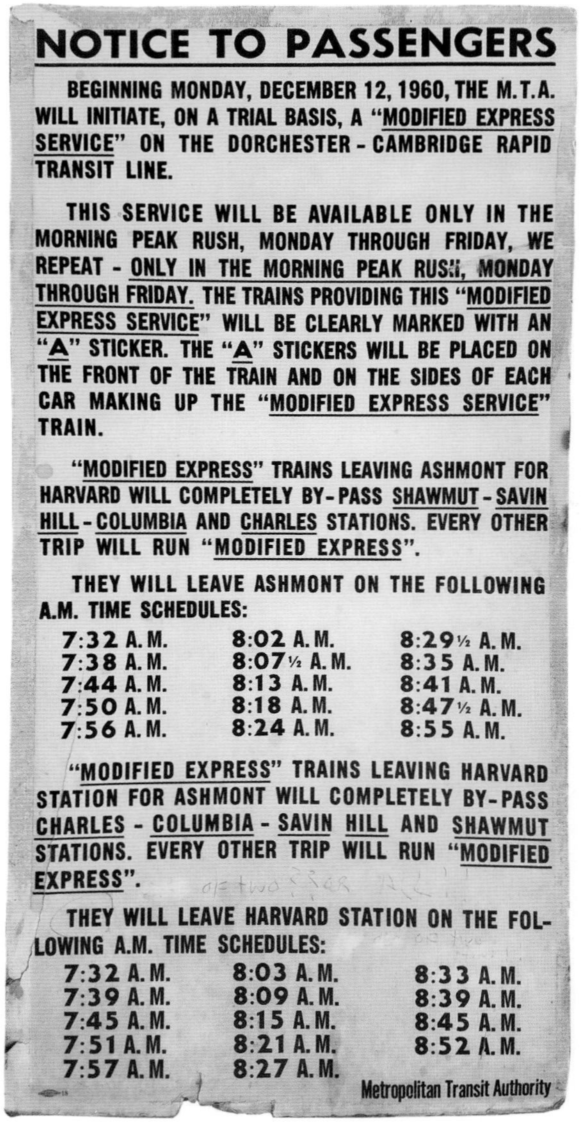

Figure 8.35 MTA Modified Express Service Poster, 1960
A poster explains one of the MTA's service experiments, "modified express service" implemented on what is now the Red Line. Under the service, sometimes referred to as skip-stop service, certain trains stopped at every other station along the line. These trains then ran express through unserved stations. As reflected by vintage graffiti on the poster, some riders were confused by the service. Modified express service lasted less than a year.

Figure 8.36 MTA Trolley Bus at Fields Corner Station, 1948
A trackless trolley purchased new by the MTA was one of a batch that received numbers 8330–8572. Complementing the new trolley buses were others purchased used, out of Providence, Rhode Island. The MTA renumbered the ex-Providence trackless trolleys 8573–8610.

of its customer base as enemies, the MTA pursued a multi-prong battle plan. First, the MTA reduced the frequency of service on routes with low ridership. In some cases, routes with significantly low ridership were eliminated entirely. Less than ten persons per trip was one threshold applied in 1954. One specific change that led to significant savings for the MTA was its stoppage of rapid transit trains and streetcars and the exclusive use of only eighteen buses for the 1:30 a.m. to 5:00 a.m. Owl Service during 1955. Five years later the MTA eliminated Owl Service entirely, generating further cost savings. Also in 1960, the MTA enacted a four percent overall reduction in service and reduced operating expenses through hiring freezes and economizing internal operations.

Along with trimming service along routes with low ridership, the MTA introduced new service to increase ridership and better serve modern travel patterns. The MTA aggressively pursued the addition of new routes beyond the BERy's former service area in order to serve Boston's growing suburban population, a significant portion of which was migrating from the urban core to outlying areas not previously served by the BERy. The Revere Extension and the Highland Branch were examples

of MTA suburban commuter outreach capital projects.

Additional prongs in the MTA's battle plan included: marketing transit services to the driving public, mostly in newspapers and on the radio; improving the public experience with fresh paint and new lighting at existing stations; upgrading existing equipment; leasing space at stations for concessions; and purchasing new vehicles, including diesel buses, trackless trolleys, and rapid transit cars. New vehicles put into service by the MTA included trackless trolleys (Figure 8.36), East Boston Tunnel Type 3 rapid transit cars, Cambridge-Dorchester Type 5 rapid transit cars, Main Line Elevated Type 11 rapid transit cars, and a plethora of buses.

Just as electric streetcars replaced horsecars in Boston by the end of 1900, trackless trolleys and buses replaced electric streetcars in the middle of the twentieth century. In eastern Massachusetts, the conversion from tracks to tires was not exclusive to the BERy nor the MTA. During the 1940s, the Eastern Massachusetts Street Railway Company (Eastern Mass) was busy converting from trolley service to bus operations. When the Eastern Mass's route from Field's Corner in Dorchester to the Fore River Shipyard in Quincy was converted

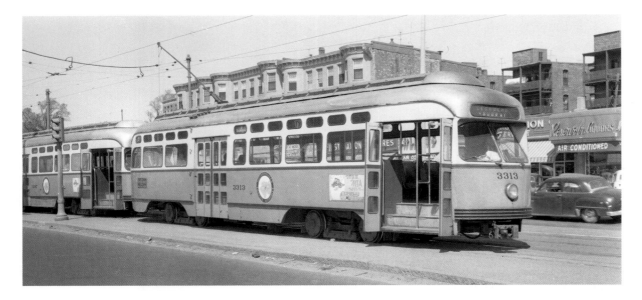

Figure 8.37 Four-year-old MTA Picture Window PCC Car #3313 at Cleveland Circle, May 20, 1955

from electric trolleys to buses in 1948, regular operations of its namesake vehicles came to an end for the Eastern Mass.

The MTA received fifty "picture window" PCCs, numbered 3272–3321 (Figure 8.37), in 1951. The vehicles featured a second set of windows, running high along both sides of each car. At the end of the 1950s, the MTA purchased twenty-five, double-ended PCCs from operators in Dallas, Texas. The majority of Boston's PCC cars were phased out of revenue service or were scrapped by the early 1980s. Today, ex-MTA PCC cars, with numbers in the 3320s–3340s, ply the Mattapan High Speed Line for the MBTA. Beyond Boston, the only American cities with significant operational fleets of PCC cars in regular revenue service are San Francisco and Philadelphia.

Park & Ride

One of the most creative and successful parts of the MTA's battle plan was its establishment of an unprecedented number of parking lots for automobile commuters at Greater Boston's transit stations, turning the competing mode of transportation, the automobile, into an extension of its network. Just as streetcars once collected suburbanites and connected them with the BERy's rapid transit stations, parking lots drew cars of mid-twentieth century suburbanites to the lines of the MTA. While the MTA established the majority of its parking lots along newer and outlying lines, such as the Highland Branch, the MTA established some in downtown Boston; the MTA acknowledged that the personal automobile had infested the city just as much as it bred freely in the suburbs. The MTA's parking program was extremely successful, with the numbers of cars parked each year at MTA lots practically doubling from over 515,000 in 1955 to just over 1,000,0000 in 1963.

Initially, parking at an MTA lot was free of charge; the MTA was grateful to attract riders who might otherwise have driven to their destination. With finances getting tighter in 1953, the MTA abolished free parking and implemented a fifty-five cent combo fare. The combo fare included one day of parking and a round-trip ride on the MTA (Figure 8.38). The daily Park & Ride cost increased to sixty five cents by 1956. The MTA advertised that the public would save time and money by using Park & Ride lots instead of commuting by car (Figure 8.39). The MTA continued to tweak parking fees throughout the 1950s and into the early 1960s, lowering the parking fee at certain lots to ten cents by 1963. The reduction was an attempt to attract more patrons, even though it caused the MTA to take a hit against parking revenue. Harkening to the past, for at time MTA parking lot claim checks featured a rendering of a horse-drawn streetcar (Figure 8.40).

The parking lots established by the MTA became the genesis of the network of lots and multi-story garages assembled by the MBTA. Parking facilities for automobile commuters remain vital in making public transportation accessible to citizens living beyond a reasonable walking distance or out of range of a bus ride to a transit station. Before the MTA, the BERy experimented with

Figure 8.38 MTA Combo Tickets, Circa late 1950s
The MTA sold tickets for a day of parking combined with round-trip fare from and back to one of its lot.

Figure 8.39 MTA Print Advertisement, Circa 1950s

Figure 8.40 MTA Parking Lot Claim Check, Undated

Figure 8.41 MTA Fare Map, 1949

The MTA prepared a map to explain a complicated fare system implemented in August 1949. Thick black lines represent rapid transit and streetcar subway lines. Surface lines connecting with rapid transit lines are thin lines. Surface lines not connecting with rapid transit lines are lines with small dots. The "Fare Schedule Table" (bottom right) explains how to calculate a fare.

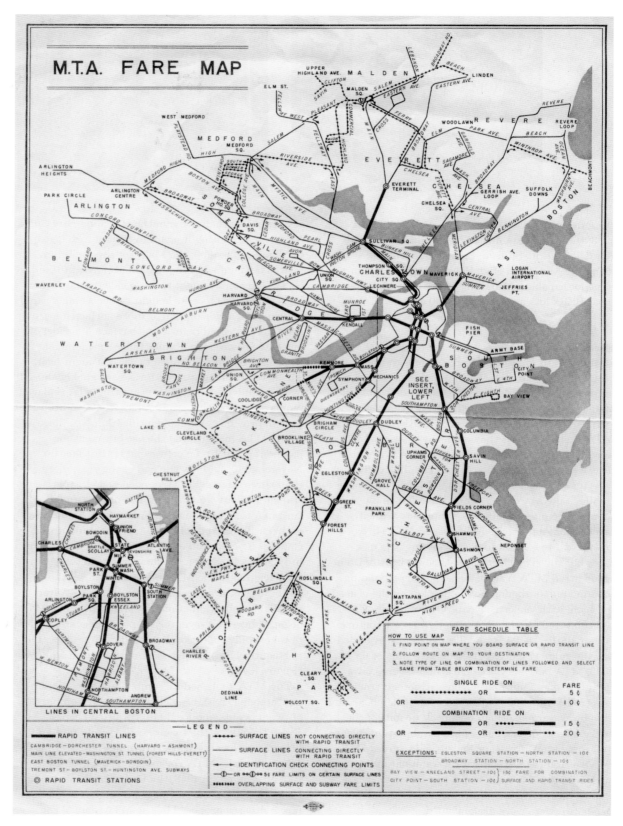

Figure 8.42 MTA Old and New Turnstiles, 1952
Within a year of the MTA accepting tokens at rapid transit stations, a General Electric passimeter (left) and a newer Perey passimeter (right) were photographed by the MTA. The Perey model protects the Chauncy Street entrance to Washington Station.

accommodations for the automobile. As early as 1933, the BERy established free parking areas at Kendall Station, Sullivan Square Station, and stops along the Mattapan High Speed Line. Except for a large lot capable of handling 220 cars at Mattapan, most BERy lots held less than 100 cars each.

Fares on the MTA

In addition to promoting Park & Ride, another tactic employed by the MTA to tackle decreasing ridership and address increasing costs was the adjustment of fares. Throughout 1947 the regular fare for most trips on either the BERy or the MTA was a dime. At the end of the year, the MTA amended its fare structure to include a five cent fare, a five cent pupil fare, a six and a half cent joint fare, and special streetcar and bus fares. Just after its 1947 takeover of the BERy, the MTA implemented the most significant changes to transit fares. That August, the MTA issued *MTA Fare Guide No. 1* to explain in detail not only the new fares but the six collection methods being used. The guide listed MTA transit lines and corresponding inbound and outbound fare collection methods used for each, with various caveats. Over a dozen pages were devoted to explaining the new fare structure. A map of the "MTA Rapid Transit Lines" rounded out the guide (Figure 8.41). Effective August 6, 1949, MTA patrons were charged: five cents for a local ride on all but four surface streetcar, trackless trolley, and bus routes; ten cents when boarding at subway, tunnel, elevated railway, or four of the surface lines; fifteen cents for a combination surface and rapid transit ride, or for any ride during Owl Service; and twenty cents for a combination of a surface, a rapid transit, and a second surface ride. Pupils' fares remained unchanged at a nickel and paper transfers were discontinued.

Within less than five months of issuing *Fare Guide No. 1*, the MTA sought again to restructure fares. On January 28, 1950, the MTA set the minimum fare at ten cents and the maximum fare at fifteen cents. Ten cents bought a single ride on the surface lines while fifteen cents bought either a single rapid transit ride, a ride on two or more surface lines, a combination rapid transit and surface line ride, or one Owl Service ride. Pupils' tickets remained at five cents, but paper transfers were brought back. The lower rate for student fares was quickly abused by non-students, so much so that the MTA replaced pupils' tickets with a student pass that required the user to provide personal identification.

The MTA inaugurated the use of tokens for payment of its fifteen cent rapid transit fare on November 10, 1951. By the end of the year, more than three quarters of fares collected at rapid transit stations were tokens, not nickels and dimes. An MTA token is shown in Figure 8.21. Two types of turnstiles used by the MTA, one manufactured by General Electric and one built by Perey, are shown in Figure 8.42. Ever since its introduced tokens in the early 1950s, the MTA pushed for the exclusive use of tokens as a means of eliminating the often unreliable collection of nickels and dimes. The MTA began converting seventeen rapid transit stations to token-only collection in 1961. The first station to be entirely converted was South Station Under (Figure 8.44).

The MTA abolished its complicated fare system on October 1, 1955, replacing it with "system fares" of twenty cents and local fares of fifteen cents. Paper tickets for the twenty cent system fare and fifteen cent local fare are shown in Figure 8.43.

Not all of the MTA's proposed fare increases made it to customers. In 1953, the Department of Public Utilities (DPU), the state agency which reviewed fare increases proposed by the MTA, denied the

Figure 8.43 MTA Fifteen Cent and Twenty Cent Tickets, 1955

Figure 8.44 Turnstiles at South Station Under, 1961

In 1961, as part of the MTA's efforts to improve the aesthetics of existing transit stations, South Station Under was repainted, received new advertisement boards, and was converted to token-only collection.

MTA's request to adjust rapid transit fares from fifteen to twenty cents with transfers, local surface line fares without transfers from ten to fifteen cents, and pupils' tickets from five to seven and a half cents. The DPU approved an MTA fare increase on April 6, 1954, allowing the MTA to bring in badly needed additional revenue.

In 1962, the MTA commissioned the production of 50,000 "token strips," each of which included five tokens (Figure 8.45). The program allowed the MTA to pre-sell fares. In return, customers were provided with a convenient, pocket-sized means of carrying tokens and a discounted purchase price. Each set of one dollar's worth of tokens cost only ninety cents. The MTA made token strips available to the public on Monday, December 6, 1962. By the evening of Wednesday December 8, the supply sold out.

Figure 8.45 MTA Token Strip, 1962

Both sides of an MTA token strip are branded with stylized MTA logos. The card stock strip was sold with five MTA tokens.

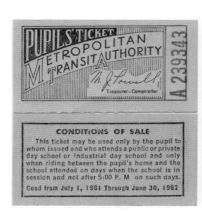

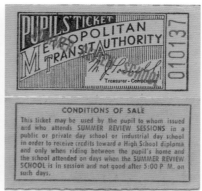

Figure 8.46 MTA Pupils' Tickets, Circa 1955–1961

From top to bottom are: the front and rear faces of an MTA pupils' ticket for daytime school, valid from July 1, 1961 through June 30, 1962; pupils' tickets valid for travel to and from schooling after 5:00 p.m.; and the front and rear face of a pupils' ticket valid for summer school. These ticket formats were in use from the 1950s into the early 1960s.

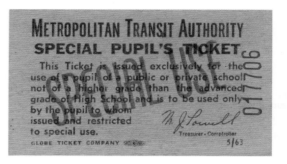

Figure 8.47 Typical MTA Special Pupil's Ticket, 1963–64

Figure 8.48 MTA Pupils-Children ID Checks, 1961–62

The MTA sold pupils-children identification checks at discounted rates. They were "issued for use by children between the ages of five and eleven inclusive, and by pupils when riding between the pupil's home and school attended when school is in session." The transfers were valid for either morning or afternoon travel. Each consisted of two parts, each valid for travel on either a rapid transit line or a surface line. Shown are afternoon checks valid in December 1961 (top) and morning checks valid in April 1962 (bottom).

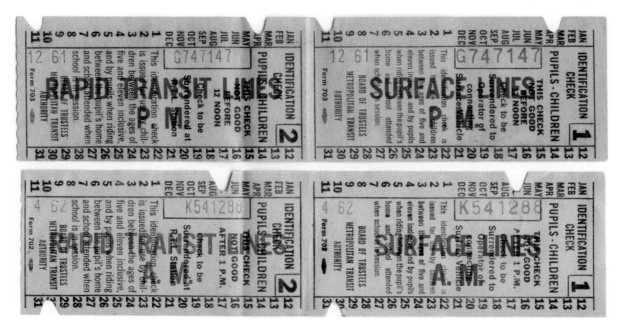

The MTA sold various types of pupils' tickets (Figure 8.46), reduced rate tickets intended for the exclusive use of students. Standard pupils' tickets were valid for one school season, typically July 30 through July 1 and only during daytime. Other pupils' tickets were valid for travel to night school and summer school. Others were "special pupil's tickets" (Figure 8.47).

Beyond simple pupils' tickets were pupils-children identification checks, a system of discounted tickets intended for use on a single day. Pupils-children identification checks were issued in sets, stapled together, and stamped with a month and year in which they were valid (Figure 8.48). If a student's route to school required travel on both rapid transit and surface lines, that student used two "A.M." tickets, one for the rapid transit portion and another for the surface line portion for their trip.

Returning home from school in the afternoon, the student used both rapid transit and surface line "P.M." tickets.

Abuse of pupils' tickets was rampant throughout both the eras of the BERy and the MTA. The MTA began to address the abuse of the pupil's fare with the creation of a ten cent children's fare and increase of the pupils' fare to ten cents, effective on May 15, 1961. The increase of the pupils' fare was the first since the fare type was established in 1919 by the BERy. Looking to finally curtail abuse of pupil's tickets, the MTA replaced paper pupil's tickets with badges in 1962.

Before the end of 1961, the MTA adjusted regular fares again. Effective October 28, surface fare became ten cents, rapid transit fare became twenty cents, and the Highland Branch maximum zone fare became forty cents. In the early 1960s, the MTA

Figure 8.49 MTA Identification Warrants, 1962–63

To receive a warrant, a rider first deposited ten, fifteen, or twenty cents into a fare box, and then, respectively, handed an additional five, ten, or twenty cents to the operator of the vehicle being boarded. If the rider alighted from the vehicle prior to a set point, the rider presented the warrant to the operator, who then returned the second payment made by the rider when obtaining the warrant.

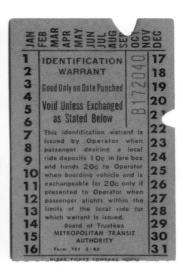
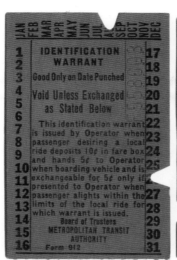

issued warrants (Figure 8.49) to riders who pre-paid a higher fare than their ride might require.

Ads on the MTA

As the BERy had before it, the MTA actively sought to increase ridership though the use of print advertising. Ads celebrated destinations accessible by taking the MTA, including Revere Beach and Franklin Park Zoo (Figure 8.50).A series of 1952 print ads featured seasonal messages including "For Fall Shopping Ride the MTA" and "Shop Early" with an image of Santa holding an ornament and reading "Season's Greetings, MTA" (Figure 8.51).

Figure 8.50 MTA Zoo Advertisement Graphic, 1952

Figure 8.51 MTA Advertisement Graphics, 1952

Explosion on the El

On the afternoon of June 11, 1959, an explosion ripped through North Station on the Main Line Elevated. Much of the station's head house was blown outwards and onto the elevated tracks over Causeway Street. Debris rained down onto Haverhill, Canal, and Causeway Streets below. An MTA inspector was killed and thirty-eight others, some of whom were MTA employees, were injured. Within minutes of the blast, hundreds of strangers, first responders, and MTA employees raced to the site of the devastation (Figure 8.52). After casualties were aided, the MTA set to work fixing severed signal lines, damaged tracks, and the partially destroyed station. By the morning of June 12, less than twenty-four hours after the explosion, the MTA performed safety tests and rapid transit service resumed through North Station on the el. The cause

of the blast was determined to have come from approximately twenty-five pounds of black powder stored in a locker.

Civil Defense

In 1961, with the Cold War intensifying and just months before the Cuban Missile Crisis amplified nuclear fears across America, the MTA coordinated with Boston to utilize MTA tunnels for emergency preparedness or in the case of a nuclear attack. The MTA estimated that one million people could be sheltered in its tunnels. The MTA received approximately $1 million worth of federal Civil Defence survival equipment and rations in 1963 alone (Figure 8.53). The allocation was a first for a transit agency in America. After the MTA tucked the supplies away in three downtown subways, the Massachusetts Civil Defence Agency ordered the establishment of an underground hospital, with 200 beds. Though there is little evidence that the subway hospital was ever established, the stashes of Civil Defense supplies remained at the ready for decades, long after the MTA and the Cold War both expired. Fortunately, none of the Civil Defense supplies in Boston's subways were used for their intended purposes. Instead, over recent decades, they have posed more of a disposal challenge than offering life-preserving aid.

A Last Big Push

After the departure of Edward Dana, the MTA ramped up efforts to improve a public transit system hobbled by increasing costs and depressed ridership and revenue. In its 1961 annual report the MTA listed its accomplishments for the year, including the "biggest face lift in the history of the transit system." The face lift included rethinking haphazardly installed and visually distracting advertising signage and the installation of both a lunch counter (Figure 8.54) and bakery concession (Figure 8.55) at Park Street Station. South Station Under, besides being the first station to be converted to token-only fare collection, was one of the first to be totally repainted and receive reconfigured advertising displays.

Beyond undertaking the face lifts, the MTA, in their own words, "institute[d] major economies, the most drastic in the history of the Authority," including reduction of payroll by over 300 positions and continued elimination of "poorly patronized" or "historic," but no longer financially viable, routes. The changes launched by the MTA in 1961, along with continued adjustments of fares and service levels, led to a first time reduction in the MTA's deficit and its first revenue increase after a decade of yearly revenue declines.

The MTA continued to fine tune services in the early 1960s, making specific adjustments to

Figure 8.54 Lunch Counter at Park Street Station, 1961
The MTA sanctioned the installation of an eighty-foot-long food concession along the eastern edge of the northbound platform at Park Street Station.

Figure 8.55 Bakery at Park Street Station, 1961
As part of the MTA's early 1960s station improvement program, a bakery concession was installed at Park Street Station.

streetcar subway service in 1961, including the turning at North Station of northbound cars running from Beacon Street through the Tremont Street Subway. As well, cars running from Commonwealth Avenue into the subway began to be turned at Park Street Station. In 1961 the MTA cut back rush hour service to Everett by fifty percent, terminating every other elevated train at Sullivan Square Station. By 1963 the MTA suspended service to Everett Terminal after 8:00 p.m. on weekdays and Saturdays. Service was discontinued entirely on Sundays and holidays.

A major part of the MTA's last big push included the 1961 purchase of 125 new diesel buses and ninety-two new rapid transit cars for the Cambridge-Dorchester line. On the cover of its 1962 annual report the MTA featured lively renderings of its new rapid transit cars and buses. The renderings were accompanied by the optimistic caption "The Wheels of the NEW Boston!" (Figure 8.1). The buses, built by General Motors (GM), entered service in late 1961 and early 1962. Seventy five of the new buses replaced seventy-five gasoline buses retired by the MTA. As part of the MTA's 1960s-era mission to eliminate trackless trolleys from its rosters, it deployed fifty of the new buses to replace trackless trolleys.

The MTA designated its new rapid transit cars as Cambridge-Dorchester Type 5 models and assigned them 1400-series numbers. The cars were built by

Figure 8.56 Cambridge-Dorchester Type 5 Cars, March 1961
An exterior elevation (top), a plan showing ceiling elements dashed (middle), and a longitudinal section (bottom), articulate the dimensions, configurations, and major components of the MTA's Cambridge-Dorchester Type 5 rapid transit cars. Ninety-two of the cars, also known as "Blue Birds," were put into service in the early 1960s.

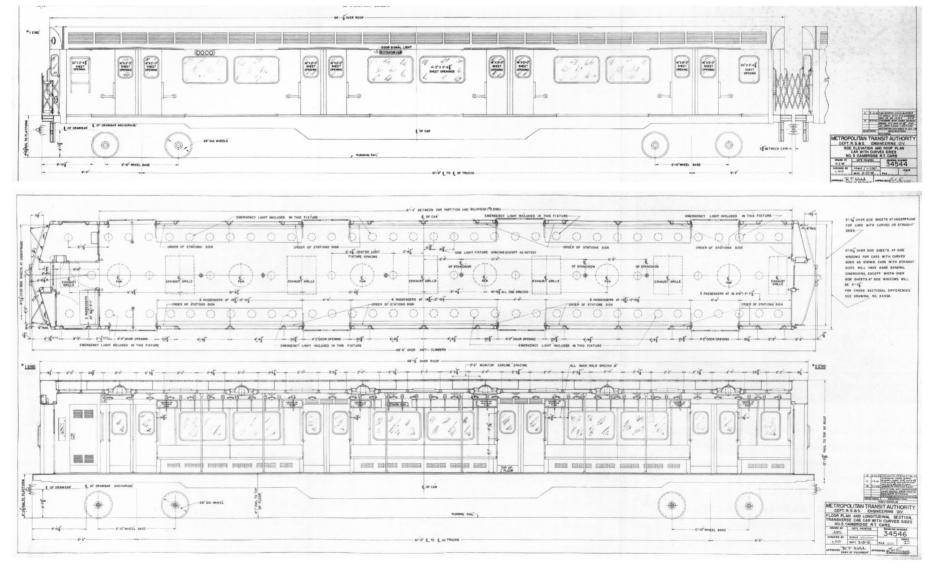

Figure 8.57 "Blue Bird" Cars, September, 1972
A train of 1400-series Cambridge-Dorchester cars arrives at Charles Station. The ten-year-old cars wear both their original MTA-era paint scheme and the MBTA's logos.

Figure 8.58 MTA "Blue Bird" Rapid Transit Car, Circa 1963
A staged photograph reveals the brightly lit interior of a new Cambridge-Dorchester Type 5 rapid transit car. A backlit Order of Stations sign is mounted above the seated passenger.

Figure 8.59 MTA "Blue Bird" Order of Stations Sign, 1962
A plastic Order of Stations sign from a Cambridge-Dorchester Type 5 rapid transit car lists stations from Harvard to Ashmont.

Pullman-Standard in 1962–63 (Figure 8.56) and measured nearly seventy feet in length. Each car featured bench-style seating and stainless steel hand-holds for standees. Four pairs of doors on each side expedited loading and unloading. The exteriors of Type 5 cars were painted blue and gold, colors used on the state seal and flag of the Commonwealth of Massachusetts. Blue was used on the lower portion and white on the upper portion of the cars. Along the sides of each car a gold stripe separated the blue and white areas. At the ends of each car, the gold expanded into a double wing-like shape (Figure 8.57). The winged paint scheme helped Type 5 rapid transit cars gain the nickname "Blue Birds."

The Blue Birds entered service with updated versions of Order of Stations signs featuring black sans-serif lettering printed onto translucent plastic (Figure 8.58). Each sign was backlit by electric light (Figure 8.59). Gone were the metal Order of Stations signs found in older rapid transit cars. When the Blue Birds entered service in 1962–63,

the Cambridge-Dorchester rapid transit line was operational between Harvard Square and Ashmont. All stops between Harvard Square and Ashmont, including both termini, were displayed on each 1962 Order of Stations sign.

The MTA formally unveiled the Blue Birds on April 24, 1963. Despite being the first new rapid transit cars constructed for the Cambridge-Dorchester rapid transit line since 1928, the Blue Birds were known to have uncomfortable seating, be hot in the summer, and make excessive noise all of the time. As a cost saving measure, upholstered seats and air conditioning were value engineered out of the cars during their design phase. By the end of 1963, service on the Cambridge-Dorchester rapid transit line was mostly provided with Blue Birds. The iconic cars were mostly out of service by the mid-1990s, though the MBTA upgraded a handful of the vehicles in 1995. No Blue Birds remain in regular service today.

Figure 8.60 The MTA's Safety Patrol Car, 1962

Complementing new revenue vehicles deployed by the MTA in the early 1960s was the Authority's "safety patrol car," a sedan, complete with a rotating light on its roof (Figure 8.60). From the MTA's 1962 annual report:

> The driver, covering approximately 200 miles each 24 hours inspects rolling stock while in operation; checks personnel; observes and corrects traffic and operating irregularities and generally promotes a better and safer operation. Plans for the future: More of the same.

The Reading Extension

In 1961 the MTA applied for federal grants to fund the removal of Boston's elevated railway lines and the construction of a new rapid transit line from Boston to the town of Reading. The removal of the els was mandated by the legislature. The Reading Extension was proposed by transportation planners as early as 1926 (Figure 6.19). It also showed up on the 1945 map of the Metropolitan Transit Recess Commission (Figure 6.75). As proposed by the MTA in 1961 (Figure 8.61), the Reading Extension was to run northward from downtown Boston, through Charlestown, along the eastern edge of Medford, and then through the cities of Malden, Melrose, and Wakefield. The MTA proposed a terminus for the line in Reading, at Massachusetts Route 128 (now Interstate 95), Boston's first circumferential highway. The Reading Extension was to be the first rapid transit line to extend beyond the MTA's fourteen-city service area.

Following the Highland Branch template for the conversion of a railroad right-of-way into a transit line to collect riders from an expanding suburbia, the MTA proposed the Reading Extension follow a Boston & Maine Railroad (Boston & Maine) right-of-way. North of Sullivan Square, the MTA proposed three intermediate stations, one each for Malden, Melrose, and Wakefield. All of the stations, along with a terminal at Route 128, were to have a Park & Ride lot. The Reading Extension was never realized as laid out by the MTA. Instead, a truncated version, an extension of the MBTA's Orange Line rapid transit line from North Station to northern Malden, was opened by the MBTA in the mid-1970s.

Real Estate Consolidations

Two significant aspects of the MTA's final push were its consolidation of real estate holdings and the construction of a new headquarters building. Located along the Arborway in Boston's Jamaica Plain neighborhood, the new MTA headquarters allowed the MTA to become its own landlord and eliminate the leasing costs of its downtown offices, inherited from the BERy. Before moving to the Arborway, the MTA was based in the Park Square Building at 31 Saint James Avenue in Boston. There, the MTA's predecessor, the BERy, had established its offices by 1923. The Park Square Building and the neighboring Hotel Statler (now the Park Plaza Hotel) opened in 1927 on lands made available after the 1909 demolition of the Boston & Providence Railroad's Park Square depots.

In 1962, the MTA solicited bids for the purchase of nearly half a million square feet of its land occupied by Bennett Street Yards in Harvard Square. The land was no longer needed for the MTA's small streetcar fleet and the Authority was in the process of relocating its Bennett Street bus and trackless trolley storage and maintenance facilities. In time, the MBTA completed the sale of not only the Bennett Street lands, but also that of neighboring Eliot Square rapid transit facilities. The MTA undertook additional consolidations of facilities in 1963, when it closed car houses at Clarendon Hill (Somerville), Union Square (Somerville), and Everett.

The 1963 Ten-Year Plan

During the last complete calendar year of its existence, 1963, the MTA presented a "Ten-Year Plan" at a Boston College Citizens' Seminar. Boston College started the seminars in 1954 as roundtables for civic discussion. With its Ten-Year Plan, the MTA proposed: constructing the Reading Extension; extending the Huntington Avenue Subway westward, to the Museum of Fine Arts; extending the Boylston Street Subway to the Cottage Farm Bridge (a.k.a. the Boston University Bridge); augmenting

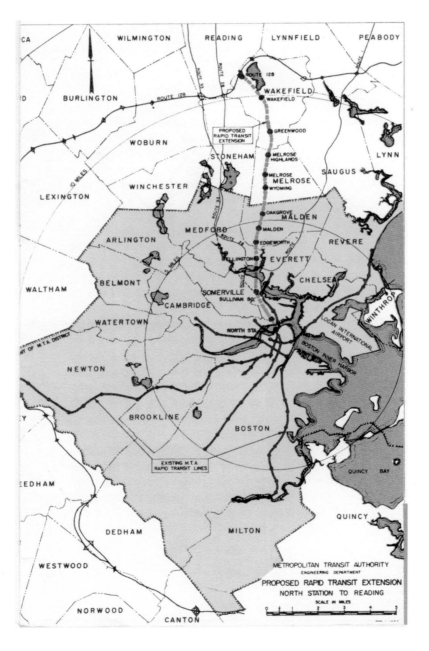

Figure 8.61 Mapping the Reading Extension, 1961
The MTA's proposed Reading Extension is highlighted as a dashed red line running north from Boston. Existing MTA rapid transit and high speed trolley lines are represented as black lines. The MTA's service area is highlighted in yellow.

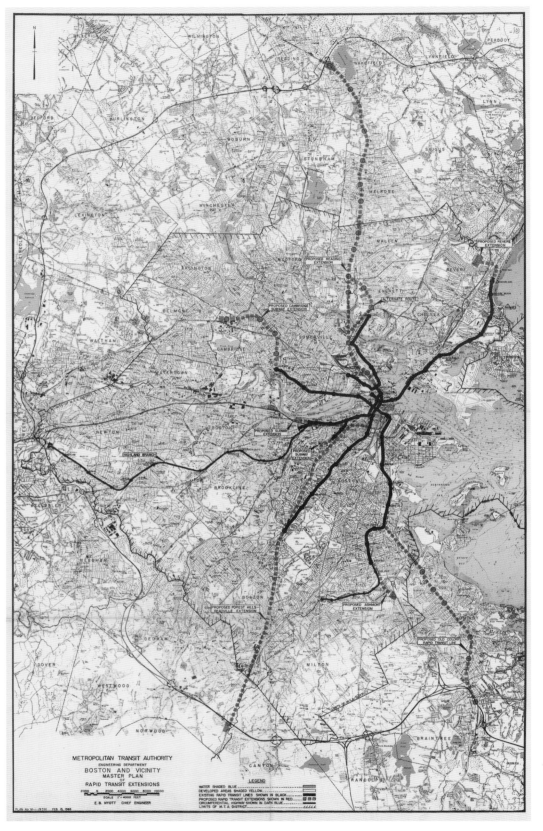

Figure 8.62 The MTA's Ten-Year Master Plan Map, 1963
Existing rapid transit, streetcar subway, and high speed trolley lines (thick black lines) are augmented by proposed extensions (dashed red lines).

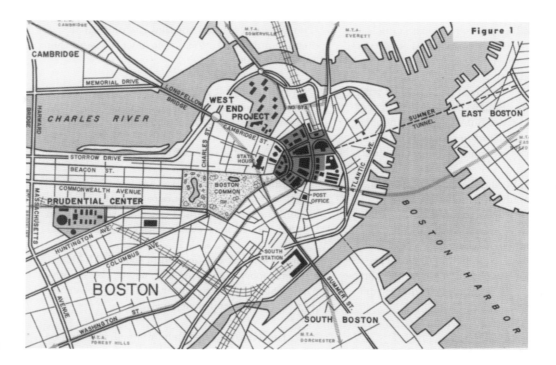

Figure 8.63 Locating the Government Center Project, 1959

the Washington Street Tunnel with a new rapid transit line running from downtown to the town of Westwood; extending the Revere Extension to a new parking lot and terminus beyond Wonderland Terminal; and extending the Cambridge-Dorchester rapid transit line northward, into North Cambridge, and southward, through Quincy and into Braintree. The proposed expansions were mapped for presentation at the seminar (Figure 8.62).

The Ten-Year Plan was ambitious in scope, perhaps encouraged by a potential new source of funding, federal urban mass transit funds. Before the U.S. Department of Transportation became a chief distributor of federal funds for public transportation in America, the U.S. Urban Mass Transportation Administration (UMTA) was the main source of federal funding for public transit projects. Late in 1963, the Commonwealth authorized further study of some of the extensions proposed in the MTA's Ten-Year Plan. Massachusetts also approved the acceptance of federal grant money for early planning of some of the projects.

The MTA continuously sought to corral new automobile commuters throughout 1963, making forays beyond simple parking lots at stations. The MTA's Park & Ride Program, a later phase of the 1963 MTA-MTC experimental bus route program (see Chapter 5), encouraged commuters to park at specific drive-in theaters during the day. MTA buses then collected commuters from the drive-ins

(Figure 7.72). The drive-in program never caught on and did not last. Patrons preferred parking directly at a station.

Government Center Station

The MTA broke ground on the renovation of Scollay Square and Scollay Under Stations on February 12, 1963. The work took place below ground, while above, a massive urban renewal project remade the cityscape. The station upgrades were funded by federal urban mass transit funds, administered to the MTA through the Boston Redevelopment Authority (now the Boston Planning & Development Agency). At street-level, around Scollay Square, the wholesale demolition of a portion of Boston's historic downtown was also paid for with federal dollars, in the form of urban renewal funds. Scollay Square and surrounding acres of urbanity were replaced with Government Center, a series of towers and office blocks, many containing federal, state, and city offices (Figure 8.63). At the heart of the renewal area, a new city hall rose for Boston in the middle of a vast open plaza.

As part of the Government Center project, the MTA made significant changes to the Tremont Street Subway. The tunnels running from Scollay Square Station to Haymarket Station via Adams Square Station, tunnels through which northbound trolleys ran under Cornhill since 1898, were mostly demolished. The MTA replaced the lost tunnels with a new tunnel for northbound cars, constructed using the cut and cover method. At Haymarket Station, the central two of the station's four streetcar tracks were removed and replaced with a new platform. Adams Square Station was severed from the Tremont Street Subway and abandoned. Though Brattle Street Station was eliminated, the Brattle Loop was reconfigured to maintain its overall function.

The MTA retired Scollay Square and Scollay Under Stations' names on October 10, 1963. Government Center Station opened to the public on October 28, 1963. All work on the station was complete by the middle of 1964, mere weeks before the MBTA would take over the MTA. Government Center Station opened with a new head house (Figure 8.64) as well as renovated escalators and interiors (Figure 8.65).

Strong Words

Despite its efforts during the early 1960s, the MTA was unable to definitively overcome ridership declines, financial problems, and a limited service area. In its annual report for 1962, the MTA's Board of Trustees wondered, after citing an almost fifty-four percent drop in ridership from 1946:

> What happened to the happy commuter of 1946? What punctured the popularity of the commuting service he used?

The Trustees pointed out that the municipalities around the San Francisco bay area were then investing $800M:

> …to build what essentially, Boston and the M.T.A. district already owns—one of the finest mass transportation systems in the country.

The MTA sought to bring to the public's attention:

> …what is missing [in Boston] thus far, is an absolute, clear-cut mandate from the citizenry and their representatives…as to the direction… that the Authority henceforth set its course.

In a "Declaration" printed in the MTA's 1963 annual report, the Board of Trustees begged for the creation of a new, larger, and more powerful regional transit authority, writing:

> …the M.T.A. by itself and in itself, is facing no transportation problem. It was set up to serve fourteen cities and towns, no one of which suffers a transportation problem - or if it does, an easily adjusted bus or rapid transit schedule will rectify the matter. THE CRISIS EXISTS BEYOND THE M.T.A.'S BORDERS. THE M.T.A. CANNOT, ON ITS OWN, ACT TO HELP THESE PEOPLE. THE M.T.A. CAN ONLY SUGGEST, OR PROD OR URGE. Others must provide the real, physical help which these people so desperately need.

Figure 8.64 Government Center Station Head House, 1963
The bunker-like head house for Government Center Station squats at the edge of the sea of brick that is City Hall Plaza. The head house was demolished in 2014.

Figure 8.65 Government Center Station Interior, 1963
Escalators and stairs lead up to street-level from the streetcar platform at Government Center. The escalator and stairs lead into the station's 1963 head house (Figure 8.64).

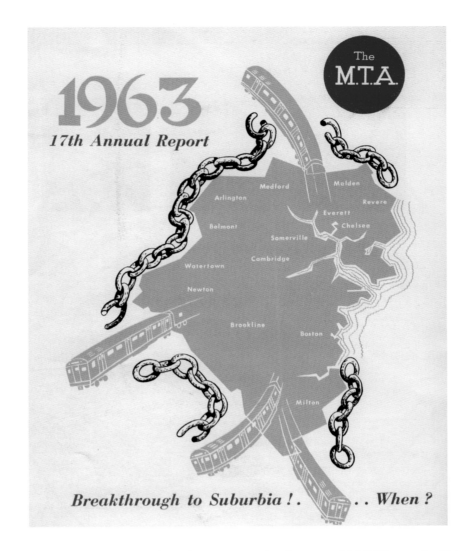

Figure 8.66 The MTA's Seventeenth Annual Report, 1963

To accompany and reinforce its strong words, the MTA published a striking image on the cover of its 1963 annual report, rapid transit trains forcefully breaking through chains surrounding the MTA's service area (Figure 8.66). Within a year of the report's issuance, the chains were indeed broken, but not by the MTA. They were snapped by the Commonwealth's replacement for the MTA, the MBTA.

At the End of the MTA-era

At the end of 1963, and six months before it was taken over by the MBTA, the MTA counted seven garages, two car houses, three rapid transit car houses, and the centralized shops at Everett among it holdings. An inventory of MTA vehicles listed: 793 buses, over 700 of which were diesel-powered; 160 trackless trolleys; 306 rapid transit cars; and 344 PCC cars. An October 23, 1963 map shows the MTA's routes and trackage, along with headways for transit vehicles that travelled along each (Figure 8.67).

By the end of 1963, the MTA was well aware of the problems that an automobile-centric landscape coupled with a decentralized population had brought to Greater Boston. The MTA's service area limited the Authority's ability to serve Greater Boston's exploding suburban population. Enabled by federally subsidized highways, area commuters were living further and further afield from Boston's historic core. In addition, the railroads connecting Boston with its expanding suburbia were seeking permission to discontinue money-losing passenger services throughout the region. If the railroads ceased commuter rail operations, the MTA would not be able to replace those services nor even reach most of the customers.

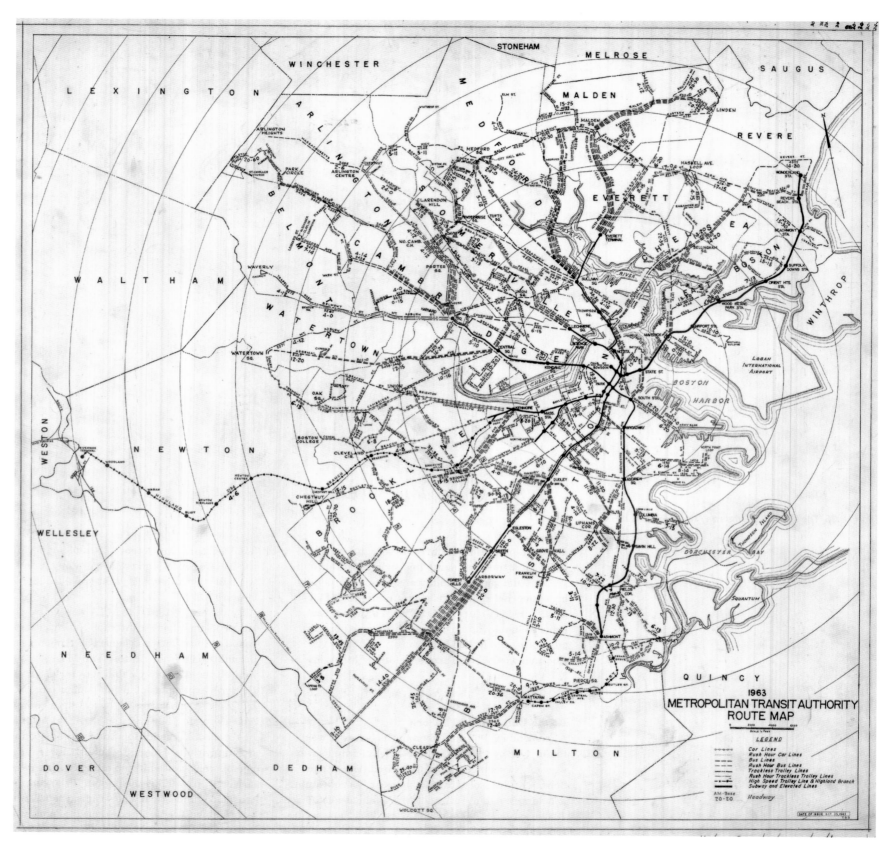

1963
METROPOLITAN TRANSIT AUTHORITY
ROUTE MAP

LEGEND

Car Lines
Rush Hour Car Lines
Bus Lines
Rush Hour Bus Lines
Trackless Trolley Lines
Rush Hour Trackless Trolley Lines
High Speed Trolley Line & Highland Branch
Subway and Elevated Lines

AM-Base
70-70   Headway

Figure 8.67 (Opposite) MTA Route Map, October 23, 1963
A 1963 map shows the streetcar, bus, trackless trolley, high speed trolley, and rapid transit lines of the MTA. Different line types distinguish regular and rush hours services. Headway times are shown for each surface line.

Figure 8.68 (Below) MTA Route Schedule Cards, Spring 1964
Examples from one of two editions of MTA pocket-sized route schedule cards. The MBTA continued to revise and reissue route cards with this format until the late 1970s.

During the late 1950s and early 1960s, the Commonwealth did what it historically did when public transportation for Greater Boston was in crisis: it created commissions and inspired studies to be undertaken. The most significant commission was the Massachusetts Rapid Transit Recess Commission (MTRC). The MTRC presented an optimistic view of suburbia, claiming Boston's suburbs were where the city's future lay. The MTRC reported that public transit service between Boston and the suburbs could be financially self-sustaining if the geographic area of the MTA, or a replacement for it, was made large enough. Responding to the MTRC's recommendations, the General Court approved the creation of the largest public entity

to ever oversee public transportation in Massachusetts, the MBTA.

The MTA did not exist in vain. It was Massachusetts' first venture into complete public ownership and operation of public transportation for Greater Boston. The MTA pushed the Commonwealth to understand that public transportation for Boston was a regional concept. The MTA was a stepping stone towards something larger; it was a bridge between privately developed and publicly operated transportation and publicly owned, subsidized, and operated transit for Greater Boston. Of the MTA's final productions and printed legacies was a series of pocket-sized route schedule cards for spring 1964 (Figure 8.68). Months after the cards were released, the MTA ceased to exist.

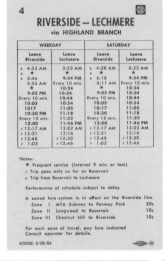
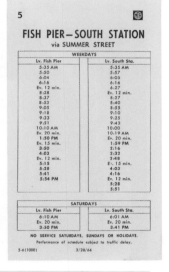
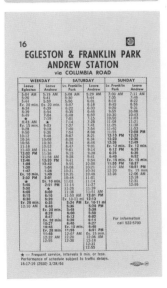
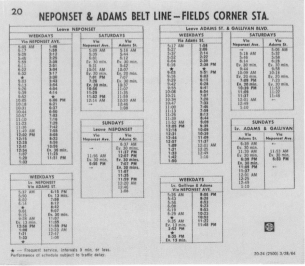

FIRST ANNUAL REPORT 1965
MASSACHUSETTS BAY TRANSPORTATION AUTHORITY

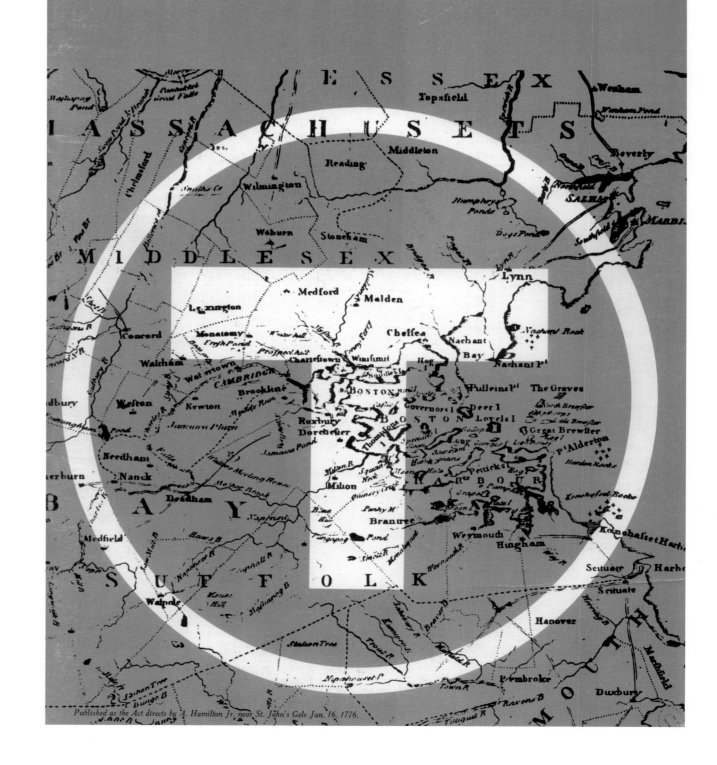

CHAPTER 9

The Massachusetts Bay Transportation Authority

Enter the MBTA

334 years after Boston's founders first established transportation for the public, the Massachusetts Bay Transportation Authority arrived to take the reins of public transit for the city. Chapter 563 of the Acts of 1964 created Chapter 161A of the General Laws of the Commonwealth. This legislation dissolved the Metropolitan Transportation Authority (MTA) and established its replacement, the Massachusetts Bay Transportation Authority (MBTA; T; the Authority). The T took over the geographically-constricted MTA and established a broader service area of seventy-eight cities and towns, all contiguous around Massachusetts Bay. The MBTA's mission was made clear by its establishing legislation:

> The [MBTA] shall have the duty to develop, finance and operate the mass transportation facilities and equipment in the public interest... and to achieve maximum effectiveness in complementing other forms of transportation in order to promote the general economic and social well-being of the area and the Commonwealth.

At the time of the MBTA's creation, the president of the American Transit Association described Chapter 563 as, "unquestionably the most daring and provocative legislative action ever taken by a state government in support of transit."

The MBTA came to life overseen by a Board of Directors and an Advisory Board. Shortly after 5:00 p.m. on August 3, 1964, the first Board of Directors was sworn in by Governor Endicott Peabody. On

the following day, the headline of the *Boston Globe* morning edition read: "MBTA Sworn In—$225 Million Transport Plan Starts—MTA Dead." On August 5, the MBTA Board of Directors held its first formal meeting. The five-person group consisted of one chairman and four members, all appointed by the governor. The MBTA Advisory Board, composed of representatives from each of the MBTA's constituent municipalities, provided public oversight of MBTA expenditures, consulted with the Authority to maximize the quality of service, and assisted in coordinating capital planning.

As required by its initiating legislation, the MBTA became an active participant in Boston's regional planning process. The Authority collaborated with entities including the Boston Redevelopment Authority (BRA; now Boston Planning and Development Agency) and the Metropolitan Area Planning Council (MAPC) (Figure 9.2). The BRA, established by the city of Boston and the Commonwealth in 1957, became Boston's planning and development arm in 1960. MAPC was created by the Commonwealth in 1963 as the regional planning entity for Greater Boston. The collaborative actions of the MBTA were recognized by the federal government in 1967, when the U.S. Department of Housing and Urban Development (HUD) issued an award to the MBTA for "outstanding contributions to intergovernmental relations." Since inception, the MBTA has participated in countless transportation planning studies, proposals, and collaborations.

In the same year that the MBTA came into existence, the federal Urban Mass Transportation Act of 1964 took effect. The Act was an early meaningful

Figure 9.1 (Opposite) The MBTA Arrives, 1965
The MBTA's logo lies superimposed upon a 1776 map of Greater Boston and Massachusetts Bay.

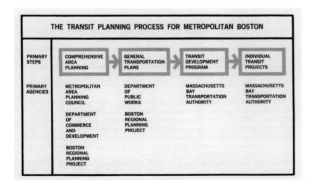

Figure 9.2 Transportation Planning Structure, 1965
A chart articulates Boston's planning entities, roles, and hierarchical relationship at the dawn of the MBTA era.

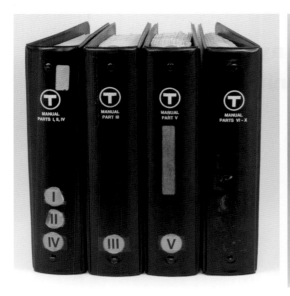

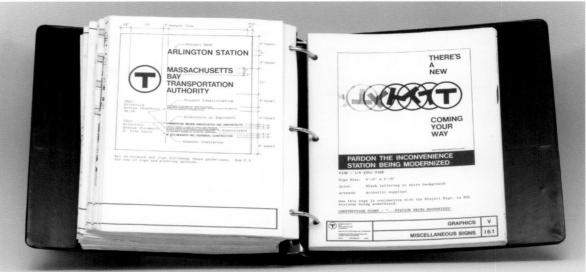

mechanism for the distribution of federal funding for public transportation, then referred to as mass transit. The first federal grant made to a mass transit system under the Urban Mass Transportation Act went to the MBTA.

Since 1964, MBTA operations and capital improvements have been funded from a variety of sources, including fare revenue, federal grants, state allocations, bonds, assessments upon constituent municipalities, and non-fare revenue. Non-fare revenue includes that collected from advertising, the sale and leasing of Authority property, and the licensing of MBTA trademarks. The MBTA issued its first bonds in 1967. Municipal assessments initiated by the MTA were continued and evolved by the MBTA.

A young MBTA described the cost of operations that exceeded available funding as its "net cost of service," much of which was billed to constituent communities as assessments. The MBTA argued:

> The Net Cost of Service to the Communities reflects the reality that public transportation service is essential to the economic health of the metropolitan area, and should no more be expected to return a "profit" than other essential services such as police, fire, and public works.

The Manual of Guidelines and Standards

Within its first eighteen months, the MBTA engaged Cambridge Seven, a Cambridge-based architecture firm, to redesign the public face of the Authority. Cambridge Seven analyzed existing conditions and proposed improvements for everything public-facing, including: branding, signage, maps, wayfinding devices, lighting, colors, vehicle aesthetics, and station architecture.

Cambridge Seven codified their vision for the MBTA into a ten-part set of documents, the *Manual of Guidelines and Standards* (Figure 9.3). The *Manual* contained thousands of specifications, diagrams, plans, and design directives. The "General Introduction" of the *Manual* confirmed its raison d'etre as "the need for orientation. The rider must not only be physically comfortable, he must know in the full sense where he is and where he is going." A memorandum signed by MBTA General Manager Rush B. Lincoln, Jr. on December 1, 1966 formalized the *Manual of Guidelines and Standards* for "the use of all Authority departments and outside consultants who are involved in modernization and expansion programs."

In Section III of the *Manual*, Cambridge Seven documented the existing conditions of all but three of the forty stations the MBTA sought to modernize. Drawings recorded inefficient pedestrian circulation, outdated lighting, and messy interiors. Correspondingly, the designers laid out proposals for streamlining circulation, upgrading lighting, and improving interiors for stations. Pairs of drawings, each composed of one "existing" conditions and one "proposed" architecture (Figure 9.4), served to document where the T was and serve as road maps of where the Authority should go as it embarked on the largest station modernization program in Boston's history.

Figure 9.3 Manual of Guidelines and Standards
A well-used copy of the *Manual of Guidelines and Standards* was photographed in 2014.

Figure 9.4 Preparing to Improve Harvard Station, 1966
Drawings document existing (top) and proposed (bottom) conditions at the uppermost of the two underground levels at Harvard Station. Dotted lines mark circulation paths of pedestrians, entering, exiting, and transferring at the station. Elevations show cluttered (before) and streamlined (after) interiors.

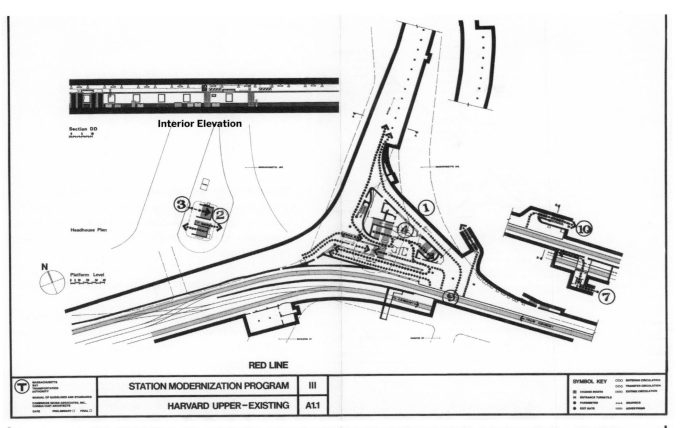

Interior Elevation

Section DD

Headhouse Plan

N

Platform Level

RED LINE

MASSACHUSETTS
BAY
TRANSPORTATION
AUTHORITY

MANUAL OF GUIDELINES AND STANDARDS

CAMBRIDGE SEVEN ASSOCIATES, INC.,
CONSULTANT ARCHITECTS

DATE   PRELIMINARY ☐   FINAL ☐

STATION MODERNIZATION PROGRAM | III

HARVARD UPPER–EXISTING | A1.1

SYMBOL KEY

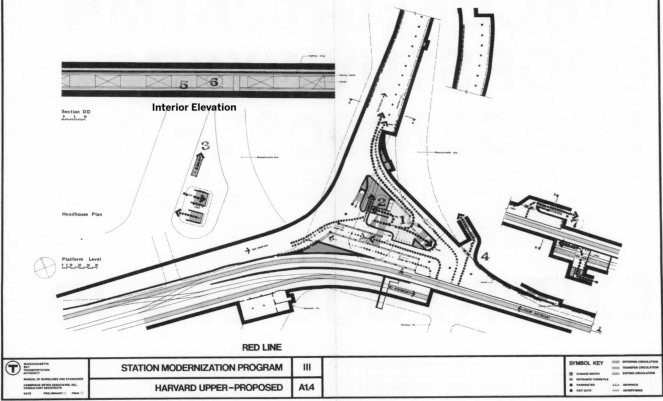

Interior Elevation

Section DD

Headhouse Plan

Platform Level

RED LINE

MASSACHUSETTS
BAY
TRANSPORTATION
AUTHORITY

MANUAL OF GUIDELINES AND STANDARDS

CAMBRIDGE SEVEN ASSOCIATES, INC.,
CONSULTANT ARCHITECTS

DATE   PRELIMINARY ☐   FINAL ☐

STATION MODERNIZATION PROGRAM | III

HARVARD UPPER–PROPOSED | A1.4

SYMBOL KEY

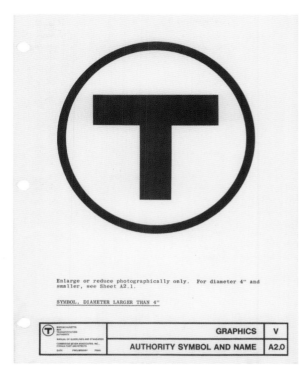

Enlarge or reduce photographically only. For diameter 4" and smaller, see Sheet A2.1.

SYMBOL, DIAMETER LARGER THAN 4"

	GRAPHICS	V
MASSACHUSETTS BAY TRANSPORTATION AUTHORITY / MANUAL OF GUIDELINES AND STANDARDS / CAMBRIDGE SEVEN ASSOCIATES, INC., CONSULTANT ARCHITECTS / DATE PRELIMINARY FINAL	AUTHORITY SYMBOL AND NAME	A2.0

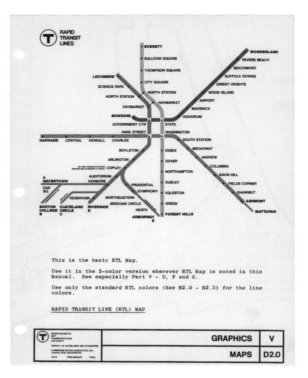

This is the basic RTL Map.

Use it in the 5-color version wherever RTL Map is noted in this Manual. See especially Part V - D, F and G.

Use only the standard RTL colors (See B2.0 - B2.3) for the line colors.

RAPID TRANSIT LINE (RTL) MAP

	GRAPHICS	V
MASSACHUSETTS BAY TRANSPORTATION AUTHORITY / MANUAL OF GUIDELINES AND STANDARDS / CAMBRIDGE SEVEN ASSOCIATES, INC., CONSULTANT ARCHITECTS / DATE PRELIMINARY FINAL	MAPS	D2.0

Figure 9.5 (Left) MBTA Symbol Master Sheet, 1966

The team at Cambridge Seven included brothers Peter and Ivan Chermayeff. After his work on the T's logo in the 1960s, Ivan went on to create iconic logos for Pan American Airways, NBC, and the United Nations.

Figure 9.6 (Right) MBTA Rapid Transit Lines Map, 1966

Figure 9.7 (Below) Lettering Specification Sheet, 1966

"Alphabet and Spacing Rules for Opaque Lettering" serve as some of the guidelines for the most minute portions of the MBTA's redesign.

LETTER SPACING

A-A = 1 units
A-C = 2 units
A-S = 3½ units
C-C = 4 units
C-S = 5 units
S-S = 7 units

(A = angle letter, C = curve letter, S = straight letter)

WORD SPACING

A-A = 14 units
A-C = 15 units
A-S = 17 units
C-C = 18 units
C-S = 19 units
S-S = 22 units

SCALE OF SPACING UNITS
32 UNITS = CAP HEIGHT

Use clear film sheet with scales for various letter heights, C4.0.

SPECIAL SPACING CONDITIONS - See C2.1 and C2.2

This alphabet is "Helvetica" medium. For applications requiring small sizes, type or proofs can be ordered from most compositors.

Alphabets also available in wax transfer letters by "Letraset" Co. from most artists' or architects' suppliers, and in pre-cut films for pressure sensitive exterior and interior applications.

OPAQUE SIGNS - ALPHABET AND SPACING RULES

	GRAPHICS	V
MASSACHUSETTS BAY TRANSPORTATION AUTHORITY / MANUAL OF GUIDELINES AND STANDARDS / CAMBRIDGE SEVEN ASSOCIATES, INC., CONSULTANT ARCHITECTS / DATE PRELIMINARY FINAL	LETTERING	C 2.0

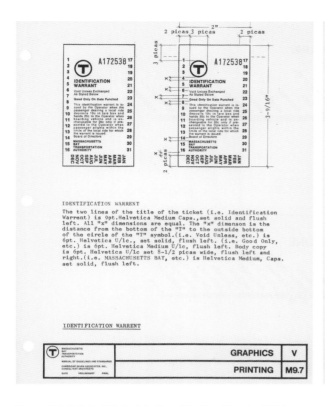

Figure 9.8 Printed Materials Specification Sheets, 1966
Specifications for identification warrants (left), letterhead (middle), and business cards (right) were codified in the *Manual of Guidelines and Standards*.

Section V of the *Manual* was packed with specifications for what the MBTA would need to communicate graphically, including: the Authority symbol (Figure 9.5), a rapid transit map (Figure 9.6), fonts and lettering (Figure 9.7), tickets, letterhead, business cards (Figure 9.8), vehicle painting (Figure 9.9), station signage (Figure 9.10), and transit line maps (Figure 9.11).

The Authority's symbol, designed by Cambridge Seven and codified in the *Manual*, was a black circle

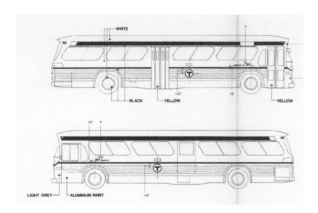

Figure 9.9 Vehicle Painting Diagrams for Buses, 1966

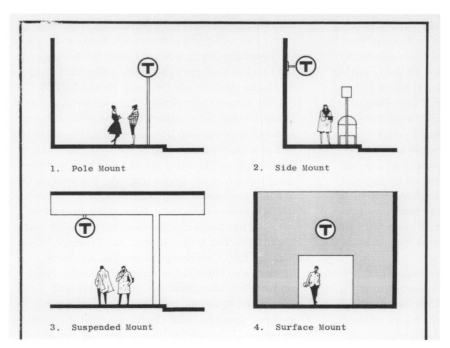

Figure 9.10 Locations for "T" Station Signage, 1966

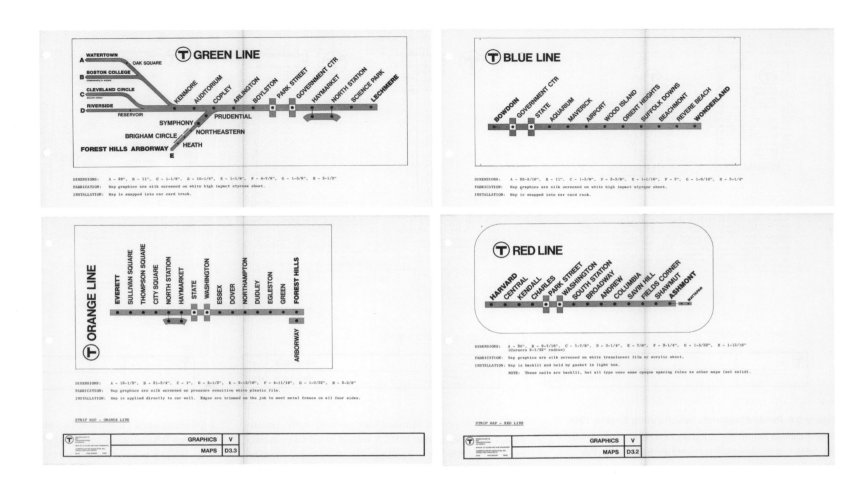

GREEN LINE · **BLUE LINE** · **ORANGE LINE** · **RED LINE** strip maps

Figure 9.11 MBTA Line Maps, 1966

The *Manual of Guidelines and Standards* contained "Strip Maps" for the MBTA's newly colored lines. Each map was designed to be printed onto panels to be installed within revenue vehicles of a corresponding line. The Red Line strip map (bottom right), with its chamfered edges, was printed onto translucent acrylic to replace Order of Stations panels in "Blue Bird" rapid transit cars.

enclosing a truncated and capitalized Helvetica "T." It was an identifying mark of supreme clarity with which the MBTA continues to brand itself. The catalog from 1967's "Design In Transit" exhibit at Boston's Institute of Contemporary Art (ICA) explained that the logo was based on then existing transit system symbols, including those of the Montreal Metro, the Stockholm Tunel-Banan, and the London Underground. The ICA's exhibit catalog went so far as to propose that the T could become a universal symbol for public transit around the world. While it may not have become an international standard, the T did become an undisputed icon in Boston. The ability to use phrases such as "ride the T," and the fact that the words transportation, tunnel, tube, and transit all begin with the letter, fortified the T as the symbol for public transit in Boston.

Section V of the *Manual* included another iconic graphic for the MBTA, a diagrammatic rapid transit line map (Figure 9.6). With its clean lines, each drawn in one of four vibrant colors, uncluttered capitalized Helvetica Medium text, and a stark white background, the map epitomized mid-twentieth century modernist graphic design. The map was graphically austere, lacking relative geography and topographic content. It harkened back to the groundbreaking work of Henry Beck mapping the London Underground in the 1930s (See Chapter 6). Cambridge Seven's 1966 map for the MBTA quickly gained the nickname "the spider map," as it loosely resembled a spider's construction, with four stations in downtown Boston holding the center of a web of transit lines radiating out to invisible points of attachment. An early printed and widely circulated version of the spider map was featured on the MBTA's first wallet map (Figure 9.12).

The colors of each line on the spider map were assigned by Cambridge Seven in consultation with the MBTA. The trolley lines of the Tremont Street Subway, East Cambridge Extension, Kenmore Subway, and Huntington Avenue Subway, as well as the Watertown, Boston College, Cleveland Circle, and Riverside branches, were collectively assigned green because the lines served the western streetcar suburbs with their tree-lined streets.

Figure 9.12 MBTA Wallet Map, Circa 1966
The MBTA's first wallet map features a spider map on one face (top) and an early MBTA slogan on the other (bottom).

The East Boston Tunnel Line and Revere Extension received a blue designation, reflecting the line's routing beneath Boston Harbor and along Revere Beach. The Cambridge-Dorchester rapid transit line was assigned a deep red, echoing the official crimson of Harvard College. Though a distinct streetcar line and not part of the Cambridge-Dorchester rapid transit line, the Mattapan High Speed Line received Red Line designation in mid-1965. The Charlestown Elevated, Washington Street Tunnel, Washington Street Elevated, and Forest Hills Extension were collectively assigned orange. The Orange Line followed Washington Street, a section of which, along with a string of connecting streets following the old Boston Neck, had long ago been renamed from Orange Street, to commemorate George Washington's first visit to Boston as President of the United States.

The *Manual* contained master sheets for each of the MBTA's first set of official colors (Figure 9.13). The now-familiar yellow accents for buses, purple for the commuter rail, and silver for the Silver Line came later. While the colors for the rapid transit lines assigned in 1966 remain in use, two dull grays initially intended for revenue service vehicles were short-lived. After only a handful of vehicles received the uninspiring tones, the MBTA began color-coding vehicles with their respective lines. A few vehicles that paraded around in the late 1960s dour gray schemes were referred to as "gray ghosts," due to their color as well as their rarity of being sited. In time, gray ghosts were repainted or decommissioned.

Section V of the *Manual* called for the installation of new signage throughout both existing and new transit stations. Horizontal ribbons of signage, each divided horizontally into at least two sections

Figure 9.13 MBTA Colors Master Sheets, 1966
Each of the first batch of official MBTA colors was specified by its own master sheet within the *Manual of Guidelines and Standards*. Green was for trolley lines. A Red, Blue, and Orange were assigned to a corresponding rapid transit line. A yellow-orange (top right) was for service vehicles and highlighting doors on revenue vehicles. One of two different shades of gray (bottom right; only one shown) were intended for most revenue vehicles but did not see widespread or long term application.

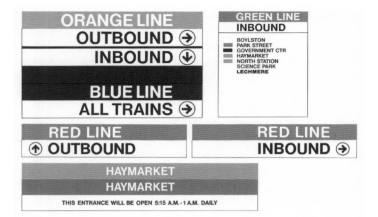

Figure 9.14 Prototypical MBTA Station Signage, 1966
The uppermost portion of each signage "ribbon" was reserved for white text of a station or line name set on a background color of the appropriate transit line. Below each ribbon's colored section was a white portion of varying height. The height was a factor of the function of the particular sign. Black text, smaller than that of the station or line name above, was used in the lower white portion. The black text clarified a station's secondary name—"Washington" beneath "Downtown Crossing," for example—or provided directional information—"exit to street," "outbound," etc. Variants of ribbons for transfer stations featured two colored portions stacked.

Figure 9.15 Station Wall Panel Specification Sheet, 1966

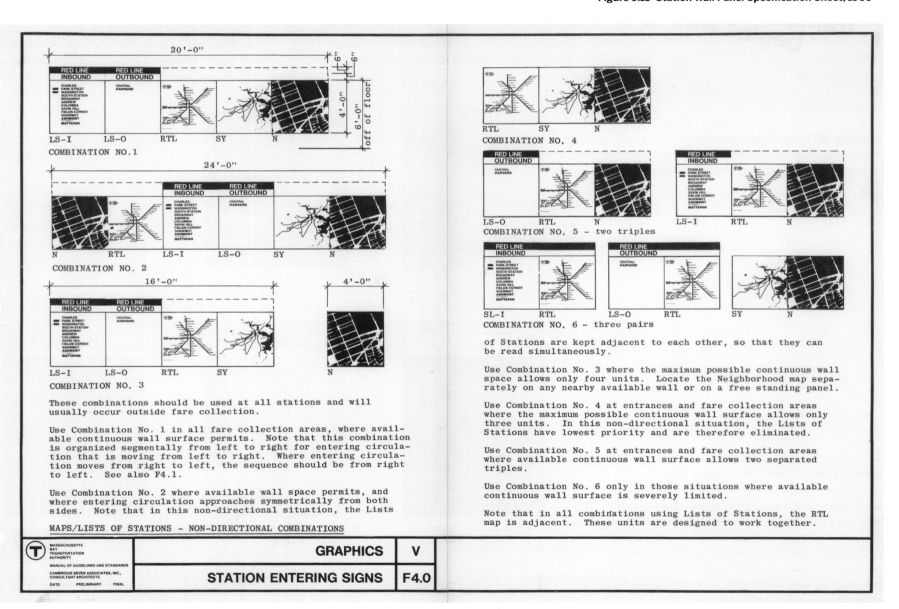

Figure 9.16 Station Signage Locations, 1966

A diagram specifies locations of different types of signage for transit patrons entering a prototypical MBTA station.

SIGN TYPE KEY

1. T Symbol
    Street Sign

2. Station Name
    Street Sign

3. Line Identification

4. Maps/Lists of Stations
    Outside Fare Collection
    (Non-directional)

5. Maps/Lists of Stations
    Inside Fare Collection
    (directional)

6. Line/Direction Sign

7. Inbound-Outbound Color Coding
    End Walls

8. Maps/List of Stations
    Platform

DIAGRAMMATIC ILLUSTRATION - SIGN TYPES

| | GRAPHICS | V |
| MASSACHUSETTS BAY TRANSPORTATION AUTHORITY — MANUAL OF GUIDELINES AND STANDARDS. CAMBRIDGE SEVEN ASSOCIATES, INC., CONSULTANT ARCHITECTS. DATE PRELIMINARY FINAL | STATION ENTERING SIGNS | F1.1 |

Figure 9.17 Prototypical MBTA Bus Signage, 1966

The *Manual of Guidelines and Standards* specified a prototypical bus stop sign (left), to be pole-mounted, and prototype rollsign curtain sections (right), to be displayed by rubber-tired transit vehicles. On the signage, route numbers, destinations, and route information stand out in white. The color of each background indicates the rapid transit line served by a particular bus or trolley route. The background for a route not connecting with a rapid transit station (96 Medford Sq) is black.

(Figure 9.14), helped the MBTA redefine wayfinding signage for public transit in Boston. Section V also specified the installation of informative wall panels at key points within each station (Figure 9.15 and Figure 9.16). Major wall panel types, each tailored to a particular station and capped by ribbons, included a list of outbound stations, a list of inbound stations, a map of the rapid transit lines, a geographically accurate system map, and a neighborhood map. The informative panels allowed a transit user to orient themselves along a line, confirm their location within the larger transit system, and locate themselves in a neighborhood.

Beyond specifying wayfinding signage and maps, Section V described visual art panels to be installed on station platforms. Intended to be seen by a rider arriving into a station on a transit vehicle, the art panels featured photographs, artwork, or images of a landmark of the neighborhood outside of the station in which they were installed. Section V also re-envisioned signage for bus and trackless trolley routes (Figure 9.17). Neither the bus stop signs nor the bus rollsign curtains specified in Section V saw long-term or complete implementation.

Test Case Arlington

In the first half of 1966, the *Manual of Guidelines and Standards* existed only on paper, remaining untested on any large scale. Before embarking on its first system-wide station modernization program, the MBTA opted to renovate a single station as a test case. The T selected Arlington Station on the Boylston Street Subway to undergo a pilot renovation and receive the complete treatment called for in the *Manual of Guidelines and Standards* (Figure 9.18). Renovations of Arlington Station began in June 1966. A "before" photograph (Figure 9.19) captures the station's original tiled walls, limited signage, outdated lighting, and lack of maps. An "after" photograph (Figure 9.20) reveals new wayfinding and orientation devices, station name ribbons, clock, lighting, and finishes. All of the new, wall-mounted panels were porcelain on steel, designed to withstand the extreme conditions of a busy transit station. A renovated Arlington Station opened to the public on August 17, 1967.

A few months after Arlington Station reopened, a second venue popped up where the public could review the new aesthetics of the MBTA. From September 30 to November 12, 1967, "Design In Transit" took place at Boston's Institute of

Contemporary Art (ICA). The exhibit showcased the architectural, wayfinding, and graphic design work that Cambridge Seven and other designers undertook for the MBTA. The T was recognized for its work to improve the face of transit for Boston, receiving an award from HUD "For Excellence in Comprehensive Design for System Redevelopment" in March 1968.

A Better Way

The MBTA released its first Comprehensive Program for Mass Transportation Development, its first Capital Improvement Plan (CIP), in May 1966. The 1966 CIP was the T's first formal road map for improvements for public transportation across Greater Boston. The ambitious plan called for the construction of twenty-five new rapid transit stations, all to be constructed along "five, new rapid transit extensions totalling 29 miles." The 1966 CIP also called for the renovation of existing rapid transit and streetcar subway stations. In its 1966 annual report, the MBTA argued:

> ... improvements must be made now. The new T will be one of the key factors in determining how successfully metropolitan Boston and the Commonwealth compete with other metropolitan areas in the next few decades. Improved mass transit will make it easier for people to reach the various business, shopping, cultural and recreational centers through the MBTA

Figure 9.18 (Above) Redesigning Arlington Station, 1966
A redesign for the wall along the inbound streetcar platform envisions a new neighborhood map, key to lines, and spider map (left), a new art panel depicting a landmark outside of the station (right), and new station ribbon signage (top and bottom).

Figure 9.19 (Below, Left) Arlington Station "Before," 1966
The MBTA inherited Arlington Station with limited improvements since opening in the 1920s. Shown is the outbound platform before the station was first renovated by the T.

Figure 9.20 (Below, Right) Arlington Station "After," 1967
The outbound platform after the first real world application of the MBTA's *Manual of Guidelines and Standards*.

district—thereby making this a highly attractive place to live.

"What About Money?" asked the MBTA in its 1966 annual report. Answering its own question, the T proposed funding capital improvement projects by leveraging state-sanctioned bonding, state cigarette tax revenue, and federal grants.

In 1968, the MBTA completed a self-described:

> Comprehensive transportation planning requirements of the Federal Urban Mass Transit Administration ... with the Authority thus becoming eligible to apply for two-thirds grants for future projects and to receive funding withheld on previously approved projects.

After unlocking federal funding, the MBTA quickly became a champion at soliciting and receiving federal funds. The Authority received nearly $40.5 million in federal grants in fiscal 1968 alone. The T updated and re-released its 1966 CIP in 1968, and then again in 1971 as its Program for Mass Transportation (PMT). In that later year, Massachusetts opened the floodgates of state funding for public transportation, designating over $100 million for MBTA capital projects.

During its first decade, the MBTA worked diligently to communicate to its constituency its intentions to remake public transportation with public dollars (Figure 9.21). The Authority's "We have a better way" slogan pushed an optimistic message (Figure 9.22). At the end of its first decade, in 1973, the MBTA converted its 1971 PMT into a multi-year master plan. This allowed the Authority to meet new federal guidelines and apply for additional federal funding. Since the 1970s, the T has prepared a plethora of capital investment and improvement plans.

A Period of Newness

The MBTA's first decade was marked by earnest efforts to improve the image, infrastructure, vehicles, and financial situation of public transportation for Greater Boston. The T described its first eighteen months as a "period of newness." During that time, the Authority restructured the vestiges of the MTA, implemented a self-described "modern management organization" and instituted cost controls over appropriations, manpower, overtime, and inventory. The Authority undertook value engineering and detailed analyses of existing programs. It commenced the construction of extensions of existing lines and ordered new transit vehicles. The Authority described all of these as "visible action."

Improvements continued into the late 1960s, with the T placing 210 new buses into service and

Figure 9.21 A Better Way, 1972
Black and white pictures of well-worn transit infrastructure and vehicles are offset by a colorful rainbow of the MBTA's railed transit lines. Beyond the cover, the brochure presented to the public a comprehensive list of improvements being pursued by the T.

Figure 9.22 "We Have a Better Way" Stickers, Early 1970s
The early years of the MBTA were an optimistic time, full of ambitious projects, ample federal funding, and strong government support for public transportation.

ordering an additional 125 air-conditioned buses in 1967 alone. During the following year, the Authority approved the $3.6 million purchase of forty buses from the Flxible Company (Flxible) and sixty buses from General Motors (GM).

At the dawn of the 1970s, the MBTA operated 1,226 buses, 356 rapid transit cars, 343 streetcars, and fifty-eight trackless trolleys. To oversee the safe movement of these thousands of vehicles, in 1970 the MBTA opened its first purpose-built operations center (Figure 9.23). Located at 45 High Street in downtown Boston, the center included electronic monitoring systems and dispatching stations (Figure 9.24). After many upgrades and improvements, including a complete rebuild and the addition of five new floors in the early 1990s, the MBTA's High Street facility now houses the Authority's Operations Control Center (OCC) (Figure 9.25). At the OCC, managers and dispatchers continue to oversee the operation of and react to changing conditions across the T.

The T's optimism of the 1960s continued into the early 1970s, with the Authority describing 1971 as a "year of innovation and renovation." The year saw the T open the first segment of the Red Line's South Shore Extension, christen a new bus maintenance garage in Charlestown, and implement an exact-fare system for streetcars, buses, and trackless trolleys. At the end of January, the Authority completed the relocation of its administrative headquarters from 150 Causeway Street, near North Station, to a new structure at 500 Arborway, in Boston's Jamaica

Plain neighborhood (Figure 9.26). The T has since mostly vacated its Arborway offices. Currently, its main offices, along with those of MassDOT and the Central Transportation Planning Staff (CTPS), occupy much of the Massachusetts Transportation Building, erected by the Commonwealth at Park Plaza in the early 1980s.

Early MBTA Station Modernization Programs

After completing the pilot modernization of Arlington Station, the T set its sights on improving additional aging stations. The MBTA funded the $9 million first phase of its station modernization program with $6 million from a HUD capital grant, $2.7 million from the Commonwealth, and $300,000 from Authority coffers. By the end of summer 1966, design work was underway for nine stations.

The first station to be modernized and presented to the public after Arlington Station was Aquarium Station, renamed from Atlantic Station effective February 13, 1967. Aquarium Station reopened on November 15, freshly adorned with maps and signage following the Arlington Station prototype. The project was completed three months early.

Besides Atlantic Station, other stations also received new names in 1967. Summer and Winter Stations became Washington Station (January 23), Milk and Devonshire Street Stations became State Station (January 25), and Union and Friend Stations became Haymarket Station (January 26). In its 1967 annual report, the MBTA justified the

Figure 9.23 MBTA Operations Center, 1970
The concrete and brick architecture of the MBTA's newly opened MBTA's Operations Center at 45 High Street echo that of Boston City Hall, just a short walk away.

Figure 9.24 Inside the MBTA Operations Center, 1970
An MBTA employee mans the Rapid Transit Control desk at 45 High Street.

Figure 9.25 MBTA Operations Control Center, 2000
A wall of screens provides constantly updated information to dispatchers and managers within the OCC, at the MBTA's 45 High Street building.

name changes: " … station names [were] changed to end confusion and create a cohesion attuned to our new color coding system for rapid transit lines." As part of its 1967 renaming program, the T removed "Street" from the official names of stations, except at Park Street and Green Street Stations.

Airport and Bowdoin Stations were the next to be modernized, both reopening in 1968. In the first quarter of 1969, the MBTA completed modernizing Government Center Station and began upgrading Copley, Prudential, and Haymarket Stations. The T spread the word about its improvement work via various publications (Figure 9.27 and Figure 9.28). 1970 saw the Authority complete modernizations of Copley, Kenmore, Prudential, Columbia, Fields Corner, Maverick, and Orient Heights Stations. Kenmore Station was last of fourteen stations modernized in phase one of the station modernization program. Stations that did not receive a complete modernization received minor upgrades.

To increase public engagement in its station modernization program, the MBTA held a competition for artwork to be printed onto new porcelain panels for Kenmore Station. The winning art was created by three local art school students. A competition organized by the T and the ICA in 1971 called for mural art to be installed at State Station. The competition and installation were funded by the Rockefeller Foundation. The winning entry was described by the T:

> Timed-lighting was installed in a newly-painted rainbow-colored archway in the pedestrian passageway connecting the State Orange Line Station and the State Blue Line Station.

Station modernizations continued throughout the 1970s. Work commenced in 1971, under a $6 million federal grant, to modernize twenty-six stations, including Wonderland Station. The federal Urban Mass Transportation Administration (UMTA) awarded the MBTA a $9.6 million grant towards the $14.3 million second phase of the station modernization program in 1972. The second phase targeted Ashmont, Auditorium (now Hynes Convention Center), Essex (now Chinatown Orange Line northbound), Haymarket (Orange Line only), Park Street, State, and Washington (now Downtown Crossing) Stations. The T completed phase one of the station modernization program in 1973. Modernizations wrapped up at Auditorium and Haymarket Green Line Stations in 1977.

Figure 9.26 The T's Arborway Headquarters, 1974
The cover of the December 1974 "T Times" brochure features a rendering of the Authority's Arborway headquarters in its modernist suburban glory.

Figure 9.27 MBTA Station Modernization Brochure, 1970
Markings on a brochure map indicate station modernizations complete at Arlington, Bowdoin, Government Center, Aquarium, and Airport Stations; modernizations were still underway at eleven other stations.

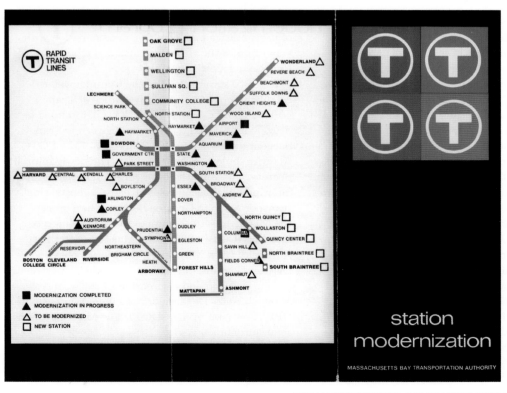

Figure 9.28 Station Modernization Round Up, 1970
A brochure promotes late 1960s renovations of existing stations with the application of designs from the *Manual of Guidelines and Standards*.

Early Fiscal Problems

After spending hundreds of millions of capital investment dollars expanding its system, modernizing infrastructure, and investing in new vehicles in the 1960s, the T found itself operating at a loss at the end of the decade. In early 1970, Governor Francis Sargent, the MBTA Advisory Board, and leadership from the General Court convened a summit to discuss the T's projected $45 million debt. The group reviewed a then $25 million statutory limit on MBTA debt, potential state tax sources to devote to the T, the issuance of bonds to fund further capital projects, and how to address communities that no longer desired Authority service. Later in 1970, the governor's transportation task force released a report highly critical of the MBTA, describing service as "noisy, dirty, unreliable." The report singled out conditions at the Authority's back-of-house facilities: "The awful obsolescence and squalor of the existing facilities tend greatly to inflate operating costs and depress employee morale." The report called out a history of deficit operation, political interference in decision making, decades of neglect

of preventative maintenance, preoccupation with expansion to the virtual exclusion of efficient operations, and superfluous unions jobs.

The 1970 summit lead to the Commonwealth's establishment of an Executive Office of Transportation and Construction (EOTC), intended to provide more MBTA oversight. Governor Francis Sargent swore in the first Secretary of the EOTC, Alan Altshuler, on June 21, 1971. The newly minted Secretary became the overseer of an entity complimenting multiple agencies already orchestrating transportation in Greater Boston. These were the Massachusetts Turnpike Authority (merged into MassDOT in 2009), the Massachusetts Port Authority (now Massport), the Metropolitan District Commission (merged into the Department of Conservation and Recreation in 2003), and the Massachusetts Department of Public Works (state DPW; now part of MassDOT). The MBTA remained semi-autonomous.

1970 also brought continued federal funding to the T. Congress's passage of the Urban Mass Transit Assistance Act provided Massachusetts with

Figure 9.29 The T's First Folding System Route Map, 1965
The MBTA's first edition of the Lufkin Format folding system map is an updated version of the MTA's 1964 edition (Figure 6.57), itself a revision of a map first issued by the BERy in 1936 (Figure 6.53). The T's 1966 folding system route map, virtually identical to the 1965 edition, was simultaneously rolled out with Cambridge Seven's new rapid transit "spider" map. Since 1966, the MBTA has regularly revised and reissued both a geographically accurate system map, akin to Lufkin Format maps, along with a more abstract line map, like the spider map. A non-Lufkin Format system map did not appear until 1967, when the T released a map prepared for it by the Boston Redevelopment Authority (Figure 9.30).

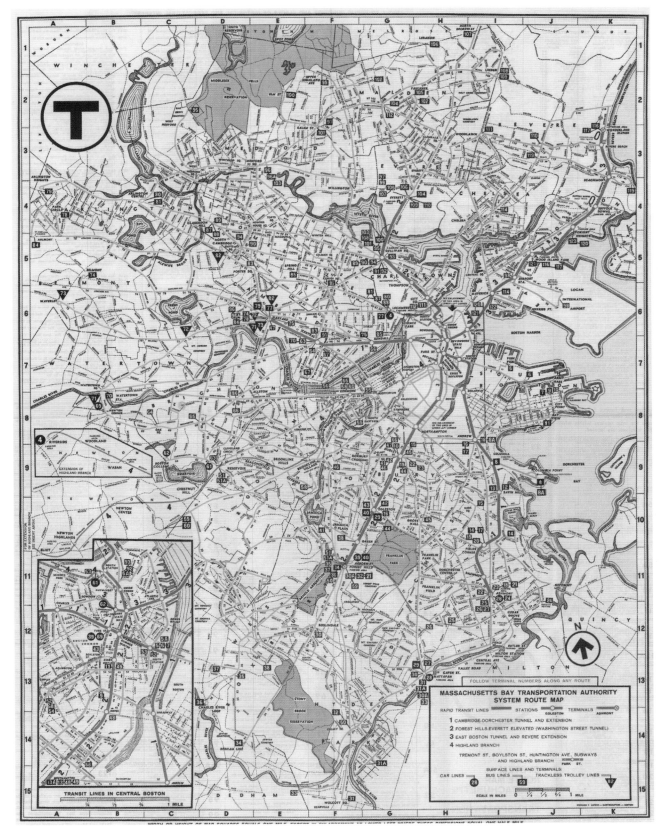

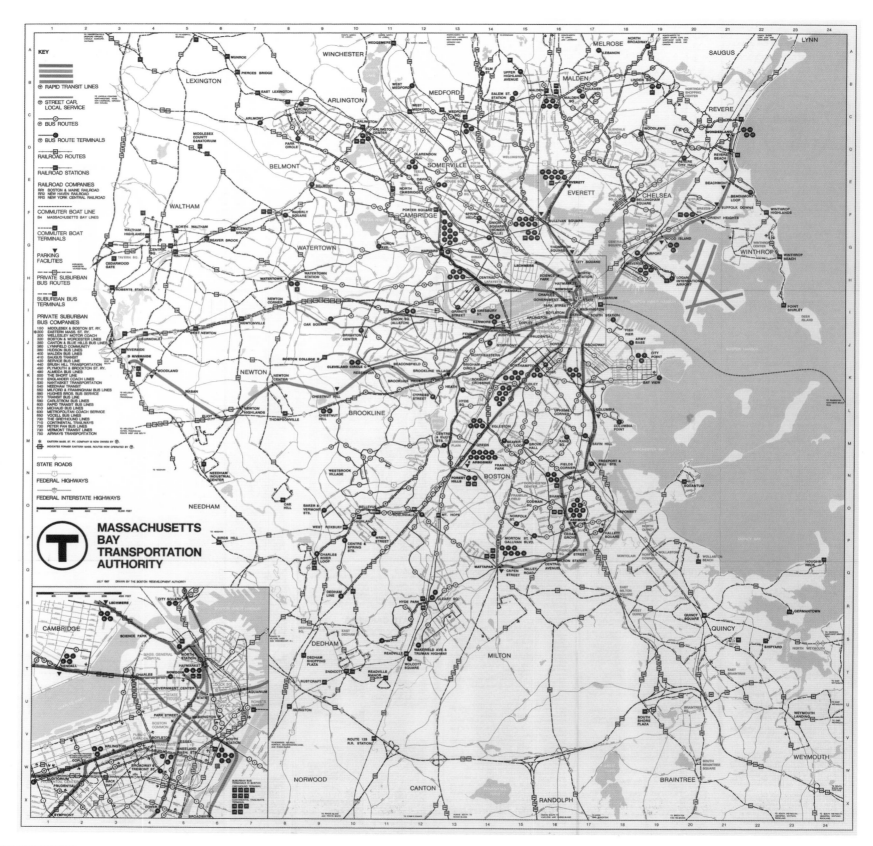

$400 million, a sizable portion of the $3.1 billion initially allocated for the entire nation. The federal funding was soon augmented at the state level. In 1971, the Massachusetts legislature received a petition signed by 100,000 citizens asking that the Commonwealth lift the prohibition of using state highway funds, which were mostly derived from state gasoline taxes, for public transportation. Two years later, the MBTA stated that 1973 "should stand out as a major bench mark in the history of transportation in the Boston Metropolitan Area." The T announced optimistically:

> ...[T]he Highway Trust Fund will be opened up for mass transit projects....Fifty percent of the MBTA's net cost of service will be assumed by the Commonwealth....Fares on rapid transit lines will be lowered....Plans for proposed highways will be scrapped, and new transit facilities substituted for them.

Before the state highway fund could be tapped to fund the T, the Authority's financial woes of 1970–71 came to a head. During the final hours of the General Court's session for 1972, the legislature passed an emergency funding measure submitted by Governor Sargent, preventing a shut down of the MBTA.

As funding from the Commonwealth kept the T solvent in the early 1970s, the federal tap continued to provide. In 1975 alone the Authority received a then record $109.6 million in federal funds. Justifying its use of federal and state dollars, the T shared in its annual report for the year: "Public transportation in the Boston area hasn't "paid for itself" since the end of 1943, when automobiles weren't being manufactured and gasoline was closely rationed." Indeed, Boston's first public transportation deficit was in 1912, under the BERy. The T continued, explaining that its twenty-five cent fare would cost one dollar without public subsidies.

Since the early 1970s, the Commonwealth has funded the T by allocating state tax revenues, approving the issuance of bonds, and passing legislative acts. In 1980, Massachusetts passed the Management Rights Act, allowing the MBTA to begin outsourcing some of its labor. Quickly, the outsourcing led to yearly costs savings of millions of dollars. Governor Michael Dukakis filed legislation in 1987 to provide $800 million for MBTA capital improvements. The governor's legislation arrived during a time of dwindling federal funding for public transportation.

As the end of the 1980s neared and President Ronald Regan continued to oversee cuts to federal funding for public transportation, the T sent an envoy to Washington. MBTA General Manager James O'Leary testified before the House Transportation Sub-Committee in April 1988. O'Leary was critical of Reagan's proposed 1989 budget, which called for a nearly sixty percent reduction in federal funding for public transportation. Despite the T's efforts, the Reagan administration continued to scale back funding for public transportation.

As federal funding continued to dry up, Massachusetts increasingly stepped in to financially assist the T. Throughout the late 1980s and into the 1990s, the MBTA was essentially kept whole by the Commonwealth. In 1988 alone, Governor Dukakis signed a $3.1 billion transportation bond bill which called for hundreds of millions of dollars for commuter rail improvements.

Fiscally conservative Governor William Weld reluctantly signed a massive transportation bond bill in 1991. The bill funded a laundry list of MBTA capital projects, including the purchase of hundreds of new vehicles, modernization of Blue Line stations, work on the Silver Line, improvements and extensions to commuter rail lines, and operation of commuter boats. The "Act Providing for an Accelerated Transportation Development and Improvement Program for the Commonwealth," a.k.a. the "Transportation Bond Bill of 1991," included authorization for the MBTA to borrow just over a billion dollars for capital improvements. Beyond the T, the bill authorized nearly $43 million for capital improvements for Massachusetts' Regional Transit Authorities (RTAs). The RTAs were in need of new vehicles and facilities, and like the T, were suffering under declining federal funding. Since the 1990s, the Commonwealth has approved various bond bills and measures that have funded both MBTA and RTA capital projects.

Addressing Public Safety

During 1965 and 1966, Boston provided a contingent of thirty-five officers to patrol portions of the MBTA's system located within the city. After a series of it drivers were physically attacked and stabbed during its first eighteen months, the MBTA set its eyes on establishing its own police force, one with powers across the multiple jurisdictions where it operated.

Massachusetts' Chapter 664 of the Acts of 1968 established the MBTA's police department,

Figure 9.30 MBTA System Map, July 1967
The 1967 system map was designed by the Boston Redevelopment Authority for the MBTA. The map is square and covers a larger geographic area than previous Lufkin Format system maps (Figure 9.29). The larger area needed for the map reflects the increased size of the service area of the MBTA over that of the MTA. Colored lines trace the T's rapid transit and trolley lines. Black lines mark bus routes. Black numbers set within white circles call out MBTA bus route designations. Black numbers set within black squares call out private carrier bus route designations. Thirty different private companies are keyed to bus routes on the map.

granting MBTA Transit Police with full police powers throughout the Authority's service area. The MBTA's first contingent of officers were trained by the FBI and took over for Boston officers. By July 1969, the T's force consisted of thirty-five persons. After establishing a headquarters at Dudley Station, Transit Police effected a sixty-five percent reduction of crime at the busy station. Still, crime remained a serious issue, with an average of 100 MBTA operators assaulted or robbed in 1969, and then again in 1970. With Transit Police unable to be on every bus or trolley at all times, the T addressed the issue by installing lockable fare boxes on vehicles and switching to exact change fare collection.

In the early 1970s, acts of sabotage were regular occurrences along MBTA rights-of-way. Vandals zeroed in on the Riverside Line, where they blocked tracks with automobiles, barrels, and other debris. On the southern portion of the Red Line, vandals regularly tossed items onto the third rail. As the 1970s progressed, frequent robberies continued to take place at transit stations. In response, the MBTA began to install bulletproof collector's booths in 1975.

Transit Police came into their own in the 1970s. At the time, Boston was on the national stage for its federally-mandated program to racially integrate its public schools through the use of buses. Bostonians protesting the bussing, attacked MBTA buses. Responding to the crisis, the T recalled:

> ...[The Authority] moved to alleviate racial tensions, which had prompted attacks on both white and black bus drivers and passengers, by organizing a joint management-union meeting with commuter leaders in Roxbury and South Boston. It stepped up a program to equip buses with two-way radios, and began the process of establishing a computerized safety alarm system for buses.

In time, bussing protest ebbed. In the meantime, Transit Police reported their sixty-four-person team reducing transit crimes by thirty-eight percent in 1976 over 1975. Since then, MBTA Transit Police has made countless improvements of safety and security for those who work and ride on the T.

MBTA Transit Police received national accreditation in 1987, validating the force and their decades of hard work. Transit Police continues to prevent, investigate, and respond to crimes across the MBTA.

Saving the Day, Saving the Future

On Tuesday, November 9, 1965, a significant part of the Northeastern United States, along with much of the Canadian Province of Ontario, was plunged into a blackout. The power outage struck Boston at approximately 5:15 p.m., just at the height of the evening commute. On that November day, the MBTA became a literal beacon of light in Boston and Eastern Massachusetts. After some hiccups during the first few hours of the crisis, the MBTA had its services up and running by 7:00 p.m. Throughout much of the over twelve-hour-long blackout, the Authority's tunnels and stations maintained power and lighting.

After the blackout, and after finally being permitted by the state to close its power stations, the MBTA shed its last power plant (South Boston Power Station) in the later part of the twentieth century. Today, the MBTA purchases electricity from commercial power companies and no longer generates its own. Across the T, a network of substations transforms electricity from alternating current (AC), from the grid, to direct current (DC), for distribution along wires and third rails. The T is the largest consumer of electricity in Massachusetts.

The MBTA came to the rescue again, on March 30, 1966, when railroad workers across America went on strike at midnight. Shortly thereafter, the MBTA orchestrated substitute transportation for commuters who would awake to discover a complete absence of Boston & Maine Railroad commuter rail service. The MBTA worked with local bus companies, police departments, and the Boston Traffic Commission to ensure additional transit options were available to commuter rail patrons during the strike.

Beyond saving the day on a local level, the MBTA stepped onto the national security stage in the late 1960s. With the cold war in full swing, the Authority got involved to protect Boston's citizenry, should a nuclear attack befall the city. In 1966 alone, the Authority stashed enough medical supplies to serve 120,000 people for thirty days. The supplies consisted of four hundred medical kits tucked away at Broadway Station in South Boston. The T coordinated with Massport to establish procedures for evacuating Logan Airport and sheltering civilians in MBTA tunnels during a nuclear attack.

Boston's civil defense materials were never needed, with many caches being forgotten and abandoned in place. Over the last six decades, the MBTA and its contractors have uncovered multiple

Figure 9.31 MBTA Pupil's Badge, 1965

Figure 9.32 Books of MBTA Pupils and Children Tickets, 1965
Tickets with a blue T logo (top) were good before 1:00 p.m. Checks with a red T logo (bottom) were good after 12:00 p.m. One half of each check was good for either a single rapid transit or one surface line trip.

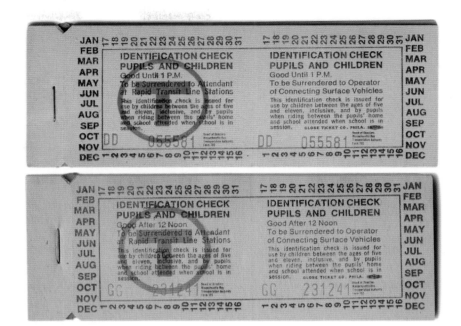

Figure 9.33 Promotional Pin for Ten Cent T Fares, 1973–74

stashes of Civil Defense supplies rotting in place, most recently while reconstructing Government Center Station.

Fares and Passes in the 1960s and 1970s

When it took over for the MTA in 1964, the T continued it predecessor's practice of offering a reduced fare for students (Figure 9.31 and Figure 9.32). On December 1, 1968, the MBTA raised regular bus fare from ten to twenty cents and increased rapid transit fare from twenty to twenty-five cents. The T began to issue identification cards for patrons sixty-five years of age or older on August 1, 1969. The Authority also began implementing a system of exact fares for bus and trackless trolley lines in the later half of 1970.

In fall 1971, the MBTA completed a significant revamping of transit fare pricing and collection techniques. The Authority attempted to set surface line fare at twenty-five cents, lowering suburban bus fare from thirty cents and increasing city bus fare from twenty cents. Transfers, discounted tokens, and discounted tickets were eliminated. Children and students paid fifteen cents while seniors paid a dime. At Quincy Red Line stations, fifty cents paid for a ride into Boston while a quarter covered a trip exclusively within Quincy.

The revised fares were accompanied by physical changes made to fare collection. The MBTA removed fare boxes from which Authority employees made change for riders. The older fare boxes were replaced with new, locked boxes, which only accepted incoming payment. The switch, intended to reduce crime and theft, virtually eliminated onboard robberies of the fare box. As part of the $1.5 million fare collection system, the MBTA constructed nearly twenty fare box vault rooms at its bus garages and streetcar facilities. The Authority purchased five revenue collection trucks and invested in modern coin sorting and counting machines.

Exact change fare collection ended the practice of drivers making change on board. To address patrons boarding a vehicle with more than exact fare, the T instituted an oddly inconvenient, two-part paper receipt system. On each half of a receipt, an Authority employee punched out the amount remitted by the rider. With the amount remitted, one half of the receipt went into the locked fare box with payment and the other half was retained by the rider. If the customer wished to reclaim their change, they needed to travel to the MBTA's Arborway headquarters, a short walk from Forest Hills Station.

The MBTA launched a self-described "novel marketing program to increase ridership in the off-peak hours" in 1973. "Dime Time" allowed riders to travel for a mere ten cents on weekdays, between 10:00 a.m. and 1:00 p.m., on the Blue, Orange, and Red Lines. Under Dime Time, the fare from Quincy Red Line stations was cut in half, from fifty cents to a quarter. By the end of 1973, Dime Time increased daytime ridership by approximately fifteen

percent and promotional pins touted the service (Figure 9.33). In 1974, the MBTA expanded Dime Time until 2:00 p.m. on weekdays and all day on Sundays, but after losing a couple of million dollars in revenue by offering Dime Time, and concluding that the discounts were "more a gift to regular riders than a major attraction for new riders," the T suspended Dime Time indefinitely on August 1, 1975.

The first MBTA monthly passes were introduced in 1974. They were available only to select private sector employees to purchase from a handful of employers, John Hancock Insurance Company being one of the first. Three types of passes were available in 1974, each imprinted with a single-fare value of either twenty-five, forty-five, or fifty cents, and costing $105, $189, or $210 a year, respectively (Figure 9.34). At the end of the first year of the monthly pass program, twenty companies were participating and approximately 7,000 people procured passes through their employers.

Though the MBTA's monthly passes were a new concept in 1974, monthly passes for local rail travel had been around for over a century, ever since railroad monthly commutation tickets appeared in the nineteenth century (See Chapter 1). Coordinating with the arrival of MBTA passes, the Boston & Maine advertised "Unlimited Ride Tickets" (essentially monthly commutation tickets) with the slogan "Here are some new ideas to save you time and headaches commuting via the B&M" (Figure 9.35). Another of the Boston & Maine's "new ideas" was an updated zone fare system. On July 1, 1974, standard Boston & Maine commuter rail fares became

based on one of five zones, each capturing stations a certain distance from Boston. The MBTA still uses a similar, distance-based zone fare system.

In fall 1974, the fare for MBTA surface routes remained twenty cents and the fare for rapid transit lines remained twenty-five cents. Children and seniors paid a dime. Riverside express bus service cost seventy-five cents. Other express bus runs cost fifty cents. Fares on former Eastern Massachusetts Street Railway Company (Eastern Mass) routes, taken over by the MBTA in 1968, were twenty-five cents in cash. A dollar purchased four Eastern Mass tokens. Fares on ex-Eastern Mass routes were good for travel within one of multiple zones. Children paid half fare. Ten cent transfers were available with conditions. Fares on Middlesex & Boston Street Railway Company (Middlesex & Boston) routes subsidized by MBTA in 1964 were twenty, forty, and sixty cents, each based on one of three zones.

The MBTA finally succeeded in increasing regular bus fare from twenty to twenty-five cents on September 1, 1975. In October, one-way fares on the Boston & Maine increased within a revised zone-based fare system, featuring eight different fare zones. By 1976, the Authority was collecting over one million dollars a week in fare revenue.

1977 brought expansion and upgrades to the T's monthly pass program, with six pass types being made available (Figure 9.36). In April, the MBTA added a twenty-five cent rapid transit pass to the back of commuter rail monthly commutation tickets. The augmented passes allowed free transfers between commuter rail and rapid

Figure 9.34 Brochure Advertising the First T Passes, 1974

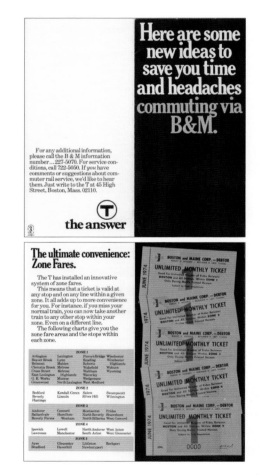

Figure 9.35 Commuter Rail Zone Fares Brochure, 1974

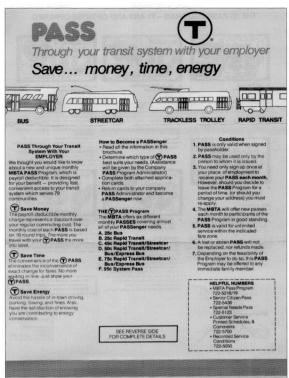

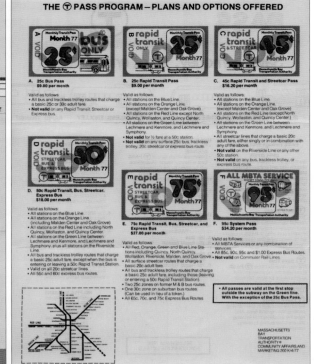

Figure 9.36 MBTA Pass Pamphlet, 1977

The MBTA marketed six types of passes in 1977. Type A was valid for twenty-five cent bus fare. Type B was valid for twenty-five cent rapid transit fare. Type C covered the forty-five cent combo fare for rapid transit and streetcar service. Types D and E, good for fifty cent and seventy-five cent fares, respectively, were valid for travel on all rapid transit, streetcar, bus, and express bus service. Type F, good for ninety-five cent fare, was valid for travel on any MBTA service except commuter rail.

transit stations in downtown Boston. By 1979, the Authority sought to eliminate the rapid transit pass from the back of commuter rail passes. It estimated losing over $500,000 annually by offering the free transfers.

In 1977, employees of the John Hancock Mutual Life Insurance Company were the first to be able to purchase a new type of T pass. Referred to as "Automatic Passes" by the MBTA, each featured a coded magnetic strip, a technological advancement for T passes. As of April 1, Automatic Passes could

be used exclusively at the Berkeley Street entrance of Arlington Station. There, a swipe of an Automatic Pass through a reader attached to a turnstile allowed a turnstile to turn and a person to pass.

After four years of increasing sales of passes exclusively through employers, on December 26, 1978 the T made passes available for general purchase. Bus cards advertised T passes to the general public (Figure 9.37). Figure 9.38 shows a variety of T passes from the late 1970s.

Figure 9.37 Car Card Advertisement for MBTA Passes, 1978

1978 closed out with no fewer than seven pass types available. A twenty-five cent surface vehicle or a twenty-five rapid transit pass cost $9. A forty-five cent rapid transit and streetcar pass cost just over $16. A fifty cent combo pass sold for $18. The T offered two types of express bus passes, one with a fifty-five cent value and another with a sixty cent value. A seventy-five cent combo pass was good for travel on rapid transit, streetcars, and most buses, including many express buses. The highest value pass was a ninety-five cent system pass, costing just over $34, good for unlimited travel for one calendar month.

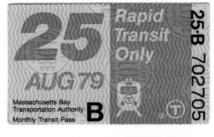

Goodbye to the A Branch

Streetcar service between downtown Boston and Watertown Square passed in succession from the West End Street Railway Company (West End) to the BERy, then to the MTA, and finally, to the MBTA. In the later half of the 1960s, the T branded trolley service between Park Street Station and Watertown Square as the A Branch of its Green Line.

On May 7, 1969, the MBTA Board of Directors approved an eleven week trial substitution of buses for A Branch Green Line trolley service from Packard's Corner (the intersection of Commonwealth and Brighton Avenues) to Watertown Square. The Authority replaced A Branch streetcar service with the Route 57 bus. The T was not excited about operating trolleys along tracks that were not separated from regular street traffic. The last A Branch trolley to operate in revenue service, MBTA Presidents' Conference Committee (PCC) car number 3126, ran on June 21, 1969 (Figure 9.39). Later that year, in December, the MBTA declared the bus substitution permanent.

Throughout the 1970s and 1980s, activist groups fought the good fight to convince the T to restore trolley service to Watertown Square. A Newton group went so far as to argue for the establishment of a new intermodal transit terminal at Newton Corner, to be served by trolleys from Watertown, Newton, and Brighton. The Newton project was never realized.

After the termination of revenue streetcar service along the A Branch, until spring 1994, MBTA trolleys in non-revenue moves used A Branch tracks to reach the Watertown Car House. The T removed the streetcar tracks from Packard's Corner to Watertown in the mid-1990s. The Watertown Car House remains, albeit very quiet, no longer a hub of trolley maintenance.

Saving the Eastern Massachusetts and the Middlesex & Boston Street Railway Companies

Concurrent with the birth of the MBTA, private carriers across America were rapidly getting out of the business of providing public transportation. Railroad companies were petitioning the federal government to eliminate passenger and commuter rail routes. Streetcar and city bus operators were being consolidated, going out of business, or falling under the thumb of public control. The Commonwealth and the MBTA saw the writing on the wall for local bus companies serving Eastern

Massachusetts. In a report to the MBTA Advisory Board, the T's Board of Directors argued:

> Our authority to regulate and our duty to sustain private carriers, taken together with our mandate to supply transportation, embraces an unprecedented range of jurisdiction over private and public enterprise.

At the end of 1964, the MBTA approved the execution of agreements with two private carriers, the Boston & Maine, provider of commuter rail service north of Boston, and the Eastern Massachusetts Street Railway Company (Eastern Mass), operator of Eastern Massachusetts' largest bus network outside of those of the MBTA. These landmark agreements prevented the loss of potentially irreplaceable public transit services and allowed the MBTA, following its mandate to plan for the future, to keep options available for possible public transit improvements and extensions.

The agreement between the MBTA and the Middlesex & Boston put the Authority entirely in charge of the bus company. It also put the MBTA on the hook for the bus company's costs not covered by revenue, with the T agreeing to guarantee profit for Middlesex & Boston stockholders. The first eighteen months of operating the Middlesex & Boston cost the MBTA approximately $220,000. Despite the cost, without the takeover, public bus service to sixteen cities and towns northwest of Boston would have been decimated.

After gaining experience overseeing and subsidizing the Middlesex & Boston, the MBTA absorbed other bus companies. It also proceeded to subsidize bus routes of private carriers. In spring 1968, the T contracted with Rapid Transit Incorporated (RTI) to operate bus service between the Winthrop and Orient Heights Station. In February 1975, the T absorbed the vehicles, equipment, and employees of Service Bus Line, a company providing service in Malden, Melrose, Lynn, Revere, Saugus, and Winthrop. In 1977, the Authority contracted out bus service for Hingham and Hull to Hudson Bus Lines, and for Salem and Peabody to Michaud Bus Lines. The two companies began operating MBTA-subsidized buses in 1978. The MBTA continues to contract out bus service to multiple private carriers. Recent examples included service from Orient Heights Station to and within Winthrop, operated by Paul Revere Transportation, and MBTA bus routes 710, 714, and 716, operated by Joseph's Transportation.

Figure 9.38 (Opposite) MBTA Passes of the Late 1970s

Last Trip

was a passenger on the Last Revenue Service Trolley to run on the MBTA

Watertown - Park St. Sta. Line

Saturday, June 21, 1969

Figure 9.39 "A Branch" Last Trip Souvenir Card, 1969

After its takeover of the Middlesex & Boston, the T made an even larger move to preserve bus transit around Massachusetts Bay. On February 9, 1968, the shareholders of the Eastern Mass approved the sale of their company's intrastate bus operations to the MBTA for $6.5 million. Omitted from the sale were Eastern Mass-controlled operations in New Bedford, Massachusetts and Portland, Maine. At the end of its life, the Eastern Mass served nineteen cities and fifty-five towns from four bus garages, one each in Lynn, Brockton, Quincy, and Tewksbury. The MBTA's purchase of the Eastern Mass preserved public bus service far north and south of Boston. A fleet of approximately 300 diesel buses, over 400 Eastern Mass employees, and complex timetables were assimilated by the MBTA. The ex-Eastern Mass president became the T's Director of Operations.

The MBTA formalized its purchase of the Eastern Mass on March 29, 1968. The next morning, twenty-one cities and towns outside of the T's service area had to decide if they wanted to contribute to the MBTA and allow former Eastern Mass service to continue in their communities. Immediately, Andover, Methuen, Taunton, and Raynham said no to paying for MBTA-subsidized bus service. Some of the objecting municipalities went so far as to prohibit Authority buses from running through their communities, even if the vehicles did not make any stops. By the end of 1968, seventeen communities rejected the MBTA's continuation of ex-Eastern Mass service. In response, the MBTA cut back ex-Eastern Mass routes from those communities.

Regional Transit Authorities

Reacting in part to the 1968 rejection of MBTA-operated bus service by municipalities formerly served by the Eastern Mass, but also recognizing the novel availability of ample federal dollars for mass transit, the MBTA encouraged the Commonwealth to create Regional Transit Authorities, essentially mini-MBTAs, to serve metropolitan areas within the Commonwealth but outside of the T's service area. Governor Francis Sargent proposed the Massachusetts Regional Transit Development Act in 1971, which, when formalized into law, led to the creation of a mechanism for the Commonwealth to preserve, expand, fund, plan, and regulate public transit services in various regions of the state.

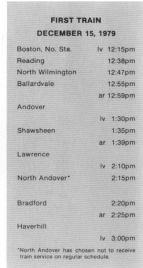

Figure 9.40 MVRTA Haverhill Timetable, 1979
A timetable produced by the Merrimack Valley Regional Transit Authority celebrates the return of passenger rail service between Boston and Haverhill, operated by the MBTA.

Figure 9.41 Boston & Maine Timetables, 1968
Passenger train timetables for the Boston & Maine service to Beverly (left), to Reading (middle), and on all lines (right) are all of series number seventeen, effective April 28, 1968.

Figure 9.42 New Haven Railroad Timetable Graphics, 1968

Massachusetts' first batch of RTAs consisted of eight entities. The Southeastern RTA served South Coast communities, including Fall River and New Bedford. The Montachusetts RTA provided service in and around the cities of Leominster and Fitchburg. The Merrimack Valley RTA served Greater Lawrence and Haverhill (Figure 9.40). The Berkshire RTA operated within Berkshire County, Massachusetts' most western county. The Lower Pioneer Valley RTA provided service in and around the city of Springfield. The Brockton, Lowell, and Worcester RTA's served their respective metropolitan areas. As of 2018, there were fifteen RTAs providing public transportation within Massachusetts. Less than three dozen of the 351 cities and towns within the Commonwealth were not served by either an RTA or the MBTA.

Preserving Commuter Rail

After being unprofitable since 1958, the Boston & Maine Railroad morphed into the Boston & Maine Corporation (Boston & Maine) and entered into its first agreement with the MBTA in 1964. The agreement required the T to subsidize operation of Boston & Maine commuter rail trains within the T's service area for three years, with an option for subsidies to be extended for an additional two years. It was the T's largest move yet to preserve existing private carrier commuter rail service for Greater Boston. Shortly after the T and the Boston & Maine entered into their agreement, the Interstate Commerce Commission (ICC) issued an order in response to a request of the Boston & Maine, allowing the railroad to cease providing passenger train service within Massachusetts. The 1964 agreement prevented commuter rail service from disappearing from the northern half of the T's service area. After the ICC order was issued, a majority of cities and towns in Massachusetts that relied on the Boston & Maine opted for the continuation of commuter rail service under the MBTA, assessments and all. By 1967, the T agreed to subsidize commuter rail operations of the Boston & Maine until June 30, 1968 (Figure 9.41).

After preserving commuter rail north of Boston, the T turned to saving commuter rail west and south of the city. In December 1965 the MBTA formalized a contract with the New York, New Haven & Hartford Railroad (New Haven). The contract included a $2.5 million purchase of the former Old Colony Railroad (Old Colony) line from the Fort Point Channel to South Braintree.

As well, it required MBTA subsidization of New Haven commuter rail service within the T's service area, at a cost of $1.5 million. Similar to the Boston & Maine agreement inked a year prior, the New Haven contract provided the MBTA with options for purchasing the New Haven's lines. The T also approved an option to purchase the New Haven's Cape Cod Branch.

In early 1968, the General Court passed legislation providing ninety percent state funding for commuter rail service subsidized by the MBTA. The funding kept Boston & Maine and New Haven (Figure 9.42) commuter rail trains running through July 31, 1969. The legislation also required that the MBTA look beyond simple subsidies, and explore long-term means for maintaining or entirely replacing commuter rail services for Boston. The Authority responded by outlining three options in January 1969. The first was a minimal investment option. The second was an audacious proposal to replace all commuter rail service with bus service. The third was a maximum investment option, calling for the purchase of railroad rights-of-way and equipment. After the MBTA Advisory Board approved a plan for minimum commuter rail investment, the T issued $10 million in bonds and requested that the General Court extend formulas used by the MBTA to assess its constituent municipalities the cost of subsidizing commuter rail service.

Complementing the three commuter rail options proposed in 1969, the MBTA recommended that the Commonwealth begin railbanking railroad lines no longer used nor wanted by private railroad companies. To railbank a line, the Commonwealth or the MBTA would purchase a railroad right-of-way to preserve it for future use. Many railroad lines within Massachusetts have been railbanked, with some converted into use for non-motorized travel, and others recycled into new transit lines. The Minuteman Commuter Bikeway is an example of the former; the Revere Extension is an example of the latter. Since the 1960s, the Commonwealth has approved the railbanking of hundreds of miles of railroad rights-of-way, and by doing so, has preserved irreplaceable transportation corridors.

On January 1, 1969, the 1,500 mile railroad network of the New Haven became the New Haven Region of the Penn Central Transportation Company (Penn Central). Penn Central was the result of a federally-overseen 1968 merging of the bankrupt Pennsylvania and New York Central Railroads. At inception, Penn Central was the

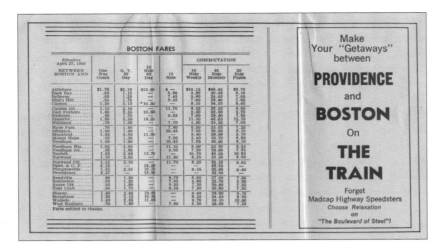

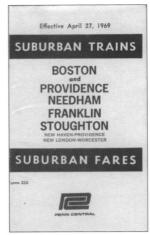

world's largest railroad company. The Boston & Albany Railroad (Boston & Albany), merged into the New York Central in 1961, became part of Penn Central. This put MBTA-subsidized commuter rail trains operated by the Boston & Albany into the hands of Penn Central (Figure 9.43, Figure 9.44, and Figure 9.45).

Months after the Penn Central merger, the Commonwealth renewed its ninety percent funding commitment to commuter rail, but capped it at $13 million and assigned it a sunset of July 31, 1970. With just one day remaining before commuter rail subsidies would end, the General Court approved a continuation of ninety percent public subsidies for commuter rail. The new agreement to subsidize the Boston & Maine and Penn Central was limited to $18.8 million and was set to end on July 31, 1971.

Before 1970 wrapped up, both the Boston & Maine and Penn Central filed for bankruptcy protection. In Boston, the financially crippled Penn Central looked to shed any saleable assets. The situation created an opportunity for the MBTA to begin its transition from commuter rail subsidizer to commuter rail owner. On December 19, 1969, the MBTA Advisory Board approved the T's purchase of approximately two dozen acres of the Penn Central's Dover Street Yards. The approval permitted the Authority to apply to the federal government for assistance in funding the construction of new yards and shops for the Red Line as well as a new major bus garage to serve the central portion of the Authority's district, both planned for the Dover Street Yards site.

After a decade of railroad companies going bankrupt or otherwise ceasing to provide passenger service across America, Congress brought to life the National Railroad Passenger Corporation (Amtrak) in 1971. The federal government created Amtrak to take over America's intercity passenger trains,

Figure 9.44 Penn Central/MBTA Rail Diesel Car, Early 1970s
A self-propelled RDC-1 wears logos of both the Penn Central, the vehicle's operator, and the MBTA, subsidizer of the car's operation.

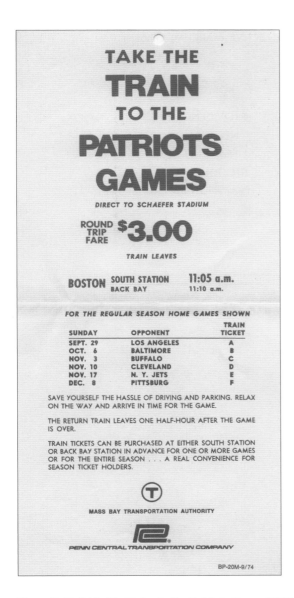

TAKE THE
TRAIN
TO THE
PATRIOTS
GAMES

DIRECT TO SCHAEFER STADIUM

ROUND
TRIP **$3.00**
FARE

TRAIN LEAVES

BOSTON SOUTH STATION **11:05 a.m.**
        BACK BAY   **11:10 a.m.**

FOR THE REGULAR SEASON HOME GAMES SHOWN

SUNDAY	OPPONENT	TRAIN TICKET
SEPT. 29	LOS ANGELES	A
OCT. 6	BALTIMORE	B
NOV. 3	BUFFALO	C
NOV. 10	CLEVELAND	D
NOV. 17	N. Y. JETS	E
DEC. 8	PITTSBURG	F

SAVE YOURSELF THE HASSLE OF DRIVING AND PARKING. RELAX ON THE WAY AND ARRIVE IN TIME FOR THE GAME.

THE RETURN TRAIN LEAVES ONE HALF-HOUR AFTER THE GAME IS OVER.

TRAIN TICKETS CAN BE PURCHASED AT EITHER SOUTH STATION OR BACK BAY STATION IN ADVANCE FOR ONE OR MORE GAMES OR FOR THE ENTIRE SEASON . . . A REAL CONVENIENCE FOR SEASON TICKET HOLDERS.

Ⓣ

MASS BAY TRANSPORTATION AUTHORITY

PENN CENTRAL TRANSPORTATION COMPANY

BP-20M-9/74

Figure 9.45 "Take the Trains to the Patriots Games," 1974
A flyer advertises six trains connecting Boston's South Station with Schaefer Stadium (later, Foxboro Stadium). The facility was home to the New England Patriots from 1971 until 2002, when the team relocated to the newer Gillette Stadium.

operations on the verge of disappearing due to multiple railroads going bankrupt or seeking to get out of the money-losing business of transporting the public. Even though the T had been subsidizing commuter rail service for over five years, Boston's railroads continued to drop passenger service. The Boston & Maine discontinued commuter rail service on its Sudbury Branch on November 26, 1971, despite earnest efforts by riders and the T to entice more riders onto Sudbury trains. The same year of Amtrak's creation, the Commonwealth re-authorised ninety percent funding for commuter rail service through the end of July 1972.

Massachusetts purchased, and in 1973 the MBTA took ownership of, 145 miles of former Penn Central railroad lines. The $19.5 million purchase included: the portion of the former New Haven main line from South Station to the Rhode Island border; Back Bay and 128 Stations; the Franklin Line; the Needham/Millis Line; the former Old Colony Lines from Braintree to Campello, and from Braintree to Plymouth; and the former Boston & Albany main line from Riverside to Framingham. The Commonwealth then committed to fund one hundred percent of the cost of commuter rail service, with a $7.6 million cap, from August 1, 1972 to August 1, 1973.

MBTA-subsidized commuter rail trains operated by the Boston & Maine and Penn Central moved a daily average of 16,000 commuters in 1973. That same year, the T began subsidizing Penn Central service to Framingham and purchased 145 miles of Penn Central rights-of-way and property. The Authority also applied for approximately $13 million in federal UMTA funding to purchase a portion of the Boston & Maine's Reading Branch, from Charlestown to Wilmington Junction.

The rainbow of MBTA transit modes expanded in 1974, when the Authority selected purple as the official color for its commuter rail service. Though the color has many symbolic associations, including one with royalty, purple provided a vibrant color to stand out from the blue, red, green, orange, and yellow already in use for other MBTA lines and modes. The first commuter rail vehicle to receive the new color was a Boston & Maine Rail Diesel Car (RDC), to which the MBTA applied a wide stripe of purple on either side and purple panels on each end. The T advertised the new color as not just a surface-level rebranding:

The color scheme signals the beginning of a new era for commuter rail passengers, a new era that

will soon include new and better equipment and vastly improved service.

As the 1970s progressed, the MBTA continued to invest in commuter rail infrastructure, committing in 1975 to a massive $39.5 million purchase of Boston & Maine properties, lines, and equipment, including over two hundred miles of railroad rights-of-way. The Boston & Maine was bankrupt and seeking to get out of providing passenger rail service. All together, the T's commitment to purchase came after its 1973-adoption of the Dyer Report, a 1972 consultant-prepared plan recommending the public acquisition and use of private railroad rights-of-way serving Greater Boston.

The T's 1975 annual report listed twenty-three locomotives, eighty-four coaches, and ninety-two RDCs moving 4.5 million and 2.9 million passengers on the lines of the Boston & Maine and Penn Central, respectively. On December 27, 1976, the MBTA finalized its purchase of nearly 280 miles of lines, over eighty RDCs, and acres of railroad facilities from the Boston & Maine. The Authority applauded its $39.5 million purchase, writing in 1977:

Boston's commuter rail network, which had been permitted to decay over the past three decades as a matter of national policy of stressing the automobile over railroads, finally came completely under public control.

After the T became the owner of the Boston & Maine's Greater Boston trackage and commuter rail equipment, the Authority hired the railroad to continue to operate Boston's commuter rail trains.

In spring 1976, the Consolidated Rail Corporation (Conrail) was created by the federal government to preserve the freight operations of failing railroad companies operating in a raft of contiguous states, from Massachusetts to Illinois. A headstrong Boston & Maine elected to not become part of Conrail. Still, the Boston & Maine didn't last long on its own, especially after years of mismanagement. In 1983, whatever the Boston & Maine had not sold off or abandoned was acquired by Guilford Transportation Industries Incorporated (Guilford). Guilford became PanAm Railways in 2006. South of the Boston & Maine's territory, Conrail took over Penn Central's remaining infrastructure, equipment, and freight operations.

In April 1976, the T approved the purchase of eight RDCs, 103 passenger coaches, and thirty-two locomotives, all ex-Penn Central equipment, from Conrail. After taking over the commuter rail operations of Penn Central, Conrail had a short lived tenure in Boston, a mere eleven months (Figure 9.46). As orchestrated by the MBTA, Conrail's Boston commuter rail operations were taken over by the Boston & Maine on March 15, 1977. The takeover occurred after Conrail confirmed it would be forced to suspend commuter rail operations unless it received a nearly one hundred percent increase in MBTA subsidies.

A spring 1977 extension of zone fares from north-side to southside trains brought, for the first time in Boston's history, all commuter rail trains under a uniform fare structure, a single operator, and a single owner. The Boston & Maine operated all of Boston's commuter rail trains while the MBTA owned virtually all commuter rail lines, facilities, and equipment. MBTA ownership allowed the T to adjust and improve commuter rail services with more economy, power, and speed than ever before. One example was the T's teaming up with Tufts University to reopen Tufts University Station on the Lowell Line. Commuter rail service returned to the station with MBTA-owned RDCs on September 1, 1977 (Figure 9.47). Tufts contributed approximately half of the approximately $4,500 cost to reopen the bare bones station, a first-of-a-kind collaboration for MBTA commuter rail.

The T commenced other improvements to its commuter rail network in 1977. On August 8, Governor Dukakis attended a formal kick off for improvements to be made along the South Acton Line (now Fitchburg Line). On August 25, Thomas

P. "Tip" O'Neill III oversaw the commencement of improvements along the Franklin Line. The September/October *Rollsign* quoted "Tip:"

The long-awaited rehabilitation of commuter rail lines, from roadbed and track work to refurbishment of rolling stock, all of which has suffered for some 30 years for lack of capital investment, will bring a turn-around in ridership. Suburbanites will find they have a fast comfortable and convenient alternative to their automobiles.

A major source of funding for the year's commuter rail upgrades was the UMTA, administered through the MBTA's Commuter Rail Improvement Program (CRIP). Under the CRIP, the T upgraded fifty-three commuter rail stations, various parking lots, and miles of trackage. Work along commuter rail lines included the installation of new track, ties, ballast, signals, and communication equipment. At the end of the year, the MBTA served ninety commuter rail stations and had 259 miles of commuter rail track under direct ownership.

Commuter rail improvements continued in 1978, when the MBTA ordered a handful of new locomotives and contracted Pullman-Standard Car Manufacturing Company (Pullman-Standard) to fabricate a batch of new commuter rail coaches, the T's 300-series coaches (Figure 9.48).

Type 6 Streetcar
At the end of 1969, the MBTA's Green Line fleet consisted exclusively of PCC cars, some purchased

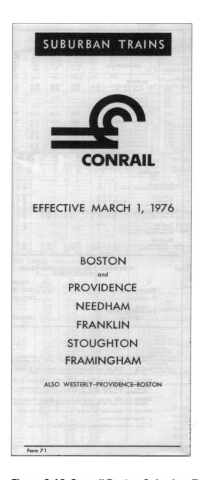

Figure 9.46 Conrail Boston Suburban Trains Timetable, 1976

Figure 9.47 Tufts University Station, September 15, 1977
A Boston & Maine RDC arrives at the ceremonial reopening of Tufts University Station. The stop opened to the public two weeks before the photograph was taken. It has since closed.

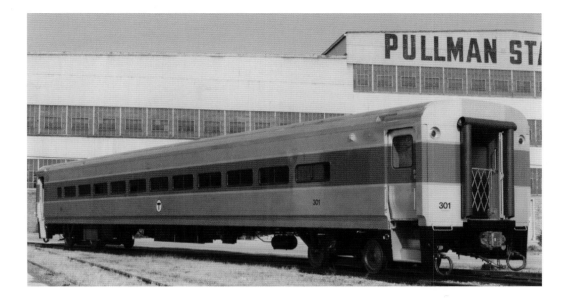

Figure 9.48 MBTA Commuter Rail Coach #301, Circa 1978
A new coach poses outside the shops of its manufacturer, Pullman-Standard.

secondhand by the MTA in the late 1950s. Partially because America had not seen the regular commercial production of streetcars for over fifteen years, spare parts for the PCCs were difficult to find, if existent at all. Over the years, as it continues to do, the MBTA regularly fabricated its own replacement parts. Knowing the long term viability of a PCC-only fleet for the Green Line was untenable, the Authority commissioned the design of a new trolley for Boston, the MBTA Type 6 streetcar. A full-scale partial mock-up of a Type 6 was displayed at the 1970 meeting of the American Transit Association (now American Public Transit Association). The mock-up lives on in Maine (Figure 9.49).

The T designed the Type 6 to be ten and a half feet tall, just under nine feet wide, and fifty feet long. It was three feet longer than a typical Boston PCC car. Specifications for the Type 6 called for air-conditioning (a first for a new streetcar in Boston), four 600 volt DC traction motors (each rated at 100 horsepower), an operational speed of fifty-five miles per hour, and the ability to accelerate from zero to forty miles per hour in half the time of a PCC car. Each Type 6 was designed to carry 264 people, with ninety seated and 174 standing. The MBTA never commissioned a production run of Type 6 streetcars. Instead, yielding to strong encouragement from the federal government, the T pursued Boston's first Light Rail Vehicles (LRVs).

Figure 9.49 MBTA Type 6 Streetcar Mock-up, 2014
The MBTA's 1970 mock-up of a never-realized trolley design resides at the Seashore Trolley Museum in Maine.

Fresh Paint
On December 13, 1971, the MBTA posed a two-car train, composed of PCC cars #3250 and #3256, at Government Center Station. The two streetcars were freshly painted in gray, green, and white, a color scheme that replaced the legacy orange of the BERy and MTA. The PCC repainting was part of a half million dollar streetcar renovation project. The Authority continued to bring the branding of its fleet into coordination with the *Manual of Guidelines and Standards*, as mentioned in its 1971 annual report:

> [The T adopted] a new color scheme for all revenue vehicles, giving them 30-inch wide bands of strong, bright line colors which reinforce the Authority's overall color scheme for graphics and design at new and modernized stations ... Rapid transit cars and streetcars use line identifying colors while the buses, because they connect with the rail lines, use a bright golden yellow, offset with narrow black stripes at the top and bottom.

Other aspects of the new color schemes called for upper bodies of buses to be painted white, with the lower bodies of buses to remain natural aluminum and the bodies of rapid transit cars to be painted gray (Figure 9.50).

Upgrades of trains and buses continued into the mid-1970s, with the T completing the renovation of thirty-eight Blue Line rapid transit cars. In 1975, the MBTA put into service 125 new buses, including seventy-five "kneeling buses" and fifty turnpike express buses. The Authority also began refurbishing Boston & Maine RDCs, initiated dispatcher-control, via radio, of train movements on the Orange and Blue Lines, and repainted 100

Figure 9.50 Train at City Square Station, September 14, 1972
A two-car train of 1957-built Orange Line Type 11 rapid transit cars pauses at City Square Station on the Charlestown Elevated. Above spans a green segment of elevated highway connecting the Mystic River Bridge (now the Maurice J. Tobin Memorial Bridge) with the Central Artery. The car wears a paint scheme adopted by the T in 1971, gray body paint with an orange stripe along the side.

Orange Line cars. In 1976, the T tested a Fiat-built RDC on Boston & Maine lines. The car was smaller and lighter than the Boston & Maine's ubiquitous Budd-built RDCs. The test was a first for the vehicle in America.

Towards the end of the 1970s, the MBTA tapped federal UMTA funds to kick off the refurbishment of an additional fifty PCC cars and eighty-eight Red Line cars. It also pushed forward with new uniforms for employees, a first since it took over from the MTA in 1964. Navy blue duds replaced dated gray designs inherited from the MTA.

The SOAC

In the early 1970s, the UMTA launched a program to develop a rapid transit car and a standard Light Rail Vehicle (SLRV) of unprecedented economy, reliability, safety, and comfort for America. The UMTA awarded management of the rapid transit program to Boeing Vertol, which in turn contracted the Saint Louis Car Company to fabricate two prototype cars, each branded a "State-Of-The-Art-Car" (SOAC) (Figure 9.52). The two cars were tested together as a short train on various American public transit systems. A UMTA press release announced:

> ...[The] two-car train will be unveiled to the Boston public and the press on Monday, August 19....The State-of-the-Art vehicle is designed to incorporate into one vehicle the best in available off-the-shelf technology. The SOAC train...has clocked more than 8,000 miles of revenue service in New York....After revenue testing in Boston,

SOAC will continue to Cleveland, Chicago, and Philadelphia for additional revenue operation.

The MBTA operated the SOAC train on the Red Line between Ashmont and Harvard Stations, carrying over 150,000 riders in revenue service. An invitation to the SOAC's inaugural Boston Run mentioned a reception for VIPs at the Parker House Hotel (Figure 9.51). During its visit to Boston, the SOAC train was displayed in City Hall Plaza for the public to walk through. The tradition continued in 2017 and 2018, when the T placed mock-ups of its latest Red and Orange Line cars in the plaza. The SOAC train still exists, albeit in static display at the Seashore Trolley Museum (Figure 9.53).

Boston's Boeing LRVs

In the middle of the twentieth century, after streetcars had mostly disappeared from the American landscape, a new vehicle arrived to transport the public along urban and suburban rails—the Light Rail Vehicle. LRVs differ from streetcars in that they are typically larger, of more robust construction, more powerful, and commonly operate along dedicated rights-of-ways. The MBTA was one of the first transit agencies in America to employ a significant fleet of LRVs as a replacement for streetcars.

The MBTA and the San Francisco Municipal Railway (MUNI) agreed in 1971 to prepare a joint-purchase order for new LRVs. The placement of a single large order, a strategy encouraged by the UMTA, allowed the MBTA-MUNI team to seek a lower per-vehicle purchase price. The UMTA provided $32.8 million in grants towards the 1973

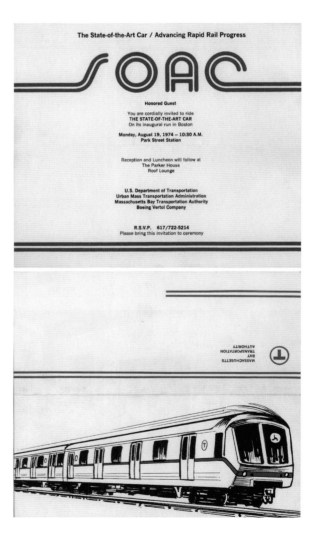

Figure 9.51 SOAC's Inaugural Boston Run Invitation, 1974

Figure 9.52 "SOAC is the Now Car!" Brochure, 1974

The State-Of-The-Art-Car train was composed of two similar prototypical rapid transit cars. One car was a high-density model that seated seventy-two and had a maximum capacity of 300 people. The other car, a low-density model, seated sixty-two and had a capacity of 220.

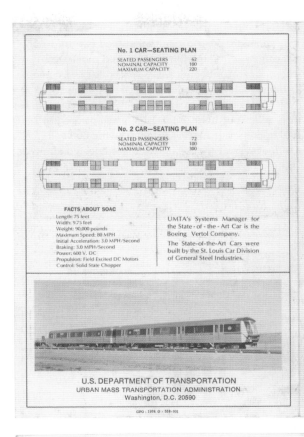

No. 1 CAR—SEATING PLAN

SEATED PASSENGERS	62
NOMINAL CAPACITY	100
MAXIMUM CAPACITY	220

No. 2 CAR—SEATING PLAN

SEATED PASSENGERS	72
NOMINAL CAPACITY	100
MAXIMUM CAPACITY	300

FACTS ABOUT SOAC

Length: 75 feet
Width: 9.75 feet
Weight: 90,000 pounds
Maximum Speed: 80 MPH
Initial Acceleration: 3.0 MPH/Second
Braking: 3.0 MPH/Second
Power: 600 V. DC
Propulsion: Field Excited DC Motors
Control: Solid State Chopper

UMTA's Systems Manager for the State-of-the-Art Car is the Boeing Vertol Company.

The State-of-the-Art Cars were built by the St. Louis Car Division of General Steel Industries.

U.S. DEPARTMENT OF TRANSPORTATION
URBAN MASS TRANSPORTATION ADMINISTRATION
Washington, D.C. 20590

SOAC
IS
THE NOW
CAR!

The STATE-OF-THE-ART CAR a program of The URBAN MASS TRANSPORTATION ADMINISTRATION

Figure 9.53 The SOAC Train, 2018

Faded by years of exposure, a U.S. Department of Transportation logo (center) brands one car of the aging SOAC train. A rollsign curtain displays "Service to Harvard," as it did during the SOAC train's brief 1974 stint in Red Line service.

UMTA... The U.S. Department of Transportation's Urban Mass Transportation Administration brings you SOAC... the State-of-the-Art Car. It's an entirely new concept in rail rapid transit.

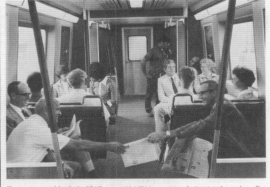

SOAC is the NOW car!

It's the first long step in making urban rail travel attractive again. Safe, Operational And Comfortable, SOAC is ready to move people conveniently, reliably and rapidly through the ever-mounting congestion of our major cities.

SOAC is a car for ALL seasons

It has the most modern controls to climatize its spacious interior for maximum comfort. The sounds, the smells and the smog of the cities cannot intrude on your smooth, quiet SOAC ride as you speed through the city faster, safer and more relaxed than in your own auto.

SOAC is the "people-car."

Lighting, climate control, quality of ride and noise control create an entirely new standard in rail car design. We call it a "creature-comfort" standard, because SOAC was designed to fulfill the needs of people. Comfort, convenience and environment coupled with success-ful, advanced, *AVAILABLE* technology make SOAC the NOW car.

The interior sound level of a SOAC train at 60 MPH is as quiet as the interior of a modern office building and normal conversations can be carried on in relaxing comfort within the speeding cars.

STATE-OF-THE-ART

In 1973, the SOAC completed initial testing at the U.S. Department of Transportation's High Speed Ground Test Center in Pueblo, Colorado. Now SOAC is being demonstrated to the industry and the public on transit lines in New York, Boston, Chicago, Cleveland and Philadelphia. At Pueblo, UMTA has had a chance to evaluate the technology. During these operational demonstrations, the transit industry will have a chance to evaluate its efficiency. But most important, YOU, the riding public will have a chance to enjoy its quality. We'll leave the riding to you!

joint-purchase of LRVs from Boeing Vertol, a division of the aerospace behemoth Boeing. With the support of the UMTA, Boeing Vertol marketed it's vehicle as the SLRV for America (Figure 9.54).

In Boston, Boeing Vertol-built SLRVs became known as Boeing LRVs (Figure 9.56). They arrived on the heels of the T's 1974 testing of the SOAC train. Boston's Boeing LRVs were slightly different from their MUNI brethren. While the

MUNI vehicles had a single aisle with pairs of seats on each side, Boston's units featured two-and-one seating, a configuration that offered more standing room. Boston's Boeing LRVs seated fifty-two people.

Boeing LRVs were designed to run in multiple unit (MU) operation and were rated to travel up to fifty miles per hour. Each LRV was powered by two 210 horsepower motors, each drawing 600 volts DC from overhead wire. An articulated design allowed

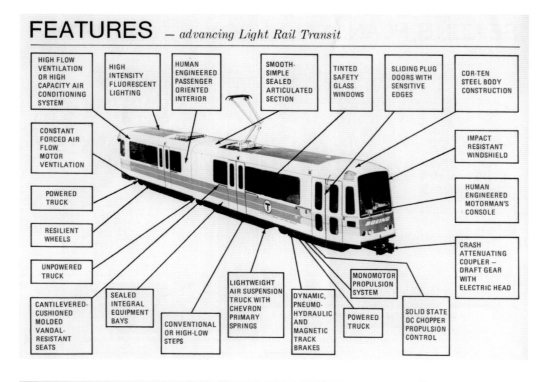

Figure 9.54 Feature Diagram for Boeing Vertol's LRV, 1975

Figure 9.55 "I Ride the LRV" Pin, Circa Late 1970s

Figure 9.56 Boston's Boeing LRV #3400, Circa 1975
The Boeing Vertol Company posed one of its LRVs manufactured for the MBTA at the U.S. Government's railroad and transit vehicle testing facility in Pueblo, Colorado.

each seventy-one-foot-long LRV (nearly twice as long as a typical streetcar) to navigate the tight turns in Boston's streetcar tunnels and turning loops. Each half of a Boeing LRV was designated either the A or B section and had an operator's cab, allowing the vehicle to be driven in either direction along a given track.

Boston's first Boeing LRV, number 3402, arrived in March 1976 and made a promotional run along the Riverside Line. After additional test runs, the car returned to Boeing for adjustments. A few months before the Boeing LRV promotional run, the T dedicated a new $10 million maintenance and repair facility for LRVs at Riverside. Still in use, the facility opened with office space, a car washer, and a 107,000 square foot car house with eleven run-through tracks.

During a massive snow storm on December 30, 1976, the MBTA pressed its first four new LRVs into service on the Riverside Line. In and out of the storm, the new vehicles were mechanically troublesome. Each LRV had three pairs of bizarrely complicated doors, assembled from hundreds of parts. The exterior mounting of the doors begged for malfunctions during bad weather and heavy use in an urban subway. In time, the MBTA replaced the troublesome doors with bi-fold types of far simpler design. To fund in-house redevelopment of its LRVs, the MBTA applied for eighty percent UMTA funding.

The August 3, 1978 *Boston Globe* reported a decreasing percentage of LRVs available for revenue service, from eighty-three percent in January, to sixty-four percent in July. Derailments and increasing failures of the vehicles' air conditioning units contributed to more LRVs being unavailable as summer progressed. By the end of the year, the T had received 135 LRVs, thirty-five of which it wanted to return to the manufacturer, citing continued failures of air conditioning systems and overly complicated doors, electronics, and traction systems. Internally, union workers protested to MBTA management and even threatened a system-wide strike if the T sent the partially disassembled trolleys back to Boeing for manufacturer-funding repair and reassembly. The union saw working on the repairs as their right.

LRV woes continued for the T with local media blasting the Authority, along with the UMTA and Boeing Vertol, for bringing an under-cooked trolley design to Boston and wasting millions of taxpayer dollars on repairs that might have been mitigated by better design and engineering prior

to manufacturing. Local media accused the UMTA, under President Richard Nixon, of forcing the SLRV upon Boston and San Francisco, despite the fact that both cities were in the process of working on what might have been better designs for new trolleys.

A resolution of Boston's Boeing LRV problems began to take shape in 1979, when the MBTA and Boeing Vertol reached agreement. The manufacturer committed to returning $40 million to the MBTA and cancelling a remaining forty cars on order, without penalty to the Authority. Boeing Vertol further agreed to repair up to thirty-five trolleys at its cost and provide the T with repair and upgrade kits to address the mechanical deficiencies of the vehicles already accepted by the T.

By the middle of 1982, over 100 Boeing LRVs were available for revenue service. At the end of the year, three of the four Green Line branches saw service exclusively provided by Boeing LRVs. For twenty-five years, Boeing LRVs were ubiquitous across the Green Line. The last Boeing LRV to operate in regular revenue service ran on March 16, 2007. Most of the retired vehicles were scrapped at Riverside Yard.

The Haymarket-North Extension

The Haymarket-North Extension was a scaled-back version of the Reading Extension proposed by the MTA in 1961 (See Chapter 8). It replaced the Charlestown Elevated, bringing the Orange Line along a new alignment through Charlestown, across the Mystic River, and into Medford and Malden (Figure 9.57). From South to North, the Haymarket-North Extension consisted of a new rapid transit station and tunnel under the south-west corner of Haverhill and Canal Streets, a new two-track tunnel under the Charles River, and new above-ground stations at the Prison Point Bridge (now Gilmore Bridge), Sullivan Square, Wellington Circle (Medford), Malden Center, and Oak Grove (Malden). North of the Charles River, the Haymarket-North Extension followed an existing Boston & Maine right-of-way.

After a September 22, 1966 groundbreaking ceremony, work commenced on the first segment of the Haymarket-North Extension, a two-track subway tunnel with station, all constructed using the cut and cover method. The tunnel and station (North Station) were threaded through a web of existing underground utilities and infrastructure, where builders tediously identified and relocated existing

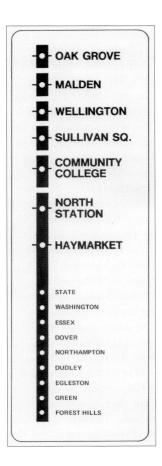

Figure 9.57 Building the Haymarket Extension, 1970
On an Orange Line map, the new stations of the Haymarket Extension are highlighted in larger text.

Figure 9.58 North Station on the Orange Line, 1975
Completed in 1971, the rapid transit station opened along with the majority of the Haymarket-North Extension in 1975.

sewers, cables, and other utilities. They located, underpinned, and trimmed hundreds of underground footings and piers that supported the North Station Office Building, North Station commuter rail terminal, and Central Artery elevated highway. The tangle of sub-surface elements gained the nickname "bucket of worms." The southernmost station of the Haymarket-North Extension, North Station was completed in 1971 and opened to Orange Line trains on April 4, 1975 (Figure 9.58).

North of North Station, the Haymarket-North Extension's Charles River tunnel consisted of two tubes, each 232 feet long, thirty-seven-and-a-half feet wide, and twenty-two-and-a-half feet high. Each tube was fabricated from plate steel in Maryland, before being floated up the East Coast to Boston. The tubes were sunk into the bed of the Charles River (Figure 9.59), where they were connected to each other and lined with reinforced concrete. Massive steel coffer dams protected workers connecting the ends of the river tubes with the fixed tunnels (Figure 9.60). The installation of sunken tubes with coffer dams, a technique pioneered in Boston on the Haymarket-North Extension, were used again in the city during construction of the Ted Williams Tunnel.

Immediately to the north of the Charles River, the double-track Haymarket-Extension emerged into daylight. There, work commenced from the Charles River to the north side of Sullivan Square in June 1969. This segment was triple-tracked, initially to allow trains to terminate at the first stations to open, and later, to allow parallel operation of express and local trains. The first station north of the river was located where the Haymarket-North

Extension passed beneath the Prison Point Bridge. Located next to the soon-to-be-completed Bunker Hill Community College, the station received the name Community College. North of Community College Station, the Haymarket-North Extension passed along a new viaduct over the tracks of the Boston & Maine's Mystic Division, before returning to grade and passing through a new Sullivan Square Station. Most of the viaduct and station were constructed contemporaneously with, and sat beneath, the superstructure of an elevated portion of Interstate 93. A bus boarding area and large parking lot rounded out Sullivan Square Station. Orange Line trains began serving Community College and Sullivan Square Stations on April 7, 1975.

From Sullivan Square Station northward, the Haymarket-North Extension followed the right-of-way of the Boston & Maine's Reading Branch. The extension and parallel railroad line crossed the Mystic River between the cities of Somerville and Medford on a new two-part bridge. One portion of the span carried three tracks of the Orange Line, another, a single track for freight and commuter rail trains. Construction of the bridge commenced on September 24, 1969 and reached completion on July 14, 1972. In December, Boston & Maine trains began using the new structure and demolition loomed for the neighboring, older, and newly redundant railroad drawbridge. On June 15, 1973, the new bridge was dedicated to honor Edward Dana, former head of both the BERy and the MTA.

The northernmost segment of the Haymarket-North Extension ran from the Mystic River to northern Malden. Just north of the river was

Figure 9.59 Sinking a Tunnel Tube, Circa 1970
One of two massive prefabricated steel tunnel tubes lies mostly submerged in the waters of the Charles River. The tube is being prepared to be sunk to the river bottom. There, it will form one half of a tunnel to carry Orange Line trains beneath the river along the Haymarket-North Extension.

Figure 9.60 Beneath the River's Shore, Circa 1970
Working at the bottom of a massive coffer dam on the north bank of the river, builders address where the northern end of a sunken tunnel tube will connect with the rest of the extension.

MALDEN CENTER STATION 1975

Figure 9.61 Malden Center Station Opening Brochure, 1975

Figure 9.62 Oak Grove Station, Circa 1976
The northernmost station of the Haymarket-North Extension remains the northern terminus of the Orange Line.

Wellington Station and Wellington Shops and Yard, all constructed during 1973–75. The shops were enclosed by a main building, with a length of 460 feet and a width of 242 feet, that sheltered nine tracks. The shops included facilities for the heavy maintenance, inspection, and washing of Orange Line cars. Wellington Yard opened with no fewer than fourteen tracks, each approximately 700 feet long. Wellington Shops and Yard remains the central storage, repair, inspection, and maintenance facility for Orange Line cars. Wellington Station opened with three tracks and two platforms. The station, complemented by a busway and parking areas capable of holding 1,000 automobiles, opened for revenue service on September 6, 1975.

North of Wellington Station, the Haymarket-North Extension served two new stations, both in Malden. Malden Center and Oak Grove Stations featured what the MBTA called "kiss-and-ride" areas, places where automobile commuters could be dropped off or picked up. Busways and parking areas rounded out each station. After being formally dedicated on October 23, 1975, Malden Center Station opened for revenue service on December 27 (Figure 9.61).

Friday April 4, 1975 was marked by a day of ceremonies along the Haymarket-North Extension. Governor Dukakis celebrated the opening of Sullivan Square, Community College, and North Stations by touring the line in a special four-car train. At the end of service, the MBTA permanently ceased Orange Line revenue train movements over the Charlestown Elevated and began work to tie the new extension into the existing Orange Line at Haymarket Station. After approximately three quarters of a century, rapid transit trains disappeared from Causeway Street, the Charlestown Bridge, Main Street in Charlestown, and the arched shed of the BERy's 1901 Sullivan Square Terminal.

On Saturday, April 5, buses that previously served Sullivan Square Station on the Charlestown Elevated, began to serve Sullivan Square Station on the Haymarket-North Extension. On Monday, Orange Line trains traveling north of Haymarket Station began to operate along the Haymarket-North Extension.

A ceremony on August 21, 1975, held in Charlestown's City Square, marked the beginning of the demolition of the Charlestown Elevated. People smashed bottles of champagne against the doomed structure. The entire el and its intermediate stations were dismantled in less than four months. Thompson Square Station lingered until April 19, 1976, when it was destroyed by fire. The station had been disconnected from the el and relocated to ground level, where it was awaiting potential reuse as a restaurant. The removal of the elevated railways and their trains from Charlestown ended decades of oppressive noise and opened streets to light and air. Rapid transit service previously available at City and Thompson Squares was relocated out of the neighborhood and consolidated at Community College Station. North Station on the el

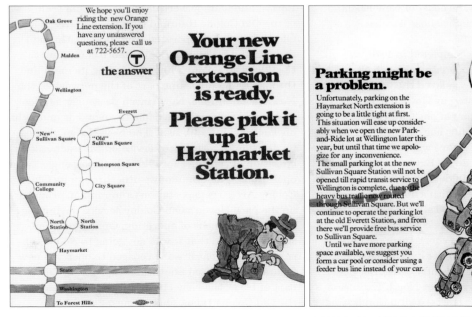

Figure 9.63 Haymarket-North Extension Brochure, Circa 1975

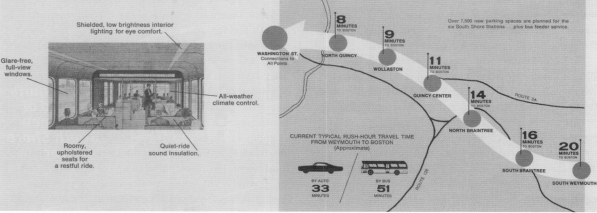

Figure 9.64 South Shore Extension Brochure, Late 1960s
Before putting shovel to earth, the MBTA published a brochure touting a proposed southern expansion of the Red Line, as far as South Weymouth. A rendering of the vision of architects at Cambridge Seven for new Red Line cars (top) is joined by a map (bottom) ticking off anticipated travel times from proposed stations to Downtown Crossing.

and the BERy's Sullivan Square Station succumbed to the wrecking ball in 1976.

At least one piece of the Charlestown Elevated remains. Tower C, which perched over the intersection of Causeway Street and the Boston approach to the Charlestown Bridge for three quarters of a century, made its way up the coast of New England to its final destination, the Seashore Trolley Museum in southern Maine.

Oak Grove Station was completed in 1976 (Figure 9.62) but did not open until March 19, 1977; additional land use studies delayed the opening. Oak Grove Station was dedicated by Governor Dukakis on March 21, 1977. Speakers at the Oak Grove ceremony confirmed that further extension of the Orange Line beyond Oak Grove was no longer being pursued by the T. The Reading Extension was not going to make it beyond Malden. The $8.5 million Oak Grove complex opened with a 500-car parking lot, which initially offered $1.00 all-day parking for commuters. After 9:30 a.m., the cost dropped to fifty cents, allowing a discount on short-term parking for mid-day shopping trips into the city. Orange Line fare for a ride into Boston was fifty cents. Service along the $165 million Haymarket North Extension commenced with four-car trains, a situation lasting

until the entire Orange Line was updated to accommodate longer trains.

The South Shore Extension
The first passengers to ride the rails between Boston and Quincy were carried on steam trains of the Old Colony Railroad (Old Colony). By 1845, Old Colony trains operated from Boston, through Quincy, and beyond, to South Shore communities. The Old Colony's lines, including its main line through Quincy, became part of the network of the New Haven in 1893. New Haven passenger service on the Old Colony Lines came to an end at midnight on Tuesday, June 30, 1959. The New Haven blamed its decision to terminate service on Massachusetts' cessation of subsidies for Old Colony passenger train operations. The Commonwealth, through its Old Colony Area Transportation Commission, propped up the New Haven's Old Colony service during the last twelve months of operation. Once Massachusetts confirmed that it was not going to renew the subsidies and that it was prepared to open the new federally-subsidized Southeast Expressway (now part of I-93), the New Haven called it quits along the Old Colony Lines. Quincy lacked a regular

Figure 9.65 South Shore Car Mock-up, Late 1960s

Figure 9.66 The South Shore Extension Opens, 1971
The cover of the *Commuter* newsletter shows a train of Red Line Type 1 rapid transit cars crossing the Neponset River.

Figure 9.67 South Shore Extension Medallion, 1971
A two-sided medallion commemorating the opening of the South Shore Extension shows a Red Line Type 1 rapid transit car (left) and car traversing the Anderson Bridge (right).

Figure 9.68 Wollaston Station Design, Circa 1968–69

passenger rail connection with Boston for over a decade, until the South Shore Extension of the Red Line opened in 1971.

Massachusetts proposed extending rapid transit service from Boston into neighboring Quincy as early as 1926. The MTA proposed an extension of the Cambridge-Dorchester rapid transit line through Quincy to Braintree in 1963. After taking over the MTA, the T proposed a new extension of the Red Line to not only serve Quincy and Braintree, but to Weymouth. The T's proposed new Red Line branch was the South Shore Extension.

When planning the South Shore Extension, the MBTA's selection of electric rapid transit trains was not a forgone conclusion. The Authority studied the feasibility of various modes for the new line, including running buses along a paved right-of-way and a monorail. Approximately one year after taking over from the MTA, the MBTA selected electric rapid transit trains, vehicles Boston transit operators had decades of experience with. Opting for the same type of vehicle already in use along the Red Line would, in time, eliminate the need for riders to change between modes if travelling between Boston and the South Shore.

To provide service along the South Shore Extension, the MBTA needed to augment the existing Red Line car fleet. To envision new cars, the T turned to Cambridge Seven, the designers behind the rebranding of the T and creation of the spider map. Cambridge Seven came up with a futuristic-looking rapid transit vehicle with rounded edges and large windows (Figure 9.64). A full size mock-up of a portion of one of the cars was posed for promotional photographs (Figure 9.65). The car's interior featured spider maps on the walls and a line map of the Red Line mounted at ceiling level. Transit car manufacturers deemed the design, especially the curved glazing and rounded car shape, not economically feasible nor technically practical for mass production. Hence, Cambridge Seven's design never saw a production run.

Construction of the South Shore Extension commenced on August 18, 1966, when a ceremony kicked off work on a new bridge over the Neponset River. The George L. Anderson Bridge was a nearly $2 million span built to replace a New Haven Railroad bridge damaged by fire. The Anderson Bridge featured massive steel spans supported by nine reinforced concrete piers. It carried Red Line tracks approximately three stories above the tidal waters of the river (Figure 9.66). With approaches included, the bridge was approximately 3,000 feet long. The scene of a four-car train of Red Line Type 1 rapid transit cars crossing the new bridge was memorialized on commemorative medallions (Figure 9.67). The Anderson Bridge remains in daily use by Red Line trains crossing between Dorchester and Quincy.

The MBTA recorded a project cost of $75.4 million, $35.2 million of which was funded by UMTA grants, for the six-and-a-quarter-mile-long South Shore Extension and its three stations, North Quincy, Wollaston (Figure 9.68), and Quincy Center

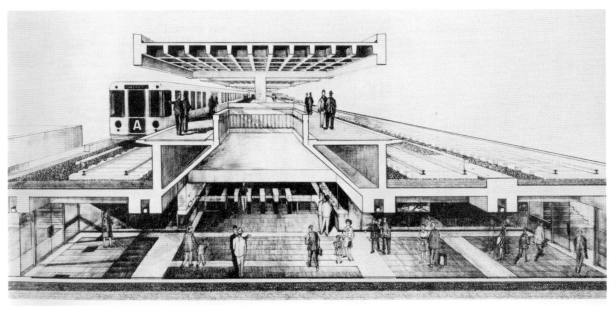

(Figure 9.69). Each station opened with a central platform served by northbound and southbound trains. Stairs and escalators carried people to ticket lobbies below (Wollaston Station) or above (North Quincy and Quincy Center Stations). Quincy Center Station opened with a five-story 800-car parking garage, multiple busways, and its own kiss-and-ride area.

Seventy-four years to the day after revenue service commenced within the Tremont Street Subway, on September 1, 1971, the MBTA opened the South Shore Extension (Figure 9.71). The extension ran from Columbia Junction (near JFK/UMass Station) in Dorchester to the southern portion of Quincy Center. The opening day program listed Joseph C. Kelly, General Manager of the MBTA, as Master of Ceremonies. Addresses were called for various pols and VIPs, including U.S. Secretary of Transportation John A. Volpe. Before serving as the second U.S. Secretary of Transportation from 1969 to 1973, Volpe served as governor of the Commonwealth from 1961 to 1963, and again, from 1965 to 1969. Edward Dana, Mr. Transit himself, rode on the inaugural train. Bands played as the train arrived at each station.

The September 2, 1971 edition of the *Quincy Sun* was peppered with advertisements encouraging transit riders to "celebrate T days" with special offers at local businesses. Mayor McIntyre officially opened Quincy Center Station and declared the

Figure 9.69 Constructing Quincy Center Station, 1970
A spiral parking garage ramp towers over the right-of-way being prepared for Red Line and commuter rail tracks along the South Shore Extension.

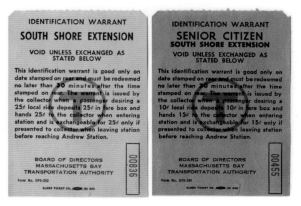

Figure 9.70 South Shore Extension Tickets, Circa 1971
"Identification Warrants" sold at Quincy's new South Shore Extension stations included a regular ticket (left) and a "Senior Citizen" ticket (right). Both were valid for thirty minutes. Half of the fare paid for each ticket was returned to the ticket holder if they detrained at another station within Quincy. The full fare was retained by the T if the ticket holder continued into Boston.

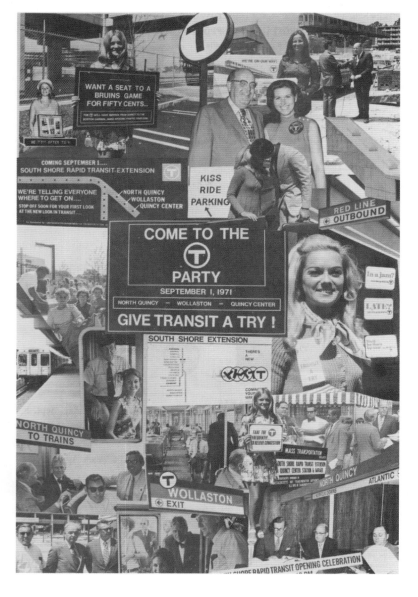

Figure 9.71 "Welcome to The T Party," 1971
A boisterous collage filled an entire page of the September 1, 1971 edition of the MBTA's *Commuter* newsletter.

day a city holiday. The MBTA provided free rides between the new Quincy stations and Columbia Station.

Regular revenue service along the South Shore Extension commenced on September 2, 1971. The day was marked by increasing delays because the new computer-controlled Red Line trains kept stopping for longer periods between stations. Opening day glitches were eventually sorted out, but larger technical problems remained, causing the T to spend years and millions of dollars improving

train control and signaling systems along the South Shore Extension.

To both encourage ridership and educate the public about the new South Shore Extension service, the MBTA produced a pocket-sized folding schedule card with the title "Give Transit a Try!" (Figure 9.72). Early ridership counts on the South Shore Extension exceeded the T's projections. More than two million revenue riders travelled the line between September 2 and December 31. Many of the line's new riders arrived by car or walked to the

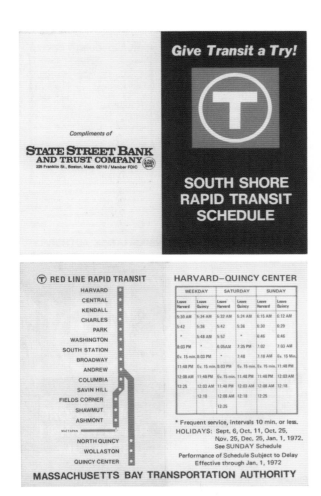

Figure 9.72 Red Line Schedule Card, 1971
Coinciding with the opening of the South Shore Extension to Quincy Center, the T issued pocket-sized schedule cards.

Figure 9.73 South Shore Extension Brochure, Circa 1970
A bright yellow exterior (left) features a collage of photographs cataloging the annoyances of driving in Boston. The brochure unfolds to reveal (right) the trains, stations, and technology—TRANSIT—as the antidote to the hassles of driving.

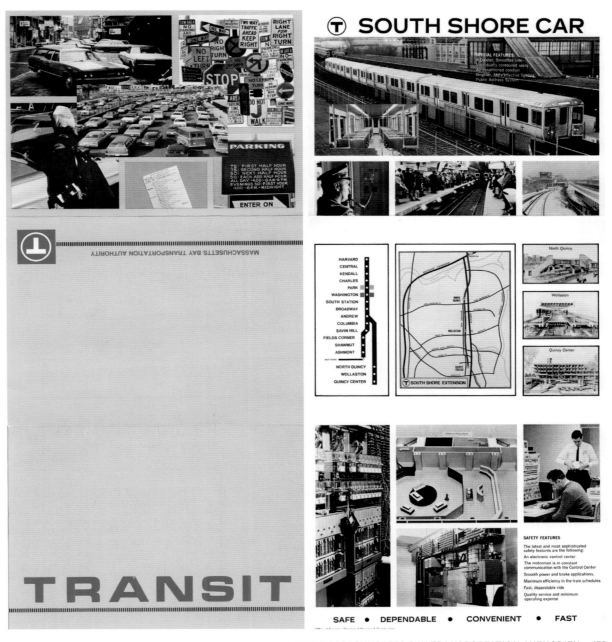

new stations, allowing the MBTA to reduce local bus service and associated costs.

Silver Birds for the Red Line

In 1968, the MBTA entered into a $13 million contract with Pullman-Standard for the production of seventy-six new Red Line rapid transit cars. The order consisted of twenty-four single cars and twenty-six "married" pairs. The single cars received 01500-series numbers. The paired cars received 01600-series numbers. When configured as a mated pair, each of the 01600-series' cabs faced one of two possible directions of travel. The first completed mated pair, numbered 01600–01601 (Figure 9.74), arrived at the T for testing in fall 1969. The MBTA recognized the 01500 and 01600-series cars as Red Line Type 1 rapid transit cars. They quickly became known as South Shore Cars.

The specifications for Red Line Type 1 cars called for some standard features that were firsts for new rapid transit cars in Boston, including aluminum body construction, air-conditioning, rubber flooring, radios, public address systems, and tinted safety glass. The MBTA boasted that its South Shore Cars featured "a satin-smooth brushed aluminum exterior, the first of its kind in the U.S. transit industry." Their aluminum skins earned Type 1 cars the moniker "Silver Birds." Each car measured just under seventy feet long and a bit less than ten feet wide (Figure 9.75). *Railway Age* magazine called the cars "the longest in transit service anywhere in the U.S." Four 100 horsepower DC traction motors powered each Silver Bird to a top rated speed of seventy miles per hour. Each car featured dynamic braking, a process through which the car's traction motors worked to slow the car to approximately fifteen miles per hour, at which point automatically applied air brakes completed the stopping of the car. Each car seated sixty-four passengers and was rated for a maximum capacity of 239 people. Initially, interiors of Type 1 cars featured transverse seating (Figure 9.76). In time, the T converted the seating within all Type 1s, save for a few seats at the extreme end of some cars, to longitudinal configurations (Figure 9.77).

With less than a year to go before the opening of the South Shore Extension, in early 1971, the MBTA

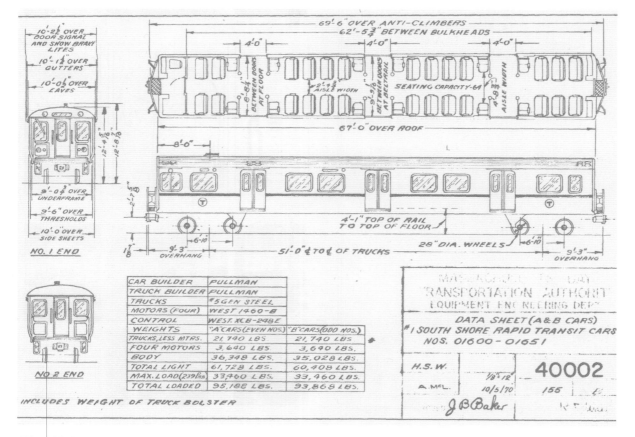

Figure 9.74 Red Line "Silver Birds," Circa 1969

A brand new married pair of Red Line Type 1 rapid transit cars is led by number 01600.

Figure 9.75 01600-Series Red Line Rapid Transit Car, 1970

A data sheet articulates dimensions and specifications for Pullman-Standard-built 01600-series Red Line cars. Each 01600-series car featured one operator's cab (left side of plan) and was designed to operate when mated to another 01600-series car.

Figure 9.76 Red Line Type 1 Car Interior, September 5, 1971
On "Silver Bird" Red Line cars, bench seating was the norm for years.

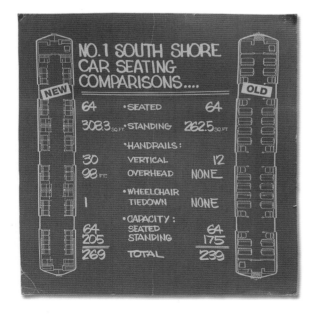

Figure 9.77 Red Line Type 1 Car Seating Comparisons
When the T began to update seating within "Silver Birds" from mostly transverse to a mix of transverse and longitudinal configurations, it posted car cards to quantify the changes.

opened a facility to train operators on the operation of the new Type 1 cars. The heart of the facility was a simulator with a full-size car operator's cab. In the simulator, a trainee operated a realistic bank of controls while facing moving images simulating a driver's view of travel along the Red Line.

The inaugural trip for Red Line Type 1 cars took place on September 25, 1969, when a four-car train ran from Eliot Square Shops in Cambridge to Codman Yard in Dorchester. The return of the train to Harvard Square was celebrated with a reception at Cambridge's Sheraton Commander Hotel attended by representatives of Pullman-Standard and the MBTA. By the end of 1969, four-car trains of Silver Birds were in regular revenue service.

From Eliot Square to Cabot Yard

As 1968 kicked off and construction entered a second year along the South Shore Extension, the MBTA sought a site for a new Red Line maintenance facility and storage yard. The forty-five year old Eliot Square Car House and Yard in Cambridge was becoming inadequate and would not be viable once the Red Line fleet became swollen with Silver Birds. The MBTA formalized the sale of its Bennett Street and Eliot Square properties in Harvard Square on February 15, 1968. Purchasers included an entity seeking to use a portion of the property as the site for the presidential library of John. F. Kennedy. The MBTA received just shy of $6.1 million from the Commonwealth for approximately

ten acres. The Authority received $1.33 million for nearly two-and-a-quarter acres deeded to the Kennedy Library project.

With a sale of its Bennett/Eliot properties in the bag, the T stepped up its efforts to establish a location for a new Red Line facility. Concurrently, in March 1968, the MBTA approved an extension of Red Line rapid transit service from Ashmont to Mattapan. The estimated $12 million project called for rapid transit service to replace streetcar service along the Mattapan High Speed Line. The T proposed closing four of the seven streetcar stations and establishing new rapid transit stations at Butler Street, Central Avenue, and Mattapan Square. In addition to proposing a new terminal station with a parking garage, the T also proposed to establish at Mattapan Square its new Red Line rapid transit car maintenance facility and storage yard.

The Mattapan rapid transit project, especially the proposed shops and yard for rapid transit cars, was aggressively opposed by Milton, the town abutting Mattapan Square. Despite the local objections, and months before his December appointment by President Nixon to U.S. Secretary of Transportation, Governor Volpe signed off on the rapid transit conversion of the High Speed Line and relocation of Harvard Square Red Line facilities to Mattapan. Though the MBTA prevailed in the courts, by the end of 1969, and facing continued local opposition, the T abandoned its plan to bring rapid transit to Mattapan. After Milton fought to subvert relocation of Red Line maintenance and storage facilities to Mattapan, communities south of Quincy, soon to be served by the South Shore Extension, joined the chorus of opposition. Local objections at South Braintree foiled the T's attempt to establish a new Red Line shops and yard there as well.

With Mattapan and South Braintree out as sites for its new Red Line facility, and its Eliot Square lands under agreement, the MBTA zeroed in on land that it just agreed to purchase in South Boston, two dozen acres of the Penn Central's Dover Street Yards. The Dover Street land complimented a neighboring parcel of nearly nine acres, a one-time Old Colony coach yard, already owned by the T. On December 19, 1969, the MBTA Advisory Board approved a $7.5 million purchase of Dover Street Yards, applying $7 million from the sale of its Bennett-Eliot properties towards the purchase.

As the MBTA began demolishing disused railroad structures at Dover Street Yards in 1971, the authority finalized plans to erect its South Bay Maintenance Center on the site. Along with new shops and storage yard for Red Line cars, the T planned to open a new bus garage at the center. U.S. Secretary of Transportation (and former Massachusetts Governor) John Volpe attended a groundbreaking for the $37 million facility in 1972. Over $19 million of the funding came from the UMTA. The MBTA dedicated its South Bay Maintenance Center as the Charles C. Cabot Transportation Center in June 1974. Cabot was a former chairman of the MBTA Board of Directors.

The Cabot Transportation Center opened with a 200-bus garage and central maintenance, inspection, and storage facility for the Red Line rapid transit car fleet. Today, facilities at Cabot include a rapid transit car house with nine run-through tracks, a massive bus garage that also houses the T's safety and training departments, and a fueling area for MBTA compressed natural gas (CNG) buses. Adjacent to the Cabot Transportation Center is an MBTA commuter rail maintenance and service facility. Immediately to the south of the commuter rail facility is Amtrak's Southampton Street Maintenance Facility, a place of layover, inspection, and workshops for Amtrak locomotives and coaches, including Acela Express equipment.

Ambitious Plans: Governor Sargent's 1972 Address

As the 1970s got underway, continued expansion of the interstate highway system finally hit some serious bumps in the road, not due to a lack of funding or federal commitment, but because people living in neighborhoods found a common voice. In Boston, activist groups consisting of residents whose neighborhoods were threatened by the construction of the region's next expressway united and spoke out against replacing city blocks with breakdown lanes and median strips. The Commonwealth's chief executive acknowledged the work of Boston's activist citizenry in 1972, calling for a re-calibration of transportation planning, funding, and construction in Massachusetts.

Governor Francis Sargent delivered a televised speech on November 30, 1972 in which he put forth a stunning vision for transportation in the Commonwealth. The Governor proposed that public transportation no longer be considered an afterthought:

> …We have been caught in a vicious cycle. More cars meant more highways, which meant more traffic jams, more traffic jams meant the need for more highways, which meant more traffic jams—and the need for super highways.

The Governor reminded those watching of his decision, "[to call] a halt to most of the highway construction within the Route 128 area." He continued:

> I called for a complete review and then for the development of plans suitable to the space age we have entered, plans providing a balance of transportation for the years ahead. The study we undertook—a balanced transportation planning review—was the first such in America, and became the most comprehensive the nation has yet seen

> It is 33 months since that study began….Shall we build more expressways…through cities? Shall we forge new chains to shackle us to the mistakes of the past? No.

After acknowledging that investment in an adequate road network for Greater Boston was indeed critical, Sargent shared his vision for robust public transportation:

> Mass transit is no good today because it was ignored yesterday—and all the years before yesterday. Tonight a declaration to end all of that.

The governor referred to the results of studies championed by his office:

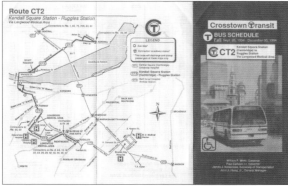

Figure 9.78 Crosstown Bus Route Schedules, Fall 1994

The first paper schedules for the MBTA's three "CT" bus routes feature maps of each initial route. CT1 (top) commenced with termini at Central Square, in Cambridge, and Boston University Medical Center, in Boston's South End. CT2 (middle) linked Kendall Square, MIT, Longwood Medical Area, and Ruggles Station. CT3 (bottom) circulated between Longwood Medical Area, Boston University Medical Center, and Andrew Station.

Contained here is the documentation for what will become the most imaginative and creative new system of people transportation to be seen anywhere in this country.

He declared: "We will buy new cars, improve railroad beds and signal systems and layout new transit routes to take people where they want to go." The Governor listed a series of transportation improvement projects, including: new transit lines in Boston and Cambridge; an upgrade of transit between Dudley Square and Mattapan; an extension of the Southwest Corridor to Canton and Needham; and "a circumferential transit system unlike anything so far imagined." Sargent also shared that the North-South Rail Link along with what became the Central Artery / Third Harbor Tunnel Project (The Big Dig) were both being considered by state planners.

Governor Sargent proposed big funding for his bold proposals, including $800 million for public transportation, $400 million for roads, and $70 million for commuter rail. Sargent proposed to offset the burden of cities and towns served by the MBTA by having the Commonwealth pick up half of the tab for the Authority's net cost of service.

The "documentation" referred to by Sargent in his speech was a set of three regional transportation planning studies prepared by the Boston Transportation Planning Review (BTPR). Each study featured analyses of existing conditions and detailed proposals for improving transportation for a specific region of Greater Boston. The Southwest and North Shore Reports were completed in 1972. The Northwest Report was completed in 1973. The Southwest report contained early conceptualization of what became the Southwest Corridor and Silver Line Projects. The Northwest Report laid out a conceptualization for the Green Line Extension (GLX) Project and Northwest Extension of the Red Line. Both the Southwest and Northwest reports contained studies for circumferential transit lines around the core of the MBTA's service area. These were built upon by later studies for what became known as the Urban Ring.

Another significant regional transportation planning report appeared in 1973. Orchestrated by the MBTA, a consultant created a plan looking at optimal uses for railroad rights-of-way between Boston and the city's outer circumferential highway, Interstate 495. The report addressed how to optimize commuter rail operations and utilize existing railroad rights-of-way for public transit. Provocatively, the report explored a $60 million

electrification of Boston's commuter rail network, something again being talked about today. The BTPR reports, along with others of the early 1970s, became the foundation for future transportation proposals and spawned over four decades of MBTA capital expansion projects.

The Urban Ring

Fifteen years after Sargent delivered his 1972 address in which he touted "a circumferential transit system," the MBTA released its Circumferential Transit Feasibility Study. The study examined ways to relieve pressure on Boston's hub-and-spoke rapid transit and light rail network through analyzing existing infrastructure and proposing improvements. The study presented options for improving transit connections between places within Boston and ten surrounding communities, specific locations around the downtown core, including Logan Airport, the Longwood Medical Area, the South Boston Seaport, the campus of UMass Boston, and various commercial nodes. The fruits of the study were a series of proposed transit improvements that formed a belt around downtown Boston. The new transit belt, referred to as the Urban Ring, was laid out to provide new connections to not only reduce the number of trips into and out of the hub, but to also shorten travel times and improve connections between nodes.

The first significant augmentations of the T's network that came out of the 1987 Circumferential Transit Study were three crosstown bus routes. These new routes featured limited stops and launched on September 26, 1994 with the designations CT1, CT2, and CT3 (Figure 9.78). "CT" was short for "crosstown." The MBTA branded existing RTS buses with new CT graphics. Signage was added at bus stops to indicate which were served by a crosstown route.

A decade after undertaking the 1987 Circumferential Transit Study, the MBTA got to work on a follow up. Completed in 2001, the Authority's Urban Ring Major Investment Study (Urban Ring MIS) was more prescriptive than the 1987 study, laying out three distinct phases for circumferential transit improvements. Phase I called for improvements and additions to both crosstown and express bus services. Phase II called for new bus rapid transit (BRT) service running along a mixture of city streets, bus lanes, and dedicated rights-of-way (Figure 9.79). The BRT service was proposed to link points around the Urban Ring, including

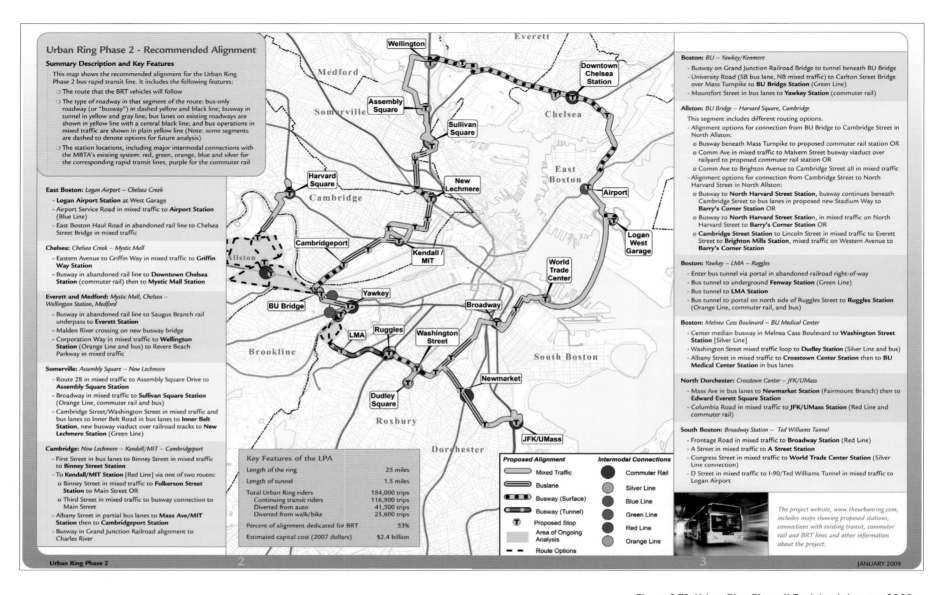

commuter rail stops proposed at Sullivan Square, Gilman Square, and Union Square. The latter two squares, both in Somerville, are currently slated to receive Green Line service as part of the ongoing GLX Project. Phase II also called for improvements at Yawkey (now Lansdowne), Ruggles, Uphams Corner, and Chelsea commuter rail stops. Chelsea Station received a reworking as part of the extension of the Silver Line into Chelsea in 2018. The portion of the Silver Line running from the Airport into Chelsea is essentially a segment of the Urban Ring laid out in 2009.

Phase III of the Urban Ring called for new rapid transit service along the most heavily travelled segment of the Urban Ring, from Assembly Square in Somerville to Dudley Square in Roxbury.

Complete circumferential BRT or rapid transit services have yet to be realized.

Rapid Transit to Braintree

In the early 1970s, before the Red Line reached Quincy Center, the MBTA sought to extend the Red Line as far south as Weymouth, or possibly even Holbrook. By late 1976, design and engineering work was underway for an extension only as far as South Braintree. The majority of the project was funded by UMTA grant money. During design, the site of the extension's lone intermediate station (now Quincy Adams Station) was shifted out of Braintree and into the southern part of Quincy. After relocating the intermediate station, the MBTA shortened

Figure 9.79 Urban Ring Phase II Explained, January 2009
A map from "2009 Urban Ring Phase 2 Fact Sheet," by the Massachusetts Executive Office of Transportation and Public Works, lays out the scope of Phase II. Highlighted in yellow, a proposed belt of transit service links transit nodes and neighborhoods around Boston's urban core. The only aspects of Phase II currently in operation are those provided by Silver Line service. The majority of Urban Ring Phase II remains on paper only.

the name of the extension's terminal station from South Braintree to Braintree Station.

Groundbreaking for the three-and-a-quarter-mile-long Braintree Extension took place on July 13, 1977. The extension's terminal station opened in March 1980 with a 1,200 car garage and a daily parking fee of $2.

The first revenue train traversed the Braintree Extension on the morning of March 22, 1980, when a Red Line train departed Braintree bound for Harvard Square. The standard entrance fare at Braintree was seventy-five cents and was part of a complex fare structure. A person riding from Braintree Station to any of the three stations in Quincy paid seventy-five cents and picked up a paper warrant. Upon exiting at any other station in Quincy, the rider surrendered the warrant to a fare collector who then provided the patron with a fifty-cent refund. A customer boarding at any station north of Quincy and exiting at any station within Quincy or Braintree paid a quarter entrance fare as well as a fifty cent exit fare. Exit fares, the bane of poor Charlie back in the MTA-era, endured in Braintree until the arrival of the MBTA's electronic fare cards in the mid-2000s.

A $33 million Quincy Adams Station opened in September 1983, over two years after Braintree Station. Quincy Adams opened with a five-level garage with a capacity of 2,000 cars. The garage was linked directly to U.S. Route 3 with new highway ramps. A translucent roof spanned from the garage and high above the platform served by Red Line trains (Figure 9.80). Alongside the outbound rapid transit track, a non-electrified track allowed commuter rail trains to run through the station.

By the end of the 1980s, the garages at Braintree and Quincy Adams Stations regularly reached capacity by 8:00 a.m. The MBTA addressed the situation in 1988 by restriping parking at the garages to increase capacity by over five percent.

JFK/UMass Station

The MBTA approved the renaming of Columbia Station to JFK/ UMass Station on December 2, 1982. The new name affirmed the station's location near the institutions on nearby Columbia Point, including UMass Boston, the John F. Kennedy Presidential Library and Museum, and the Massachusetts State Archives. The MBTA added the secondary station name "Columbia" to the official name of JFK/UMass Station on June 26, 1985.

As early as 1973, the MBTA studied the feasibility of adding a rapid transit station along the South Shore Extension at Columbia Station (now JFK/UMass Station) on the Red Line's Ashmont Branch. In 1978, an outside consultant recommended that the MBTA expand the station by adding it as a stop along the South Shore Extension. After years of dragging its feet, in 1979 the MBTA pushed the station expansion project forward.

Ground was broken on a $13.5 million reconstruction of JFK/UMass Station on July 16, 1987. The project brought to the station new platforms for Braintree Red Line trains, a new platform for Old Colony commuter rail trains, as well as a bus loop, elevated lobby, and elevators. The station opened to South Shore Extension Red Line trains in mid-December 1988. Select Old Colony commuter rail trains began to serve JFK/UMass Station as early as April 2001. Greenbush Line trains began serving the station in 2007.

Mapping the T in the 1970s

A new format for the MBTA's folding system map appeared in 1974. It was prepared by Cities Incorporated (Cities Inc.) and went through multiple editions. Unfolding the 1974 map revealed a large regional transit map (Figure 9.81), the opposite side of which was covered with schedules of frequency for transit lines, multiple neighborhood–scale maps, a commuter rail network map, and a large-scale transit map of central Boston (Figure 9.82). The 1974 map's earth-tone color palette, fashionable at the time, was a significant departure from the aesthetics of previous folding system maps. The 1974 map was an evolution of the Lufkin Format, with its combination of a large regional map paired with a smaller, inset map focusing on a particular neighborhood. In the case of the Cities Inc. format, multiple inset maps appeared, features that permeated subsequent system maps.

The 1974 folding system map included, for the first time on a system map, a commuter rail map with lines represented in purple. The commuter rail map was tangled with an inelegant rendition of the spider map and was accompanied by the logos of the Boston & Maine and Penn Central Railroads, then, operators of MBTA-subsidized commuter rail service.

The cover of the 1974 folding system map displayed the T's logo with the assertive subtext "The Answer." In the middle of a decade known for energy crises and increasing traffic on American

Figure 9.80 Quincy Adams Station, 1983
Captured on the cover of the MBTA's 1983 Annual Report, a train of "Silver Birds" pauses within a newly-opened Quincy Adams Station on the Braintree Extension.

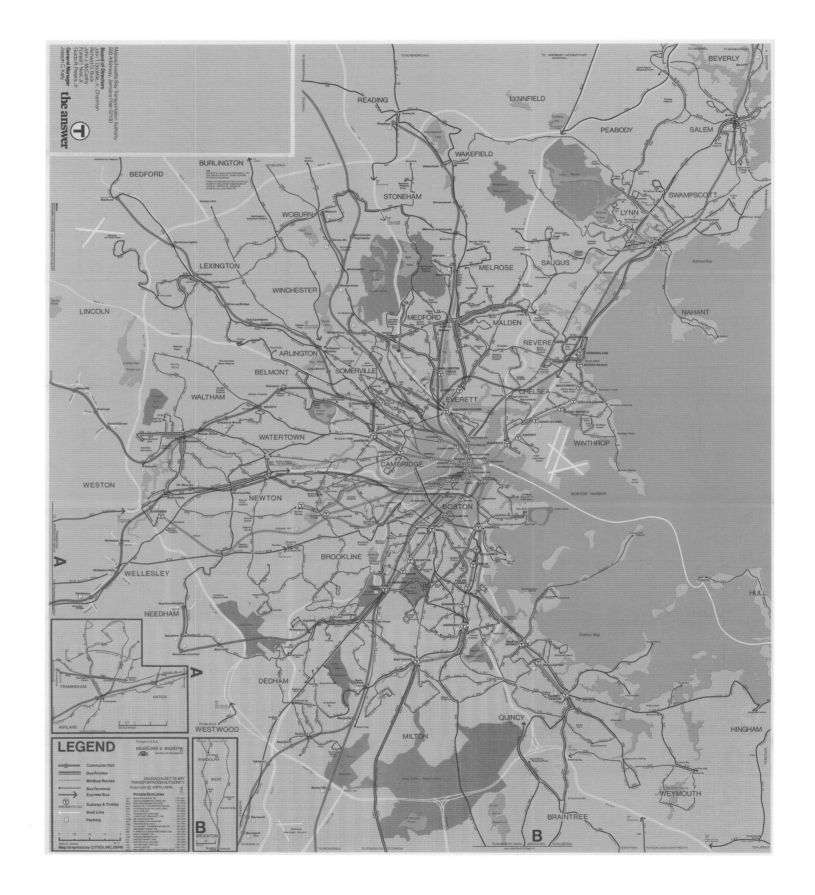

LEGEND

Commuter Rail
Bus Routes
Minibus Routes
Bus Terminal
Express Bus
Ⓣ Subway & Trolley
Boat Line
Parking

MASSACHUSETTS BAY
TRANSPORTATION AUTHORITY
Copyright © MBTA (1974)

Private Bus Lines

Printed in U.S.A.
BRADFORD & BIGELOW

Map Graphics by CITIES, INC. (1974)

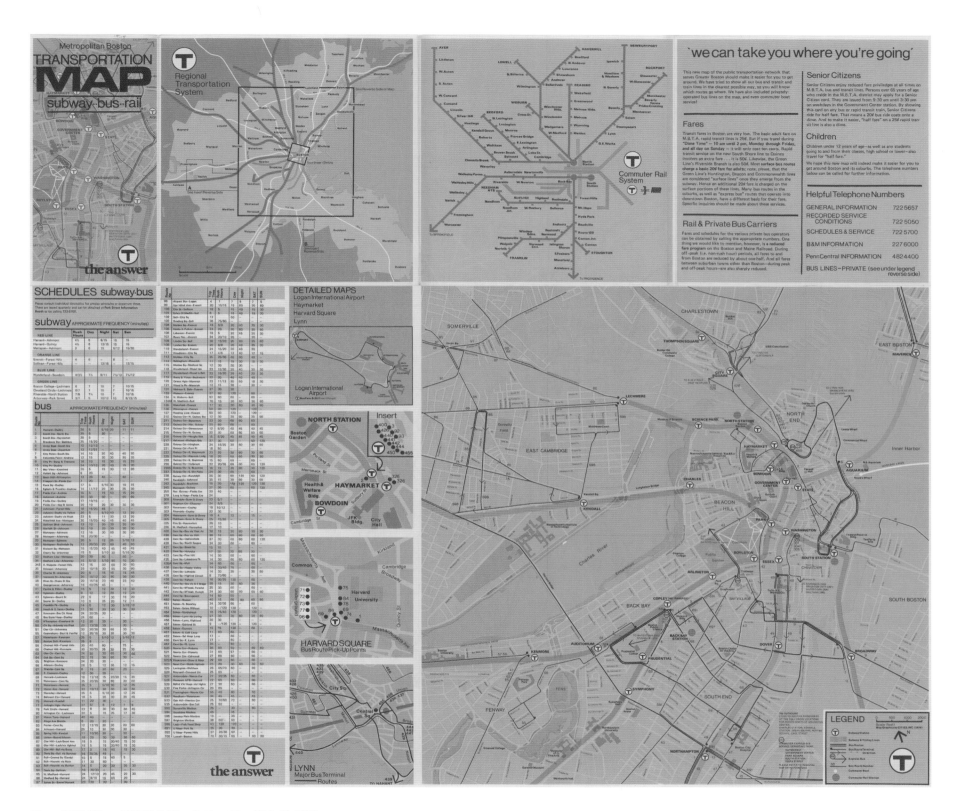

Figure 9.82 (Above) MBTA Folding System Map (Side A), 1974

Figure 9.81 (Opp.) MBTA Folding System Map (Side B), 1974

BLUE LINE
WONDERLAND—BOWDOIN STA.
via EAST BOSTON RAPID TRANSIT

WEEKDAY		SATURDAY		SUNDAY	
Leave Wonderland	Leave Bowdoin	Leave Wonderland	Leave Bowdoin	Leave Wonderland	Leave Bowdoin
5:13 AM	5:27 AM	5:13 AM	5:27 AM	5:58 AM	6:20 AM
3:25	3:35	3:25	5:45	6:15	6:50
3:35		Ev. 12 min.	5:45	6:45	7:15
		6:01	6:12	6:45	
8:05 PM	8:25 PM	6:12	6:32	7:00	7:26
Ev. 11 min.	Ev. 11 min.	6:22	6:42	Ev. 12 min.	
12:05 AM	12:05 AM	11:56 PM	11:54 PM	10:10 AM	10:30 AM
12:18 AM	12:18	12:07 AM	12:06 AM		
		12:18	12:19	11:13 PM	11:33 PM
				11:23	11:43
				11:34	11:54 PM
				11:45	12:05 AM
				11:56 PM	12:07 AM
				12:07 AM	12:18
				12:18	

98
AIRPORT STA. — LOGAN AIRPORT

WEEKDAY		SATURDAY		SUNDAY	
Leave Airport Sta.	Leave Airport	Leave Airport Sta.	Leave Airport	Leave Airport Sta.	Leave Airport
5:35 AM	5:30 AM	5:35 AM	5:30 AM	6:36 AM	6:30 AM
11:51 PM	11:51 PM	11:51 PM	11:51 PM	11:55 PM	11:55 PM
12:02 AM	12:06 AM	12:02 AM	12:06 AM	12:14	12:04
12:14	12:11	12:14	12:11	12:14	12:11
12:27	12:23	12:27	12:23	12:31	12:25
12:41	12:35	12:41	12:35	12:41	12:31
12:56	12:47	12:56	12:47	12:45	
				12:56	

Notes:
- ✱ — Frequent service, intervals 10 min. or less.
- g — Government Ctr. to Wonderland, does not stop at Aquarium Sta.
- h — Orient Hts. to Bowdoin. → To Maverick Square via Airport.

HOLIDAYS:
April 15 — see SATURDAY service.
May 27 — see SUNDAY service.

Blue-98-MAP (4M) Effective 3/23/74

BLUE LINE & 98
AIRPORT SHUTTLE

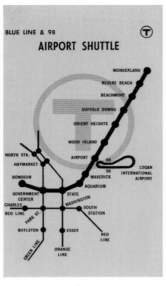

ORANGE LINE
EVERETT—FOREST HILLS
via WASHINGTON STREET TUNNEL & ELEVATED

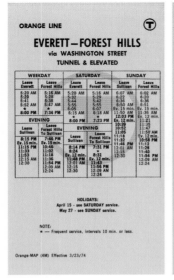

WEEKDAY		SATURDAY		SUNDAY	
Leave Everett	Leave Forest Hills	Leave Everett	Leave Forest Hills	Leave Sullivan	Leave Forest Hills
5:20 AM	5:16 AM	5:20 AM	5:16 AM	6:07 AM	6:02 AM
5:29	5:23	5:29	5:29	6:23	6:30
5:41	5:38	5:41	5:42	6:30	6:36
5:53	5:47 AM	5:55	6:45	6:50 AM	6:51
6:05	6:07	6:15 AM	6:07	11:36 AM	11:36
8:00 PM	7:34 PM			11:50 AM	11:40
				12:03 PM	11:52
EVENING		EVENING		Ev. 12 min.	
Leave Sullivan	Leave Forest Hills	Leave Sullivan	Leave Forest Hills		
8:15 PM	7:46 PM	8:14 PM	7:31 PM	11:21	
9:15	10:46	8:24		11:28	
11:15 PM	11:02	8:31	Ev. 12 min.	11:40	
11:53	11:18	11:46 PM	11:43 PM	11:52 PM	
12:15 AM	11:48	12:01 AM	11:43	12:04 AM	
12:30	11:54 PM	12:09 AM	11:56 PM	12:09 AM	
	12:24	12:30	12:09 AM	12:24	
			12:24		

NOTE:
✱ — Frequent service, intervals 10 min. or less.

HOLIDAYS:
April 15 — see SATURDAY service.
May 27 — see SUNDAY service.

Orange-MAP (4M) Effective 3/23/74

ORANGE LINE
EVERETT—FOREST HILLS
via WASHINGTON STREET TUNNEL & ELEVATED

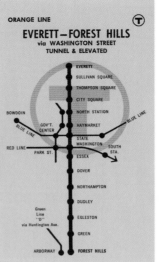

RED LINE
HARVARD—ASHMONT
via CAMBRIDGE — DORCHESTER RAPID TRANSIT

WEEKDAY		SATURDAY		SUNDAY	
Leave Harvard	Leave Ashmont	Leave Harvard	Leave Ashmont	Leave Harvard	Leave Ashmont
5:24 AM	5:17 AM	5:24 AM	5:17 AM	6:03 AM	6:03 AM
5:30	5:23	5:36	5:36	5:25	6:21
6:12 AM	5:41 AM	5:59	5:40 AM	6:12	6:30
	5:59			7:05	7:01
8:40 PM	7:46 PM	8:40 PM	8:10 PM	Ev. 15 min.	
11:55 PM	8:10	11:55 PM		11:55 PM	11:55 PM
12:17 AM	Ev. 15 min.	12:17 AM	Ev. 15 min.	12:17 AM	12:10 AM
12:32	8:40	12:32		9:32	12:24

HARVARD — QUINCY
RAPID TRANSIT

WEEKDAY		SATURDAY		SUNDAY	
Leave Harvard	Leave Quincy	Leave Harvard	Leave Quincy	Leave Harvard	Leave Quincy
5:32 AM	5:24 AM	5:32 AM	5:24 AM	6:15 AM	6:12 AM
5:42	5:36	5:42	5:36	6:30	6:36
5:54	5:48 AM	5:52	5:48 AM	Ev. 15 min.	7:01 AM
	6:05 AM	6:05 AM		7:48	7:18
8:03 PM	8:03 PM	7:48	7:35 PM	Ev. 15 min.	Ev. 15 min.
11:48 PM	Ev. 15 min.	11:48 PM	Ev. 15 min.	11:48 PM	11:48 PM
12:08 AM	12:03 AM	12:08 AM	12:03 AM	12:17 AM	12:10 AM
12:25	12:18	12:25	12:18	12:28	12:24

✱ — Frequent service, intervals 10 min. or less.

HOLIDAYS:
April 15 — see SATURDAY service.
May 27 — see SUNDAY service.

Red Line MAP (6M) Effective 3/23/74

RED LINE
HARVARD — QUINCY
RAPID TRANSIT

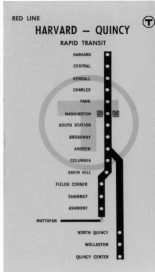

B
BOSTON COLLEGE LECHMERE
via COMMONWEALTH AVE.

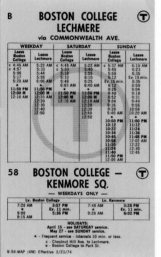

WEEKDAY		SATURDAY		SUNDAY	
Leave Boston College	Leave Lechmere	Leave Boston College	Leave Lechmere	Leave Boston College	Leave Lechmere
c 4:46 AM	5:22 AM	4:48 AM	5:22 AM	5:45 AM	6:23 AM
4:57	5:33	5:44	5:33	5:45	6:23
5:06	5:44	6:06 AM	5:44	Ev. 15 min.	6:25
5:28 AM	6:06 AM	5:48	6:25	6:03 AM	6:40
			6:40		
11:50 PM	11:50 PM	11:50 PM	11:50 PM	11:50 PM	11:50 PM
12:00 M	12:00 M	12:00 M	12:00 M	12:00 M	12:00 M
12:10 AM	12:10 AM	12:10 AM	12:10 AM	12:10 AM	12:10 AM
		12:40	12:40	12:40	12:40
		12:50	12:50	12:50	12:50

58
BOSTON COLLEGE — KENMORE SQ.
WEEKDAYS ONLY

Lv. Boston College		Lv. Kenmore	
7:20 AM	3:57 PM	7:48 AM	3:28 PM
9:00	Ev. 11 min.		Ev. 11 min.
9:15 AM	5:36 PM		6:02 PM

HOLIDAYS:
April 15 — see SATURDAY service.
May 27 — see SUNDAY service.
- ✱ — Frequent service - intervals 10 min. or less.
- c - Chestnut Hill Ave. to Lechmere.
- e - Boston College to Park St.

B-58-MAP (4M) Effective 3/23/74

B
BOSTON COLLEGE NORTH STATION
via COMMONWEALTH AVE.

D
RIVERSIDE to NORTH STATION
via HIGHLAND BRANCH

WEEKDAY		SATURDAY		SUNDAY	
Leave Riverside	Leave North Sta.	Leave Riverside	Leave North Sta.	Leave Riverside	Leave North Sta.
4:51 AM	5:19 AM	5:00 AM	5:27 AM	5:51 AM	6:16 AM
c 5:05	5:33	5:33	6:03	6:13	6:40
5:23	5:44	6:00 AM	6:19	6:13	7:10
5:43	6:00 AM		6:36	6:45 AM	7:27 AM
5:53			6:36		
6:03	11:42 PM	11:52 PM	11:52 PM	11:57 PM	8:01
11:00 PM	12:04 AM	12:04 AM	12:02 AM		
11:53	12:38	12:22	12:22		
12:03 AM		12:40	12:40		

HOLIDAYS:
April 15 — see SATURDAY service.
May 27 — see SUNDAY service.
Notes:
- a - North Sta. to Riverside
- b - Reservoir to North Sta.
- c - Riverside to North Sta.
- d - Riverside to Reservoir
- e - Reservoir to Gov't. Ctr.

For information call 722-5000
- ✱ — Frequent service, intervals 10 min. or less.

Average Running Times:
Riverside to: North Sta.
Newton Ctr. 10 min.   North Sta. 5 min.
Kenmore 26 min.   Kenmore 15 min.
Park St. 35 min.   Newton Ctr. 30 min.
North Sta. 40 min.   Riverside 40 min.

D-MAP (5M) Effective 3/23/74

D
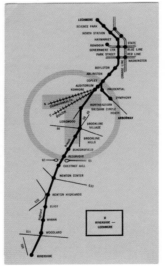

E
ARBORWAY—PARK STREET
via HUNTINGTON AVE.

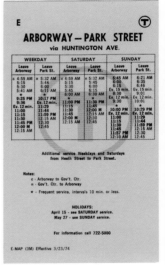

WEEKDAY		SATURDAY		SUNDAY	
Leave Arborway	Leave Park St.	Leave Arborway	Leave Park St.	Leave Arborway	Leave Park St.
c 4:59 AM	5:32 AM	4:59 AM	5:32 AM	5:45 AM	6:21 AM
5:19	5:44	5:19	5:45	6:30	6:30
5:41 AM	6:03 AM	5:41 AM	6:03 AM	Ev. 12 min.	Ev. 12 min.
9:25 PM	10:17 PM	9:25 PM	10:00 PM	9:30	10:01
9:36	Ev. 12 min.	11:30	11:45	Ev. 12 min.	
11:00	11:30	11:30	11:45	11:45	
11:15	11:59 PM	11:45		11:45	11:59 PM
11:30	12:00 M	12:00 M		11:57 PM	12:30
12:00 M	12:45	12:15 AM		12:15 AM	12:30
12:15 AM					

Additional service Weekdays and Saturdays from Heath Street to Park Street.

Notes:
- c - Arborway to Gov't. Ctr.
- n - Gov't. Ctr. to Arborway
- ✱ - Frequent service, intervals 10 min. or less.

HOLIDAYS:
April 15 — see SATURDAY service.
May 27 — see SUNDAY service.

For information call 722-5000

E-MAP (3M) Effective 3/23/74

E
ARBORWAY—PARK STREET
via HUNTINGTON AVE.

1
HARVARD SQ.—DUDLEY STA.
via MASS. AVE.

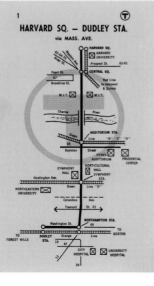

WEEKDAY		SATURDAY		SUNDAY	
Leave Harvard	Leave Dudley	Leave Harvard	Leave Dudley	Leave Harvard	Leave Dudley
5:10 AM	4:44 AM	5:10 AM	4:44 AM	5:50 AM	5:30 AM
5:30	5:04	5:20	5:04	Ev. 30 min.	Ev. 30 min.
5:50	5:20	5:50	5:20	Ev. 20 min.	
6:05	5:40	5:50	5:35		
6:30 AM	6:35	6:20	5:50	12:05	
		6:50 AM	6:14		
7:08 PM	6:15 PM	7:03	6:25	12:52	12:52
7:20	6:50	9:48	7:03	1:03	1:03
7:35	7:07	Ev. 11 min.	6:01 PM	Ev. 11 min.	7:01 PM
7:50	7:20	9:00	Ev. 11 min.	6:15	7:15
Ev. 20 min.	7:30	7:15	6:22	6:35	
11:50 PM	7:35	5:08 PM	6:35	6:35	
12:00 M	12:00 M	Ev. 20 min.	8:50 PM	12:30 AM	1:00
1:00	12:30 AM	12:00 M	12:00 M		1:25
1:25	1:00	8:40	6:23		
	1:25	Ev. 20 min.			

- ✱ — Frequent service, intervals 10 min. or less.

Performance of schedule subject to traffic delay.

HOLIDAYS:
April 15 — see SATURDAY service.
May 27 — see SUNDAY service.

For information call 722-5000

1-MAP (4M) Effective 3/23/74

1
HARVARD SQ. — DUDLEY STA.
via MASS. AVE.

2
SOUTH STATION NORTH STATION
via POST OFFICE SQUARE

WEEKDAYS	
Lv. South Station	Lv. North Station
6:35 AM	6:49 AM
	7:00
9:05	9:05
9:30 AM	9:42
Ev. 30 min.	Ev. 30 min.
3:00 PM	10:50
3:30	2:42 PM
3:35	3:15
3:35	3:30
6:00 PM	3:36
	6:00
	6:17

3
SOUTH STATION HAYMARKET SQUARE
via ATLANTIC AVE.

WEEKDAY	
Lv. South Station	Lv. Haymarket
6:20 AM	6:45 AM
Ev. 20 min.	6:35
9:00 AM	7:00
	9:20 AM
3:20 PM	3:40 PM
Ev. 20 min.	Ev. 20 min.
5:40 PM	6:00 PM

- ✱ — Frequent service, intervals 10 min. or less.

Performance of schedule subject to traffic delay.
NO SERVICE SATURDAY, SUNDAY OR HOLIDAYS.
For further information call 722-5000

2-3-MAP (3M) Effective 3/23/74

2
SOUTH STA. — NORTH STA.
via POST OFFICE SQUARE

3
SOUTH STA. — HAYMARKET
via ATLANTIC AVENUE

20
FIELDS CORNER STA. NEPONSET & ADAMS BELT LINE

LEAVE FIELDS CORNER STATION					
WEEKDAY		SATURDAYS		SUNDAYS	
Via Neponset Ave.	Via Adams St.	Via Neponset Ave.	Via Adams St.	Via Neponset Ave.	Via Adams St.
5:20 AM	5:28 AM	5:20 AM	Ev. 30 min.	6:30 AM	Ev. 30 min.
5:40	Ev. 12 min.	6:28	6:30 AM	8:15 AM	11:30
6:00	6:40	8:00 AM	Ev. 30 min.	11:30	Take Neponset
Ev. 12 min.	7:28	Ev. 30 min.	6:30 PM	6:30 PM	Ave. Bus
7:20	7:50	11:30 PM	6:15 PM	6:30 PM	
9:55	7:50	12:00 M			
9:02	9:55	12:00 M			
Ev. 12 min.	12:05 AM	12:40		12:40	
12:05 AM	1:01	1:01		1:01	
12:16 AM					
Via Adams & Hilltop Sts.					
2:00 PM					
2:50					
Ev. 12 min.					
5:00					
6:10					
6:23					
6:40					
Ev. 30 min.					
11:00					
11:32 PM					
12:16 AM					
a 1:01					

HOLIDAYS:
April 15 — see SATURDAY service.
May 27 — see SUNDAY service.

Notes: ✱ — Frequent service, intervals 10 min. or less.

For information call: 722-5000 or 472-3450

- a - To Neponset via Adams Ave.
- g - Operates thru to Quincy Center Sta.

12
HALLET SQ. — ASHMONT

WEEKDAYS ONLY		WEEKDAYS ONLY	
Lv. Hallet Sq.		Lv. Ashmont	
6:04 AM	4:35 PM	6:13 AM	4:25 PM
Ev. 20 min.	Ev. 20 min.	Ev. 20 min.	Ev. 20 min.
8:44 AM	6:15 PM	8:33 AM	6:25 PM

12-20-MAP (4M) Effective 3/23/74

20
FIELDS CORNER STA. NEPONSET & ADAMS BELT LINE

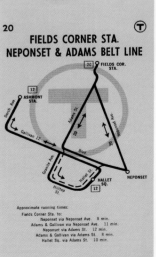

Approximate running times:
Fields Corner Sta. to:
Neponset via Neponset Ave. 8 min.
Adams & Gallivan via Neponset Ave. 11 min.
Neponset via Adams St. 12 min.
Adams & Gallivan via Adams St. 8 min.
Hallet Sq. via Adams St. 10 min.

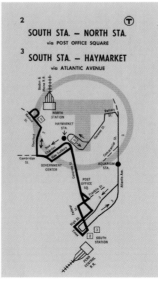

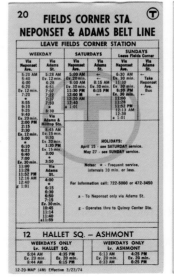

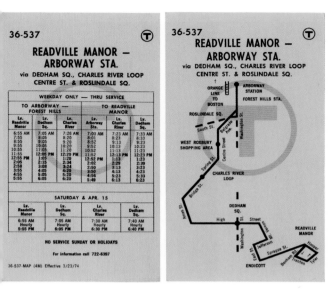

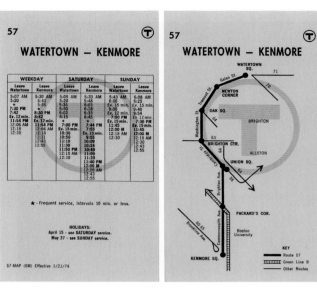

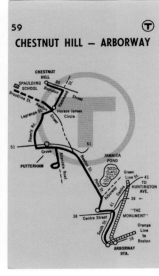

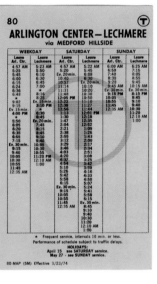

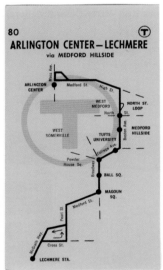

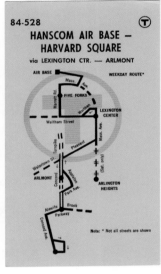

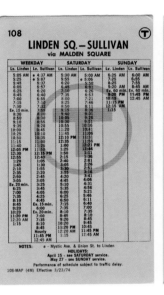

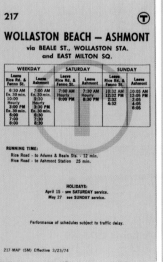

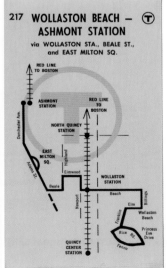

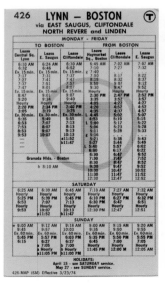

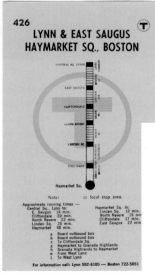

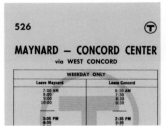

Figure 9.83 MBTA Route Schedule Cards, 1974

Each schedule cards reveals a timetable on one face (left in each pair) and, for the first time on the majority of the set of route schedule cards issued by either the MTA or the MBTA, a route map on the opposite face (right in each pair). MBTA schedule cards issued before 1973 followed a timetable-only format, one started by the MTA in spring 1964 (Figure 8.68).

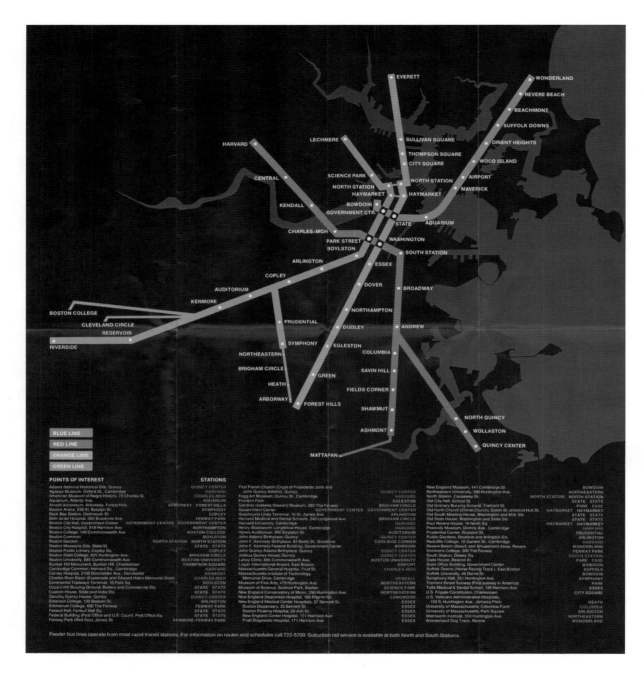

Figure 9.84 MBTA Color Brochure, 1974

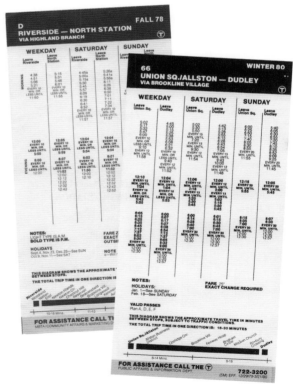

highways, "The Answer" to unreliable availability of gasoline for private commuting and worsening traffic jams was a ride on the T. "The Answer" appeared on other MBTA publications of the mid-1970s (Figure 9.84).

Beyond "The Answer" publications, 1973–74 saw the MBTA release route schedule cards in a fresh format (Figure 9.83). From 1978 through 1980, the T produced schedule cards in an awkwardly tall format (Figure 9.85). In 1981, schedule cards returned to a more pocket-friendly format. These

lasted until 1991, when folding paper schedules replaced card stock schedule cards for good.

The MBTA zeroed in on Lynn in 1975 with the production of a folding map dedicated to lines and routes serving the city (Figure 9.86). Moving on from Lynn, the Authority released the third, fourth, and final iterations of the Cities Inc. format system map for spring, summer, and fall 1976, respectively (Figure 9.87). The 1977 folding system map was an updated version of the 1976 Cities Inc. format, but was produced by the General Drafting Company.

Figure 9.85 MBTA Tall Format Schedule Cards, 1978–80

Figure 9.86 MBTA Lynn Transportation Map, 1975

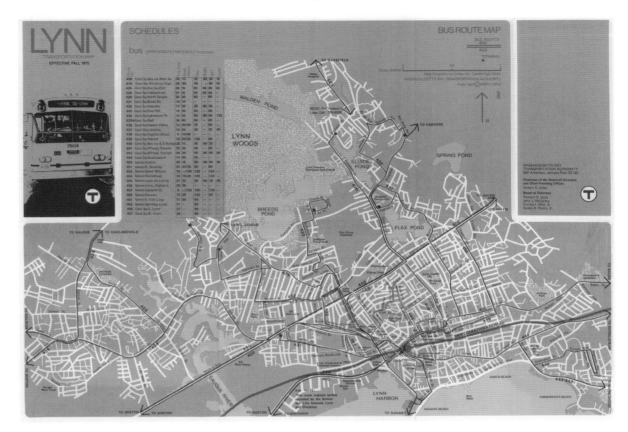

Figure 9.87 System Map Covers, Fall 1976; 1977; 1978–79

Figure 9.88 "Music Under Boston" Print Ad, 1977

Though the cover of the 1977 map read "Spring-Summer 1977," the map was the only edition of 1977, a year that also saw the T release a rapid transit map in Chinese. The MBTA continues to furnish information in various languages.

In 1977 the T launched "Music Under Boston" (Figure 9.88), a program of "live music at three subway stations which was a national first for Boston and since duplicated in several other cities." After a successful initial run during summer 1977, Music Under Boston continued through September 1, 1978, with musicians and performance artists performing during morning and evening rush hours in Government Center, Harvard, and Park Street Stations. The tradition of MBTA-sanctioned live music in subway stations continues, with musicians regularly performing, most after obtaining MBTA approval and utilizing marked performance spaces.

Bicentennial Year Lows, Highs, and More Paint

The United States celebrated its two-hundredth birthday in 1976, a year packed not only with countless bicentennial celebrations, but a few highs and lows for the MBTA. A series of severe storms during the winter of 1975–76, compounded by electrical and switching breakdowns, periodically overwhelmed service on both the Blue and Red Lines. The MBTA did not fully recover until the following spring.

Another low hit during summer 1976, when the T slashed bus service to keep operations within budget and workforce limitations, resulting in a twenty percent reduction in service. Soon after full bus service was restored in September, trouble returned to the rapid transit lines. On September 13, an axle broke under a Red Line Blue Bird, causing the car to derail. Another Blue Bird axle failed on October 5, causing the MBTA to pull all Blue Birds from the Red Line that night. After inspecting each and every axle, a service plan was implemented; cars with defective axles were gradually repaired and returned to revenue service.

Another MBTA high of 1976 occurred in the realm of funding, with the Authority receiving a record $345.9 million in federal funds during 1975–76.

Figure 9.89 MBTA PCC Car #3252, 1976
MBTA PCC cars numbered 3252 (shown at Riverside), 3262, and 3264 were painted white and emblazoned with an American flag on their sides and a "Boston 200" icon on their noses to celebrate America's bicentennial.

Figure 9.90 Boston & Maine Locomotive #200, 1975
To mark America's bicentennial, the Boston & Maine repainted and renumbered locomotive number 2120 to 200.

Complementing statewide bicentennial celebrations, the MBTA painted three of its PCC cars (Figure 9.89) and six of its buses with patriotic color schemes. The Boston & Maine joined the fun with the application of a patriotic paint scheme to one of its locomotives (Figure 9.90). Prior to 1976, from April 19–28, 1975, the nationally-touring American Freedom Train paused in Boston. The train was headed by a steam locomotive and included ten cars, each packed with exhibits celebrating the history and bicentennial of the United States. Tickets allowed visitors to access the exhibits on the special train at its Boston stop (Figure 9.91).

During America's bicentennial year, the MBTA painted two Blue Bird cars with a new, red color scheme, furthering its mission to color code its vehicles per the *Manual of Guidelines and Standards*. The freshly painted cars entered service on August 23. Nicknamed "Red Birds," the cars joined Silver Birds already sporting red stripes. Within the

upgraded Blue Birds, the 1963-era back-lit order of stations signs were replaced with Red Line maps and rapid transit spider maps (Figure 9.92).

The Southwest Corridor Project

A proposed extension of Interstate 95 (I-95), from Massachusetts Route 128 in Canton, through Boston's Hyde Park, Roxbury, and South End neighborhoods, was laid out by transportation planners as early as 1948. By the mid-1960s, with property taking and land clearing for the highway extension underway, public protests against the project had become a regular occurrence. At the time, plans called for the Orange Line to be relocated from the Washington Street Elevated into the median of the interstate. The contiguous highway and rapid transit line was to replace the former Boston & Providence line from Back Bay Station to Forest Hills. Governor Sargent's 1970 moratorium on

Figure 9.91 American Freedom Train Boston Ticket, 1975

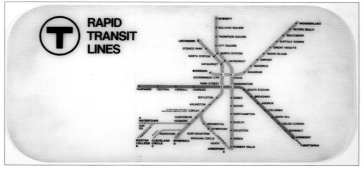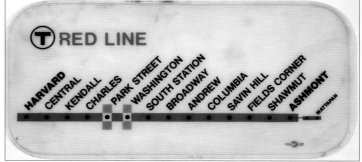

Figure 9.92 Maps from Red Line "Blue Bird" Cars, Mid-1970s
An acrylic Red Line map (right) and a rapid transit lines map
(left) replaced 1960s-era Order of Station signs (Figure 8.59)
inside "Blue Bird" cars transformed into "Red Birds."

new highway construction within Boston's inner circumferential highway, Massachusetts 128, killed the extension of I-95 from Canton into Boston. Two years after the highway moratorium was enacted, a revised study of the project, by then known as the Southwest Corridor Project, was undertaken by the BTPR.

In 1973, the Governor appointed a Southwest Corridor Coordinator to, as described by the MBTA, "bring the public agencies together with citizens groups to plan for transportation and development needs of the corridor." During planning of the Southwest Corridor Project, the MBTA recorded "sponsoring over 1,000 community meetings to discuss planning, design, construction and traffic concerns." The T circulated its award-winning *Southwest Corridor Project Newsletter* to approximately 12,000 residents around the project area. Community input significantly informed the project. For example, a proposed 500-car parking garage was eliminated from the design of a new Forest Hills Station.

After Governor Dukakis formalized the removal of an interstate highway from the Southwest Corridor Project in mid-1975, the Commonwealth diverted, under the 1973 Federal Highway Act, federal funding for the scuttled highway to redevelopment and public transportation along the corridor. The MBTA noted the diversion of funds as "the first time in the United States that a major expressway had been scrapped and funding converted to mass transportation."

During planning of the Southwest Corridor Project, the MBTA took the opportunity to explore extending the Orange Line beyond Forest Hills, working up plans in the 1970s for an Orange Line extension into Needham. The proposed Needham Extension was laid out to follow the Penn Central's Needham Branch and would have served Boston's Roslindale and West Roxbury neighborhoods. In lieu of extending the Orange Line to Needham, the

Authority upgraded the railroad line for commuter rail service. During 1985–87, the T rebuilt tracks, signals, and stations along the Needham Line, a line that had been out of service since October 13, 1979. Nearly eight years to the day later, on October 19, 1987, rail service resumed between South Station and multiple stops in Needham.

Multiple public entities collaborated on the planning and funding of the Southwest Corridor Project, including the MBTA, the city of Boston, the Commonwealth, Amtrak, and the Federal Railroad Administration (FRA). While the MBTA and state DPW oversaw the design and construction of transportation infrastructure, various state agencies worked to develop housing and recreational facilities along the corridor. Boston oversaw the development of schools, housing, civic buildings, and an area for new industries. Massachusetts approved the construction of Roxbury Community College on land initially cleared for I-95. Much of the funding for the Southwest Corridor Project was administered through the MBTA or the FRA's Northeast Corridor Improvement Project (NCIP).

A groundbreaking ceremony for the Southwest Corridor Project took place on December 3, 1979. The T described the $740 million Southwest Corridor Project as "the largest construction ever undertaken in the history of the Commonwealth… funded by one of the largest federal grants ever awarded to a transit project." The grant was nearly half a billion dollars.

The final configuration of the Southwest Corridor Project included: a new, two-track rapid transit subway which extended the Washington Street Tunnel to Back Bay Station; new, parallel rapid transit and railroad trackage from Back Bay Station to Forest Hills Station; and the removal of the Washington Street Elevated after relocation of the Orange Line into the Southwest Corridor. The extension of the Washington Street Tunnel was the South Cove Tunnel project, the first phase of which

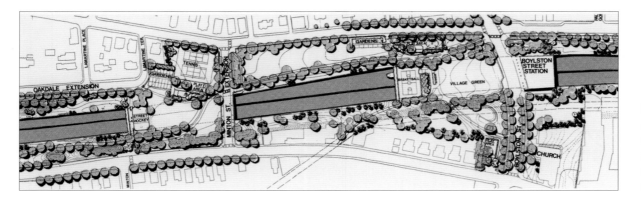

commenced in the late 1960s and was substantially
completed in 1971. Groundbreaking for the second
phase of the South Cove Tunnel, which included a
two-track incline for Orange Line trains to travel
between the tunnel and the surface on the southern
side of the Massachusetts Turnpike, took place
in January 1978. The tunnel included a new rapid
transit station at New England Medical Center
(now Tufts Medical Center).

The Back Bay to Forest Hills segment of the
Southwest Corridor featured a pair of rapid transit
tracks for use by Orange Line trains and three
parallel tracks for use by MBTA commuter rail
and Amtrak trains. The new tracks, along with
the station platforms they served, were installed
below street level, within a purpose-built trench.
Some portions of the trench were covered, creating
short tunnels; other sections remained open to the
sky. Road bridges, station head houses, and new
parkland were built atop portions of the trench
(Figure 9.93). The parkland formed a mostly

continuous, fifty-two-acre, pedestrian-friendly
greenway, the Southwest Corridor Park.

As the Boston Transit Commission (BTC) had
done with construction of the Tremont Street
Subway in the 1890s (See Chapter 3), the MBTA
broke down the Southwest Corridor Project into
sections (Figure 9.94), each assigned to a different
designer and contractor. Section One, which
consisted of 1.1 miles of line from the South Cove
Tunnel and included Back Bay and Massachusetts
Avenue Stations, was complicated by a high water
table, nearby ongoing construction of Copley Place,
and the need to maintain the operation of freight,
Amtrak, and MBTA trains through the site. Where
a high water table and soft soil prevented cut and
cover construction, builders of Section One used a
then-novel technique, slurry wall construction. The
method commenced with excavation of trenches for
tunnel sidewalls. As earth was removed, a dense,
mud-like slurry of bentonite was pumped into
the excavation. The slurry prevented earth from
caving in on the excavations. Once the trench was

Figure 9.94 The Orange Line on the Southwest Corridor, 1982

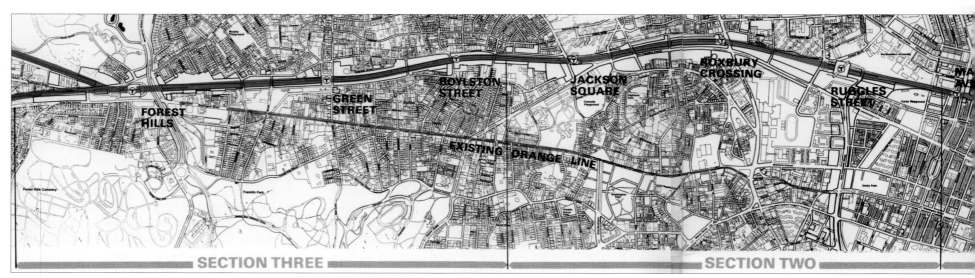

Southwest
Corridor
Project

Massachusetts Bay
Transportation
Authority
October, 1982

Figure 9.95 Building the Southwest Corridor Project, 1982
The cover of a 1982 project update brochure captures much of section two during the height of construction. Temporary roads circle around the site of Roxbury Crossing Station (center). Fresh concrete reflects brightly from the trench being constructed for trains. Roxbury Community College has yet to rise along the grassy area to the right of the trench.

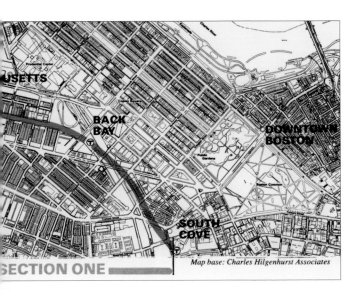

excavated to depth, steel reinforcing was lowered into the hole. Concrete was then pumped into the trench and around the reinforcing. As concrete filled the trench from the bottom up, the slurry was pushed up, out of the hole, and recovered. Beyond the Southwest Corridor Project, slurry wall construction was employed by the T on the Northwest Extension of the Red Line. After local success with the technique on MBTA projects, the Commonwealth approved the large-scale use of slurry wall construction for The Big Dig.

Back Bay Station of the Southwest Corridor Project replaced a passenger depot opened in 1929 by the New Haven, purchased by the Commonwealth in 1971, and received by the MBTA in 1973 (See Chapter 4). Below street-level, former Boston & Albany and New Haven tracks and platforms were separated by new tracks and platform for the

Orange Line. The T approved "South End" as the official secondary station name for Back Bay Station in 1985.

Section Two of the Southwest Corridor Project was the central 1.4 miles running through Roxbury (Figure 9.95). It included Roxbury Crossing, Jackson Square, and Ruggles Street Stations, along with new arterial roads. Section Three was the southernmost 2.2 miles of the project. It was anchored by a new Forest Hills Station, a replacement for the BERy's 1909 Forest Hills Station and the neighboring railroad depot of the same name. The MBTA's station consolidated both older ones into a new intermodal complex.

Over a decade of construction along the Southwest Corridor brought nine stations to the southern portion of the Orange Line. These opened as New England Medical Center (now Tufts Medical

Center), Back Bay, Massachusetts Avenue, Ruggles, Roxbury Crossing, Jackson Square, Stony Brook, Green Street, and Forest Hills Stations. The T described each station being "conceived as a bold symbol of its respective neighborhood and a place of public gathering." The main hall in Back Bay Station echoed the sky-lit carriageway of the New Haven's 1899 Back Bay Station (See Chapter 4). The vaulted concourse with retail storefronts at Ruggles attempted to establish a vibrant link between Boston's Fenway and Roxbury neighborhoods (Figure 9.96). The open steel framework of the clock

tower atop Forest Hills Station stood as a modern civic marker.

In the first hours of the early morning of May 1, 1987 the last Orange Line train to carry paying passengers along the Washington Street Elevated trundled through the South End. By sunrise, any remaining Orange Line cars had departed from the Washington Street Elevated and Forest Hills Extension. At Dudley Station the upper level closed forever, while the lower level remained open until June 21, 1991. The T prepared its riders for the

Figure 9.98 Large Format Southwest Corridor Token, 1987
Oversize tokens were distributed by the MBTA to commemorate the opening of the Orange Line on the Southwest Corridor.

Figure 9.99 Southwest Corridor Token, 1987
Produced at the dimensions of a standard MBTA token, a Southwest Corridor white metal token was valid where T tokens were accepted.

relocation of the Orange Line with a myriad of advertisements, including car cards (Figure 9.97).

Opening ceremonies for the Southwest Corridor Project commenced on the morning of May 2, 1987. The public was joined by a slew of VIPs, including MBTA General Manager O'Leary, state Secretary of Transportation Frederick Salvucci, Governor Dukakis, Senate President William Bulger, Boston Mayor Raymond Flynn, and UMTA Regional Administrator Richard Doyle. The celebrations, branded "Across the Neighborhood: Celebrating our New T," featured over fifty performance groups, many from neighborhoods along the corridor. Balloons, banners, music, and free rides were orders of the day. The American Society of Civil Engineers awarded its 1988 outstanding civil engineering achievement award to the Southwest Corridor Project.

To celebrate the opening of the project, the MBTA produced oversized (Figure 9.98) and standard-sized (Figure 9.99) commemorative tokens. While the larger tokens were merely mementos, the standard-sized tokens were usable at turnstiles. Car cards and posters (Figure 9.100) announced the opening to transit riders. Regular Orange Line service along the 4.75 mile long Southwest Corridor commenced on May 4, 1987. On October 5, Attleboro/Stoughton and Franklin Line commuter rail trains began traversing the corridor.

The relocation of the Orange Line from the Washington Street Elevated and Forest Hills Extension allowed the MBTA to dismantle aging elevated railways running through the South End and Roxbury. The high cost of maintenance, lack of accessibility, and available federal funding for demolition made the elevated railways appealing targets. The demolition of the Washington Street Elevated commenced in the later half of 1987. While most of the structure

was cut up and sold for scrap, a few components were preserved. A portion of Dudley Station was recycled into a shelter for MBTA buses at Dudley Square. Much of Northampton Station was transported in 1900 to Kennebunkport, Maine, where it lies in state in the parking lot of the Seashore Trolley Museum.

Hawker-Siddeley Rapid Transit Cars
Vehicle purchases made by the MBTA in the 1970s brought entirely new fleets to both the Orange and Blue Lines. In 1976, the T approved an initial contract with Hawker-Siddeley of Canada for the purchase of seventy new cars for the Blue Line and 120 new cars for the Orange Line (Figure 9.101). The UMTA provided eighty percent funding for the new vehicles. The MBTA touted: "The procurement of 70 Blue Line and 120 Orange Line cars, at a cost of $115 million, is the largest single procurement contract ever issued by the MBTA." Each Blue Line car cost $540,000, sat forty riders, and carried just over 100 standees. Each Orange Line car cost $550,000 and was rated to carry fifty-eight people seated with 162 standing.

While both the Orange Line and Blue Line Hawker-Siddeley cars were similar in general layout and aesthetics, the Blue Line cars were approximately fifteen feet shorter than the sixty-five-foot-long Orange Line models. The reduced length of the Blue Line cars was required for the cars to navigate the tight radii of East Boston Tunnel trackage, a legacy of the line's genesis as a streetcar subway (See Chapter 5). All of the Hawker-Siddeley cars featured paddles for picking up third-rail DC power, but Blue Line models were also equipped with roof-mounted pantographs, needed for making contact

Figure 9.100 Southwest Corridor Poster, 1987

The New Orange Line...Now Boarding!

with overhead wire along the Revere Extension (Figure 9.102).

The Blue Line Hawker-Siddeley cars, designated as East Boston Tunnel Type 4s, brought some firsts to the Blue Line, including air suspension instead of steel springs, vertical grab poles instead of ceiling grab handles, two-way radio communications, and public address systems. Mated-pair 0600–0601 arrived in October 1978 at Orient Heights Car House, where the MBTA held an open house to show off the new vehicles. Both the Blue and Orange Line cars featured backlit maps (Figure 9.103), improvements upon older Order of Stations signs of the BERy and MTA eras and unique on MBTA vehicles.

When the Type 4s entered revenue service on July 16, 1979, they began replacing a motley fleet of aging vehicles, some placed into service by the BERy in the early 1920s. At the end of July 1981, nearly seventy of the new cars were in service. Soon, Blue Line service was exclusively provided by Hawker-Siddeley cars. The 0600-series cars remained in service for decades, until their retirement, back

to where they first arrived, Orient Heights Yard. There, in 2012, a scrapping contractor's massive hydraulic shears cut into the decommissioned cars, rendering them out of existence.

On the Orange Line, the first six Hawker-Siddeley cars entered revenue service in February 1981. By the end of the year, at least 100 of the new cars were in regular service. The new cars, designated as Orange Line Type 12s (Figure 9.104 and Figure 9.105), replaced older cars, many constructed in 1957. The remaining Orange Line Hawker-Siddeley cars are currently living their final years running between Oak Grove and Forest Hills. The first of their successors, Orange Line Number 13 rapid transit cars, entered service in 2019.

The Blizzard of '78

On Monday, February 6, and Tuesday, February 7, 1978, America's East Coast from New Jersey to Maine was pummeled by heavy wet snow, multiple high tides swollen with storm surge, and hurricane-force winds. In Boston, the Blizzard of

Figure 9.102 Blue Line Hawker-Siddeley Cars
A train of East Boston Tunnel Type 4 cars operates just north of Wonderland Station. In the distance, the lead car of the train has its pantograph raised to make contact with overhead power wire.

Figure 9.103 Orange Line Car Map Lens, April 7, 2018
All of the MBTA's Orange and Blue Line Hawker-Siddeley cars featured maps adhered to plastic lenses backlit by fluorescent lighting.

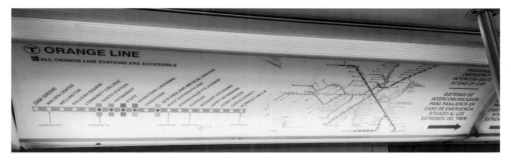

Figure 9.104 Train of Orange Line Hawker-Siddeley Cars
An inbound train of Orange Line Type 12 cars at Massachusetts Avenue Station on the Southwest Corridor.

Figure 9.105 Orange Line Hawker-Siddeley Car Interior, 1987

'78 arrived just days after an earlier storm deposited over twenty-one inches of snow. The February storm dumped over twenty-seven inches atop what already lay on the ground, paralyzing Greater Boston, and with it, the MBTA.

The Blizzard of '78 arrived in Massachusetts Bay with a vengeance. Mid-day on Monday, February 6, snow and ice accumulating along the Revere Extension brought a Blue Line train to a halt, and with it, service to Wonderland. In the early afternoon, two Orange Line trains collided at Sullivan Square Station, injuring nearly thirty people. By late afternoon, extreme measures were being taken. Along the Blue Line, MBTA employees cut through fences to clear a path for passengers emerging from a stalled train. Multiple Red Line trains became bogged down along surface tracks in Dorchester and Quincy. At least one train was evacuated with the assistance of the Quincy Fire Department. So many transit patrons were leaving stalled trains and walking down rapid transit rights-of-way that the T was forced to cut third rail power.

By Monday evening, all regular MBTA rapid transit, streetcar, trackless trolley, and bus service, except for some operations protected within tunnels, was rendered inoperable by the storm. On the roads, the situation turned deadly. On local highways, automobile commuters were immobilized within their vehicles by high drifting snow. People abandoned their cars to seek shelter in local businesses or were rescued by first responders using snowmobiles. Approximately a dozen people succumbed to carbon monoxide poisoning after their cars' exhaust systems were blocked by accumulating snow.

On Tuesday, February 7, Greater Boston awoke to not only an unnavigable road network, but a paralyzed public transit system. Over a dozen of the T's PCC cars sat in a frozen train along Commonwealth Avenue. Rapid transit trains remained motionless amidst towering snow drifts in Quincy and Revere. Buses were entombed in ice at bus yards. The MBTA documented that the blizzard, in combination with the previous storm of January 20, "devastated the commuter rail fleet" and that "almost every bus suffered damage during the two storms."

Responding during the crisis, Governor Dukakis closed all roads within the Commonwealth. Exceptions were made for emergency vehicles and snow removal equipment. Revenue public transit service vehicles were prohibited from operating on the roads. During the travel ban, the MBTA operated emergency buses to serve hospitals and evacuate people from coastal communities devastated by the onslaught of wind, snow, ice, and sea.

After the storm, the Governor's driving ban was lifted in stages. The MBTA operated buses along rapid transit and light rail lines still being dug out and yet to reopen. When rapid transit service resumed, the MBTA bore the weight of over double its typical daily ridership. It took the better part of a week for the T to bring most bus, trolley, and rapid transit services back to pre-storm levels. Commuter Rail service came back slowly, with only a quarter of regular trains operating during the first few days of restarted operations. Within a week of the storm, the T recorded that commuter rail service was operating with only fourteen locomotives (down from a pre-storm count of twenty), with only fifty-one coaches (down from seventy-nine), and with thirty-two RDCs (down from sixty-three). Commuter rail service was not fully restored until May 1978.

The summer after the blizzard, the MBTA caught its breath and reevaluated its snow-fighting capabilities. During the Blizzard of '78, the T fought along its rails with antiquated equipment, including snow plow-equipped trolleys dating from the first decade of the twentieth centuries (Figure 9.106). Seeking to be better prepared to clear its rails of snow in the future, the Authority approved spending nearly $200,000 on a pair of jet snow blowers, each powered by vintage jet engines and built by Portec Incorporated of Pittsburgh. Both machines survived into the twenty-first century. As recent as 2018, one machine, nicknamed Snowzilla, was surviving with most of its original parts (Figure 9.107). The other had been rebuilt.

Out of Cash and Out of Control

After over a decade of improving the aesthetics, operations, and equipment of public transportation in Greater Boston, the MBTA suffered some major setbacks, initially from the harsh light of a critical media expose, then later, from repeated lack of funds, and finally, from a criminal corruption scandal. First came the media expose.

A 1979 *Boston Globe* Spotlight investigation revealed blatant waste and mismanagement at the MBTA. Reporters documented workers not putting in full shifts, despite receiving full pay as if they did. The Spotlight series was merely the first of two punches to the gut of the Authority in 1979. By early winter, the T was on the verge of running out of funds and the Advisory Board refused to approve

increases in municipal assessments. Passed into law earlier in the year, the Commonwealth's "Proposition 2 1/2" property tax cap began to severely limit the previously deep pool of municipal tax revenues available for public transportation. Attempting to address the MBTA's financial crisis head on, Governor King took control of the T for the last weeks of the year. On Saturday December 6, the Authority's budget ran dry, and lacking the funding to operate, the MBTA shut down operations. After the Commonwealth stepped in with emergency funding legislation, the T reopened on December 7.

The crises of late 1979 inspired Governor King to convene a task force, reminiscent of the earlier governor's committee of 1972. The 1979 task force released a report in April 1980 recommending that the T increase fares, but only after the Commonwealth established dedicated funding for the T from increases in state gasoline taxes, highway tolls, or local parking fees. The report called for a reduction of Advisory Board authority along with significant MBTA management reorganization. The Authority responded to the report by approving a twenty-five cent rapid transit fare increase. Meanwhile, the governor proposed legislation to, among other things, see the Commonwealth entirely take over funding of MBTA commuter rail, rapid transit, and express bus service. The state funding takeovers did not happen.

History repeated itself on November 18, 1980, when again the MBTA ran out of authorized funds, and again Governor King seized control of the T. This time, the Governor's move was aggressively fought by the Advisory Board. Ten days after the takeover, the Massachusetts Supreme Judicial Court ruled King's action illegal; without authorized funds from the Commonwealth, the MBTA would be required to shut down. The court set a deadline of midnight at the end of Friday, December 5 for the state to approve a funding package for the T. During Friday's final hours, the MBTA got wind that the General Court was not going to come through before midnight and began to shutter operations. Bostonians awoke on Saturday, December 6 to an absence of MBTA service.

After twenty-four hours without the MBTA serving Boston, in the wee hours of Monday, December 7, the General Court passed Chapter 581 of the Acts of 1980, allowing the T to reopen. Beyond providing funding for the Authority through the end of 1980, Chapter 581 mandated that the Massachusetts Secretary of Transportation begin to serve concurrently as the MBTA Chairman, and

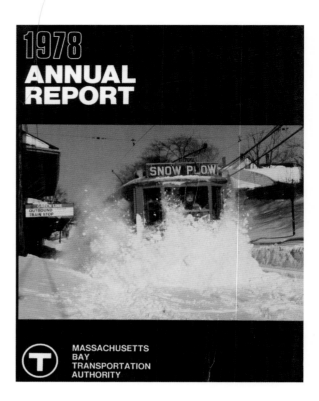

Figure 9.106 Digging Out Along the Line, 1978
Streetcar #5123, a Type 3 semi-convertible first used in 1907 by the BERy and later rebuilt into a snow plow, blasts through snow drifts deposited by the Blizzard '78. The car took six hours to plow from Kenmore Square to Newton Highlands.

Figure 9.107 Snowzilla Ready to Melt Some Snow, 2011
The Portec RMC Hurricane Jet Snow Blower Model RP-3 (a.k.a. Snowzilla) was purchased by the MBTA shortly after the Blizzard of '78.

required that the Authority recreate the position of General Manager. Chapter 581 was referred to as the Management Rights Act because it allowed the T to begin outsourcing labor, initially cleaners, janitor, and watchmen. MBTA unions fought unsuccessfully to have it struck down in the courts. The legislation allowed to T to save $50 million in 1981 and nearly $60 million in 1982.

Belt tightening continued at the T into the early 1980s. After the Advisory Board's approval of a 1981 budget with slightly less funding than 1980, the T slashed services. Hundreds of employees were laid off. Bowdoin and Symphony Stations closed on January 3, 1981. Select entrances at three other downtown Green Line stations were shuttered. Bus service was reduced and some routes were outsourced. The T worked to save $1.1 million alone by closing nine commuter rail stations, reducing the number of commuter rail trains by ten percent, and slashing Saturday and Sunday commuter rail service. Commuter rail service to Woburn ceased entirely. The changes on the commuter rail network took effect during January and February 1981. Additional cost savings proposals made by the T at the time included replacing Mattapan High Speed Line streetcar service with buses, eliminating over a dozen school bus routes, and closing Arlington Heights Bus Yard, Arborway Car House, and South Boston Power Station. All but the replacement of the Mattapan trolleys took place.

Amidst the 1981 cost cutting, another scandal hit the T. On May 2, 1981, Barry Locke, then Secretary of Transportation and MBTA Chairman, was suspended pending an investigation for corruption. Locke, his brother, and seven others were indicted by a grand jury on multiple accounts of wrongdoing, including participating in multiple kickback schemes. Locke was convicted and sentenced to seven-to-ten years for taking bribes. After receiving a sentence reduction, Locke was released on parole in 1984.

In 1982, the Commonwealth passed legislation requiring Massachusetts to fund the balance of MBTA municipal assessments that exceeded a newly capped amount. Massachusetts essentially provided the T with a blank check, allowing the Authority to balance its budget each year. The blank check funding mechanism came to an end on July 1, 2000, when new legislation established a new funding source for the MBTA, a dedicated portion of Massachusetts sales tax revenue. After sales tax revenue failed to meet projections, the Authority's ability to balance its budget again fell into jeopardy.

The Northwest Extension: Planning & Preparation

During the seventy years after the BERy's 1912 launch of rapid transit service between Boston and Cambridge, various proposals for extending the Cambridge Subway beyond Harvard Square were explored. In 1945, the Metropolitan Transit Recess Commission (MTRC) proposed extending the Cambridge Subway through Watertown, to a terminus in Arlington Heights. The MTA proposed an extension to North Cambridge in its 1963 Ten-Year Plan. In the early 1970s, the BTPR laid out its own options for extending the Red Line beyond Harvard Square. As early as 1972, the MBTA approved the study of an extension passing through Davis Square, Somerville. Before the Davis Square routing became its preferred option, the T studied running the extension along Cambridge's Garden Street, avoiding Somerville altogether.

As plans for a Red Line extension began to gel in 1976, the MBTA described the project as the Northwest Extension, a 6.4-mile-long line from Harvard Square to Arlington Heights. The T proposed rapid transit stations at Porter Square, Davis Square, Alewife Brook Parkway, Arlington Center, and Arlington Heights. The stations at Alewife Brook Parkway and Arlington Heights were each to include an above-ground parking garage to collect suburban commuters. Proposals for extending the Red Line beyond Arlington Heights to Massachusetts Route 128 (now Interstate 95) continued to be considered (Figure 9.108), but only for a little while longer.

In the end, the Red Line never made it to Route 128, nor even into Arlington. In 1977, residents of Arlington voted in a non-binding referendum and rejected the T's proposal to extend the Red Line into their community. Citizens voted over four to one against the project. Had the Northwest Extension continued into Arlington, it would have run northward from Alewife Brook Parkway, depressed in a trench along the Boston & Maine's Lexington Branch.

With the Red Line stopped at the Arlington Line, the Bedford Branch right-of-way from Cambridge to Railroad Street in Bedford became the Minuteman Commuter Bikeway. After two decades of planning, the paved, multi-use path for non-motorized vehicles was dedicated on October 3, 1992. The Minuteman Bikeway was the first major example of a railroad right-of-way owned by the MBTA to be converted into a rail trail. Just after the turn of the millennium, the MBTA formalized a process through which cities and towns could

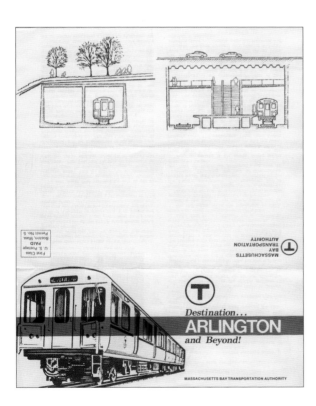

Figure 9.108 Red Line to Arlington and Beyond, Early 1970s
A mailer announces the T's intensions to extend the Red Line into Arlington, and possibly beyond.

more easily coordinate with the T and construct rail trails along MBTA-owned rights-of-way. Since the 1990s, the T and the state have entered into leases and agreements allowing the conversion of miles of railroad rights-of-way into multi-use trails.

The Northwest Extension moved into the schematic design phase in late 1976 (Figure 9.109), with major construction contracts going out the following year. The project proceeded without the portion serving Arlington because Arlington still had not approved the project and federal funds were ready and available for proceeding in Cambridge and Somerville.

The final design of the Northwest Extension became a nearly three-mile-long, two-track extension of the Red Line, featuring: a complete reconstruction of Harvard Station; a cut and cover tunnel from Harvard Square to Cambridge Common; a deep bore tunnel from Cambridge Common following Massachusetts Avenue, under Porter

Figure 9.109 Stations of the Northwest Extension, 1976
A pamphlet circulated by the MBTA explains the locations and designs of proposed stations of the Northwest Extension.

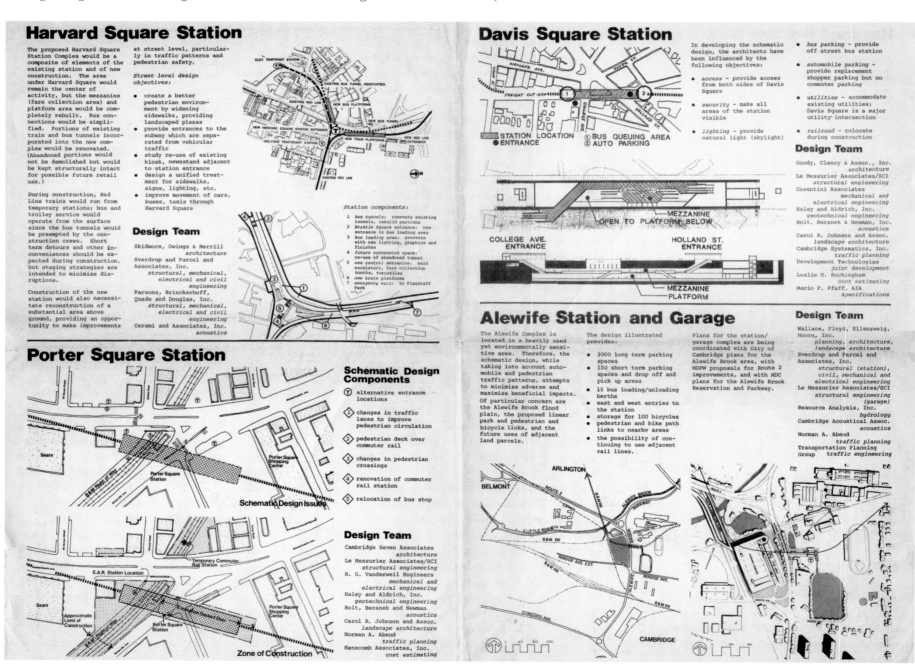

Figure 9.110 The Northwest Extension of the Red Line, 1978
A plan (top) and section (bottom) lay out the Northwest Extension of the Red Line, from Harvard Square (right) to Alewife (left).

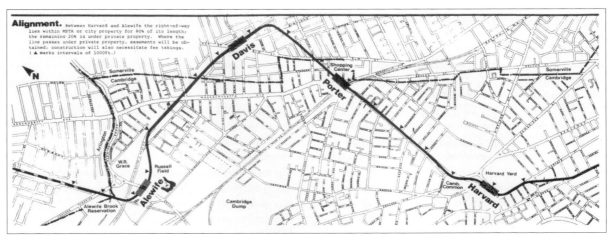

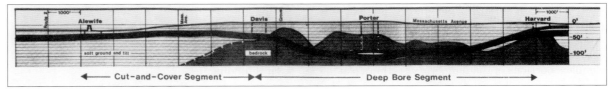

Square, and to the eastern side of Davis Square; new stations at Porter and Davis Squares; a cut and cover tunnel through Davis Square westward, following the disused right-of-way of the Fitchburg Freight Cut-Off to Alewife Brook Parkway; and a terminal station with a parking garage where Massachusetts Route 2 intersected with Alewife Brook Parkway (Figure 9.110). The deep bore tunnel, consisting of a pair of parallel tubes, each approximately twenty-two feet in diameter and enclosing one track, was required where the extension passed under the MBTA's South Acton (now Fitchburg) commuter rail line and private property in Cambridge and Somerville. All stations along the Northwest Extension were designed with platforms long enough to accommodate six-car trains.

To maintain Red Line service to Harvard Square during construction of the Northwest Extension (Figure 9.111), two temporary Red Line stations were constructed to serve Harvard Square.

Figure 9.111 Harvard Station During Reconstruction, 1982
The rebuilding of Harvard Station and maintenance of service through the site required a careful sequencing of work on multiple subterranean levels.

Figure 9.112 Construction at Harvard Square, 1979
With the March 24 doomsday date prominently featured on its cover, a brochure provides information in advance of temporary transit changes to be made around Harvard Square to accommodate construction of the Northwest Extension.

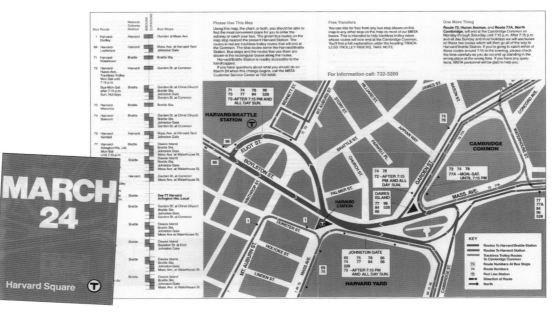

Harvard/Brattle Temporary Station (Harvard/Brattle), erected on the western edge of the Eliot Square Shops and Yard, opened on March 24, 1979. Harvard/Brattle, which served as the temporary northern terminus of the Red Line (Figure 9.113), was accessed from Eliot Square. There, where buses and trackless trolleys temporarily terminated while Harvard Station's underground busways were rebuilt. Another temporary bus and trackless trolley terminal area was located along Garden Street.

Harvard/Holyoke Temporary Station was carved out of the eastern end of the 1912 Harvard Station. The temporary station featured two entrances, one near Dunster Street and one near Holyoke Street. With the early 1981 opening of Harvard/Holyoke, the 1912 Harvard Station closed for its rebuild. Though much of Harvard/Holyoke was absorbed back into the new Harvard Station complex, portions of the temporary station's platforms remain visible beyond the eastern end of Harvard Station. Ghost platforms, one alongside the outbound track and one alongside the inbound track, can be seen from trains by eagle-eyed Red Line riders. Each platform is on the right side of the direction of train travel.

During planning and construction of the Northwest Extension, the MBTA made concerted efforts to involve and inform communities that would be impacted by the project. Thousands of citizens attended hundreds of planning meetings and information sessions. The final designs of the extension's stations were affected by the input from the citizenry, neighborhood groups, and business associations. Complementing meetings held and surveys conducted, numerous flyers, pamphlets, and brochures kept stakeholders abreast of the project's status and upcoming phases. The MBTA printed 90,000 copies of each edition of "Red Line News." The Authority organized an information hotline with the telephone number "MBTA RED."

The Northwest Extension: Construction & Opening

The creation of the deep-bore tubes and Porter Station demanded perhaps the most intensive of techniques, starting with the excavation of vertical shafts into bedrock. The shafts not only allowed engineers to evaluate and confirm underground conditions, they became starting points for lateral excavations (Figure 9.114). Tunneling for the two deep bore tubes proceeded at an average of sixty feet per week in 1981. To bore the tubes, the Perini

Corporation deployed the Atlas Copco Hydraulic Drill Jumbo, a rock drilling machine then on the cutting edge of American deep tunnel construction. The semi-automated machine deployed three large drills like arms of a spider to simultaneously drill multiple and approximately ten-foot-deep holes into bedrock. The drills were then withdrawn and the holes filled with explosives. Controlled explosions loosened ancient bedrock for removal and the process was repeated.

Spoils from tunnel excavations were transported along a specifically built haul road paralleling the Fitchburg Commuter Rail line from Porter Square to Cambridge's recently closed city dump. The MBTA and Cambridge coordinated the capping of the landfill, upon which Cambridge constructed a fifty-acre public park (now Danehy Park). Much of the cost of the Northwest Extension, including the capping of Cambridge's landfill, was covered by federal funding.

In 1981, Harvard Stations's 1929 head house, itself a replacement for the station's 1912 head house, was moved off-site for renovation. The 1929 head house, added to the National Register of Historic Places in 1978, returned to Harvard Square in 1984. The historic structure was converted into a newsstand and installed next to the station's third head house, a glass, steel, and brick structure that opened on March 2, 1985. The pair of structures were accompanied by a new elevator kiosk and improved pedestrian plaza. Red Line service between Harvard Square and Quincy Adams Station commenced in September 1983.

The Northwest Extension brought with it a plethora of public art through "Arts on the Line," a program launched in 1978 by the USDOT to bring high quality artwork to American public transit projects. The USDOT teamed up with the Cambridge Arts Council (CAC) who, together with the MBTA, took the federal pilot project and ran with it. The T approved $400,000 for the program in 1979 alone. Early on, Arts on the Line funded the exhibition of construction photographs and design drawings. The lasting legacy of the program was the commissioning and installation of dozens of permanent art pieces at stations along the Northwest Extension.

On December 8, 1984, ceremonies marked the openings of $44.9 million Porter Station (Figure 9.115) and $29 million Davis Station. The platforms at Porter Station, offset horizontally and vertically from each other, occupied an oddly

Figure 9.113 Harvard/Brattle Temporary Station, Circa 1980
Open for only a few years during construction of the Northwest Extension, Harvard/Brattle was constructed mostly of wood. Skylights bring natural light onto a train of Silver Birds.

Figure 9.114 Building the Northwest Extension, 1982
At the bottom of an access shaft lies one of two deep bore tunnels being constructed to bring the Red Line through North Cambridge.

Figure 9.115 Porter Station Opening Day, December 8, 1984
Attempting to bring natural light into the deepest station on the T, the station's architects coordinated the installation of an intricate mobile, hung from the underside of the station's steel and glass roof structure. The mobile never reflected much light down to the platforms and was removed after a small portion of it fell to the ground.

Figure 9.116 A Brand New Davis Station, 1984

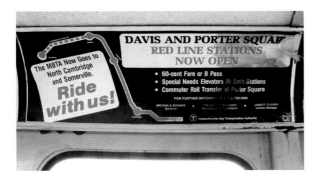

Figure 9.117 Northwest Extension Car Card
Captured in 2014, a worn car card from 1984–85 continues to advertise the openings of Davis and Porter Stations.

maritime-themed cavern carved out of bedrock and some 120 feet below ground.

After five years of construction, Davis Station opened to the public with two head houses, one to the east and another to the west of its namesake square. A new busway opened alongside the eastern head house. To the middle of Davis Square, the station brought a new park, punctuated by a linear skylight bringing natural light into the station. Below ground, the station featured a single center platform (Figure 9.116). Stretching westward from Davis Square to Harvey Street, a linear park atop a cut and cover segment of tunnel was dedicated on October 17, 1985.

By early February 1985, the MBTA recorded that Porter and Davis Stations were each serving approximately 10,000 riders per day, and that usage of Harvard Station had dropped by approximately 6,000 persons. The net increase of 4,000 riders confirmed studies that predicted the entire Northwest Extension would serve more riders than Harvard Station alone. Coinciding with its opening of Porter and Davis Stations, the MBTA produced car cards encouraging people to "Ride with us!" (Figure 9.117).

Alewife Station was the final station to open along the Northwest Extension. Governor Dukakis, Massachusetts Secretary of Transportation Frederick Salvucci, U.S. House Speaker Thomas F. "Tip" O'Neill Jr., and the UMTA Administrator opened the station to the public on March 30, 1985. Underground, Red Line trains arrived and departed alongside a broad central platform. Above the station sat a massive parking garage for 2,000 vehicles. Below the garage and above the Red Line platforms was a twelve-berth busway. Massive concrete cylinders enclosing ramps for automobiles wore multi-story T logos beckoning automobile commuters into four levels of parking. Under a steel and glass-roofed atrium, escalators transported people from the parking decks to the turnstiles (Figure 9.118). Arts on the Line appeared at Alewife in various forms, including a giant T logo sculpture by Toshihiro Katayama.

After completing the Northwest and Braintree Extensions in the 1980s, the MBTA continued to upgrade the Red Line. From June 1981 through January 1982, the Authority undertook a seven-month reconstruction of Mattapan High Speed Line trackage, tunnels, and right-of-way infrastructure. Ashmont and Shawmut Stations received upgrades. The Mattapan High Speed Line reopened on January 16, 1982 with a fleet of a dozen rebuilt PCC cars, formerly used on the Arborway Line. The Red Link I and II projects brought additional improvements to the Braintree branch. Upgrades also came to the Orange Line. In the early 1980s, the Authority invested $35 million into a rehabilitation of Everett Shops.

Red Birds and Longer Trains

The MBTA began rush hour operation of five-car trains between Braintree and Park Street Stations on November 30, 1981. The new service was a step towards regular six-car operation on the Red Line. Lacking enough cars to make six-car operation the norm, the T developed specifications for a new Red Line car in 1983. A year later, the Authority ordered fifty-eight of the cars and assigned them 01700-series numbers and designated them as Red Line Type 2 rapid transit cars (Figure 9.119). The vehicles were constructed by Canada's Urban Transportation Development Corporation in 1987–89. The first handful of 01700s entered service in 1987. The 01700s were similar to Red Line 01600s and 01500s. All three car types were essentially interchangeable and regularly operated together.

In the early 1980s, the MBTA began returning to service its 01400-series Blue Bird cars, rebuilt by the T and GE. Next, the entire fleet of nearly seventy-five Silver Bird cars was rebuilt during 1984–87. Again, GE worked on the rebuilds. The cars, with freshly white and red painted car bodies, returned to service as Red Birds.

Renaming Kendall—Twice

The MBTA renamed Kendall Station to Cambridge Center / MIT in 1982. The new name was a combination of the moniker for a contiguous urban redevelopment project and the acronym for the neighboring Massachusetts Institute of Technology. Cambridge Center, located one stop away from Central Station, also in Cambridge, did not keep its name for long. The T approved revision of the name back to Kendall, along with the addition of the secondary station name "MIT" on June 26, 1985. Since then, signage and maps regularly depict the station's name as Kendall/MIT.

Longer Platforms and More Art

In the mid-1980s, the MBTA embarked on an $80 million modernization program for Orange Line and Red Line stations at the core of its system. The Authority targeted seven stations along the Red Line (Central through Andrew Stations) and three along the Orange Line (State through Essex Stations). Each station received upgraded lighting, finishes, and wayfinding signage. Platforms were lengthened to accommodate six-car trains. By the end of 1986, all of the Red Line modernizations were complete. All Orange Line stations in the program were complete and being served by six-car trains by the end of 1988. Regular operation of six-car trains on the Red Line began on March 28, 1988.

The Red and Orange Line station modernization and platform lengthening programs brought a new batch of public art underground. This time, the art came through ArtStops, an extension of Arts on the Line and a continued collaboration between the MBTA and the Cambridge Arts Council. Through

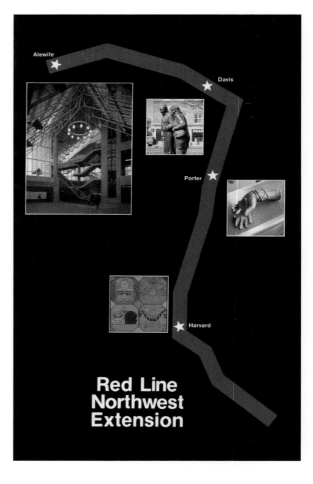

Figure 9.118 Northwest Extension Brochure, Circa 1985
A photograph of the great hall of Alewife Station (top left) and images of Arts on the Line commissioned art pieces pepper the cover of a Northwest Extension brochure.

Figure 9.119 Train of 01700-series Cars, March 12, 2019
A Red Line train has just departed from Charles Station onto a freshly rebuilt Longfellow Bridge.

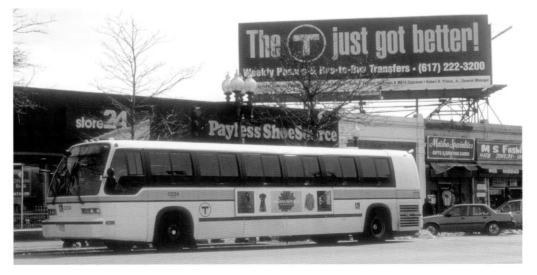

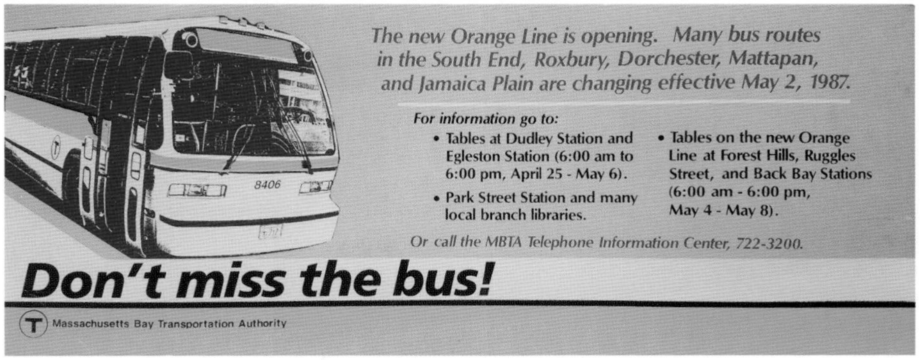
The new Orange Line is opening. Many bus routes in the South End, Roxbury, Dorchester, Mattapan, and Jamaica Plain are changing effective May 2, 1987.
For information go to:
• Tables at Dudley Station and Egleston Station (6:00 am to 6:00 pm, April 25 - May 6).
• Park Street Station and many local branch libraries.
• Tables on the new Orange Line at Forest Hills, Ruggles Street, and Back Bay Stations (6:00 am - 6:00 pm, May 4 - May 8).
Or call the MBTA Telephone Information Center, 722-3200.
Don't miss the bus!
Massachusetts Bay Transportation Authority
8406

Figure 9.120 RTS Bus on a Car Card, Circa Early 1987

ArtStops, site-specific art installations appeared at each modernized station. Examples included the "Imagination Chamber" at Chinatown Station and "The Kendall Band" at Kendall Station. The Kendall Band, designed by Paul Matisse of Groton, consisted of three "instruments," each triggered by either a passing train or a person operating a mechanism on the platform. Central Station reopened with twelve-by-four-foot murals of glazed wall tiles by Elizabeth Mapelli. Broadway Station featured "Domestic Objects and Tools of the Trade," a composition of black and white aluminum forms by Jay Coogan. Essex Station reopened with "Colors on the Line" by Toshihiro Katayama. Downtown Crossing Station reopened with thirty-one fanciful benches designed by Buster Simpson.

Double Deck, Flyer, and RTS Buses

In addition to ordering hundreds of new buses and rebuilding scores of existing vehicles throughout the 1980s, the MBTA supported various experiments in public bus transit. The Authority approved the private operation of double-deck buses to connect Boston's downtown shopping districts in 1982. Each of the initial fleet of six buses seated sixty passengers. The UK-built buses served a loop connecting the Back Bay, Downtown Crossing, and Quincy Market. The service was marketed to shoppers and advertised a fare of fifty cents.

The first of the T's 9400-series Flyer-built buses arrived in 1982, the same year that the Authority netted $1.27 million from the sale of its Brockton Garage, Somerville (Union Square) Garage, and Lincoln Wharf Power Station. In 1983, the T tested a fifty-eight-foot articulated bus, significantly longer than non-articulated models of the time.

The MBTA invested $51 million into its revenue vehicle fleet in 1985 alone. Among its purchases in 1985 were nearly two hundred of what the T called "Advanced Design" or RTS buses (Figure 9.120). Constructed by GM and other manufacturers, RTS buses quickly became the backbone of the MBTA's bus fleet for decades (Figure 9.121).

The T just got better!
Weekly Passes & Bus-to-Bus Transfers • (617) 222-3200
store 24
Payless ShoeSource
0224

Figure 9.121 RTS Bus at Mattapan Square, Circa 1998–99
The early paint scheme for MBTA RTS buses featured a broad yellow stripe over a thin black stripe (shown). Later paint schemes featured yellow and blue stripes. Above the bus, a billboard touts the MBTA's weekly passes and bus-to-bus transfers.

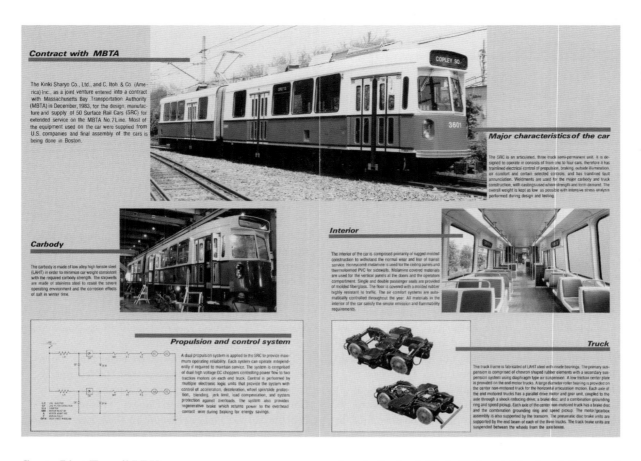

Green Line Type 7 LRVs

In 1983, the T awarded a $52.1 million contract to Kinki Sharyo for fifty MBTA Type 7 LRVs, the newest LRV for the Green Line (Figure 9.122). Kinki Sharyo was a joint venture between the Kinki Sharyo Company of Japan and C. Itoh & Company of New York. The 1983 contract was the first of multiple, which in total netted the MBTA 220 Type 7s (Figure 9.123). Final assembly of the Type 7s took place in Boston's Hyde Park neighborhood. Scores of Type 7s entered service throughout 1986 and 1987. Nearly 100 of the trolleys were in regular service at the end of 1989.

Beginning in 2012, the MBTA approved multiple contracts, with initial ones totalling $220 million, with Alstom Transport (now Siemens Alstom) for the modernization of eighty-six of its remaining Type 7 LRVs and seventy-four aging commuter

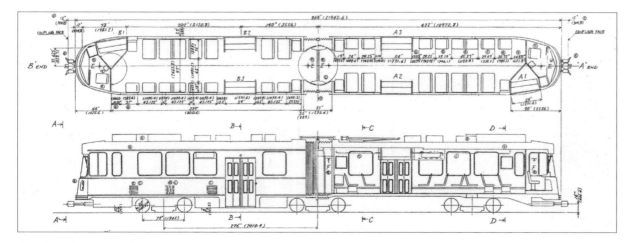

Figure 9.123 Type 7 LRV Dimensional Drawings, 1984

A plan (top) and side elevation (bottom) depict a Type 7, a seventy-two-foot-long attenuated vehicle with a 201-person capacity

rail coaches. The Type 7s received new propulsion systems, climate control systems, and refreshed interiors. The commuter rail coaches, all bi-level Kawasaki-constructed models built in 1990–91, received brake overhauls, new controls, new information displays, and new seating, among other upgrades. The work on both the Type 7s and commuter rail coaches took place at Alstom's facility in Hornell, New York. The same facility is currently constructing the next generation of train set for Amtrak's Acela service.

Commuter Rail Goes Purple

At the end of the 1970s, the MBTA's commuter rail fleet was far from homogeneous. A motley collection of Locomotives from the 1950s, 1960s, and 1970s, including an E8, various GP7s, F40-PH-2s, and F3s rebuilt into F10s (Figure 9.124 and Figure 9.125), pulled a rainbow of passenger equipment. Coaches included models built in 1908–16 for the Pennsylvania Railroad (rebuilt in 1966 and still retaining steam heating systems), over fifty coaches leased from Ontario, Canada's Go Transit (Figure 9.126), and relatively new, single level Pullman-Standard-built coaches. Complimenting the disparate array of locomotives and coaches were various types of Rail Diesel Cars (RDCs), including RDC-1s, RDC-2s, RDC-3s, RDC-4s, and RDC-9s. The first coaches to wear the MBTA's commuter rail purple were Boston & Maine RDC number 6448 and Penn Central coach number 2591. Purple stripes appeared on the two coaches in 1974.

At the tail end of 1978, the first of sixty new commuter rail coaches from manufacturer Pullman-Standard arrived. Fifteen featured a controller-cab with train operation and braking controls at one end. As it still does, the MBTA typically operated its commuter rail trains with a locomotive at the outbound end and a controller-cab

Figure 9.124 Commuter Rail at North Station, October, 1982
MBTA locomotive number 1112 heads a commuter rail train alongside platforms yet to be rebuilt into high-level types. The elevated highway structure and the former Boston & Maine office building (both in the background) were demolished for The Big Dig.

Figure 9.125 Commuter Rail on the Southside, March, 1979
MBTA locomotive 1100 pulls a train of Go Transit coaches.

Figure 9.126 Go Transit Coach in Boston, March 23, 1979
Cab-controller coach number 107 wears a temporary T logo.

Figure 9.127 Controller-Cab #1301, May 25, 1985
An MBTA commuter rail train lead by a controller-cab coach heads through East Fitchburg towards Boston.

coach at the inbound end of the train. The push-pull configuration kept the loud and fume-belching locomotives as far as possible from the concourses at North and South Stations. Outbound trains were operated in pull mode, with the engineer operating the train from the locomotive's cab and pulling coaches. The engineer operated inbound trains in push mode from the controller-cab of the push-pull coach, with the locomotive providing propulsion from the rear and pushing the train back to Boston (Figure 9.127).

The MBTA's order for push-pull coaches was among the last to be fulfilled by Pullman-Standard,

a company formed by a 1930s merger of the Standard Steel Car Company (Standard) and Pullman. In 1910, Standard acquired the Osgood Bradley Company (Osgood), a Worcester company launched as a builder of carriages in 1820. Over the centuries, in turn, Osgood, Standard, and Pullman-Standard were each manufacturers of vehicles used in public transportation for Greater Boston. The former Osgood complex in Worcester closed in 1960. Despite being ravaged by fire in the mid-1990s, the massive Osgood Bradley Building, located steps away from Worcester Union Station, remains a

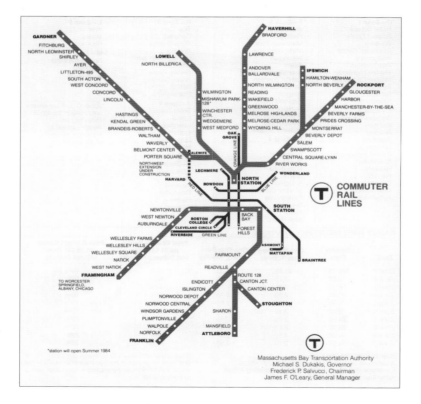

Figure 9.128 Commuter Rail Brochure, 1983

Figure 9.129 MBTA Ski Train Ad, 1982

monument to over 150 years of public transit vehicle production in Massachusetts.

Commuter Rail Expansions and Contractions in the 1970s and 1980s

Commuter rail service returned to Haverhill in 1979. Three years earlier, the MBTA had stopped running trains to the city. Andover and North Andover had stopped paying for MBTA service in 1976 and 1974, respectively. Service to Haverhill recommenced with five daily weekday trains on December 17, 1979. Weekend trains returned to Haverhill in spring 1980.

A month after restoring service to Haverhill, the T extended service westward beyond South Acton, to the city of Fitchburg, and beyond, to Gardner. A special train with four new Pullman-Standard coaches marked the opening of the extension on January 12, 1980. The next day, regular service began with four inbound and three outbound daily trips. Travel time from Boston to Gardner was approximately two hours with a one-way fare of $3.50.

The MBTA faced significant funding and equipment shortages as it entered the 1980s. Ontario reclaimed its loaner Go Transit coaches and the T's program to rebuild its RDCs was stalled, waiting on federal funding. To cut costs, in 1981 the T cut back commuter rail service by approximately ten percent, terminated service on the Woburn Branch, and raised commuter rail fares. Despite decreased service and higher fares, overall ridership remained generally constant. Riders effectively paid more money to share fewer trains. Despite cutting back service, the T worked hard to keep the trains it did operate running on time.

The MBTA described 1982 as "A Year of Historic Firsts," celebrating its deployment of thirty-two RDCs, freshly rebuilt by Morrison-Knudsen into push-pull coaches. The T assigned rebuilt RDC controller-cabs 1400-series numbers and non-controller-cabs units 400-series numbers. The cost of the rebuilds was two thirds of that for new coaches.

In 1982, commuter rail revenue was up nearly eighteen percent and ridership across the T's 280-mile commuter rail system exceeded ten million riders for the first time. West Natick Station opened on August 23. It was the first new MBTA commuter rail station to open in over five years. 1982 also brought a new operating agreement between the MBTA and the Boston & Maine.

In 1984, the Mishawam Station opened along the Lowell Line in Woburn. A map within a 1983 "Going Your Way" commuter rail brochure noted the station as "opening soon" (Figure 9.128).

Serving the Slopes

A high point of commuter rail operations during the early 1980s was the Saturday December 27, 1980 departure of the T's first Ski Train. A joint effort of the MBTA and the Montachusett Regional Transit Authority (MRTA), the Ski Train operated on winter weekends out of North Station. At the far end of the Fitchburg Line, each ski train connected with dedicated buses serving alpine ski areas at Wachusett Mountain and Mount Watatic. The round-trip fare, including a lift ticket, was approximately $15. The Ski Train continued to operate through the 1982–83 ski season (Figure 9.129). From 2006 to 2016, the MBTA again ran weekend ski trains between North Station and Fitchburg Station. The trains coordinated with shuttle bus service to Wachusett Mountain only.

A recent iteration of MBTA service to the slopes kicked off for the 2016–17 ski season. From December through March, a train outfitted with ski and snowboard racks left Boston each weekend morning for the T's newest commuter rail station, Wachusett Station. Included in the twenty-six-dollar round-trip fare was a shuttle bus transfer between Wachusett Station and Wachusett Mountain, thirteen miles away. Each weekend evening, the ski train returned to North Station. The special service to Wachusett Station expanded during the 2017–18 ski season to include a round-trip each Wednesday. The fare was $23 round-trip.

Fires on the Northside

A low-point for commuter rail service in the 1980s occurred on the northside, where two fires devastated MBTA commuter rail bridges in 1984. At North Station, approximately one hundred feet of wood trestle burned at the drawbridges carrying trains across the Charles River. The damage severed the platform tracks at North Station from the rest of the commuter rail network. While the T worked to repair the damaged Charles River crossing, it established shuttle bus service between North Station and temporary platforms at the Boston Engine Terminal. The Authority increased service at Oak Grove and Sullivan Square Stations to accommodate northside commuter rail passengers

COMMUTER RAIL NEWS

Special Issue 1985 • Published by the Massachusetts Bay Transportation Authority • Vol. II No. 3

Beverly-Salem Drawbridge Reopens

On December 1, 1985, the first passenger train crossed the Beverly-Salem Drawbridge since fire destroyed it just over a year ago. Commuter Rail trains are running once again from North Station to points north of the bridge, allowing over 3000 daily passengers direct access into Boston.

(See story on page 2)

Figure 9.130 Danvers River Bridge Damage and Repairs, 1985
A photograph shows twisted and severed tracks dangling across the fire-damaged remains of the Beverley-Salem Drawbridge (middle).

transferring to rapid transit and bus services. Service over the damaged Charles River crossing into North Station was restored in 1985.

Just as the T was getting its temporary service and bridge reconstruction program underway at North Station, another trestle fire stuck northside tracks. On November 16, 1984, a massive blaze decimated the trestle and drawbridge that carried trains across the Danvers River, between Salem and Beverly (Figure 9.130). Some 2,500 daily riders were immediately affected. In short order, the MBTA wrangled private carriers to provide shuttle bus service between points north of the Danvers River and stations in Salem, where commuter rail service continued to operate to and from Boston. Upon arriving in Boston, and until the broken Charles River span was repaired, rail passengers transferred to a shuttle bus to make it over the Charles and into North Station. The loss of the Beverley-Salem Drawbridge trapped some of the T's commuter rail equipment north of the newly-formed gap. At least one MBTA locomotive was transported out of the zone on a flat bed truck navigating local roads. The T moved quickly to award demolition and reconstruction contracts for the Danvers River Bridge. The new bridge reopened less than a year after the fire.

Improving Commuter Rail in the Late 1980s

1986 was a busy year for commuter rail upgrades. Construction commenced on a new station to replace an aging Boston & Maine facility at Salem. Preliminary studies were under way for restoring service to Rowley and Newburyport on the northside, and to South Shore communities along Old Colony Lines on the southside. The T purchased eighteen new F-40 locomotives from General Motor's Electromotive Division (GM-EMD). Under a $45 million contract with the MBTA, Messerschmitt-Bolkow-Blohm (MBB) of West Germany built sixty-seven new coaches in 1987–88. MBB controller-cab units received 1500-series numbers (Figure 9.131) and non-controller-cab coaches received 500-series numbers.

As 1986 turned into 1987, the MBTA was in dire need of commuter rail coaches it ordered but had yet to receive. As a stopgap measure, the T leased nine coaches from the New Jersey Transit Corporation (NJ Transit). Improvements continued in 1987 with the deployment of seventy new commuter rail coaches and eighteen new locomotives. Construction commenced on new stations at Lynn and South Attleboro, as well as a new, three-and-one-half-mile extension of the Franklin Line. A new Forge Park/495 Station opened for Commuter Rail service in summer 1988.

Figure 9.131 Commuter Rail Coach #1504, March 12, 1989
A relatively new, MBB-built 1500-series controller-cab coach leads a train at Lawrence.

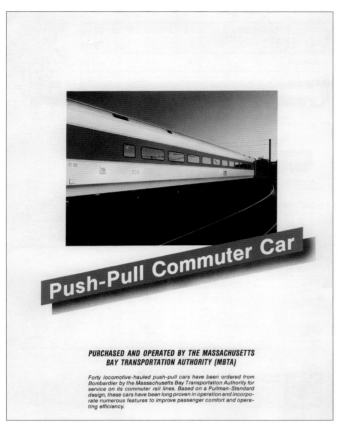

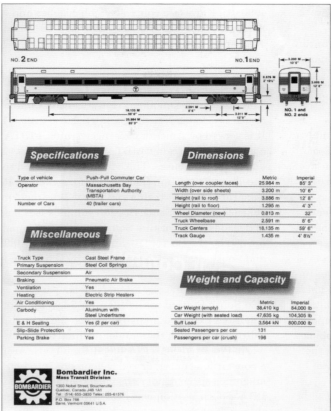

Figure 9.132 MBTA 600-series Push-Pull Coaches, Circa 1989

Figure 9.133 Fenway Flyer Schedules, Circa 1988; 1995

The Boston & Maine's final contract to operate commuter rail service on behalf of the MBTA expired on December 31, 1986. On the next day, January 1, 1987, Amtrak took over MBTA commuter rail operations. The operator of America's passenger rail network experienced a rocky start in Boston. During Amtrak's first few months, trains were regularly standing room only and there was an approximately ten percent drop in on-time performance. Throughout the rest of the late 1980s, MBTA commuter rail coaches, especially those in service on the southside, were increasingly at, or over, capacity.

Seeking to address the problem of overcrowded coaches, the MBTA ordered an initial batch of fifty single-level commuter rail coaches from Bombardier. Each coach seated 120 riders in a three-plus-two seating configuration (Figure 9.132). Controller-cab units received 1600-series numbers and non-controller-cab coaches received 600-series numbers. Over 100 Bombardier-built coaches were delivered to the MBTA by mid-1990.

Parking at virtually all MBTA commuter rail surface parking lots was free of charge before 1989. At the end of the year, and seeking to increase revenue at the end of a decade of fiscal stress, the MBTA began charging $1 daily for a day of parking at commuter rail lots. During winter 1989–90 and spring 1990, the T phased in the new fee across nearly 11,000 parking spaces. The Authority had wanted to charge $2 per day, but backed down after receiving objections from the public.

The Fenway Flyer

MBTA commuter rail service to Yawkey Station (now Lansdowne Station) commenced on April 29, 1988. The stop opened with mostly at-grade platforms and was served by Framingham Line trains. Trains arrived and departed approximately a half hour before and after each game at Fenway Park. In 1989, Framingham Line trains served Fenway Park Station on weekday game days, and Attleboro Line trains served the station on weekend game days.

Game day service in the early 1990s was branded the "Fenway Flyer." High level platforms appeared at the station during that time. The MBTA issued special printed commuter rail schedules for Fenway Park service (Figure 9.133). Yawkey Station was rebuilt in 2012–14 to include a new pedestrian bridge. After Boston's renaming of Yawkey Way back to Jersey Street in early 2018, the fate of Yawkey Station's name remained in question until early 2019, when the T announced it would rename Yawkey Station to Lansdowne Station.

Commuter Rail Rises to New Heights

At the end of the 1980s, the MBTA sought to add its first bi-level coaches to its commuter rail fleet. If the T replaced a single-level coach with a bi-level coach on a given train, more passengers could be carried with that train, without increasing that train's length. Higher capacity without a longer train saved the massive expenses of lengthening station platforms wherever the train would stop.

In early 1989, the T confirmed a $149 million purchase of 126 coaches, including seventy-five bi-level models, all from a division of Kawasaki of Japan (Figure 9.134 and Figure 9.135). Assembly in the U.S. was required if the MBTA was to apply federal funding towards its purchase of the vehicles. Accordingly, the manufacturer agreed to have the coaches assembled at a former General Electric facility in Pittsfield.

The first bi-level coaches arrived for testing and an August VIP run to South Station in 1990. Each new coach carried fifty percent more seated passengers than a typical MBTA single-level model. The bi-level coaches featured a two-plus-three seating configuration. Constructed during 1990–91, Kawasaki controller-cab coaches and non-controller-cab coaches received 1700-series and 700-series numbers, respectively.

South Station Transportation Center

The Michael S. Dukakis Transportation Center at South Station is New England's busiest transit hub. It is served by Amtrak passenger trains, MBTA commuter rail trains, MBTA buses, and intrastate and interstate buses. The center is connected to the T's underground South Station, served by Red Line rapid transit trains and Silver Line dual-mode vehicles. Today's South Station complex is the result of decades of reworking South Station Terminal, opened by the Boston Terminal Company in 1898, and South Station Under, opened by the BERy in 1917.

In 1965, a financially ailing New Haven Railroad sold South Station to the BRA for $6.95 million. The BRA explored many reuses for the sprawling railroad terminal, then under-utilized and well worn. Potential reuses included a multi-use arena, a convention center, or redevelopment into hotel and office space. Under the custodianship of the BRA, South Station was heavily downsized. More than half of the main head house was demolished. A portion of the head house was replaced with a modernist office tower erected by Stone & Webster, an engineering company behind the design, construction, and operation of hundreds

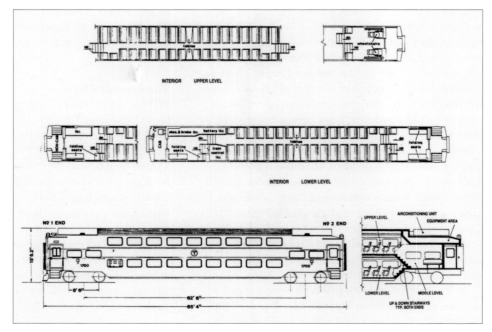

Figure 9.134 The T's First Bi-level Coach, Circa 1990

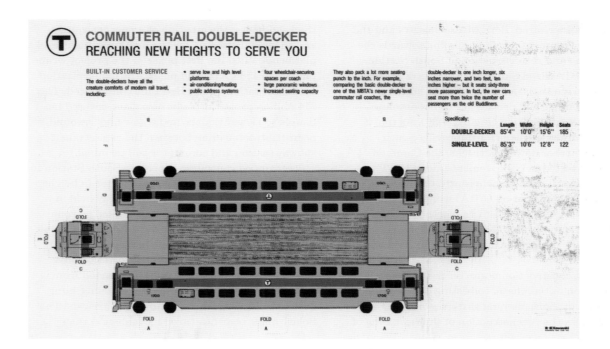

Figure 9.135 Paper Bi-level Train, Circa 1990

The T promoted its first bi-level commuter rail coaches, 0700 and 1700-series units, with cut-out paper trains.

of infrastructure and transit projects around the world, including dozens of electric street railway networks. The office tower, 245 Summer Street continues to stand where patrons once packed South Station's lunch counters and dining rooms.

In July 1978, Governor Dukakis signed off on legislation leading to the creation of the multi-modal transportation center that now bears his name. The Commonwealth and the BRA then agreed that the MBTA should become the custodian of South Station. In October, a purchase and sale agreement was formalized between the BRA and the MBTA. Using state monies allocated in the Commonwealth's 1977 Passenger Rail Transportation Fund, the MBTA paid $4.4 million in cash.

An additional $2 million was "paid" by the T in the form of the Authority bearing the cost of new foundations for potential public or private air-rights developments over South Station. After the BRA deeded South Station to the MBTA in 1979, both of Boston's commuter rail terminals were under MBTA control for the first time.

The South Station purchased by the MBTA was a mere shell of the grand terminal opened by the Boston Terminal Company in 1898. A truncated head house was served by only ten tracks, down from twenty-eight in place in 1898. South Station had lost tracks, platforms, and its entire Dorchester Avenue wing to a hulking U.S. Postal Service facility. Most of the wing along Atlantic Avenue

Figure 9.136 South Station Redevelopment Model, Circa 1981

A scale model lays out a massive mixed use complex replacing much of South Station Terminal. The view is of the north side of the complex, facing Atlantic Avenue. The bus station and parking garage (right) came into being in the 1990s. Only recently has work begun on a private office tower (center) between the bus and train terminals.

has also disappeared. Both Massachusetts and the federal government directed funding towards the rethinking and reconstruction of South Station.

The MBTA hired Skidmore, Owings & Merrill (SOM) to study the addition of a bus station, parking garage, and private air-rights development for South Station (Figure 9.136). As the MBTA worked up plans for improving South Station, farther down the tracks, the Commonwealth invested in improvements along the T's commuter rail lines. Concurrently, the Federal Railway Administration (FRA) worked on intercity rail improvements through its Northeast Corridor Improvements Project (NECIP), authorized by the Railroad Revitalization and Regulatory Reform Act of 1976.

In 1984, construction began on South Station's $49 million initial phase, consisting of: the rehabilitation of the remaining eastern portion of the head house; the reconstruction of the west wing of the head house; the creation of a new concourse; and the installation of, for the first time, high-level platforms. With the first phase of the project wrapping up in 1988, a second phase, the modernization of South Station on the Red Line commenced. The $14 million project brought new glass-covered head houses to Dewey Square and a new underground pedestrian connection between the rapid transit subway station and commuter rail terminal.

A revamped concourse opened at South Station in 1988. The multi-story space made up for in height what the original South Station midway held in acreage. The new concourse was flanked by renovated head house wings housing a food court, retail space, and office space. A multi-story glazed wall separated the concourse from platforms where commuter rail trains arrived and departed from eleven numbered tracks. A massive, ceiling-hung board displayed train departures and arrivals. The Solari-made board featured movable text that

Figure 9.137 Nantasket Steamboat Co. Schedule Card, 1934

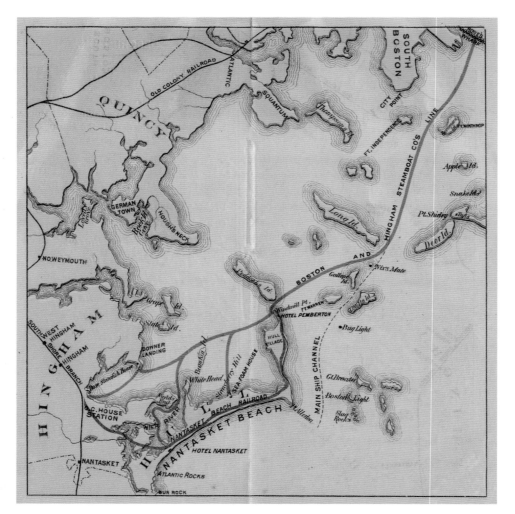

Figure 9.138 Hull & Hingham Ferry Timetable, 1881

A timetable advertises not only the Boston & Hingham Steamboat Company, but the Nantasket Beach Railroad Company. While the steamboat company linked Boston with Hull and Hingham, the railroad traversed Hull, stopping at ferry landings and connecting with the Old Colony Railroad in Hingham.

Figure 9.139 Water Transportation Schedule, July 1985
Two faces of a pocket-sized schedule card list timetables for MBTA commuter boats operating between Boston and Hingham, Hull, and North Quincy.

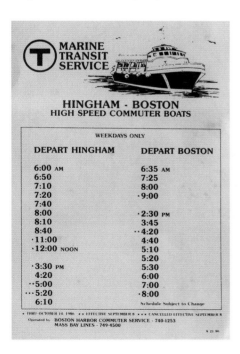

Figure 9.140 (Left) Hingham Ferry Schedule Card, 1986

made an attention-grabbing clicking sound every time it was updated. The sound of the updating Solari board, as it did at many train stations around the world during the twentieth century, directed waiting rail travelers to look up to the board for the latest update on train departures and arrivals. The board has since been decommissioned, auctioned off, and replaced by LED boards.

On November 13, 1989, a week of celebratory events at South Station was punctuated by a ceremony to rededicate the complex. Governor Dukakis and his Secretary of Transportation Frederick Salvucci, together a juggernaut behind many transit improvements for Greater Boston, joined the FRA's Chief Executive, Amtrak's President, and the BRA's Director for speeches at South Station. Train-shaped cakes, a flag waving crowd, and the blasting of train horns rounded out the celebration.

In 1989 and 1990, designs were finalized for the third and final phase of the redevelopment of South Station, which included the construction of a new bus terminal and parking garage atop the far ends of the terminal's platforms. Early designs called for a covered connection with moving sidewalks linking the bus and train stations, berths for forty-five buses, and parking for 500 cars. The final design, approved by the MBTA in late 1990, and for which construction commenced in late 1992, featured two levels, a lower concourse level with bus berths, and an upper level with public parking spaces. Only the lower level of the new bus terminal was enclosed.

On October 28, 1998, regular operations commenced at the $82 million South Station bus terminal, Boston's first, consolidated terminal for all interstate bus carriers. The bus terminal opened with a multi-story main entrance on Atlantic Avenue. New ramps expedited the movement of motor coaches between the terminal's twenty-nine numbered gates and nearby Interstates 90 and 93. The bus terminal project brought with it an additional two numbered commuter rail tracks and platforms to South Station below.

The MBTA Sets Sail

For hundreds of years before the arrival of the MBTA, Boston was served by various ferries, including the Charlestown Ferry, the Winnisimmet Ferry, and the East Boston Ferries (See Chapter 1). The T's first public system map to depict a commuter ferry was released in 1967 (Figure 9.30). In that year, a Massachusetts Bay Lines commuter boat connected Boston's Rowe's Wharf with Hull's

Pemberton Point. Ferry service between Rowe's Wharf and Hull was nothing new. The Nantasket Steamboat Company, along with others, provided links for decades before the MBTA (Figure 9.137).

Two ferries appeared on the T's 1978 system map. One, connecting Long Wharf with Hull's Pemberton Point, was operated by Massachusetts Bay Lines. Another, funded by the EOTC, linked Long Wharf with the shuttered Hingham Shipyard. Ferries linking Rowe's Wharf with Hingham and Hull existed since the 1900s (Figure 9.138).

In 1984, a planned reconstruction of Boston's Southeast Expressway (now part of Interstate 93) was about to put some major kinks into the trips of automobile commuters driving between Boston and the South Shore. Anticipating a potential traffic nightmare, the federal government and the Commonwealth stepped in to increase bus and commuter boat options for South Shore commuters. Increased private bus service to Boston as well as hourly commuter boat service between Hingham and downtown Boston were launched.

After the Southeast Expressway rebuild wrapped up, the T continued to subsidize the Hingham Ferry. In 1985, a pair of boats, the Chimera and the Dragonfish, were joined by the Captain Joseph. The latter was a seventy-eight-foot vessel with a 149-passenger capacity. By the end of the year, a small fleet of five boats made forty trips and carried an average of 1,600 riders daily (Figure 9.139). Two private contractors, Boston Harbor Commuter Service and Massachusetts Bay Lines, provided seventeen daily round-trips in 1986 (Figure 9.140). A third contractor and a sixth boat joined the fleet of the Hingham Ferry in 1989. In that year, a one-way ticket for the ten-mile journey cost $3.00. A ten-trip book cost $27.50. Patrons praised the service, as reported in the July/August 1989 *Rollsign*:

> Passengers boarding at Rowe's Wharf on a steamy summer afternoon bore little resemblance to typical end-of-the-day, exhausted, often irritable bus or subway commuters. Spotless, sleek blue and white vessels attended by smiling crew welcome all comers.

At the end of the 1980s, Massport completed a report exploring the creation of a network of sixteen ferry terminals around Boston Harbor. The report predicted as many as 4,000 daily riders by 1995 and a set-up cost of between $2 and $4 million. The study followed on the heels of both Massport's launching of inner harbor water shuttles and the T's late 1980s establishment of a Charlestown to Long Wharf ferry.

During the 1990s, provide companies experimented with various Boston Harbor ferry services. A pair of vessels operated by Fort Point Associates linked Rowe's Wharf and Chelsea in 1990. One vessel carried sixty passengers, the other, forty-nine. Picking up where the Winnisimmet Ferry left off in 1917, the Chelsea Ferry departed every twenty minutes each morning and evening. A round-trip ticket, including the cost of parking in Chelsea, was $7.50. Round-trip fare without parking was $4.00. On September 30, 1991, a new company launched ferry service between Rowe's Wharf and Hull's Nantasket Pier. After only a few months of operation, the service, provided with a single boat, succumbed to financial difficulties exacerbated by bad weather.

1992–94 saw Boston Harbor Cruises operate a new subsidized ferry between Long Wharf and the John F. Kennedy Presidential Library and Museum (JFK Library) in Dorchester. The seasonal ferry service was complemented on land by shuttle buses operating between the library, the neighboring campus of UMass Boston, and JFK/UMass Station. With a one-way fare of $2.00, the JFK Library ferry took three quarters of an hour to travel between its terminal points.

After some three decades of subsidizing harbor ferries, the MBTA and the Commonwealth worked to provide ferries linking Boston with points beyond Boston Harbor. In 1995, the state funded a short-lived, experimental commuter boat to test the demand for mid-day service between Boston and the North Shore. From January 16 to March 16, one daily round-trip was made. Regular ferry service between Boston and the North Shore returned in June 2006, with the launch of the seasonally-operated Salem Ferry. Since 2012, Boston Harbor Cruises has operated the Salem Ferry since 2012 with the Nathaniel Bowditch, a ninety-two-foot high-speed catamaran purchased by the City of Salem. The boat was named after the Salem native son famed as a pioneer of modern ocean navigation.

Throughout the early to mid-1990s, MBTA commuter boats connected Rowe's Wharf with the Hingham Shipyard and Long Wharf with the Charlestown Navy Yard (Figure 9.142). The Hingham Ferry operated on weekdays only. At the end of the 1990s, The Big Dig brought increased public funding for alternative transit modes to Boston. In August 1995, Boston Harbor Cruises assigned one boat to a subsidized rush hour ferry

linking Long Wharf with East Boston. Boats operated from 6:30 a.m. to 9:00 a.m., and from 3:30 p.m. to 6:40 p.m. The service kicked off with twenty minute headways and a one-way fare of $1.00. Mid-day and weekend service to East Boston was also provided by the MBTA's Charlestown Ferry. By 1996, the T was subsidizing a variety of harbor ferries, including routes linking: Long Wharf and Charlestown Navy Yard; Long Wharf and Hull; and Rowe's Wharf and Hingham Shipyard. A ferry linking downtown, East Boston, and Marina Bay in Quincy did not endure beyond the mid-1990s. The operation wrapped in fall 1997, when the T withdrew its subsidy after Big Dig dollars dried up.

The last year of the twentieth century brought notable changes to MBTA ferry service. During summer 1999, the Hingham Ferry began to provide limited weekend service. A weekday ferry operated by Harbor Express connected Long Wharf with Quincy and Hull's Pemberton Point.

Boston Harbor Cruises inked a $2.3 million contract in 1999, funded by Big Dig dollars, to continue operating two harbor ferry routes. One connected Lovejoy Wharf, situated along the eastern flank of North Station, with the Charlestown Navy Yard and Long Wharf. The other route served Lovejoy Wharf, Fan Pier, and the World Trade Center, in the South Boston Seaport. The routes were administered by the MBTA. Prior to receiving the 1999 contract, Boston Harbor Cruises operated MBTA ferries serving the Navy Yard (since 1987) and Lovejoy Wharf (since 1996). Citing low ridership numbers of less than one hundred passengers per day, the MBTA decided to terminate ferry service from Lovejoy Wharf in 2004. After The Big Dig wrapped up, the T balked at picking up the over $700,000 yearly cost of service. The last MBTA-subsidized ferry from Lovejoy Wharf departed on January 21, 2005.

On April 10, 2002, the MBTA took over the operations of Harbor Express, a ferry linking Long Wharf, Logan Airport, Hull, and Quincy. The T bought out the equipment and dock leases of Water Transportation Alternatives, maintaining the company as operator of Harbor Express. With the takeover, the T became the proud owner of two catamarans, each capable of carrying nearly 150 passengers. The MBTA added two new vessels to its fleet of Authority-owned vessels in 2017, the high-speed catamarans "Champion" and "Glory," each 150-passenger crafts with an individual cost of $5.7 million.

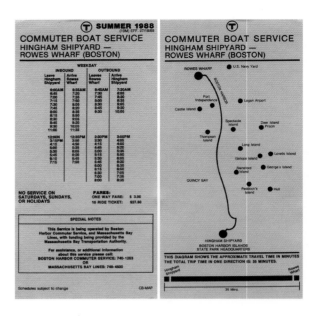

Figure 9.141 Hingham Ferry Schedules Card, 1988

Figure 9.142 MBTA Commuter Boat Schedule Covers, 1992

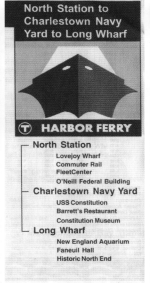
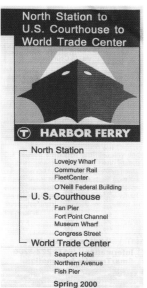

Figure 9.143 MBTA Boat and Ferry Schedules, Spring 2000
With the issuance of its 1999 ferry schedules, the MBTA began differentiating Commuter Boat from Harbor Ferry service. Commuter Boats connected Boston with Hingham, Quincy, and Hull. Harbor Ferries linked inner harbor points, including the Charlestown Navy Yard, Lovejoy Wharf, and Long Wharf.

Figure 9.144 MBTA Ferry Schedules, Fall 2002
A schedule for Harbor Ferries F3, F4, F5, and F5X (left) maps service connecting Charlestown, North Station, Long Wharf, and the South Boston Seaport. A schedule for Commuter Boats F1, F2, and F2H (right) maps service linking Boston with Quincy, Hull, and Hingham.

With the issuance of its fall 2002 ferry schedules, the MBTA began to assign its ferries alphanumeric designations F1 through F5 (Figure 9.144). The T dropped F3 and F5 in 2005. In 2013, Boston Harbor Cruises, operator of F1 and F4, added F2 and F2H to its fleet, becoming the sole operator of MBTA ferries.

Mapping the T in the 1980s
The MBTA's 1980 folding system map (Figure 9.145 and Figure 9.146) was a revised version of previous editions. It included a commuter rail map showing the Lowell Line extending to Nashua, Manchester, and Concord, all cities in New Hampshire. Trains ran from January 20, 1980 until February 28, 1981, when, after the federal government cut funding, the MBTA stopped the interstate service.

The T redesigned its folding system and wallet-sized rapid transit maps in 1981, releasing both the following year. The T sold space on the map to advertiser in an effort to offset the costs of producing and publishing the folding system map. Further seeking to reduce production costs, the T released the map with a recommended price of seventy-five cents. The 1982 system map was not

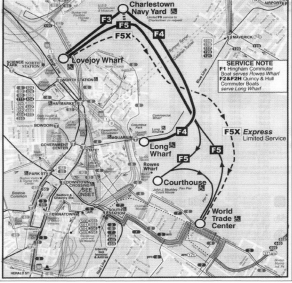
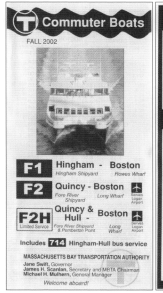
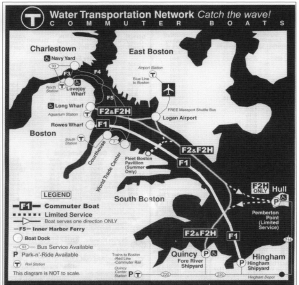

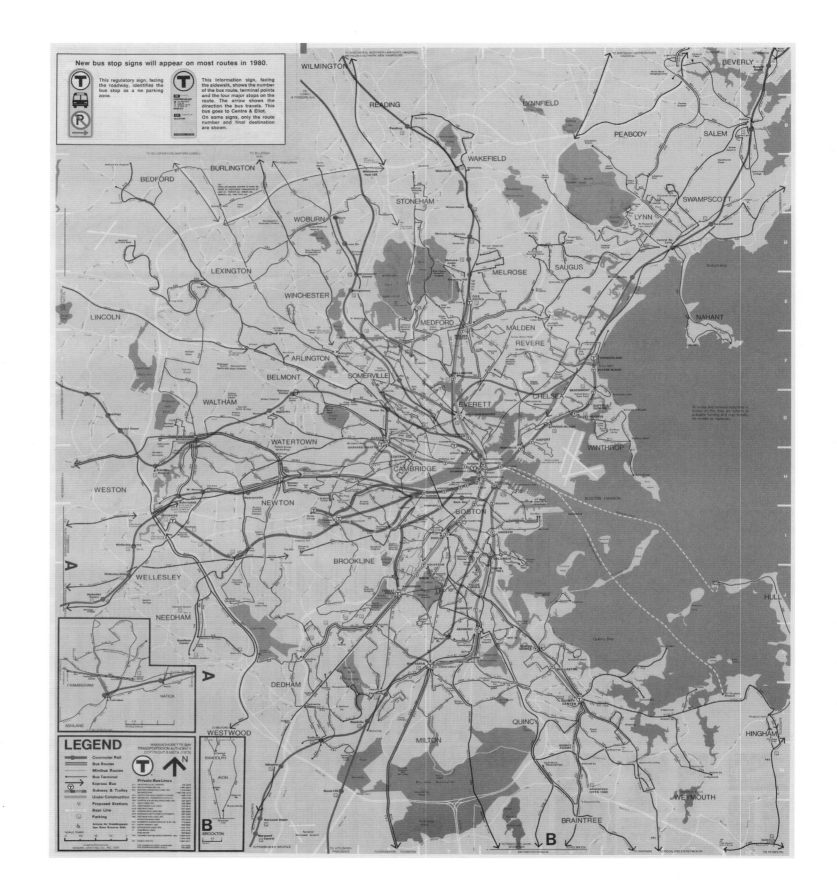

Figure 9.145 MBTA Folding System Map (B Side), 1980

Figure 9.146 MBTA Folding System Map (A Side), 1980

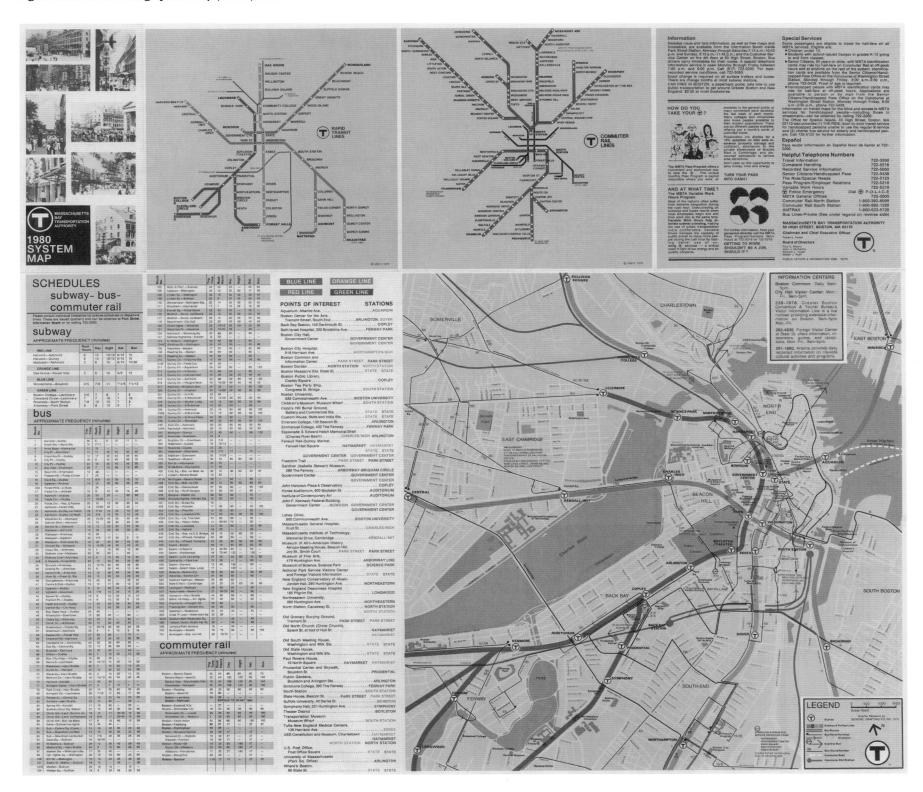

widely distributed until 1986, by which time much of the schedule and fare information was out of date. Instead of revising the map and paying for a costly new print run, the Authority included a pink paper slip listing the latest fares and other updated information. After its 1986 issuance of the 1982 map, the T did not release a folding public system map until 1988.

In the late 1980s, the in-station maps, wall panels, and ribbons across the T were of various vintages. Over two decades of system expansions, station modernizations, map redesigns, and incomplete signage upgrades contributed to a discordant collection of wayfinding signage. The May/June 1988 *Rollsign* recorded:

Figure 9.147 "Trolleys & Trains: A Kid's T Guide," 1987

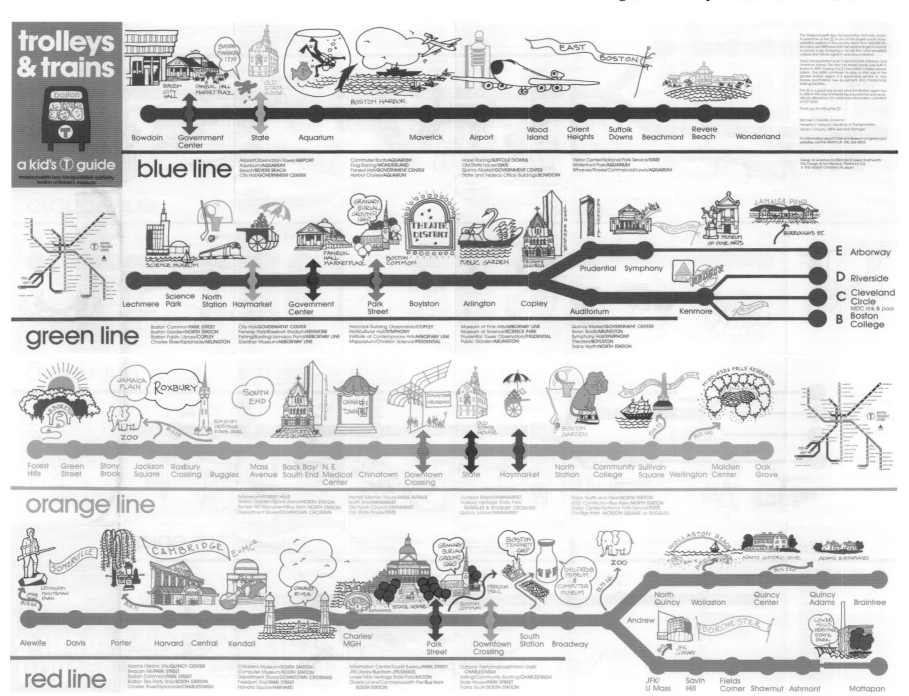

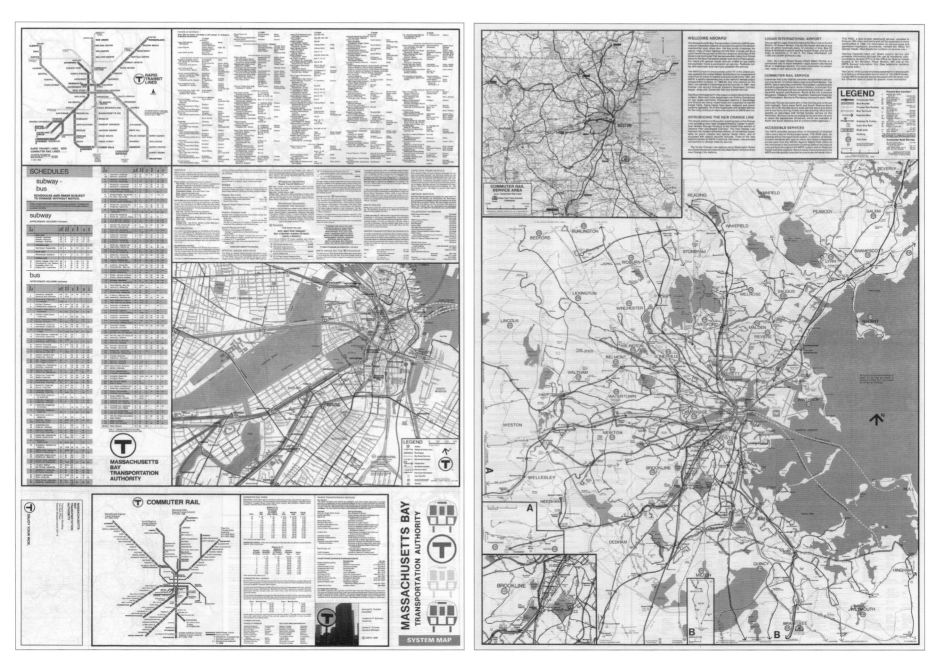

Figure 9.148 MBTA Folding System Map, 1988

The 1988 folding system map is packed with information for MBTA riders, including a spider map (top left), a downtown transit map (left middle), a commuter rail map (bottom left), a regional transit map (right) and a far-regional map (top middle). Route and fare information occupies spaces between the maps. The white background replaces the 70s-era earth tones of previous editions.

Officials of the MBTA Advisory Board ... have chided the MBTA for allowing so many signs to become inaccurate.... An April survey from the *Boston Globe* found 47% of the signs at the system's 10 busiest stations were then in some way out of date, with a few signs dating to 1967.

Responding to the criticism, the MBTA invested over half a million dollars to identify existing wayfinding inconsistencies and to commission fabrication and installation of revised maps and

signage. Many of the replacement maps and wall panels were vandal-resistant sheet enamel panels screwed into and secured over existing, heavy-weight panned-steel panels. The T committed to the installation of nearly 400 spider maps and nearly 250 line maps.

In August 1987, the MBTA released a little something for the kids, a folding map titled "Trolleys & Trains: A Kid's T Guide" (Figure 9.147). A year later, the T released a revised system map (Figure 9.148), an enlarged and revised version of

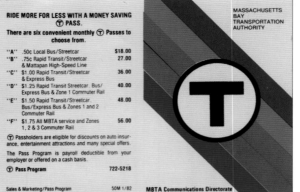

Figure 9.149 MBTA Folding Pocket Map, 1982

The T followed its first pocket map card, characterized by a simple map on one side and slogan on the other (Figure 9.12), with a larger format card (shown). Measuring 3.5" x 5", it folded in half and contained more information than earlier cards, including a list of five different MBTA monthly passes.

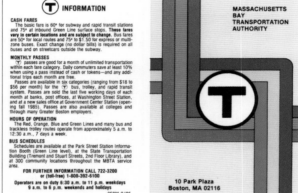

Figure 9.150 MBTA Folding Pocket Map, 1985

On the rapid transit map (left) of the 1985 pocket map, a dashed line alongside the southern half of the Orange Line hints at the 1987-opening of the Southwest Corridor.

Cities Inc. format in use since 1974. The MBTA issued various editions of a pocket-sized rapid transit map throughout the 1980s (Figure 9.149 and Figure 9.150). The 1989 edition featured a tri-fold format (Figure 9.151). Complementing pocket-sized rapid transit maps were portable commuter rail maps.

Figure 9.151 (Below) MBTA Folding Pocket Map, 1989

A late 1980s MBTA pocket map is packed with information, including advertisements for the T's Boston Passport" tourist pass. The map has been reduced in size from earlier pocket maps to accommodate paid advertising.

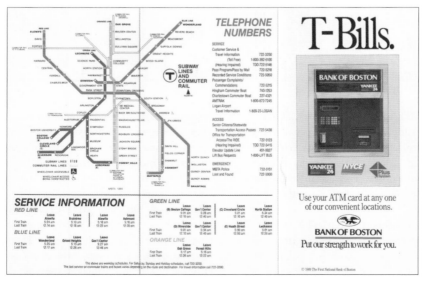

North Station Subway and Super Station

In the mid-1980s, the MBTA completed studies for the replacement and relocation of not only Lechmere Station, but much of the northern portion of the Green Line, from the Haymarket Incline to Science Park Station. The Authority studied replacing the Causeway and West End streetcar elevated railways with either a new tunnel running beneath North Station or a new el running around North Station and along the shore of the Charles River. The tunnel plan won out.

By the late 1980s, the MBTA moved forward with constructing the North Station Subway, a two-track streetcar tunnel running from Haymarket Station, beneath North Station, and to an incline linking it with the existing elevated streetcar tracks to the south of Science Park Station. The subway project included the expansion of North Station on the Orange Line into a "super station."

Early designs for the North Station super station called for a multi-level, multi-modal facility (Figure 9.152). At street-level, new busways were to replace the Green Line North Station surface stop, opened as the Canal Street streetcar stop and loop in 1898. The loop was converted to stub-end tracks in 1977. Final designs of both the North Station Subway and super station were in place by the end of 1988. The projects were coordinated with the anticipated construction of a new arena and commuter rail terminal, both planned to rise directly behind the Boston Garden, closed in 1995 and demolished in 1998.

In the first half of 1988, the MBTA granted the city of Boston air rights over its commuter rail tracks and platforms behind the Boston Garden. In turn, the city assigned the air rights to a private developer. Cooperatively, the MBTA and the new arena's private developer undertook the single largest improvement to North Station since the Boston & Maine opened its North Station complex in the late 1920s. As 1989 rolled around, $400 million of work overseen by the MBTA was underway. Below ground, the T coordinated the construction of a five-level 1,300-car parking garage and the North Station Subway. As part of its subterranean scope, the MBTA orchestrated the construction of foundations upon which the private developer would later erect their arena. On the ground floor, the developer established new ticketing and waiting facilities for commuter rail patrons on the ground floor of the arena. The T constructed new commuter rail platforms atop the new garage, making all of the terminal's platforms high-level for the first time. The platforms served ten numbered tracks and extended far from the concourse, allowing locomotives to remain attached to their trains but out from beneath the soon-to-be-constructed arena.

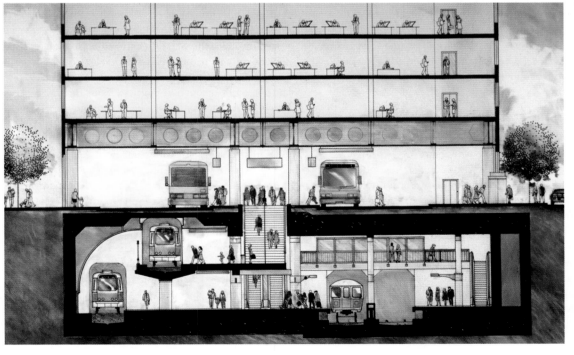

Figure 9.152 Designing a Super Station, Circa mid-1980s
A design drawing for North Station super station shows a multi-floor office building (top) and sheltering busways (middle). Below the busways is an underground transit station (bottom) served by Green Line LRVs (left) and Orange Line Trains (right). The station is an expansion of the existing North Station on the Orange Line.

Figure 9.153 The Green Line at North Station, Circa 2010
A southbound train of Green Line trolleys picks up passengers on the lower level of North Station super station.

Figure 9.154 The Orange Line at North Station, Circa 2010
A northbound train of Hawker-Siddeley Orange Line cars arrives at the lower level of North Station super station. In the distance, Green Line platforms lie beyond the stairs.

The last day of Green Line service along the Causeway Street and West End elevated railways was June 25, 2004. Until the North Station Subway was tied into the East Cambridge Extension near Science Park Station, shuttle buses transported riders between North Station and Lechmere. Regular Green Line service between the super station and Lechmere commenced on November 12, 2005. An inbound Green Line track (Figure 9.153) served the super station's lowermost level and shared a platform with inbound Orange Line trains (Figure 9.154). The outbound Green Line track ran one level above, alongside an expanded station mezzanine.

The Arborway Saga
When the MBTA took over from the MTA in 1964, the latter's Arborway Line ran beyond Heath Street, through Boston's Jamaica Plain neighborhood, and to a terminus at Arborway, a short walk from Forest Hills Station. The T rebranded the Arborway Line to the E Branch of the Green Line in the late 1960s. Some years later, in 1980, the Authority temporarily closed the line between Brigham Circle and Arborway, rebuilding the line's trackage for street-running trolleys. During the closure, the MBTA operated substitute bus service along the line (Figure 9.155). The last stop along the rehabilitated E Branch reopened on June 26, 1982.

Symphony Station, closed on January 3, 1981 for upgrading, reopened at the same time as the rebuilt E Branch. Afterwards, MBTA trolleys served the E Branch from Park Street Station to Arborway for three years. Then, to accommodate road work along Huntington and South Huntington Avenues, as well as replacement of rail within the subway, on December 28, 1985, the T suspended E Branch service. At the same time, the last of the PCCs to provide Green Line service retired from the line.

In July 1986, the MBTA restored E Branch service only as far as Brigham Circle. Concurrently, the Authority pondered what to do with the yet-to-be-reopened portion, from Brigham Circle to Arborway. Hesitant to redeploy trolleys where tracks ran in the middle of city streets, the T presented the public with more bus options than LRV alternatives, arguing that light rail was too costly, streets were too narrow for the safe operation of trolleys, and restoration of rail service would fail to meet accessibility requirements. The mayor, city council, local state representatives, business groups, neighborhood groups, and environmental advocates voiced support for the return of trolleys. Attempting to address the T's concerns, Boston proposed a series of roadway improvements, including constructing new safety islands, consolidating the number of stops, establishing priority street signaling for trolleys, and increasing traffic and parking enforcement. Despite agreeing in 1989 to work together and share the costs of making improvements along the Arborway Line, Boston and the MBTA failed to adequately provide for accessibility. In response, accessibility advocates argued that the T could not re-open the line without making it accessible.

On November 4, 1989, the MBTA restored E Branch service as far as Heath Street. The new terminus at Heath Street received a $3.5 million upgrade that included accessibility improvements. Extension of service all the way to Arborway was hindered by a $12 million estimated cost, a pending lawsuit over accessibility along the line, and the T's reluctance to have street-running trolleys mixing with general traffic along congested streets.

The 1990s brought with them not only continued battles over the restoration of trolley service to Arborway, but a new set of conflicts surrounding the T's proposal to construct new vehicle maintenance and storage facilities at Arborway. In 1990, the Authority sought designs for a new complex at Arborway to accommodate the maintenance, inspection, and storage of a couple hundred buses, over two dozen LRVs, and a handful of trolleys.

Throughout the 1990s, citizen coalitions, business groups, and politicians worked and clashed with the MBTA, and sometimes each other, over the restoration of Arborway trolley service and the scope of the planned Arborway maintenance complex. At the end of the decade, the MBTA released "The Arborway Study," providing an analysis of a half dozen options for Arborway service. After studying one LRV, one trackless trolley, and four bus options, the Authority recommended deploying sixty-foot buses powered by compressed natural gas (CNG). Like trackless trolleys, new CNG buses would be cleaner than diesel-powered buses. Buses, which were more nimble than either trackless trolleys or LRVs in city traffic, could also meet accessibility requirements. The report noted restoration of accessible trolley service would require a reduction in stops then served by route 39 buses. The reduction in stops was predicted to cause a decline in ridership below that which would justify the cost of LRVs over buses. Constructing accessible LRV stops would cause the permanent loss of a significant amount of street parking, something local businesses objected to. With its recommendation for CNG buses, the T proposed a new CNG storage and fueling facility to be part of its proposed Arborway Yard maintenance complex. Many constituents rejected the T's recommendation for buses and continued to fight for LRVs.

Light again shone through the window of restoration of trolley service to the Arborway, when in 2001, the MBTA announced it was being required by the Massachusetts Department of Environmental Protection (MassDEP) to restore nearly two miles of street running trolleys along the E Branch at an estimated cost of $80 million. Supporters were jubilant. The Arborway Rail Restoration Project Advisory Committee (ARR-PAC) spread the word, worked on maps, and circulated newsletters. The T held public meetings at which the community shared concerns about traffic, parking, and construction sequencing. While groups like the ARR-PAC and the Arborway Committee supported restoration, another group, Better Transit Without Trolleys, drawing from local businesses, argued against restoration. Though many local residents were supportive, the city was no longer one hundred percent behind full trolley restoration. Boston

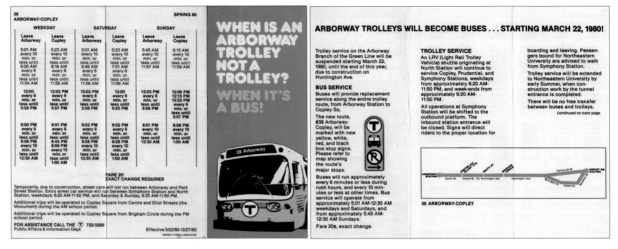

Figure 9.155 Arborway Bus Substitution Brochure, 1980
A brochure advertising the replacement of Green Line trolleys to the Arborway with service of Bus Route 39.

Mayor Thomas Menino, the Boston Police Department, and the Boston Fire Department voiced concerns over traffic safety and parking.

In 2003, the *Boston Globe* summed up the conflict: "Trolleys and only trolleys should be considered in the restoration of the Arborway line in Jamaica Plain, according to a key ruling on June 24, 2003, by the state's top environmental official." The newspaper continued: "State Secretary of Environmental Affairs Ellen Roy Herzfelder said she will not consider substituting buses that burn natural gas for trolleys on the route..." The *Boston Globe* pointed out: "The MBTA is required by law to restore light rail to this corridor and has been required to do so for over a decade."

The Arborway saga peaked in early 2005, when a coalition of groups announced plans to sue the MBTA to restore trolley service with LRVs. But by then, CNG buses were already providing service along route 39. Two issues reached a state of resolution in 2006. First, for the Arborway Line the Commonwealth dropped its mandate that the MBTA restore service with LRVs. Second, in November, a revised settlement between Massachusetts and the Conservation Law Foundation (CLF) over Big Dig mitigation projects no longer required the MBTA to restore complete Arborway trolley service. While the CLF agreement did require the T to continue to study the best transit options for the E Branch, LRVs were no longer a must. For the proposed Arborway Yard facility, the MBTA finally had an agreement in place with its neighbors regarding a scope of work and a mitigation package. The Arborway Committee continued to fight, suing the Commonwealth in state court, but that battle was lost.

The July/August 2008 *Rollsign* memorialized the death of Arborway trolley service:

> ...[O]n July 31, when the federal government quietly approved new state regulations that killed the idea.

> In 2008, the state announced that it would simply rewrite environmental regulations to get out of restoring the service. The new regs replace the air-quality benefits of trolleys with new parking lots and commuter rail improvements elsewhere.

Earlier that summer, Boston had already begun the process of paving over the unused streetcar tracks between Heath Street and Arborway. By the end of the 2000s, and after over a dozen years of negotiations, disputes, and planning, the MBTA had yet to erect much of the new facilities it planned for Arborway Yard. An exception was a CNG bus fueling facility, erected as "temporary" in 2003. Still in use, the facility was required after the MBTA shuttered its Bartlett bus maintenance facility near Dudley Square.

The Restoration of Old Colony Service

For over a century, commuter trains connected Boston with South Shore communities, until 1959, when the New Haven discontinued passenger service along its Old Colony Lines. Commuter rail service between South Station and the South Shore did not return for nearly forty years. The MBTA got serious about bringing back the trains with its 1984 submittal of the Old Colony Feasibility Study. The year-long study confirmed that rehabilitation of the Old Colony Lines to Scituate, Plymouth, and Middleboro was indeed feasible, with ridership projected to be on par with comparable existing commuter rail lines. By 1986, the T was studying possible locations for stations.

As the 1980s became the 1990s, a critical link between South Station and the Old Colony Lines remained missing, a bridge across the Neponset River between Dorchester and Quincy. Soon after the New Haven's 1959 cessation of passenger service along the Old Colony Lines, a fire destroyed the railroad's bridge that provided the link. During the late 1980s, and amidst a shortage of federal funding for a new Neponset River Bridge, the MBTA proposed restoring the Old Colony Lines from the South Shore, but only as far north as Quincy. Without funding for a new bridge, the T proposed that commuter rail riders arriving from South Shore communities transfer to the Red Line at Braintree. Braintree opposed the idea, citing potential increases in traffic with no discernible local benefit. Quincy objected to all the extra commuters simply passing through its city, especially if Red Line trains would be more crowded.

By the end of the 1980s, citing increasing traffic on Massachusetts Route 3 south of Boston, and after studying various alternatives including providing additional bus service or expanding South Shore highways, the Commonwealth and the MBTA made restoration of commuter rail service to the South Shore a priority (Figure 9.156). Complementing the T's internal planning team was the Old Colony Citizens Advisory Committee, a group of nearly two dozen elected officials and residents from communities along the Old Colony Lines.

While communities to be served by the lines to Lakeville and Plymouth mostly supported the restoration of commuter rail service, many residents to be served by the branch to Scituate were strongly opposed to a return of trains. Resumption of commuter rail service along the Lakeville branch would not be such a shock to lineside communities there, since freight trains never stopped running through the area. But, along the line to Scituate, which saw passenger service disappear in 1959, many residents had become lulled into thinking that trains would never again traverse the tracks in their backyards.

Facing local opposition, as well as further environmental review, along the Scituate branch, the MBTA segmented the restoration of Old Colony service into two projects. The first consisted of the lines to Lakeville and Plymouth. The second was the branch to Scituate—the Greenbush Line. While moving forward with design and construction of the Lakeville and Plymouth branches, the Authority worked towards settling legal opposition and undertaking environmental reviews hindering progress on the Greenbush Line. The MBTA received final environmental approvals to proceed with work on the Lakeville and Plymouth branches in 1992. Funding came from the federal government, the Commonwealth, and the MBTA.

An initial groundbreaking for the Old Colony Lines project occurred on November 20, 1992. The location was one of a handful of railroad bridges to be reconstructed in Dorchester. Construction soon

Figure 9.156 Old Colony Restoration Brochure, Circa 1989

A brochure articulates a problem—South Shore commuter traffic—and a corresponding solution—the restoration of commuter rail service along the Old Colony Lines. A commuter rail map (left) depicts proposed Old Colony Lines as dashed. A companion map (middle) reveals tendrils of proposed-to-be-restored Old Colony Lines reaching throughout South Shore communities.

THE PROBLEM: TRAFFIC

The South Shore and Southeastern Massachusetts are the most rapidly growing areas of the Commonwealth, with many residents traveling to work in downtown Boston.

The roadways serving the area are not adequate to meet the region's growing transportation needs. Motorists are confronted with daily traffic jams and gridlock. Commuter boats are a help, but are not an appropriate solution for many people in the region. The Red Line is another alternative, but is not convenient for everyone. Increasing demand and inadequate parking limit the Red Line's ability to serve.

COMMUTER RAIL SERVICE TODAY

Commuter rail provides a valuable option to existing overburdened modes of transportation and relieves congestion on metropolitan Boston highways, local streets, and rapid transit facilities.

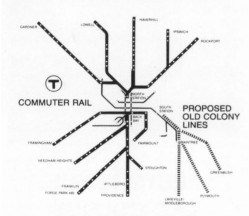

The MBTA operates over 360 train trips daily on its 11-line network that stretches from the southern border of Massachusetts to the New Hampshire line, and as far west as Fitchburg. The only area not served by commuter rail is the quickly developing South Shore and southeastern part of the state.

"I love my commute. I've been a commuter rail rider for more than 20 years. I moved to Stoughton because it had commuter rail to Boston. I can relax, talk or read. There is no better way to go."

—Ed Hoffman
Commuter Rail rider for more than 20 years
Stoughton, Stoughton Line

Because commuter rail service is so successful and acceptable, the MBTA is now being asked by various local officials and resident groups to explore expansion of the existing network to Newburyport, Worcester, New Bedford/Fall River, and Bellingham/I-495.

ONE SOLUTION:
RESTORE OLD COLONY

The MBTA is considering the restoration of commuter rail to Southeastern Massachusetts on the three branches of the Old Colony Railroad because it is a viable transportation service that could greatly improve the quality of life in the Old Colony area. Several alternatives to commuter rail restoration are also being examined.

"We generally support MBTA commuter rail service, service improvements and expansions. It is an excellent system that serves the Commonwealth well by moving more than 33,000 commuters a day to and from Boston, and by reaching out beyond the limits of the rapid transit and MBTA bus network. Commuter rail works."

—Representative Stephen J. Karol, Attleboro
Chairman, Joint Transportation Committee

On all four branches of the Old Colony System, the rights-of-way are currently in rail transportation use. In Boston, Quincy and Braintree, the Old Colony Main Line right-of-way is already within the parameters of the existing Red Line right-of-way. On the Middleborough, Plymouth and Greenbush Lines, the railroad track is in place on 85 percent of the 80 miles of track included in the MBTA study. Most of this track is presently used for non-commuter and limited passenger service.

"Commuter rail is an important plus for our community. It helps improve our air quality. It creates no noise problems. Even with five busy grade crossings, we have little traffic disruption from the train service. As a matter of fact, commuter rail will be our critical link to Boston during the Central Artery work."

—The Honorable John J. Brennan, Jr.
Mayor, City of Chelsea

"The train service fits right into our beautiful and unique community. There is one problem with MBTA commuter rail service. We can't get enough of it!

—Suzanne Noble
Selectwoman, Manchester

Today's commuter rail equipment is clean and efficient. This type of service promotes improved air quality by reducing the volume of auto emissions and their known dangerous pollutants.

The new diesel locomotives are designed for quieter, more efficient operation. They are substantially lighter than the equipment used when the former Old Colony service was operating.

New welded rail eliminates the "clickety-clack" noise reducing the vibration impact of former days and providing passengers with a smooth, quiet ride.

Grade crossings are protected by automatic gate, light and bell systems for maximum safety. Where appropriate, the right-of-way is protected by fencing.

Commuter rail stations today feature canopy-type shelters, platform ramps for access by people with special needs, paved parking areas, extensive lighting, drainage and landscaping. The stations are designed to be as unobtrusive, attractive, and serviceable as possible.

Commuter rail is different from rapid transit service. It runs less frequently; usually service on a line will be once a half hour during the rush hours and once every two hours off-peak. In terms of technology, commuter rail does not require a third rail or permanent overhead wires.

"I remember what the old rail service was like years ago. It was good and we liked it. But it wouldn't hold a candle to what I've seen of the new commuter rail system. Today it's better in every way—cleaner, quieter, more dependable..."

—Bill Parmenter
Former Commuter Rail Rider
Cohasset

ramped up along the branches to Lakeville and Plymouth. To carry Old Colony Line trains between Dorchester and Quincy, the MBTA constructed the needed new bridge across the Neponset River. In 1995, the new commuter rail bridge was completed alongside the George L. Anderson Bridge, opened for Red Line trains in 1971. The T produced bumper stickers (Figure 9.157) and car cards (Figure 9.158) announcing the imminent return of commuter rail trains along the Old Colony Lines.

Commuter rail service returned between South Station and stations along Old Colony Lines to Lakeville, Kingston, and Plymouth in 1997. On September 26, two trains packed with politicians and decked out with balloons, banners, pennants (Figure 9.159), and marching bands made their way into South Station. A 1997 brochure mapped the open Old Colony Lines, listing four morning and four evening trains (Figure 9.160). Service was quickly expanded. Early December schedules listed twenty weekday and seven weekend round-trips along the Middleboro/Lakeville Line, and fifteen weekday and eight weekend round-trips along the Kingston/Plymouth Line. Suburban commuters took advantage of the new trains, filling parking lots at stations as early as 8:00 a.m. The MBTA's pre-opening estimates for ridership numbers along the Lakeville and Plymouth lines were quickly exceeded. Before the arrival of bi-level commuter coaches in early 1998, many rush-hour trains were standing room only.

Early impacts of the opening of the MBTA's Middleboro/Lakeville and Kingston/Plymouth Lines were reported in the *Patriot Ledger*: "The Old Colony Railroad dramatically reshaped the transportation and economic landscape of the South Shore in 1998, its first full year of operation." The project "helped boost home construction and sales in the towns

they serve." While ridership was strong and reviews were positive for restored service to Lakeville and Plymouth, dark clouds had gathered over the future of the yet-to-be completed Greenbush Line.

The Greenbush Saga

In the 1980s and 1990s, opposition to the MBTA's restoration of commuter rail service to Scituate was most intense in Hingham. There, the T faced strong resistance at all levels. Local residents who feared reductions in their property values and whom had not seen passenger trains pass through town for decades displayed flags with an image of a train crossed out. Though local business owners were divided on their support for the return of trains, many were accustomed to using the railroad right-of-way for parking, storage, and other extensions of their private property. Residents and business owners formed groups to oppose commuter rail service and the damage they feared trains would cause to local structures, many of which were historic and sat just feet from the right-of-way. Hingham also objected to the restoration of service citing potential degradation of the nearby seacoast environment.

The MBTA announced in October 1995 that it had selected full restoration of commuter rail service as its preferred alternative for expanding public transportation to Scituate. By end of the year, the Commonwealth and the MBTA opted to fund restoration of the Greenbush Line, but without the use of federal dollars. Without federal funding, the project was exempted from most federal environmental reviews. This stung Hingham. The town had hoped that an intense federal environmental review process might slow or kill the Greenbush Line. A detailed federal review would have also been required if federal funds were to be deployed

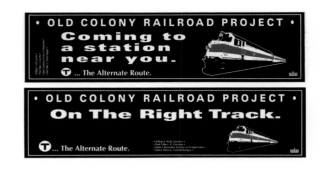

Figure 9.157 Old Colony Project Bumper Stickers, Mid-1990s

Figure 9.158 New Old Colony Railroad Car Card, Circa 1995
A car card predicts commuter rail service would be restored to Middleboro and Plymouth by the end of 1996.

to rebuild the rail line through the Lincoln Historic District in Hingham's town center.

With the MBTA and the Commonwealth advocating for the Greenbush Line and federal review formally limited, in 1996, Hingham raised the stakes and took the MBTA to court. The town accused the T of opting out of using federal dollars in order to avoid delays that federal environmental reviews might cause. Just before Hingham took the T to court, the tide turned against the Greenbush Line in Scituate, where citizens voted in a non-binding referendum, 1,163 against and 798 in support of the project. By 1998, a federal judge was reviewing the entire history of the T's planning for the Greenbush Line and Hingham's formal objections. While Hingham's suit made its way through the federal courts, all parties waited for the Greenbush Line to receive final regulatory approvals, including a key approval from the United States Army Corps of Engineers (USACE).

As 1999 dawned, neither the MBTA nor Hingham could agree on how to settle things without court intervention. Summer brought with it a USACE report that was favorable for the MBTA. By the end of the year, the courts confirmed that the MBTA was correct in its assertion that it did not have to submit to federal environmental review.

A final settlement was reached between Hingham and the MBTA on May 15, 2000. In return for the town's dropping of legal objections to the Greenbush Line, the Authority agreed to build an over $40 million tunnel through Hingham's town center. As well, the Commonwealth agreed to contribute $1.35 million "to a historic preservation trust fund that Hingham can use to mitigate the trains' effects after service begins." As with most settlements, both sides won and lost. The MBTA was finally able to build its rail line, but with the addition of an expensive tunnel. Hingham kept trains from rumbling along the surface next to its historic

Figure 9.159 Old Colony Lines Opening Day Pennant, 1997
A pennant commemorates opening day of the first two branches of the T's "New Old Colony Railroad."

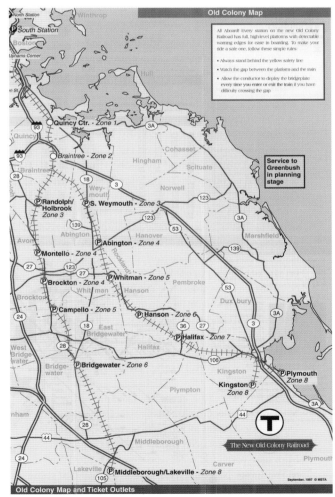

Figure 9.160 "New Old Colony Railroad" Map, 1997
A late 1990s brochure maps the first two branches of the Old Colony Lines to be restored, one to Lakeville, and another to Kingston and Plymouth. The map notes: "Service to Greenbush in planning stage."

downtown buildings, but trains returned to town. The addition of the Hingham tunnel, coupled with delays in the commencement of full construction, saw cost estimates for the Greenbush Line approximately double, from $215 million to over $400 million.

Upon receipt of approval of the project from the Commonwealth's EOEA on August 20, 2001, the MBTA was free to begin early work on the seventeen and a half mile Greenbush Line, the third and final branch of the T's Old Colony Lines. South of Quincy, the MBTA finalized Greenbush Line station locations at Weymouth Landing, East Weymouth, West Hingham, Nantasket Junction, Cohasset, North Scituate, and Greenbush. Hingham's village center did not receive a station. Land takings and early preparation work commenced in 2002, but progress was not without issue. A brief cessation of work during which various permitting and costing issues were sorted out occurred in 2003. The following year, opponents in Cohasset rose up and fought the project in court. The MBTA partially satisfied Cohasset by striping the Cohasset Station parking lot spaces wider-than-standard to accommodate oversize suburban-sized SUVs. Cohasset Station was located north of its former downtown location. Various homes along the line received soundproofing to the cost of $2 million. A few mitigation requests were rejected by the T, including the purchase of antidepressants for a resident's dog bothered by train horns. In the later half of 2004, the USACE granted the Greenbush Line its final federal approval and construction was able to proceed full steam ahead.

The final cost for the Greenbush Line tallied approximately $408 million. A decade after commuter rail trains returned to the first two branches of the Old Colony Lines, on October 30, 2007, a train carrying VIPs traversed the Greenbush Line. The Greenbush Line was then opened for regular service. The first MBTA Greenbush schedule, effective October 31, 2007, listed a dozen weekday and eight weekday round-trips (Figure 9.161). A one-way ride from Greenbush to South Station cost $7.75. A day of parking at one of the 3,100 spaces along the line cost $2.00.

T Tokens

Metal tickets first appeared for use on Boston's transit lines in the 1830s (see Chapter 1). After taking over from the MTA in 1964, the MBTA continued to circulate and accept its Series-of-1951

MTA tokens (See Chapter 8). The T changed tack and focused on accepting coins instead of tokens at turnstiles in 1968. Twelve years later, the MBTA switched back to tokens, deploying millions of stockpiled MTA tokens.

By the late 1980s, the quantity of MTA tokens in circulation on the MBTA was dangerously low. 100,000 tokens issued by the T to commemorate the opening of the Southwest Corridor in 1987 (Figure 9.99) did not make a dent. The Authority became so concerned about running out of tokens after long holiday weekends that it staffed overtime workers to sort and return tokens into circulation before commuters arrived on the next business day. To address the token crisis, the T commissioned a California company to produce three million brass tokens, the MBTA's first of its own design. Each Series-of-1988 MBTA token featured the T's logo on one face and a rapid transit car on the other (Figure 9.163).

As the T took in approximately one and a half million tokens each week during the early 1990's, the overall amount of tokens in circulation dropped by a few hundred thousand. Tokens were lost to damage, non-use, and souvenir seekers. The Authority needed to mint more tokens, and fast. As it planned to purchase three million new tokens in 1992, the T began to install token vending machines at busy stations. The machines accepted cash and dispensed tokens and change. By 1995, over forty machines were in service and the T was deploying additional units. Around the same time, the MBTA developed a roll of ten tokens for sale at a discount (Figure 9.162).

The MBTA celebrated Boston's 1992 Tall Ships event by issuing its second commemorative token, a brass token featured "Sail Boston 1992" with a stylized flag on one face and the T's logo and name on the other (Figure 9.164). The third and final commemorative token issued by the MBTA arrived at the turn of the millennium. During the last week of 1999 and the first week of 2000, the T sold gold-plated tokens marking the turn of the century (Figure 9.165). Sold for $2 a piece, millennium tokens were souvenirs only. They could not be used at turnstiles.

Rollsign magazine recorded the sale of the last MBTA token occurring just after 10:30 a.m. on December 2, 2006 at Government Center Station. Local media was on hand as the T's General Manager provided a certificate and a $100 fare card to the lucky patron. After discontinuance of their use, most MTA and MBTA tokens were taken out of

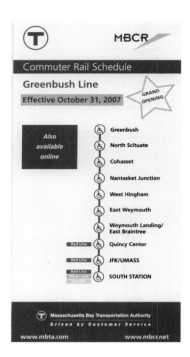

Figure 9.161 Greenbush Line Commuter Rail Schedule, 2007
The first folding paper schedule for Greenbush Line service is marked with a star labeled "Grand Opening."

Figure 9.162 MBTA Roll of Ten Tokens, Circa mid-1990s

Figure 9.163 MBTA Series-of-1988 Token

Figure 9.164 MBTA Sail Boston 1992 Token

Figure 9.165 MBTA Millennium Token

Figure 9.166 MBTA Type B Passes, 1980–82

In 1981, six pass types were available. Type A, costing $18, was a fifty cent local bus and streetcar pass. Type B (shown), costing $27, was a combination rapid transit, streetcar, and Mattapan trolley pass. Types C, D, and E were combination passes that were valid, respectively, on express buses, zone one of the commuter rail, and zones one and two of the commuter rail. Type F, costing $56, was valid on all modes of the MBTA and zones one through three of the commuter rail.

circulation by the T and sold for scrap. A few thousand were salvaged for sale as collectors' items.

Fares and Passes Evolve in the 1980s and 1990s

The MBTA significantly restructured and increased fares twice in 1980–81. During that time, the fare for zone one, which covered the core of the T's system, increased from a quarter to seventy-five cents. At the northern end of the Haymarket Extension, Oak Grove and Malden Center moved into zone one. Travel within zone two increased from twenty-five cents with a warrant to fifty cents without a warrant. Travel between zones two and three, essentially travel between Quincy stations and Braintree, increased from twenty-five to fifty cents. Travel between zones one and three increased from seventy-five cents to one dollar.

The T increased commuter rail fares an average of nineteen percent. Commuter rail fare increases went into effect in mid-July 1981. On August 1, the cost of a token increased from fifty to seventy-five cents. After announcing the token cost increase in June, and to curb hoarding of tokens, the MBTA limited the purchase of tokens to four at one time. Token sales continued to be brisk, so much so that the Authority reduced the individual limit per purchase to two tokens. In conjunction with the 1980–81 fare increases, the MBTA consolidated its offering of non-commuter rail passes from seven to six types. All passes enabled a bearer to bring, at no additional cost, a second person with them on Sundays.

In the early 1980s, the MBTA began to issue passes with magnetic strips and install magnetic card readers at turnstiles. The magnetic reader system was developed and deployed by MBTA employees. The system replaced the practice of patrons having to flash their pass at transit employees for passage through turnstiles. A selection of passes from 1981 and 1982 are shown in Figure 9.166.

The MBTA consolidated and redesigned its passes in 1989. The new passes arrived on the heels

Figure 9.167 MBTA Passes, 1988–1992
Effective July 1, 1989, four monthly pass types were available for non-commuter rail travel. The Local Bus pass, good for travel on local buses and surface-running streetcars, sold for $18. The Subway pass, costing $27, was valid at all rapid transit stations (except Quincy Adams or Braintree), along all light rail lines (except stops in Newton), and for commuter rail zones 1A and 1B. The Combo pass, costing $40, was valid on local bus routes, at rapid transit stations (except Quincy Adams or Braintree), at light rail stations, and on certain express bus routes. A second version of the Combo pass, costing $48, was also good for select express bus routes added.

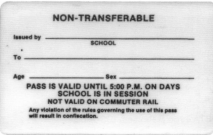

of double-digit increases in commuter rail fares and the increase of the surcharge for on-board commuter rail fare purchases from twenty-five to fifty cents. The surcharge was paid by riders who purchased fares after boarding a train where tickets were available for off-board purchase.

As The Big Dig was ramping up and consuming massive amounts of transportation funding in the early 1990s, and after encouragement from Governor Weld, the MBTA approved a fare increase over cutting services. Effective September 3, 1991, rapid transit fare increased from seventy-five to eighty-five cents; Green Line Riverside Branch inbound service became $2 at Riverside through Chestnut Hill Stations, and $1 at Reservoir through Fenway Stations; and local bus fare increased from fifty to sixty cents. Senior passes, express bus fares, and commuter rail fares increased as well. The revised fare structure led to some buses becoming newly classified as local buses, with fares dropping from seventy-five to sixty cents. In fall 1992, the

MBTA upgraded to passes that were thinner and more economical to produce. A selection of T passes from 1988–92 are shown in Figure 9.167.

New fare boxes began to show up on MBTA buses, trackless trolleys, and streetcars in 1992. By the end of the year, at least 1,800 were installed, replacing worn out models. The new fare boxes were electronic (Figure 9.169), collecting fare payment statistics and equipped with readers for magnetic strips soon to become standard on passes. The boxes produced electronic beeps confirming if a fare was paid or not.

Throughout the 1980s and 1990s, as it continues to do, the MBTA offered various promotional fare programs, special passes, and discount fares. The Authority launched its Boston Passport program on July 1, 1989 (Figure 9.170). The "Sizzlin' Summer" program of July and August of 1989 and 1990 allowed the holder of any type of T pass to travel on any MBTA service, including commuter rail. An echo of the program was 2018's kick off of a $10

Figure 9.168 MBTA September 1989 Student Pass
The first year during which elementary and high school students were offered MBTA monthly passes was 1986. Student passes (like the one shown above) costing $10 a month, replaced pupil badges which had secured a fifty percent discount for the bearing student.

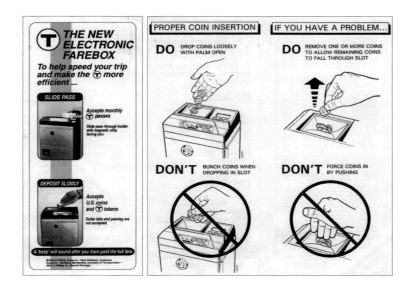

Figure 9.169 Electronic Fare Box Instructions, 1993

Figure 9.170 MBTA "Boston Passport" Brochure, 1989
Available for $8 and $16, respectively, three-day and seven-day Boston Passport passes allowed unlimited travel on rapid transit lines, light rail lines, and commuter rail trains within zones 1A and 1B. The passes were available in two formats, a three-day and seven-day, costing $9 and $18 each, respectively. Kid's passes were available for half of adult prices.

fare allowing unlimited commuter rail travel on select summer weekends. $10 unlimited weekend commuter rail fares reappeared in 2019, becoming a fixture that same year.

Mapping the T in the 1990s
By the end of the 1990s, signage and maps across the T's system had again become inaccurate and inconsistent. Responding to the problem in 1989, the T awarded a contract to a Nashville company for the production of over a thousand porcelain on steel and fiberglass signs and maps. The updated signs and maps were installed in the early 1990s.

Complementing refreshed station signs and maps of the early 1990s, new pocket-sized schedules were released in 1990–91 (Figure 9.171). The new paper format folded down to pocket-size and allowed the inclusion of more information than had been possible on previous schedule cards (Figure 9.83 and Figure 9.85). For the first time, public schedules were produced from computerized data sets and inclusive of the latest MBTA maps. Updated folding paper schedules based on the 1990–91 format continue to be circulated by the Authority.

After updating signage, in-station maps, and paper schedules, the MBTA released an updated system map. The 1992 folding paper system map (Figure 9.172) was the first to be produced by CTPS,

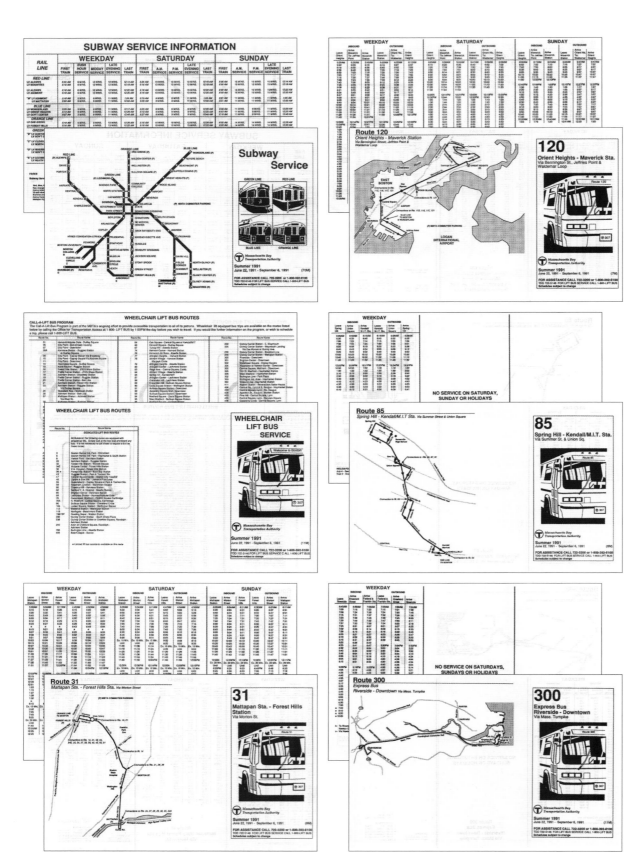

Figure 9.171 MBTA Folding Schedules, 1991

1991 was the first year that the MBTA issued folding paper schedules in the now-familiar format.

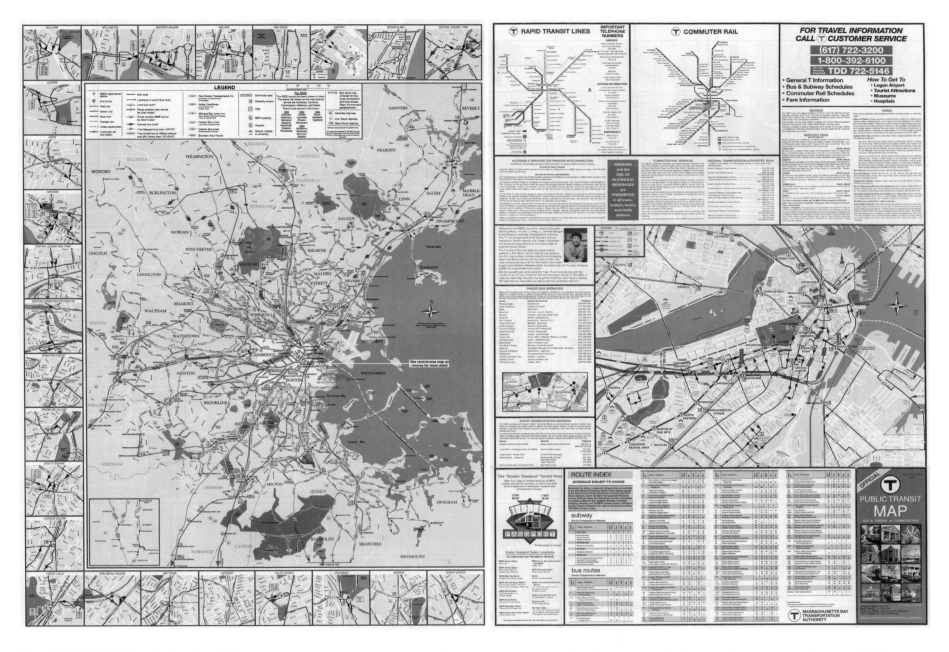

Figure 9.172 MBTA Folding System Map, 1992

The 1992 folding system map was the first to be produced entirely electronically. A graphic designer at CTPS, and the hand behind MBTA maps since 1988, tapped then-state-of-the-art technology to produce the 1992 map. Using a giant digitalization tablet, the designer traced hundreds of scale miles of roads from paper DOT and MBTA maps. He formalized the vector information with CAD software. The process took months. The MBTA released its 1992 folding system map with a retail price of $2.50.

the entity that continues to oversee the production of maps for the MBTA.

The next major edition of the MBTA folding system map came out in 1996 (Figure 9.173 and Figure 9.174), the same year in which the T launched MBTA.com. Before it ever appeared in stations, a rotated spider map was first printed on the 1996 folding system map. For the first time, the spider map was entirely reconstructed from scratch; the square formed by the four key downtown stations was rotated forty-five degrees to become a diamond. The rapid transit map also

received water features, shorelines, and highways. The commuter rail map received similar revisions and was also featured on the 1996 folding system map.

Red Line Type 3 Cars

The MBTA's Red Line Type 3 cars were Boston's first rapid transit cars to feature automated station announcements and in-car electronic displays. The cars were constructed by Bombardier, a builder of commercial jets in addition to transit and rail

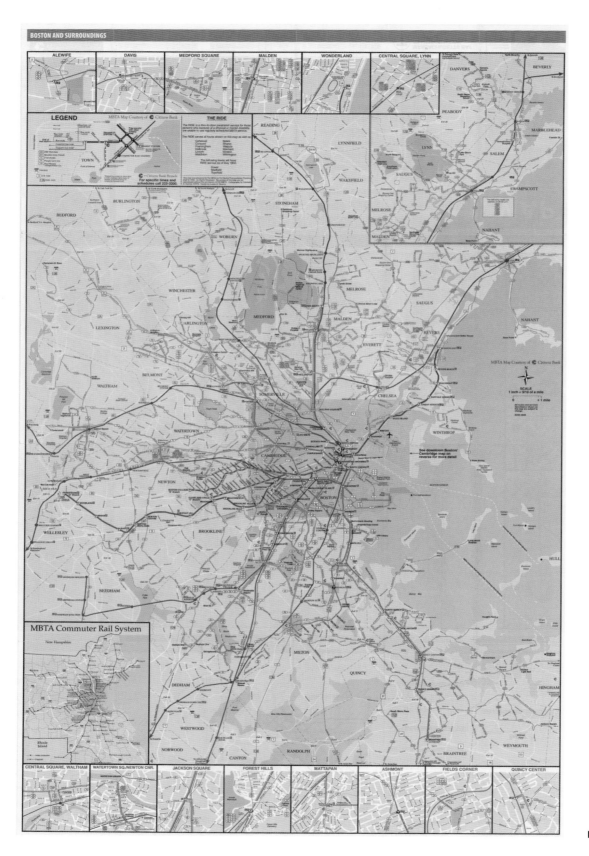

Figure 9.173 MBTA Folding System Map (Side B), 1996

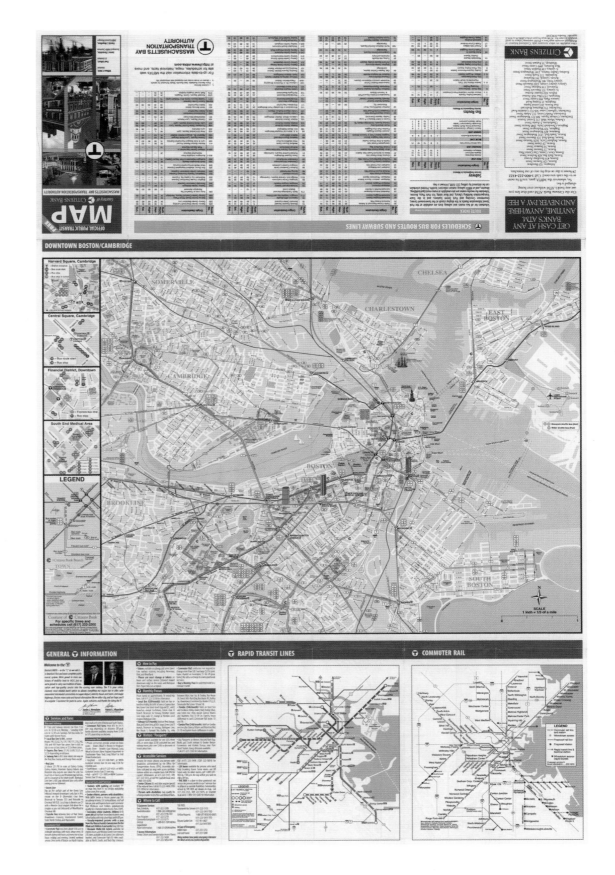

Figure 9.174 MBTA Folding System Map (Side A), 1996

Figure 9.175 Red Line Type 3 Pamphlet, 1992

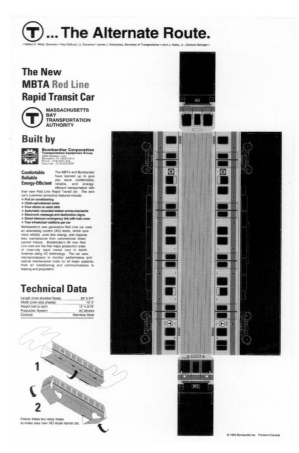

Figure 9.176 Pop-up Red Line Car, 1993
Canada's Bombardier, manufacturer of Red Line Type 3 cars, produced card stock sheets from which a model of one of the new cars could be popped out and folded in miniature.

vehicles. The company produced promotional brochures (Figure 9.175) and card-stock cut-out versions of Type 3s (Figure 9.176). The MBTA assigned the cars 01800-series numbers. Their arrival allowed the T to provide rush hour crowds with consistent six-car service as well as sideline aging 01400-series Red Line cars. The last Type 3 Red Line cars entered regular service in March 1995.

Moving the People at Wellington

When a groundbreaking took place for a massive new parking garage next door to Wellington Shops on May 8, 1996, an odd little mode of transit was about to be added to the T. The garage, constructed by a private developer who leased spaces to the MBTA, was linked to Wellington Station by an elevated people mover. Designed by the Otis Elevator Company, the people mover was formally opened at a ribbon cutting on October 23, 1997. Each car of the people mover transported forty-five passengers across the tracks of Wellington Yard. It travelled at twenty-five miles per hour, back and forth between the garage and station. The free journey took just less than a minute in each direction. The unique

horizontal transportation mode endured for less than a decade. After years of breakdowns, the people mover was dismantled in the later half of 2006. Its elevated superstructure was converted into an enclosed pedestrian walkway that remains in use today.

New Digs for Commuter Rail

The MBTA's work in the 1980s and 1990s to improve North and South Stations was complimented by a major back-of-the-house project to modernize the Authority's Boston Engine Terminal (BET). Kicking off in 1989 and lasting nearly a decade, the BET project brought the replacement of railroad facilities that the MBTA purchased in the mid-1970s from the Boston & Maine. Across the former Boston & Maine BET complex, aspects of which dated back to the era of steam railroading, the T invested approximately $230 million to replace outdated facilities for the storage, inspection, and heavy maintenance of commuter rail locomotives and coaches.

The centerpiece of the BET upgrades was a new commuter rail maintenance building (Figure 9.178).

Figure 9.177 1800-series Red Line Cars, March 15, 2018
A northbound train of Red Line Type 3 rapid transit cars pauses at Charles/MGH Station.

Taking three years to complete, the building covered more than eight acres and was adorned with bright commuter rail-inspired colors. Outside of the shops, the T installed a new six-track yard. The MBTA's Commuter Rail Maintenance Facility, still referred to as the BET, officially opened on March 26, 1998.

The new BET rose on the northside of the T's bifurcated commuter rail network. To limit the movement of commuter rail equipment from the southside to the northside for minor inspections and daily maintenance, the MBTA established a service and inspection facility on the southside. Groundbreaking on the southside project took place on February 15, 1989. At sixty-thousand square feet, the $31.3 million commuter rail maintenance building was a fraction of the size of the BET. The southside complex was in full operation by the early 1990s with two run-through tracks enclosed beneath a finished second story. Pits below the tracks allowed workers space to service locomotives and coaches from below. By 1996, it was complemented by additional shops at layover facilities at Readville.

From Toxic to Transit

Along a stretch of the Lowell Line in Woburn, the federal government and the Commonwealth joined forces to oversee the remediation of a 250-acre toxic waste site and turn much of it into a multi-modal transit hub. In 1983, Woburn's Industri-plex site was added to the federal Environmental Protection Agency (EPA) Superfund list of contaminated sites prioritized for clean up. An approximately thirty-five acre portion of the Industri-plex site was rehabilitated into a new intermodal transit facility, a first of its kind transformation for a Superfund

site. The EPA worked with private companies on the hook for the clean up of toxic areas. The Commonwealth oversaw the design and construction of the new intermodal station as well as parking lots, an access road, and ramps to link the station with nearby Interstate 93. The station's sprawling parking lots became the topmost layer of an engineered cap that sealed away toxic deposits not feasible to be removed.

Construction on the new intermodal station, Metro North Center Station (now Anderson Regional Transportation Center), was under way at the end of the 1990s. The project brought a new station to the Lowell Line and a greatly expanded location for Logan Express's Woburn operation. The MBTA, Massport, and MassHighway split $10 million in project costs. The T invested an additional $7 million in commuter rail infrastructure.

The Anderson Regional Transportation Center (Anderson RTC) was opened on May 16, 2001 by a cadre of VIPs, including the EPA Administrator and local resident Anne Anderson. Ms. Anderson's son Jimmy succumbed to Leukemia on January 18, 1981. His illness was the impetus for a lawsuit that led to judgements against Industri-plex polluters as well as the site's cleanup. The story was chronicled in the book and motion picture, *A Civil Action*.

Commuter Rail Returns to Worcester

The 1990s was a decade of multiple commuter rail upgrades and expansion studies. In the early part of the decade, the MBTA rebuilt the Rockport/Ipswich Line. Studies were underway for extensions of the Framingham Line to Worcester and the Stoughton Line to Taunton, New Bedford, and Fall River. South Attleboro Station opened in summer 1990. Commuter rail schedules published from the

Figure 9.178 MBTA Boston Engine Terminal, Circa 1998
The sprawling structure encloses thirteen run-through tracks and two stub-end tracks. Initially, three tracks were designated for service and inspection of a locomotive and train consisting of up to nine cars in length. Two tracks were designated for inspection and ten were designated for repair work. The building houses various machine shops, storage areas, and offices.

mid-1990s through the early 2000s featured handsome line-specific watercolor views (Figure 9.179, Figure 9.180, Figure 9.181, and Figure 9.182).

The Massachusetts Transportation Secretary announced in fall 1992 that the T was pursuing an approximately $120 million, twenty-three mile extension of the Framingham Line westward, to Worcester. Two years later, trains began to roll. MBTA commuter rail trains began limited service between South Station and downtown Worcester on September 26, 1994. Three days earlier, during a ceremony marking the start of service, Governor Weld remarked that MBTA commuter rail should be extended west of Worcester to Springfield. Such

an extension continues to be discussed by politicians and planners.

Service to Worcester quickly expanded. By the end of 1994, a full weekday schedule was in place. On December 14, 1996, weekend service commenced. After a July 2000 reopening of a restored Worcester Union Station, MBTA commuters were provided with a grand terminal that continues to mark the western end of the Worcester Line. Intermediate stations did not appear between Framingham and Worcester until the early 2000s. Grafton Station opened in February 2000. Southborough and Westborough Stations, each costing just shy of $5 million, opened on June 22, 2002. Ashland Station opened on August 24, 2002.

Figure 9.179 (Left Pair) Worcester Line Schedules, 1994; 1995
The covers of paper schedules before (left) and after (right) the opening of MBTA commuter rail service to Worcester.

Figure 9.180 (Right Pair) North Shore Schedules, 1993; 1998
Before the MBTA extended service to Newburyport (right), the line terminated at Ipswich (left).

Figure 9.181 (Left Pair) Northside Schedules, 2004; 1999
Commuter rail schedules for the Fitchburg Line (left) and Lowell Line (right) feature line-specific artwork.

Figure 9.182 (Right Pair) Southside Schedules, 1999, 1998
A modest platform (left) and the Canton Viaduct (right) grace the covers of southside MBTA commuter rail schedules.

As work was nearing completion on the Worcester Extension, planning was under way to upgrade Route 128 Station on the Providence Line. The T approved over $40 million for the project in 1997. Construction commenced in summer 1998 on a new parking garage and enclosed ticketing and waiting areas for passengers of both MBTA and Amtrak trains.

The Newburyport Extension

After over a decade of planning, permitting, and design, on May 12, 1997 the MBTA oversaw groundbreaking ceremonies for two new commuter rail stations in the North Shore, one in Rowley and another in Newburyport. In addition to the new stations, the extension of the Rockport/Ipswich Line included new trackage, signals, and a four-track layover yard for commuter rail trains to Newburyport. The nearly nine mile Newburyport Extension followed a portion of the one-time main line of the Eastern Railroad, a route opened in the first half of the nineteenth century. Before the opening of the Newburyport Extension, the last passenger service

along the line, an MBTA-subsidized single, weekday round-trip, ceased in 1976.

On October 23, 1998, an inaugural train chock full of federal, state, and local politicians traveled from Ipswich to Newburyport. Rowley and Newburyport Stations opened with parking lots for automobile commuters. Regular service commenced on October 26, with a dozen round-trips each weekday and five round-trips each Saturday. Trains making the one hour journey between Newburyport and North Station reached speeds of seventy miles per hour. Figure 9.180 shows commuter rail schedules from the 1990s, before and after the opening of the Newburyport Extension.

Sail Boston 1992

In the middle of July 1992, the MBTA carried over eight million passengers during Sail Boston. The six day event's 250 visiting ships drew massive crowds to viewing and boarding points around Boston Harbor. The MBTA posted car cards informing riders how to leverage the T to get around during the festivities (Figure 9.183). According to the

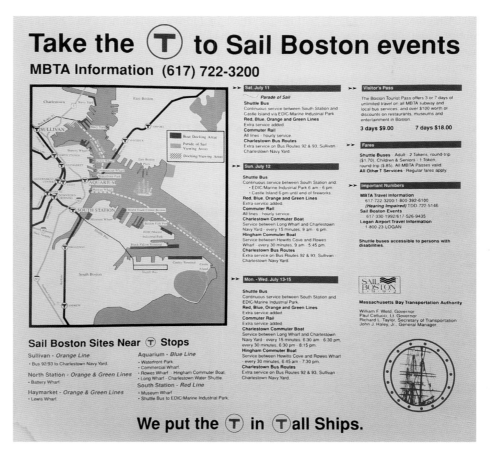

Figure 9.183 Sail Boston 1992 Car Card

September/October 1992 *Rollsign*, the MBTA carried approximately two million riders on Saturday July 11, and then again, on Sunday July 12. The MBTA next set a one-day ridership record on July 17, 1997, when Sail Boston cruised back into town.

To transport people to and from Sail Boston 1992, the T increased the frequency of service on all rapid transit and trolley lines. Special commuter rail and commuter boat runs brought people to and from the city on the weekend. Even with hourly service on some lines, commuter rail trains were so jammed that some trains resorted to skip-stop service. During the height of the festivities, from Sunday through Wednesday, the Hingham Ferry operated with half hour headways. Ferries connected Long Wharf and Charlestown Navy Yard with fifteen minute headways. No commuter boats operated on Saturday or Thursday, days when ships moved into and out of the harbor.

With portions of Charlestown, East Boston, the North End, and Downtown closed to non-resident vehicular traffic, the T deployed some 250 extra buses to shuttle people around. Using a temporary dedicated bus lane, approximately 150 shuttle buses moved between South Station and South Boston each weekend day. The MBTA memorialized Sail Boston 1992 with the production and distribution of 300,000 commemorative tokens (Figure 9.164). The tokens, viable for use like standard tokens, were available for purchase as early as July 8.

a plethora of upgrades, rebuilds, and improvements along the Green Line. Ancient infrastructure has been upgraded. Surface branches have had tracks and stops rebuilt. Tunnel stations have been modernized. Accessibility has been improved. Revenue vehicles have been replaced.

Improvements in the 1980s included the 1984 opening of the new $11 million Reservoir Car House. The new LRV storage and maintenance facility was complemented by a rebuilt Reservoir Station, renovated at the cost of $7 million. The late 1980s saw the completion of an MBTA-commissioned study of Green Line accessibility. The year-long study resulted in the Authority moving ahead with massive improvements to accessibility along its least accessible line. In the early 1990s, a multi-million dollar modernization of Park Street Station brought improved lighting, signage, entrances, and, for the first time, elevators to the historic station.

Significant Green Line improvements in the 2000s and 2010s included the construction of a new busway at Kenmore Station, and major renovations of Copley, Arlington, and Science Park / West End Stations. The largest Green Line capital improvement project currently underway is the GLX Project, which includes a replacement for Lechmere Station. When complete, the GLX will bring Green Line trolleys north of Lechmere for the first time. Stations are planned across Somerville and into Medford.

Green Line Improvements Since 1980

Since taking over the streetcar subways and surface routes of the MTA in 1964, the MBTA has overseen

Green Line Type 8 LRVs

By the 1990s, the MBTA acknowledged that full Green Line accessibility could only be achieved

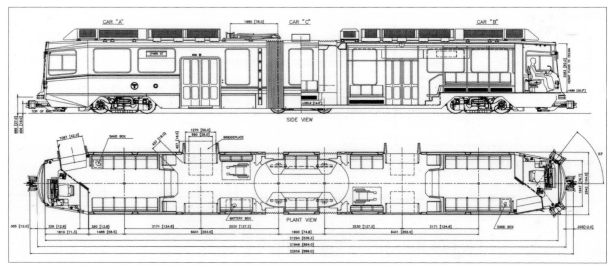

Figure 9.184 MBTA Type 8 LRV Dimensional Drawings, 1996

Figure 9.185 Trolleys at Packard's Corner, February 2011
An MBTA Type 8 LRV leads a two-car train towards Boston College Station. The second car is a Type 7 LRV, lacking the low-floor found in the Type 8.

through the deployment of new LRVs with floors aligned with platforms. Stairs at doors of Boeing and Type 7 LRVs prevented persons of limited mobility from boarding without a lift or a high-level platform with a bridge plate; low-floor trolleys were needed on the Green Line.

On February 8, 1995, the MBTA awarded an initial $215 million contract to Breda Costruzioni Ferroviarie (Breda) of Italy for the construction of 100 Type 8 trolleys, Boston's first, low-floor LRVs. Not only did the new trolleys bring increased accessibility to the Green Line, the Type 8s began replacing aging Boeing LRVs, in service since the late 1970s. Each Type 8 measured seventy-two feet long and seated forty-six passengers (Figure 9.184). Low floors aligned with station platforms and AC traction motors, both firsts for Green Line trolleys, were standard to each Type 8. In February 1999, the MBTA and Breda celebrated the establishment of an LRV-finishing plant in Littleton, where final assembly of each car took place. The cars' bodies were manufactured in Italy.

The first two Type 8s entered service on the Green Line at the end of March 1999. By fall of that year, Breda had delivered only thirteen of the forty-two cars anticipated by the MBTA; the Authority was not happy. After finding less than half of the batch of thirteen acceptable, the T froze payments to Breda and directed the manufacturer to resolve issues with the cars already on Authority property before it would pay out any more money. By the end of 1999, braking problems during wet conditions caused the T to pull from service all five Type 8s it had accepted.

The Breda woes continued into the 2000s as breaking problems persisted and serious derailments occurred. In early 2001 the MBTA's entire fleet of fifteen Type 8s was sidelined. After spending over $5 million to improve trackage in an attempt

to stop the derailments, the T put the Type 8s back into service during summer 2001, but the vehicles did not last long. At the end of August, and after over a half dozen Type 8s derailed in revenue service, the Breda-built cars were again pulled from the Green Line. They remained out of service throughout the rest of 2001 and all of 2002.

In early 2003, the MBTA committed to a nearly $4 million plan to get the Type 8s back on the tracks. That spring, the new trolleys operated for less than two months before yet another derailment occurred, this time within the Boylston Street Subway. Again, the MBTA halted payments to the manufacturer. The Breda problems were summed up in a late 2004 *Boston Globe* article which tabulated that the MBTA spent nearly $10 million on reworking Green Line trackage and Type 8 wheels to prevent derailments. The article mentioned the T stabling forty-seven Type 8s and refusing delivery on the remaining fifty-three of its 100-vehicle order. To the *Boston Globe*, MBTA General Manager Michael Mulhern admitted, "we bought a lemon." Fingers were pointed all around. The Authority accused Breda of poor design. The manufacturer blamed derailments on the T's failure to provide accurate track specifications during design of the cars. In the end, the MBTA and Breda agreed to a final production run of ninety-five vehicles, eighty-five in 2005, and an additional ten in 2007. As more rectified Type 8s entered regular service, and more importantly stayed on the tracks, the MBTA was finally able to complete the retirement of its Boeing LRVs. The last Boeing LRV operated in regular revenue service on March 16, 2007.

As they have since their arrival, Type 8 LRVs regularly operate in two-car trains, each regularly attached to an older, non-low-floor Type 7 (Figure 9.185). The mixed trains allow the MBTA to maximize its mixed-fleet of Green Line LRVs while providing low-floor accessibility on most trips.

Rebuilding the Blue Line

The MBTA approved a massive, multi-phase Blue Line reconstruction program in spring 1989 (Figure 9.186). One phase included stations west of Aquarium Station. Another phase covered stations in Revere and East Boston, except for Airport Station. Work on Aquarium Station, which was integrated with Big Dig work, composed a third phase. The reconstruction program brought to the Blue Line lengthened platforms to accommodate six-car trains, new mechanical and electrical systems, new elevators and ramps for improved accessibility, upgraded escalators, and new fare collection equipment. The program also brought new maps, signage, lighting, public art, landscaping, and furnishings to Blue Line stations. New entrances were carved out of existing buildings to improve access to both State and Aquarium Stations. In the early 1990s, the T added a wholesale replacement of Airport Station to the $500 million dollar Blue Line upgrade program.

Wonderland, Revere Beach, Beachmont, and Suffolk Downs Stations closed for a year on June 25, 1994. Within two years, the four stations reopened. During its renovation, Wood Island Station lost its upper busway, replaced by a surface busway along Bennington Street. Work on Aquarium Station commenced in 1996. In October 2000, the station closed for a year so the T could complete the $72 million renovation. Aquarium Station reopened in October 2001 with new entrances on State Street. Work was underway at Maverick and Airport Stations by 2002 with Maverick Station receiving a new head house.

Airport Station was razed and replaced with a sparkling new structure. A ceremony marked the reopening of the $23 million station on June 3, 2004. Light filled spaces featured luggage slides and flight information monitors for airport travelers. Massport shuttle buses linked the station with Logan Airport terminals.

The completion of $68 million in improvements at State Station, including the opening of two new accessible entrances, was celebrated on May 26, 2011. The Old State House, which served as the station's head house since it opened as Devonshire Street Station in 1905, was too historic and small to accommodate work required to make the station fully accessible. 2011 also brought with it the beginning of a $15 million complete reconstruction

of Orient Heights Station. A new Orient Height Station opened on November 26, 2013.

Amidst the ongoing modernization of the Blue Line in the fall of 2001, the MBTA approved a $172 million purchase of ninety-four new Blue Line rapid transit cars (Figure 9.187). Remembering the not-so-smooth arrival of Breda's Type 8 LRV's on the Green Line, the Authority rejected the low bid from Breda and selected Siemens Transportation Systems (Siemens) to produce the Blue Line cars. Unfortunately, the Siemens cars ended up arriving with their own problems. Production ran behind for years because of faults with the first cars produced. Doors leaked and air conditioning systems smoked. At a point of frustration, MBTA General Manager Daniel Grabauskas wrote in a letter to Siemens: "It appears to me that your company is far more interested in demanding money for work you have not performed, rather than completing the job." By the end of 2007, the total cost for the new Blue Line cars, including spare parts, rose to $200 million. The kinks were eventually worked out.

The T assigned the Siemens-built Blue Line cars 0700-series numbers and designated them as Number 5 East Boston Tunnel cars (Figure 9.188). Initially, only a handful of six-car trains of 0700 cars entered regular service, but as each new train replaced a shorter existing four-car train, that train's capacity was increased by fifty percent. At the end of 2017, the MBTA's Blue Line revenue fleet became the homogenous stable of ninety-four 0700-series cars it remains.

Beyond Wonderland

Proposals for extending rapid transit service north of Revere, and into neighboring Lynn have existed since the first half of the twentieth century. The Metropolitan Transit Recess Commission (MTRC) mapped an extension of rapid transit service through Revere's Point of Pines neighborhood and into downtown Lynn in 1945. In the 1970s, the MBTA and regional planning authorities conducted studies for extending the Blue Line beyond Wonderland. A proposed Blue Line extension to Lynn underwent environmental and federal review in the early 1980s. The proposal was scuttled by Revere's objection to a routing through Point of Pines and by a federal government unwilling to provide funding for both a new Lynn commuter rail station as well as a parallel extension of the Blue Line. In the early 1990s, a Blue Line extension continued to be explored in conjunction with proposals to extend

Figure 9.186 Blue Line Reconstruction Program Graphic

Figure 9.187 New Cars for the Blue Line, Circa Early 2000s
Labeled "Exterior Concept C," renderings envision what became the newest cars for the Blue Line, 0700-series, Number 5 East Boston Tunnel cars.

the Orange Line from Sullivan Square into Chelsea, and possibly as far as Lynn.

A Blue Line extension was again being studied in the early 2000s, this time as part of a larger planning initiative for the North Shore. A draft environmental impact statement depicting eight options for extending the Blue Line to Lynn and Salem received some support, including a potential funding commitment from the Commonwealth. Governor Patrick included funds for planning of Blue Line augmentations in a nearly $3 billion transportation bond bill in late 2004. Options studied included a rapid transit extension to Lynn, an improved connection between Wonderland Station and the nearby North Shore commuter rail line, and improvements to bus and commuter rail service

in lieu of a rapid transit extension. Lynn typically supported the T's proposals to bring rapid transit service to its city. Farther north, Salem's representatives in Congress pushed to secure federal funding for a Blue Line extension deeper into Essex County.

The MBTA stopped pursuing a northern extension of the Blue Line as a priority capital project by 2010. The math did not work when the Authority compared the project's massive capital cost with low estimated increases in ridership. Instead, the T made improvements to Wonderland Station. The opening ceremony for the Wonderland Intermodal Transit Center was held on June 30, 2012. The $54 million project added a 1,500-car parking garage and sheltered busways to Wonderland Station. A new elevated plaza and grand stairway linked the

Figure 9.188 0700-series Blue Line Cars, January 5, 2018
Two trains of Number 5 East Boston Tunnel cars meet on a wintery day at Wood Island Station.

improved station with nearby Revere Beach. The project became a successful catalyst for redevelopment of the surrounding neighborhood.

Mitigating The Big Dig

Few transportation infrastructure projects affected Boston like The Big Dig. The $14 billion highway project bought an extension of Interstate 90 through the South Boston Seaport, under Boston Harbor, and into East Boston. It also brought the replacement of an elevated segment of Interstate 93 running through downtown Boston (the Central Artery) with tunnels below the city. Over a decade of construction brought massive and perpetually changing disruptions to downtown Boston and the South Boston Seaport.

While The Big Dig was on the drawing board in the late 1980s, the Commonwealth and the MBTA began to strategize transit improvements in advance of the massive traffic congestion that construction of the project would bring. It was then that the T began to seriously consider extending the Blue Line, from Bowdoin Station to Charles Station on the Red Line. While it studied options for a Blue to Red Line connection, the T responded more immediately to Big Dig traffic concerns by increasing Blue Line, Orange Line, and select Commuter Rail service.

Thinking big picture, activists felt simple increases in service were inadequate. They felt Boston would need more than a handful of extra trains on existing lines, especially taking into account the billions about to be spent giving Boston open heart surgery to add more roadways. Boston's Conservation Law Foundation (CLF) took up the bullhorn, threatening to file a lawsuit challenging billions of funding for The Big Dig unless the Commonwealth committed to undertake a series of public transportation improvements, many already on the boards but not yet guaranteed to come to life. The threat worked.

The Commonwealth and the CLF entered into a series of initial agreements mandating Massachusetts facilitate a laundry list of transportation improvements and deadlines, including: a carpool lane would be added to the Southeast Expressway by 1993; new tracks and a new intercity bus terminal at South Station would be completed by 1993; new commuter boat service would be established between Lovejoy Wharf, Charlestown, Logan Airport, and South Boston Seaport by 1994; commuter rail service would be extended from

Ipswich to Newburyport by 1994; service would return along the Old Colony Lines to the South Shore by 1996; what became Phase II and Phase I of the Silver Line would be completed before the end of the 1990s; tens of thousands of new Park & Ride and commuter rail parking lot spaces would be established in Boston's suburbs by 1996–98; Blue Line trains would increase from four to six cars; the Blue to Red Line connection would be completed by 2001; the T would cap fares; and highways serving Boston would not be widened within Massachusetts Route 128. Additionally, the agreements required that the MBTA and the Commonwealth study: the restoration of commuter rail service between Boston and Worcester; the construction of the North-South Rail Link; a new water shuttle between Boston and the North Shore; and new carpool lanes for existing highways.

The CLF had to light a fire under the MBTA again, suing the Authority in 1998. The CLF protested that the T had not yet added 400 buses promised by 1993, Phase II of the Silver Line remained incomplete, Blue Line trains were not yet up to six-cars, and Green Line service was not yet restored to Arborway. The Commonwealth responded, agreeing on September 1, 2000 to a consent order clarifying the delivery of nearly $2 billion in transportation projects, many to be provided by the MBTA. The new consent order called for, among other action items, the retrofitting of existing buses with emissions controls, completion of a Major Investment Study for the Urban Ring by mid-2001, completion of Silver Line Phase II by 2002, the addition of four new commuter rail stations along the Worcester Line by late 2004, the addition of 18 cars to the Orange Line fleet by late 2004, and completion of Silver Line Phase III by late 2010.

The CLF and the Commonwealth agreed to a revised scope in 2006. The MBTA now only had to complete studies for restoration of Green Line service to the Arborway and construction of the Blue Line to Red Line extension. The T was taken off the hook for constructing either project. At the end of 2006, and in an attempt to head off additional CLF suits, Governor Mitt Romney agreed to push forward with the GLX, reconstruction of the Fairmount Line, and the addition of parking spaces to commuter rail lots.

Most Big Dig mitigation projects agreed to by the Commonwealth and the MBTA came into being. The carpool lane, a.k.a. "the zipper lane," opened in 1995. Additional tracks and the new bus terminal at

South Station were operational in late 1998. Lovejoy Wharf commuter boats operated from the late 1990s into the mid-2000s. Commuter rail service returned to the Old Colony Lines in late 1997 and 2007. Commuter rail trains reached Newburyport in October 1998 and Worcester in September 1994. Silver Line Phase I and Phase II opened in July 2002 and December 2004, respectively. Six-car trains became the norm along the Blue Line in the late 2000s. The Salem Ferry began to link Boston with the North Shore in 2006.

The largest unbuilt Big Dig mitigation projects, including some for which only study was required, include the Blue to Red Line connector, Silver Line Phase III, the GLX, and the North-South Rail Link. The latter was a tunnel to allow commuter rail trains to pass beneath downtown Boston through a tunnel between the north and south sides of Greater Boston's bifurcated commuter rail network. Early designs for The Big Dig called for the railroad tunnel to be constructed beneath and concurrently with the highway project. But by the time The Big Dig was tearing Boston apart, the North-South Rail Link had been eliminated from the project as a cost savings measure. Of unbuilt Big Dig mitigation projects, only the GLX is currently in construction.

MBTA Accessibility

Accessibility for all riders has been a decades-long work-in-progress at the MBTA. Early in its tenure, the T received a massive push from the federal government to improve accessibility. Building upon its work to protect civil rights in the 1960s, in the early 1970s, the U.S. government enshrined into law guaranteed protections for persons with disabilities. Section 504 of the Rehabilitation Act of 1973 prohibited an entity receiving federal financial assistance from discriminating against a person with a disability. The MBTA, with its building of new lines and purchasing of new vehicles with massive amounts of federal funds, was subject to the new law. Responding to the federal legislation, the Authority established its Office of Special Needs in 1974. A year later, the T launched a reduced fare program for riders with select needs.

In the 1970s, the MBTA worked with the Commonwealth and private advocacy groups to explore potential improvements for transit users with physical challenges. After consulting with and receiving a grant from the Massachusetts Commission for the Blind, the MBTA commissioned the production of a map for the blind and visually impaired. Released in 1976, the braille map was a letter-size piece of plastic on which the rapid transit lines were both printed in color as well as embossed. The coloring was intended for those with partial sight while the embossing allowed persons without sight to trace each line with their fingers. Alongside each line on the map were braille codes, each representing a particular station. Accompanying the map were four-pages of braille instructions with a list of the station codes and corresponding full station names for each. The plastic maps were designed to be resilient, water-resistant, and preserve the embossed lines and raised braille cells. Braille cells are subject to flattening, thereby becoming illegible when embossed into regular paper.

The T's production and distribution of the 1976 braille map was a follow up to its 1974 commissioning of a braille rapid transit map. Both the 1974 and 1976 maps were designed and manufactured by Gilligan Tactiles, of West Newton, Massachusetts. Additional MBTA maps for the visually impaired

Figure 9.189 Early MBTA Lift-Equipped Vehicles, 1981
Mechanical lifts extend from a first-generation MBTA lift-equipped van (left) and bus (right). The lifts raised and lowered riders needing such access between ground level and the interior level of each vehicle.

appeared in 1979, when the T issued a series of ten bus maps, each featuring braille and large print. Again, the MBTA worked with Gilligan Tactiles to produce the maps.

The MBTA began purchasing buses equipped with lifts for wheelchairs in the early 1980s. By the middle of the decade, it had yet to procure enough lift-equipped buses to provide accessible service every day on every route. To optimize when and along which route it deployed one of its lift-equipped buses, the MBTA launched its Call-A-Lift-Bus program in January 1986. Throughout that year, over 1,000 people dialed a dedicated phone number and requested a lift-equipped bus be assigned to a route they planned to use on a particular upcoming day. By the end of the year, the program was available on 140 bus routes (Figure 9.190). The program was a stop gap measure, put in place until additional accessible buses could be purchased and deployed system-wide. That purchase came in 1988, when a portion of 1988 state transportation bond funding approved by Governor Dukakis was applied to the purchase of 200 lift-equipped buses. In mid-1989, twenty-one bus routes were completely served by lift buses.

Since the 1980s, the MBTA has undertaken multiple station, vehicle, and wayfinding modernization programs which have improved accessibility. The T doubled these efforts after Congress' 1991 passing of the Americans with Disabilities Act (ADA). Unlike the federal legislation of 1973, which focused on entities receiving federal funding, the ADA extended broad protections throughout the public and private sectors for persons with disabilities. Massachusetts augmented the ADA with regulations of the Commonwealth's Architectural Access Board. At the time of the ADA's passage in 1991, only twenty-six of fifty-one rapid transit stations and thirty-five of 121 MBTA commuter rail stops were entirely or mostly accessible. No Green Line station or stop was fully accessible due to stairs present at the entrances of all trolleys. Of the Authority's approximately 1,025 buses, only 473 were lift-equipped. Despite incomplete system-wide accessibility, the T did provide paratransit service with 121 lift-equipment vans.

As 1991 turned into 1992, the MBTA worked to designate nearly eighty stations as "key stations," stops at which it planned to improve accessibility. The initial list of key stations included nearly two-dozen stops along commuter rail lines, nearly thirty stops along the Green Line, and twenty-seven rapid transit stations. Each Green Line key station

upgrade included the raising of a station's platforms to align with soon-to-arrive low-floor LRVs. Before the arrival of low-floor trolleys, the MBTA fitted out select Green Line stations with short stretches of high-level platforms and mechanical wheelchair lifts. The work was coordinated with Type 7 LRVs configured to receive wheelchair-bound riders from the high-level platforms. Accessibility improvements came to buses as well. The MBTA tested a New Flyer-built low-floor bus with a ramp in January 1992. In time, low-floor buses with extendable ramps became standard equipment.

As the 2000s got underway, and despite bringing many improvements across its system, the MBTA had a long way to go in making its system universally accessible. Seeking to push the T along, eleven MBTA users and the Boston Center for Independent Living (BCIL) filed a class action lawsuit in 2002. The suit resulted in the MBTA signing a landmark agreement in 2006, the MBTA/BCIL Settlement Agreement. The agreement legally bound the Authority to move forward with improving accessibility across all aspects of its system, including wayfinding, vehicle access, station access, and communications. After the settlement, the MBTA established a Department of System-Wide Access in 2007. The Authority continues to work to comply fully with both federal and state accessibility requirements, guidelines, rulings, and agreements. Most recently, starting in 2019, downtown stations have seen complete upgrading of their signage, maps, and lighting.

The Ride

The MBTA describes The Ride as its "door-to-door, shared-ride paratransit service…operated in compliance with the Americans with Disabilities Act (ADA)." Each trip on The Ride is booked in advance and does not follow a fixed route. The T subsidizes The Ride significantly more so than typical modes.

The Ride has its roots in a pilot program launched in 1977 to service Allston, Brighton, Brookline, the Fenway, and part of the South End. To establish The Ride, the T needed to assemble a new fleet of vehicles—its existing rubber-tired buses and trackless trolleys could not operate on non-fixed routes and also meet ADA requirements. The MBTA purchased its first pair of specially equipped vans in 1976. When The Ride kicked off in April 1977, the T's fleet of six vans included models it had to lease. A year later, the Authority purchased six more vans, doubling its fleet.

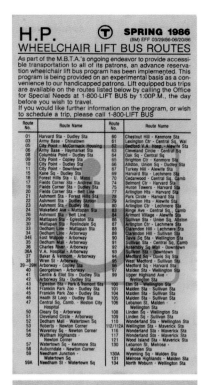

Figure 9.190 Lift Bus Routes Schedule Card, Spring 1986
A two-sided schedule card lists MBTA bus routes offering Call-A-Lift-Bus service.

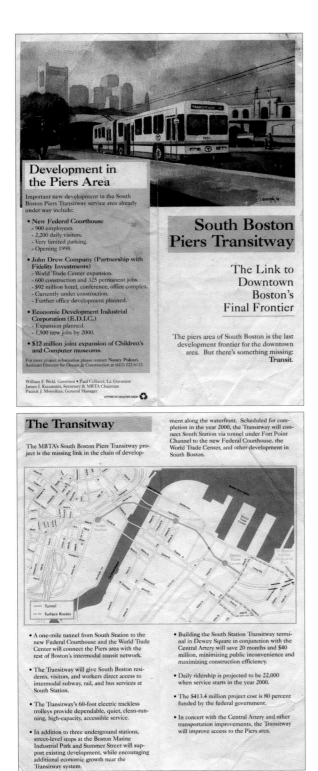

Development in the Piers Area

Important new development in the South Boston Piers Transitway service area already under way include:

- **New Federal Courthouse.**
  - 900 employees.
  - 2,200 daily visitors.
  - Very limited parking.
  - Opening 1998.
- **John Drew Company** (Partnership with Fidelity Investments)
  - World Trade Center expansion.
  - 600 construction and 325 permanent jobs.
  - $92 million hotel, conference, office complex.
  - Currently under construction.
  - Further office development planned.
- **Economic Development Industrial Corporation (E.D.I.C.)**
  - Expansion planned.
  - 1,500 new jobs by 2000.
- **$12 million joint expansion** of Children's and Computer museums.

For more project information please contact Nancy Pokrati, Assistant Director for Design & Construction at (617) 222-6122.

William F. Weld, Governor • Paul Cellucci, Lt. Governor
James J. Kerasiotes, Secretary & MBTA Chairman
Patrick J. Moynihan, General Manager

printed on recycled paper

South Boston Piers Transitway

The Link to Downtown Boston's Final Frontier

The piers area of South Boston is the last development frontier for the downtown area. But there's something missing: **Transit.**

The Transitway

The MBTA's South Boston Piers Transitway project is the missing link in the chain of develop- ment along the waterfront. Scheduled for completion in the year 2000, the Transitway will connect South Station via tunnel under Fort Point Channel to the new Federal Courthouse, the World Trade Center, and other development in South Boston.

- A one-mile tunnel from South Station to the new Federal Courthouse and the World Trade Center will connect the Piers area with the rest of Boston's intermodal transit network.
- The Transitway will give South Boston residents, visitors, and workers direct access to intermodal subway, rail, and bus services at South Station.
- The Transitway's 60-foot electric trackless trolleys provide dependable, quiet, clean-running, high-capacity, accessible service.
- In addition to three underground stations, street-level stops at the Boston Marine Industrial Park and Summer Street will support existing development, while encouraging additional economic growth near the Transitway system.
- Building the South Station Transitway terminal in Dewey Square in conjunction with the Central Artery will save 20 months and $40 million, minimizing public inconvenience and maximizing construction efficiency.
- Daily ridership is projected to be 22,000 when service starts in the year 2000.
- The $413.4 million project cost is 80 percent funded by the federal government.
- In concert with the Central Artery and other transportation improvements, the Transitway will improve access to the Piers area.

Figure 9.191 South Boston Transitway Pamphlet, Late 1980s
Before becoming Phase II of the Silver Line, a proposed transitway linking South Station and the South Boston Seaport was known as the South Boston Piers Transitway.

A year after it started, The Ride served approximately 800 users. It had expanded into Back Bay, parts of Cambridge, and parts of Roxbury. The T mentioned: "During its first 15 months of operations, handicapped persons have used the seventy-five-cent fare service over 16,000 times." The Ride expanded to South Boston and East Boston in 1979. Scheduling a ride on one of twenty vans or four small buses, available seven-days a week, was a phone call away.

At the end of 1985, over sixty vans worked a service area of over 200 square miles, up from a mere twelve square miles in 1977. Two years later, The Ride boasted a fleet of eighty-seven vans and provided approximately 600 daily trips across two dozen municipalities. The service area expanded as far north as Danvers and as far south as Holbrook in late 1988. By the mid-1990s, the T figured out how to provide many more vehicles for The Ride. In 1996, the Authority approved $1.54 million for the purchase of 100 sedans for The Ride. Each sedan provided paratransit for the nearly three-quarters of The Ride users who were ambulatory and did not require a lift.

Since launching The Ride in 1977, the MBTA has contracted operation of the paratransit service out to various private companies. By 1989, multiple contractors and sub-contractors provided service 365 days a year, from 6:00 a.m. to 1:00 a.m. A one-way trip cost only three quarters.

The Ride's 2018 service area was composed of four, smaller service areas. The "north area" covered communities north of Boston and along the North Shore. The "west area" covered the north-western suburbs, as far as Concord. The "south area" covered the southern suburbs, from Medfield to Cohasset. A "shared area" consisted of Boston, Brookline, Cambridge, and Somerville.

Genesis of the Silver Line

The Silver Line was Boston's first transit line to feature dual-mode vehicles, transit vehicles that could operate under power from either on-board internal combustion engines or electricity drawn from overhead wires. Beyond its novel vehicles, the Silver Line as a route came out of the mutual need of the MBTA and the city of Boston to provide solutions for multiple transit problems facing the city in the mid-1980s. One was the need for a replacement for rapid transit service along the Washington Street Corridor, lost after the Orange Line was relocated to the Southwest Corridor. Another was the need to

improve transit to the South Boston Seaport District, a neighborhood for which millions of square feet of new urbanity was being planned.

For the Washington Street Corridor, the MBTA evaluated three potential replacements for lost Orange Line service between Downtown Crossing and Dudley Square: light rail, trackless trolleys, and buses. Light rail, with its fixed tracks, stations, and vehicles was the most expensive option, but it could allow a direct connection with the existing Green Line subway, and with that link, a single-fare ride between Dudley Square and downtown. LRVs would also not contribute to neighborhood pollution, as diesel buses would. Trackless trolley service was less expensive than and had similar environmental benefits to light rail, but it would be subject to street traffic. Buses were the least expensive option but came with significant drawbacks. They lacked a potential for a direct connection to the central subway, would become stuck in city traffic, and would increase local air pollution.

Around Dudley Square and along the Washington Street Corridor, neighborhood groups and business associations correctly decried buses as slow, polluting, and nowhere near the quality of service provided by the Orange Line that once served their neighborhood. While final replacement for Washington Street Corridor service was being debated, the T's substitute bus service was forcing former Orange Line riders to pay two fares, one to ride the bus from Dudley to downtown, and then a second, to board the subway downtown. Activists criticized the T for increasing the financial burden for residents of a neighborhood most in need of subsidized public transportation and least likely to be able to bare a permanent two-fare burden.

Concurrent with the MBTA's exploration for permanent replacement service along the Washington Street Corridor in the mid to late 1980s, Boston pushed for transit improvements to serve the South Boston Seaport. Proposals for transit to serve the area included a new loop branch of the Red Line. The branch was proposed as a $200 million two-track tunnel running from South Station, through the Seaport, and to Broadway Station in South Boston. One or more new stations were proposed to serve the South Boston Seaport. Another option for Seaport transit was an estimated $250–$400 million transit link from South Station, through the Seaport, continuing beneath Boston Harbor to Logan Airport. This option, the South Boston Piers Transitway (Figure 9.191), evolved to become Phase I of the Silver Line.

Planners refined ideas for transit to the South Boston Seaport in 1988. On the table then were a $170 million shuttle bus network as well as a $190 million light rail system to be constructed in two phases, one from South Station to Fan Pier, and a second from South Station to North Station along the route of The Big Dig. Also considered was a $390 million underground people mover and a $395 million underground light rail line from Boylston Street Station, past South Station, and into the Seaport. The latter would have become a new branch of the Green Line. A $300 million Red Line loop continued to be considered.

In late 1989 and early 1990, the MBTA began to clarify its preferred options for not only transit to the Seaport, but along the Washington Street Corridor. In early 1990, the T presented its latest plan for service along the corridor, recommending sixty-foot articulated trolley buses running with six-minute rush hour headways. Recognizing the two fare and two ride situation in place from Dudley Square since closure of the el, the T proposed a free transfer from trolley bus service to the Orange Line at New England Medical Center Station (now Tufts Medical Station Center). The Washington Street Corridor Coalition continued to advocate for light rail and the MBTA continued to push for less expensive trackless trolleys. South End and Lower Roxbury neighborhood groups continued to fight for light rail throughout the 1990s.

Dudley Square Station

A new transit hub opened on the site of Dudley Station on November 19, 1993, when a ribbon cutting marked the completion of Dudley Square Station

(now Nubian Station). The new station opened for regular service on November 21. The $10 million project supported bus service after the cessation of Orange Line service to Dudley Square (now Nubian Square). The massive, copper-clad roof of the BERy's Dudley Station was brought down from high upon the el and converted into a busway shelter. Tower F was lowered from the el and repurposed at ground-level.

Alongside the recycled pieces of the el, the T constructed entirely new sheltered busways (Figure 9.192). For a time, these were intended to be served by trackless trolleys, which the T planned to run from downtown to Dudley Square, and potentially beyond, to Mattapan or even Jamaica Plain. No trackless trolleys arrived. Instead, a decade after its completion, the new busway became the southernmost terminal for Silver Line service.

The Silver Line Arrives

Portions of the Silver Line began to take shape in the mid-1990s, when federal and state agencies coordinated to reconstruct South Station on the Red Line concurrently with The Big Dig. Work at the subway station included the addition of transitways and turning loops for forthcoming Silver Line vehicles and a reconstruction of the station's ticket lobby. Meanwhile, along the Washington Street Corridor, in 1996, and despite the Commonwealth approving a bond bill to fund LRVs for the corridor, the T continued to push for trackless trolleys. That October, the MBTA confirmed that the South Boston Piers Transitway was to be known as the Silver Line.

Figure 9.192 Silver Line at Dudley Square, July 20, 2002
A New Flyer model C40 CNG-powered bus serves Dudley Square Station on the first day of Silver Line service.

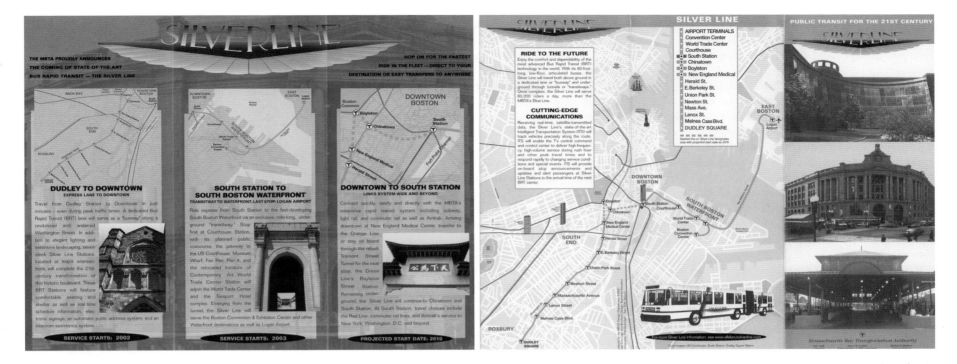

Figure 9.193 Silver Line Brochure, Circa 2000

A brochure breaks down the original three phases of the Silver Line: Phase I, from Dudley Square to downtown; Phase II, from South Station to the Airport; and Phase III, a direct connection between Phases I and II, perhaps a tunnel, to allow uninterrupted Silver Line Service between Roxbury and Logan Airport. Phase III was never constructed.

In late 1997, the MBTA announced plans to operate alternative fuel, low-floor, ramp-equipped, articulated buses to not only along the truncated E Branch of the Green Line to Arborway, but also along the Washington Street Corridor. The plans ruled out LRVs to either Arborway or Dudley Square. That fall, the T tested a New Flyer-built sixty-foot articulated bus on Route 39 to Arborway and along the Washington Street Corridor.

Following the launch of the Federal Alternative Fuels Initiative Program, which encouraged public transit agencies to test and gain familiarity with alternative fuels, including ethanol and CNG, in early 1998, the MBTA applied for a $3.2 million federal grant to test a handful of CNG and ethanol-powered vehicles. This foray allowed the MBTA to gain confidence in the operation and maintenance of CNG buses, vehicles that would soon become the core of its Silver Line fleet serving Washington Street.

The Silver Line came into full focus just before the turn of the millennium. In 1999, the MBTA notified the Commonwealth of its intention to alter the scope of the Washington Street Corridor replacement service project by combining it with the ongoing South Boston Piers Transitway project. The state's Executive Office of Environmental Affairs approved the combined project as the Silver Line.

Beyond addressing both transit for Washington Street and the Seaport, the Silver Line also addressed Massport's efforts to provide improved transit links between Logan Airport and downtown. Throughout the 1980s and 1990s, Massport studied the creation of people movers and bus systems following raised transitways, dedicated busways, and public roadways. Massport's goal was to circulate people efficiently, not only around airport terminals, but to Airport Station on the Blue Line, and potentially to a to-be-determined transit station in downtown Boston. In 1998, Massport's proposed Airport Intermodal Transit Connector (AITC) called for transit to link Airport Station, Logan Airport terminals, and South Station. Massport intended to use improved airport roadways, an extension of Interstate 90, and the third harbor tunnel (now Ted Williams Tunnel), all being constructed as part of The Big Dig to facilitate its new service. The AITC became realized in parts, initially as shuttle buses linking Airport Station with Logan's terminals, and later, as Phase II of the Silver Line.

The Silver Line project consisted of three distinct phases (Figure 9.193). Phase I linked Dudley Square with Downtown Crossing, via the Washington Street Corridor. Phase II linked South Station with Logan Airport, via the Seaport, and was designed for sixty-foot, articulated dual-mode vehicles. From South Station to Silver Line Way, Phase II was a dedicated transitway through the South Boston Seaport, mostly enclosed within a tunnel. Silver Line vehicles used surface roads and the Ted

Williams Tunnel to travel between Silver Line Way and terminals at the airport. Phase II included a new maintenance and storage yard for Silver Line vehicles.

The MBTA planned to connect Phases I and II with Phase III, a transit tunnel between South Station and the Park Plaza area. The T anticipated upgrading Phase I from CNG-powered buses to dual-mode vehicles after completion of Phase III. If the tunnel was constructed, overhead wire for dual-mode vehicles might have been extended from South Station, to the Park Plaza end of the tunnel, and then above ground, potentially as far as Dudley Square. Phase III remains unbuilt, killed in 2005 by a $1 billion price tag and a lack of finality for its routing.

Silver Line Phase I opened to the public on July 20, 2002. It was served by CNG-powered, forty-foot-long, low-floor buses constructed by New Flyer (Figure 9.192). These 6010-series buses were joined along the Washington Street Corridor by sixty-foot, 1000-series articulated CNG buses (Figure 9.194). Between Dudley Square and Temple Place at Downtown Crossing, Silver Line buses served stops at Melnea Cass Boulevard, Lenox Street, Massachusetts Avenue, Newton Street, Union Park Street, East Berkeley Street, Herald Street, New England Medical Center, Chinatown Station (inbound trips only) and Boylston Station (outbound trips only). A stop at Worcester Square opened shortly after the others. Intermediate stops south of the medical center received kiosks clad in porcelain panels celebrating local civic leaders and the history of the neighborhoods along the line. Silver Line vehicles, though they were supposed to enjoy the freedom of a dedicated bus lane along Washington Street, became tangled with general traffic that mostly ignored bus-only lane markings and signage.

With Silver Line Phase I up and running, the MBTA turned its attention to Phase II. By 2003, contractors were executing contracts for Phase II, including: a station and underground loop at South Station; a tunnel beneath Fort Point Channel; tunnels and a station near the federal courthouse at Fan Pier; tunnels and a station near the World Trade Center; and the Sliver Line's Southampton Street support facility. A previously proposed extensions of the Silver Line westward, within a tunnel to Boylston Street Station, was no longer part of the project. The underground transitway of Phase II came to the surface just east of World Trade Center Station. Between there and the terminals at Logan Airport, Silver Line vehicles utilized public

streets, the Ted Williams Tunnel, and airport roadways.

On December 17, 2004, ceremonies held inside a gleaming Courthouse Station marked the opening of Silver Line Phase II. Service commenced with a group of 1400-series trackless trolleys that the T temporarily relocated from North Cambridge. The vehicles were rebranded for the Silver Line and provided service between South Station and Silver Line Way, where overhead wire ended. The trackless trolleys served as stand-ins until the arrival of the Silver Line's bespoke vehicles, articulated dual-mode vehicles with 1100-series numbers (Figure 9.195). When operating from South Station to Silver Line Way, dual-mode vehicles, constructed by Neoplan of Colorado, operated like trackless trolleys, drawing power from overhead wire. Where no overhead wire existed, between Silver Line Way and Logan Airport, the 1100s were powered by their internal combustion engines.

The Silver Line Evolves

The MBTA kicked off a program to rebuild its fleet of dual-mode Silver Line vehicles in 2017. A year later, the T added its first extended-range dual-mode vehicle to the Silver Line. Batteries allowed the vehicle's engine to remain off for longer periods of time when not connected to overhead wires.

When Phase I of the Silver Line opened, the route lacked the "SL" route designations in use today. Silver Line buses running between Dudley Square and Downtown Crossing simply displayed "Downtown," "Dudley Square," or "Silver Line." After Phase II opened, Silver Line dual-mode vehicles began displaying SL1, SL2, and SL3 designations, in 2005. SL3 ran between South Station and City Point until being cancelled in spring 2009. On October 13, 2009, Silver Line SL4 service commenced, and SL5 appeared for the first time. SL4, a variant of SL5, linked Dudley Square with South Station. SL4 buses enjoyed a new dedicated bus lane along Essex Street, from Washington Street to South Station. South of Essex Street, both SL5 and SL4 served the Washington Street Corridor.

The Commonwealth's commitment to extend the Silver Line to Chelsea was formally announced by Governor Deval Patrick on October 30, 2013. At the time, the governor proposed a $82.5 million package, including $20 million for upgrades at the existing Chelsea commuter rail stop. The MBTA approved a final routing to Chelsea in 2014.

Figure 9.194 Silver Line Bus #1003, Circa 2000s
Number 1003 was among the earliest attenuated Silver Line buses to serve the Washington Street Corridor.

Figure 9.195 Silver Line at Chelsea Station, April 21, 2018
The first Silver Line vehicle to provide revenue service along the SL3 branch was dual-mode vehicle #1102, shown here at the Northern end of the line.

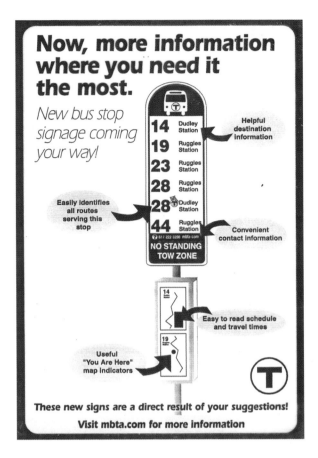

Figure 9.196 MBTA Bus Stop Signage Info-graphic, 2001
The MBTA introduced an augmentation for bus stop signage in 2001. That December, the Authority revealed a new bus stop sign and cube-shaped schedule display. The T's iconic tombstone-shaped metal bus stop sign was updated to feature a list of numbered routes along with a corresponding destination for each. Night Owl Service was called out by a friendly owl icon. Below each tombstone was a new, four-sided box with route maps and timetables protected behind transparent plastic.

The newest extension of the Silver Line, designated SL3, opened to the public on Saturday April 21, 2018. The extension linked Logan Airport with Chelsea Station on the commuter rail. Along the way, three new Silver Line stations opened, Bellingham Square (initially called Downtown Chelsea), Box District, and Eastern Avenue. Between Box District and Chelsea Stations, SL3 and its parallel shared-use path follow former and active railroad rights-of-way.

Better Buses and Trackless Trolleys

Since 1990, the MBTA has added a range of new buses to its fleet. It ordered 150 vehicles from Nova Bus Incorporated (Nova) of Roswell, New Mexico in 1995. In 2001, the T approved a $60 million purchase of 175 low-emission buses, most of which were constructed by North American Bus Industries (NABI) in 2003–04. As new bus models hit the streets, the MBTA retired older, less efficient, and worn out models. On October 16, 1994, a fond farewell was granted to the fishbowls with a special trip by bus number 6169. At the end of service on December 29, 2017, the T retired the last of its workhorse RTS buses.

In the early 1990s, the MBTA embarked on a mission to install air conditioning onto hundreds of buses lacking the convenience. Buses newly retrofitted with air conditioning wore a blue "Ice T" logo and the MBTA confirmed that air conditioning would be a standard feature on new buses.

After nearly forty years of operating a bus fleet composed of exclusively diesel-powered buses, the MBTA introduced its first CNG models in the early 2000s. The T followed Massport's mid-1990s introduction of CNG buses to serve terminals at Logan Airport. The T's vehicles were constructed by Neoplan. Before the company went bankrupt, Neoplan manufactured hundreds of vehicles for the MBTA, including articulated and non-articulated CNG buses, low-emission diesel buses, dual-mode vehicles, and trackless trolleys.

The MBTA unveiled its first low-floor trackless trolleys in 2004. The 4100-series trolley buses (Figure 9.197) featured extendable ramps, making them the T's most accessible trackless trolleys yet. The forty-foot Neoplan-built vehicles featured AC propulsion, automatic stop announcements, and location displays. Security cameras began to appear in MBTA buses at the end of the 2000s.

During the early 2010s, the Authority began to pursue its Key Bus Route Improvement Program. The T targeted its fifteen busiest bus routes, which included routes 1, 15, 22, 23, 28, 32, 39, 57, 66, 71, 73, 77, 111, 116, and 117. Through the program, the T worked to improve the overall customer experience, reduce travel times, enhance bus stop amenities, increase reliability, improve signage, improve accessibility, and optimize bus stop locations.

In 2014, the MBTA ordered sixty "Xcelsior" buses from New Flyer and assigned them 1400-series numbers. Each forty-foot model seated thirty-seven and featured a "clean diesel-electric hybrid" system. The system was composed of a diesel engine,

Figure 9.197 4100-series Trackless Trolleys, March 15, 2019
Two Neoplan-built trolley buses head out from their yard and shops in North Cambridge.

AC traction motor, energy storage system (for acceleration and climbing), and energy control system. In June 2015, the T approved an order for over 300 diesel-electric hybrid and CNG buses, all from New Flyer (Figure 9.198). The diesel-electric hybrid models replaced older CNG buses. At the end of 2017, the MBTA's active fleet included nearly 1,000 buses, thirty-two dual-mode vehicles, and twenty-eight trackless trolleys.

Recent MBTA efforts to improve bus operations include its ongoing "Better Bus" program and establishment of bus-only lanes along busy commuting corridors. As the T increasingly looks to its constituent communities to assist in the betterment of bus service, municipalities have coordinated with the T and converted stretches of on-street-parking and road travel lanes into lanes dedicated for bus and bicycle traffic. Successful bus-only lanes, some initially set up with cones during rush hours, were established along Broadway in Everett, in 2016, and Washington Street leading to Forest Hills, two years later. The Forest Hills conversion became permanent in 2018. Additional lanes have since appeared in Cambridge and elsewhere around the T's service area.

The Return of Owl Service

Late night bus service returned to the streets of Boston on September 7, 2001 with the T's kickoff of a one-year, $2.8 million pilot program. On early Saturday and early Sunday mornings, MBTA Night Owl buses served ten routes, each following a subway line, light rail line, or one of seven bus routes (Figure 9.199). After regular service ceased around 12:30 a.m., Night Owl buses operated until 2:30 a.m. The T recorded over 6,000 riders opting for the service during its first two-day period. After a few months, ridership exceeded estimates by more than thirty percent. Night Owl buses prowled Greater Boston streets until 2005, when, on June 26, the service succumbed to budget cuts and ceased operating. At the end, Night Owl buses operated along thirteen routes. The *Boston Globe* reported the T was facing a $20 million shortfall and when it eliminated Night Owl service, the service had a per rider subsidy of $7.53, versus a weekday rider subsidy of $1.37.

Just shy of a decade after the demise of its Night Owl service, the MBTA brought late night buses back to Boston yet again. March 28, 2014 saw the launch of a one-year pilot program, dubbed Late Night Service. Funded by private sponsors, Late Night Service buses served select bus routes until 2:30 a.m. on Saturday and Sunday mornings. On June 27, 2015, the T cut the service back until 2:00 a.m. and terminated five low-ridership routes. On September 2, 2018, late night bus service was expanded to run from 10:00 p.m. until 3:00 a.m. every night, except for some Sunday exceptions. Thirteen late night bus routes were in operation at the beginning of 2018. On April 1 of that year, the MBTA expanded early morning operation of many bus routes. A handful were scheduled to begin service as early as 3:20 a.m. While full

Figure 9.198 MBTA Bus #1845, September 22, 2018
With a bicycle rack mounted to its front, a New Flyer-built model XDE40 departs the Kenmore Square bus shelter.

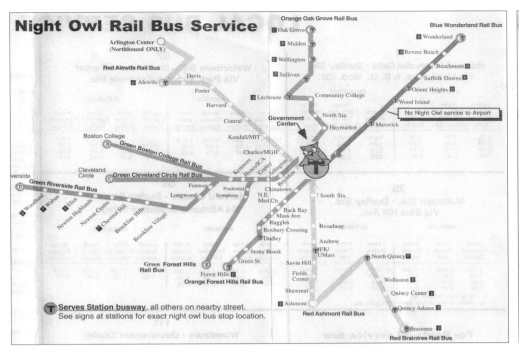

Figure 9.199 MBTA Night Owl Service Schedule, 2002

around-the-clock service does not yet exist, late night and early morning operation of select bus routes brings the T closer to providing for twenty-four-hour bus service.

Logan Express

The roots of Logan Express, the Massport-subsidized bus service connecting suburban parking areas with Logan Airport, are found in Quincy. As early as 1986, Massport-subsidized buses operated between Logan Airport and a then-new Quincy Adams Station. In 1988, the fare was $4 each way with parking at Quincy Adams costing an additional $1.50.

In the early 1990s, Logan Express opened its first suburban terminal, a massive parking lot at the shuttered Braintree's South Shore Twin Drive-In. Logan Express arrived in Woburn, where on November 16, 1992, buses operated by Peter Pan Bus Lines began running between Mishawum Station on the T's Lowell Line and Logan Airport.

On January 14, 1993, Logan Express buses operated by Fox Bus Lines commenced service from Framingham's Shoppers World. Massport has since opened a parking garage in Framingham and relocated its Woburn operations to Anderson RTC. In 2001, Massport invested $3 million to establish a new Logan Express site in Peabody, alongside U.S. Route 1. In the mid-2010s, Logan Express

buses began connecting the Airport with the Hynes Convention Center, in Boston's Back Bay.

Beyond Logan Express, other non-MBTA-subsidized bus services operate within Boston. EZ-Ride links North Station with sites around the eastern portion of Cambridge. The service launched on January 14, 2002 with funding from the Federal Highway Administration's Congestion Mitigation Air Quality Program. Recent funding for EZ-Ride comes from entities it services, including private employers and condominium associations. Complimenting a myriad of public and privately funding bus and shuttle operations serving Greater Boston are Longwood Medical Area (LMA) shuttles, overseen by the Medical Area and Scientific Community Organization (MASCO), linking the MBTA with points around Boston, Cambridge, and Chestnut Hill.

Upgrading the Red Line

Major improvements came to the Red Line in the first decade of the new millennium. Charles/MGH Station closed for a significant rebuild in the early 2000s. The station reopened in 2007 with new elevators, escalators, and a multi-story glass-enclosed lobby. An $80 million modernization of the Ashmont Branch commenced in fall 2003. Savin Hill, Fields Corner, Shawmut, and Ashmont Stations were modernized and made fully accessible.

Fields Corner and Ashmont Stations were rebuilt from the ground up. Savin Hill Station reopened in August 2005. Ashmont Station reopened by the end of 2008. In conjunction with the reconstruction of Ashmont Station, the Mattapan High Speed Line closed for an approximately eighteen-months-long upgrade. The Mattapan High Speed Line reopened on December 22, 2007 with six PCC cars providing service. All stations along the Ashmont Branch were back in service by the end of 2008.

As recommended by 2009's D'Alessandro Report, which outlined a myriad of immediate infrastructure repairs and upgrades needed across the MBTA, the T commenced the Floating Slab Replacement project along the Red Line. The ongoing project replaces failing portions of track infrastructure in tunnels of the Northwest Extension. A recently completed reconstruction of the Longfellow Bridge kicked off in 2013.

From Amtrak to Keolis

The early 2000s saw MBTA commuter rail operations transition out of Amtrak's hands. In 2002, the T put out to bid a billion dollar contract for the operation of its commuter rail network, America's fourth largest under a single operator. Only a handful of entities made presentations for the T. Guilford Rail System (Guilford; now Pan Am Railways) made a pitch to operate commuter rail as the Boston & Maine Railroad, a corporate entity purchased by Guilford in 1983. Guilford's $2 billion dollar bid was double that of the only other complete bid received by the MBTA. Amtrak declined to bid, with its president David Gunn citing years of excessive MBTA staffing requirements, high overtime costs, and an inordinate amount of workplace injury claims made by its Boston employees.

With Amtrak's contract set to expire on June 30, 2003, in December 2002, the MBTA awarded a five-year $1.07 billion contract for operation of its commuter rail network to the Massachusetts Bay Commuter Railroad Company (MBCR). The MBCR was a collaboration of Canada's Bombardier, France's Connex (then owned by Vivendi Universal), and a newly-formed, Boston-based transportation consulting firm. The head of the Boston firm was former MBTA General Manager James F. O'Leary. Initially, MBCR's managing director was John K. Leary, Jr., former head of the Southeast Pennsylvania Transportation Authority (SEPTA). MBCR took over from Amtrak on July 1, 2003, before

receiving contract extensions in the late 2000s and early 2010s.

MBCR's tenure lasted until 2014, when on July 1, Keolis America (Keolis) took the helm of the T's commuter rail system. Two years earlier, the MBTA received only two bona fide bids, one from MBCR and one from Keolis. Approved January 8, the Keolis contract was worth over $2.6 billion, had a term of eight years, and included options to extend for an additional four years. It was Massachusetts' largest contract. Thus far, commuter rail operations under Keolis have been far from smooth. The company has experienced equipment shortages, regularly cancelled scheduled trains, reworked schedules to limit the number of cancellations, dealt with crushing weather events, and has been fined by the MBTA for failure to meet certain benchmarks.

Commuter Rail Highlights in the 21st Century

The MBTA announced in 2006 that the owner of the TD Banknorth Garden (now TD Garden), Delaware North Companies, would fund a doubling of the size of the cramped commuter rail concourse at North Station. When completed, the expanded concourse brought higher ceilings, more seating, and expanded concessions. Recent improvements for commuter rail patrons of North Station were revealed in 2019, with completion of a portion of The Hub on Causeway development project.

Wi-Fi began to appear on commuter rail coaches in early 2008. Around the same time, the MBTA awarded a $170 million contract to Hyundai Rotem for the construction of seventy-five commuter rail coaches. Quiet cars appeared on most rush hour commuter rail trains in 2011. In 2013, Massachusetts purchased the Worcester Line from freight railroad company CSX. MBCR took over dispatching of all trains along the line and Worcester Line commuter rail trains were given priority, ending decades of delays due to CSX dispatching. To facilitate the planned South Coast Rail Project, the Commonwealth purchased approximately thirty miles of rail lines from CSX in Massachusetts' South Coast communities.

Ongoing MBTA commuter rail capital investment projects include the installation of federally-mandated Positive Train Control (PTC) and the replacement of the Gloucester Drawbridge. Another long-term, multi-billion dollar capital project continues to loom large for the MBTA. South Coast Rail calls for the restoration of commuter rail service between Boston and the cities of Fall River

Figure 9.200 MBTA Locomotive #2001, October 2013
The T received the first of forty model HSP-46 locomotives, constructed by Wabtec, a subsidiary of MPI, of Boise, Idaho, on October 24, 2013. Two years before the arrival of locomotive number 2001, in July 2011, the T allowed the public to vote on options for the paint scheme for the HSP-46s.

Figure 9.201 Blue Hill Avenue Station, January 2019
Opened as part of the rehabilitation of the Fairmount Line, a freshly completed Blue Hill Avenue Station is ready for service.

and New Bedford. South Coast Rail has remained a goal of the Commonwealth for decades with some preliminary work already underway. While the project currently has strong support from Governor Charlie Baker, most of the project remains on paper.

Reaching Wachusett and Wickford Junction

At the end of the 2000s, the MBTA kicked off a massive, years-long project to modernize the infrastructure along the Fitchburg Line. On October 18, 2010, the T held a groundbreaking for a four-and-a-half-mile-long extension of the Fitchburg Line, to a new terminal station and layover facility in the southwestern portion of Fitchburg. With limited service, Wachusett Station opened at the end of the nearly $60 million extension on September 30, 2016. By the end of the year, regular service to Wachusett Station was up and running.

MBTA revenue commuter rail service commenced at Rhode Island's Green Airport Station on December 6, 2010. Construction of the nearly $225 million station started in mid-2006. The station opened with a 1,000-car parking garage spanning the railroad right-of-way. A skyway provided an enclosed connection between the station and Rhode Island's major aerodrome. Before the airport station opened, MBTA commuter rail trains served Rhode Island's capital for decades, except during a suspension of service from 1981 to 1988 brought on by Rhode Island's failure to pay its share of funding for the service. The Ocean State's third MBTA commuter rail station, Wickford Junction Station, opened on April 23, 2012. The $44 million station, complete with requisite commuter parking garage, is the southernmost station of the T's commuter rail network.

Rebuilding the Fairmount Line

The Fairmount Line is the only MBTA commuter rail line to exclusively serve one city, Boston. The nine-and-a-quarter-mile line runs from South Station, through Dorchester, to a terminus at Readville Station in Hyde Park. The New Haven terminated regular passenger service along the line in 1944. Later, the T restored limited commuter rail service. As early as 2000, residents clamored for the T to reopen two of the line's shuttered stations. In response, in 2002, the MBTA announced that it would increase service levels, add four new stations, and seek funding to rebuild much of the existing line.

Work commenced on the multi-phase Fairmount Line reconstruction project in 2005. Along the line, bridges were rebuilt, existing stations were improved, and four new stations were added. The final names of the new stations were Newmarket, Four Corners / Geneva, Talbot Avenue, and Blue Hill Avenue. The $15.9 million Talbot Avenue Station opened on November 12, 2012. Newmarket and Four Corners / Geneva Stations opened on July 1, 2013. Blue Hill Avenue Station opened March 2019 as Boston's newest commuter rail stop (Figure 9.201).

Convention Security and Terrorism

The MBTA has endured various stress tests, including weather events, blackouts, mechanical failures, financial crises, and management scandals. Recent events, one planned, others unanticipated, tested the Authority in unique ways.

Since the terrorist attacks of September 11, 2001, the T has worked to keep its facilities, stations, and vehicles secure. Immediate responses to 9/11 included the deployment of bomb-proof trash cans, locking down of non-public facilities, and investment in training and security.

Boston hosted the 2014 Democratic National Convention (DNC) during July 26–29. The T spent months coordinating with federal, state, and local agencies for the main event at Boston's Fleet Center (now TD Garden), directly atop the T's North Station commuter rail terminal. Fresh in the T's mind as it prepped for the DNC were the Madrid train bombings of March 11, 2004.

On the T, from July 22–30, the Authority implemented various service changes and security checks. Transit Police began random bag inspections on July 22. The most significant service changes were related to a temporary closure of North Station. To protect the convention, the T cut commuter rail, rapid transit, and bus service short of a "hard security zone." Some exceptions were made, including for the operation of Orange Line trains reserved for DNC attendees departing North Station and travelling to Back Bay Station at the end of each night's festivities. Before conventioneers boarded a train, it was swept for explosives. The late night trains were free of charge for convention attendees.

On the afternoon of Monday April 15, 2013, terrorism struck home in the form of the Boston Marathon Bombing. For days after the event, MBTA bus routes were reconfigured around the expansive crime scene. Thursday evening, the two bombers, after murdering an MIT police officer, were boxed in on a Watertown street. As the pair of terrorists unleashed bullets and homemade bombs, law enforcement from around the region put the two men in their sights. The confrontation in Watertown left one terrorist dead and a Transit Police officer wounded by gunfire. After the gunfight, law enforcement officials searched throughout the night for the second bomber.

The following morning, on Friday April 19, Boston awoke to an eerie silence. Just before dawn, Governor Patrick gave an unprecedented shelter-in-place order for areas where police continued to search for the missing terrorist. At 5:30 a.m., the T tweeted: "The MBTA is SUSPENDED on ALL modes until FURTHER NOTICE." Following the MBTA's lead, most other transit agencies and operators in the area, including Amtrak and intercity bus lines, suspended their service in the Boston area all day. Governor Patrick lifted the shelter-in-place order at 6:00 p.m. Soon thereafter, the MBTA prepared to restart operations. The missing terrorist was located in Watertown and taken into custody shortly before 9 p.m.

For weeks after the bombing, destination signs on MBTA buses displayed messages of solidarity, including "Boston Strong" and "We Are One Boston." Authority employees installed stickers and banners with the similar messages. Yellow ribbon stickers graced T vehicles for months.

After 9/11, the DNC, and the Boston Marathon Bombing, the MBTA has worked continuously to improve the security of its system. Cameras are becoming standard on new revenue vehicles. Non-public areas within stations are protected by alarms and key-pad-secured doors. Perimeter fencing and electronic gates surround most yards, shops, and other back-of-house facilities. The T's "See

Something, Say Something" campaign asks transit users to be a million sets of eyes and ears. A Transit Police app allows transit uses to anonymously report suspicious activity via their mobile device.

Government Center Station Reconstruction

The reconstruction of Government Center Station evolved out of the MBTA's plans to upgrade the station as part of the Blue Line improvement program in combination with the Authority's ongoing efforts to satisfy federally-mandated accessibility requirements. During the decade spanning from 2003 to 2013, designs evolved into a gut renovation of the busy station. A notable change in the scope of the project was the jettisoning of a second head house, once proposed for Cambridge Street when the T was considering a permanent closure of Bowdoin Station.

On March 22, 2014, the MBTA closed Government Center Station for its two year makeover. The long closure allowed for a faster completion of the renovation over keeping the station open and phasing the work over a longer period of time. During the closure, Blue Line trains and Green Line trolleys ran through Government Center Station without stopping. Within the station, Blue and Green Line levels received entirely new stairs, escalators, elevators, lighting, mechanical systems, and finishes. New elevators, escalators, and stairs linked the station's subterranean spaces with a new glass-enclosed head house standing tall in Government Center Plaza. The 1963-built bunker-like head house and aging internal stairways (Figure 9.202) became a thing of the past.

A gleaming Government Center Station reopened to the public in March 2016. Natural light flooded down from the airy head house into

Figure 9.202 (Left) Gov't Center Station, December 12, 2012
As late as 2012, the station's interior and signage looked little changed since is mid-century redo. The view is of the stairs and escalators linking the Green Line platform with the head house.

Figure 9.203 (Right) Gov't Center Station, March 2019
A newly renovated station features the latest MBTA wayfinding signage, maps, and countdown clocks. The view is the same as one taken just over six years earlier (Figure 9.202).

Figure 9.204 Scollay Under Mosaic Tiles, September 2015
A mosaic spelling out the former name of the lower level at Government Center Station dates from the early twentieth century. Scollay Under is now the Blue Line level of Government Center Station.

a station refreshed with white tile walls, bright terrazzo floors, updated wayfinding signage, and the latest MBTA maps (Figure 9.203). Throughout the station, the MBTA conserved bits of history. 120-year-old "Scollay Under" tile mosaics were preserved and restored to locations of prominence (Figure 9.204).

Fares and Passes in the Early 2000s

As the first year of the new millennium got underway, the MBTA had not raised fares for nearly a decade. Fares were essentially the lowest amongst comparable American public transit systems. Effective September 18, 2000, fares went up. Rapid transit fare increased from eighty-five cents to one dollar. Local bus fare increased by fifteen cents, to seventy-five cents. All commuter rail zone fares increased. The Hingham Ferry increased from

$4–$5 dollars each way. Passes reflected new rates, with a monthly bus pass increasing from $20 to $25, and a monthly subway pass going from $27 to $35. The increases were partially due to the Commonwealth's cessation of issuing a yearly "blank check" to cover MBTA operating losses. The Commonwealth's replacement funding mechanism, a dedicated portion of state sales tax revenue, did not provide predicted nor adequate funds to prevent sooner-than-expected fare increases.

Additional fare hikes took place in January 2004, when the MBTA sought additional revenue of approximately $25 million to maintain service and meet its financial obligations. Rapid transit fare jumped to $1.25. Bus fare rose to ninety cents. Fares increased for commuter rail, commuter boat, and The Ride. Multiple fare increases have occurred since.

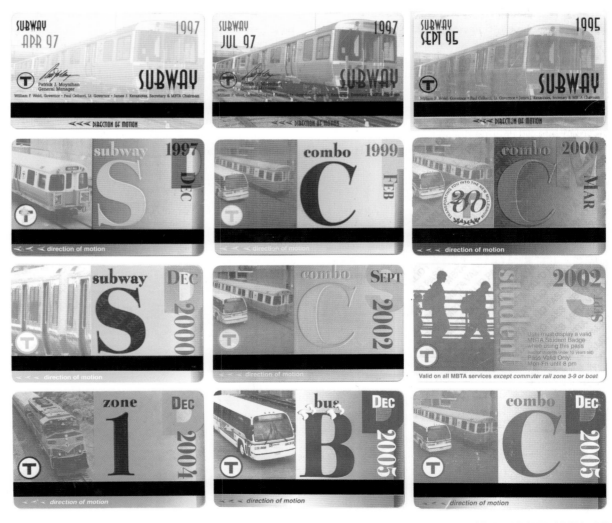

Figure 9.205 MBTA Passes, 1997–2005

Figure 9.206 (Left) CharlieCard

Figure 9.207 (Middle) CharlieTicket, 2019

Figure 9.208 (Right) Zone 1A Pass, September 2018

The MBTA continued to issue monthly passes into the 2000s (Figure 9.205). By then, the flexible passes featured a magnetic stripe for use at turnstiles and entry to certain revenue vehicles. Pass types included "Subway," "Bus," "Combo," and "Student." Combo passes allowed travel on rapid transit, streetcar, and most bus routes. Zone passes were available for use on the commuter rail.

Charlie Returns

In 2004, the MBTA announced that Charlie would finally be making his way out of the subway. His fate became known when he became the namesake for the T's first stored-value transit passes, CharlieCards (Figure 9.206) and CharlieTickets (Figure 9.207). CharlieCards were Boston's first RFID-equipped passes. They replaced older passes, with their credit-card-like magnetic strips. Once loaded, a simple tap of a CharlieCard at a turnstile or on an MBTA vehicle allowed the user to pay their fare faster than ever before (Figure 9.209). With Charlie's arrival, the MBTA eliminated exit fares. The entire reason why poor Charlie was unable to leave the subway—his lack of a nickel for exit fare—finally became moot.

New 2007 Fares and Passes

① NEW! Best Deal!
Monthly LinkPass
Passes are the best deal! Our new monthly LinkPass offers unlimited travel on our entire local bus and rapid transit network - linking you everywhere in the Metro-Boston area.

②
Use a CharlieCard to get the lowest fare!
If you don't use a pass, use a CharlieCard to lower your fare.

③ NEW!
Inner Express and Outer Express Bus Pass
Our new Inner Express and Outer Express Bus Passes offer unlimited travel on our entire local bus and rapid transit network PLUS Express Buses. You're covered from your home bus stop to Boston and back!

Inner Express Bus Pass includes routes: 170, 325, 326, 351, 424, 426, 428, 434, 441, 442, 448, 449, 450, 455, 459, 501, 502, 503, 504, 553, 554, 556 and 558.

Outer Express Bus Pass includes routes: 352, 354, 355, 500 and 505.

④ Coming in 2007!
Commuter Rail, Commuter Boat, Express Bus, One and Seven Day Pass holders
Continue to use tickets or CharlieTicket passes until further notice.

⑤ NEW!
Multi-day LinkPass
New, One or Seven Day LinkPasses lets you start on a day of your choice, with unlimited bus and rapid transit use. Great for weekly riders and visitors!

NEW!
Children 11 and under ride free with a paying adult!

Fares			Passes
Type of Travel	CharlieCard Fare ②	CharlieTicket Fare (or cash on board)	On either a CharlieTicket or CharlieCard
Local Bus	$1.25	$1.50	$40.00
Rapid Transit	$1.70	$2.00	$59.00 ①
Local Bus + Rapid Transit	$1.70	$3.50	
Senior/T.A.P.	40¢ Bus, 60¢ Subway		$20.00
Type of Travel	CharlieCard Fare	CharlieTicket Fare	Passes on a CharlieTicket Only
Inner Express Bus	$2.80	$3.50	$89.00 ③
Outer Express Bus ④	$4.00	$5.00	$129.00
Commuter Rail			
Zone 1A	Not applicable	$1.70	$59.00
Zone 1	Not applicable	$4.25	$135.00
Zone 2	Not applicable	$4.75	$151.00
Zone 3	Not applicable	$5.25	$163.00
Zone 4	Not applicable	$5.75	$186.00
Zone 5	Not applicable	$6.25	$210.00
Zone 6	Not applicable	$6.75	$223.00
Zone 7	Not applicable	$7.25	$235.00
Zone 8	Not applicable	$7.75	$250.00
Interzone 1	Not applicable	$2.00	$65.00
Interzone 2	Not applicable	$2.25	$77.00
Interzone 3	Not applicable	$2.50	$89.00
Interzone 4	Not applicable	$2.75	$101.00
Interzone 5	Not applicable	$3.00	$113.00
Interzone 6	Not applicable	$3.50	$125.00
Interzone 7	Not applicable	$4.00	$137.00
Interzone 8	Not applicable	$4.50	$149.00
Commuter Boat	Not applicable	$6.00	$198.00
Inner Harbor Ferries	Not applicable	$1.70	$59.00
One Day Unlimited Travel	Not applicable		$9.00 ⑤
Seven Day Unlimited Travel	Not applicable		$15.00
The RIDE	$2.00		Not applicable
Student	60¢ Bus, 85¢ Subway		$20.00

Introducing the new plastic CharlieCard.
Just tap and go – and save money!

Discover the convenience and ease of the new CharlieCard on all buses and subways starting in January.

What's the benefit of using the new plastic CharlieCard versus the paper CharlieTicket?

• **It's free** – we're giving them away in stations, at retail outlets wherever T passes are sold, and online at mbta.com beginning December 4th.

• **Using it gets you the lowest fare.**

• **It's simple to use** – just tap it on the black target at our fare vending machines, bus fareboxes or any fare gates – to get going.

• **It's permanent** – when you get it, keep it to use over and over again. It will last for years.

Who should get a CharlieCard?

• **Subway and Bus pass holders** – if you buy your pass online or receive your T pass

through an employer or at a T Pass Sales Office or local store – your January '07 Bus, Link, or Senior/T.A.P. pass can be loaded on a CharlieCard.

• **Subway and Bus cash or token users** – put money on a CharlieCard to get the lowest fare.

Who doesn't need a CharlieCard in January?

• **Commuter Rail, Boat, Express Bus, One and Seven Day Pass holders** – coming in 2007!

Senior/T.A.P. Customers: If your Senior/T.A.P. ID doesn't look like this, it's time for a new one. Whether you ride the subway, bus, commuter rail or boat, you still need a valid ID. Get yours at Back Bay Station or Downtown Crossing today!

Figure 9.209 CharlieCard Information Pamphlet, Fall 2006
Along with Charlie came some revisions to the T's fare structure. By the end of 2006, CharlieCard users were charged bus fare of $1.25 and subway fare of $1.70. CharlieCard holders received free transfers from rapid transit or light rail to buses or trackless trolleys. Commuter rail fares increased an average of approximately twenty-five percent. Commuter rail zone 1B disappeared, merging into zone 1A. Children under twelve accompanied by an adult rode for free.

Figure 9.210 Electronic Fare Brochure, April 2005

A detailed brochure provides instructions for use of the MBTA's first electronic fare system, including CharlieCards, CharlieTickets, and new electronic turnstiles and fare vending machines.

CharlieTickets, unlike rigid PVC CharlieCards, were made of treated paper, and featured a magnetic stripe long used on T passes. Each paper CharlieTicket was fed into a turnstile or fare box. The ticket was returned to the user after electronic deduction of appropriate fare. Each CharlieTicket reader required a user to insert their ticket and then wait for it to be read before it was returned. This process made CharlieTickets slower to use than CharlieCards, with their tap-and-go functionality. Monthly T passes were initially produced as CharlieTickets. Later, they were issued in the faster-to-use, RFID-equipped CharlieCard format (Figure 9.208).

A year after Charlie arrived, the MBTA began its final push to equip all stations and vehicles with Charlie-capable fare vending or collection equipment. The first rapid transit station to receive new electronic fare collection gates, along with new fare machines, was Airport Station. On May 17, 2005, the MBTA staged a ribbon cutting to celebrate the replacement of the old "click-clunk" sound of a person depositing a token and then pushing through a turnstile, with the "tap-beep" of a CharlieCard being registered and the "swish-swoosh" of an electric fare gate opening and closing. New fare machines allowed CharlieCard holders to add funds to their card from a credit card or cash. Today, beyond CharlieCards, a monthly, senior, student, multi-day "LinkPass," disabled persons pass, or youth pass can be paid for directly at MBTA fare vending machines.

As 2006 rolled around, automated fare collection machines and gates appeared at more and more stations (Figure 9.210). Meanwhile, Charlie himself became a living mascot of sorts. MBTA marketing staff wore a costume based on Charlie at special events. The Authority unveiled a Charlie-branded truck in 2006. In 2014, the MBTA opened its CharlieCard Store, the latest iteration of an MBTA pass sales office and customer service counter. Opened in the Downtown Crossing concourse above the Red Line, the CharlieCard Store replaced the aging pass sales offices at Government Center and Downtown Crossing Stations.

The MBTA stopped accepting tokens in exchange for fare value in July 2006, though fare machines at some stations continued to accept tokens and apply fare value to CharlieCards and CharlieTickets. On the commuter rail, electronic ticketing arrived in November 2012. The mTicket app allowed users to purchase commuter rail tickets on their mobile phone for the first time. With the appearance of mTicket, conductors were able to check more tickets in less time. For most transactions, a quick glance at a rider's phone displaying a valid ticket replaced the time consuming handling of cash and punching of a paper ticket. mTicket eventually expanded to cover all commuter rail routes.

On October 29, 2018, "Perq for Work" became the MBTA's program for employees to purchase monthly T passes through employers with pre-tax dollars. The rebranding came with improved features for online management of monthly passes.

Keolis' "fare is fare" program kicked off in 2018 with Keolis staff checking commuter rail customers' tickets, passes, and mobile device tickets before each patron boarded trains at North and South Stations. Furthering a mission to more consistently collect fares from all riders, Keolis is working towards installing fare gates for commuter rail passengers to pass through at North and South Stations.

On the rapid transit and light rail network, the MBTA is currently working towards implementation of its "Automated Fare Collection 2.0 Project." The new fare system has a current price tag of over a billion dollars.

Assembly and Boston Landing Stations

On August 20, 2008, the MBTA announced a public/private partnership that led to the opening of Boston's first new rapid transit station in nearly three decades. Located along the Orange Line between Sullivan Square and Wellington Stations, Assembly Station opened on September 2, 2014. Its construction was funded in part by developers converting former industrial properties at Assembly Square into Somerville's newest mixed-use neighborhood.

Boston's newest commuter rail station opened on May 17, 2017, when, after a year and a half of construction, the $20 million Boston Landing Station opened in Brighton. The station was the result of a 2012 agreement inked between MassDOT and New Balance, owner and developer of lands contiguous with the station site. New Balance paid for the design, construction, operation, and maintenance of Boston Landing Station, the T provided the trains.

Green Line Type 9 LRVs

When the GLX opens, more trolleys will be needed to serve an extended Green Line. In 2014, Mass-DOT committed to the purchase of two dozen Type 9 LRVs. The new trolleys are being constructed by CAF of Spain, with vehicle shells constructed in Europe and final assembly taking place in Elmira, New York. Though a Type 9 features approximately the same number of seats as a Type 8, each new car offers a ten percent increase in capacity. Type 9s feature additional low-floor space for increased accessibility over existing trolleys.

Figure 9.211 Type 9 LRV Mock-up Interior, April 22, 2017

Figure 9.212 Type 9 LRV at North Station, December 21, 2018
Green Line LRV number 3900 arrives at North Station to pick up the first paying passengers to ride in a Type 9.

Figure 9.213 Type 9 LRV at North Station, December 21, 2018
The doors close on the first revenue service trip of a Type 9.

Figure 9.214 (Left) Orange Line Interior Mock-Up, 2017
For the first time, Orange Line cars will feature electronic maps and station signage.

Figure 9.215 (Right) Orange Line Car Mock-up, 2017
A mock-up of a new Orange Line car body sits ready for inspection at Wellington Shops.

A full-scale mock-up of a Type 9 was received by the MBTA in 2017 (Figure 9.211). At the end of the year, the Green Line active revenue fleet included eighty-one active Type 7s and eighty-six active Type 8s. A pilot Type 9 arrived for inspection and testing by the MBTA in June 2018. The first Type 9 entered revenue service on December 21, 2018 (Figure 9.212 and Figure 9.213). Beyond its Type 8 and Type 9 LRVs, the MBTA is planning the next generation of LRV for the Green Line, the Type 10. The MBTA plans to replace all current Green Line trolleys with Type 10s and possibly retire the Type 9s to the Mattapan High Speed Line.

New Fleets for the Red and Orange Lines
The last decade has seen the Red and Orange Lines increasingly become subject to service interruptions, whether they be caused by fires, equipment breakdowns, signal problems, trespassers, or derailments. Trains on both lines regularly operate beyond capacity. But a solution is in the works—fleets of new trains.

New fleets of rapid transit cars are currently in production for both the Orange and Red Lines. A Chinese company, CRRC, is manufacturing new Orange Line Number 13 cars and new Red Line Number 4 cars. Massachusetts required assembly of the cars in the state, so final assembly of the vehicles is taking place at a nearly $100 million, purpose-built facility in Springfield. The cost for the new vehicles was approximately $850 million. The new cars and associated upgrades to facilities and infrastructure were funded by $1.3 billion in bonding approved by the Commonwealth. In October 2015, the MBTA got the public involved by allowing them to vote on paint scheme options for the new vehicles.

The T displayed a mock-up of a new Orange Line car body in 2017 (Figure 9.214 and Figure 9.215). The following year, the Authority did the same with a Red Line car body mock-up (Figure 9.216 and Figure 9.217). A test train of new Orange Line

Figure 9.216 Red Line Car Mock-up Exterior, 2018
Promotional material features a photograph of a mock-up of a Red Line Number 4 car body, complete with its LED destination sign illuminated for Ashmont.

Figure 9.217 Red Line Car Mock-up Interior, 2018
Boston's newest Red Line cars feature increased capacity, wider doors, and better informational displays. Technology includes LED lighting, redundant climate control systems, and regenerative breaking.

cars began operating along the Haymarket-North Extension in 2018. In that year, the T anticipated total replacements of both the Orange Line and Red Line fleets to be complete by 2023.

The new cars will allow the MBTA to replace its entire existing fleets on both the Orange and Red Lines. The fleets will also grow, from 120 to 152 cars on the Orange Line, and from 218 to 252 cars on the Red Line. Once all existing cars are replaced with new vehicles, each line will have a fleet of cars of a single type and age. The homogeneity and newness will ease maintenance needs, lower operational costs, and allow the deployment of more trains at once, all contributing to more reliable service.

Maps and Wayfinding for the 21st Century

The first decade of the new millennium brought with it new MBTA maps. The opening of the Silver Line between Downtown Crossing and Dudley Square caused the T to revise rapid transit and system maps for 2002. The updated maps began to appear at stations in 2005. The MBTA continues to update wall maps in many stations by simply

printing new maps, adhering them to sheets of aluminum, and installing them behind clear acrylic. This installation is far less expensive than porcelain on steel used consistently for decades and in new stations. Older sheets of maps are removed and recycled or sold as souvenirs by the MBTA's Merchandise Program, MBTAgifts.

Beginning in 2007, rapid transit maps in stations were joined by neighborhood and bus connection wall maps (Figure 9.218). Laid out by CTPS, each neighborhood map detailed the streets and urbanity surrounding a particular station or stop. Each bus connection map showed bus and transit connections available at a particular station.

Building upon the 2006 MBTA/BCIL Settlement Agreement, in fall 2009, MassDOT and the MBTA announced an initiative to improve public wayfinding, signage, and maps across the T. Key bus routes appeared on the rapid transit map for the first time (Figure 9.219). Additional neighborhood and bus connection maps, accompanied by augmented Rapid Transit with Key Bus Routes Maps, were installed at stations and stops. Government Center Station was the first to receive all

Figure 9.218 Neighborhood and Bus Connections Maps, 2012
The neighborhood map for Dudley Square Station (left) details the streets, landmarks, and transit services within a ten minute walk of the station. The bus connections map for Dudley Square Station (right) explains bus routes linking the station with destinations farther afield. Each map was installed and displayed at four feet square.

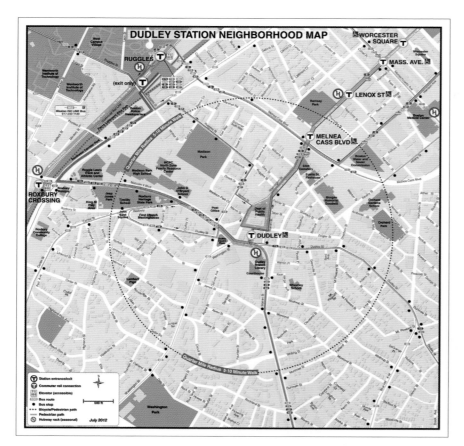

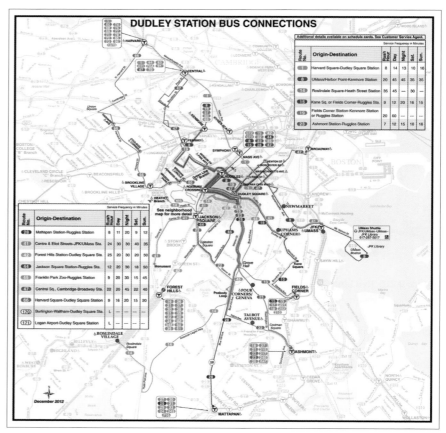

Figure 9.219 Rapid Transit / Key Bus Routes Map, Nov. 2010

three. Inside of revenue service vehicles, old maps were replaced with updated ones. A new Commuter Rail map entered development at CTPS.

The most significant aspect of the T's late 2000s wayfinding improvement initiative was its commencement of the implementation of new signage standards designed by BIA.studio, a Boston architecture firm. BIA.studio's creation of new MBTA system-wide signage guidelines was a multi-year undertaking, echoing work undertaking by Cambridge Seven in the 1960s. BIA.studio cataloged and analyzed existing signage and station configurations across the T, taking over 8,500 photographs

(Figure 9.220 and Figure 9.221). After identifying deficiencies and inconsistencies, the designers worked with stakeholders to establish new guidelines for the visual identity, wayfinding signage, and maps of the MBTA (Figure 9.222 and Figure 9.223). The firm then created bespoke resources, including Sign Maker TB software and a Digital Signage Manual. The manual informed the MBTA what existed, what was deficient, and what new signage guidelines should be for a given station or stop. The software and manual remain tools for the layout, production, and tracking of signage and maps, all with levels of consistency, speed, and compliance

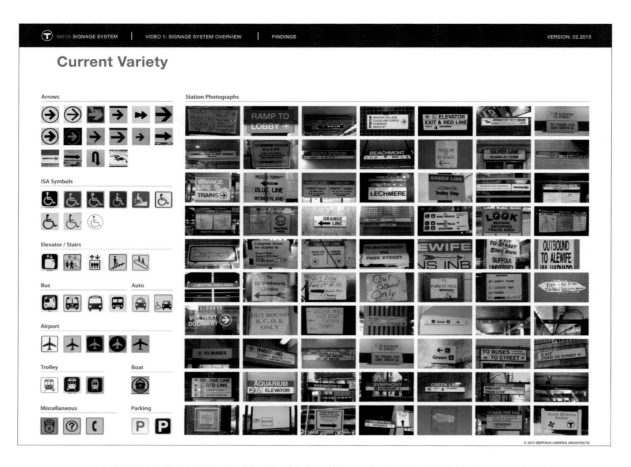

Figure 9.220 Survey of MBTA Station Signage, 2015
A bewildering amount of variations of MBTA sign icons (left) and texts (right) is currently being homogenized with new standards designed by Boston architecture firm BIA.studio. The architects prepared this assemblage of examples from thousands of photographs taken of existing MBTA signs.

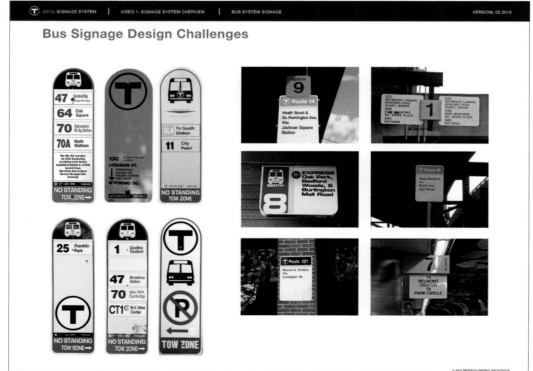

Figure 9.221 Survey of MBTA Bus Signage, 2015
A photo survey reveals many variants of bus stop signage (left) and bus berth signs (right) deployed across the MBTA's service area.

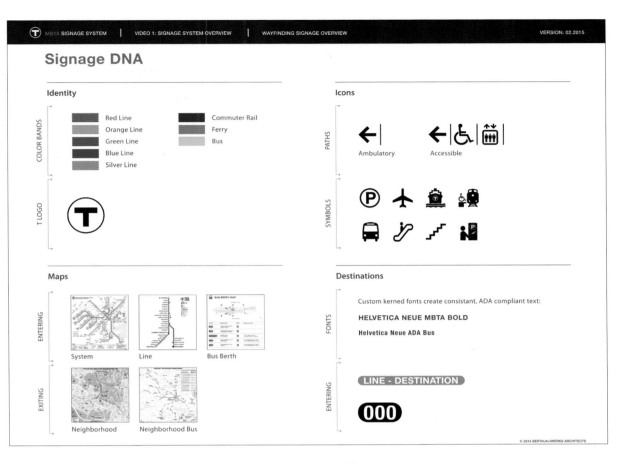

Figure 9.222 Signage DNA, 2015

For the first time since the MBTA's 1966 adoption of the *Manual Guidelines and Standards*, the Authority has a coherent visual identity, ready to be applied to signage and maps across its system. This graphic breaks down the MBTA's "Identity" as its color brands and logo. A concise set of icons, typography, and maps complete the "Signage DNA."

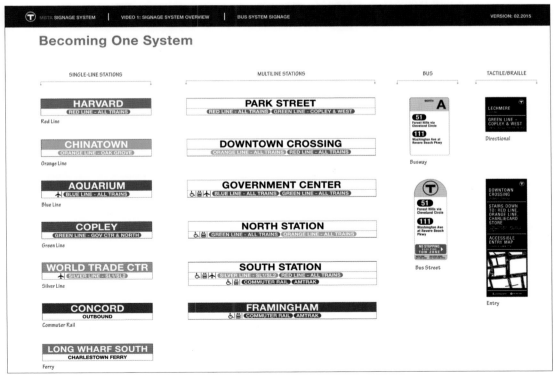

Figure 9.223 MBTA Station and Bus Stop Signage, 2015

Under the title "Becoming One System," are prototypical signs for single-line stations (left), mainline stations (middle left), bus stops (middle right), and tactile boards (right). The MBTA is currently updating signage across the system to coordinate with these examples.

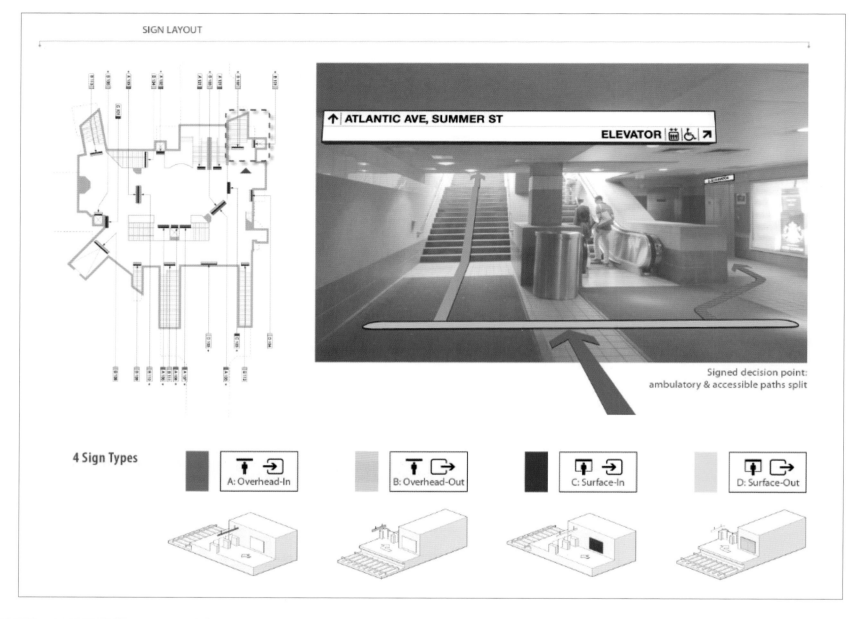

SIGN LAYOUT

↑ ATLANTIC AVE, SUMMER ST

ELEVATOR 🛗 ♿ ↗

Signed decision point:
ambulatory & accessible paths split

4 Sign Types

A: Overhead-In

B: Overhead-Out

C: Surface-In

D: Surface-Out

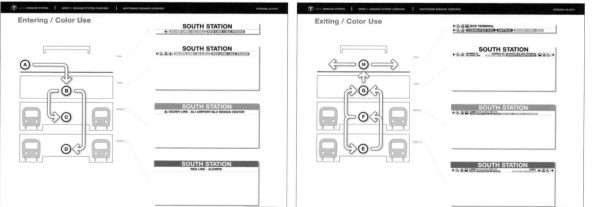

Figure 9.224 Prototypical Station Signage Arrangement, 2015
A series of diagrams explain the locations and types of signage to be installed in a MBTA station.

Figure 9.225 Arrangement of Sequential Signage, 2015
A pair of graphics specify the locations and types of signs to be installed for people entering (left) and existing (right) a station. The example given is South Station.

Figure 9.226 Existing (left) and Proposed (right) Signs, 2015
Across the T, the signage ribbons codified in 1966 by Cambridge Seven (left) are to be replaced with those designed by BIA.studio (right).

with accessibility standards than had been previously possible (Figure 9.224 and Figure 9.225).

During 2012–14, the MBTA applied the new standards, with pilot projects at Orient Heights, Science Park, Wonderland, and South Weymouth Stations. Prior to that, BIA.studio produced before and after examples for MBTA review (Figure 9.226 and Figure 9.227). Beyond signage, the architects vetted MBTA maps for consistency with the new standards and compliance with accessibility requirements.

BIA.studio's work for the MBTA was the first time that all MBTA maps and wayfinding signage were wholesale upgraded since Cambridge Seven created the *Manual of Guidelines and Standards* in 1966. An obvious visual change from Cambridge Seven's sign designs are BIA.studio's inclusion of lozenges and ovals that enclose destinations and trains only, important visual cues for color-impaired users. The architects' standards also significantly reduced the use of and increased the consistency of signage iconography.

Figure 9.227 Application of New Signage Standards, 2015
A composite image shows a specific application of the new MBTA Signage Standards to a location within South Station. The station's name and directional signage brackets a commuter rail map, Silver Line map, station plan, and bus connections map.

The T upped its informational outreach game in early 2008 with its first use of automated text messaging and email alerts. The Authority continues to conveys information about service and schedules via text, email, social media, apps, and in-station monitors. In 2012, countdown clocks, a presence on heavy-rail rapid transit lines for some previous years, began to appear at Green Line stations. By 2013, fifty-one of fifty-three non-Green Line rapid transit stations had countdown clocks functioning. The clocks are now ubiquitous across the T.

In 2013, the MBTA took creative steps to seek a new design for its rapid transit map, holding an open competition to solicit map design ideas from anyone and anywhere. The Authority received a wide range of designs, from maps drawn with crayons by children to elegant compositions constructed by graphic design professionals. Competition submissions were reviewed by a jury (which included this book's author) that selected six finalists (Figure 9.228). In 2014, the MBTA selected the winning entry (Figure 9.229), submitted by information designer Michael Kvrivishvili of Moscow, Russia. The T turned Kvrivishvili's submission over to CTPS for conversion into the MBTA's newest rapid transit map (Figure 9.230).

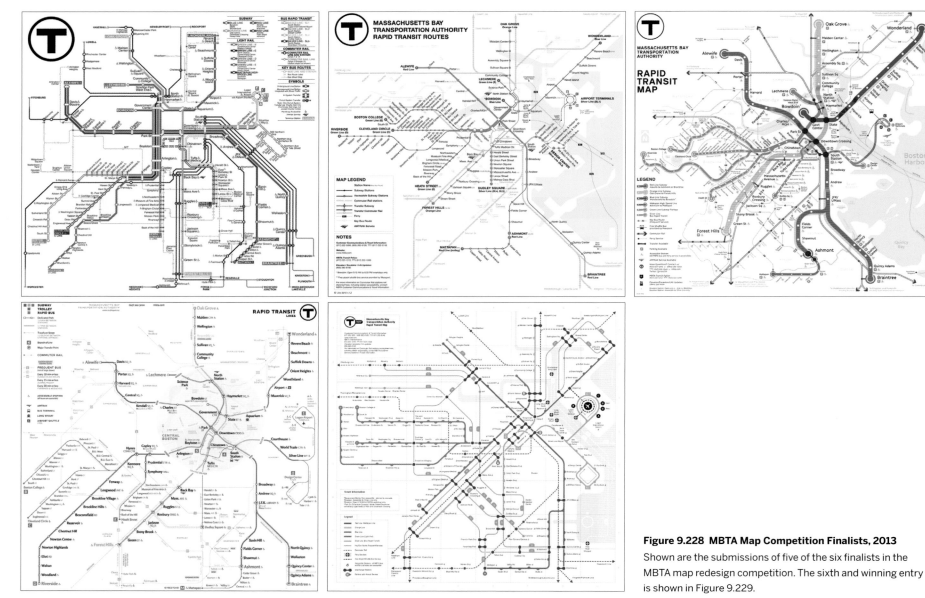

Figure 9.228 MBTA Map Competition Finalists, 2013

Shown are the submissions of five of the six finalists in the MBTA map redesign competition. The sixth and winning entry is shown in Figure 9.229.

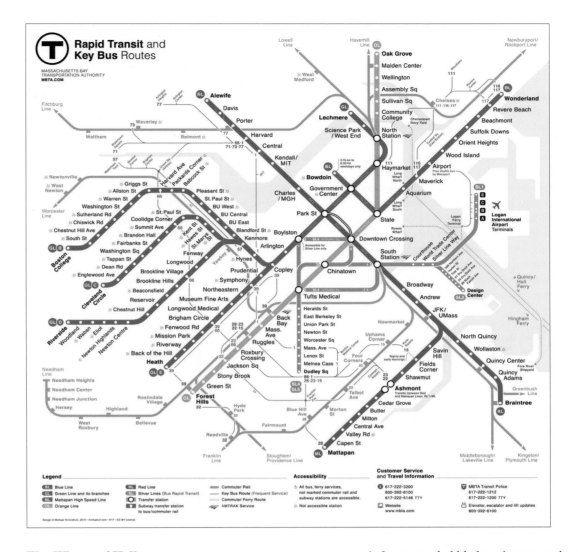

Figure 9.229 The Winning Map, 2013
The winning map of the MBTA's map competition was submitted by Michael Kvrivishvili. The map works within restrictions placed by the MBTA, including requirements that the map be square in format as well as depict, for the first time, all stops along the western branches of the Green Line. Kvrivishvili's map became the genesis for the most recent MBTA Rapid Transit Maps, the first of which was released in April 2014 (Figure 9.230).

The Winter of Hell

Not many events had as intense and long lasting impacts on the MBTA as 2014–15's "Winter of Hell." The second half of the winter pummeled the T with repeated snow storms, each lacking a thaw period between. Nearly 100 inches of snow fell during January and February alone. On the T, snow, ice, and cold met unpreparedness, failing infrastructure, and outdated equipment, leading to a massive breakdown of MBTA operations. Essentially, the Authority was brought to its knees. Rapid transit cars broke down after their motors became clogged with snow. Track switches froze across the rapid transit, light rail, and commuter rail networks. Heroic efforts made by MBTA employees to dig out and thaw their equipment were rendered futile not just by the punishing weather, but a lack of winterized and modernized equipment. Entire lines were closed to allow for removal of snow and ice as well as wait for storm-hobbled equipment to be repaired. Bus routes were regularly redirected or had service severely cut back. "Bustitution" was a prolonged occurrence along rapid transit and light rail lines.

Throughout the crisis, and for weeks after the storms abated, the Authority published, updated, and republished schedules and maps listing what services, lines, routes, and stations would reopen and when. For long weeks, MBTA users waited eagerly to see their route or station move from the "suspended" to "operating" column at MBTA.com. The MBTA came back to life gradually. Regular service did not return across the entire system until late spring 2015.

Reacting to the T's breakdown earlier in the year, on July 17, 2015, Governor Charlie Baker established the five-member Fiscal and Management Control Board (FMCB). Three of the members of the MassDOT board served on the FMCB. The establishment of the FMCB followed not only the Winter of Hell, but years of analyses and studies, including 2009's D'Alessandro Report and an April 2015 peer review of MBTA winter practices by the American Public Transit Association (APTA), both of which were highly critical of the MBTA.

The mission of the FMCB was massive. In its own words, the FMCB sought to address the MBTA's "unsustainable operating budget, under investment in infrastructure, difficulty completing projects, ineffective workplace practices, lack of long-term vision and strategy, and lack of customer focus." Segments of FMCB meetings open to the public were often characterized by board members grilling MBTA brass who came before them to request approvals or present information.

While the long term impact of FMCB oversight of the MBTA is not yet known, the board has already

hailed improvements made during its watch. The FMCB hailed spending $100 million in "winter resiliency upgrades," ordering new rapid transit cars for the Red and Orange Lines, overseeing "replacement of 1/3 of the bus fleet with 375 new hybrid and CNG vehicles," and resetting the GLX project.

390 Years and Counting

Public transportation has been critical for Boston, ever since the city's founding in 1630. Public ferries arrived with English colonists. Horse-drawn coaches, then steam railroads, and later, omnibuses, evolved to support a burgeoning city. Horse railroads and electric streetcar lines appeared in the nineteenth century, allowing the city to densify and early suburbs to sprout. Unification, initially by private hands and later, under public management,

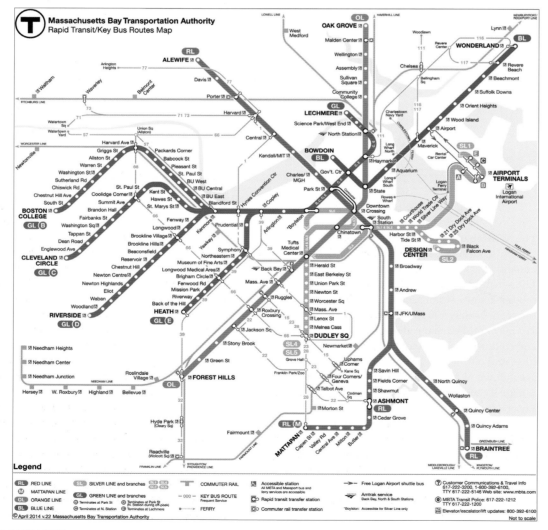

Figure 9.230 Rapid Transit / Key Bus Routes Map, 2014
Released in April 2014, version 22 of the Rapid Transit / Key Bus Routes Map was based on the winning map design of Michael Kvrivishvili (Figure 9.229). The map incorporates the standards developed by BIA.studio. Details new to an MBTA rapid transit map included termini capsules, a "not to scale" notation, and representation of all Green Line stops.

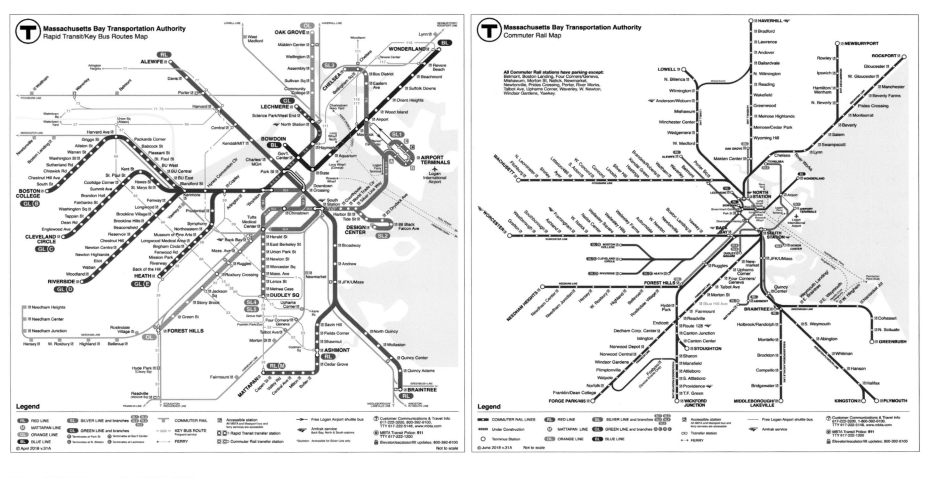

Figure 9.231 Mapping the MBTA, 2018
The MBTA's Rapid Transit / Key Bus Route Map (left) and Commuter Rail Map (right) reveal the scope of the MBTA's railed transit lines in 2018.

lead to the multi-modal, regional public transportation network in place today.

Boston evolved from a settlement of a few hundred Europeans with a single public ferry, to a metropolitan region of millions, connected by the T's hundreds miles of commuter rail line, hundreds of rapid transit trains, scores of trolleys, handful of streetcars, small fleet of ferries, and over a thousand buses and trackless trolleys. For over three and a half centuries, Boston was on the forefront of public transportation development, being an early adopter of new technologies and new modes of transit, all to connect more people together and improve the quality of service. Until the later half of the twentieth century, the historical highs mostly outnumbered the lows.

Today, we are amidst a period of many lows in public transportation for Boston, with aging infrastructure, worn-out vehicles, inadequate funding, and inconsistent political will. Though the arrival of new vehicles and delivery of capital expansion projects remain imminent, the future quality, consistency, and reliability of public transportation for Greater Boston remains unclear.

Public transportation in Boston has a history longer and more impactful than that of any other city in North America. We've been at it a long time, bringing America its first subway along the way. Today, more than a million riders rely on the MBTA each day. The T's over 8,000 bus stops and approximately 300 commuter rail, rapid transit, light rail, and bus rapid transit stations are spread across nearly 200 municipalities. The T's network, complemented by those of the Commonwealth's RTA's, ties together and remains vital to the health and growth of Greater Boston and the entire state of Massachusetts.

As Boston moves forward and seeks to maintain its vitality and importance, both regionally and globally, consistent political and financial commitment to public transportation is required. Whether it is overseen by the MBTA, another public entity, or a mixture of public and private operators, Boston's lifeblood that is public transportation must continue to evolve for another 390 years.

List of Figures

Bibliography & Sources

ABC Pathfinder Railway Guide. New England Railway Publishing Co., no. 792, Dec. 1905.

"All Aboard!" *Boston Daily Globe*, 10 Jun. 1901. p. 1.

Allison, Robert J. *A Short History of Boston*. Commonwealth Editions, 2004.

Anderson, Edward A. "The Subway at Government Center Revisited." *Rollsign*, vol. 47, no. 7–8, July./Aug. 2010, pp. 3–16.

---, "PCC Cars of Boston: 1937–1967." Boston Street Railway Association, Inc., 1968.

Appleton's Illustrated Railway and Steam Navigation Guide. D. Appleton & Co., Jun. 1860.

"Atlantic-Av Loop of the Elevated Railroad Will Open Tomorrow for Public Travel." *Boston Daily Globe*, 21 Aug. 1901, p. 2.

Bacon, Edwin M. *King's Dictionary of Boston*. Moses King, Cambridge, MA, 1883.

Badger & Porter's Stage Register, no. LXVI, Oct.–Nov. 1836.

Baedeker, Karl, editor. "Boston: Railway Stations;" "Tramways." *The United States with an Excursion into Mexico*. New York, Charles Scribner's Sons, 1893. pp. 72–73.

---, editor. "Boston: Railway Stations;" "Boston: Tramways." *The United States with an Excursion into Mexico*. New York, Charles Scribner's Sons, 1899. pp. 81–82.

---. "Introduction III: Railways;" "Steamers;" "Coaches;" "Tramways." *The United States with Excursions to Mexico, Cuba, Porto Rico [sic], and Alaska*. New York, Charles Scribner's Sons, 1909. pp. xv–xix.

Bahne, Charles. MBTA Celebrates Subway Centennial. *Rollsign*, vol. 34, no. 11/12, Nov./Dec. 1997, p. 3.

---. "MBTA Spider Map Redesigned," *Rollsign*, vol. 34, no. 5/6, May/Jun. 1997.

Barber, John Warner. "Boston." *Historical Collections...Relating to the History of Antiquities of Every Town in Massachusetts....* Worcester, MA, Warren Lazell, 1844, pp. 534–538.

Barrett, Richard C. *Boston's Depots and Terminals: A History of Downtown Boston's Railroad Stations*. Railroad Research Publications, 1996.

Beacon Street: Its Improvement in Brookline by Connection with Commonwealth Avenue. The Chronicle Press, Cambridge, MA, 1887.

Boeing Vertol Company. *Light Rail Vehicle*. Jun. 1975. Marketing brochure.

The Boston Almanac & Business Directory. George Coolidge, 1867; 1870.

---. Sampson, Davenport & Co., 1876; 1884.

---. Sampson, Murdock & Co., 1886; 1890–91.

Boston and Maine Railroad. "Summary of Equipment." 1 Nov. 1959.

The Boston Directory. Edward Cotton, 1806

---. George Adams, 1852.

---. John West, 1796; 1798; 1800; 1803.

The Boston Elevated As You Should Understand It: Radio Talks by Edward Dana, General Manager. Boston Elevated Railway Co. Circa 1924.

Boston Elevated Railway Co. *Annual Reports*. 1898–1946.

---. "A Decade of The Bus on The 'EL' V - The Evolution of the Motor-Coach." *Co-Operation*, vol. 12, no. 2, Apr. 1933, pp. 19–23.

---. "A Decade of The Bus on The 'EL' VI - Facilities for Passenger Interchange Between Motor Coaches and Rail Lines." *Co-operation*, vol. 12, no. 3, Jul. 1933, pp. 35–39.

---. *Instructions: Car Equipment and Signal System - Rapid Transit Lines*. Apr. 1919.

---. "Rapid Transit Extension Completed." *Co-operation*, vol. 8, no. 12, Dec. 1929, pp. 189–190.

---. "Recent 'El' Advertising." *Co-operation*, vol. 10, no. 11, Nov. 1931, pp. 172–173.

---. *Rules for Trainmen and Other Employes of the Rapid Transit Lines*. Mar. 1944.

Boston Evening Mercantile Journal, Jul. 1835, p. 1.

"Boston Has Longest Boat Trip in the World for a Penny." *Boston Daily Globe*, 6 Oct. 1946, p. 5.

"Boston L Road Opened Today." *The Boston Post*. Morning edition, 10 Jun. 1901, p. 1.

The Boston Horse and Street Railroad Guide. Boston, Edward E. Clark, 1887.

"Boston is Getting its First Air-Conditioned Transit Cars." *Railway Age*, vol. 167, no. 9, 1 Sep. 1969, pp. 14–18.

Boston Pocket Manual: Boston Terminal Guide, vol. II, no. 21, 24 Jul. 1899.

Boston Street Railway Association, Inc. "Celebrating the MBTA's Golden Anniversary." *Rollsign*, vol. 51, no. 11–12, Nov.–Dec. 2014, pp. 2–15.

---. "The Governor's Transportation Program." *Rollsign*, vol. 9, no. 11, Nov. 1972, pp. 2–5.

---. "MBTA Power Facilities." *Rollsign*, vol. 7, no. 11, Nov. 1970, pp. 2–8.

---. "New Braille Transit Map Demonstrated." *Rollsign*, vol. 13, no. 11/12, Nov./Dec. 1976. p. 10.

---. 'South Shore Opening Day.' *Rollsign*, vol. 8, no. 8/9, Aug./Sep. 1971, pp. 2–6.

Boston Transit Commission. *Annual Reports.* 1895–1917.

Boston Transit Department. *Annual Reports.* 1918–34.

---. *Dorchester Rapid Transit: Official Inspection Trip, Friday, November 4, 1927.* Pamphlet.

"Boston's Omnium-gatherum." *Trains*, vol. 8, no. 11, Sep. 1948, pp. 14–17.

"Bostonians Developing the L Voice." *Boston Daily Globe*, 26 Aug. 1901, p. 6.

Bahne, Charles. "Boston Transit Station Names Through the Years." *Rollsign*, vol. 29, no. 3–4, Mar.–Apr. 1992, pp. 10–15.

---. "The East Boston Suspension Railroad of 1834." *Rollsign*, vol. 21, no. 3–4, Mar.–Apr. 1984, p. 18.

---. "A History of BERy, MTA, and MBTA System Maps." *Rollsign*, vol. 30, no. 3–4, Mar. 1993, pp. 13–15.

Bechtel Civil & Minerals, Inc. "Red Line Extension Northwest: Progress Report, October, 1982." Massachusetts Bay Transportation Authority, 1982.

Bechtel, Inc. and David A. Crane & Partners. "Red Line Extension NW, Harvard to Alewife: Going Underground, August 1978 Update." Massachusetts Bay Transportation Authority, 1978.

Bradlee, Francis B. C. *The Boston and Lowell Railroad, the Nashua and Lowell Railroad, and the Salem and Lowell Railroad.* Panorama Publications, 1972. Originally published by The Essex Institute, 1918.

"The Cambridge Horse Railroad." *Ballou's Pictorial*, vol. x, no. 23, 7 Jun. 1856, p. 1.

Campbell, Robert, and Peter Vanderwarker. "Meigs Elevated Railway: Changing Tracks." *Boston Globe*, 23 Feb. 1992, p. 20.

Carlson, Stephen P., Compiler. *Boston PCC Memories.* The Friends of the Boston Transit Museum Inc., Jun. 1983.

Casaburi, Victor F. *A Colonial History of Noddle's Island.* 1975.

Catalogue of the Exhibitors in the United States Sections of the International Universal Exposition, Paris, 1900. pp. 160–161.

Cheney, Frank. *Boston's Red Line: Bridging the Charles from Alewife to Braintree.* Arcadia Publishing, 2002.

---. *Boston's Blue Line.* Arcadia Publishing, 2003.

Cheney, Frank, and Anthony Mitchell Sammarco. *When Boston Rode the EL.* Arcadia Publishing, 2000.

---. *Boston in Motion.* Arcadia Publishing, 1999.

---. *Trolleys Under the Hub.* Arcadia Publishing, 1997.

Chiasson, George. "Boston's Main Line EL: The Formative Years 1879–1908." *Headlights: The Magazine of Electric Railways*, 1987.

Chronology of America's Railroads. Association of American Railroads, circa 1988.

Clark, Norton D, and Thomas J. Humphrey. *Boston's Commuter Rail: Second Section.* Boston Street Railway Assoc., Inc., 1986.

---. *Boston's Commuter Rail: The First 150 Years.* Boston Street Railway Association, Inc., 1985.

Clarke, Bradley H. "A Century of Streetcars on Beacon Street." *Rollsign*, vol. 26, no. 1–2, Jan.–Feb. 1989, pp. 3–30.

---. *The Boston Rapid Transit Album.* Boston Street Railway Assoc., Inc., 1981.

---. *The Boston Transit Album.* Boston Street Railway Assoc., Inc., 1977.

---. *South Shore: Quincy–Boston.* Boston Street Railway Assoc., Inc., 1972.

---. "Southwest Corridor Opening Revisited." *Rollsign*, vol. 54, no. 5/6, May/Jun. 2017.

---. *Streetcar Lines of the Hub: The 1940s Heyday of Electric Transit in Boston.* Boston Street Railway Assoc., Inc., 2003.

---. *The Trackless Trolleys of Boston.* Boston Street Railway Assoc., Inc., 1970.

---. *Transit Boston 1850–1970.* Boston Street Railway Assoc., Inc., 1970.

---. *Tremont Street Subway – A Century of Public Service.* Boston Street Railway Association, Inc., 1997.

Coffee, John M. and Harold V. Ford, compilers and editors. *The Atwood-Coffee Catalogue of United States and Canadian Transportation Tokens - Sixth Edition.* The Catalogue Committee of the American Vecturist Association, 2007, pp. 271–284.

Boston Massachusetts. Boston Chamber of Commerce Convention Bureau, 1928.

Coolidge & Wiley. *The Boston Almanac.* B. B. Mussey & Co. and Thomas Groom, 1850.

Cox, Harold E, and O. R. Cummings. *Surface Cars of Boston 1903–1963.* Harold E. Cox, 1963.

Crocker, George G. "The Passenger Traffic of Boston and the Subway." *Rollsign*, vol. 34, no. 9–10, Sep. 1997, pp. 6–15.

Cudahy, Brian J. *Change At Park Street Under.* The Stephen Greene Press, 1972.

Cummings, O.R. *Central Power Station, Albany St. Shops and Yard, Albany Garage.* 2005. Unpublished manuscript.

---. "The Massachusetts Electric Companies - 1899–1919." *Rollsign*, vol. 50, no. 3–4, Mar.–Apr. 2013, pp. 5–15.

---. *Street Cars of Boston Vol. 1: Closed and Electric Cars 1887 – 1900.* Harold E. Cox, 1973.

---. *Street Cars of Boston Vol. 2: Open Horse and Electric Cars.* Harold E. Cox, 1973.

---. *Street Cars of Boston Vol. 3: Closed and Semi-Convertible Cars 1903–1908.* Harold E. Cox, 1975.

---. *Street Cars of Boston Vol. 4: Type 4 Semi-Convertibles and Trailers 1911–1952.* Harold E. Cox, 1976.

---. *Street Cars of Boston Vol. 6: Birneys, Type 5 Semiconvertibles, Parlor, Private, and Mail Cars.* Harold E. Cox, 1980.

Damrell & Moore, and George Coolidge. *The Boston Almanac.* B. B. Mussey & Co., 1852.

---. *The Boston Almanac.* Brown, Taggard & Chase, 1860.

---. *The Boston Almanac.* John P. Jewett & Co., 1853–4; 1857.

Dana, Edward. "Buses Supplement Rail Transportation System In Boston." *Electric Railway Journal*, vol. 67, no. 18, 1 May 1926, pp. 92–93.

---. "Five and Ten-Cent Boston Fares." *Electric Railway Journal*, 9 July 1921, pp. 757–759.

---. "Metropolitan Transit Authority, Boston, Mass.: Riverside Line Extension, 1959." *Transportation Bulletin*, no. 65, National Railway Historical Society, Connecticut Valley Chapter, Oct. 1960 – Jul. 1961.

Dickinson, S. N. *The Boston Almanac.* Thomas Groom, 1840–44; 1846.

---. *The Boston Almanac.* Mussey, B.B. and Thomas Groom, 1847.

Dobbin, Claire. *London Underground Maps: Art, Design and Cartography.* Lund Humphries, 2011.

Drake, Samuel G. *The History and Antiquities of the City of Boston.* Luther Stevens, 1854.

Dumas, Ken, Central Transportation Planning Staff. 2 Apr. 2014. Interview with Author.

Dunbar, Seymour. *A History of Travel in America.* The Bobs-Merrill Co., 1915. 4 vols.

Eastern Massachusetts Street Railway Company. *Report of the Public Trustees.* 1930; 1932; 1935; 1941.

"East Boston Ferry Big Thrill to Kids." *Boston Daily Globe*, 5 Sep. 1937, p. 1.

East Boston Tunnel Extension Official Inspection Trip, Friday, March 17, 1916. Boston Elevated Railway Co., 1916. Pamphlet.

"Eight Minutes to Harvard Sq." *Boston Daily Globe*, 24 Mar. 1912, p 24.

Elder, Andrew, and Jeremy C. Fox. *Boston's Orange Line.* Arcadia Publishing, 2013.

Electric Railway Engineering. International Textbook Co., 1925.

"Ferry House Destroyed by Three-Alarm Fire." *Boston Daily Globe*, 21 Nov. 1961, p. 3.

Fifty Years of Unified Transportation in Boston. Boston Elevated Railway Co., 1938.

"Firemen Barely Escape...." *Boston Daily Globe*, 9 Apr. 1941, p. 4.

"First of 24 New Green Line Cars Has Arrived." *Boston Globe*, 25 Mar. 2018.

Forbes, Allan and Ralph M. Eastman. *Taverns and Stagecoaches of New England.* State Street Trust Co., 1953.

---. *Taverns and Stagecoaches of New England Volume II.* State Street Trust Co., 1954.

Frazier, P. W. *Rapid Transit Cars In Boston.* Boston Street Railway Assoc., Inc., 1964.

---. *Rapid Transit Lines In Boston.* Boston Street Railway Assoc., Inc., 1964

Garfield, Simon. "The Biggest Map of All: Beck's London Tube." *On The Map.* Gotham Books, 2013, pp. 307–326.

Hall, Fred E. *"Under The Hub" Subway Souvenir.* Boston Engraving Co., 1899.

Hearld, Bruce D., Ph.D. *Boston & Maine in the 19th Century.* Arcadia Publishing, 2001.

Heinen, Roger J. *The Street Railway Post Offices of Boston.* Mobile Post Office Society, 1981.

"Improvements of the Boston Elevated System." *Electric Railway Journal*, 1 Mar. 1913, pp. 357–.

Kelville, Francis M. *The Building of a Transit Line: The Massachusetts Bay Transportation Authority's Haymarket-North Extension Project.* Massachusetts Bay Transportation Authority.

King's Handbook of Boston. Moses King, 1881.

---. 4th ed., Moses King, 1885.

---. 9th ed., Moses King Corporation, 1889.

Krieger, Alex, and David Cobb with Amy Turner, Editors. *Mapping Boston.* The MIT Press, 1999.

Kuttner, Peter. 17 Oct. 2014. Interview with author.

Lenihan, Daniel T. "A History of the Development of Route Numbers on the MBTA and its Predecessors." *Rollsign*, vol. 20, no. 1–2, Jan. 1983, pp. 8–9.

"Light-weight Coaches Delivered to the Boston & Maine." *Railway Age*, 13 Apr. 1935, pp. 562–566.

MacPherson, John N. "Seventy-Five Years of Local Transportation - I." *Co-operation*, vol. 9, no. 12., Dec. 1930, pp. 197–198.

Manley, Laurence B. "The Stations of the Washington St. Tunnel, Boston, Mass." *Engineering News*, 7 Oct., 1909.

Massachusetts Bay Transportation Authority. *Annual Reports.* 1965–2016.

---. *An Interim Review of the MBTA Late-Night Service Pilot Program.* 11 Feb. 2005.

---. *New Orange Line, The.* 1987.

---. *Northwest Extension Report.* Aug. 1978.

---. Press releases. 2000–19, www.MBTA.com.

---. *Project Information: T South Shore Rapid Transit Extension.* 1971.

---. *Red Line News.* No. 1, Dec. 1976.

---. *Southwest Corridor Development Plan.* Fall 1989.

---. *Southwest Corridor Project.* Oct. 1982.

Massachusetts, Commonwealth of. "Southwest Development Report Summer 1974." 1974.

"MBTA Sworn In...." *Boston Globe.* Morning edition, vol. 168, no. 35, 4 Aug. 1964, p. 1.

"Metropolitan Horse Railroad." *Ballou's Pictorial*, 13 Dec. 1856, p. 1.

Metropolitan Transit Authority. *Annual Reports.* 1947–63.

---. "Buses Roll Up 39 Years on System." *Co-operation*, vol. 31, no. 1, Apr. 1952, pp. 11–13.

---. "East Boston Transit Extension Opened." *Co-operation*, vol. 31, no. 1, Apr. 1952, p. 15.

---. "Suffolk Downs Station." *Co-operation*, vol. 31, no. 2, Jul. 1952, p. 43.

---. "Today, It's Tokens." *Co-operation*, vol. 31, no. 1, Apr. 1952, pp. 16–17.

"Metropolitan Transit Authority." CBTDB Wiki. https://cptdb.ca/wiki/index.php/Metropolitan_Transit_Authority. Accessed 7 Apr. 2019.

Meigs, Joe Vincent. *The Meigs Railway.* Boston, C. H. Whiting, 1887.

"Monster Crowds Swamp L Riders." *The Boston Post.* Morning edition, 11 Jun. 1901, p. 1.

Most, Doug. *The Race Underground: Boston, New York, and the Incredible Rivalry that Built America's First Subway.* St. Martin's Press, 2013.

Myer, Balthasar Henry, et al. *History of Transportation in the United States before 1860.* Peter Smith, 1948.

"Nearly 1500 Feet Completed." *Boston Daily Globe*, 27 Aug. 1901, p. 9.

"North Ferry Closes Career of 79 Years." *Boston Daily Globe*, 30 Apr. 1933, p. A6.

O'Regan, Gerry. "MBTA Fare Collection." *www.nycsubway.org.* www.nycsubway.org/wiki/MBTA_Fare_Collection. Accessed 23 Jun. 2015.

"Only Test Trips Now." *Boston Daily Globe*, 3 Jan. 1889, p. 8.

"Open Car, Metropolitan Horse Railroad." *Ballou's Pictorial*, 25 Apr. 1857, p. 1.

Osgood, James R. "Boston: Horse-cars; Omnibuses; Carriages." *New England: A Handbook for Travellers.* James R. Osgood and Co., 1873, p. 6.

Packard, Aaron. "The Roxbury Coaches & Its Omnibus Tokens." *Nova Numistics*, 24 Mar. 2013, www.novanumistics.com/numismatic-research/the-roxbury-coaches-omnibus-its-tokens. Accessed spring 2015.

Palmer, Foster M. "Horse Car, Trolley, and Subway." *Cambridge Historical Society Proceedings*, vol. 39, 1961–63, pp. 78–107.

Palmer, Howard S. *New England in National Leadership, 1895, The First Team Railroad Electrification!* The Newcomen Society of England, American Branch, 1945.

Palmer, Thomas C., Jr. "On 100th Anniversary, T Celebrates its Past and Embraces Future." *The Boston Globe*, 23 Oct. 1997, p. C19.

Phelps's Travellers' Guide Through the United States. Ensign & Thayer, New York, 1850.

Porter, Horace. "Railway Passenger Travel." Scribner's 1888. *Railway Passenger Travel 1825–1880*, Americana Review, 1962.

Prescott, Michael R. *Boston Transit Equipment: 1979–2006.* The Boston Street Railway Assoc., Inc., 2009.

Proceedings of the Brookline Historical Society at the Annual Meeting. 21 Jan. 1913.

"Protest Closing of North Ferry." *Boston Daily Globe*, 1 Oct. 1930, p. 10.

Quincy, Josiah. *A Municipal History of the Town and City of Boston, During Two Centuries. From September 17, 1630, to September 17, 1830.* Charles C. Little and James Brown, 1852.

"Rapid Transit: Subway." *Architectural Record*, Jul. 1979, pp. 122–125.

"Recent Improvements of the Boston Elevated System." *Electric Railway Journal*, vol. XLI, no. 10, 8 Mar. 1913, pp. 408–414.

Red Line Fact Sheet." Cambridge Commuter Development Department. Circa 1976. Unpublished draft memo.

Report of the Board of Commissioners of Internal Improvement in Relation to the Examination of Sundry Routes for a Railway from Boston to Providence. Board of Commissioners of Internal Improvements, 1828.

Report of the Board of Directors of Internal Improvements of the State of Massachusetts on the Practicability and Expediency of a Rail-Road from Boston to the Hudson River and from Boston to Providence. Board of Directors of Internal Improvements, 1829.

Reps, John W. *Bird's Eye Views: Historical Lithographs of North American Cities.* Princeton Architectural Press, 1998.

Rollsign, vol. 4, no. 12, Dec. 1967 – vol. 54, nos. 11/12, Nov./Dec. 2017.

Russell's Horse Railroad Guide for Boston and Vicinity. Boston, Benjamin B. Russell, 1862.

Rutman, Darrett B. *Winthrop's Boston: Portrait of a Puritan Town 1630–1649.* The University of North Carolina Press, 1965.

Sammarco, Anthony Mitchell. *Cambridge.* Arcadia Publishing, 1999.

Sachs, Joseph. "Conduit Versus Trolley." *Electric Power*, Jan.–Jun. 1895.

Sanborn, George M. *A Chronicle of the Boston Transit System.* Massachusetts State Transportation Library, 1993.

Scharfenberg, David. "The MBTA's Long, Winding, Infuriating Road to failure." *The Boston Globe*, 15 Feb. 2015.

Simms, Wilfrid. *Railways of Boston: The Massachusetts Bay Transportation Authority System.* Wilfrid S. Simms, 1999.

"Snowzilla vs. Winter's Furry." *The Boston Globe*, 23 Jan. 2011.

Spalding, Henry Curtis. *Local Transportation at Boston. Comprising Swift Transit by Tunnel Railways Connecting Together the Tracks of all the Steam Railroads and Rapid Transit by the Aid of Subways....* 1891.

"The Sprague Electric Road at Boston." *The Street Railway Journal*, vol. V, no. 2, Jan. 1889, pp. 5–7.

Stanley, Robert C. "The Maine Line 'El' Part 2: Notes on Rolling Stock." *Rollsign* vol. 14, no. 7/8, Jul./Aug. 1977, pp. 14–23.

---. *Narrow Gauge: The Story of the Boston, Revere Beach & Lynn Railroad.* The Boston Street Railway Assoc., Inc., 1980.

Stark, James H. *Antique Views of ye Towne of Boston.* Morse-Purce Co., 1907.

State Street Trust Co. "The First Stage-Coach Line Out of Boston." *Some Events of Boston and its Neighbors.* State Street Trust Co., 1917, pp. 30–32.

---. "The Harvard College Ferry." *Some Events of Boston and its Neighbors.* State Street Trust Co., 1917, pp. 14–16.

---. "West End Street Railway." *Other Industries of New England.* State Street Trust Co., 1924, pp. 47–59.

Steward, H. M. "Points in Motor Coach Garage Design." *Railway Age*, vol. 85, no. 17, 27 Oct. 1929, pp. 845–849.

Stimpson's Boston Directory. Stimpson & Clapp, 1832.

---. Charles Stimpson Jr., 1835–36.

"Story of the Explosion." *Boston Daily Globe.* 5 Mar. 1897, p. 3.

Stranger's Illustrated Guide to Boston and its Suburbs; with maps of Boston and the Harbor. Photo-Electrotype Co., 1881.

The Stranger's New Guide Through Boston and Vicinity. A. Williams & Co., 1869.

Taft, Herbert C. "Early Days of Railroading: A paper ready before the Lowell Historical Society, March 2, 1909, Lowell, Mass." *Contributions to the Lowell Historical Society*, vol. I, pt. III, 1913. Pamphlet reprint.

"Ten-Cent Fares and 7-Cent Tickets: How They Are Being Collected and Registered on the City and Interurban Lines of the Bay State Street Railway." *Electric Railway Journal*, vol. 53, no. 17, 26 Apr. 1919, pp. 831–832.

"To Open Elevated Tomorrow." *Boston Daily Globe*, 9 Jun. 1901, p. 1.

Tomkavage, Nick. "MBTA Emergency Training Center." *Rollsign*, vol. 50, no. 5–6, May–Jun. 2013, pp. 8–13.

Throm, Edward L., Editor. *Popular Mechanics' Picture History of American Transportation.* Simon and Schuster, 1952.

Trumbull, J. Hammond, Esq. Letter to Charles Folsom Esq. regarding Shawmut, recorded in *Proceedings of the Massachusetts Historical Society*, vol. 9, 1866–67, pp. 376–279.

Urban Mass Transportation Administration, U. S. Department of Transportation. *The State-of-the-Art-Car: Advancing Rail Rapid Transit.* 1974.

"Urban Ring Phase 2 - Recommended Alignment." *Urban Ring Phase 2 Fact Sheet.* Executive Office of Transportation, Jan. 2009.

Vandervoort, Bill. *Boston Transit: Early Street Railway Companies (North Suburbs).* www.chicagorailfan.com/boshisn.html.

---. *Boston Transit: Early Street Railway Companies (South Suburbs).* www.chicagorailfan.com/boshiss.html.

Walton Advertising & Printing Co. *The Quarries of the Granite Railway Company.* Granite Railway Co., 1928.

Wheildon, William W. *Curiosities of History: Boston September Seventeenth, 1630–1880.* 2nd ed., Lee and Shepard, 1880.

"West End Railway." *Boston Daily Globe*, 18 Jan. 1889, p. 3.

"West End Railway Notes." *Boston Daily Globe*, 13 Jan. 1889, p. 2.

West End Street Railway Co. *Annual Reports.* 1883–1921.

---. "Strangers' Guide to the Streetcar System of the West End Street Ry." Circa 1890. Facsimile published by Boston Street Railway Assoc., Inc., 1973.

"When the Subway's Done!" *Boston Daily Globe*, 17 Nov. 1895, p. 36.

Whitney, Henry M. *History of the West End Street Railway.* Louis P. Hager, 1892.

"Why the Horses Shrieked." *Boston Daily Globe*, 10 Apr. 1889, p. 4.

Winsor, Justin, Editor. *The Memorial History of Boston, Including Suffolk County, Massachusetts. 1630–1880.* James R. Osgood and Co., 1882–83.

Zaitzevsky, Cynthia. "Frederick Law Olmsted in Brookline: A Preliminary Study of His Public Projects." *Proceedings of the Brookline Historical Society*, fall 1977, pp. 42–65.

Index

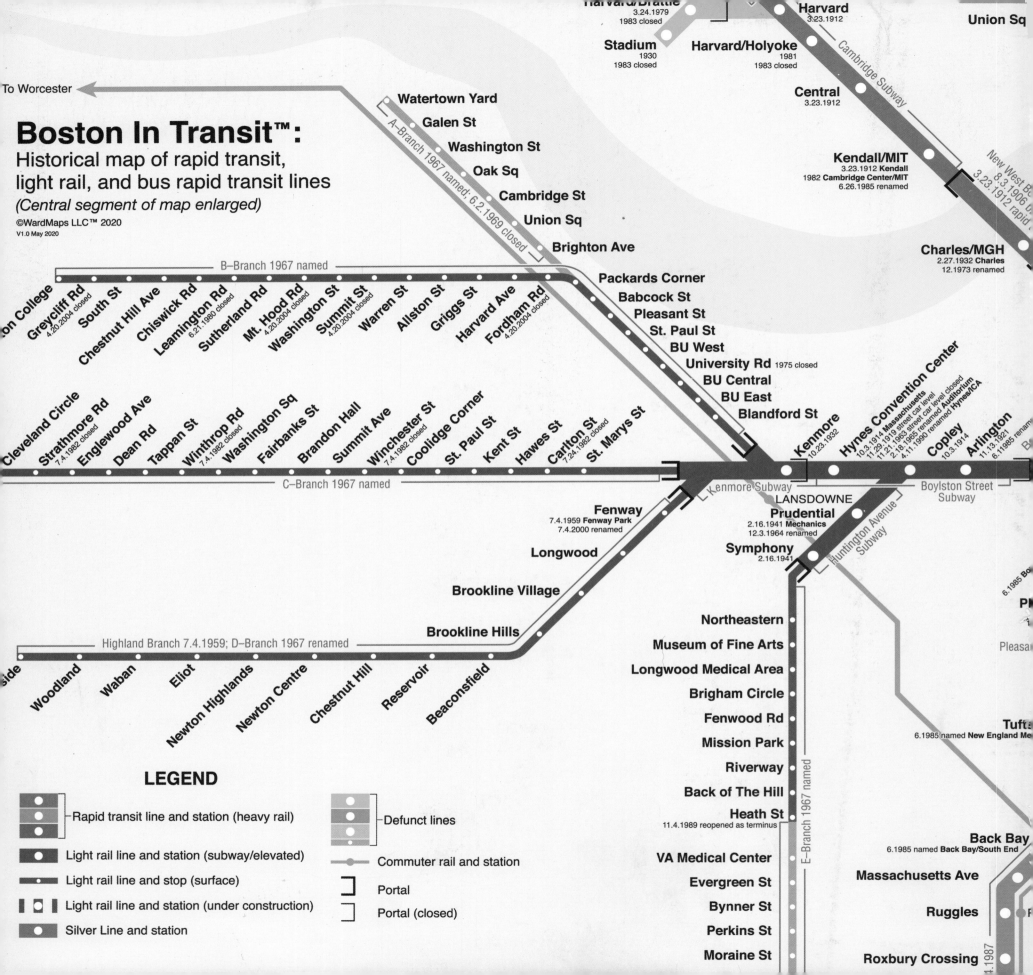

Boston In Transit™:

Historical map of rapid transit,
light rail, and bus rapid transit lines
(Central segment of map enlarged)

©WardMaps LLC™ 2020
V1.0 May 2020

To Worcester

Harvard/Brattle
3.24.1979
1983 closed

Stadium
1930
1983 closed

Harvard/Holyoke
1981
1983 closed

Harvard
3.23.1912

Union Sq

Cambridge Subway

Central
3.23.1912

Kendall/MIT
3.23.1912 **Kendall**
1982 **Cambridge Center/MIT**
6.26.1985 renamed

New West B
8.3.1906 U
3.23.1912 rapid

Charles/MGH
2.27.1932 **Charles**
12.1973 renamed

Watertown Yard
Galen St
Washington St
Oak Sq
Cambridge St
Union Sq
Brighton Ave

A–Branch 1967 named; 6.2.1969 closed

B–Branch 1967 named

ton College
Greycliff Rd
4.20.2004 closed
South St
Chestnut Hill Ave
Chiswick Rd
Leamington Rd
Sutherland Rd
6.21.1980 closed
Mt. Hood Rd
4.20.2004 closed
Washington St
Summit St
4.20.2004 closed
Warren St
Allston St
Griggs St
Harvard Ave
Fordham Rd
4.20.2004 closed

Packards Corner
Babcock St
Pleasant St
St. Paul St
BU West
University Rd 1975 closed
BU Central
BU East
Blandford St

Cleveland Circle
Strathmore Rd
Englewood Ave
7.4.1982 closed
Dean Rd
Tappan St
Winthrop Rd
7.4.1982 closed
Washington Sq
Fairbanks St
Brandon Hall
Summit Ave
Winchester St
7.4.1982 closed
Coolidge Corner
St. Paul St
Kent St
Hawes St
Carlton St
7.24.1982 closed
St. Marys St

C–Branch 1967 named

Kenmore
10.23.1932

Hynes Convention Center
10.3.1914 **Massachusetts**
11.29.1919 street car level closed
11.21.1963 street car level closed
2.18.1965 renamed **Auditorium**
4.11.1990 renamed **Hynes/ICA**

Copley
10.3.1914

Arlington
11.13.1921
6.11985 renamed

Bo

6.1985 Bo

Kenmore Subway

LANSDOWNE

Boylston Street
Subway

Fenway
7.4.1959 **Fenway Park**
7.4.2000 renamed

Prudential
2.16.1941 **Mechanics**
12.3.1964 renamed

Longwood

Symphony
2.16.1941

Huntington Avenue
Subway

Brookline Village

Northeastern

PI

Pleasa

side
Woodland
Waban
Eliot
Newton Highlands
Newton Centre
Chestnut Hill
Reservoir
Beaconsfield

Brookline Hills

Highland Branch 7.4.1959; D–Branch 1967 renamed

Museum of Fine Arts

Longwood Medical Area

Brigham Circle

Fenwood Rd

Mission Park

Riverway

Back of The Hill

Heath St
11.4.1989 reopened as terminus

E–Branch 1967 named

Tuft
6.1985 named **New England Me**

Back Bay
6.1985 named **Back Bay/South End**

VA Medical Center

Evergreen St

Bynner St

Perkins St

Moraine St

Massachusetts Ave

Ruggles

Roxbury Crossing

1987

LEGEND

Rapid transit line and station (heavy rail)

Light rail line and station (subway/elevated)

Light rail line and stop (surface)

Light rail line and station (under construction)

Silver Line and station

Defunct lines

Commuter rail and station

Portal

Portal (closed)